Parimal Sanskrit Series No. 35

THIRTY MINOR UPANIṢADS

REVISED EDITION INCLUDES SANSKRIT TEXTS

ENGLISH TRANSLATION BY

K. NARAYANASVAMI AIYAR

PARIMAL PUBLICATIONS

DELHI

Published by

PARIMAL PUBLICATIONS

Office : 27/28, Shakti Nagar, Delhi-110007 (INDIA)

Retail Outlet : 22/3, Shakti Nagar, Delhi-110007 (INDIA)

ph. : +91-11-23845456, 47015168

e-mail : order@parimalpublication.com

url : http://www.parimalpublication.com

Third Reprint Edition : Year 2016

ISBN : 978-81-7110-137-5

Price : ₹ 300.00

Printed at

Vishal Kaushik Printers

Jagat Puri Vistar, Delhi

TO

THE ṚṢIS OF INDIA

WHO BY TREADING THE PATH

OF

THE UPANIṢADS HAVE PERFECTED THEMSELVES

AND

REALISED THE GOAL

Contents

Sanskrit Text

Foreword

For the first time it is, I believe, that the English translation of so many as 30 *Upaniṣads* is being put forth before the public in a collected form. Among the, Hindu Scriptures, the Vedas hold the pre-eminent place. The *Upaniṣads* which are culled from the *Āraṇyaka*-portions of the Vedas— So-called because they were read in the *Araṇya* (forest) after the learner had given up the life of the world— are regarded as the *Vedānta*, or the end or final crown of the Vedas. *Vedānta* is also the end of all knowledge, since the word Vedas means according to its derivation 'knowledge'. Rightly were the *Upaniṣads* so considered, since their knowledge led a person to *Ātmā*, the goal of life. The other portion of the Vedas, *viz.*, *Saṁhitās* and *Brāhmaṇas*, conferred upon a man, if he should conform to the requisite conditions, the mastery of the Universe only which is certainly inferior to *Ātmā*. It is these *Upaniṣads* that to the western philosopher Schopenhauer were the "Solace of life".

There are now extant, in all, 108 *Upaniṣads*, of which the principal or major 12 *Upaniṣads* commented upon by Śrī Śankarācārya and others were translated into English by Dr. Roer and Rāja Rājendra Lal Mitra and re-translated by Max Müller in his "Sacred Books of the East", together with one other *Upaniṣad* called *Maitrāyaṇī*. Of the rest, 95 in number, two or three *Upaniṣads* have appeared in English up to now, but never so many as are here presented to the public, so far as I am aware.

Many years ago, the late Sundara Śāstri, a good *Sanskrit* Scholar and myself worked together to put into English garb the *Upaniṣads* that had not been attempted before, and succeeded in publishing most of those which are here gathered in the monthly issues of *The Theosophist*. The *Kārmic* agents willed that my late co-worker should abandoned his physical garment at a premature age. Then I resolved upon throwing up my worldly business of pleading the cause of clients before the bench for that of pleading the cause of God before the public. The incessant travel in that cause since then for over 18 years from place to place in all parts of India left me no leisure until now to republish all the above translations in a book form. But when this year a little rest was afforded me, I was able to revise them as well as add a few more. I am conscious of the many faults from which this book suffers and have no other hope in it than that it will serve as a piece of pioneer work, which may induce real *Yogins* and scholars to come into the field and bring out a better translation.

There are many editions of the *Upaniṣads* to be found in Calcutta, Bombay, Poona, South India and other places. But we found that the South Indian editions, which were nearly the same in *Telugu* or *Grantha* Characters, were in many cases fuller and more intelligible and significant. Hence we adopted for our translation South Indian editions. The editions of the 108 *Upaniṣads* which the late Tukārāma Tātya of Bombay has published in *Devanāgarī* Characters approaches the South Indian edition. As the South Indian edition of the *Upaniṣads* is not available for the study of all, I intend to have the recessions of that edition printed in *Devanāgarī* characters, so that even those that have a little knowledge of *Sanskrit* may be able to follow the original with the help of this translation.

The Order of the Upaniṣads

The *Upaniṣads* translated have been classified under the headings of (1) *Vedānta*, (2) Physiology, (3) *Mantra*, (4) *Sannyāsa* and (5) *Yoga*. But these are not hard and fast divisions. For instance in the *Sannyāsa* and *Yoga Upaniṣads*, *mantras* also are given. But in the *Māntric Upaniṣads* alone are given.

Vedānta and Yoga Upaniṣads

The *Upaniṣads* that come under the headings of *Vedānta* and *Yoga* are the most important. But it is the latter *Upaniṣads* that are most occult in their character, since it is they that give clues to the mysterious forces located in nature and man, as well as to the ways by which they may be conquered. With reference to *Vedānta*, the ancient teachers thereof have rightly ordained that none has the right to enter upon a study of it unless he has mastered to a slight degree at least the *Sādhana-Catuṣṭaya*, or four means of salvation. He should not only be convinced in theory of the fact that *Ātmā* is the only Reality, and all else are but the ephemeral things of the world, but he should also have outgrown in practice the craving for such transitory worldly things : besides he should have developed a fair mastery over the body and the mind. A non-compliance with these precedent conditions leads men into many anomalies. The orthodox and the clever without any practice are placed in a bad predicament through a study of these *Upaniṣads*. In such *Upaniṣads* as *Maitreya* and others, pilgrimages to holy places, the rituals of the Hindus, ceremonial impurities at the time of birth and death, *Mantras*, etc., are made light of. To the orthodox that are blind and strict observers of rites and ceremonies, statements like these give a rude shock. Hence *Upaniṣads* are not meant for persons of this stamp. Nor are they intended for mere intellectual people who have no knowledge of practice about them, and are immersed in the things of the world. Some of us are aware of the manner in which men with brains alone have made a travesty of the doctrine of *Māyā*. Not a few clever but unprincipled persons actually endeavour to justify arguments of all kinds of dissipations and wrong conduct by the assertion that it is all *Māyā*. The old *Ṛṣi* were fully aware of the fact that *Vedānta* would be desecrated by those that had not complied with its precedent conditions. Only when the desires and the self are overcome and the heart is made pure, or as *Upaniṣ adic* writers put it, the heart-knot is broken, only then the *Ātmā* in the heart will be truly realised : and then it is that the *Ātmā* in all universe is realised also, the universe being then seen as *Māyā*. But so long as the *Ātmā* in the heart is not realised through living the life, the universe will not be realised as *Māyā*, and "God everywhere" will be but in words.

One special point worthy of notice in the *Upaniṣads* is that all the knowledge bearing upon a subject is not put forward in one and the same place. We have to wade through a mass of materials and a number of *Upaniṣads*, ere we can have a connected view of a subject. In modern days when a subject is taken up, all the available information is given in one place in a systematic manner. But not so in the *Upaniṣads*. Take the subject of *Prāṇas* which refer to life itself. In one *Upaniṣad*, one piece of information is given, another in another and so on. And unless we read them all together and reconcile the seemingly discrepant statements, we cannot have a complete and clear knowledge of the subject. This process was adopted by the *Ṛṣis*, probably because they wanted to draw out thereby the intellectual and spiritual faculties latent in the disciple, and not to make him a mere automation. In these days when knowledge is presented in a well-assimilated form, it is no doubt taken up easily but it does not evoke the latent reasoning power so much. When therefore, the disciple went in the ancient days to the teacher for the solution of a difficulty, having been unable to find it himself after hard thinking, it was understood easily and permanently because of the previous preparation of the mind, and was also reverently appreciated as a boon and godsend, because of the difficulty previously experienced. The function of the teacher was not only to explain the difficult points to the taught, but also to make him realise those things of which understanding was sought. As an illustration, we might take the case of the soul. The *Guru* not only explained the difficult passages of points relating to the soul, but also made the disciple leave the body or bodies and realise himself as the soul. As we cannot get such *Gurus* in the outer world now a days, the only thing left to do instead is to secure the publication of simple treatises on matters of *Vedānta* and *Yoga* for the benefit of the public. I hope, I shall before long be able to make a start in this direction.

In studying the *Upaniṣads* on *Vedānta* and *Yoga*, we find certain peculiarities which throw a light on their greatness. Both of them lay stress upon certain centres in the human body for development. The 12 major *Upaniṣads* as well as the *Vedānta*, *Upaniṣads* herein published deal with the heart and the heart alone; while the *Yoga Upaniṣads* treat of many centres including the heart. For the purpose of simplification, all the centres may be divided under the main headings of head, heart and the portion of the body from the navel downwards.

But why ? The key which will unlock these secrets seems to be this. All religions postulate that the real man is the soul, and that the soul has to reach God. Christianity states that God created the soul in His own image and that the soul has to rise to the full stature of God in order to reach Him. Hinduism says that *Jīvātmā* (the human soul) is an *Aṁśa* or portion of *Paramātmā*, or God, which is to eventually unfold the powers of God, and compares it with a ray of the sun of God, or a spark out of the fire of God. In all religions, there is an unanimity of opinion that the soul is a likeness of God, having God's powers in latency to be unfolded hereafter. Let us therefore first understand the attributed of God. He is said to have omnipresence, omniscience and omnipotence. Hinduism translates these ideas into *Sat*, *Cit* and *Ānanda*. They are eternal existence, infinite knowledge, and unlimited power. The soul identifying itself with the body thinks it lives for the life-term of the body only; cooped up by the brain, it imagines, it has only the knowledge circumscribed by the brain; carried away by the pleasures of the senses, it whirls about in the midst of them as if they constituted the Real Bliss. But when it wakes up from the dream of the lower things of the body and glances upwards to the higher world of Spirit, it discovers its delusions and finds itself to be of the same nature as the God above, who is eternal, all-knowing and all-powerful. And this discovery has to be made by each soul in the human body, in which it is functioning, through the three main centres of head, heart and navel. Through the heart, it cuts the heart-knot and realises its all-pervading character when it realises its eternity of existence; through the brain, it rises beyond it through its highest seat, *viz.*, *Sahasrāra* which corresponds to the pineal gland in the physical body, and obtains its omniscience; through the navel, according to the *Upaniṣads*— It obtains a mastery over that mysterious force called *Kuṇḍalinī* which is located therein, and which confers upon it an unlimited power— that force being mastered only when a man arises above *Kāma* or passion. Psychologists tell us that desires when conquered lead to the development of will. When will is developed to a great degree, naturally great power, or omnipotence, ensues : our statement is that *Kuṇḍalinī* when conquered leads to unlimited powers and perfections, or *Siddhis* like *Aṇimā*, etc., and that *Kuṇḍalinī* can only be conquered through rising above the desires of the senses.

From the foregoing it is clear that the *Vedānta Upaniṣads* are intended only for those devotees of God that want to have a development of the heart mainly, and not of the brain and the navel, and that the *Yogic Upaniṣads* are intended for those that want to have an all-round development of the soul in its three aspects. Here I may remark that Śrī Śaṅkarācārya and other commentators commented upon the 12 *Upaniṣads* only, since other *Upaniṣads* treating of *Kuṇḍalinī*, etc., are of an occult character and not meant for all, but only for the select few who are fit for private initiation. If they had proceeded to comment upon the minor *Upaniṣads* also, they would have had to disclose certain secrets which confer powers and which are not meant, therefore, for all. It would be nothing but fatal to the community, were the secrets leading to the acquisition of such powers imparted indiscriminately to all. In the case of dynamite, the criminal using it may be traced, since it is of a physical nature, but in the case of the use of the higher powers, they are set in motion through the will, and can never be traced through ordinary means. Therefore in the *Upaniṣads* called *Yoga-Kuṇḍalinī*, the final truths that lead to the realisation of the higher powers are said to be imparted by the *Guru* alone to the disciple who has proved himself worthy after a series of births and trials.

In order to expound the *Upaniṣads*, especially those that bear upon *Yoga*, some one who is a specialist in *Yoga*— better still, if he is an Adept— should undertake the task of editing and translating them. The passages in *Yoga Upaniṣads* are very mystic sometimes; sometimes there is no nominative or verb, and we have to fill up the ellipses as best as we can.

One more remark may be made with reference to the *Upaniṣads*. Each *Upaniṣad* is said to belong to one of the Vedas. Even if we take the 12 *Upaniṣads* edited by Max Muller and others, we find some of them are to be found in the existing Vedas and other not. Why is this? In my opinion this but corroborates the statement made by the *Viṣṇu-Purāṇa* about the Vedas. It says that at the end of each *Dvāpara Yuga*, a Veda-Vyāsa, or compiler of the Vedas, incarnates as an *Avatāra* of Viṣṇu — a minor one— to compile the Vedas. In the *Yugas* preceding the *Kali Yuga* we are in, the Vedas were "one" alone through voluminous. Just before this *Kali Yuga* began, *Kṛṣṇa-Dvaipāyana* Veda-Vyāsa incarnated, and, after withdrawing the Vedas that were not fit for this *Yuga* and the short-lived people therein, made with the aid of his disciples a division of the remaining portions into four. Hence perhaps we are unable to trace the Vedas of which some of the extant *Upaniṣads* form part.

Adyar,
March 1914

K. Narayanaswami

Muktikopaniṣad

OF

ŚUKLA-YAJURVEDA

Adhyāya I

Addressing with devotion and obedience Śrī-Rāma— the Lord Hari, at the end of his *Samādhi*, who being Himself changeless is the witness of the thousands of changes of *Buddhi*, and who ever rests in *Svarūpa-Dhyāna* (the meditation on Reality) while seated under the bejewelled dome of the palace in the lovely city of *Ayodhyā*, in the midst of Sītā, Bharata and Soumitri (Lakṣmaṇa) Śatrughna and others, eulogised day and night by Sanaka and other hosts of *Munis*, as well as by Vasiṣṭha, Śukra, and other devotees of Viṣṇu— Hanumān, after praising them, asked : "O Rāma, Thou art *Paramātmā* of the nature of *Saccidānanda*. O foremost of the family of Raghu, I make prostrations to Thee again and again. O Rāma, I wish to know for the sake of emancipation, Thy nature as it really is. O Rāma, be Thou gracious enough to tell me that by which I shall be easily released from the bondage of mundane existence and by which I shall attain salvation."

(Śrī Rāma replied :) "O mighty-armed one, well as led: hearken then to the truth uttered by Me. I am well established in *Vedānta* (or the end of Vedas or knowledge). Have thou recourse to *Vedānta* well."

(Hanumān again asked :) "O foremost of Raghus, what are *Vedāntas*? where do they abide? Pray enlighten me". (Śrī-Rāma replied :) "O Hanumān, listen to me. I shall truly describe to you the nature of *Vedānta*. Through the expiratory breath of Myself— Viṣṇu, the Vedas were generated as many. Like the oil in the *sesamum* seeds, *Vedānta* is well established (or latent in the Vedas".

(Hanumān asked again :) "O Rāma, how many are the Vedas and their branches? O Rāghava, what are the *Upaniṣads*? Please, through Thy grace, tell me truly."

(Śrī-Rāma said :) "Through the divisions of *Ṛgveda* and others, the Vedas are said to be four in number. Their branches are many. So also the *Upaniṣads*. In *Ṛgveda*, there are branches, 21 in number. O son of *Vāyu*, there are 109 branches in *Yajurveda*. O conqueror of enemies, there are 1,000 branches in *Sāmaveda*, O best of Monkeys, there are 50 branches in *Atharvaveda*. In each branch, there is one *Upaniṣad*. Whoever with devotion to Me studies even one of the *Ṛks* (hymns) in these attains the state of absorption, rare for the *Munis* to attain."

(Hanumān asked :) "O Rāma, some excellent *Munis* have said there is one kind of salvation only, while other [stated that salvation is attained] through the uttering of Thy name or the initiation into *Tāraka* (*Om*) at *Kāśī* (Varanasi); others through *Sāṁkhya-Yoga*, others through the *Yoga* of Devotion; other *Maharṣis* through the meditation upon the meaning of *Mahāvākyas* (the sacred sentences of the Vedas). Salvation is stated to be of four kinds through the divisions of *Śālokya* and others."

(Śrī-Rāma replied :) "There is only one true emancipation. O *Kapi* (Monkey), even a person addicted to evil practices attains the salvation of *Sālokya* (My world) through the uttering of My name, but not of other worlds. Should one die in *Brahma-nāḷa* (the lotus-stalk— also street)[1] in *Kāśī*, he attains My *Tāraka* (Mantra). Such a person attains salvation without any rebirth; wherever he may die in *Kāśī*, *Maheśvara* initiates him by whispering My *Tāraka* (*Mantra*) into his right ear. Such person, freed from all sins, attains my *Svarūpa* (Form). It is this that is termed *Sālokya-Sārūpya* salvation. The twice-born who is of virtuous conduct and who without diverting his intelligence on any other, meditates upon Me, the All-*Ātmā*, attains *Sāmīpya* (nearness) to Me.

"It is this that is termed *Sālokya-Sārūpya-Sāmīpya* salvation. The twice-born who according to the path opened by the teacher, meditates upon My immutable Reality attains *Sāyujya* (absorption) into Me, like the caterpillar into the wasp. This is the *Sāyujya* salvation which is productive of Brahmic bliss and auspicious. Thus these kinds of salvation arise through the *Upāsanā* (worship) of Me.

"The only means by which the final emancipation is attained is through *Māṇḍūkya-Upaniṣad* alone, which is enough for the salvation of all aspirants. If *Jñāna* is not attained thereby, study the 10 *Upaniṣads*; thou shalt soon attain *Jñāna*, and then My Seat. O son of *Añjanā*, if thy *Jñāna* is not made firm, practise (study) well the 32 *Upaniṣads*. Thou shalt get release. If thou longest after *Videhamukti* (or disembodied salvation), study the 108 *Upaniṣads*. I will truly state in order the (names of the) *Upaniṣads* with their *Śānti* (purification *Mantras*). Hearken to them. (They are :) *Īśa*, *Kena*, *Kaṭha*, *Praśna*, *Muṇḍa*, *Māṇḍūkya*, *Tittiri*, *Aitareya*, *Chāndogya*, *Bṛhadāraṇyaka*, *Brahma*, *Kaivalya*, *Jābāla*, *Śvetāśvatara*, *Haṁsa*, *Āruṇi*, *Garbha*, *Nārāyaṇa* (*Parama*), *Haṁsa*, (*Amṛta*)-*Bindu*, (*Amṛta*)-*Nāda*, (*Atharva*)-*Śira*, (*Atharva*)-*Śikhā*, *Maitrāyaṇī*, *Kauṣitaki*, (*Bṛhat*)-*Jābāla*, (*Narasiṁha*)-*Tāpanī*, *Kālāgnirudra*, *Maitreyī*, *Subāla*, *Kṣurikā*, *Mantrikā*, *Sarvasāra*, *Nirālamba*, (*Śuka*)-*Rahasya*, *Vajrasūchikā*, *Tejo*-(*Bindu*), *Nāda*-(*Bindu*), *Dhyāna*-(*Bindu*), (*Brahma*)-*Vidyā*, *Yoga-Tattva*, *Ātmabodhaka*, *Parivrāt* (*Nārada-Parivrājaka*), (*Tri*)-*Śikhī*, *Sītā* (*Yoga*)-*Cūdā*-(*Maṇī*) *Nirvāṇa*, *Maṇḍala*-(*Brāhmaṇa*), *Dakṣiṇā*-(*Mūrti*), *Śarabh-Skands*, (*Tripādvibhūtī*)-

---

1. There is a street in *Kāśī* called *Brahma-nāḷa*.

Mahā-Nārāyaṇa, Advaya-(Tāraka), (Rāma)-Rahasya), (Rāma)-Tāpanī, Vāsudeva, Mudgala, Śāṇdilya Paiṅgala, Bhikṣu, Mahat-Śāriraka, (Yoga)-Śikhā, Triyatīta, Saṁnyāsa, (Paramahaṁsa)-Parivrājaka, Akṣamālikā, Avyakta, Ekākṣara, (Anna)-Pārṇa, Sūrya, Akṣi, Adhyātma, Kuṇdikā, Sāvitri, Ātmā, Pāśupata, Parabrahma, Avadhūta, Tripuratapaṇī, Devī, Tripura, Kara, Bhāvanā, (Rudra)-Hṛdaya (Yoga)-Kuṇḍalinī, Bhasma-(Jābāla) Rudrākṣa, Gaṇapati, Darśana, Tārasāra, Mahāvākya, Pañcabrahma, (Prāṇa)-Agnihotra, Gopāla,-Tāpanī, Kṛṣṇa, Yājñavalkya, Varāha, Śātyāyanī, Hayagrīva, Dattatreya, Garuḍa, Kali-(Santāraṇa), Jābāla, Soubhāgya, Sarasvatī-rahasya, Bahvrica, and *Muktika*. These 108 (*Upaniṣads*) are able to do away with the three *Bhāvanās* [of doubt, vain thought, and false thought], conferring *Jñāna* and *Vairāgya*, and destroying the three *Vāsanās* [of book-lore, world and body].

"The twice-born— after learning the 108 *Upaniṣads*, together with the *Śāntī* as prescribed both before and after from the mouth of a *Guru* well versed in the observances of Vedic knowledge and study— become *Jīvanmuktas* till the destruction of their *Prārabdha*; in course of time as *Prārabdha* is destroyed, they attain My disembodied salvation. There is no doubt of it. O son of *Vāyu*, these 108 *Upaniṣads*, which are the essence of all the *Upaniṣads*, and are capable of destroying all sins through their mere study, have been imparted by Me to you as a disciple. This science of the 108 *Upaniṣads* taught by Me, is occult one, and will free persons from bondage, whether they read them with or without knowledge. To gratify the desire of a supplicant, a kingdom may be given or wealth, but never shall the 108 *Upaniṣads* be imparted to an atheist, an ungrateful person, one intent on vicious actions, one having no devotion towards Me, or one who loses his path in the cave of books. On no account shali they be given to one devoid of devotion. O Māruti, it is only after a thorough examination that they should be imparted to a disciple doing service (to a *Guru*), to a well-disposed son, or to one devoted to Me, following good observances, belonging to a good family, and being of good intelligence. Whoever studies or hears the 108 *Upaniṣads* attains Me. There is no doubt of this. This is stated in the *Ṛk* (verse) thus— *Vidyā* (Sarasvatī) went to a *Brāhmaṇa* (and addressed him) thus : 'Protect me. I shall be thy treasure. Do not confide me to the envious, to one not treading the right path, or to the rogue. Then I shall be potent'. Impart this *Ātmaniṣtha-Vidyā* relating to Viṣṇu to one after well examining him who had studied much, is alert, intelligent, observant of the vow of celibacy, and serving [the *Guru*]."

Then Hanumān asked Śrī-Rāmacandra to relate the *Śānti* of each *Upaniṣad* according to the divisions of *Ṛgveda* and others to which they belong. To which Śrī-Rāma replied: "*Aitareya, Kauṣītakī, Nāda-(Bindu), Ātmā-Bodha, Nirvāṇa, Mudugala, Akṣamālikā, Tripurā, Saubhāgya* and

Bahvṛca— these 10 *Upaniṣads* are of *Ṛgveda* and have the *Śānti* beginning with '*Vāṅme-Manasi*, etc.'. *Īśā, Bṛhadāraṇyaka, Jābāla, Haṁsa, (Parama)-Haṁsa, Subāla, Mantrikā, Nirālamba, Triśikhī Brāhmaṇa, Maṇḍala-Brāhmaṇa, Advaya-Tāraka, Paiṅgala, Bhikṣu, Turīyātīta, Adhyātma, Tārasāra, Yājñavalkya, Śātyāyanī,* and *Muktika*— these 19 *Upaniṣads* are of *Śukla Yajurveda* and have the *Śānti* beginning with '*Pūrṇamada*, etc'.

"*Kaṭha, Tittiri, Brahma, Kaivalya, Śvetāśvatara, Garbha, Nārāyaṇa,* (*Amṛta*)-*Bindu*, (*Amṛta*)-*Nāda, Kālāgnirudra, Kṣurikā, Sarvasāra, Śukrarahasya, Tejo*-(*Bindu*), *Dhyāna*-(*Bindu*), (*Brahma*)-*Vidyā, Yoga-Tattva, Dakṣiṇā*-(*Mūrti*), *Skanda-Śārīraka*, (*Yoga*)-*Śikhā, Ekākṣara, Akṣi, Avadhūta, Kara,* (*Rudra*)-*Hṛdaya*, (*Yoga*)-*Kuṇḍalinī, Pañcabrahma,* (*Prāṇa*)-*Agnihotra, Varāha, Kali*-(*Santāraṇa*), and *Sarasvatīrahasya*,— These 32 *Upaniṣads* are of *Kṛṣṇa Yajurveda* and have the *Śānti* beginning with '*Sahanāvavatu*, etc.'

"*Kena, Chāndogya, Āruṇi, Maitrāyaṇī, Maitreyī, Vajrasūcikā,* (*Yoga*)-*Cūdā*-(*Maṇi*), *Vasudeva, Mahat-Sannyāsa, Avyakta, Kuṇḍikā, Sāvitrī, Rudrākṣa, Jābāla, Darśana*, and *Jābāli*,— these 16 *Upaniṣads* are of *Sāmaveda* and have the *Śānti* beginning with '*Āpyāyantu*, etc.'

"*Praśna, Muṇḍaka, Māṇḍūkya,* (*Atharva*)-*Śira*, (*Atharva*) *Śikhā,* (*Bṛhat*)-*Jābāla*, (*Nṛsiṁha*)-*Tāpanī*, (*Nārada-Parivrājaka Sītā, Śarabha, Mahā-Nārāyaṇa,* (*Rāma*)-*Rahasya*, (*Rāma*)-*Tāpani, Śāṇḍilya,* (*Paramahaṁsa*)-*Parivrājaka*, (*Anna*)-*Pūrṇā, Sūrya Ātmā, Pāśupata, Parabrahma, Tripuratāpanī, Devī, Bhāvanā, Bhasma*-(*Jābāla*), *Gaṇapati, Mahāvākya, Gopāla-Tāpanī, Kṛṣṇa, Hayagrīva, Dattātreya,* and *Garuḍa*,— These 31 *Upaniṣads* on *Atharvaveda* have the *Śānti* commencing with '*Bhadram-Karṇebhih*, etc'.

"Persons desirous of emancipation and having developed the four means of salvation should, with presents in then hands, approach a *Guru* full of faith, of good family, proficient in Vedas, scripture-loving, of good qualities, straightforward, intent upon the welfare of all beings, and an ocean of compassion; and after studying under him, according to the rules, the 108 *Upaniṣads*, he should ever be going through the process of studying, thinking and reflecting upon them. With the cessation of the three bodies through the destruction of *Prārabdha*, they attain the state of Plenum without any *Upādhis* like the ether in the pot (after the pot is broken). This is the embodied salvation, this is the final emancipation. Therefore even those in *Brahmaloka* through the studying of *Vedānta* from the mouth of Brahmā attain with Him the final emancipation. Hence to all these is stated the final emancipation through the *Jñāna* path, and not through *Karma, Sāṁkhya-Yoga*, and other *Upāsanās*. Thus is the *Upaniṣad*."

Adhyāya II

Again Māruti (Hanumān) addressed Śrī-Rāmacandra thus : "What is *Jīvanmukti*? what is *Videhamukti*? what is the authority therein? what about its perfection? what is the object of such a perfection?"

(Śrī-Rāma replied :) "The *Dharma* of a man's *Citta* that has the characteristics of agency and enjoyment is fraught with pains and hence tends towards bondage. The control of it (the *Citta*) is *Jīvanmukti*. *Videhamukti* follows when through the extinction of *Prārabdha*, the removal of the vehicles [of the bodies] takes place like the ether in the pot [after the pot is broken]. The authority on the points of *Jīvanmukti* and *Videhamukti* is the 108 *Upaniṣads*. Its object [of perfection] is the attaining of eternal bliss through the removal of the pains of agency, etc. This has to be achieved through human efforts. Like progeny obtained through the *Putrakāmeṣṭi* sacrifice, wealth in trade, or heaven through the *Jyotiṣṭoma* sacrifice, so *Jīvanmukti* is gained through *Samādhi* arising through Vedāntic study, and accomplished through human efforts. It has to be won through the extinction of all *Vāsanās*. Regarding it, there are verses thus : "The efforts of man are stated to be of two kinds, those that transcend scriptures and those that are according to scriptures. Those that transcend scriptures tend to harn while those that are according to scriptures tend to Reality.' To men, true *Jñāna* does not arise through the *Vāsanās* of the world, scripture and body. *Vāsanā* is divided into two, the pure and the impure. If thou art led by the pure *Vāsanās*, thou shalt thereby soon reach by degrees My Seat. But should the old impure *Vāsanās* land thee in danger, they should be overcome through efforts. This river of *Vāsanās* towards objects, which flows in the pure and impure paths, should be diverted to the pure path through human efforts. The impure ones have to be transmuted into the pure. That which is diverted from the impure turns towards the pure. So also the reverse. This child, *Citta* has to be fondled through human efforts. O killer of enemies, it is only when through means of practice both *Vāsanās* quite abandon thee, that thou wilt be able to realise the effects of [such] practice. Even in the case of doubt, the pure *Vāsanās* alone should be practised.

"O son of *Vāyu*, there is nothing wrong in the increase of the pure *Vāsanās*. The extinction of *Vāsanās*, *Vijñāna* and the destruction of *Manas* [as these three] when practised together for a long time are regarded, O great and intelligent one, as fruitful. So long as these are not equally practised again and again, so long the [Supreme] Seat is not attained, even after the lapse of hundreds of years. Even should one of these [three] be practised for a long time, it will not yield its fruit like a *Mantra* imperfectly done. Through the practice of these for a long time, the firm knots of the heart are cut, without doubt, like the breaking of the threads in a lotus-stalk rent in twain. The illusory *Sāmsārika Vāsanā* that has arisen through the practice of [many] hundreds of lives never perishes except through the practice of *Yoga* for a long time. Therefore, O *Somya* [disciple], after having put away to a distance the desire of enjoyment through discriminative human effort, resort to these three alone. The wise know that a mind associated with *Vāsanā* tends to bondage, while a mind well freed from *Vāsanā* is said to be an emancipated one. O *Mahā-kapi* [great Monkey] practise the state of a mind devoid of *Vāsanā*. *Vāsanā* perishes through well-conducted deliberation and truth. Through the absorption of *Vāsanās*, *Manas* attains quiescence like a lamp [without oil]. He whose mind, devoid of destruction, is [centred] on Me as of the nature of *Cinmātra* [consciousness alone], abandoning the *Vāsanās*, is no other than Myself of the nature of *Saccidānanda*. Whether *Samādhi* and *Karma* are performed or not, one who has a supreme *Citta* with a heart devoid of all desires is an emancipated person. He whose mind is freed from *Vāsanās* is not subject to the fruits arising from the performance or non-performance of actions, or *Samādhi* of *Jñāna*. Except through the entire giving up of *Vāsanā*s and through *Mouna* [the observance of silence towards objects], the Supreme Seat is not attained. Though devoid of *Vāsanās*, the eye and other organs are involuntarily prompted to their (respective) external objects through habit. Just as the eye without any desire sees without any effort the objects that fall on it, so also the undaunted man of intelligence enters into the affairs [of the world] without any desire. O Māruti, the *Munis* know that as *Vāsanā* which is manifested through the consciousness of objects, which is of the nature of the object itself, and which is the cause of the origination and absorption of *Citta*. This excessively fluctuating *Citta* is the cause of birth, dotage and death, due to the identification of itself with objects practised firmly [for a long time]. Like the analogy of the seed and the tree, the variation of *Prāṇa* arises through *Vāsanā* and *(vice versa)* the *Vāsanā* through the former— these forming the need of *Citta*. To the tree of *Citta*, there are two seeds: the vibration of *Prāṇa* and *Vāsanā*. Should either of them perish, both perish soon. Through the actions of the world being done without attachment, through the abandoning of the [thought of the] reality of the universe and the conviction of the distractibility of the body, *Vāsanā* does not arise. Through the complete giving up of *Vāsanā*. *Citta* becomes not-*Citta*. When the mind does not think at all, being completely devoid of *Vāsanā*, then dawns the state of mindlessness which confers the great peace. So long as you are without a mind of [true] discrimination and are not a knower of the Supreme Seat, so long should you follow whatever has been decided by the teacher and the authorities of the sacred books. When your sins are burnt up and you are a knower of the Reality without any anxiety then all the good *Vāsanās* even should be given up.

"The destruction of *Citta* is of two kinds, that with form and that without form. [The destruction of] that with form is of the *Jīvanmukta*;

(the destruction of), that without form being of the *Videhamukta*. O son of *Vāyu*, hearken to [the means of] the destruction of *Citta*. That is said to be destruction of *Citta* when it, associated with all the attributes of *Maitrī* (friendship) and others, becomes quiescent [without any resurrection]. There is no doubt of it. Then the *Manas* of a *Jīvanmukta* is free from fresh rebirth; to him, there is the destruction of *Manas* with form. But to the *Videhamukta*, there is the destruction of *Manas* without form. It is *Manas* that is the root of the tree of *Saṁsāra* with its thousands of shoots, branches, tender, leaves and fruits. I think it to be *Saṅkalpa* alone. In order that the trees of *Saṁsāra* may wither soon, dry up its root through the quiescence of *Saṅkalpa*. There is only one means to control one's mind. That is to destroy the mind as soon as it rises. That is the (great) dawn. In the case of the wise, the mind is destroyed : but in the case of ignorant, it is indeed a fetter. So long as the mind is not destroyed through the firm practice of the One Reality, so long as *Väsanās* are prancing about in the heart like *Vetāla* (goblin) in the night-time. The *Vāsanās* of enjoyment of one who has destroyed the egoism of *Citta* and controlled organs, the enemies, decay like lotuses in mid-winter. Pressing one hand against the other, setting teeth against teeth, and forcing one limb against the order, he should first conquer his mind.

"It is not possible on the part of the one-thoughted to control the mind by sitting up again and again except through the approved means. As a vicious rutting elephant is not subject to control except through the goad, so in the matter of the control of the mind, the effective means are the attainment of spiritual knowledge, association with the wise, the entire abdication of all *Vāsanās* and the control of *prāṇas*. While such are the [prescribed] means, should persons try to control the mind through violence, they are like those that search in darkness, having thrown aside the light (in their hands). Those who endeavour to control the mind through force are but trying to bind a mad elephant with the filaments of a lotus-stalk.

To the tree of the mind having the ever-growing branches of modifications, there are two seeds. One is the fluctuation of *Prāṇa*, and the other is the firmness of *Vāsanā*. The [One] All-pervading Consciousness is agitated by the fluctuation of *Prāṇas*. The means of *Dhyāṇa* by which [the one] *Jñāna* is attained through the one-pointedness of the mind is now imparted to you after duly resolving back the things originated [in the universe] with all their changes, meditate upon that which remains— [viz.], *Cinmātra* (the consciousness alone), which is also *Cidānada* (conscious-bliss). The wise say that the interval experienced by *Yogins* after the inspiration and before the (next) expiration is (the internal) *Kumbhaka* (cessation of breath); while the interval of complete equilibrium after expiration and before the next inspiration is the external

Kumbhaka. Through the force of the practice of *Dhyāna*, the current of the modification of *Manas* devoid of Self that is of Brāhmic nature is said to be *Samprajñāta Samādhi*, while the mind with the utter quiescence of modifications that confers upon the supreme bliss is said to be *Asamprajñāta-Samādhi* that is dear into *Yogins*. This [state] that is devoid of light, *Manas* and *Buddhi*, and that is of the nature of *Cit*. (consciousness merely) is styled by the *Munis Atadvyāvṛtti Samādhi* (a *Samādhi* that does not care or require the aid of another). It is Plenum above, below and in the middle, and is of the nature of Śiva (suspiciousness). This noumenal (of occult) *Samādhi* is itself *Vidhi-Mukha* (sanctioned by books of Brahmā).

"The clinging to objects without previous or subsequent deliberation through intense though [or longing] is stated to be *Vāsanā*. O chief of Monkeys, whatever is meditated upon by a person with ardent impetuosity without any other *Vāsanā*— that he soon becomes. A person that is entirely subject to *Vāsanā* becomes of the nature of that. When he regards this [universe] as *Sat* [the Reality], then he is subject to delusion. Because of the many strong *Vāsanā*, he does not abandon the nature of the universe. This person of wrong vision sees everything under infatuation like one deluded. *Vāsanās* are of two kinds— the pure and the impure. The impure ones are the cause of rebirth, while the pure are the destroyers of it. The impure are said by the wise to be of the nature of intense *Ajñāna*, associated with the great *Ahaṁkāra* and generative of rebirth. Of what avail is the chewing again and again of the many Śāstric stories to one that has abandoned the seed of re-birth, having turned it into a burnt one? O Māruti, thou shouldst with effort seek the effulgence within. O tiger of Monkeys, whoever, after having abandoned the visible and the invisible, is as the One alone is not a mere knower of *Brahman* but is *Brahman* itself. One who having studied the four Vedas and the various books does not cognize the reality of *Brahman* is like the ladle ignorant of the taste of the dainty. Therefore what other advice of indifference can be imparted to a person that has not attained the indifference can be imparted to a person that has not attained the indifference to the impure *Vāsanā* of delusion [or body]? This body is very impure while the one [*Ātmā*] that dwells in it is very pure. When the differences between the two are [thus] known, what then may be ordained as the purification? The bondage of *Vāsanā* is the [real] bondage, while the destruction of *Vāsanā* is salvation. After wholly abandoning the *Vāsanās*, give up even the desire for salvation. After first giving up the *Vāsanā* of objects dependent upon the *Vāsanā* of the mind, attract unto the pure *Vāsanās* associated with *Maitrī* [friendship] and others. Though engaged in the world with these pure *Vāsanās*, give up them too and retire within the quiescent desires and become of the form of the longing after

Cit alone. Then, O Māruti ! giving up that also associated as it is with *Manas* and *Buddhi*, mayst thou now left alone become firm in Me in *Samādhi*. O son of *Vāyu* ! always worship My Reality that is destructive of pains, without sound, touch, form, decay taste, destruction or smell, and without name and *Gotra* [clan]. I am that non-dual One (*Brahman*) that is of the nature of the visible (*Jñāna*), like unto the *Ākāśa*, supreme, always shining, without birth, non-dual, without destruction, without attachment and pervading all. I am the All, and of the nature of salvation. One should ever meditate upon Me thus : 'I am of the form the visible [*Jñāna*] the, pure, of changeless nature and have really no objects in Me. I am the ever-full *Brahman*, transverse and across, up and down. Also meditate upon Me thus : 'I am birthless, deathless, ageless, immortal, self-shining, all-pervading, destructionless, causeless, pure beyond the effect (of the universe) and ever content.' When one's becomes a prey to time, he gives up the state of *Jīvanmukti*, as the wind attains the motionless state.

"The following is said in the *Ṛg* [-*Veda*] also : Like the eye which is spread in the *Ākāśa* (seeing all things without any obstacle), so the wise ever see the Supreme Seat of Viṣṇu. The *Brāhmaṇas* that have ever the Divine vision praise in diverse ways and illumine the Supreme Seat of Viṣṇu."

Om-Tat-Sat is the Upaniṣad

Sarvasāra Upaniṣad[1]

OF

KṚṢṆA-YAJURVEDA

[In the text, all the questions are given first and then the answers follow. But the following arrangement is adopted to facilitate reference.]

1. What is *Bandha* (bondage).

Ātmā [the Self] falsely superimposing the body and others which are non-Self upon Himself, and identifying Himself with them— this identification forms the bondage of the Self.

2. What is *Mokṣa* [emancipation]?

The freedom from the [identification] is *Mokṣa*].

3. What is *Avidyā* (Nescience)?

That which cause this identification— that indeed is *Avidyā*.

4. What is *Vidyā* (knowledge)?

That which removes this identification is *Vidyā*.

5. What are (meant by) the states of *Jāgrata* [the waking], *Svapna* [the dreaming], *suṣupti* [the dreamless sleeping] and *Turīya* [the fourth]?

Jāgrata is that [state] during which *Ātmā*[2] enjoys the gross objects of senses as sound, etc., through the 14 organs as *Manas*, etc., having the sun and the rest as their presiding deities.

Svapana is that [state] during which *Ātmā* experiences, through the 14 organs associated with the *Vāsanās* (affinities], of the waking condition, sound and other objects which are of the form of the *Vāsanās* created for the time being, even in the absence of [the gross] sound and the others. *Ātmā* experiences *Suṣupti* when it does not experience sound and other objects of sense from the cessation of the functions of the 14 organs, there being no special enjoying consciousness on account of the absence of these organs.

Turīya is that state during which *Ātmā* is a witness to the existence of the above-mentioned three states, thought it is in itself without (their) existence and non-existence and during which it is one uninterrupted *Caitanya* (consciousness) alone. And that *Caitanya* is that which is connected with the three states, which is without the three states, and which is pure.

---

1. This *Upaniṣad* and the next form a glossary of some of the terms of Vedānta. '*Sarva-Sāra*' is all-essence or quintessences.
2. They are the 5 organs os sense, the 5 organs of action and the 4 of *Antaḥkaraṇa* (the internal organ, *viz., Manas*, *Buddhi*, *Citta* and *Ahaṁkāra*. Each is animated by a *Devatā* or intelligential principle.

6. What are the *Annamaya, Prāṇamaya, Manomaya, Vijñānamaya* and *Ānanḍamaya Kośas* (sheaths)?

Annamaya sheath is the aggregate of the materials formed by food. When the ten *Vāyus* (Vital airs), *Prāṇas* and others, flow through the *Annamaya* sheath, then it is called the *Prāṇamaya* sheath. When *Ātmā* connected with the above two sheaths performs the functions of hearing, etc., through the 14 organs of *Manas* and others, then it is called *Manomaya* Sheath.

When in the (*Antaḥ-Karaṇa*) internal organs connected with the above three sheaths, there arise the modifications of contemplation, meditation, etc., about the peculiarities of the sheaths, then it is called *Vijñānamaya* sheath.

When the self-cause *Jñāna* is in its self-bliss like the banyan tree in its seed, though associated with these four sheaths caused by *Ajñāna*, then it is called *Ānandamaya* sheath. *Ātmā* which is associated with the *upādhi* [vehicle] of these sheaths is figuratively called *Kośa*.

7. What is meant by *Kartā* (actor), *Jīva, Pañcavarga* (the five groups], *Kṣetrajña* (the lord of the place), *Sākṣi* [the witness], *Kūtastha* and *antaryāmin* (the latent guide)?

Kartā (the actor) is the one who possesses the body and the internal organs through their respective desires proceeding from the idea of pleasure and pain. The idea of pleasure is that modification of the mind known as love.The idea of pain is that modification of the mind know as hate. The cause of pleasure and pain are sound, touch, form, taste and odour.

Jīva is that *Adhyāsi* [deluded one] that thinks that this body, which is obtained through the effects of good and bad *Karmas*, is one not so obtained.

Pañcavarga (the five groups) are (1) *Manas, viz., Manas, Buddhi, Citta* and *Ahaṁkāra* (creating uncertainly, certitude, flitting thought and egoism), (2) *Prāṇa, i.e., Prāṇa. Apāna, Vyāna Samāna* and *Udāna*, (3) *Sattva, i.e., Sattva, Rajas,* and *Tamas*. (4) the [five] elements : earth, water, fire, *Vāyu* and *Ākāśa* and (5) *Dharma* and its opposite *Adharma*.

The original *Avidhyā* which has the characteristics of the above 5 groups, which does not perish without *Ātma-Jñaña*, which appears eternal through the presence of *Ātmā* and which is the vehicle for [the manifestation of] *Ātmā*, is the seed of the *liṅga* [subtle] body. It is also called *Hṛdaya-granthi* [the heart-kont].

The *Caitanya* [consciousness] which is reflected and shines in it is *Kṣ etrajña*.

Sākṣi [the witness] is that conscious one that is aware of the appearance and disappearance [of the three states] of the knower, the knowledge and the known, who is himself without [or not affected by] this appearance and disappearance, and who is self-radiant.

Kūṭastha is he who is found without exception in the *Buddhi* of all creatures from Brahmā down to ants, and who is shining as *Ātmā* and dwells as witness to the *Buddhi* of all creatures.

Antaryāmin is the *Ātmā* that shines as the Ordainer, being within all bodies like the thread [on which] beads [are strung] and serving to know the cause of the several differences of *Kūṭastha* and others associated with him.

8. Who is *Pratyagātmā*?

He is of the nature of truth, wisdom, eternity and bliss. He has no vehicles of body. He is abstract wisdom itself, like a mass of pure gold that is devoid of the changes of bracelet, crown, etc. He is of the nature of mere consciousness. He is that which shines as *Caitanya* and *Brahman*. When He is subject to the vehicle of *Avidyā* and is the meaning of the word "*Tvam*" ('Thou' in "*Tattvamasi*"), then He is *Pratyagātmā*.

9. Who is *Paramātmā*?

It is He who is associated with truth, wisdom, eternity, bliss, omniscience, etc., who is subject to the vehicle of *Māyā* and who is the meaning of the word "*Tat*" (or 'That' in "*Tattvamasi*").

10. What is *Brahman* ?

Brahman is that which is free from all vehicles, which is the Absolute Consciousness devoid of particularities, which is *Sat* (Be-ness), which is without a second, which is bliss and which is *Māyā*-less. It is different from characteristics of that expressed by the word "*Tvam*" (Thou) subject to *Upādhis* (vehicles), or the characteristics of '*That*' expressed by the word "*Tat*" subject to *Upādhis*. It is itself differenceless and is seen as the Seat of everything. It is the pure, the noumenal the true and the indestructible.

And what is *Satya* (the true) ?

It is the Sat (Be-ness) which is the aim pointed out by the Vedas. It is that which cannot be said to be *Asat* (non-Be-less). It is that which is not affected by the three periods of time. It is that which continues to exist during the three periods of time. It is that which continues to exist during the three periods of time. It is that which is. It is one without a second. It has not the differences of similarity or dissimilarity; or it is that which is the source of all ideas. It is that which does not perish even though space, time, matter, cause, etc., perish.

And what is *Jñāna* (wisdom) ?

It is self-light. It is that which illuminates all. It is that Absolute Consciousness which is without any obscuration. It is that Consciousness which has no beginning or end, which is perpetual and which is the witness to all modifications and their opposites.

And what is *Ananta* (the eternal) ?

It is that which is without origin and destruction. It is that which is not subject to the six changes (*viz.*, birth, growth, manhood, decay, old age and death). It is free from all *Upādhis*. It is that Consciousness which, being all full and without destruction, permeates the created universe composed of *Avyakta* and others, like the earth in the modifications of clay, the gold in the modifications of gold. and thread in the modifications of thread.

And what is *Ānanda* (bliss) ?

It is the seat of all sentient beings, like the ocean of the water, is eternal, pure, partless and non-dual, and is the sole essence of *Cidānanda* (consciousness-bliss).

11. Of how many kinds are substances ?

There are three kinds, *Sat* (Bee-ness), *Asat* (not-Be-ness) and *Mithyā* (Illusion).

Sat alone is *Brahman*. *Asat* is that which is not. *Mithyā* is the illusory ascription to *Brahman* of the universe that is not.

What is fit to be known is *Brahman*, the *Ātmā* alone.

Brahma-Jñāna is the rooting out of all— bodies and such like— that are not Self, and the merging in *Brahman*, the *Sat*. The universe of *Ākāśa* and others including *Jīva* is not-*Ātmā*.

12. What is *Māyā* ?

The root of this not-*Ātmā* is *Māyā*. She appears in *Brahman* life clouds, etc., in the sky. She has no beginning but has an end. She is subject to proof and not-proof. She neither is; nor is not; nor is she a combination of both (*Sat* and *Asat*). Her seat is indescribable. She has the varieties of differences as extolled by the wise. It is she that truly is not. Her nature is *Ajñāna*. She appears as *Mūlaprakṛti*[1], *Guṇa-Sāmya* (a state where the three *Guṇas* are found in equilibrium), *Avidyā* (Nescience) and other forms, transforming herself into the form of the universe. Thus does a knower of *Brahman* cognize her.

Thus ends the Upaniṣad

1. This refers to that slumbering or latent state of the universe—called also *Mahā-Suṣupṭi* when the *Guṇas* are in equilibrium; on re-awakening into activity when the *Guṇas* are disturbed, *Mūlaprakṛti* is called by the different names of *Māyā*, *Avidhyā*, *Tamas*, etc.

Nirālamba[1]-Upaniṣad

OF

ŚUKLA-YAJURVEDA

Hariḥ-Om. I shall relate in the form of a catechism whatever should be known for the removal of all miseries that befall these ignorant creatures (men).

What is *Brahman*? Who is *Īśvara*? Who is *Jīva*? What is *Prakṛti*? Who is *Paramātma*? Who is *Brahmā*? Who is *Viṣṇu*? Who is *Rudra*? Who is *Indra*? Who is *Yama*? Who is *Sūrya*? Who is *Candra*? Who are *Devas*? Who are *Rākṣasas* ? Who are *Piśācas*? Who are *Manuṣyas*? Who are Women? Who are *Paśus*, etc.? What is *Sthāvara*? Who are *Brāhmaṇas* and others? What is *Jāti* (caste)? What is *Karma*? What is *Akarma*? What is *Jñāna*? What is *Ajñāna*? What is *Sukha*? What is *Duḥkha*? What is *Svarga*? What is *Naraka*? What is *Bandha*? What is *Mokṣa*? Who is *Upāsya*? Who is *Vidvān*? Who is *Mūḍha*? What is *Āsura*? What is *Tapas*? What is *Paramapada*? What is *Grāhya*? What is *Agrāhya*? Who is *Sannyāsi*? Thus are the questions.

1. What is *Brahman*?

It is the *Caitanya* that appears, through the aspects of *Karma* and *Jñāna*, as this vast mundane egg composed of *Mahat*' *Ahaṁkāra* and the five elements, earth, water, fire, *Vāyu* and *Ākāśa*— that is secondless—that is devoid of all *Upādhis* [vehicles], that is full of all *Śaktis* [potencies], that is without beginning and end, that is described as pure, beneficial, peaceful, and *Guṇa*-less and that is indescribable.

2. Who is *Īśvara*? and what are His characteristics? *Brahman* itself, having through His *Śakti* called *Prakṛti* (matter) created the worlds and being latent in them, becomes the ruler of *Buddhi* and *Indriyas* (organs of sense and action) as well as Brahmā (the creator) and others, Hence he is named *Īśvara*.

3. Who is *Jīva*?

Īśvara Himself, subject to the false superimposition upon Himself [or the idea] "I am the gross" through the [assumption of the] names and forms of Brahmā, Viṣṇu, Rudra, Indra, and others is *Jīva*s Though one, he appears as many *Jīvas*, through the force of the different *Karmas* originating the bodies.

4. What is *Prakṛti* (matter)?

---

1. Lit,—without support.

It is nothing else but the *Śakti* [potency] of *Brahman* which is of the nature of *Buddhi* that is able to produce the many motley worlds by virtue of the mere presence of *Brahman*.

5. What is *Paramātmā*? The supreme *Ātmā* or soul.

It is *Brahman* alone that is *Paramātmā* as it (the former) is far superior to bodies and others.

6. Who is *Brahmā* [the creator]?
7. Who is *Viṣṇu* [the preserver]?
8. Who is *Rudra* [the destroyer]?
9. Who is *Indra*?
10. Who is *Yama* [the angel of death]?
11. Who is *Sūrya* [the Sun]?
12. Who is *Candra* [the Moon]?
13. Who are *Devas* [the Angels]?
14. Who are *Asuras* [the Demons]?
15. Who are *Piśācas* [the evil spirits]?
16. Who are *Manuṣyas* [the men]?
17. Who are women?
18. What are beasts, etc.?
19. What are the *Sthāvaras* [fixed ones]?
20. Who are *Brāhmaṇas* and others?

That *Brahman* is Brahmā, Vishṇu, Rudra and Indra, Yama, Sun and Moon, Devas, Asuras, Piśācas, men, women, beasts, etc., the fixed ones, Brāhmans and others. Here there is no manyness in the least degree: all this is verily *Brahman*.

21. What is *Jāti* (caste)

It cannot refer to the skin, the blood, the flesh or the bone. There is no caste for *Ātmā*; caste is only conventional.

22. What is *Karma*?

Karma is that action alone which is performed by the organs and ascribed to *Ātmā*; as "I do" (*viz.*, agency being attributed to *Ātmā*).

23. What is *Akarma* [or non-*Karma*]?

Akarma is the performance, without any desire for the fruits, of the daily and occasional rites, sacrifices, vows, austerities, gifts and other actions that are associated with the egoism of the actor and the enjoyer, and that are productive of bondage, rebirth, etc.

24. What is *Jñāna*?

It is the realisation by direct cognition of the fact that in this changing universe there is nothing but *Caitanya* [the one life] that is Consciousness, that is of the form of the seer and the seen, pervading all things, that is the same in all, and that is not subject to changes like pot, cloth, etc. This realisation is brought about by means of the subjugation of the body and the senses, the serving of a good *Guru* (teacher), the hearing of the exposition of Vedāntic doctrines and constant meditation thereon.

25. What is *Ajñāna*?

It is the illusory attribution, like the snake in the rope, of many *Ātmās* (souls) through the diverse *Upādhis* [or vehicles] of the angels, beasts, men, the fixed ones, females, males, castes and orders of life, bondage and emancipation, etc., to *Brahman* that is secondless, all-permeating and of the nature of all.

26. What is *Sukha* (happiness)?

It is a state of being of the nature of bliss, having cognized through experience the Reality of *Saccidānanda* [or that which is be-ness, consciousness and bliss].

27. What is *Duḥkha* (pains)?

It is the mere *Saṅkalpa* [or the thinking] of the objects of mundane existence [or of not-Self according to the Bombay Edition].

28. What is *Svarga* (heaven)?

It is the association with *Sat* [either good men or *Brahman* which is *Sat*, the true].

29. What is *Naraka* (hell)?

It is association with that which brings about this mundane existence which is *Asat* [the false].

30. What is *Bandha* [bondage]?

Such *Saṅkalpas* [thoughts] as "I was born," etc., arising from the affinities of beginningless *ajñāna* from bondage.

The thought obscuration [or mental ignorance] of the mundane existence of "mine" in such as father, mother, brother, wife, child, house, gardens, lands, etc., are bondages.

The thought of I-ness as actor, etc., are bondage.

The thought of the development in oneself of the eight *siddhis* (higher psychical powers) as *Aṇimā* and others[1] is bondage.

The thought of propitiating the angels, men, etc., bondage.

The thought of going through the eight means of Yoga[2] practice, *Yama*, etc., is bondage.

The thought of performing the duties of one's own caste and order of life is bondage.

The thought that command, fear and doubt are the attributes of [or pertain to] *Ātmā* is bondage.

The thought of knowing the rules of performing sacrifices, vows, austerity and gift is bondage. Even the mere thought of desire for *Mokṣa* (emancipation) is bondage. By the very act of thought, bondage is caused.

31. What is *Mokṣa* [emancipation]?

Mokṣa is the (state of) the annihilation, through the discrimination of the eternal from the non-eternal, of all thoughts of bondage, like those of "mine" in objects of pleasure and pain, lands, etc., in this transitory mundane existence.

---

1. There are 18 siddhis, 8 higher and 10 lower.
2. They are *Yama, Niyama*, etc.

32. Who is *Upāsya* [or fit to be worshipped]?

That *Guru* (or spiritual instructor) who enables (the disciple) to attain to *Brahman*, the Consciousness that is in all bodies.

33. Who is *Śisya* (the disciple)?

The disciple is that *brahman* alone that remains after the consciousness of the universe has been lost (in him) through Brāhmic wisdom.

34. Who is *Vidvān* (the learned)?

It is he who has cognized the true form (or reality) of his own consciousness that is latent in all.

35. Who is *Mūḍha* [the ignorant]?

He who has the egoistic conception of the body, caste, orders of life, actor, enjoyer and others.

36. What is *Āsura* [the demoniacal]?

It is the *Tapas* [austerity] practised by one inflicting trouble on the *Ātmā* within through *Japa* (or inaudible muttering of *Mantras*], abstinence from food, *Agnihotra* [the performance of the worship of fire], etc., attended with cruel desire, hatred, pain, hypocrisy and the rest for the purpose of acquiring the powers of Viṣṇu, Brahmā, Rudra, Indra and others.

37. What is *Tapas*?

Tapas is the act of burning— through the fire of direct cognition of the knowledge that *Brahman* is the truth and the universe, a myth— the seed of the deep-rooted desire to attain the powers of Brahmā, etc.

38. What is *Paramapada* [the supreme abode]?

It is the seat of the eternal and emancipated *brahman* which is far superior to *Prāṇas* (the vital airs), the organs of sense and actions, the internal organs (of thought), the *Guṇas* and others, which is of the nature of *Saccidānanda* and which is the witness to all.

39. What is *Grāhya* [or fit to be taken in]?

Only that Reality of Absolute Consciousness which is not conditioned by space, time or substance.

40. What is *Agrāhya*?

The thought that this universe is truth— this universe which is different from one's Self and which being subject to *Māyā* (or illusion) forms the object of (cognition of) *Buddhi* and the organs.

41. Who is the *Sannyāsī* [ascetic]?

A *Sannyāsī* is an ascetic who having given up all the duties of caste and orders of life, good and bad actions, etc., being freed from [the conception of] "I" and "mine" and having taken his refuge in *Brahman* alone, roams at large practising *Nirvikalpa Samādhi* and being firmly convinced of "I am *Brahman*" through the realisation of the meaning of such sacred (Vedic) sentences as "Thou are *That*" "All this is verily

Brahman" and "Here there is no manyness in the least". He only is an emancipated person. He only is fit to be adored. He only is a *Yogin*. He only a *Paramahaṁsa*. He only is an *Avadhūtc*. He only is a *Brahman*. Whoever studies the *Nirālamba-Upaniṣaḍ* becomes, through the grace of *Guru*, pure like fire. He becomes pure like *Vāyu* (air). He does not return. He is not born again: may he is not born again.

Such is the Upaniṣaḍ

Maitreya-Upaniṣad

OF

SĀMAVEDA

A King named *Bṛhadratha*, thinking this body to be impermanent and having acquired indifference (to objects), retired to the forest, leaving his eldest son to rule over (his) kingdom. With hands uplifted and eyes fixed on the sun, he performed a severe *Tapas* (or religious austerity). At the end of a thousand days, the Lord Śākāyanya Muni, a knower of *Ātmā*, who was like fire without smoke, and who was as scorching fire with his *Tejas* (spiritual lustre) approached (him) and addressed the King thus: "Rise, rise and choose a boon." The King prostrated before him and said: "O Lord, I am not an *Ātmavit* (or knower of *Ātmā*). Thou art a *Tattvavit*, we here, Please enlighten me about *Sattva* (the state of *Sat* or *Brahman*)." (To which the Muni replied thus: "O thou that art born of the race of *Ikṣ vāku*: To begin with, your question is difficult (or explanation) : do not question me. Ask for any other thing you desire." Thereupon the King touched the feet of *Śākāyanya* and recited the (following) verse:

"What is the use of these to me or any other? Oceans dry up Mountains sink down. The positions of *Dhruva* (the Polar Star) and of trees change. Earth is drowned. The *Suras* (angels) run away, leaving their (respective) places. (While such is the case), I am He in reality. Therefore of what avail to me is the gratification of desires since one who clings to the gratification of desires is found to return again and again to this *Saṁsāra* (mundane existence). Thou art able to extricate me (out of this *Saṁsāra*). I am drowned like a frog in a dry well. Thou art my refuge.

"O Lord! this body was the result of sexual intercourse. It is without wisdom; it is hell (itself). It came out through the urinary orifice. It is linked together by bones. It is coated over with flesh. It is bound by skin. It is replete with faeces, urine, *Vāyu* (air), bile, phlegm, marrow, fat, serum and many other impurities. O Lord ! to me in such a foul body (as this), thou art my refuge."

Thereupon Lord *Śākāyanya* was pleased and addressed the King thus: "O *Mahārāja*, *Bṛhadratha*, the flag of the *Ikṣvāku* race, thou art an *Ātmajñānī*. Thou art one that has done his duty. Thou art famous by the name of *Marut*." At which the King asked: "O Lord ! in what way, can you describe *Ātmā*?" To which he replied thus: "Sound, touch, and others which seem to be *Artha* (wealth) are in fact *Anartha* (evil). The *Bhūtātmā* (the lower Self) clinging to these never remembers the Supreme Seat.

Through *Tapas*, *Sattva* (quality) is acquired; through *Sattva*, a (pure) mind is acquired; and through mind, (*Parama-*) *Ātmā*, (the higher Self) is reached.Through attaining *Ātmā*, one gets liberation. Just as fire without fuel is absorbed into its own womb, so *Citta* (thought) through the destruction of its modifications is absorbed into its own womb (source). To a mind that has attained quiescence and truth, and which is not affected by sense-objects, the events that occur to it through the bondage of *Karma* are merely unreal. It is *Citta* alone that is *Saṁsāra*. It should be cleansed with effort. Whatever his *Citta* (Thinks), of that nature he becomes. This is an archaic mystery. With the purifying of *Citta*, one makes both good and bad *Karmas* to perish. One whose mind is thus cleansed attains the indestructible Bliss (through his own Self). Just as *Citta* become united with an object that comes across it, so why should not one (be released) from bondage, when one is united with *Brahman*. One should meditate in the middle of the lotus of the heart, *Parameśvara* (the highest Lord) who is the witness to the play of *Buddhi*, who is the object of supreme love, who is beyond the reach of mind and speech, who has no beginning or end, who is *Sat* alone being of the nature of light only, who is beyond meditation, who can neither be given up nor grasped (by the mind), who is without equal or superior, who is the permanent, who is of unshaken depth, who is without light or darkness, who is all-pervading, changeless and vehicleless, and who is wisdom of the nature of *Mokṣa* (salvation). I am He— that *Paramātmā* who is the eternal, the pure, the liberated, of the nature of wisdom, the true, the subtle, the all-pervading, the secondless, the ocean of bliss, and one that is superior to *Pratyagātmā* (the lower Self). There is no doubt about it. How will calamity *or bondage) approach me who am depending upon my own bliss in my heart, who have put to shame the ghost of desires, who look upon this universe as (but) a jugglery and who am not associated with anything. The ignorant with their observance of the castes and orders of life obtain their fruits according to their *Karmas*. Men who have given up all duties of castes, etc., rest content in the bliss on their own Self. The distinctions of caste and orders of life have divisions among them, have beginning and end, and are very painful. Therefore having given up all identification with sons and as well as body, one should dwell in that endless and most supreme Bliss."

Adhyāya II

Then Lord Maitreya went to *Kailāśa* and having reached it asked Him thus: "O Lord ! Please initiate me into the mysteries of the highest *Tattva*." To which Mahādeva replied: "The body is said to be a temple. The *Jīva* in it is Śiva alone. Having given up all the cost-off offerings of *Ajñāna*, one should worship Him with So'ham (I am He). The cognition of everything as non-different from oneself of *Jñāna* (wisdom).

Abstracting the mind from sensual objects is *Dhyāna* (meditation). Purifying the mind of its impurities is *Snāna* (bathing). The subjugation of the *Indriyas* (sensual organs) is *Śauca* (purification). One should drink the nectar of *Brahman* and beg food for maintaining the body. Having one (though) alone, he should live a solitary place without a second. The wise man should observe thus: then he obtains Absolution.

"This body is subject to birth and death. It is of the nature of the secretion of the father and mother. It is impure, being the seat of happiness and misery. (Therefore) bathing is prescribed for touching it. It is bound by the *Dhātus* (skin, blood, etc.), is liable to severe diseases, is a house of sins, is impermanent and is of changing appearance and size. (Therefore) bathing is prescribed for touching it. Foul matter is naturally oozing out always from the nine holes. It (body) contains bad odour and foul excrement. (Therefore) bathing is prescribed for touching it. It is connected (or tainted) with the child-birth impurity of the mother and is born with it. It is also tainted with death impurity. (Therefore) bathing is prescribed for touching it. (The conception of) "I and mine" is the odour arising from the besmeared dung and urine. The release from it is spoken of as the perfect purification. The (external) purification by means of water and earth is on account of the worldly. The destruction of the threefold affinities (of *Śāstras*, world and body) generates the purity for cleansing *Citta*. That is called the (real) purification which is done by means of the earth and water of *Jñāna* (wisdom) and *Vairāgya* (indifference to objects).

"The conception of *Advaita* (non-dualism) should be taken in as the *Bhikṣā* (alms-food); (but) the conception of *Dvaita* (dualism) should not be taken in. To a *Sannyāsī* (ascetic), *Bhikṣā* is ordained as dictated by the *Śāstra* and the *Guru*. After becoming a *Sannyāsī*, a learned man should himself abandon his native place and live at a distance, like a thief released from prison. When a person gives up *Ahaṁkāra* (I-am-ness) the son, wealth the brother, delusion the house, and desire the wife, there is no doubt that he is an emancipated person. Delusion, the mother is dead. Wisdom, the son is born. In this manner while two kinds of pollution have occurred, how shall we (the ascetics) observe the *Sandhyās* (conjunction periods)? The *Cit* (consciousness) of the sun is ever shining in the resplendent *Ākāśa* of the heart. He neither sets nor rises; while so, how shall we perform the *Sandhyās*? *Ekānta* (solitude) is that state of one without second as determined by the words of a *Guru*. Monasteries or forests are not solitudes. Emancipation is only for those who do not doubt. To those who doubt, there is no salvation even after many births. Therefore one should attain attain faith. (Mere) abandoning of the *Karmas* or of the *Mantras* uttered at the initiation of a *Sannyāsī* (ascetic) will not constitute *Sannyāsa*. The union of *Jīva* (*-Ātmā*) (the lower self) and *Parama* (*-Ātmā*) (the higher Self) at the two *Sandhis* (morning and evening) is termed *Sannyāsa*. Whoever has a nausea for all *Īśaṇā* (desires) and the rest as for vomited food, and is devoid of all affection for the body, is qualified for *Sannyāsa*. At the moment when indifference towards all objects arises in the mind, a learned person may take up *Sannyāsa*. Otherwise, he is fallen person. Whoever becomes a *Sannyāsī* on account of wealth, food, clothes and fame, becomes fallen in both (as a *Sannyāsī* and as householder); (then) he is not worthy of salvation.

"The thought of (contemplation upon) *Tattvas* is the transcendental one; that of the *Śāstras*, the middling, ant that of *Mantras*, the lowest. The delusion of pilgrimages is the lowest of the lowest. Like one, who, having seen in water the reflection of fruits in the branches of trees, tastes and enjoys them, the ignorant without self-congnition are in vain overjoyed with (as if they reached) *Brahman*. That ascetic is an emancipated person who does not abandon the internal alms-taking (*viz.,* the meditation upon the non-dual), generating *Vairāgya* as well as faith the wife, and wisdom the son. Those men (termed) great through wealth, age, and knowledge, are only servants to those that are great through their wisdom as also to their disciples. Those whose minds are deluded by My *Māyā*, however learned they may be, do not attain Me, the all-full *Ātmā*, and roam about like crows, simply for the purpose of filling up their belly, well burnt up (by hunger, etc.). For one that longs after salvation, the worship of images made of stone, metals, gem, or earth, is productive of rebirth and enjoyment. Therefore the ascetic should perform his own heart-worship alone, and relinquish external worship in order that he may not be born again. Then like a vessel full to its brim in an ocean, he is full within and full without. Like a vessel void in the ether, he is void within and void without. Do not become (or differentiate between) the *Ātmā* that knows or the *Ātmā* that is known. Do become of the form of that which remains, after having given up all thoughts. Relinquishing with their *Vāsanās* the seer, the seen and the visual, worship *Ātmā* alone, the resplendent supreme presence. That is the real supreme State wherein all *Saṅkalpas* (thoughts) are at rest, which resembles the state of a stone, and which is neither waking nor sleeping."

Adhyāya III

"I am "I" (the Self). I am also another (the not-Self). I am *Brahman*. I am the Source (of all things). I am also the *Guru* of all worlds. I am of all the worlds. I am He. I am Myself alone. I am *Siddha*. I am the Pure. I am the Supreme. I am. I am always He. I am the Eternal. I am stainless, I am *Vijñāna*. I am the Excellent. I am Soma. I am the All. I am without honour or dishonour. I am without *Guṇas* (qualities). I am Śiva (the auspicious). I am neither dual or non-dual. I am without the dualities (of heat or cold, etc.) I am He. I am neither existence nor non-existence. I am without language. I am the Shining. I am the Glory of void and non-void. I am the good and the bad. I am Happiness. I am without grief. I am

Caitanya. I am equal (in all). I am the like and the non-like. I am the eternal, the pure, and the ever felicitous. I am without all and without not all. I am *Sāttvika*. I am always existing. I am without the number one. I am without the number two. I am without the difference of *Sat* and *Asat*. I am without *Saṅkalpa*. I am without the difference of manyness. I am the form of immeasurable Bliss. I am one that exist not. I am the one that is not another. I am without body, etc. I am with asylum. I am without asylum. I am without support. I am without bondage or emancipation. I am pure *Brahma*. I am He. I am without *Citta*, etc. I am the supreme and the Supreme of the supreme. I am ever of the form of deliberation and yet am without deliberation. I am He. I am of the nature of the *Akāra* and *Ukāra* as also of *Makāra*. I am the earliest. The contemplator and contemplatior I am without. I am One that cannot be contemplated upon.

Am He. I have full form in all. I have the characteristics on *Saccidānanda*. I am of the form of places of pilgrimages. I am the higher Self and Śiva. I am neither the thing defined nor non-defined. I am the non-absorbed Essence. I am not the measurer, the measure or the measured. I am Śiva. I am not the universe. I am the Seer of all. I am without the eyes, etc. I am the full grown. I am the Wise. I am the quiescent. I am the Destroyer. I am without any sensual organs. I am the doer of all actions. I am One that is content with all *Vedāntas* (either books or *Ātmic* Wisdom). I am the easily attainable. I have the name of one that is pleased as well as one that is not. I am the fruits of all silence. I am always of the form of *Cinmātra* (Absolute consciousness). I am always *Sat* (Be-ness) and *Cit* (Consciousness). I am one that has not anything in the least. I am not one that has not anything in the least. I am without the heart-Granthi (knot). I am the Being in the middle of the lotus. I am without the six changes. I am without the six sheaths and without the six enemies. I am within the within. I am without place and time. I am of the form of happiness having the quarters as My garment. I am the emancipated One. Without bondage. I am without the "no". I am of the form of the partless. I am the partless. I have *Citta*, though released from the universe. I am without the universe. I am of the form of all light. I am the Light (*Jyotis*) in *Cinmātra* (Absolute Consciousness). I am free from the three periods (of time past, present, and future). I am without desires. I am without body. I am One that has no body. I am *Guṇaless*. I am alone. I am without emancipation. I am the emancipated One. I am ever without emancipation. I am without truth or untruth. I am always One that is not different from *Sat* (Be-ness). I have no place to travel. I have no going, etc. I am always of the same form. I am the Quiescent. I am *Puruṣottama* (the Lord of Souls). There is no doubt that he who has realised himself thus is Myself. Whoever hears (this) once becomes himself *Brahman*, yea, he comes himself *Brahman*. Thus is the *Upaniṣad*."

Kaivalya[1]-Upaniṣad

OF

KṚṢNA-YAJURVEDA

Hariḥ-Om. Then[2] *Āśvalāyana* went to Lord *Parameṣṭī* (Brahmā) and addressed Him thus: "Please initiate me into *Brahmavidyā* (Divine Wisdom), which is the most excellent, which is ever enjoyed by the wise, which is mystic, and by which the learned, after having soon freed themselves from all sins, reach *Puruṣa*, the Supreme of the supreme."

To him the Grandfather (thus) replied: "Know (It) through *Śraddhā* (faith), *Bhakti* (devotion), *Dhyāna* (meditation), and *Yoga*. Persons attain salvation not through *Karma*, progeny or wealth but through *sannyāsa* (renunciation) alone. Ascetics of pure mind through (the realisation of) the meaning well-ascertained by *Vedānta-Vijñāna* and through *Saṁnyāsa-Yoga* enter into That which is above *Svaṛga* (heaven) and is in the cave (of the heart). They all attain *Paramātmā* in the *Brahma*-world and are (finally) emancipated.

"Being seated in a pleasant posture in an unfrequented place with a pure mind, and with his neck, head, and body erect, having given up the duties of the (four) orders of life, having subjugated all the organs, having saluted his *Guru* with devotion, having looked upon the heart (-lotus) as being free from *Rajoguṇa* and as pure, and having contemplated in its (heart's) centre *Parameśvara* who is always with His consort *Umā*, who is pure and free from sorrow, who is unthinkable and invisible, who is of endless forms, who is of the nature of happiness, who is very quiescent, who is of the form of emancipation, who is the source of *Māyā*, who has no beginning, middle or end, who is One, who is All-Pervading, who is *Cidānanda* (Consciousness-Bliss), who is formless, who is wonderful, who is the Lord (of all), who has three eyes, who has a blue neck, (*Nīlakaṇṭha*), and who is serenity (itself)— the Muni attains *Paramātmā*, the womb of all elements, the All Witness, and above *Tamas*. He only is Brahmā. He only is Śiva. He only is Indra. He only is the indestructible. He only is the Supreme. He only is the Self-Shining. He only is Viṣṇu. He only is *Prāṇa*. He only is Time. He only is *Agni* (fire). He only is the moon. He only is all things that exist or will hereafter exist. He only is eternal. Having known Him, one crosses death. There is no other path to

---

1. Lit., isolation-or emancipation-*Upaniṣad*.
2. After attaining *Sādhana-Catuṣṭaya* or the four means of salvation.
3. *Hiraṇyagarbha* or the higher Self.

salvation. He only attains *Parabrahman* who sees in himself all elements and himself in all elements. There is no other means. Having constituted his body an *Araṇi* (the lower attritional piece of wood) and *praṇava* (*Om*), the upper *Araṇi*, a wise man burns *Ajñāna* by the churning of meditation.

"It is only He (*Paramātmā*) who, deluded by *Māyā*, assumes a body with the internal organs and does everything. It is only He who in the waking state is gratified with women, food, drink, and other diverse enjoyments. In the dreaming state, the *Jīva* enjoys pleasures and pains in the several worlds which are created by His *Māyā*. In the dreamless sleeping state when all are absorbed, He, replace with *Tamas*, attains the state of happiness. Then through the force of the *Karmas* of previous births, the *Jīva* again wakes up and goes to sleep. All the diversified objects (of the universe) emanate from the *Jīva*, who sports in the three bodies (gross, subtle and casual). The three bodies are finally absorbed in Him who is the source of all, who is Bliss, and who is Absolute Wisdom. From Him, arise *Prāṇa*. *Manas*, all the organs of sense and action *Ākāśa*, *Vāyu*, *Agni*, water and earth supporting all. *Parabrahman*, which is of all forms, which is the Supreme Abode of this universe, which is the most subtle of the subtle and which is eternal, is only yourself. You are only That. One who knows himself to be that *Parabrahman* that shines as the universe in the waking, dreaming, dreamless and other states, will be relieved from all bondage. I am that *Sadāśiva*, (or the eternal happiness) who is other than the enjoyer, the enjoyed, and the enjoyment in the three seats (or bodies), and who is witness and *cinmātra*. All emanate from me alone. All exist in Me alone. All merge into Me alone. I am that non-dual *Brahman*. I am the atom of atoms; so am I the biggest (of all). I am this diversified universe. I am the oldest of all. I am *Puruṣa*. I am *Īśa* (the Lord). I am of the form of *Jyotis* (light) and of the form of happiness. I have neither hands nor feet. I have power unthinkable. I see without eyes. I hear without ears. I am omniscient. I have one kind of form only. None is able to know Me fully. I am always of the form of *Cit*. I am the One that should be known through all the Vedas. I am the *Guru* who revealed the *Vedānta*. I am only He who knows the true meaning of *Vedānta*. I have no sins or virtues. I have no destruction. I have no birth, body, organs of sense or action, or *Buddhi*. To me there is no earth water or fire. There is no *Vāyu*; there is no *Ākāśa*. He who thinks *Paramātmā* as being in the cave (of the heart), as having no form, as being secondless, as being the witness of all and as being neither *Sat* nor *Asat*, attains the pure form of *Paramātmā*.

"Whoever recites this *Upaniṣad* belonging to *Yajurveda* he becomes as pure as *Agni* (fire). He becomes purified from the sins of theft of gold. He becomes purified from the sins of drinking alcohol. He becomes purified from the sins of murder of a *Brahman*. He becomes purified from the sins of commission (of those that ought not to be done) and the sins of omission (of those that ought to be done). Therefore he becomes a follower of *Brahman*. Were one who has stepped beyond the duties of the four orders of life to recite (this *Upaniṣad*) always or even once, he acquires the wisdom that destroys the ocean of *Saṁsāra*. Therefore having known Him, he attains the *Kaivalya* State (or state of isolation or emancipation)— yea, he attains the *Kaivalya* State."

Om-Tat-Sat

Amṛtabindu[1]-Upaniṣad

OF

KṚṢṆA-YAJURVEDA

Om. *Manas* (mind) is said to be of two kinds, the pure and the impure. That which is associated with the thought of desire is the impure, while that which is without desire is the pure. To men, their mind alone is the cause of bondage or emancipation. That mind which is attracted by objects of sense tends to bondage, while that which is not so attracted tends to emancipation. Now inasmuch as to a mind without a desire for sensual objects there is stated to be salvation, therefore an aspirant after emancipation should render his mind ever free from all longing after material objects. When a mind freed from the desires for objects and controlled in the heart attains the reality of *Ātmā*. Then is it in the Supreme Seat. Till that which arises in the heart perishes, till then it (*Manas*) should be controlled. This only is (true) wisdom. This only is true *Dhyāna* (meditation). Other ways are but long or tedious. It (*Brahman*) is not at all one that can be contemplated upon. It is not one that cannot be contemplated upon. It is not capable of contemplation, (and yet) it should be contemplated upon. Then one attains *Brahman* that is devoid of partiality. *Yoga* should be associated with *Svara* (sound, accent). (*Brahman*) should be meditated upon without *Svara*. By meditating without *Svara* upon *Brahman*, that which is cannot become non-existent. Such a *Brahman* is partless, devoid of fancy and quiescent (or free from the action of mind). Whoever cognizes "I" to be that *Brahman* attains certainly *Brahman*. A wise man having known that *Brahman*, that is without fancy, without and without cause, or example, beyond inference and without beginning, is emancipated. There is (for him then) no destruction, no creation, no person in bondage, no devotee, no aspirant for salvation, no emancipated person. This is the truth. *Ātmā* that should be contemplated upon is One is (the three states), the waking, the dreaming, and the dreamless sleep. There is no rebirth to him who goes beyond the three states. The one *Bhūtātmā* of all beings is in all beings. Like the moon (reflected) in water, he appears as one and as many. While a pot is being carried (from one place to another), the *Ākāśa* (ether) that is within it is not carried (along with it). As the pot alone is carried, *Jīva* (within the body) may be likened to the *Ākāśa*. Like the pot, the body has various kinds of forms. The body which perishes again and again is not conscious of its own destruction. But he (the *Jīva*) knows (it)

---

1. Lit., the immortal germ.

always. He who is enveloped by the *Māyā* of sound, is never able to come to (or see) the sun (of *Parabrahman*) from the darkness (of ignorance). Should such darkness be cleared, then he alone sees the non-dual state. *Parabrahman* is *Śabdākṣara*[1]. What remains after the cessation of *Śabda*-Vedas, that is *Akṣara*. (indestructible), should be meditated upon by a learned man who wishes to secure quiescence to his *Ātmā*.

Two *Vidyās* (sciences) are fit to be known, *viz.*, *Śabdabrahman* and *Parabrahman*. One who has completely mastered *Śạbdabrahman* attains *Parabrahman*. Having studies well the books, the learned man should perservere studiously in *Jñāna* (the acquisition of knowledge) and *Vijñāña* (Self-realisation according to such knowledge). Then he should discard the whole of the books, as a person in quest of grain gives up the straw. Though there are cows of different colours, yet their milk is of the same colour. Like milk is seen *Jñāna*, and like cows are seen the different kinds of forms (in the universe). As ghee is latent in milk, so is *Vijñāña* (Self-realisation) latent in every being. Through churning always the *Manas* with the churning-stick of *Manas* and the string of *Jñāna*, *Parabrahman* that is partless, calm and quiescent should be brought out like fire from the wood. I am the *Brahman*. That *Vāsudeva* who is support of all beings, who lives in all and who protects all creatures is Myself. That *Vāsudeva* is Myself.

Such is the *Upaniṣad*.

Om-Tat-Sat

1. It is the indestructible known through the sound or the Vedas.

Ātmabodha[1]-Upaniṣad

OF

ṚGVEDA

Om. Prostrations of Nārāyaṇa wearing conch, discus, and mace,[2] by whom the *Yogī* is released from the bondage of the cycle of rebirth through the utterance of Him who is of the form of *Praṇava*, the *Om*, composed of the three letters A, U, and M, who is the uniform bliss and who is the *Brahmapuruṣa* (all-pervading *Puruṣa*). *Om*. Therefore the reciter of the *Mantra* "*Om-namo-Nārāyaṇa*" reaches the *Vaikuṇṭha* world. It is the heart-*Kamala* (lotus), *viz.*, the city of *Brahman*. It is effulgent like lightning, shining like a lamp. It is *Brahmaṇya* (the presider over the city of *Brahman*) that is the son of *Devakī*. It is *Brahmaṇya* that is *Madhusūdna* (the killer of *Madhu*). It is *Brahmaṇya* that is *Puṇḍarīkākṣa* (lotus-eyed). It is *Brahmaṇya*, Viṣṇu that is acyuta (the indestructible). He who meditates upon that sole Nārāyaṇa who is latent in all beings, who is the causal *Puruṣa*, who is causeless, who is *Parabrahman*, the *Om*, who is without pains and delusion and who is all-pervading— that person is never subject to pains. From the dual, he becomes the fearless non-dual. Whoever sees this (world) as manifold (with the difference of I, you, he, etc.), passes from death to death. In the centre of the heart-lotus is *Brahman*, which is the All, which has *Prājña* as Its eye and which is established in *Prajñāna*[3] alone. To creatures, *Pranjñāna* is the eye of *Prājña* is the seat. It is *Prajñāna* alone that is *Brahman*. A person who meditates (thus), leaves this world through *Prajñāna*, the *Ātmā* and ascending attains all his desires in the Supreme *Svarga* deathless. Oh! I pray Thee, place me in that nectar-everflowing unfailing world where *Jyotis* (the light) always shines and where one is revered. (There is no doubt) he attains nectar also. *Om-namaḥ*.

I am without *Māyā*. I am without compare. I am solely the thing that is of the nature of wisdom. I am without *Ahaṁkāra* (I-am-ness). I am without the difference of the universe, *Jīva* and *Īśvara*. I am the Supreme that is not different from *Pratyagātmā* (individual (*Ātmā*). I am with ordinances and prohibitions destroyed without remainder. I am with

---

1. This *Upaniṣad* treats of Ātomic instruction.
2. The three symbols stand for *Ākāśa*, *manas*, and *Buddhi*.
3. In the *Māṇḍūkya upaniṣad*, *Prajñā* is said to be the *Jīva* in the third state and *Prajñāna* is its attribute. *Prajñāna* is *Prakarṣa Jñāna* or special wisdom, *viz.*, of looking over the past and the future.

Āśramas (observances of life) well given up. I am of the nature of the vast and all-full wisdom. I am one that is witness and without desire. I reside in My glory alone. I am without motion. I am without old age— without destruction— without the differences of My party or another. I have wisdom as chief essence. I am the mere ocean of bliss called salvation. I am the subtle. I am without change. I am *Ātmā* merely, without the illussion of qualities. I am the Seat devoid of the three *Guṇas*. I am the cause of the many worlds in (My) stomach. I am the *Kūtastha-Caitanya* (supreme Cosmicmind). I am of the form of the *Jyotis* (light) free from motion. I am not one that can be known by inference. I alone am full. I am of the form of the stainless salvation. I am without limbs or birth. I am the essence which is *Sat* itself. I am of the nature of the true wisdom without limit. I am the state of excellent happiness. I am One that cannot be differentiated. I am the all-pervading and without stain. I am the limitless and endless *Sattva* alone. I am fit to be known through *Vedānta.* I am the one fit to be worshipped. I am the heart of all the worlds. I am replete with Supreme Bliss. I am of the nature of happiness, which is Supreme Bliss. I am pure, secondless, and eternal. I am devoid of beginning. I am free from the three bodies (gross, subtle, and causal). I am of the nature of wisdom. I am the emancipated One. I have a wondrous form. I am free from impurity I am the One latent (in all). I am the equal *Ātmā* of eternal *Vijñāna*. I am the refined Supreme Truth. I am of the nature of Wisdom-Bliss alone.

Through I cognize as the secondless *Ātmā* by means of discriminative wisdom and reason, yet is found the relation between bondage and salvation. Though to Me the universe is gone, yet it shines as true always. Like the truth in the (illusory conception of a) snake, etc., in the rope, so the truth of *Brahman* alone is, and is the substratum on which this universe is playing. Therefore the universe is not. Just as sugar is found permeating all the sugar-juice (from which the sugar is extracted), so I am full in the three worlds in the form of the non-dual *Brahman*. Like the bubbles waves, etc., in the ocean, so all beings, from Brahmā down to worm, are fashioned in Me; just as the ocean does not long after the motion of the waves, so to Me, there is no longing after sensual happiness, being Myself of the form of (spiritual) Bliss. Just as in a wealthy person the desire for poverty does not arise, so in Me who am immersed in Brāhmic Bliss, the desire for sensual happiness cannot arise. An intelligent person who sees both nectar and poison rejects poison; so having cognized *Ātmā*. I reject those that are not *Ātmā*. The sun that illuminates the pot (both within and without) is not destroyed with the destruction of the pot; so the *Sākṣhī* (witness) that illuminates the body is not destroyed with the destruction of the body. To Me there is no bondage; there is no salvation, there are no books, there is no *Guru*; for these shine through *Māyā* and I have crossed them and am secondless. Let *Prāṇas* (vital airs) according to their laws be fluctuating. Let *Manas* (mind) be blown about by desire. How can pains affect me who am by nature full of Bliss? I have truly known *Ātmā*. My *Ajñāna* has fled away. The egoism of actorship has left Me. There is nothing I should yet do. *Brahman*'s duties, family. Gotra (clan), name, beauty, and class— all these belong to the gross body and not to Me who am without any mark (of body). Inertness, love, and joy— these attributes appertain to causal body and not to Me, who am eternal and of changeless nature. Just as an owl sees darkness only in the sun, so a fool sees only darkness in the self-shining Supreme Bliss. Should the clouds screen the eyesight a fool thinks there is no sun; so an embodied person full of *Ajñāna* thinks there is no *Brahman*. Just as nectar which is other than poison does not commingle with it, so I, who am different from inert matter, do not mix with its stains. As the light of a lamp, however small, dispels immense darkness, so wisdom, however slight makes *Ajñāna*, however immense, to perish. Just as (the delusion) of the serpent does not exist in the rope in all the three periods of time (past, present, and future), so the universe from *Ahaṁkāra*. (down) to body does not exist in Me who am the non-dual One. Being of the nature of consciousness alone, there is not inertness in Me. Being of the nature of Truth, there is not non-truth to me. Being of the nature of Bliss, there is not sorrow in Me. It is through *Ajñāna* that the universe shines as truth.

Whoever recites this *Ātmabodha-Upaniṣad* for *Muhūrta* (48 minutes) is not born again— Yea, is not born again.

Thus ends the Upaniṣad

Skanda[1]-Upaniṣad

OF

KṚṢṆA-YAJURVEDA

Om. O Mahādeva (Lord of Devas), I am indestructible through a small portion of Thy grace. I am replete with *Vijñāna*. I am Śiva (Bliss). What is higher than It? Truth does not shine as such on account of display of the *antaḥkaraṇa* (internal organs). Through the destruction of the *antaḥkaraṇa*, Hari abides as *Samvit* (Consciousness) alone. As I also am of the form of *Samvit*. I am without birth. What is higher than It? All inert things being other (than *Ātmā*) perish like dream. That acyuta (the indestructible or Viṣṇu), who is the seer of the conscious and the inert, is of the form of *Jñāna*. He only is Mahādeva. He only is *Mahā-Hari* (*Mahā-Viṣṇu*). He only is the *Jyotis* of all *Jyotis* (or Light of all lights). He only is Parameśvara. He only is *Parabrahman*. That *Brahman* I am. There is no doubt (about it). *Jīva* is Śiva. Śiva is *Jīva*. That *Jīva* is Śiva alone. Bound by husk, it is paddy; freed from husk, it is rice. In like manner *Jīva* is bound (by *karma*). If *karma* perishes, he (*Jīva*) is *Sadāśiva*. So long as he is bound by the bonds of *karma*, he is *Jīva*. If freed from its bonds, then he is *Sadāśiva*. Prostrations on account of Śiva who is of the form of Viṣṇu, and on account of Viṣṇu who is of the form of Śiva. The heart of Viṣṇu is Śiva. The heart of Śiva is Viṣṇu. As I see no difference[2] (between these two), therefore to me are prosperity and life. There is no difference— between Śiva and *Keśava* (Viṣṇu). The body is said to be the divine temple. The Śiva (in the body) is the God *Sadāśiva*[3] (in the temple).

Having given up the cast-off offerings of *ajñāna*, one should worship Him with the thought "I am He". To see (oneself) as not different (from Him) is (*jñāna*) wisdom. To make the mind free from sensual objects is *dhyāna* (meditation). The giving up of the stains of the mind is *Snāna* (bathing). The subjugation of the senses is *śouca* (cleansing). The nectar of *Brahman* should be drunk. For the upkeep of the body, one should go about for alms and eat. He should dwell alone in a solitary place without a second. He should be with the sole thought of the non-dual One. The wise

---

1. Skanda is the son of Śiva and is represented on earth by *Sanatkumāra*.
2. This will give a rude shock to the followers of Śiva and Viṣṇu in India, who wage useless war as to the supremacy of Viṣṇu and Śiva.
3. *Sadāśiva*, lit., eternal bliss. This is one of the names applied to Śiva as also Mahādeva,

person who conducts himself thus, attains salvation. Prostrations on account of *Sarīmat Param-Jyotis* (Supreme Light) abode ! May prosperity and long life attend (me). O *Narasiṁha*![1] O Lord of Devas ! through Thy grace, persons cognize the true nature of *Brahman* that is unthinkable, undifferentiated, endless, and immutable, through the forms of the Gods, Brahmā, Nārāyaṇa, and Śaṅkara.

Like the eye (which sees without any obstacle the things) spread in the *ākāśa* so the wise always see the supreme abode of Viṣṇu. *Brahmans* with divine eyes who are always spiritually awake, praise in diverse ways and illuminate the supreme abode of Viṣṇu. Thus is the teaching of the Vedas for salvation.

Thus is the Upaniṣad

1. *Narasiṁha*, Lit., Man-lion. This refers to one of the incarnations of Viṣṇu when he killed the evil power *Hiraṇyakasipu*.

Paiṅgala-Upaniṣad[1]

OF

ŚUKLA-YAJURVEDA

Adhyāya-I

Om. *Paiṅgala*, having served under Yājñavalkya for twelve years, asked him to initiate him into the supreme mysteries of *Kaivalya*. To which *Yājñavalkya* replied thus : "O gentle one, at first, this (universe) was *Sat* (Bee-ness) only. It (*Sat*) is spoken of as *Brahman* which is ever free (from the trammels of matter), which is changeless, which is Truth, Wisdom, and Bliss, and which is full, permanent, and one only without a second. In It, was like a mirage in desert, silver in mother-of-pearl, a person in the pillar, of colour, etç., in the crystals, *mūlaprakṛti*, having in equal proportions the *guṇas*, red, white, and black, and being beyond the power of speech. That which is reflected in it is *Sākṣi-Caitanya* (lit., the witness-consciousness). It (*mūlalprakṛti*) undergoing again change becomes with the preponderance of *Śattva* (in it), *Āvaraṇa Śakti* names *avyakta*. That which is reflected in it (*Avyakta*) is *Īśvara-Caitanya*. He (*Īśvara*) has *Māyā* under his control, is omniscient, the original cause of creation, preservation, the dissolution, and the seed of this universe. He causes the universe which was latent in Him. To manifest itself through the bonds of *karma* of all creatures like a painted canvas unfurled. Again through the extinction of their *karmas*, he likes it disappear. In Him alone is latent all the universe, wrapped up like a painted cloth. Then from the supreme (*āvaraṇa*) *Śakti*, dependent on (or appertaining) to *Īśvara*, arose, through the preponderance of *Rajas*, *Vikṣepa*[4] *Śakti* called *Mahat*. That which is reflected in it is *Hiraṇyagarbha-Caitanya*. Presiding (as He does) over *Mahat*, He (*Hiraṇyagarbha*) has a body, both manifested and unmanifested. From *Vikṣepa Śakti* of *Hiraṇyagarbha* arose, through the preponderance of *Tamas*, the gross *Śakti* called *ahaṁkāra*. That which is reflected in it is *Virāṭ-Caitanya*. He (*Virāṭ*) presiding over it (*anaṁkara*) and possessing a manifested body becomes Viṣṇu, the chief *Puruṣa* and

---

1. This *Upaniṣad* so called after the questioner.
2. *Rajas*, *Sattya* and *Tamas* colours.
3. *Āvaraṇa*, *Śakti* literally means the veiling or contracting power. This is it that produces egoism. It may be called the centripetal force.
4. *Vikṣepa Śakti* (lit.,) is the expanding power, It may be called the centrifugal force.
5. The account given here though differing form that in other books may be justified.

protector of all gross bodies. From that *Ātmā* arose *ākāśa*; from *ākāśa* arose *vāyu*, from *vāyu agni*, from *agni apas*, and from apas *Pṛthivī*. The five *tanmātras* (rudimentary properties) alone are the *guṇas* (of the above five). That generating cause of the universe (*Īśvara*) wishing to create and having assumed *tamoguṇa*, wanted to convert the elements which were subtle *tanmātras* into gross ones. In order to create the universe, he divided into two parts each of those divisible elements; and having divided each moiety into four parts, made a fivefold mixture, each element having moiety of its own original element and one-fourth of a moiety of each of the other elements, and thus evolved out of the fivefold classified gross elements, the many myriads of *Brahmāṇḍas* (Brahmā's egg or macrocosm), the fourteen worlds pertaining to each sphere, and the spherical gross bodies (microcosm) fit for the (respective) worlds. Having divided the *Rajas*-essence of the five elements into four parts, He our of three such parts created (the five) *prāṇas* having fivefold function. Again out of the (remaining) fourth part, He created *Karmendryas* (the organs of action). Having divided their *Sattva*-essence into four parts, He out of three such parts created the *antaḥkaraṇa* (internal organ) having fivefold function. Out of the (remaining) fourth part of *Sattva*-essence, He created the *jñānendriyas* (organs of sense) Out of the collective totality of *Sattva*-essence, He created the *devatās* (deities) ruling over the organs of sense and actions. Those (*devatās*) He created. he located in the spheres (pertaining to them). They through His orders, began to pervade the macrocosm. Through His orders, *Viraṭ* associated with *ahaṁkāra* created all the gross things. Through His orders, *Hiraṇyagarbha* protected the subtle things. Without Him, they that were located in their spheres were unable to move or to do anything. Then he wished to infuse *Cetanā* (life) into them. Having pierced the *Brahmāṇḍa* (Brahmā's egg or macrocosm) and *brahmarandhras* (heads-fontanelle) in all the microcosmic heads, he entered within. Though they were (at first) inert, they were then able to perform *karmas* like beings of intelligence The omniscient *Īśvara* entered the microcosmic bodies with a particle of *Māyā* and being deluded by that *Māyā*, acquired the state of *Jīva*. Identifying the three bodies with Himself, He acquired the state of the actor and enjoyer. Associated with the attributes of the states of *Jāgrat*, *svapna*, *suṣupti*, trance, and death and being immersed in sorrow, he is (whirled about and) deluded like water-lift of potter's wheel, as if subject to birth and death.

Adhyāya II

Paiṅgala again addressed Yājñavalkya thus : "How did *Īśvara*, who is the creator, preserver, and destroyer and the Lord of all the worlds, acquire the state of *Jīva*?" To which Yājñavalkya replied : "I Shall tell in detail the nature of *Jīva* and *Īśvara*, together with a description of the

1. They are sound, touch, form, taste, and odour.

origin of the gross, subtle, and *Kāraṇa* (causal) bodies. Hear attentively with one-pointed mind.

"*Īśvara* having taken a small portion of the quintuplicated *mahābhūtas*, (the great elements), made in regular order the gross bodies, both collective and segregate. The skull, the skin, the intestines, bone, flesh, and nails are of the essence of *pṛthivī*. Blood, urine, saliva, sweat and others are of the essence of *āpas*. Hunger, thirst, heat, delusion, and copulation are of the essence of *agni*. Walking, lifting, breathing and others are of the essence of *vāyu*. Passion, anger, etc., are of the essence of *ākāśa*. The collection of these having touch and the rest is this gross body that is brought about by *karma*, that is the seat of egoism in youth and other states and that is the abode of many sins. Then he created *prāṇas* out of the collective three parts of *Rajas*-essence of the fivefold divided elements. The modifications of *prāṇa* are *prāṇa*, *apāna*, *vyāna*, *udāna*, and *samāna*; *nāga*, *kūrma*, *kṛkala*, *devadatta* and *dhanañjaya* are the auxiliary *prāṇas*. (Of the first five), the heart, anus, navel, throat and the whole body are respectively the seats. Then He created the *karmendriyas* out of the fourth part of the *Rajas-guṇa*. Of *ākāśa* and the rest the mouth, legs, hands, and the organs of secretion and excretion are the modifications. Talking, walking, lifting, excreting, and enjoying are their functions. Likewise out of the collective three parts of *Sattva*-essence, He created the *antaḥkaraṇa* (internal organ). *Antaḥkarana*,[1] *manas*, *buddhi*, *Citta*, and *ahaṁkāra* are the modifications. *Saṅkalpa* (thought), certitude, memory, egoism, and *anusandhāna* (inquiry) are their functions. Throat, face, navel,[2] heart, and the middle of the brow are their seats. Out of the (remaining) fourth part of *Sattva*-essence, He created the *Jñānendriyas* (organs of sense). Ear, skin, eyes, tongue, and nose are the modifications. Sound, touch, form, taste, and odour are their functions. *Dik* (the quarters), *Vāyu*, *Arka* (the sun), Varuṇa, *Aśvini Devas, Indra, Upendra, Mṛtyu* (the God of death), Prajāpati, the Moon, Viṣṇu, the four-faced Brahmā and Śambhu (Śiva) are the presiding deities of the organs. There are the five *kośas* (sheaths), *viz.*, *annamaya*, *prāṇamaya*, *manomaya*, *vijñānamaya*, and *ānandamaya*. *Annamaya*, sheath is that which is created and developed out of the essence of food, and is absorbed into the earth which is of the form of food. It alone is the gross body. The prāṇas with the *karmendriya* (organs of action) is the *prāṇamaya* sheath. *Manas* with the *jñānendriyas* (organs of sense) is the *manomaya* sheath. *Buddhi* with the *jñānendriyas* is the *vijñānamaya* sheath. These three sheaths constitute the *liṅgaśarīra* (or the subtle body). (That which tends to) the *ajñāna* (ignorance) of the Reality (of *Ātmā*) is the *ānandamaya* sheath. This is the *kāraṇa* body. moreover the five

---

1. The fifth aspect of *antaḥkaraṇa* is made to be itself, having the function of *anusandhāna* or inquiry through others call it otherwise.
2. Navel is the seat of *Citta*.

organs of sense, the five organs of action, the five *prāṇas* and others, the five *ākāśa* and other elements, the four internal organs, *avidyā*, passion, *karma*, and *tamas*— all these constitute this town (of body).

"*Virāṭ*, under the orders of *Īśvara* having entered this microcosmic body, and having *buddhi* as his vehicle, reaches the state of *Viśva*. Then he goes by the several names of *Vijñānātma*, *Cidābhāsa*, *Viśva*, *Vyāvahārika*, the one presiding over the waking gross body and the one generated by *karma*. *Sūtrātmā*, under the orders of *Īśvara*, having entered the micro-cosmic subtle body, and having *manas* as his vehicle, reaches the *Taijasa* state, Then he goes by the names of *taijasa*, *prātibhāsika* and *svapnakalpita* (the one bred out of dream). Then under the orders of *Īśvara*, he who is coupled with *avyakta*, the vehicle of *Māyā* having entered the microcosmic *kāraṇa* body, reaches the state of *prajñā*. He goes then by the names of *prājña*, *avicchinna*, and *pāramārthika* and *sus upti-abhimānī* (the presider over *suṣupti*). Such sacred sentences, as *Tattvamasi* (That art thou) and others, speak of the identify with the *Brahman* of the *Pāramārthika-Jīva* enveloped by *ajñāna*, which is but a small particle of *avyakta*; but not *vyāvahārika* and *prātibhāsika* (*Jīvas*). It is only that *caitanya* which is reflected in *antaḥkaraṇa* that attains the three states. When it assumes the three states of *jāgrat*, *svapna*, and *suṣ upti*, it is like a water-lift as if grieved, born and dead. There are five *avasthās*— *jāgrat*, *Svapna*, *suṣupti*, *mūrchā* (trace), and death. *Jāgrat avasthā* is that in which there is the perception of objects, of sound, etc. through the grace of the *devatā* presiding over each of them. In it, the *Jīva*, being in the middle of the eyebrows and pervading the body from head to foot, becomes the agent of actions, such as doing, hearing, and others. He becomes also the enjoyer of the fruits thereof; and such a person doing *karma* for the fruits thereof goes to other worlds and enjoys the same there. Like an emperor tired of worldly acts (in the waking state), he strives to find the path to retire into his abode within. The *svapna avasthā* is that in which, when the senses are at rest, there is the manifestation of the knower and the known, along with the affinities of (things enjoyed in) the waking state, In this state *Viśva* alone, its actions in the waking state having ceased, reaches the state of *Taijasa* (of *tejas* or effulgence), who moves in the middle of the *nāḍīs* (nerves), illuminates by his lustre the heterogeneity of this universe which is of the form of affinities, and himself enjoys according to his wish. The *suṣupti avasthā* is that in which the *citta* is sole organ (at play). Just a bird, tired of roaming, flies to its nest with its stomach filled, so the *Jīva* being tired of the cations of the world in the waking and dreaming states, enters *ajñāna* and enjoys bliss. Then trance is attained which resembles death, and in which one with his collection of organs quails, as it were, through fear and *ajñāna*, like one beaten unexpectedly by a hammer, club or any other weapon. Then death *avasthā* is that which is other than the *avasthās* of *jāgrat*, *svapna*, *suṣupti*, and trance, which produces fear in all *Jīvas* from

Brahmā down to small insects and which dissolves the gross body. The *Jīva*, that is surrounded by *avidyā* and the subtle elements, takes with it the organs of sense and action, their objects, and *prāṇas* along with the *kāmic karmas* and goes to another world, assuming another body. Through the ripening of the fruits of previous *karmas*, the *Jīva* has no rest like an insect in a whirlpool. It is only after many births that the desire of emancipation arises in man through the ripening of good *karma*. Then having restored to a good *Guru* and served under him for a long time, one out of many attains *mokṣa*, free form bondage. Bondage is through non-inquiry and *mokṣa* through inquiry. Therefore there should always be inquiry (into *Ātmā*). The Reality should be ascertained through *adhyāropa* (illusory attribution) and *apavāda* (withdrawal or recession of that idea). Therefore there should be always inquiring into the universe, *Jīva* and *paramātmā*. Were the true nature of *Jīva* and the universe known, then there remains *Brahman* which is non-different from *Pratyagātmā*."

Adhyāya III

Then *Paiṅgala* asked Yājñavalkya to offer an exposition on the *mahāvākyas* (sacred sentences of the Vedas). to which Yājñavalkya replied : "One should scrutinise (the sacred sentences), *Tattvamasi* (That art thou), *Tvamtadasi* (Thou art That), *Ṭvambrahmāsi* (Thou art *Brahman*) and *Ahambrahmāsmi* (I am *Brahman*). The word 'Tat' denotes the cause of the universe that is variegated beyond perception, has the characteristics of omniscience, has *Māyā* as His vehicle and has the attributes of *Saccidānanda*. It is He that is the basis of the notion 'I' which has the differentiated knowledge produced by *antaḥkaraṇa*; and it is He that is denoted by the word "*Tvam*" (Thou). That is the undifferentiated *Brahman* which remains as the aim (or meaning) of the words *Tat* and *Tvam* after freeing itself from *Māyā* and *Avidyā* which are respectively the vehicles of *Paramātmā* and *Jīvātmā*. The inquiry into the real significance of the sentences *Tattvamasi* and *aham brahmāsmi* forms (what is called) *śravaṇa* (hearing— the first state of inquiry). To inquire in solitude into the significance of *śravaṇa* is *manana*. The concentration of the mind with one-pointedness upon that which should be sought after by *śravaṇa* and *manana* is *nididhyāsana*. *Samādhi* is that state in which *Citta* having given up (the conception of the difference of) the meditator and the meditation, becomes of the form of the meditated like a lamp in place without wind. Then arise the modifications pertaining to *Ātmā*. Such (modifications) cannot be known; but they can only be inferred through memory (of the *samāḍhi* state). The myriads of *karmas* committed in this beginningless cycle of rebirths are annihilated only through them. Through proficiency in practice, the current of nectar always rains down

---

1. It is said that in *samādhi* astral nectar flows from the head down which the *Yogins* are said to drink and which gives them infinite bliss.

in diverse ways. Therefore those who know *Yoga* call this *Samādhi*, *ḍharma-megha* (cloud). Through these (modifications of *Ātmā*), the collection of affinities is absorbed without any remainder whatever. When the accumulated good and bad *karmas* are wholly destroyed, these sentences (*Tattvamasi* and *Aham brahmāsmi*), like the myrobalan in the palm of the hand, bring him face to face with the ultimate Reality, though It was before invisible. Then he becomes a *Jīvanmukta*.

"*Īśvara* wished to produce non-quintuplication (or involution) in the fivefold differentiated elements, Having drawn into their cause Brahmā's egg and its effects of worlds, and mixed together the subtle organs of sense and action and the four internal organs and dissolved all things composed of the elements into their cause, the five elements, he then caused *Pṛthivī* to merge into water, water into *agni*, *agni* into *vāyu*, and *vāyu* into *ākāśa, ākāśa* into *ahaṁkāra*, *ahaṁkāra* into *mahat*, *mahat* into *avyakta*, and *avyakta* into *puruṣa* in regular order. *Virāṭ*, *Hiraṇyagarbha* and *Īśvara* being freed form the vehicle of *Māyā*, are absorbed into *Paramātmā*. This gross body composed of the five differentiated elements and obtained through accumulated *karma*, is merged into its subtle state of non-quintuplicated elements, through the extinction of (bad) *karma* and increase of good *karma*, then attains its *kāraṇa* (causal) state and (finally) is absorbed into its cause, (*viz*.,) *Kūṭastha-Pratyagātmā*. *Viśva* and *Taijasa* and *Prājña*, their *upādhi* (of *avidyā*) having become extinct, are absorbed in *Pratyagātmā*. This sphere (of universe) being burnt up by the fire of *Jñāna* is absorbed along with its cause into *Paramātmā*. Therefore a *Brāhmaṇa* should be careful and always meditate upon the identity of *Tat* and *Tvam*. Then *Ātmā* shines, like the sun freed from the (obscuration of the) clouds. One should meditate upon *Ātmā* in the midst (of the body) like a lamp within a jar.

"*Ātmā*, the *Kūṭastha*, should be meditated upon as being of the size of a thumb, as being of the nature of the jyotis (light) without smoke, as being within, illuminating all and as being indestructible. That Muni (sage) who meditates (upon *Ātmā* always) until sleep or death comes upon him passes into the state of *Jīvanmukti*) emancipation like the immovable state of the wind. Then there remains the One (*Brahman*) without sound, touch, free from destruction, without taste or odour, which is eternal, which is without beginning or end, which is beyond the *Tattva* of *Mahat*, and which is permanent and without stain or disease."

Adhyāya IV

Then *Paiṅgala* addressed Yājñavalkya thus : "To the wise, what is their *karma*? And what is their state?" To which Yājñavalkya replied: "A lover of *mokṣa*, having humility[1] and other possessions (or virtues),

---

1. Humility and other virtues twenty in number are decribed in *Bhagavad-Gitā*, Chapter-XIII.

enables twenty-one generations to cross (to *Ātmā*). One through his being a *Brahmavit*[1] alone enables 101 generations to cross. Know *Ātmā* to be the rider and the body as the chariot. Know also *buddhi* as the charioteer and *manas* as the reins. The wise say the organs are the horses, the objects are the roads (through which the horses travel) and the hearts are the moving balloons. *Maharṣis* say that *Ātmā*, when associated with the sense organs and means, is the enjoyer. Therefore it is the actual Nārāyaṇa alone that is established in the heart. Till his *prārabdha karma*[2] is worn out, he exists (in his body) as in the (case-off) slough of a serpent (without any desire for the body.) An emancipated person having such a body roves about like a moon-gladdening all with no settled place of abode. He given up his body whether in a sacred place, or in a *caṇḍāla*'s (out-caste's) house (without any distinction whatever), and attains salvation. Such a body (when seen by a person) should be offered as a sacrifice of *dik* (the quarters) or should be buried (undergrund). It is only to *Puruṣa* (the wise) that the *sannyāsa* (renunciation) is ordained and not to others. In case of the death of an ascetic who is of the form (or has attained the nature) of *Brahman*, there is no pollution (to be observed); neither the ceremonies of fire (as burning the body, *homa* etc.,); nor the *piṇḍa* (balls of rice), nor ceremonies of water nor the periodical ceremonies (monthly and yearly). Just as a food once cooked is not again cooked, so a body once burnt (by the fire of wisdom) should not be burnt (or exposed to fire) again. To one whose body was burnt by the fire of wisdom there is neither *śrāddha*[3] (required to be performed), nor (funeral) ceremony So long as there is the *upādhi* (of non-wisdom) in one, so long should he serve the *Guru*. He should conduct himself towards his *Guru*'s wife and children as he does to his *Guru*. If being of a pure mind, of the nature of immaculate *cit* and resigned, and having the discrimination arising from the attainment of wisdom "I am He", he should concentrate his heart on *Paramātmā* and obtain firm peace in his body, then he becomes of the nature of Jyotis, void of *manas* and *buddhi*. Of what avail is milk to one content with nectar? Of what avail are the Vedas to him who has known his *Ātmā* thus? For a *Yogin* content with the nectar of wisdom, there is nothing more to be done. If he has to do anything, then he is not a knower of *Tattva*. *Pratyagātmā* though far (or difficult of attainment), is not far; though in the body, he is devoid of it (since) he is all-pervading. After having purified the heart and contemplated on the One without disease (*viz., Brahman*), the cognizing of 'I' as the supreme and the all is the highest bliss. Like water mixed with water, milk with milk, and ghee with ghee, so *Jīvātmā* and *Paramātmā* are without difference. When the body is rendered bright through wisdom and the

1. There are four classes of *Brahmajñāna* or initiates of whom this is one.
2. That portion of past *karma* which is being enjoyed in this life.
3. The yearly ceremonies in honour of the dead.

buddhi becomes of the partless One, then the wise man burns the bondage of *karma* through the fire of *Brahmajñāna*. Then be becomes purified, of the nature of the non-dual named *Parmeśvara* and the light like the stainless *ākāśa*. Like water mixed with water, so *Jīva*(-*Ātmā*) becomes *upādhi*-less (or freed from the bonds of matter). *Ātmā* is invisible like *vāyu*. Though he is within and without, he is the immovable *Ātmā*. Through the torch of wisdom, the internal *Ātmā* sees (or knows).

"A wise man, in whatever place or manner he dies, in absorbed in that place like the all-pervading *ākāśa*. It should be known that *Ātmā* is absorbed as truly as the *ākāśa* in the pot (when broken). Then he attains the all-pervading wisdom-light that is without support. Through men should perform tapas standing on one leg for a period of 1,000 years, it will not in the least, be equal to one-sixteenth part of *dhyānayoga*. One desirous of knowing what *jñāna* (wisdom) and *jñeya* (the object to be known) are, will not be able to attain his desired end, even though he may study the *Śāstras* for 1,000 years. That which is alone should be known as the indestructible. That which exists (in this world) is only impermanent. (therefore) after having given up (the study of) the many *Śāstras*, one should worship that which is *satya* (truth). The many *karmas*, purity (of mind and heart), *japa* (the muttering of *mantras*), sacrifice and pilgrimages— all these should be observed till *Tattva* is known. For *Mahātmans* (noble souls) to be always in (the conception of) 'I am *Brahman*' conduces to their salvation. There are two causes (that lead) to bondage and emancipation. They are 'mine' and 'not mine'. Through 'mine' creatures are bound, whereas through 'not mine' they are released from bondage. When the mind attains the state of *Unmani* (above *manas*, *viz.*, when it is destroyed), then there is never the conception of duality. When the *Unmani* state occurs, then is the supreme-Seat (attained). (After which) wherever the mind goes, there is the supreme Seat (to it, *viz.*, the mind enjoys salvation wherever it is). That which is equal in all is *Brahman* alone. One may attain the power to strike the *ākāśa* with his fist; he may appeases his hunger by eating husks (of grain), but never shall be attain emancipation who has not the self-cognition, 'I am *Brahman*'.

"Whoever recites this *Upaniṣad* becomes as immaculate as *Agni*. He becomes as pure as Brahmā. he becomes as pure as *Vāyu*. He becomes like one who has bathed in all the holy waters. he becomes like one who has studied all the Vedas. He becomes like one that has undergone all vedic observances. He obtains the fruit of the recitation of *Itihāsas*[1], *Purāṇas* and *Rudramantras* a lakh of times, He becomes like one that has pronounced *Praṇava* (*Om*) ten thousand times. He purifies his ancestors ten degrees removed and is descendants ten degree removed. he becomes purified of all those that sit with him for dinner. He becomes a great personage. He becomes purified from the sins of the murder of a

---

1. *Itihāsas* are the *Rāmayaṇa* and the *Mahābhārata*.

Brāhmaṇa, the drinking of alcohol, theft of gold, and sexual cohabitation with *Guru*'s wife, and from the sins of associating with those that commit such sins.

"Like the eye pervading the *Āsās* (seeing without effort everything above), a wise man sees (always) the supreme Seat of Viṣṇu. The *Brāhmaṇas* who have always their spiritual eyes wide open prise and illuminate in diverse ways the supreme Seat of Viṣṇu. *Om* : This *Upaniṣ ad* is truth."

Thus ends the Upanișad

Adhyātma[1]-Upaniṣad

OF

ŚUKLA-YAJURVEDA

The One *Aja* (unborn) is ever located in the cave (of the heart) within the body. (*Pṛthivī*) the earth is His Body; though he pervades the earth, it does not know Him. The waters are His body; though He pervades the waters, they do not know Him. *Agni* is His body; though He pervades *agni*, it does not know Him. *Vāyu* is His body: though the pervades *vāyu*, it does not know Him. *Ākāśa* is His body; though He pervades *ākaśa*, it does not know Him. *Manas* is His body; though He pervades *manas*, it does not know Him. *Buddhi* is His body; though he pervades *buddhi*, it does not know him. *Ahaṁkāra* is His Body; though He pervades *ahaṁkāra*, it does not know Him *citta* is His body; though He pervades *Citta*, it does not know Him. *Akṣara* is His body; though He pervades *avyakta*, It does not know Him. *Akṣara* is His body; though He pervades *akṣara*, it does not know Him. *Mṛtyu* is His body; though He pervades *Mṛtyu*, it does not know Him. He who is the inner soul of all creatures and the purifier of sins, is the one divine Lord Nārāyaṇa.

The wise should through the practice of deep meditation of *Brahman* leave off the (recurrent) conception of 'I' and 'mine' in the body and the senses which are other than *Ātmā*. Having known himself as *Pratyagātmā*, the witness of *buddhi* and its actions, one should ever think "So'ham" ("I am That") and leave off the idea of *Ātmā* in all others. Shunning the pursuits of the world, the body and the *Śāstras*, set about removing the false attribution of self. In the case of a *Yogin* staying always in his own *Ātmā*, his mind perishes, having known his *Ātmā* as the *Ātmā* of all, through inference, Vedas and self-experience. Never giving slightest scope to sleep, worldly talk, sounds, etc., think of *Ātmā*, (in yourself) to be the (supreme) *Ātmā*. Shun at a distance like a *caṇḍāla* (the thought of) the body, which is generated out of the impurities of parents and is composed of excreta and flesh. then you will be become *Brahman* and be (in a) blessed (state). O Sage, having dissolved (*Jīva-*) *Ātmā* into *parmātmā* with the thought of its being partless, like the ether of a jar in the universal ether, be ever in a state of taciturnity. Having become that which is the seat of all *Ātmās* and the self-resplendent, give up the macrocosm and microcosm like an impure vessel. Having merged into *Cidātmā*, which is ever blissful, the conception of "I" which is rooted in

---

1. This *Upanṣad* is also called *Turīyātīta Avadhūta Upaniṣad.*

the body, and having removed the (conception of) *Liṅga* (here the sign of separateness), become ever the *Kevala* (alone). Having known "I am that *Brahman*" in which alone the universe appears like a town in a mirror, become one that has performed (all) his duty, O sinless one. The ever-blissful and the self-effulgent One being freed from the grip of *ahaṁkāra* attains its own state, like the spotless moon becoming full (after eclipse).

With the extinction of actions, there arises the extinction of *cintā*. From it arises the decay of *vāsanās*; and from the latter, arises *mokṣa*; and this is called *Jīvanmukti*. Looking upon everything in all places and times as *Brahman* brings about the destruction of *Vāsanās* through the force of *vāsanās* of *sāttvika* nature. Carelessness in *Brahmaniṣṭhā* by (or meditation of *Brahman*) should not in the least be allowed (to creep in). Knowers of *Brahman* style (this) carelessness, in Brāhmic science, as death (itself). Just as the moss (momentarily) displaced (in a tank) again resumes its original position, in a minute, so *Māyā* envelops even the wise, should they be careless (even for a moment). He who attains the *Kaivalya* state during life becomes a *Kevala* even after death of his body. Ever devoted to *samādhi*, become a *nirvikalpa* (or the change-less one), O sinless one. the *granthi* (or knot) of the heart, full of *ajñāna*, is broken completely only when one sees his *Ātmā* as secondless through *nirvikalpa samādhi*.

Now, having strengthened the conception of *Ātmā* and well given up that of "I" in the body, one should be indifferent as he would be towards jars, cloth, etc. From Brahmā down to a pillar, all the *upādhis* are only unreal, hence one should see (or cognize) his *Ātmā* as all-full and existing by itself (alone). Brahmā is *Svayam* (*Ātmā*); Viṣṇu is *Ātmā*; Rudra is *Ātmā*; Indra is *Ātmā*; all this universe is *Ātmā* and there is nothing but *Ātmā*. By expelling (from the mind) without any remainder all objects which are superimposed on one's *Ātmā*, one becomes himself *Parabrahman* the full, the secondless and the actionless. How can there be the heterogeneity of the universe of *saṅkalpa* and *vikalpa* in that One Principle which is immutable formless and homogeneous? When there is no difference between the seer, the seen, and sight, there being the decayless and *Cidātmā*, full like the ocean at the end of a *Kalpa* and effulgent, all darkness, the cause of false perception, merges in it. How can there be heterogeneity in that one supreme Principle which is alike? How can there be heterogeneity in the highest *Tattva* which is One? Who has observed any heterogeneity in *suṣupti* the dreamless sleep), where there is happiness only? This *vikalpa* has its root in *Citta* only. When *Citta* is not, there is nothing. Therefore unite the *Citta* with *Paramātman* in its *Pratyāgātmika* state. If one knows *Ātmā* as unbroken bliss in itself, then he drinks always the juice (or essence) of bliss in his *Ātmā*, whether internally or externally.

The fruit of *vairāgya* is bodha (spiritual wisdom); the fruit of *bodha* is *uparati* (renunciation); *śānti* (sweet patience) is attained out of the enjoyment of the bliss of one's *Ātmā*, and this *śānti* is the fruit of *uparati*. If the latter in each of these is absent, the former is useless. *Nivṛtti* (or the return path) leads to the highest contentment and (spiritual) bliss is said to be beyond all analogy. That which has *Māyā* as its *upādhi* is the womb of the world; that true one which has the attribute of omniscience, etc. and has the variegated mystery is denoted by the word "*Tat*" (that). That is called *Apara* (the other or inferior[1]) which shines through meditation upon the idea and the world *asmat* and the consciousness of which is developed by *antaḥkaraṇa*. By separating the *upādhis Māyā* and *avidyā* from *Parā* and *Jīva* (cosmic and human *Ātmās* respectively) one realises *Parabrahman* which is partless and *saccidānanda*. Making the mind dwell upon such sentences (or ideas) as the above constitutes *śravaṇa* (hearing). It becomes *manana* (contemplation) when such ideas are quited (in one) through logical reasoning. When (their) meaning is confirmed through these (two processes) the concentration of the mind on it alone constitutes *nididhyāsana*. That is called *samādhi* in which the *citta*, rising above the conception of the contemplator and contemplation, merges gradually into the contemplated, like a light undisturbed by the wind. Even the mental states are not known (at the time when one is within the scope of *Ātmā*). But they are only inferred from the recollection which takes place after *samādhi*. Through this *samādhi* are destroyed crores of *karmas* which have accumulated during cycles of births without beginning and pure *dharma* is developed. Knowers of *Yoga* call this *samādhi*, *dharma-megha* (cloud), in as much as it showers nectarine drops of *karma* in great quantities, when all the hosts of *vāsanās* are destroyed entirely through this, and when the accumulated *karmas*, virtuous and sinful, are rooted out. Then that in which speech was hidden till now, appears no longer so, and shines as *Sat*; and direct cognition reveals itself, like the myrobalan in the palm of the hand. *Vairāgya* beings from where the *vāsanās* cease to arise towards objects of enjoyment. The cessation of the rising of the idea of "I" is the highest limit of *buddhi*; *uparati* beings from where the mental states once destroyed do not again arise. That ascetic is said to possess *Sthitaprajñā* who enjoys bliss always and whose mind is absorbed in *Brahman* that is formless and actionless. That state of mind is termed *prajñā* that realises the oneness of *Brahman* and *Ātmā* after deep inquiry, and that has the *vṛtti* of *nirvikapla* and *cinmātra*. He who possessess this always is *Jīvanmukta*. He is a *Jīvanmukta* who has neither the conception of "I" in the body and the senses of the conception of another (different from himself) in everything

---

1. I and its inflexions.

else. He is a *Jīvanmukta* who sees through his *prajña* no difference between his own *Ātmā* and *Brahman* as well as between *Brahman* and the universe, He is a *Jīvanmukta* who preserves equanimity of mind, either when revered by the good or reviled by the vicious. One who has cognized the true nature of *Brahman* is not subject to rebirth as before. But were he so subjected, then he is not a true knower, the knowing of *Brahman* being external only. A man is subject to *prārabdha*[1] so long as he is affected by pleasure, etc. The attainment of a result is always preceded by action; and nowhere is it without *karma*. Through the cognition. "I am *Brahman*" are destroyed the *karmas* accumulated during hundreds of crores of previous births, like the actions in the dreaming state (that are destroyed) during the waking state.

An ascetic having known himself as associateless and indifferent like ether, is not at all affected by any of his *karmas* at any time. Just as the ether is not affected by the alcoholic smell through its contact with a pot, so *Ātmā* is not affected by the *guṇas* produced by its *upādhi*. The *Prārabdha karma* that has begun to act before the dawn of *jñāna* is not checked by it; and one should reap its fruit, as in the case of an arrow discharged at a target. An arrow that is discharged towards an object with the idea that it is tiger, does not stop when it (the tiger) is found to be a cow; but it (even) pierces the mark through its speed, without stopping, When one realises his *Ātmā* as free from old age and death, then how will *prārabdha* affect him? *Prārabdha* accomplishes (its work) only when one considers his body as *Ātmā*. This conception of *Ātmā* as body is not at all a desirable one; so it should be given up along with *prārabdha*, since it is simply a delusion to attribute *prārabdha* to this body. How can there be reality to that which is super-imposed upon another? How can there be birth to that which is not real? How can there be death to that which is not born? How can there be *prārabdha* to that which is unreal? The Veda speaks of *prārabdha* in an external sense only, to satisfy those foolish persons that doubt, saying : "If *jñāna* can destroy all the results of *ajñāna* (such as body, etc.), then whence is the existence of this body to such a one?" But not to inculcate to the wise the existence of the body.

Ātmā is all-full, beginningless, immeasurable unchangeable, replete with *Sat*, *Cit*, and *Ānanda*, decayless, the one essence, the eternal, the differentiated, the plenum, the endless, having its face everywhere, the one that can neither be given up nor taken up, the one that can neither be supported nor be made to support, the *guṇa*-less, the actionless, the subtle, the changeless, the stainless, the indescribable, the true nature one's *Ātmā*, above the reach of speech and mind, the one full *Sat*, the self-existent, the immaculate, the enlightened, and incomparable; such is *Brahman*, one only without a second. There are not in the least many. He who knows his

1. The result of past *karma* now enjoyed.

Ātmā himself through his own cognition, as the one who is not restricted by any, is a *Siddha* (one that has accomplished his object), who has identified his *Ātmā* with the one changeless *Ātmā*. Whither is this world gone, then? How did it appear? Where is it absorbed? It was seen by me just now, but now it is gone. What a great miracle ! What is fit to be taken in? And what to be rejected? What is other (than *Ātmā*)? And what is different (from It)? In this mighty ocean of *Brahman* full of the nectar of undivided bliss, I do not see, hear, or know anything. I remain in my *Ātmā* only and in my own nature of *Sat*, *Ānandarūpa*. I am an *asaṅga* (or the associateless). I am an *asaṅga*. I am without any attributes. I am *Hari* (the Lord taking away sin). I am the quiescent, the endless, the all-full and the ancient. I am neither the agent nor the enjoyer. I am the changeless and the decayless. I am of the nature of pure enlightenment. I am the one and the perpetual bliss.

This science was imparted to *Apāntaratama* who gave it to Brahmā. Brahmā gave it to *Ghora-Aṅgiras*. *Ghora-Aṅgiras* gave it to *Raikva*, who gave it to Rāma. And Rāma gave it to all beings. This is the teaching of *Nirvāṇa*; and this is the teaching of the Vedas; yea, this the teaching of the Vedas.

Thus ends the Upaniṣad

Subāla-Upaniṣad

OF

ŚUKLA-YAJURVEDA

Khaṇḍa I

Then he (Raikva[1]) asked : "What was at first" to which (He the Lord replied :

"There was neither Sat[2] nor asat nor sat-aṣat. From it, tamas (darkness) was evolved. From tamas came *bhūtādi*;[3] from *bhūtādi* came *ākāśa*, from *ākāśa*, *vāyu*; from *vāyu*, *agni* (fire); from *agni āpas* (water); and from *āpas*, *pṛthivī* (earth). Then it became an egg. After remaining so for one divine year, it split into two and became earthbelow,[4] the *ākāśa* above and in the midst,the infinite *Puruṣa* of a divine from of myriads of heads, eyes, feet and hands. Prior to the bhūtas (elements), he had evolved *Mṛtyu* (time or death) of[5] three letters , three heads, and three feet, and having a *Khaṇḍa-paraśu*[6] (broken axe). To him, *Brahmā* (the *Puruṣa*) spoke. He entered Brahmā himself and evolved mentally the seven sons[7] and these Ḥavirāts (or sons) as well as the seven *Prajāpatis* (progenitors). *Brāhmaṇas*[8] were born from His mouth, *Kṣattryas* from His hands, *Vaiṣ yas* from His thighs, and from the feet were born the *Śudras*. The moon

---

1. In the *Chāndogya Upaniṣad Raikva* is sait to be the imparter of Samvargavidya.
2. The absolute (*Parabrahman*) is neither Sat (Be-ness) nor asat (Not-Be-ness) nor a commingling of both. It is neither spirit nor matter nor a commingling of both.
3. *Bhūtādi* is *tāmasa ahaṁkāra* according to *Viṣṇu Purāṇa*.
4. "Above and below" refers not to the position but only to the state, or matter, gross or subtle. "In the midst" implies that *ākāśa* and earth are soaked in and with spirit.
5. "This refers to the first triune manifestation of *Puruṣa* or spirit through time when only there is activity. *Mṛtyu* or *Kāla* is the first manifestation whereas *Yama* (or the God of death) is the secondary one dealing with the death of creatures lower down.
6. Khaṇḍa means divided or with parts. Parasu literally injuring an-other. Hence *Mṛtyu* with his Khaṇḍa-parasu divided eternal time into its parts and conditions the absolute through primordial matter. In the *Purāṇas* and other books, *Mṛtyu* and *Yama* are expresented as having an axe broken in a conflict.
7. This refers to the septenary manifestation from the triune one; also to the sub-septenary ones.
8. In other words beings of *Sattva*, Rajas and Tamas and an admixture of these were born.

was born from His *manas* (mind), the sun from His eyes, *vāyu* from (His) ears and *prāṇas* from (His) heart. Thus all things were born."

Khaṇḍa II

"From *apāna* came *Niṣādas, yakṣas, Rākṣasas*, and *Gandharvas*. From (His) bones, arose the mountains. From His hairs arose the herbs and the trees. From His forehead, *Rudra* was born through His anger, the breath of this great Being became the *Ṛgveda, Yajurveda, Sāmveda, Atharvaveda, Śīkṣā* (the science of the proper pronunciation and articulation of sounds) *Kalpa* (the science of methodology), *Vyākaraṇa* (grammar), *Nirukta* (glossarial explanation of absolete and other terms in Vedas), Chandas (prosody or vedic metre), *Jyotiṣa* (astronomy), *Nyāya* (logic), *Mīmāṁsā* (including rituals and *vedānta*), *Dharmaśāstras*, commentaries, glosses and all beings. This *Ātmā* (or the Self of *Puruṣa*) is *Hiraṇyajyotiṣ* (or golden or effulgent Light) into which all the universe is absorbed. He divided *Ātmā* (his Self) into two moieties; out of one moiety, the woman was created; and out of the other man. Having become a *Deva*, he created the *Devas*. Having become a *Ṛṣi*, He created the *Ṛṣis*; also He created Yakṣas, Rākṣasas, *Gandharvas*, wild and domestic beasts and others such as cows, bulls, mares and horses, she-asses and asses and *Viśvambhara* (the Supporter) and *Viśvambharā* (the earth). Becoming *Vaiśvānara* (fire) at the end (of creation), He burnt up all objects, then (in dissolution). *Pṛthivī* was absorbed in *āpas*, *āpas* in *agni*, *agni* in *vāyu*, *vāyu* in *ākāśa*, *ākāśa* in indṛyas (organs), *indṛyas* into *tanmātras* (rudimentary properties), *tanmātras* into *bhūtādi, bhūtādi* into mahat, mahat into *avyakta*, *avyakta* into *akṣara* (the indestructible), *akṣ ara* into tamas (darkness) and tamas becomes one with the supreme Lord. And then there is neither Sat nor asat, nor Sat-asat. This is the teaching of *Nirvāṇa* and this is the teaching of the Vedas. Yea, this is the teaching of the Vedas."

Khaṇḍa III

"As first, there was Asat, unborn, non-existent, unsupported, soundless, touchless, formless, tasteless, odourless, and decayless. The undaunted man never grieves, as he knows *Ātmā* to be great, all-pervading and unborn. It (*Ātmā*) is *prāṇaless*, mouthless, earless, tongueless, *manas*-less, tejas-less, eyeless, nameless, gotraless (or clanless), headless, handless, feetless, non-unctuous, bloodless, non-measurable, neither long nor short, neither gross nor atomic, neither great nor small, endless, indescribable, non-returnable, non-luminious, not hidden, having neither inside nor outside, neither eating anything nor being eaten by others. Some one (out of many) attains to this (*Ātmā*) by the six means of *satya* (truth), *dāna* (charity), tapas (religious austerities, non-injury to any creature, celibacy and complete indifference to worldly objects;[1] and there are no other means. Whoever feels happy with the thought 'I know that', that learned persons, *prāṇa* will never get out of his body at the moment of death, but will become absorbed in *Brahman*; and being absorbed in *Brahman*, he attains the state of *Brahman* Itself as he who knows this."

Khaṇḍa IV

"In the middle of the heart is a red fleshy mass in which is the *dhara*-lotus. Like the lotus, it opens into many (petals). There are ten openings in the heart. The (different kinds of) *prāṇas* are located there. Whenever the (*Ātmā*) is united with prāṇa, he sees cities with rivers and other variegated things; when united with vyāna, he sees *Devas* and *Ṛṣis*; when united with *apāna*, he sees Yakṣas, Rākṣasas and *Gandharvas*; when united with *Udāna*,he perceives the celestial world, *Devas*, *Skanda* (*Kārtikeya* or the six-faced Mars), and *Jayanta* (*Indra*'s son); when united with *samāna*, he sees the celestial world and the treasures (of Kubera); when united with *rambhā* (a *nādi* hereafter given out), he sees whatever is seen or not seen, heard or not heard, eaten or not eaten, asat or *Sat* and all else.

"There are ten *nādis*; in each of these are seventy-one. And these become 72,000 branch *nāḍis*. When *Ātmā* sleeps therein, it produces sound; but when *Ātmā* sleeps in the second *kośa* (or sheath) then it sees this world and the higher as also knows all the sounds. this is spoken of as *samprasāda* (deep sleep rest). Then *prāṇa* protects the body. The *nāḍis* are full of blood, of the colours green, blue, yellow, red, and white. Now this dahara-lotus has many petals like a lily. Like a hair divided into 1,000 parts, the *nāḍis* called hita are. The divine *Ātmā* sleeps in the *ākāśa* of the heart, in the supreme *kośa* (or *ānandamaya sheath*); sleeping there, it has no desires, no dreams, no deva-worlds, no *yajñas* or sacrificer, no mother or father, no relative, no *kinsman*, no thief, or no *Brāhman*-slayer. Its body is tejas (resplendent effulgence) and of the nature of nectar (or the immortal). It is as if in sport, a water-lotus. When he returns again to the waking state, by the same way (he quitted or went in before to the heart), he is *Samrāt*[2]. Thus says he."

Khaṇḍa V[3]

"That which joins one place (or centre) with another is the nāḍis which bind them. The eye is *adhyātmā* (pertaining to the body); the

1. The word *anāsakena* (non-injury) is repeated in the text which is wrong.
2. Lit., one producing sound.
3. In this chapter are given out the several correspondences of the devas (or the presidding spiritualeities) and of the objects of the five organs of sense, the five organs of action, and the antaḥkaraṇa (or lower mind) composed of *manas*, *buddhi*, *ahaṁkāra*, and citta.

visible objects are *ādhibhūta* (pertaining to the elements and the sun is *adhidaivata* (spiritual). The *nāḍis* form their bond (or connect them). He who moves in the eye, in the visible, in the sun, in the *nāḍis*, in *prāṇa*, in *vijñāna*,[1] in *ānanda*, in the *ākāśa* of the heart, and within all else— That is *Ātmā*. It is that which should be worshipped.It is without old age, death, fear, sorrow, or end.

"The ear is *adhyātma*, the audible *adhibhūta*, and dik (the quarters) is *adhidaivata*. The *nāḍis* bind them. He who moves in the ear, in the audible, in the quarters, in the *nāḍis*, in *prāṇa*, in *vijñāna*, in *ānanda*, in the *ākāśa* of the heart, and within all else— That is *Ātmā*. It is that which should be worshipped. It is without old age, death, fear, sorrow, or end.

"The nose is *adhyātma*, the odoriferous *adhibhūta*, and the earth is *adhidaivata*. The *nāḍīs* bind them. He who moves in the nose, the odoriferous, the earth, the *nāḍīs*, prāṇa, *vijñāna*, *ānanda*, the *ākāśa* of the heart, and within all else— That is *Ātmā*. It is that which should be worshipped. It is without old age, death, fear, sorrow, or end.

"The tongue is *adhyātma* : the tastable *adhibhūta*, and Varuṇa is *adhidaivata*. The *nāḍīs* bind them. He who moves in the tongue, the tastable, Varuṇa, the *nāḍīs*, *prāṇa, vijñāna, ānanda,* tha *ākāśa* of the heart, and within all else— That is *Ātmā*. It is that which should be worshipped. It is without old age, death, fear, sorrow, or end.

"The skin is *adhyātma*, the tangiferous *adhibhūta*, and the *vāyu* is *adhidaivata*. The nāḍis bind them. He who moves in the skin, the tangiferous, the *vāyu*, the *nāḍis, prāṇa, vijñāna, ānanda*, the *ākāśa* of the heart, and within all else— That is *Ātmā*. It is that which should worshipped. It is without old age, death, fear, sorrow, or end.

"*Vāk*.(speech) is *adhyātma*, that which is acted upon by vāk is *adhibhūta*, and *Agni* is *Adhidaivata*. The *nāḍis* bind them. He who moves in vāk, that which is acted upon by *vāk, Agni*, the nāḍis, prāṇa, *vijñāna*, the *ākāśa* of the heart, and within all else— That is *Ātmā*. It is that which should be worshipped. It is without old age, death, fear, sorrow, or end.

"The hand is *adhyātma*, that which can be handled is *adhibhūta*, and Indra is *adhidaivata*. The *nāḍis* bind them. He who moves in the hand, that which can be handled by it, Indra, the *nāḍīs*, *prāṇa*, *vijñāna*, *ānanda*, the *ākāśa* of the heart, and within all else— That is *Ātmā*. It is that which should be worshipped.It is without old age, death, fear, sorrow, or end.

"The feet is *adhyātma*, that which is walked upon is *adhibhūta*, and Viṣṇu (or Upendra) is *adhidaivata*. The nāḍis bind them. He who moves in the feet, that which is walked upon Viṣṇu, the *nāḍis*, *prāṇa*, *vijñāna*, *ānanda*, the *ākāśa* of the heart, and within all else— That is *Ātmā*. It is that which should be worshpped. It is without old age, death, fear, sorrow, or end.

---

1. Probably *prāṇa*, *vijñāna*, and *ānanda* refers to the sheaths formed by them.

"The anus is *adhyātma*, the excreta is *adhibhūta*, and *Mṛtyu* is *adhidaivata*. The *nāḍīs* bind them. He who moves the anus, the excreta, *Mṛtyu*, the *nāḍīs*, *prāṇa*, *vijñāna*, *ānanda*, the *ākāśa* of the heart, and within all else— That is *Ātmā*. It is that which should be worshipped. It is without old age, death, fear, sorrow, or end.

"The genitals is *adhyātma*, the secretion is *adhibhūta*, and Prajāpati is *adhidaivata*. The *nāḍīs* bind them. He who moves in the genitals, secretion Prajāpati, the nāḍis, *prāṇa*, *vijñāna*, *ānanda*, the *ākāśa* of the heart, and within all else— That is *Ātmā*. It is that which should be worshipped. It is without old age, death, fear, sorrow, or end.

"*Manas*[1] is *adhyātma*, the thinkable is *adhibhūta*, and the moon is *adhidaivata*. The nāḍis bind them. He who moves in the *manas*, the thinkable, the moon, the nāḍis, *prāṇa*, *vijñāna*, *ānanda*, the *ākāśa* of the heart, and within all else— That is *Ātmā*. It is that which should be worshipped. It is without old age, death, fear, sorrow, or end.

"Buddhi is *adhyātma*, the certainly knowable is *adhibhūta*, and Brahmā is *adhidaivata*. The nāḍis bind them. He who moves in *buddhi*, the certainly knowable, Brahmā, the nāḍis, *prāṇa*, *vijñāna*, *ānanda*, the *ākāśa* of the heart, and within all else— That is *Ātmā*. It is that which should be worshipped. It is without old age, death, fear, sorrow, or end.

"Ahaṁkāra is *adhyātma*, that which is acted upon by *ahaṁkāra* is *adhibhūta*, and *Rudra* is adidaivata. The nāḍis bind them. He who moves in *ahaṁkāra*, that which is acted upon by *ahaṁkāra*, *Rudra*, the *nāḍīs*, *prāṇa*, *vijñāna*, *ānanda*, the ākāśa of the heart, and within all else— That is *Ātmā*. It is that which should be worshipped. It is without old age, death, fear, sorrow, or end.

"Citta is *adhyātma*, that which is acted upon by citta (producing fluctuation of thought) is *adhibhūta*, and Kṣetrajña is *adhidaivata*. The nadis bind them. He who moves in citta, that which is acted upon by citta, Kṣetrajña, naḍīs, *prāṇa*, *vijñāna*, *ānanda*, the *ākāśa* of the heart, and within all else— That is *Ātmā*. It is that which should be worshipped. It is without old age, death, fear, sorrow, or end.

"He is the knower of all, the Lord of all, the ruler of all, the one latent in all, the one worshipped for the happiness of all, but Himself not worshipping (or seeking) any happiness, the one worshipped by all, the Vedas and other books and to which all this is food, but who does not become the food of another; moreover, the one who, as the eye, is the ordainer of all, the one who as *annamaya* is *Bhūtātmā*; the one who is prāṇ*amaya* is Indṛyātmā, the one as *manomaya* is *Saṅkalpātmā*, the one who as *vijñānamaya* is *Kālātmā*, the one who as *ānandamaya* is *Layātmā*, is one and not dual. How can it be said to be mortal? How can it be said

1. Although in the original *manas*, *buddhi*, etc., are in the middle, yet they are inserted here after the *karmendṛyas*.

that there is not immortality in It? It is neither internal *prajñā* nor external *prajñā* nor both, nor *Prajñāghana*; It is neither *prajñā* nor not-*prajñā*, it is neither known nor is it to know anything. Thus is the exposition of *Nirvāṇa*; and thus is the exposition of the Vedas; yea, thus is the exposition of the Vedas."

Khaṇḍa VI

"At first there was not anything in the least. These creatures were born through no root, no support but the Divine *Deva*, the one Nārāyaṇa[1]. The eye and the visible are Nārāyaṇa; the ear and the audible are Nārāyaṇa; the tongue and the 'tastable' are Nārāyaṇa; the nose and the 'smellable' are Nārāyaṇa; the skin and the tangible are Nārāyaṇa; *manas* and that which is acted upon by it are Nārāyaṇa; *buddhi* and that which is acted upon by it are Nārāyaṇa; *ahaṁkāra* and that which is acted upon by it are Nārāyaṇa; citta and that which is acted upon by it are Nārāyaṇa; vāk and that which is spoken are Nārāyaṇa; the hand and that which is lifted are Nārāyaṇa; the leg and that which is walked upon are Nārāyaṇa; the anus and the excreted are Nārāyaṇa; the genitals and the enjoyment of pleasure are Nārāyaṇa. The originator and the ordainer as also the agent and the causer of changes, are the Divine *Deva* Nārāyaṇa only. Ādityas, Rudras, Maruts, Vasus, *Aśvins*, the *Ṛk*, Yajus, and Sāma, Mantras, *Agni*, clarified butter and oblation— all these are Nārāyaṇa. The origin and the combination are the Divine *Deva* Nārāyaṇa only. Mother, father, brother, residence, asylum, friends and dependents are Nārāyaṇa only. The divine *nādis* known as *Virājā, Sudarśanā, Jitā, Saumyā, Moghā, Kumārā, Amṛtā, Satyā, Samadhyamā, Nāsīrā, Śiśirā, Surā, Sūryā*, and *Bhāsvatī* (fourteen *nādis* in all), that which thunders, sings and rains, *viz.*, Varuṇa, *Aryamā* (sun), Candramas (moon) *Kalā* (part), *Kavi* (*Sukra*), the creator Brahmā and Prajāpati, Indra, *Kāla* (or time) of days, half-days, *Kalpa*, the upper, and the directions— all these are Nārāyaṇa. That which was and will be is this *Puruṣa* only. Like the eye (which sees without any obstacle) the thing spread in the *ākāśa*, the wise ever see this supreme seat of Viṣṇu. *Brāhmaṇas* who are ever spiritually awake, praise in diverse ways and illuminate the suprme abode of Viṣṇu. thus is the exposition to theattaining of *Nirvāṇa*; thus is the teaching of the Vedas; yea, this is the teaching of the Vedas.

Khaṇḍa VII

"Within the body, is the one eternal Aja (unborn), located in the cave (of the heart). Earth is His body. Though He moves in the earth, earth does not know Him. Waters are His body. Though He moves in the

1. Nārāyaṇa is the Universal Self. This chapter gives out pantheistic theory that the whole universe is nothing but God Nārāyaṇa.

waters, waters do not know Him. Tejas is His body. Though He moves in tejas, tejas does not know Him. *Vāyu* is His body. Though He moves in *vāyu*, *vāyu* does not know Him. Ākāś is His body. Thought He moves in ākāśa, ākāśa does not know Him. *Manas* is His body. Though He moves in *manas*, *manas* does not know Him. *Buddhi* is his body. Though He moves in *buddhi*, *buddhi* does not know Him. *Ahaṁkāra* is His body. Though He moves in *ahaṁkāra*, *ahaṁkāra* does not know Him. Citta is His body.Though He moves in citta, citta does not know Him. *Avyakta* is His body. Though He moves in *Avyakta*, *Avyakta* does not know Him. *Akṣara* is His body. Though He moves in *Akṣara*, akṣara does not know Him. *Mṛtyu* (death) is His body. Though He moves in *Mṛtyu*, *Mṛtyu* does not know Him. Such an one is the *Ātmā* within all creatures, the remover of all sins and the Divine *Deva*, the one Nārāyaṇa.

"This knowledge was imparted (by Nārāyaṇa) to Apāntaratama who in turn imparted it to Brahmā. Brahmā imparted it to *Ghora-Aṅgiras*. He imparted it to Raikva, who in turn imparted it to Rāma. Rāma imparted it to all creatures. This is the teaching of *Nirvāṇa*; this is the teaching of the Vedas; yes, this is the teaching of the Vedas."

Khaṇḍa VIII

"The *Ātmā* of all which is immaculate, is located within the cave in the body. *Ātmā* which lives in the midst of the body filled with fat, flesh and phlegm in a seat very closely shut up with shining many-coloured walls resembling a Gandharva city and with the (subtle) essence going out of it (to other parts of the body), which seat may be likened to a plantain flower and is ever agitated like a water-bubble— this *Ātmā* is of an unthinkable form, the Divine *Deva*, associateless and pure, has tejas as its body, is of all forms, the Lord of all, the unthinkable and the bodiless, placed within the cave, immortal, shining, and bliss itself. He is a wise person who cognizes *Ātmā* thus, and not one who does not do so."

Khaṇḍa IX

Once Raikva questioned Him (Lord) thus : "O Lord, in whom does everything disappear (or merge) ?" He replied thus : "That which (or he who) disappears in the eye becomes the eye only; that which disappears in the visible becomes the visible only; that which disappears in the sun becomes sun only; that which disappears in Virāṭ becomes Virāṭ only; that which disappears in *prāṇa* becomes *prāṇa* only; that which disappears in *vijñāna* becomes *vijñāna* only; that which disappears in *ānanda* becomes *ānanda* only; that which disappears in turya becomes turya only— (all these) attain that which is deathless, fearless, sorrowless, endless, and seedless."

Then He continued : "That which disappears in the ear becomes ear itself; that which disappears in the audible becomes the audible only; that which disappears in dik (space) becomes dik only; that which disappeas in sudarśana (discus) becomes sudarśana only : that which disappears in *apāna* becomes *apāna* only; that which disappears in *vijñāna* becomes *vijñāna* only; that which disappears in *ānanda* becomes *ānanda* only; that which disappears in turya becomes turya only— (all these) attain that which is deathless, fearless, sorrowless, endless,and seedless."

Then He continued : "That which disappears in the nose becomes nose only; that which disappears in the odoriferous becomes odoriferous only; that which disappears in *pṛthivī* becomes *pṛthivī* only; that which disappears in jitam (victory) becomes victory only; that which disappears in vyāna becomes vyāna only; that which disappears in *vijñāna* becomes *vijñāna* only; that which disappears in bliss becomes bliss only; that which disappears in turya becomes turya only— (all these) attain that which is deathless, fearless, sorrowless, endless, and seedless."

Then He continued : "That which disappears in the mouth becomes the mouth only; that which disappears in the tasted becomes the tasted only; that which disappears in Varuṇa becomes Varuṇa only; that which disappears in Soumya (moon or Mercury) becomes soumya only; that which disappears in *udāna* becomes *udāna* only; that which disappears in *vijñāna* becomes *vijñāna* only; that which disappears in bliss becomes bliss only; that which disappears in turya becomes turya only— (all these) attain that which is deathless, fearless, sorrowless, endless, and seedless."

Then He continued : "That which disappears in the skin becomes the skin only; that which disappears in touch becomes touch only; that which disappears in *vāyu* becomes *vāyu* only; that which disappears in cloud becomes cloud only; that which disappears in samāna becomes samāna only; that which disappears in *vijñāna* becomes *vijñāna* only; that which disappears in bliss becomes bliss only; that which disappears in turya becomes turya only— (all these) attain that which is deathless, fearless, sorrowless, endless, and seedless."

Then He continued : "That which disappears in vāk becomes vāk only; that which disappears in speech becomes speech only; that which disappears in *Agni* becomes *agni* only; that which disappears in Kumārā becomes kumārā only; that which disappears in hostility becomes hostility itself; that which disappears in *vijñāna* become *vijñāna* only; that which disappears in bliss becomes bliss only; that which disappears in turya becomes turya only— (all these) attain that which is deathless, fearless, sorrowless, endless, and seedless."

Then He continued : "That which disappears in the hand becomes the hand only; that which disappears in that which is lifted by the hand becomes that which is lifted by the hand; that which disappears in Indra becomes Indra only; that which disappears in the nectar becomes nectar only; that which disappears in mukhya becomes mukhya only; that which disappears in *vijñāna* becomes *vijñāna* only; that which disappears in bliss becomes bliss only; that which disappears in turya becomes turya only— (all these) attain, that which is deathless, fearless, sorrowless, endless and seedless."

Then He continued : "That which disappears in the leg becomes the leg only; that which disappears in that which is walked upon becomes that which is walked upon; that which disappears in Viṣṇu becomes Viṣṇu only; that which disappears in *satya* becomes *satya* only; that which disappears in the suppression of the breath and voice becomes the suppression of the breath and voice; that which disappears in *vijñāna* becomes *vijñāna* only; that which disappears in bliss becomes bliss only; that which disappears in turya becomes turya only— (all these) attain that which is deathless, fearless, sorrowless, endless, and seedless."

Then He continued : "That which disappears in the anus becomes the anus only; that which disappears in that which is excreted becomes that which is excreted; that which disappears in *Mṛtyu* becomes *Mṛtyu* only; that which disappears in spirituous liquor becomes spiritous liquor only; that which disappears in hurricane becomes hurricane only; that which disappears in *vijñāna* becomes *vijñāna* only; that wich disappears in bliss becomes bliss only; that which disappears in turya becomes turya only— (all these) attain that which is deathless, fearless, sorrowless, endless, and seedless."

Then He continued : "That which disappears in the genitals becomes the genitals only; that which disappears in that which is enjoyed becomes that which is enjoyed; that which disappears in that which is Prajāpati becomes Prajāpati only; that which disappeas in nāsīnām becomes nāsīnām only; that which disappears in kurmira becomes kurmira only; that which disappears in *vijñāna* becomes *vijñāna* only; that which disappears in bliss becomes bliss only; that which disappears in turya becomes turya only— (all these) attain that which is deathless, fearless, sorrowless, endless, and seedless."

Then He continued : "That which disappears in *manas* becomes *manas* itself; that which disappears in the thinkable becomes thinkable itself; that which disappears in the moon becomes the moon itself; that which disappears in śiśu becomes śiśu itself; that which disappears in śyena becomes śyena itself; that which disappears in *vijñāna* becomes *vijñāna* only; that which disappears in *ānanda* becomes *ānanda* itself; that which disappears in turya becomes turya itself— (all these) attain that which is deathless, fearless, sorrowless, endless, and seedless."

Then He continued : "That which disappears in *buddhi* becomes *buddhi* itself; that which disappears in the certainly knowable becomes the certainly knowable itself; that which disappears in Brahmā becomes Brahmā himself; that which disappears in Kṛṣṇa becomes Kṛṣṇa himself;

that which disappears in Sūrya becomes Sūrya itself; that which disappears in *vijñāna* becomes *vijñāna* itself; that which disappears in *ānanda* becomes *ānanda* itself; that which disappears in turya becomes turya itself— (all these) attain that which is deathless, fearless, sorrowless, endless, and seedless."

Then He continued : "That which disappears in *ahaṁkāra* becomes *ahaṁkāra* itself; that which disappears in that which is acted upon by *ahaṁkāra* becomes that itself; that which disappears in *Rudra* becomes *Rudra* himself; that which disappears in asura becomes asura itself; that which disappears in śveta becomes śveta itself; that which disappears in *vijñāna* becomes *vijñāna* itself; that which disappears in *ānanda* becomes *ānanda* itself; that which disappears in turya becomes turya itself— (all these) attain that which is deathless, fearless, sorrowless, endless, and seedless."

Then He continued : "That which disappears in citta becomes citta itself; that which disappears in that which is acted upon by citta becoming that itself; that which disappears in Kṣetrajña becomes Kṣetrajña itself; that which disappears in bhāsvatī becomes bhāsvatī itself; that which disappears in nāga becomes nāga itself; that which disappears in *vijñāna* becomes *vijñāna* itself; that which disappears in *ānanda* becomes *ānanda* itself; that which disappears in turya becomes turya itself— (all these) attain that which is deathless, fearless, sorrowless, endless, and seedless."

"He who knows this as seedless in this manner becomes himself seedless. He is neither born, nor dies, nor is deluded nor split, nor burnt, nor cut— yea, he dos not feel angry, and hence he is said to be *Ātmā*, capable of burning all. Such an *Ātmā* is neither attained by a hundred sayings, nor by (the reading of) many scriptures, nor by mere intelligence, no by hearing from others, nor by understanding, nor by Vedas, nor by scriptures, nor by severe tapas, nor sāṁkhya, nor *yoga*, nor observances of the orders of the life, nor by any other means (than the following). Devoted *Brāhmaṇas* who repeat the Vedas according to rules and who worship Him with praise attain Him. He who is quiescent, self-controlled, indifferent to worldly objects and resigned, having centred his mind on *Ātmā* sees *Ātmā* and becomes one with the *Ātmā* of all, as also he who knows this."

Khaṇḍa X

Then Raikva asked Him : "O Lord, where do all things rest? He replied : "In the worlds of Rasātala (or nether worlds)."

"In what are these (Rasātala world) woven wrap and woof?" He replied : "In the worlds of Bhūḥ."

"In what are these (worlds of Bhūḥ) woven warp and woof?" he replied : "In the worlds of Bhuvaḥ."

"In what are these (Bhuvaḥ worlds) woven warp and woof?" "In the worlds of Suvaḥ."

"In what are these (Suvaḥ worlds) woven warp and woof?" In the worlds of Mahaḥ."

"In what are these (Mahaḥ worlds) woven warp and woof.?" "In the Janaloka."

"In what are these (Jana worlds) woven warp and woof?" "In the Tapoloka."

"In what are these (Tapolokas) woven warp and woof?" "In the *Satya* Loka."

"In what are these (*Satya* worlds) woven warp and woof." "In the Prajāpati lok."

"In what are these (Prajāpati worlds) woven warp and woof?" In the Brahmaloka."

"In what are these (Brahma worlds) woven warp and woof." "In the Sarvaloka."

"In what are these (Sarva lokas) woven warp and woof." "In *Ātmā*—which is *Brahman*, like beads (in a rosary) warp-wise and woof-wise."

Then he said : "All these rest in *Ātmā*, and he who knows this, becomes *Ātmā* itself. Thus is the exposition of *Nirvāṇa*. Thus is the exposition of the Vedas; yea, thus is the exposition of the Vedas."

Khaṇḍa XI

Again Raikva asked Him : "O Lord ! what is the seat of *Ātmā* which is replete with *vijñāna*? and how does it leave the body and pervade the universe?" To this He replied : "There is a mass of red flesh in the middle of the heart. In it, there is a lotus called dahara. It buds forth in many petals like a water-lily. In the middle of it is an ocean (samudra).[1] In its midst a *koka*[2] (bird). In it there are four nāḍis. They are ramā, aramā, *Icchā* and *punarbhava*. Of these, ramā leads a man of virtue to a happy world. *Aramā* leads one of sins into the world of sins. (Passing) through *Icchā* (*Nāḍi*), one gets whatever he remembers. Through *Punarbhava*, he splits opon the sheaths after splitting open the sheaths, he splits open the skull of the head; then he splits open pṛthvī; then *āpas*; then tejas; then *vāyu*; then *ākāśa*. Then he splits open *manas*; then bhūtādi; then mahat; then *avyakta*; then akṣara; then he splits open mrtyu and mrtyu becomes one with the supreme God. Beyond this, there is neither Sat nor asat, nor Sat-asat. Thus is the exposition of *Nirvāṇa*; and thus is the exposition of the Vedas; yea, thus is the exposition of Vedas."

1. The ocean probably refers to ākāśic space.
2. *Koka* probably refers to *Haṁsa*.

Khaṇḍa XII[1]

"*Anna* (food) came from Nārāyaṇa. It was first cooked in Brahmaloka in the *Mahā-samvartaka* fire. Again it was cooked in the sun; again it was cooked in *kravyādi* (lit., the fire that burns raw flesh, etc.); again it was cooked in *jwālakīla* (the flaming kīla); then it became pure and not stale (or fresh). One should eat whatever has fallen to his lot and without begging; one should never beg any (food)."

Khaṇḍa XIII

"The wise man should conduct himself like a lad, with the nature of a child, without company, blameless, silent and wise and without exercising any authority. This description of *Kaivalya* is stated by Prajāpati. Having found with certitude the supreme seat, one should dwell under a tree with torn cloths, unaccompanied, single and engaged in *samādhi*. He should be longing after the attaining of *Ātmā* having attained this object, he is desireless, his desires have decayed. he fears none, though he finds the cause of death in such as elephants, lions, gadflies, mosquitoes, ichneuma, serpents, *Yakṣas*, *Rākṣasas* and *Gandharvas*. He will stand like a tree. Though cut down, he will neither get angry nor tremble. he will stand (or remain) like a lotus. Though pierced, he will neither get angry nor tremble. He will stand like *ākāśa*; though struck, he will neither get angry nor tremble. He will stand by *Satya* (truth), since *Ātmā* is *Satya*.

"*Pṛthivī* is the heart (or centre) of all odours; apas is the heart of all tastes; tejas is the heart of all forms; *vāyu* is the heart of all touch; ākāśa is the heart of all sounds; *avyakta* is the heart of gītās (or sounds); *mṛtyu* is the heart of all *Sattvas*; and *mṛtyu* becomes one with the Supreme. And beyond Him, there is neither Sat nor asat, nor Sat-asat. Thus is the exposition of *Nirvāṇa*; thus is the exposition of the Vedas; yea, thus is the exposition of the Vedas."

Khaṇḍa XIV[2]

"*Pṛthivī* is the food, and *āpas* is he eater; *āpas* is the food and *jyotis* (or fire) is the eater; *jyotis* is the food, and *vāyu* is the eater; *vāyu* is the food, and *ākāśa* is the eater; and *ākāśa* is the food and the indṛiyas (organs) are the eaters; indṛyas are the food and *manas* is the eater; *manas* is the food, and *buddhi* is the eater; *buddhi* is the food, and *avyakta* is the eater; *avyakta* is the food, and akṣara is the eater; akṣara is the food, and *mṛtyu* is the eater; and *mṛtyu* becomes one with the Supreme. Beyond Him, there is neither Sat and asat, nor Sat-asat. Thus is the exposition of

1. In this chapter are related the different fires, the first or primordial anna or food-substance has to pass through in order to became the gross food.
2. The causes and effects are herein given out, cause of an effect becoming itself the effect of a higher cause.

Nirvāṇa, and thus is the exposition of the Vedas; yea, thus is the exposition of the Vedas."

Khaṇḍa XV

Again Raikva aksed : "O Lord, when this *Vijñāna*-ghana goes out (of the body or the universe), what does it burn and how?" To which He replied : When it goes away, it burns *prāṇa*. *apāna*, vyāna, *udāna*, samāna, vairambha, mukhya, antaryāma, prabhañjana, kumāra, śyena, Kṛṣ ṇa, śveta, and nāga. Then it burns *pṛthivī*, *āpas*, tejas, *vāyu*, and *ākāśa*; then it burns the waking, the dreaming, the dreamless sleeping and the fourth states as well as the maharlokas and worlds higher; then it burns the lokāloka (the highest world forming a limit to the other worlds). Then it burns dharma and adharama. Then it burns that which is beyond, is sunless, limitless, and worldless. Then it burns mahat; it burns *avyakta*; it burns akṣara; it burns *mṛtyu*; and *mṛtyu* becomes one with the great Lord. Beyond Him, there is neither Sat nor asat, nor Sat-asat. Thus is the exposition of *Nirvāṇa*, and thus is the exposition of the Vedas; yea, thus is the exposition of the Vedas."

Khaṇḍa XVI

"This Subāla-Bīja,-Brahma-Upaniṣad should neither be given out nor taught to one who has not controlled his passions, who has no sons, who has not gone to a *Guru*, and having become his disciple has not resided with him for a year, and whose family and conduct are not known. These doctrines should be taught to him who has supreme devotion to the Lord and as much to his *Guru*.Then these truths shine in his great soul. Thus is the exposition of *Nirvāṇa*; thus is the exposition of the Vedas; yea, thus is the exposition of the Vadas."

Thus ends the Upaniṣad

Tejobindu[1]-Upaniṣad

OF

KṚṢṆA-YAJURVEDA

Chapter I

Param-Dhyān (the supreme meditation) should be upon tejobindu, which is the *Ātmā* of the universe, which is seated in the heart, which is of the size of an atom, which partains to Śiva, which is quiescent and which is gross and subtle, as also above these qualities. That alone should be the *dhyāna* of the Munis as well as the men, which is full of pains, which is difficult to meditate on, which is difficult to perceive, which is the emancipated one, which is decayless and which is difficult to attain. One whose food is moderate, whose anger has been controlled, who has given up all love for society, who has subdued his passions, who has overcome all pairs (heat and cold etc.), who has given up his egoism, who does not bless anyone nor take anything from others, and also who goes where they naturally ought not to go, and naturally would not go where they like to go— such persons also obtain three[2] in the face. Hamsa is said to have three seats Therefore know it is the greatest of mysteries, without sleep and without support. It is very subtle, of the form of Soma, and is the supreme seat of Viṣṇu. That seat has three faces, three *guṇas* and three dhātus, and is formless, motionless, changeless, sizeless, and supportless. That seat is without upādhi, and is above the reach of speech and mind. It is *Svabhāva* (self or nature) reachable only by *bhāva* (being). The indestructible seat is associateless, without bliss, beyond mind, difficult to perceive emancipated and changeless. It should be meditated upon as the liberated, the eternal, the permanent and the indestructible. It is *Brahman*, is *adhyātma* (or the deity presiding as *Ātmā*) and is the highest seat of Viṣṇu. It is inconceivable, of the nature of *Cidātmā* and above the *ākāśa*, is void and non-void, and beyond the void, and is abiding in the heart. There is (in It) neither meditation nor meditator, nor the meditated, nor the non-meditated. It is not the universe. It is the highest. it is neither supreme nor above the supreme. It is inconceivable, unknowable, non-truth, and not the highest. It is realised by the Munis, but the *Devas* do not know the supreme One. Avarice, delusion, fear, pride, passion, anger, sin,

---

1. Ṭejas is spiritual light and bindu is seed; hence the seed or source of spiritual light.
2. This probably refers to the triangle appearing in the disciples.

heat, cold, hunger, thirst thought and fancy— (all these do not exist in It). (In It) there is no pride of (belonging to) the *Brāhmaṇa* caste, nor is there the collection of the knot of salvation. (In It) there is no fear, no happiness, no pains, neither fame nor disgrace. That which is without these states is the supreme *Brahman*.

Yama[1] (forbearance), *niyama* (religious observance), tyāga (renunciation), *mauna* (silence) according to time and place, *āsana* (posture), *mūlabandha*, seeing all bodies as equal, the position of the eye, *prāṇa-samyamana* (control of breath), *pratyāhāra* (subjugation of the senses), *dhāraṇā*, *ātma-dhyāna* and *samādhi*— these are spoken of as the parts (of *yoga*) in order. That is called yama in which one controls all his organs (of sense and actions) through the *vijñāna* that all is *Brahman*; this should be practised often and often. *Niyama*, in which there is the supreme bliss enjoyed through the flowing (or inclination) of the mind towards things of the same (spiritual) kind, (*viz*., *Brahman*) and the abandoning of things differing from one another is practised by the sages as a rule. In tyāga (renunciation), one abandones the manifestations (or objects) of the universe through the cognition of *Ātmā* that is *Sat* and *Cit*. This is prectised by the great and is the giver of immediate salvation. *Mauna* (the silence), in which, without reaching That, speech returns along with mind, is fit to be attained by the Yogins and should be ever worshipped by the ignorant even). How is it possible to speak of "That", from which speech returns? How should it be described as the universe as there is no word to describe it? It is "That" which is (really) called silence, and which is naturally understood (as such). There is silence in children, but with words (latent); whereas the knowers of *Brahman* have it (silence) but without words. That should be known as "the lonely seat" in which there is no man in the beginning, middle, or end, and through which all this (universe) is fully pervaded. The illusion of Brahmā and all other beings takes place within one twinkling (of His eye). That should be known as *āsana* (posture), in which one has with ease and without fatigue (uninterrupted) meditation of *Brahman*; that is described by the word *kāla* (time), that is endless bliss and that is secondless. Everything else is the destroyer of happiness. That is called *siddhāsana* (siddha-posture) in which the siddhas (psychical personages) have succeeded in realising the endless One as the support of the universe containing all the elements, etc. That is called the mūlabandha, which is the Mūla (root) of all words, and through which the root Citta is (bandha) bound. It should be always practised by the Rājayogins.

One after having known the equality of the aṅgas (or parts of *yoga*) point to one and the same *Brahman*, should be absorbed in that equal (or

1. All these parts of *yoga* are explained here from the sandpoint of *vedānta*.

uniform) *Brahman*; if not, there is not that equality (attained). Then ike a dry tree, there is straightness (or uniformity throughout). Making one's vision full of spiritual wisdom, one should look upon the world as full of *Brahman*. That vision is very noble. It is (generally) aimed at the tip of the nose; but it should be directed towards that seat (of *Brahman*) wherein the sessation of seer, the seen, and sight will take place, and not towards the tip of the nose. That is called *prāṇāyāma* (the control of breath), in which there is the control of the modifications (of mind) through the cognition of *Brahman* in all the states of citta, and others. The checking of (the conception of the reality of) the universe, is said to be expiration. The conception of "I am *Brahman*" is inspiration. The holding on (long) to this conception without agitation is cessation of breath. Such is the practice of the enlightened. The ignorant close their nose. That should be known as *pratyāhāra*, through which one sees *Ātmā* (even) in the objects of sense, and pleases citta through *manas*. It should be practised often and often. Through seeing *Brahman* wherever the mind goes, the *dhāraṇā* of mind is obtained. *Dhāraṇā* is thought of highly by wise. By *dhāraṇā* is meant that state where one indulges in the good thought, "I am *Brahman* alone," and is without any support. This *dhyāna* is the giver of supreme bliss. Being first in a state of changelessness, and then throughly forgetting (even) that state owing to the cognition of the (true) nature of *Brahman*— this is called *samādhi*. This kind of bliss should be practised or enjoyed) by a wise person till his cognition itself united in a moment with the state of pratyag (*Ātmā*). Then this King of Yogins becomes a Siddha, and is without any aid (outside himself). Then he will attain a state, inexpressible and unthinkable.

When *samādhi* is practised, the following obstacles arise with great force— absence of right inquiry, laziness, inclination to enjoyment, absorption (in material object) tamas, distraction, impatience, sweat, and absent-mindedness. All these obstacles should be overcome by inquirs into *Brahman*. Through *bhāvavṛttis* (worldly thoughts) one gets into them. Through *Śūnya-vṛttis* (void or empty thoughts), one gets into them. But through the *vṛttis* of *Brahman*, one gets fullness. Therefore one should develop fullness through this means (of *Brahman*). He who abondons this *vṛtti* of *Brahman*, which is very purifying and supreme— that man lives in vain like a beast. But he who understands this *vṛtti* (of *Brahman*), and having understood it makes advances in its, becomes a good and blessed person, deserving to be worshipped by the three worlds. Those who are greatly developed through the ripening (of their past *karmas*) attain the state of *Brahman* : others are simply reciters of words. Those who are clever in arguments about *Brahman*, but are without the action pertaining to *Brahman*, and who are greatly attached to the world— those certainly are born again and again (in this world) through their *ajñāna*; (the former) never remain, even for half a moment—without the *vṛtti* of *Brahman*, like Brahmā and others, Sanaka,[1] Śuka and others. When a cause is subject to changes, it (as an effect) must also have its cause. When the cause ceases to exist in truth, the effect perishes through right discrimination. Then that substance (or principle) which is beyond the scope of words, remains pure. After that, *vṛtti jñāna* arises in their purfied mind; through meditation with transcendental energy, there arises a firm certitude. After reducing the visible into the invisible state, one should see everything as *Brahman*. The wise should every stay in bliss with their understanding full of essence of *cit*. Thus ends the first chapter of Tejobindu.

Chapter II

Then the Kumāra[2] asked Śiva : "Please explain to me the nature of *Cinmātra*, that is the partless non-dual essence." The great Śiva replied : "The partless non-dual essence is the visible. It is the world, it is the existence, it is the Self, it is mantra, it is action, it is spiritual wisdom, it is water. It is the earth, it is ākāśa, it is the books, it is the three Vedas, it is the *Brahman*, it is the religious vow, it is *Jīva*, it is Aja (the unborn), it is Brahmā, it is Viṣṇu, it is *Rudra*; it is I, it *Ātmā*, it is the *Guru*. It is the aim, it is sacrifice, it is the body, it is *manas*, it is citta, it is happiness, it is vidyā; it is the undifferentiated, it is the eternal, it is the supreme, it is everything. O six-faced one, different form It there is nothing. None, none but It; It is I. It is gross, it is subtle, it is knowable, it is thou; it is the mysterious; it is the knower; it is existence, it is mother, it is father, it is brother, it is hushand, it is *Sūtra* (*Ātmā*), it is Virāt. It is the body, it is the head, it is the internal, it is the external, it is full, it is nectar, it is gotra (clan), it is gṛha (the house), it is the preservable, it is the moon, it is the stars, it is the sun, it is the holy seat. It is forgiveness, it is patience, it is the *guṇas*, it is the witness. It is a friend, it is a relative, it is an ally, it is the king, town, kingdom and subjects. It is Om, *japa*, meditation, the seat, the one worthy to be taken (in), the heart, the *Jyotis*, Swarga (heaven) and Self."

"All the partless and non-dual essence should be regarded as *Cinmātra*. *Cinmātra* alone is the Absolute Consciousness; and this partless non-dual essence alone is the (real) essence. All having consciousness alone except those having changes, are *cinmātra*. All this is *Cinmātra*. He is *Cinmātra*; the state of *Ātmā* is known as *Cinmātra* and the partless non-dual essence. The whole world is *cinmātra*. our state and

1. Sanaka is one of the four *Kumāras* in the *Pruāṇas* who refused to create; *Śuka* is the son of *Veda-Vyās*.
2. The Kumāra is the son of Śiva called *Kārtikēya* the six-faced, symbolising the six-faced Mars in one sense.

my state are *cinmātra*. *Ākāśa*, earth, water, *vāyu*, *agni*, Brahmā, Viṣṇu, Śiva and all else that exist or do not, are *Cinmātra*. That which is the partless non-dual essence is *Cinmātra*. All the past, present, and future are *Cinmātra*. Substance and time are *Cinmātra*. Knowledge and the knowable are *Cinmātra*. the knower is *Cinmātra*. Everything is *Cinmātra*. Every speech is *Cinmātra*. Whatever else is *Cinmātra*. Asat and Sat are *Cinmātra*. The beginning and end are Cinmāṭra; that which is in the beginning and end is *Cinmātra* ever. The *Guru* and the disciple are *Cinmātra*. If the seer and the seen are *Cinmātra*, then they are always *Cinmaya*. All things wondrous are *Cinmātra*. The (gross) body is *Cinmātra*. The (gross) body is *Cinmātra*, as also the subtle and causal bodies. There is nothing beyond *Cinmātra*. I and thou are *Cinmātra*. From and non-from are *Cinmātra*. Virtue and vice are *Cinmātra*. The body is a symbol of *Cinmātra*. *Saṅkalpa*, knowing, mantra, and others the gods invoked in mantras, the gods presiding over the eight quarters, the phenomenal and the supreme *Brahman* are nothing but *Cinmātra*. There is nothing without *Cinmātra*. *Māyā* is nothing without *Cinmātra*. Pūjā (worship) is nothing without *Cinmātra*, Mediation, turth, sheaths and others, the (eight) vasus, silence, non-silence, and indifference to objects— are nothing without *Cinmātra*. Everything is from *Cinmātra*. Whatever is seen and however seen— it is *Cinmātra* so far. Whatever exists and however distant, is *Cinmātra*. Whatever elements exist, whatever is perceived, and whatever is Vedānta— all these are *Cinmātra*. Without *Cinmātra*, there is no motion, no *mokṣa* and no goal aimed at. Everthing is *cinmātra*. *Brahman* that is the partless non-dual essence is known to be nothing but Chinmātra. Thou, O Lord, art the partless non-dual essence (stated) in the books, in me, in Thee, and in the ruler. He who thus percieves 'I' as of one homogeneity (pervading everywhere) will at once be emancipated through this spiritual wisdom. He is his own *Guru* with this profound spiritual wisdom. Thus ends the second chapter of Tejobindu.

Chapter III

The Kumāra addressed his father (again) : "Please explain to me the realisation of *Ātmā*. "To which the great Śiva said : "I am of the nature of the Parabrahman. I am the supreme bliss. I am solely of the nature of divine wisdom. I am the sole supreme, the sole quiescence, the sole *Cinmaya*, the sole unconditioned, the sole permanent and the sole *Sattva*. I am the 'I' that has given up 'I'. I am one that is without anything. I am full of Cidākāś. I am the sole fourth one. I am the sole one above the fourth (state of turya). I am the nature of (pure) consciousness. I am ever of the nature of bliss-consciousness. I am of the nature of the non-dual. I am ever of a pure nature, solely of the nature of divine wisdom, of the nature of happiness, without fancies, desires or diseases, of the nature of bliss, without changes or differentiations, and of the nature of the eternal one essence and *Cinmātra*. My real nature is indescribable, of endless bliss, he bliss above Sat and *Cit* and the interior of the interior. I am beyond reach of *manas* and speech. I am of the nature of Ātmic bliss, true bliss and one who plays with (my) *Ātmā*. I am *Ātmā* and Sadāśiva. My nature is Ātmic spiritual effulgence. I am the essence of the *jyotis* of *Ātmā*. I am without beginning, middle or end. I am like the sky. I am solely Sat. Ānanda, and Ciṭ which is unconditioned and pure. I am the Saccid*ānanda* that is eternal, enlightened and pure. I am ever of the nature of the eternal Śeṣa (serpent-time). I am ever beyond all. My nature is beyond form. My form is supreme *ākāśa*. My nature is of the bliss of earth. I am ever without speech. My nature is the all-seat (foundation of all). I am ever replete with consciousness, without the attachment of body, without thought, without the modifications of citta, the sole essence of Cidātma, beyond the visibility of all and of the form of vision. My nature is ever full. I am ever fully contented, the all, and *Brahman*, and the very consciousness; I am 'I'. My nature is of the earth. I am the great *Ātmā* and the supreme of the supreme; I appear sometimes as different from myself; sometimes as possessing a body, sometimes as a pupil and sometimes as the basis of the words. I am beyond the three periods of time, am worshipped by the Vedas, am determined by the sciences and am fixed in the citta. There is nothing left out by me, neither the earth nor any other objects here. Know that there is nothing which is out of myself. I am Brahmā, a Siddha, the eternally pure, non-dual one, *Brahman*, without old age or death. I shine by myself; I am my own *Ātmā*, my own goal, enjoy myself, play in myself, have my own spiritual effulgence, am my own greatness, and am used to play in my own *Ātmā*, look on my own *Ātmā* and am in myself happily seated. I have my own *Ātmā* as the residue, stay in my own consciousness, and play happily in the kingdom of my own *Ātmā*, Sitting on the real throne of my own *Ātmā*. I think of nothing else but my own *Ātmā*, I am Cidrūpa alone, *Brahman* alone, Saccid*ānanda*, the secondless, the one replete with bliss and the sole *brahman* and ever without anything, have the bliss of my own *Ātmā*, the unconditioned bliss, and am always *Ātma-Ākāśa*. I alone am in the heart like Cidāditya (the consciousness-sun). I am content in my own *Ātmā*, have no form, or no decay, am without the number one, have the nature of an unconditioned and emancipated one and I am subtler than *ākāśa*; I am without the existence of beginning or end, of the nature of the all-illuminating, the bliss greater than the great, of the sole nature of Sat, of the nature of pure *mokṣa*, of the nature of truth and bliss, full of spiritual wisdom and bliss, of the nature of wisdom alone, and of the nature of Saccid*ānanda*. All this is *Brahman* alone. there is none other than *Brahman* and that is 'I'.

"I am *Brahman* that is Sat, and bliss, and the sncient. The word 'thou' and the word 'that' are not different from me. I am of the nature of consciousness. I am alone the great Śiva. I am beyond the nature of existence. I am of the nature of happiness. As there is nothing that can witness me, I am without the state of witness. Being purely of the nature of *Bṛahman*, I am the eternal *Ātmā*. I alone am the Ādiśeṣa (the primeval Śeṣa)[1]. I alone am the Śeṣa. I am without name and form, of the nature of bliss, of the nature of being unperceivable by the senses, and of the nature of all beings; I have neither bondage nor salvation. I am of the form of eternal bliss. I am the primeval consciousness alone, the partless and non-dual essence, beyond reach of speech and mind, of the nature of bliss everywhere, of the nature of fullness everywhere, of the nature of earthly bliss, of the nature of contentment everywhere, the supreme nectary essence, and the one and secondless Sat (*viz.,*), *Brahman*. There is no doubt of it. I am of the nature of all-void. I am the one that is given out by the Vedas. I am of the nature of the emancipated and emancipation, of Nirvāṇic bliss, of truth and wisdom, of Sat alone and bliss, of the one beyond the fourth, of one without fancy, and ever of the nature of Aja (the unborn). I am without passion or faults. I am the pure, the enlightened, the eternal, the all-pervading and of the nature of the significance of Om, of the spotless, and of *Cit*. I am neither existing nor non-existing. I am not of the nature of anything. I am of the nature of the actionless. I am without parts. I have no semblance, no *manas*, no sense, no *buddhi*, no change, none of the three bodies, neither the waking, dreaming, or dreamless sleeping states. I am neither of the nature of the three pains nor of the three desires. I have neither śravaṇa nor manana in chidātma in order to attain salvation. There is nothing like me or unlike me. There is nothing within me. I have none of the three bodies.

"The nature of *manas* is unreal, the nature of *buddhi* is unreal, the nature of aham (the 'I') is unreal; but I am the unconditioned, the permanent and the unborn. The three bodies are unreal, the three periods of time are unreal, the three *guṇas* are unreal, but I am of the nature of the real and the pure. That which is heard is unreal, all the Vedas are unreal, the *Śāstras* are unreal, but I am the Real and of the nature of chit. The *Mūrtis* (Brahmā Viṣṇu and *Rudra* having limitation) are unreal, all the creation is unreal, all the tattvas are unreal, but know that I am the great Śadāśiva. The master and the disciple are unreal, the *mantra* of the *Guru* is unreal, that which is seen is unreal, but know me to be Real. Whatever is thought of is unreal, whatever is lawful is unreal, whatever is beneficial is unreal, but know me to be the Real. Know the *Puruṣa* (ego) to be unreal, know the enjoyments to be unreal, know things seen and heard are unreal as also the one woven warp-wise and woof-wise, *viz.,* this universe; cause and non-cause are unreal, things lost or obtained are unreal. Pains and happiness are unreal, all and non-all are unreal, gain and loss are unreal, victory and defeat are unreal. All the sound, all the touch,

1. *Śeṣa*, meaning remainder is the serpent representing time.

all the forms, all the taste, all the smell, and all *ajñāna* are unreal. Everthing is always unreal— the mundane existence is unreal— all the *guṇas* are unreal. I am of the nature of Sat.

"One should cognize his own *Ātmā* alone. One should always practise the mantra of his *Ātmā* alone the mantra (Aham-brahmāsmi) 'I am brahman' removes all the sins of sight, destroys all other mantras, destroys all the sins of body and birth, the noose of Yama, the pains of duality, the thought of difference, the pains of thought, the disease of *buddhi*, the bondage of Citta, all diseases, all griefs and passions instantaneously, the power of anger, the modifications of citta, *saṅkalpa*, crores of sins, all actions and the ajñān of *Ātmā*. The mantra 'I am brahman' gives indescribable bliss, gives the state of ajada (the non-inertness or the undecaying) and kills the demon of non-*Ātmā*. The thunderbolt 'I am *Brahman*' clears all the hill of not-*Ātmā*. the wheel 'I am *Brahman*' destroys the asuras of not-*Ātmā*. The mantras 'I am *Brahman*' will relieve all (persons). The mantra 'I am *Brahman*' gives spiritual wisdom and bliss. There are seven crores of great mantras and there are viratas (vows) of (or yielding) hundred crores of births. having given up all other mantras, one should ever practise this mantra. he obtains at once salvation, and there is not even a particle of doubt about it. Thus ends the third chapter of the Tejobinḍu Upaniṣad."

Chapter IV

The Kumāra asked the great Lord : "Please explain to me the nature of *Jīvanmukti* (embodied salvation) and *videhamukti* (disembodied salvation)." To which the great Śiva replied : "I am *cidātmā*. I am *Para-Ātmā*. I am the *Nirguṇa*, greater than the great. One who will simply stay in *Ātmā* is called a *Jīvanmukta*. He who realises : 'I am beyond the three bodies, I am the pure consciousness and I am *Brahman*', is said to be a *Jīvanmukta*. he is said to be a *Jīvanmukta*, who realises : "I am of the nature of the blissful and of the supreme bliss. and I have neither body nor any other thing except the certitude "I am *Brahman*" Only. He is said to be a *Jīvanmukta* who has not at all got the 'I' in myself, but who styas in *cinmātra* (absolute consciousness) alone, whose interior is consciousness alone, who is only of the nature of *Cinmātra*, whose *Ātmā* is of the nature of the all-full, who has *Ātmā* left over in all, who is devoted to bliss, who is undifferentiated, who is all-full of the nature of consciousness, whose *Ātmā* is of the nature of pure consciousness, who has given up all affinities (for objects), who has unconditioned bliss, whose *Ātmā* is tranquil, who has got no other thought (then Itself), and who is devoid of the thought of the existence of anything. He is said to be a *Jīvanmukta* who realises : 'I have no citta, no *buddhi*, no *ahaṁkāra*, no sense, no body at any time, no *prāṇas*, no *Māyā*, no passion and no anger, I am the great, I have nothing of these objects or of the world, and I have no sin, no characteristics, no eye, no *manas*, no ear, no nose, no tongue, no hand, no waking, no dreaming, or causal state in the least or the fourth state.' He is said to be a *Jīvanmukta*, who realises : 'All this is not mine, I have no time, no space, no object. no thought, no snāna (bathing), no sandhyās (junction-period ceremonies), no deity, no place, no sacred places, no worship, no spiritual wisdom, no seat, no relative, no birth, no speech, no wealth, no virtue, no vice, no duty, no auspiciousness, no *Jīva*, not even the three worlds, no salvation, no duality, no Vedas, no mandatory rules, no proximity, no distance, no knowledge, no secrecy, no *Guru*, no disciple, no diminution, no excess, no Brahmā, no Viṣṇu, no rudra, no moon, no earth, no water, no *vāyu*, no *ākāśa*, no *agni*, no clan, no lakṣya (object aimed at), no mundane existence, no meditator, no object of meditation, no *manas*, no cold, no heat, no thirst, no hunger, no friend, no foe, no illusion, no victory, no past, present, or future, no quarters, nothing to be said or heard in the least, nothing to be gone (or attained) to, nothing to be contemplated enjoyed or remembered, no enjoyment, no desire, no *yoga*, no absorption, no garrulity, no quietude, no bondage, no love, no joy, no instant joy, no hugeness, no smallness, neither length nor shortness, neither increase nor decrease, neither adhyāropa (illusory attribution) nor apavāḍa (withdrawal of the conception) no oneness, no manyness, no blindness, no dullness, no skill, no flesh, no blood, no lymph, no skin, no marrow, no bone, no skin, none of the seven dhātus, no whiteness, no redness, no bluness, no heat, no gain, neither importance nor non-importance, no delusion, no perseverance, no mystery, no race, nothing to be abandoned or received, nothing to be laughed at, no policy, no religious vow, no fault, no bewailments, no happiness, neither knower nor knowledge nor the knowable, no Self, nothing belonging to you or to me, neither you nor I, and neither old age nor youth nor manhood; but I am certainly *Brahman*. "I am certainly *Brahman*. I am *Cit*, I am *Cit*." He is said to be a *Jīvanmukta* who cognizes : 'I am *Brahman* alone, I am *Cit* alone, I am the supreme'. No doubt need be entertained about this : 'I am Hamsa itself, I remain of my own will, I can see myself through myself, I reign happy in the kingdom of *Ātmā* and enjoy in myself the bliss of my own Ātmā'. He is a *Jīvanmukta* who is himself, the foremost and the one undaunted person who is himself the lord and rests in his own Self.

"He is a *Videhamukta* who has become *Brahman*, whose *Ātmā* has attained quiescence, who is of the nature of Brāhimc bliss, who is happy, who is of a pure nature, and who is a great mouni (observer of silence). He is *videhamukta* who remains in *Cinmātra* alone whithout (even) thinking thus : 'I am all *Ātmā*, the Atmā that is equal (or the same) in all, the pure, without one, the non-dual, the all, the self only, the birthless and the deathless— I am myself the undecaying *Ātmā* that is the object aimed at, the sporting, the silent, the blissful, the beloved and the bondless salvation— I am *Brahman* alone— I am. *Cit* alone'. he is a *Videhamukta* who having abdandoned the thought : 'I alone am the *Brahman*' is filled with bliss. He is a *Videhamukta* who having given up the certainly of the existence of non-existence of all objects is pure Cid*ānanda* (the consciousness bliss), who having abandoned (the thought): 'I am *Brahman*' (or) 'I am not *Brahman*' does not mingle his *Ātmā* with anything, anywere or at any time, who is ever silent with the silence of *Satya*, who does nothing, who has gone beyond *guṇas*, whose *Ātmā* has become the All, the great, and the purifier of the elements, who does not cognize the change of time, matter, place, himself or other differences, who does not see (the difference of) 'I', 'thou', 'this' or 'that', who being of the nature of time is yet without it, whose Ātma is void, subtle and universal, but yet without (them), whose *Ātmā* is divine and yet without Devas, whose *Ātmā* is measurable and yet without measure, whose *Ātmā* is without inertness and within every one, whose *Ātmā* Devoid of any *saṅkalpa*, who thinks always : 'I am *Cinmātra*, I am simply Paramātman, I am only of the nature of spiritual wisdom, I am only of the nature of Sat, I am afraid of nothing in this world,' and who is without the conception of Devas, Vedas and sciences, 'All this is consciousness, etc.,' and regards all as void. He is a *Videhamukta* who has realised himself to be Caitanya alone, who is remaining at ease in the pleasure-garden own *Ātmā*, whose *Ātmā* is of an illimitable nature, who is without the conception of the small and the great, and who is the fourth of the fourth state and the supreme bliss. He is a *Videhamukta* whose *Ātmā* is nameless and formless, who is the great spiritual wisdom of the nature of bliss, and of the nature of the state beyond turya, who is neither auspicious not inauspicious, who has *yoga* as his *Ātmā*, whose *Ātmā* is associated with *yoga*, who is free from bondage or freedom, without guṇa or non-guṇa, without space, time, etc., without the witnessable and the witness, without the small or the great, and without the cognition of the universe or even the cognition of the nature of *Brahman*, but who finds his spiritual efflugence in his own nature, who finds bliss in himself, whose bliss is beyond the scope of words and mind, and whose thought is beyond and beyond. He is said to be *Videhamukta* who has gone beyond (or mastered quite) the modifications of citta, who illumines such modifications, and whose *Ātmā* is without any modifications at all. In that case, he is neither embodied nor disembodied. If such a thought in entertained (even), for a moment, then he is surrounded (in thought) by all. He is a *Videhamukta* whose external *Ātmā* invisible to others is the supreme bliss aiming at the highest vedānta, who drinks the juice of the nectar of *Brahman*, who has the nectar of *Brahman* as medicine, who is devoted to the juice of the nectar of *Brahman*, who is immersed in that juice, who has the beneficent worship of the Brāhmic bliss, who is not satiated with the juice of the nectar or *Brahman*, who realises Brāhmic bliss, who cognized the Śiva bliss in Brāhmic bliss, who has the effulgence of the essence of Brāhmic bliss, who has become one with it, who lives in the household of Brāhmic bliss, has mounted the car of Brāhmic bliss, who has an imponderable *Cit* being one with it, who is supporting (all), being full of it, who associated with me haveing it, who says in *Ātmā* having that bliss and who thinks : 'All this is of the nature of *Ātmā*, there is nothing else beside *Ātmā*, all is *Ātmā*, I am *Ātmā*, the great *Ātmā*, the supreme *Ātmā*, and *Ātmā* of the form of bliss.' He who thinks : 'My nature is full, I am the great *Ātmā*, I am the all-contented and the permanent *Ātmā*. I am the *Ātmā* pervading the heart of all, which is stained by anything, but which has no *Ātmā*; I am the *Ātmā* whose nature is changeless, I am the qiescent *Ātmā*; and I am the many Ātmā' He who does not think this is Jīvātmā and that is Paramātmā, whose *Ātmā* is of the nature of the emancipated and the non-emancipated, but without emancipation or bondage, whose *Ātmā* is of the nature of the dual and the non-dual one, but without duality and non-duality; whose *Ātmā* is of the nature of All and the non-All, but without them; whose *Ātmā* is of the nature of the happiness arising from objects obtained and enjoyed, but without it; and who is devoid of any *saṅkalpa*— such a man is a *videhamukta*. He whose *Ātmā* is partless, stainless, enlightened, Puruṣa, without bliss, etc., of the nature of nectar, of the nature of the three periods of time, but without them; whose *Ātmā* is entire and non-measurable, being subject to proof though without proof; whose *Ātmā* is the eternal and the witness, but without eternality and witness; whose *Ātmā* is nature of the secondless, who is the self-shining one without a second, whose *Ātmā* cannot be measured by vidyā and avidyā but without them; whose *Ātmā* is without conditionedness or unconditionedness, who is without this or the higher worlds, whose *Ātmā* is without the six things beginning with śama, who is without the qualifications of the aspirant after salvation, whose *Ātmā* is without gross, subtle, causal, and the fourth bodies, and without the *anna*, prāṇa, *manas*, and *vijñāna* sheaths; whose *Ātmā* is of the nature of *ānanda* (bliss) sheath, but without five sheaths; whose *Ātmā* is the nature of nirvikalpa, is devoid of *saṅkalpa*, without the characteristics of the visible or the audible, and of the nature of void, owining to unceasing *samādhi*, who is without beginning, *samādhi*, who is without beginning, middle, or end; whose *Ātmā* is devoid of the word Prajñana, who is without the idea 'I am *Brahman*,' whose *Ātmā* is devoid (of the thought) of 'thou art', who is without the thought of 'this is Ātmā'. whose *Ātmā* is devoid of that which is described by Om, who is above the reach of any speech or the three states, and is the indestructible and the *cidātmā*, whose *Ātmā* is not the one which can be known by *Ātmā* and whost *Ātmā* has neither light nor darkness. Such a personage is a *Videhamukta*. Look only upon *Ātmā*; know It as your own. Enjoy your *Ātmā* yourself, and stay in peace. O six-faced one, be content in your own *Ātmā*, be wandering in your own *Ātmā*, and be enjoying your own *Ātmā*. Then you will attain *Videhamukti*."

Chapter V

The Sage named Nīdāgha addressed the venerable *Rbhu* : "O Lord please explain to me the discrimination of *Ātmā* from non-*Ātmā*." The Sage replied thus :

"The furthest limit of all vāk (speech) is *Brahman*; the furthest limit to all the thoughts is *the Gu*ru. That which is of the nature of all causes and effects but yet without them, that which is without *saṅkalpa*, of the nature of all bliss, that which illuminates all luminaries and that which is full of the bliss of *nāda* (spiritual sound), without any enjoyment and contemplation and beyond *nādas* and kalās (parts)— that is *Ātmā*, that is the 'I', the indestructible. Being devoid of all the difference of *Ātmā* and non-*Ātmā*, of heterogeneity and homogenity and of quiescence and non-quiescence— that is the one *Jyotis* at thee and of *nāda*. Being remote from the conception of Mahā-vakyārtha (*i.e.,* the meaning of Mahā-vākyas) as well 'I am *Brahman*', being devoid of or without the conception of the world and the meaning, and being devoid of the conception of the destructible and indestructible— that is the one *Jyotis* at the end of *nāda*. Being without the conception 'I am the partless non-dual essence' or 'I am the blissful', and being of the nature of the one beyond all-that is one *Jyotis* at the end of *nāda*. He who is devoid of the significance of *Ātmā* (*viz.,* motion) and devoid of Saccid*ānanda*— he is alone *Ātmā*, the eternal. He who is undefinable and unreachable by the words of the vedas, who has neither externals nor internals, and whose symbol is either the universe or *Brahman*— he is undoubtedly *Ātmā*. He who has no body, nor is a *Jīva* made up of the elements their compounds, who has neither from nor name, neither the enjoyable nor the enjoyer, neither Sat nor asat, neither preservation nor regeneration, neither guṇa nor non-guṇa— that is undoubtedly my *Ātmā*. He who has neither the described nor description, neither śravaṇa nor manana, neither *Guru* nor disciple, neither the world of the Devas nor Devas nor Asuras, neither duty nor non-duty, neither the immaculate nor non-immaculate, neither time nor non-time neither certainty nor doubt, neither mantra nor non-mantra, neither science nor non-science, neither the seer nor the sight which is subtle, nor the nectar of time— that is *Ātmā*. Rest assured that not-*Ātmā* is a misnomer. There is no *manas* as not-Ātma. There is no world as not-Ātma. Owing to the absence of all saṅkalpas and to the giving up of all actions, *brahman* alone remains, and there is no not-*Ātmā*. Being devoid of the three bodies, the three periods of time, the three *guṇas* of *Jīva*, the three pains and the three worlds, and following the saying 'All is *Brahman*', know that there is nothing to be known through

1. Herein is given the hint as to the difference of functions between an *Iṣṭadevatā* and a *Guru*.

the absence of citta; there is no old age thrugh the absence of body; no motion through the absence of legs; no action through the absence of hands; no death through the absence of creatures; no happiness through the absence of *buddhi*; no virtue, no purity, no fear, no repetition of mantras, no *Guru* nor disciple, There is no second in the absence of one. Where there is not the second, there is no the first. Where there is truth alone, there is no non-truth possible; where there is non-truth alone, there is no truth possible. you regard a thing auspicious as inauspicious, then auspiciousness is desired (as separate) from inauspiciousness. if you regard fear as non-fear, then fear will arise out of non-fear. If bondage should become emancipation, then in the absence of bondage will be no emancipation. If birth should imply death, then in the absence of birth, there is no death. If 'thou' should imply 'I', then in the absence of 'thou' there is no 'I' if 'this' should be 'that', 'this' does not exist in the absence of 'that'. If being should imply nor being, then non-being will imply being. If an effect implies a cause, then in the absence of effect, there is no cause. If duality implies non-duality, then in the absence of duality, there is no non-deality. If there should be the seen, then there is the eye (or sight); in the absence of the seen, there is no eye. In the absence of the interior, there is no exterior. If there should be fullness, then non-fullness is possible. Therefore (all) this exists nowhere. Neither you nor I, nor this nor these exist. There exists no (object of) comparison in the true one. There is no simile in the unborn. There is (in it) no mind to think. I am the supreme *Brahman*. This world is *Brahman* only. Thou and I are *Brahman* only. I am *cinmātra* simply, and there is no not-*Ātmā*. Rest assured of it. This universe is not (really at all). It was nowhere produced and stays nowhere. Some say that citta is the universe. Not at all. It exist not. Neither the universe nor citta nor ahaṁkara nor *Jīva* exists (really). Neither the creation of *Māyā* nor *Māyā* itself exists (really). Fear does not (really) exit. Actor, action, hearing, thinking, the two *samādhis*, the measurer, the measure, *ajñāna* and *aviveka*—[1] none of these exists (truly) anywhere. Therefore the four more moving considerations and the three kinds of realationship exist not. There is no *Gaṅgā*, no *Gayā*, no *Setu* (bridge), no elements or anything else, no earth, water, fire, *vāyu*, and *ākāśa* anywhere, no Devas, no guardians of the four quarters, no Vedas, no *Guru*, no distance, no proximity, no time, no middle, no non-duality, no turth, no untruth, no bondage, no emancipation, no Sat, no asat, no happiness, etc., no class, no motion, no caste, and no worldly business. All is *Brahman* only and nothing else— all is *Brahman* only and nothing else. There exists then nothing (or statement) as that 'consciousness alone

---

1. The four moving consideration (of *vedānta*) are subject (*Brahman*), object relationship, and the qualified person.

is'; there is (then) no saying such as '*Cit* is I'. The statement 'I am *Brahman*' does not exist (then); nor does exist (then) the statement : 'I am the eternally pure'. Whatever is uttered by the mouth, whatever is thought by *manas*, whatever is determined by *buddhi*, whatever is cognized by citta— all these do not exist. there is no *Yogin* or *yoga* then. All are and are not. Neither day nor night, neither bathing nor contemplating, neither delusion nor not-delusion— all these do not exist then. Know that is no not-*Ātmā*.

"The vedas, Science, *Purāṇas*, effect and cause, Īśvara and the world and the elements and mankind— all these are unreal. There is not doubt of it. Bondage, salvation, happiness, relatives, meditation, citta, the Devas, the demons, the secondary and the primary, the high and the low— all these are uneral. There is no doubt of it. whatever is uttered by the mouth, whatever is willed by *saṅkalpa*, whatever is thought by means— all these unreal. Whatever is determined by the *buddhi*, whatever is cognized by citta, whatever is discussed by the religious books, whatever is seen by the eye and heard by the ears, and whatever exists as Sat, as also the ear, the eye, and the limba— all these are unreal. Whatever is described as such and such, whatever is thought as so-and-so, all the existing thoughts such as 'thou art I', 'that is this', and 'He is I', and whatever happens in *mokṣa*, as aslo all saṅkalpas, delusion, illusory arrtibution, mysteries and all the diversities of enjoyment and sin— all these do not exist. So is also not— all these do not exist. So is also not-*Ātmā*. Mine and thine, my and thy, for me and for thee, by me and by thee— all these are unreal. (The statement) that Viṣṇu is the preserver, Brahmā is the creator, *Rudra* is the destroyer— know that these undoubtedly are false. Bathing, uttering of mantras, *japas* (religious austerities) homa (sacrifice), study of Vedas, worship of the Devas, mantra, tantra, association with the good, the unfolding of the faults of *guṇas*, the working of the internal organ, the result of avidyā, and the many crores of mundane eggs— all these are unreal. Whatever is spoken of as true according to the verdict of all teachers, whatever is seen in this world and whatever exists— all these are unreal. Whatever is uttered by words, whatever is ascertained, spoken, enjoyed, given or done by any one, whatever action is doen, good or bad, whatever is done as truth— Know all these to be unreal. Thou alone art the transcendental *Ātmā* and the supreme *Guru* of the form of *ākāśa*, which is devoid of fitness (for it) and of the nature of all creatures. Thou are *Brahman*; thou time; and thou at *Brahman*, that is ever and imponderable. thou are of everywhere, of all forms, and full of consciousness. Thou art the truth. Thou art one that has mastered the siddhis, and thou art the ancient, the emancipated, emancipation, the nectar of bliss, the God, the quiescent, the diseaseless, *Brahman* the full, and greater than the great. Thou art impartial, Sat and the ancient knowledge, recognised by the words 'Truth, etc'. Thou art devoid of all parts. Thou art the ever-existing— thou appearest as Brahmā, *Rudra*, Indra, etc.— thou art above the illusion of the universe— thous shinest in all element— thou art without *saṅkalpa* in all— thou art known by means of the underlying meaning of all scriptures; thou art ever content and ever happily seated (in thyself): thou art without motion, etc. In all things, thou art without any characteristics; in all things thou art contemplated by Viṣṇu and other Devas at all times; thou hast the nature of *Cit*, thou art *Cinmātra* unchecked, thou stayest in *Ātmā* itself, thou art void of everything and without *guṇas*, thou art bliss, the great, the one secondless, the state of Sat and asat, the knower, the known, the seer, the nature of Saccid*ānanda*, the lord of Devas, the all-prevading, the deathless, the moving, the motionless, the all and the non-all with quiescence and non-quiescence, sat alone, Sat commonly (found in all), of the form of Nitya-Siddha (the unconditioned developed one), and yet devoid of all siddhis. There is not an atom which thou does not penetrate; but yet thou are without it. Thou art devoid of existence and non-existence as also the aim and object aims at. Thou art changelss, decayless, beyond all *nādas*, without *kāla* or kāta (divisions of time) and without Brahmā, Viṣṇu and Śiva. Thou lookest into the nature of each and art above the nature of each. thou art immersed in the bliss of Self. Thou art the monarch of the kingdom of Self, and yet without the conception of Self. Thou art of the nature of *fulln*ess and incompleteness. There is nothing that thou see which is not in thyself. Thou dose not stir out of thy nature. Thou actest accoding to the nature of each. Thou art nothing but the nature of each. Have no doubt 'thou art I'.

"This universe and everything in it, whether the seer or the seen, resembles the horns of a hare (or are illusory). Earth, water, *agni*, *vāyu*, *ākāśa*, *manas*, *buddhi*, *ahaṁkāra*, tejas, the worlds and the sphere of the universe, destruction, birth, tuth, virtue, vice, gain desires, passion, anger, greed, the object of meditation, wisdom, *Guru*, disciple, limitation, the beginning and end, auspiciousness, the past, present, and future, the aim and the object of aim, mental restraint, inquiry, contentment, enjoyer, enjoyment, etc., the eight parts of yaga, yama, etc., the going and coming (of life), the beginning, middle and end, that which can be taken and rejected, Hari, Śiva, the organs, *manas*, the three states, the twenty-four tattvas, the four means, one of the same class or different classes, Bhūh and other worlds, all the castes and orders of life with the rules laid down for each, mantras and tantras, science and nonscience, all the vedas, the inert and the non-inert, bondage and salvation, spiritual wisdom and non-wisdom, the enlightened and the non-enlightened, duality and non-duality, the conclusion of all Vedāntras and Śāstras, the theory of the existence of all souls and that one soul only, whatever is thought by citta, whatever is willed by *saṅkalpa*, whatever is determined by *buddhi*, whatever one hears and sees, whatever the *Guru* instruct. whatever is sensed by all the organs, whatever is discussed in mīmānsā, whatever is ascertained by nyāya (philosophy) and by the great ones who have reached the other side of the Vedas, the saying 'Śiva destroys the world, Viṣṇu protects it, and Brahmā creates it', whatever is found in the *purāṇas*, whatever is ascertained by the Vedas, and is the signification of all the Vedas— all these resemble the horns of a hare. The conception 'I am the body' is spoken of as the internal organ; the conception 'I am the body' is spoken of as the great mundane existence; the conception 'I am the body' constitutes the whole universe. The concepiton 'I am the body' is spoken of as the knot of the heart, as non-wisdom, as the state of asat, as nonscience, as the dual, as the true *Jīva* and with parts, is certainly the great sin, and is the disease generated by the fault of thirst after desires. That which is *saṅkalpa*, the three pains, passion, anger, bondage, all the miseries, all the faults and the various forms of time— know these to be the result of *manas*. *Manas* alone is the whole world, ever-deluding, the mudane existence, the three worlds, the great pains, the old age and others, death and the great sin, the *saṅkalpa*, the *Jīva*, the citta, the *ahaṁkāra*, the bondage, the internal organ and earth, water, *agni*, vāyū, and *ākāśa*. Sound, thoch, form, taste, and odour, the five sheaths, the waking, the dreaming, and dreamless sleeping states, the guradians of the eight quarters, vasus, Rudras, Ādityas, the seen, the inert, the pairs and non-wisdom— all these are the products of *manas*. Rest assured that there is no reality in all that is *saṅkalpa*. The whole world, the *Guru*, disciple, etc., do not exit, yea, do not exist. Thus ends the fifth chapter of this Upaniṣad."

Chapter VI

Ṛbhu continues again : "Know everything as *Saccinmaya* (full of Sat and consciousness). It pervades everything. Saccid*ānanda* is non-dual, decayless, alone and other than all. It is 'I'. It alone is *ākāśa* and 'thou'. It is I. There is (in it) no *manas*, no *buddhi*, no ahaṁkara, no citta, or the collection of these— neither 'thou' no I, nor anything else nor everything. *Brahman* alone is. Sentence, words, Vedas, letters, beginning, middle, or end, truth, law, pleasure, pain, existence, *māyā*, prakṛti, body, face, nose, tongue, plate, teeth, lip, forehead, expiration and inspiration, sweat, bone, blood, urine, distance, proximity, limb, belly, crown, the movement of hands and feet, Śāstras, command, the knower, the known, and the knowledge, the waking, dreaming and dreamless sleeping and the fourth state— all these do not belong to me. Everything is *Saccinmaya* interwoven. No attributes pertaining to body, elements and spiriti, no root, no vision, no Taijasa, no Prāṇa, no Virāṭ, no Sūtrātmā, no Īśvara, and no going or coming, neither gain nor loss, neither the acceptable nor the rejectable, nor the censurable, neither the pure nor the impure, neither the stout nor the lean, no sorrow, time, space, speech, all, fear, duality, tree, grass or mountain, no meditation, no siddhi of *yoga*, no *Brāhmana*, Kṣ atriya or *Vaiśya*, no bird or beast, or limb, no greed, delusion, pride, malice, passion, anger or others, no woman, *Śūdra*, castes or others, nothing that is eatable or enjoyable, no increase or decrease, no belief in the Vedas, no speech, no worldliness or unworldliness, no transaction, no folly, no measure or measured, no enjoyment or enjoyed, no friends, son, etc., father, mother, or sister, no birth or death, no growth, body of 'I', no emptiness or fullness, no internal organs or mundane existence, no night, no day, no Brahmā, Viṣṇu or Śiva, no week, fortnight, month, or year, no unsteadiness, no brahmaloka, Vaikunṭha, Kailāśa and others, no Swarga, Indra, *Agniloka*, *Agni*, Yamaloka, Yama, *vāyu*loka, guardians of the world, three worlds— Bhūḥ, Bhuvaḥ, Svaḥ, Pātāla or surface of earth, no science, nescience, *māyā*, prakṛti, enertness, permanency, transcience, destruction, movement, running, object of meditation, bathing, mantra or object, no adorable object, anoinment or siping, with water, no flower, fruit, sandal, light waved before god, praise, prostrations, or circumambulation no entereaty, conception of separateness even obliation of food, offered food, sacrifice, actions, abuse, praise, Gāyatrī and sandhi (period of junction, such as twilight, etc.), no mental state, calamity, evil desire, bad soul, chaṇḍāla (low caste person) pulkasa, unberableness, unspeakableness, kirāta (hunter), kaiṭava (demon), partiality, partisanship, ornament, chief, or pride, no manyness, no oneness, durability, traid, tetrad, greatness, smallness, fullness, or delusion, no kaiṭava, Benares, tapas, clan, family *sūtra*, greatness, poverty, girl, old woman or widow, no pollution, birth, introvision or illusion, no sacred sentences, identity, or the siddhis, aṇimā, etc.

"Everything being consciousness alone, there is no fault in anything. Everything being of the nature of Sat alone, is saccid*ānanda* only. *Brahman* alone is everything and there is nothing else. So 'That' is 'I' 'That' is 'I'. 'That' alone is 'I'. 'That' alone is 'I'. 'That' alone is 'I'. The eternal *Brahman* alone is 'I'. I am *Brahman* alone without being subject to mundane existence. I am *Brahman* alone without *manas*, any *buddhi*, organs or body. I am *Brahman* alone not perceivable. I am *Brahman* alone and not *Jīva*. I am *Brahman* alone and not liable to change. I am *Brahman* alone and not inert. I am *Brahman* alone and have no death. I am *Brahman* alone and have no *prāṇas*. I am *Brahman* alone and greater than the great. This is *Brahman*. Great is *Brahman*. Truth is *Brahman*. It is all-pervading. Time is *Brahman*. *Kāla* is *Brahman*. Happiness is *Brahman*. It is self-shining. One is *Brahman*. Two is *Brahman*. Delusion is *Brahman*. Śama and others are *Brahman*. Badness is *Brahman*. Goodness is *Brahman*. It is of the form of restraint, quiesence, the all-pervading and the all-powerful. the Loka (world) is *Brahman*. *Guru* is *Brahman*. Disciple is *Brahman*. It is Sadāśiva. (That which) is *Brahman*. (That which will be) hereafter is *Brahman*. Purity is *Brahman*. Auspiciousness and inauspiciousness are *Brahman*. *Jīva* always is *Brahman*. I an Saccid*ānanda*. All are of the nature of *brahman*. The universe is said to be of the nature of *Brahman*. *Brahman* is itself. There is no doubt of it. There is nothing out of itself. The letter OM of the form of consciousness is *Brahman* alone. Everything is itself. I alone am the whole universe and the highest seat, have crossed the *guṇas* and am greater than the great, the supreme *Brahman*, *Guru* of *Gurus*, the support of all and the bliss of bliss. There is no universe besides *Ātmā*. The universe is of the nature of *Ātmā*. There is nowhere (or no place) without *Ātmā*. There is not even grass different from *Ātmā*. There is not husk different from *Brahman*. The whole universe is of the nature of *Ātmā*. All this is of the nature of *Brahman*. Asat is not of the nature of *brahman*. There is not a grass different from *Brahman*. There is not a seat different from *Brahman*; there is not a *Guru* different from *Brahman*. there is not a body different froms *Brahman*. There is nothing different from *Brahman* like I-ness or you-ness. Whatever is seen in this world, whatever is spoken of by the people, whatever is enjoyed everywhere— all these are asat (unreal) only. The differences arising from the actor, action, qualities, likes, taste and gender— all these arise from asat and are (but) pleasurable. The differences arising from time, objects, actions, success or defeat and whatever else— all these are simply asat. The internal organ is asat. The organs are asat. All the *prāṇas*, the collections of all these, the five sheaths, the five deities, the six changes, the six enemies, the six seasons, and the six tastes, are asat. I am Saccid*ānanda*. The universe is rootless. I am *Ātmā* alone, *Cit* and Ānanda. The scenes of mundane existence are not different. I am the Truth of the nature of Ānanda and of the nature of the imponderable *Cit*. All this is of the nature of *jñāna*.

"I am the secondless, having *jñāna* and bliss. I am of the nature of an illuminator of all things. I am of the nature of all non-being. I alone shine always. Therefore how can I with such a nature become asat? That which is called 'thou' is the great *brahman* of the natue of the bliss of consciousness and of the nature of *Cit* having cidākāś and *cit* alone as the great bliss. *Ātmā* alone is 'I'. Asat is not 'I'. I am Kūtastha, the great *Guru* and Saccid*ānanda* alone. I am this born universe. No time, no universe, no *māyā*, no prakṛti (in me). I alone am the Hari Personally, I alone am the Sadāśiva. I am of the nature of pure consciousness. I am the enjoyer of pure *sattva*. I am the only essence full of *cit*. Everything is *Brahman* and *Brahman* alone. Everything *Brahman* and is *cit* alone. I am of the nature of all-latent and the all-witness. I am the supreme *Ātmā*, the supreme *jyotis*, the supreme wealth, the supreme goal, the essence of all vedāntas, the subject discussed in all the Śāstras the nature of yogic bliss, the ocean of the chief wisdom, the brightness of the fourth state and the non-fourth but devoid of them, the indestructible *cit*, truth, Vāsudeva, the birthless, and the deathless brahmā, Cidākāś, the unconditioned, the stainless, the immaculate, the emancipated, the utterly emancipated, the soulless, the formless and of the nature of the non-created universe.

"The universe which is assumed as truth and non-truth does not really exist. *Brahman* is of the nature of eternal bliss and is even by itself. It is endless, decayless, quiescent and of one nature only. If anything is other than myself, then it is as unreal as the mirage in an oasis. If one should be afraid of the son of a barren woman, of if a powerful elephant be killed by means of the horns of a hare, then the world (really is). If one (person) can quench his thirst by drinking the waters of the mirage, or if one should be killed by the horns of a man, then the universe really is. The universe exists always in the true Gandharva city (merely unreal). When the blueness of the sky really exists in it, then the universe really is. When the silver in mother-of-pearl can be used in making an ornament, when a man is bitten by (the conception of) a snake in a rope, when the flaming fire is quenched by means of a golden arrow, when milky food is obtained in the (barren) forest of Vindhya (mountains), When cooking can take place by means of the fuel of (wet) plantain trees, when a female (baby) just born begins to cook, when curds resume the state of milk, or when the milk (milked) goes back through the teats of a cow, then will the universe really be. When the dust of the earth shall be produced in the ocean, when the maddened elephant is tied by means of the hair of a tortoise, when (mountain) Meru is shaken by the thread in the stalk of a lotus, when the ocean is bound by its rows of tides, when the fire flames downwards, when flame shall become (really) cold, when the lotus shall grow out of flaming fire, when Indranīla (sapphire) arises in the great mountains, When Meru comes and sits in the lotus-eye, when a mountain can become the offspring of a black bee, when Meru shall shake, when a lion is killed by a gnat, when the three worlds can be found in the *space* of the hollow of an atom, when the fire which burns a straw shall last for a long time, when the objects seen a dream shall come in the waking state, when the current of a river shall stand still (of itself), when the delivery of a barren woman shall be fruitful, when the crow shall walk shall like a swan, when the mule shall fight with a lion, when a great ass shall walk like an elephent, when the full moon shall become a sun, when Rāhu (on of the nodes) shall abandon the sun and the moon, when a good crop shall arise out of the waste (burnt) seeds, when the poor shall enjoy the happiness of the rich, when the lions shall be conquered by the bravery of dogs, when the heart of Jñānīs is known by fools, when the ocean is drunk by the dogs without any remainder, when the pure ākāśa shall fall upon men, when heaven shall fall no the earth, when the flower in the sky shall emit fragrance, when a forest appearing in pure ākāśa shall move, and when reflection shall arise in a glass simply (without mercury or anything else in its back), then the world really is. There is no universe in the womb of Aja (the unborn *Brahman*)— there is no universe is the womb of *Ātmā*. Duality and non-duality, which are but the results of differentiation, are really not. All this is the result of *māyā*. Therefore, there should be *Brahma-Bhāvanā*. If misery should arise from the conception of 'I am the body', then it is certain 'I am *Brahman*'. The knot of the heart is the wheel of *Brahman*, which cuts asunder the knotof existence. When doubt arises in one, he should have faith of *Brahman*. The non-dual *brahman*, which is eternal and of the form of unconditioned bliss, is the gurad of *Ātmā* against of the chief of the form of non-*Ātmā*. Through instance like the above is established the nature of *Brahman*. *Brahman* alone is the all-abode. Abandon the name even of the universe. Knowing for certain 'I am *Brahman*', give up the 'I'. Everything disappears as the flower from the hands of sleeping person. There is neither body nor *karma*. Everything is *Brahman* alone. There are neither objects, nor actions, nor the four states. Everything which has the three charactiristics of *vijñāna* is *Brahman* alone. Abondoning all action, contemplate 'I am *Brahman*', 'I am *Brahman*'. There is no doubt of this. I am *Brahman* of the nature of *cit*— I am of the nature of sacci*dānanda*.

"This great science of Śaṅkara should never be explained to any ordinary person, to an atheist or to a faithless, all-behaved or evil-minded person. It should be, after due examination, given to the high-soul ones whose minds are purified with devotion to their *Gurus*. It should be taught for a year and a half. Leaving off thoroughly and entirely the practice recommended by the (other) Upaniṣad one should study the Tejobindū-Upaniṣad always with delight. By once studying it, he becomes one with *Brahman*. Thus ends the sixth chapter.

Thus ends the Upaniṣad

Brahmopaniṣad[1]

OF

KṚṢṆA-YAJURVEDA

[This Upaniṣad is intended to give a complete and clear idea of the nature of *Ātmā*, that has four avasthās (states of consciousness) and four seats, for the better onsummation of the *nirguṇa dhyāna*.]

Om. Śaunaka Mahāṣala questioned the holy Sage Pippalāda of the *Aṅgiras* gotra thus : "In this beautiful Brahmapura of body, the fit residence of divine beings, how are (the deitis of) vāk, etc., located ? How do they function? To whom belongs this power? He to whom this power belongs, what is He?"

Pippalāda then having deeply considered, imparted to him the *Brahmavidyā* (divine wisdom), that most excellent of all things. "It is prāṇa (*i.e.,*) *Ātmā*. It is *Ātmā* that exercises this power. It is the life of all Devas. It is their death and (their) life. *Brahman* that shines pure, niṣkala, resplendent, and all-pervading, in this divine *Brahmapura* (of body), rules (all). The *Jīva* (identifying himself with) the indṛyas, rules them like a spider. The spider throws out from a single thread out of his body a whole web, and draws it into himself by that same thread; so prāṇa, whenever it goes, draws after it the objects of its creation (vāk, etc.,). during suṣupti, (the prāṇa) goes to its seat (*Brahman*) through the nādis of which is the devatā, like an eagle, that making air as the means of communication, reaches his abode. they say, as devadatta, though beaten (during suṣupti) by a stick, etc., does not move, so also the actor does not suffer or enjoy for the merits or demerits of religious actions. Just as a child obtains happiness without desiring for it (in play), so also devadatta obtains happiness in suṣupti. He certainly knows, (being) Param-*Jyotis*, and the person desiring *jyotis*, enjoys bliss in the contemplation of *jyotis*. then he comes back to the dream-plane by the same way, like a caterpillar. It remaining on a blade of grass, first put forward its foot on another blade in front, conveys its body to it, and having got a firm hold of it. then only leaves the former and not before. So this is the jāgrata state. As this (devadatta) bears at the same time eight skulls, so this jāgrata, the source of devas and vedas, clings to a manlike the breasts in a woman. During the jāgrata avasthā. merit and demerit and postulated of this *Deva* (power); he is capable of great expansion and is the inner mover. He is

1. In this Upaniṣad, the Southern Indian edition begins later on but the other portions also are given as being fuller.

khage (bird), karakata (crab), puṣkara (ākāśa), prāṇa, pain, parāpara, *Ātmā* and *Brahman*, the supreme the support of all things, and the Kṣetrajñā. He obtains *Brahman*, the supreme, support of all things, and the Kṣetrajñā.[1]

"The Puruṣa has four seats— navel, heart, neck, and head. There *Brahman* with the four feet specially shines. Those feet are jāgrata, svapna, suṣupti, and turya. In jāgrata he is Brahmā, in svapna Viṣṇu, in suṣupti *Rudra*, and in turya the supreme *Akṣara*. He is Āditya, Viṣṇu, Īśvara, puruṣa, *Jīva*, agani, the resplendent. The Para-*brahman* shines in the midst of these. He is without *manas*, ear, hands, feet, and light.There the worlds are no worlds, Devas no Devas, Vedas no Vedas, sacrifices no sacrifices, mother no mother, father no father, daughter-in-law no daughter-in-law, Caṇḍāla no caṇdala, pulkasa no paulkasa, śramaṇa no śramaṇa, hermits no hermits; so one only *Brahman* shines as different. In the Hṛdayākāś (*ākāśa* in the heart) in the Cidākāś. That is *Brahman*. It is extermely subtle. The Hṛdayākāś can be known. This moves in it. In *Brahman*, everthing in strung. Those who thus know the Lord know everything. In him the Devas, the worlds, the Pitṛs and the *Rsis* do not rule. He who has awakened knows everything. All the Devas are in the heart; in the heart are all the prāṇa : in the heart are prāṇa, *jyotis* and that threeplied holy thread. In the heart in caitanya, it (prāṇa) is. Put on the yajñopavīta (holy thread), the supreme, the holy, which came into existence along with the Prajāpati, which gives long life and which is very excellent; let this give you strenght and tejas. The wise man having shaved his head completely, should throw away the external thread. he should wear, as the holy thread, the supreme and indestructible *Brahman*. It is called *sūtra*, because sūcanāt (indicating) (that the *Ātmā* is in the heart). *Sūtra* means the supreme abode. He who knows that *sūtra* is a vipra (*Brāhmaṇa*), he has crossed the ocean of the Vedas. On that *sūtra* (thread), everything is strung, like the beads on the thread. The yogin, well versed in *yoga* and having a clear perception of Truth, sould wear the thread. Practising the noble *yoga*, the wise man should abandon the external thread. He who wears the *sūtra*, as *Brahman*, he is an intelligent being. By wearing the sātra, he is not polluted. They whose *sūtra*, is within, whose *yajñopavīta* is *jñāna*— they only know the *sūtra*, and, they only wear the yajñopavīta in this world. Those whose tuft of hair is *jñāna*. who are firmly grounded in *jñāna* and whose *yajñopavīta* is *jñāna*, consider *jñāna* only as supreme. *Jñāna* is holy and excellent. he whose *śikhā* (tuft of hair) is *jañāna* like the *śikhi* (flame of *agni*)— he, the wise one; only wears a true śikhā; others wear a mere fuft of heair. Those *brāhmaṇas* and others who perform the ceremonies prescribed in the Vedas— they wear this thread only as a symbol of their cerermonies. Those who know the Vedas say that he only is a ture *brāhmaṇas* who

1. The South Indian Edition begins here.
2. This mantra is repeated whenever the holy thread is newly worn.

wears the *śikhā* of *jñāna* and whose *yajñopavīta* is the same (*jñāna*). This yajñopavīta (*Yajña* means Viṣṇu or sacrifice and *Upavita* is that which surrounds; hence that which surrounds Viṣṇu) is supreme and is the supreme refuge. He who wears that really knows— he only wears the *sūtra*, he is *Yajña* (Viṣṇu) and he only knows *Yajña* (Viṣṇu). One God hidden in all things, pervades all things and the Inner Life of all things. He awards the fruits of *karma*, he lives in all things, he sees all things without any extraneous help, he is the soul of all. There is nothing like him. and he is without any *guṇas* (being secondless). He is the great wise one. He is the one doer among the many actionless objects. He is always making one thing appear as several (by *māyā*) Those wise men who see him in *buddhi*, they only obtain eternal peace. Having made *Ātmā* as the upper) araṇi (attritional piece of wood) and *Praṇava* the lower araṇi, by constant practice of *dhyāna* one should see the concealed deity. As the oil in the sesamum seed, as the ghee in the curds, as the water in the rivers, and as the fire in the *araṇi*, so they who practise turth and austerities see Him in the *buddhi*. As the spider throws out and draws into itself the threads, so the *Jīva* goes and returns during the *jāgrata* and the svapna states. The heart is in the form of a closed lotus-flower, with its head-hanging down; it has a hole in the top. Know it to be the great abode of all. Know that during *jāgrata* it (*Jīva*) dwells in the eye, and during svapna in[1] the throat; during *suṣupti*, it is in the heart and during turya in the head. (Because *buddhi* units) the *Paratyagātma* with the *Paramātma*, the worship of *sandhyā* (union) arose. So we should perform sandhyāvandana (rites). The sandhyāvandana performed by *dhyāna* requires no water. It gives no trouble to the body or the speech. That which units all things in the sundhyā of the one-staffed sannyāsins). Knowing That from which speech and mind turn back without being able to obtain it and That which is the bliss of *Jīva*, the wise one is freed. The secret of Brahmavidyā is to reveal the real nature of the *Ātmā*, that is all-pervading, that is like ghee in the milk, that is the source of *ātmavidyā* and tapas and to show that everything is in essence one.

Thus ends the Upaniṣad

---

1. The five sentences from here relating to *Sandhyā* are not to be found in the South Indian Edition.

Vajrasūci[1]-Upaniṣad

OF

SĀMAVEDA

I now proceed to declare the vajrasūci— the weapon that is the destroyer of ignorance— which condemns the ignorant and praises the man of divine vision.

There are four castes— the *brāhmaṇa*, the kṣatriya, the *vaiśya*, and the śudra. Even the smṛtis declare in accordance with the words of the vedas that the *brahmaṇa* alone is the most important of them.

Then this remains to be examined. what is meant by the *brāhmaṇa*? Is it a *jīva*? Is it a body? Is it a class? is it *Jñāna*? Is it *karma*? Or is it a doer of dharma?

To begin with : is *Jīva* is the *brāhmaṇa*? No. since the *jīva* is the same in the many past and future bodies (of all persons), and since the *jīva* is the same in all of the many bodies obtained through the force of *karma*, therefore *jīva* is not the *brāhamaṇa*.

Then is the body the *brāhmaṇa*? No. Since the body, as it is made up of the five elements, is the same for all people down to *caṇḍālas*,[2] etc., since old age and death, dhrama and adharma are found to be common to them all, since there is no absolute distinction that the *brāhmaṇas* are white-coloured, the *kṣatriyas* red, the *vaiśyas* yellow, and the *sūdras* dark, and since in burning the corpse of his father, etc., the stain of the murder of a *brāhmaṇa*, etc., will accrue to the son, etc., therefore the body is not the *brāhmaṇa*.

Then is a class the *brāhmaṇa*? No. Since many great *Rsis* have sprung from other castes and orders of creation— *Rsyaṣṛṅga* was born of deer; *Kauśika*, of *Kuśa* grass; *Jāmbuka* of a jackal; Vālmīki of valmīka (an ant-hill); *Vyāsā* of a fisherman's daughter; Gautama, of the posteriors of a hare; Vasiṣṭha of *Ūrvaśi*[3]; and Agastya of a water-pot; thus have we heard. Of these, many *Ṛṣis* outside the caste even have stood first among the teachers of divine Wisdom; therefore a class is not the *brāhmaṇa*.

Is *jñāna* the *brāhmaṇa*? No. Since there were many kṣatriyas and others well versed in the cognition of divine Truth, therefore *jñāna* is not the *brāhmaṇa*.

---

1. Lit., the diamond-needle-Upaniṣad.
2. The lowest class of persons among the Hindus.
3. One of the celestial nymphs dancing in the court of India.

Then is *karma* the *brāhmaṇa*? No. Since the *prārabdha*[1], *sañcita*[2], and āgami[3] *karmas* are the same for all beings, and since all people perform their actions as impelled by *karma*, therefore *karma* is not the *brāhmaṇa*.

Then is a doer of dharma (virtuous actions) the *brāhmaṇa*? No. Since there are many *kṣatriyas*, etc., who are givers of gold, therefore a doer of virtuous actions is not the *brāhmaṇa*.

Who indeed then is *brāhmaṇa*? Whoever he may be, he who had directly realised his *Ātmā* and who is directly cognizant, like the myrobalan in his palm, of his *Ātmā* that is without a second, that is devoid of class and actions, that is free from the faults of the six stains[4] and the six changes,[5] that is of the nature of truth, knowledge, bliss, and eternity, that is without any change in itself, that is the substratum of all the kalpas, that exists penetrating all things that pervades everything within and without as *ākāśa*, that is of natue of undivided bliss, that cannot be reasoned about and that is known only by direct cognition. He who by the reason of having obtained his wishes is divoid of the faults of thirst after worldly objects and passions, who is the possessor of the qualifications beginning with *śama*[6], who is free from emotion, malice, thirst after worldly objects, desire, delusion, etc., whose mind is untouched by pride, egoism, etc., who possesses all these qualities and means— he only is the *brāhmaṇa*.

Such is the opinion of the vedas, the smṛtis, the itihāsa and the *purāṇas*. Otherwise one cannot obtain the status of a *brāhmaṇa*. One should meditate of his *Ātmā* as Saccid*ānanda*, and the non-dual *Brahman*, Yea, one should meditate on his *Ātmā* as the Saccid*ānanda Brahman*.

Thus ends the Upaniṣad

---

1. The kārmic affinities generated by us in our former lives, the fruit of which is being enjoyed in our present life.
2. The kārmic affinities generated by us in our former lives, and collected together to be enjoyed in our future lives.
3. The affinities generated by us in our present life to be enjoyed hereafter.
4. The six stains—hunger, thirst, grief, confusion, old age, and death.
5. Birth, existence, etc.
6. *Śama*, *dama*, *uparati*, *titiksā*, *samādhāna*, and *sraddhā*.

Śārīraka[1]-Upaniṣad

OF

KṚṢṆA-YAJURVEDA

Om. The body is a compound of *pṛthivī* (earth) and other *mahābhūtas* (primordial elements, as *āpas* or water, *agni* or fire, *vāyu* or air, and *ākāśa*) (in the body), that which is hard is (of the essence of) earth; that which is liquid is (of the essence of) water; that which is hot is (of the essence of) fire; that which moves about is (of the essence of) *vāyu*; that which is perforated is (of the essence of) *ākāśa*. The ear and others are the *jñānendṛyas* (organs of sense). the ear is of the essence of *ākāṣa*, the skin of the essence of *vāyu*, the eye of the essence of fire, the tongue of the essence of water, and the nose of essence of earth; sound, touch, form, taste, and odour being respectively the objects of perception for these organs. There arose respectively out of the primordial elements, beginning with earth. The mouth, the hands, the legs, the organs of excretion and the organs of generation are the *karmendriyas* (or organs of action). Their functions are respectively talking, lifting, walking, excretion, and enjoyment. *Antaḥkaraṇa* (or the internal organ) is of four kinds— *manas*, *buddhi*, *ahaṁkāra*, and *citta*. Their functions are respectively *saṅkalpa-vikalpa*, (or will thought and about), determination, egoism, and memory. The seat of *manas* is the end of the throat, that of *buddhi* the face, that of *ahaṁkāra* the heart, and that of *citta*, the navel. The bone, skin, *nādis*, nerves, hair, and flesh are of the essence of earth. Urine, phlegm, blood, *śukla* (or sperm), and sweat are of the essence of water. Hunger, thirst, sloth, delusion, and (desire of) copulation are of the essence of fire. Walking, scratching, opening and closing the gross eyes, etc., are of the essence of *vāyu*. Desire, anger avarice, delusion, and fear are of the essence of *ākāśa*. Sound, touch, form, taste, and odour are the properties of earth : sound, touch, form, and taste are the properties of water : sound, touch, and form, are the properties of fire : sound and touch are the properties of *vāyu* : sound alone is property of *ākāśa*. There are three *guṇas* (or qualities), *sāttvika*, *rājasa*, and *tāmasa*. Non-killing veracity, nor stealing, continence, non-covetousness, refraining from anger, serving the *Guru*, purity (in mind and body), contentment, right conduct, abstinence from self-praise, freedom from pompousness, firm conviction in the existence of God, and not causing any injury to others— all these are to be known as *sāttvika-guṇas* chiefly. I am the actor, I am the enjoyer, I am the speaker, and I am the egoistic— such are said by

---

1. This *Upaniṣad* treates of *Śarīra* of the body.

knowers of *Brahman* to be *rājasa-guṇas* Sleep, sloth, delusion, desire, copulation, and theft are said by expounders of the Vedas to be *tāmasa-guṇas*. Those having *sattva-guṇa* (go) up (*viz.*, higher spheres)— those having *rājasa-guṇa* (stay) in the middle (*viz.*, the sphere of earth)— those having *tāmasa-guṇa* (go) down (*viz.*, to hell, etc.,). Perfect (or divine) knowledge is of *sāttvika-guṇa*; knowledge of *dharma* is of rājasa-*guṇa*, the mental darkness is of *tāmasa*. *Jāgrata* (waking state), svapna (dreaming state), *suṣupti* (dreamless sleeping state), and turya (the fourth state beyond these three) are the four states. *Jāgrata* is (the state) having (the play of) the fourteen organs, the organs of sense (five), the organs of action (five), and the four internal organs. *Svapna* is (the state) associated with the four internal organs. *Suṣupti* is (the state) where the *citta* is the only organ. *Turya* is that state having *jīva* alone. Regarding *jīvātmā* and *Paramātmā* (enjoying the three states) of a person with opened eyes, the closed eyes, and with eyes in an intermediate state with neither, *jīva* is said to be the *kṣetrajña* (the lord of the body). The organs of sense (five), the organs of action (five), *prāṇas*, (five), *manas*, and *buddhi*— all these seventeen are said to constitute the *sūkṣma* or liṅga (*viz.*, subtle) body. *Manas*, *buddhi*, *ahaṁkāra*, *ākāśa*, *vāyu*, fire, water, and earth— these are the eight *prakṛtis* (on matter) : ear, skin, eye, toungue, nose the fifth, the orgnas of excretion, the orgnas of secretion, hands, legs, speech the tenth, sound, from, touch, taste, and odour are the fifteen modifications (of the above eight *prakṛtis*). Therefore the *tattvas* are twenty-threee. The twenty-fourth is *avyakta* (the undifferentiated matter) or *pradhāna*. *Puruṣ a* is other than (or superior to) this.

Thus ends the Upaniṣad

Garbha-Upaniṣad[1]

OF

KṚṢṆA-YAJURVEDA

Om. The body is composed of the five (elements); it exists in the five (objects of sense, etc.); it has six supports : it is associated with the six *guṇas*; it has seven *dhātus* (essential ingredients) and three malas (impurities); it has three yonis (wombs) and is formed of four kinds of food.

Why is the body said to be composed of five? Because there are five elements in this body (*viz.,*), *pṛthivī*, *āpas*, *agni*, *vāyu*, and *ākāśa*? In this body of five elements? what is the *prthivī* elements? What *āpas* ? What *agni*? what *vāyu*? and what *ākāśa*? Pṛthivī is said to be that which is hard; *āpas* is said to be that which is liquid; *agni* is said to be that which is hot; *vāyu* is that which moves; *ākāśa* is that which is full of holes (or tubes[2]). Of these, *pṛthivī* is seen in supporting (objects), *āpas* in cohesion, tejas (or *agni*) is making forms visible, *vāyu* in moving, *ākāśa* chiefly in *avakāṣa* (*viz.,* giving space). (Then what are the five objects of sense, etc.?) The ear exists in sound, the skin in touch, the eye in forms, the tongue in taste, and the nose in odour. (Then) the mouth (exists) in speech, the hand in lifting, the feet in walking, the anus in excreting, and the genitals in enjoying. (Then through *buddhi*, one knows and determines; through *manas*, he thinks and fancies; through *citta*. he recollects; through *ahaṁkāra*, he feels the idea of 'I'. thus these perform their respective functions.

Whence the six supports? There are six kinds of rasas (essence or tastes)— sweet, sour, saltish, bitter, astringent, and pungent. The body depends upon them while they depend upon the body. There are six changes of state (*viz.,*), the body exists, is born, grows, matures, decay, and dies. And there are also six cakras (wheels) depending on the *dhamani* (nerves), (*viz.,*), *mūlādhāra, svādhisthāna, maṇipūrraka*, *anāhata, viśuddhi*, and *ājñā*. Also the *guṇas* are six— *kāma* (passion) and others and *śama* (mental restraint) and others; there being properly— association (with the former) and devotion (to the latter). Then there are seven kinds of sounds, (*viz.,*). *ṣadja* (sa), *ṛṣabha* (ri), *gāndhāra* (*ga*), *madhyama* (*ma*) *pañcama* (*pa*), *daivata* (*da*), and *niṣāda* (ni), which are stated to be seven agreeable and disagreeable ones; and there are seven kinds of dhātus having seven colours, (*viz.,*) *śukla* (white), *rakta* (red), kṛṣ

---

1. The *Upaniṣad* treating of embryo, etc.
2. The Sanskrit word `suṣira' means performed or tubular.

ṇa (dark-blue or indigo), *dhūmara* (blue), *pīta* (yellow), *kapila* (orange-red), and *pāndara* (yellowish white). In whomsoever these substances arise and increase, the rasa (essence) is the cause of the one following and so on (as stated below). (These rasas are six in number; from the rasas (probably chyme) arises blood : from blood, flesh; from flesh, fat; from fat, bones; from bones, marrow; and from marrow, *śukla* (the male seminal fluid). From the union of *śukla* and śoṇita (the female vital energy), occurs *garbha* (conception in the womb). being stationed in the heart, it is led. In the heart of persons, (there is) an internal *agni*; in the seat of *agni*, there is bile; in the seat of bile, there is *vāyu*; in the seat of *vāyu*, is *hṛdaya* (heart or *Ātmā*).

Through having connection at the ṛtu (seasons) fit for raisingissues, it (the embryo formed in the womb) is like water is the first night; in seven nights, it is like a bubble; at the end of half a months, it becomes a ball. At the end of a month, it is hardened; in two months, the head is formed; in three months, the region about the feet; and in fourth month, the region about the stomach and the lions and also ankle is formed, in the fifth month, the back (or spinal) bone; in the sixth, the face of the nose, eyes, and ears; in the seventh, it becomes united with *Jīva* (*Ātmā*); in the eighth month, it becomes full (of all organs); in the ninth, it becomes fatty. *Sukla* belongs to men and *śoṇita* to women. Each (by itself) is neutral (of is powerless). (But in their combination) a son is born when the father's seed preponderates. A daughter is born when the mother's seed preponderates. Should both be equal, a eunuch is born. Since females have more of passion, on account of their deriving more pleasure (than male from sexual union), a greater number of females are born. Action corresponds to mental state (of the actor). Hence the child (born) takes after (the thought of) the parents. From parents with minds full of anxieties (at the time of union) are born and blind, the lame, the hunchback, the dwarf, and the limbless. (From impregnation) during the eclipses of the sun and the moon, children are born with defective *limba*. Increase or decrease, similarities or dissimilarities of bodies arise (in children) through the influence of time, place, action, *dravya* (substance), and enjoyment. From a well-conducted intercourse (or union), the child being born with the form of the father possesses, his qualities, just as the image in a glass reflects truly the original. When *śukla* bursts into two through the interaction (or blowing against one another) of the *vāyu* of both *śukla* and *śoṇita*, then twins (of the same sex) are born. In the same manner when the retas (the seminal fluids), *viz.*, (*śukla* and *śoṇita*) of both the parents burst into two, then mixed progeny (male and female) is the result. Among mankind, five embryos (only can be formed at a pregnancy in the womb), A womb with one embryo is common. There are some with two. Those with three are only to be found (as rarely) as one in a thousand. Where there is a frequent pouring (of seminal fluid into the womb), a greater number of limbs is produced (in the child). When the pouring (within the womb) is only once, then the child becomes dried up (or contracted). By pouring (within) more than once, couples are (sometimes) born.

Then (*viz.,* in the ninth month), this (in the body) made of five elements and able to sense odour, taste, etc., through *tejas* (spiritual fire), etc., which is also made up of the five elements— this cognizes the indestructible *omkāra* through its deep wisdom and contemplation. It cognizes as the one letter (*Om*). Then there arise in the body the eight *prakṛtis*[1] and the sixteen *vikāras* (changes). Through the food and drink of the mother transmitted through her *nādis*, the chid obtains *prāṇa*. In the ninth month, it is full of all attributes.

It then remembers its previous births, finds out what has been done and what has not been done, and discriminates between actions, right and wrong. (Then it thinks thus:) "Many thousnads of wombs have been seen by me, many kinds of food have been tasted (by me), and may breasts have been suckled (by me). All parts of the world have been my place of birth, as also my burning-ground in the past. In eighty-four lakhs[2] of wombs, have I been born. I have often born and have often died. I have been subject to the cycle of re-births very often. I have had birth and death, again birth and death, and again birth (and so on). There is much suffering whilst living in the womb. Delusion and sorrow attended every birth. In youth are sorrow, grief, dependence on others, ignorance, the non-performance of what is beneficial laziness, and the performance of what is unfavourable. In adult age, (the sources of sorrow are) attachment to sensual objects and groaning under the three kinds[3] of pain. In old age anxiety, disease, fear of death, desires, love of self, passion, anger, and non-independence— all these produce very great suffering. This birth is the seen of sorrow is unbearable. I have not attained the *dharma* of *nivṛtti*, (*viz.,* the means of overcoming the cycle of re-birht) nor have I acquired the means of *yoga* and *jñāna*. Alas ! I am sunk in the ocean of sorrow and find no remedy for it. Fie on *ajñāna* ! fie on *ajñāna* ! fie on the troubles caused by passion and anger; fie on the fetters of *saṁsāra* (the mundane existence) ! I shall attain wisdom from a *Guru*. If I get myself freed from the womb, then I shall practise *sāṁkyha yoga* which is the cause of the extinction of all evil and the bestower of the fruit of emancipation. If I get myself freed from the womb, I shall seek refuge of *Maheśvara* (the great Lord) who is cause of the extinction of all evil and bestower of the (four[4])

1. The eight *prakṛtis* are *mūlaprakṛti*, mahat, *ahaṁkāra*, and the five elements; the sixteen *vikāras* are the five organs of sense, the five organs of action, the five *prāṇas*, and *antaḥkaraṇa*.
2. The Hindus believe in so many number of wombs to be born on the earth.
3. Those that arise from the body, the elements, and the devas.
4. They are kāma (passion), artha (acquisition of wealth), *dharma* (performance of duty, and *mokṣa* (salvation).

ends of life. If I get myself freed from the womb, then I shall seek refuge in that Lord of the world who is the *cidātmā* of all śakti and the cause of all causes. If I get myself freed from the womb, then I shall seek refuge in that supreme Lord *Bhargaḥ* (Śiva or light) who is *paśupati* (the lord of *paśus* or souls), *Rudra*, *Mahādeva* (the great *Deva*) and the *Guru* of the world. If I get myself freed from the bondage of the womb, I shall perform great penances. If I get myself freed from the passage of the womb, I shall worship Viṣṇu in my heart who is the bestower of nectar, who is bliss, who is Nārāyaṇa, and who never decays. I am now confined in my mother's womb; and were I freed from its bonds, I shall please the divine *Vāsudeva* without diverting my mind Him. I am burnt through actions, good and bad, committed by me alone before for the sake of others, whilst those who enjoyed the fruits thereof have disappeared. Through non-belief (unspirituality), I formely gave up all fear (of sin) and committed[1] sins. I now reap their fruits. I shall becme a believer hereafter ."

Thus does the *Jīva* (*Ātmā*) within the (mother's womb) contemplate again and again the many kinds of miseries (it had undergone), and remembering always the miseries of the cycle or re-births, becomes disgusted (with the material enjoyments of the world), often fainting in the inmost centre (*viz.*, heart) of all creatures of (the idea of) his *avidyā*, desire, the *karma*. Then this beings, who had entered many hundreds of female wombs of beings (in the previous births), comes to the mouth of the womb wishing to obtain release. Here being pressed by the yantra (neck of the uterus), it suffers much trouble. Moreover it is much affected by parsūti (delivery) *vāyu* and ceases to remember anything of the past; it also ceases to see far and to be the cognizer of the real. Coming into contact with the earth, it becomes fiercy-eyed and debased. The evail of the eye after it if rubbed with (or cleaned by) water vanishes; and with it, vanishes memory of birth and death, good and bad actions and their affinities. Then how does he understand *vāyu*, bile, and *śleṣma* (phlegm)? When they are in their proper state, they produce health : with their disturbance, diseases are generated. It should be known that one becomes capable of knowing through a proper quantity of bile; through having a little more or a little less of it, he comes of know more. When the bile is changed (otherwise), he becomes changed and acts lik a mad man. And that bile is *agni*. *Agni* influenced by *karma* is kindled by *vāyu*, the source (or seat) of virtue and vice, fuel is kindled within (by fire) from without (by the wind).

And of how many kinds is *agni*? It has three bodies, three reatas (seeds or progeny), three puras (cities), three *dhātus*, and three kinds of

---

1. The reason why it remembers them seems to be that the *jīvātmā* is in the pineal gland then, prior to its coming down.

agni threefold. Of these three, *Vaiśvānara* is bodiless. And that *agni* becomes (or is subdivided into) *Jñānāgni* (wisdom-fire), *Darśanāgni* (eye-fire), and *Koṣṭhāgni* (digestive fire). Of these *Jñānāgni* pertains to the mind; *Daśanāgni* pertains of the senses; and *Koṣṭhāgni* pertains to dahare and daily cooks (of disgests) equally whatever is eaten, drunk, licked, or sucked through *prāṇa* and *apāna*. *Darśanāgni* is (in) the eye itself and is the cause of the *vijñāna* and enables one to see all objects of form. It has three seats, The (spiritual) eye itself being the (primary) seat, and the eyeballs being the accessory seats. *Dakśināgni* is in the heart, *Gārhapatya* is in the belly, and in the face is *Āhavanīya*. (In this sacrifices with the three *agnis*), the *Puruṣa* is himself the sacrificer; *buddhi* becomes his wife; santoṣa (contentment) becomes the *dīkṣā* (vow) taken; the mind and the organs of the senses become the sacrificial vessels; the *karmendriyas* (organs of action) are the sacrificial instruments. In this sacrifice of the body, the several devas who become the *ṛtvijas* (sacrificial priests) perform their parts following the master of the sacrifice, (*viz*., the true individuality), wherever he goes. In this (sacrifice), the body is the sacrificial place, the skull of the head is the fire-pit, the hairs are the *kuśa* grass; the mouth is the antarvedi (raised platform in sacrifice); *kāma* (or passion) is the clarified butter; the period of life is the period of sacrifice; *nāda* (sound) produced in dahara (heart) is the *sāmaveda* (recited during the sacrifice; *vaikharī* in the *yajus* (or *yajurveda* hymns); *parā*, *paśyanti*, and *madhyamā*[1] are the ṛks (or ṛgveda hymns); cruel worlds are the atharvas (*atharvaveda* hymns) and *khilas* (supplementary texts of each veda); true; words are the *vyāhṛtis*[2]. Life, strength, and bile are the *paśus* (sacrificial creatures) and death is *avabhṛta* (the bath which concludes the sacrifice). In this sacrifice, the (three) fires blaze up and then according to (the desires of) the worldly, the devas bless him. All who are living (in this world) are the sacrificers. There is none living who does not perform *yajña* (sacrifice). This body is (created) for *yajña*, and arises out of *yajña* and changes according to *yajña*. If this *yajña* is continued in a direction changed (from the right course, or is abused), then it leads to an ocean of misery.

In this body, there are sixteen side-teeth, having each a membrane (as its root) and fifteen openings. It (the body) is measured by ninety-six digits. there are in it fourteen *nādis* seats and 108 joints. There are seventy-two tubes seats with seventy-two *nādis* between them, of which three are important, *viz*., *iḍā*, *piṅgalā*, and *suṣumnā*, the fourth is purītati, and *jīvata* the fifth. Above *Jīvata* is bile and near bile is *purīati*. Above

1. *Vaikharī* and the three others are the different stages of *nāda* (sound).
2. *Vyāhṛtis* are parts of *Gāyatrī Mantra*, *viz*., *Bhuḥ*, *Bhuvaḥ*, *Svaḥ*.

the navel, two digits to the left of it, is seated the source of bile. The food taken in is divided into three parts— urine, fæces, and *sāra* (the essence of chyme). The urine dividing itself into two, spreads to the left below the navel. The fæces is in the right side and is of seven kinds. The *sāra* is of five kinds and spread itself over the body. hence the semen and blood are produced from food and drink. In this body, *vāyu* which is moving as *prāṇa* is the *Sūtrātma*. Through it, one inspires and expires and moves (his limbs). Withot it, no limb of the body will be animated. Through *vāyu*, the currênt of blood is driven into the *nādis* from the *cakra* (plexus) of the heart, and those which can be touched (on the body) are easily discernible. The juicy essences (of food) which arise out of digestion enter the womb which is suspended in the stomach of the mother and coming near the child's head nourishes the child's *prāṇa* through the *suṣumnā* (on the head or pineal gland). *Suṣumnā* is the *Brahma-nāḍī*. *Prāṇa* and others are found there. It (*prāṇa*) descends lower and lower as the time of birth approaches and settles in the heart when the child is born. Through *yoga*, it should be brought from the midle of the eyebrows to the end of *suṣumnā* (*viz.,* the pineal gland), when he becomes the cognizer of the Real like the child in the womb. In the body of this nature, *Ātmā* is latent and deathless, and is the witness and *Puruṣa*. It lives in this body, being enveloped (by *māyā*). *Prāṇi* (or the *jīva* having *prāṇa*) has *abhimāna* (identification with the body) on account of *avidyā*. *Ajñāna* which surrounds it is seed; the *antaḥkaraṇa* (internal organ) is the sprout and the body is the tree. In this tree (of body), there are eight crores of hairs, eighty hundreds of joints, nine hundreds of tendons, eight palams of heart[1], twelve palams of tongue, one *prastha* (or two palams) of bile; one *ādhaka* of phlegm, one kudupa (or 1/4 *prastha*) of *śukla* and two *prasthas* of marrow. One should consider everything as evanescent, like the child in the womb (with its *prāṇa*. etc.,) stationed in the *suśumnā* (of the head). Then he becomes freed and gets on more body. If not, an ignorant man becomes subject to the cycle of re-births, etc., is exposed like a worm to the drink of urine and fæces, and undergoes in this body the sufferings of hell. Therefore knowing all this, one should be averse to worldly objects. Thus ends the *mokṣa-śāstra* of *Pippalāda*— thus ends the *mokṣa-śāstra* of *Pippalāda*.

Thus ends the Upaniṣad

1. Eight palams are 3/5 of a lb. (avdp.)

Tārasāra-Upaniṣad[1]

OF

ŚUKLA-YAJURVEDA

Om. *Bṛhaspti* asked *Yājñavalkya* : "That which is called *Kurukṣetra* is place of the sacrifice of the *Devas* and the spiritual seat of all beings. Therefore where should one go in order that he may cognize *Kurukṣetra*, the place of the sacrifice of the *Devas* and the spiritual seat of all beings?" (To which *Yājñavalkya* replied :) "*Avimukta*[2] is *Kurukṣetra*, the place of the sacrifice of the *Devas* and of the study of *Brahman*, because it is there that *Rudra* initiates one into the *Tāraka*[3] *brahman* when *prāṇa* (life) goes out. Through this, one becomes immortal and the enjoyer of *mokṣa*. Therefore one should always be in the midst of that place *avimukta*, and should never leave, O reverend sir, *avimukta*." Thus said *Yājñavalkya*.

Then *Bhāradvāja* asked *Yājñavalkya* : "What is *tāraka*? what is that which causes one to cross (this mundane existence)." Two which *Yājñvavalkya* replied : "*Om-Namo-Nārāyaṇāya* is the *tāraka*. It should be worshipped as *Cidātma*. *Om* is a single syllable and of the nature of *Ātmā*. *Namaḥ* is of two syllables and is of the nature of *prakṛti* (matter). Nārāyaṇāya is of five syllables and is of the nature of *parabrahman*. He who knows this becomes immortal. Through *Om*, is Brahmā produced; through *Na* is Viṣṇu produced; through *Ma* is *Rudra* produced; through *Nā* is *Īśvara* produced; through *Rā* is the *Aṇḍa-Virāṭ* (or *Virāṭ* of the universe) produced; through *ya* is *Puruṣa* produced; through *Nā* is *Bhagavān* (Lord) produced; and through *Ya* is *Paramātmā* produced. This *Aṣṭākṣara* (eight syllables) of Nārāyaṇa is the supreme and the highest *Puruṣa*. Thus is the *Ṛgveda* with the first foot (or half). That which is *Om* is the indestructible, the supreme, and *Brahman*. That alone should be worshipped. It is this that is of the eight subtle syllables. And this become eight, being of eight forms. A is the first letter; U is the second; M is the third; *Bindu* is the fourth; *Nāda* is the fifth; *Kalā* is the sixth; *Kalātīta* (the beyond kalā) is the seventh; and that which is beyond these is the eighth. It is called *Tāraka*, because it enables one to cross this mundane existence. Know that *Tāraka* alone is *Brahman* and it alone should be worshipped." The (following) verses may be quoted here : "From the letter A came brahmā named *Jāmbavān*[4] (the bear). From the letter U

---

1. This *Upaniṣad* treats of the *sāra* (essence) for *tāra* (crossing).
2. It is one of the many names given to Benares.
3. *Tāraka* is *Om*—from *tṛ* to cross.
4. As the bear, Brahmā incarnated according to the '*Rāmāyaṇa*'.

came *Upendra*[1], named *Hari*. From the letter M came *Śiva*. known as Hanumān[2]. *Bindu* is named *Īśvara* and is *Śatrughna*, the Lord of the discus itself. *Nāda* should be known as the great Lord named *Bharata* and the sound of the conch itself. From *Kalā* came the *Puruṣa* himself as Lakṣ maṇa and the bearer of the earth. *Kālātīta* is known as the goddess *Sītā* Herself. that which is beyond is the *Paramātmā* named *Śrī-Rāma* and is the highest *Puruṣa*. All this is the explanation of the letter *Om*, which is the past, the present, and future, and which is other than these (*viz.,*). *Tattva, mantra, varṇa* (colour), *devatā* (deity), *Chandas* (metre), *ṛk, kāla, śakti*, and *sṛṣti* (creation). he who knows this becomes immortal. (Thus is) *Yajurveda* with the second foot."

Then *Bhāradvāja* asked *Yājñavalkya* : "Through what *mantra* is *Paramātmā* pleased and shows his own *Ātmā* (to persons) ? Please tell this." *Yājñavalkya* replied :

"(1st *Mantra*) : *Om*. He who is *Śrī-Paramātmā*, Nārāyaṇa and the Lord described by (the letter) A and is *Jāmbavān* (the bear) and *Bhūḥ, Bhuvaḥ, Svaḥ* : Salutation to Him."

"(2nd *Mantra* :) He who is *Paramātmā*, Nārāyaṇa, and the Lord described by (the letter) *U* and is *Upendra* (or) *Hari* and *Bhūḥ, Bhuvaḥ,* and *Svaḥ*) : Salutation to Him.

"(3rd *Mantra* :) *Om*. He who is *Śrī-Paramātmā*, Nārāyaṇa, and the Lord described by (the letter) M and is of the form of Śiva (or), *Hanumān* and *Bhūḥ, Bhuvaḥ,* and *Svaḥ*) : Salutation to Him.

"(4th *Mantra* :) *Om*. He who is *Śrī-Paramātmā*, Nārāyaṇa, the Lord of *Śatrughna*[3] of the form of *Bindu* and the *Bhuḥ, Bhuvaḥ* and *Svaḥ* : Salutation to Him.

(" 5th *Mantra* :) *Om*. he who is *Śrī-Paramātmā, Nārāyaṇa*, and the Lord, and is *Bharata*[4] of the form of *Nāda* and the *Bhuḥ*, *Bhuvaḥ* and *Svaḥ*. : Salutation to Him.

(6th *Mantra* :) *Om*. He who is *Śrī-Paramātmā*, Nārāyaṇa, and the Lord, and is Lakṣmaṇa of the form of *Kalā* and the *Bhūḥ*, *Bhuvaḥ*, *Svaḥ* : Salutation to Him.

("7th *Mantra* :) *Om*. He who is *Śrī-Paramātmā*, Nārāyaṇa, and the Lord, and is *Kalātīta*, the Goddess *Sītā*, of the form of *Cit* and the *Bhuḥ*, *Bhuvaḥ*, and *Svaḥ* : Salutation to Him.

(8th *Mantra* :) *Om*. he who is "*rī-Paramātmā*, Nārāyaṇa, and the Lord what is beyond that (*Kalātīta*), is the supreme *Puruṣa*, and is the ancient *Puruṣottama*, the eternal, the immaculate, the enlightened, the

---

1. As upendra, Viṣṇu incarnates in the lower tala as well in the legs in man.
2. Hanumān is the incarnation of *vāyu*, one of the elements of Śiva.
3. Bharata is rather the incarnation of discuss or consciousness and Satrughna, that of conch—*viz.*, ākāsic sound.
4. Bharata is rather the incarnation of discuss or consciousness and Satrughna, that of conch—*viz.*, ākāsic sound.

emancipated, the true, the highest bliss, the endless, the secondless, and the all-full— that *Brahman* is myself. I am Rāma and the *Bhuḥ*, *Bhuvaḥ*, and *Svaḥ* : Salutation to Him."

He who has mastered this eightfold *mantra* is purified by *Agni*; he is purified by *Vāyu*; he is purified by the sun; he is purified by Śiva; he is known by all the *Devas*. He attains the fruit of reciting *Itihāsas*, *Purāṇas*, *Rudra* (*Mantras*), a hundred thousand times. He who repeatedly remembers (or recites) the *Aṣṭākṣara* (the eight-syllabled *mantra*) of the Nārāyaṇa gains the fruit of the recitation of *Gāyatrī* hundred thousand times or of *Praṇava* (*Om*) a myriad of times. He purifies (his ancestors) ten (degrees) above and (his descendants) ten (degrees) below. He attains the state of Nārāyaṇa. He who knows this attains the state of Nārāyaṇa. He who knows this (attains the state of Nārāyaṇa).

Like the eye (which sees without any obstacle) the things spread (in the sky), the wise ever seen this supreme seat of Viṣṇu. *Brāhmaṇas* who are spiritually awake praise in diverse ways and illuminate the supreme abode of Viṣṇu. (Thus is) the *Sāmaveda* with the third foot.

Thus ends the Upaniṣad

Nārāyaṇa-Upaniṣad

OF

KṚṢṆA-YAJURVEDA

Om. Then Nārāyaṇa, the supreme *Puruṣa* desired. "I shall create offspring." From Nārāyaṇa emanates *prāṇa*, *manas*, the several organs of sense and action, *ākāśa*, *vāyu*, *agni*, *āpas* and *pṛthivī* that supports all. From Nārāyaṇa emanates Brahmā. From Nārāyaṇa emanates *Rudra*. From Nārāyaṇa emanates Indra. From Nārāyaṇa emanates Prajāpati (the divine progenitor). From Nārāyaṇa emanates the twelve *ādityas, rudras, vasus*, and all the *chanḍas* (Vedas). From Nārāyaṇa only do (all these) proceed. Through Nārāyaṇa do (they) prosper. In Nārāyaṇa (they) are absorbed. The *Ṛgveda* teaches this.

Then Nārāyaṇa is eternal. Brahmā is Nārāyaṇa, Śiva is Nārāyaṇa. *Indra* is Nārāyaṇa, *Kāla* (Time) is Nārāyaṇa, *Dik* (space) is Nārāyaṇa, the intermediate quarters also are Nārāyaṇa; that which is above is Nārāyaṇa, that which is below is Nārāyaṇa, that which is in and out is Nārāyaṇa, that whole universe which that existed and will exist is Nārāyaṇa. Nārāyaṇa is the only one that is stainless, sinless, changeless, and unnameable, and that is pure and divine. There is no second. Whoever knows Him thus, becomes viṣṇu Himself. The *Yajurveda* teaches this.

One should utter "*Om*" first, then "*namaḥ*" and then "Nārāyaṇa." "*Om*" (is) a single syllable; "*Namaḥ*" contains two syllables : Nārāyaṇaya contains five syllables. this is the sentence known as the *Aṣṭāṣara*[1] of Nārāyāṇa. Whoever studies this *Aṣṭākṣara* of Nārāyaṇa and recites it constantly, attains full life and supremacy over men, enjoys the pleasures of royalty and becomes the master of all souls. He attains *Mokṣa*; yea, he attains *mokṣa*. The *Sāmaveda* teaches this.

The *Yogin* having pronounced (the name of) Him who is complete bliss, who is *Brahma-puruṣa* and who is of the nature of *Praṇava* (*Om*)—combination of A, U, and M— is released from the bondage of birth and mundane existence. He who practises the *mantra* "*Om-Namo-*Nārāyaṇāya" reaches *Vaikuṇṭha* (the abode of Viṣṇu). It is this lotus (heart). It is replete with *vijñāna* : It has the brilliancy of lighting. The son of *Devakī* is *Brahmaṇya*[2] *Madhusūdana* is *Brahmaṇya*. Nārāyaṇa who pervades all elements, who is one only, who is the cause *Puruṣa* and who is causeless, is known as *Parabrahman*. The *Atharvaṇa Upaniṣaḍ* teaches this.

---

1. The eight syllables.
2. Means Viṣṇu or Brahmā devoted to Tapas, Truth, and *Jñāna*.

Whoever recites (the *Upaniṣad*) in the morning destroys the sins committed the night (before). Whoever recites it in the evening destroys the sins committed during the day. Whoever recites morning and evening becomes free from sins, however sinful he may be. whoever recites (it) in the noon facing the sun is freed from all the five[1] great sins as well as from the minor ones. he derives the good effects of the recitation of all the Vedas. Whoever knows thus attains *Sāyujya* of Nārāyaṇa (*viz.*, is absorbed in the essence of Nārāyana). He attains *Sāyujya* of Nārāyaṇa.

Thus ends the Upaniṣad

1. They are theft of gold, drinking alcohol, the murder of a *Brāhmana*, and unlawful union with the *Guru*'s wife and association with them.

Kalisanṭāraṇa[1]-Upaniṣad

OF

KṚṢṆA-YAJURVEDA

At the end of *Dvāpara yuga,* Nārada[2] went the Brahmā and addressed him thus : "O Lord, how shall I, roaming[3] over the earth, be able to cross *Kali*?" To which Brahmā thus replied : "Well asked. Hearken to that which all *Śrutis* (the Vedas) keep secret and hidden, through which one may cross the *saṁsāra* (mundane existence) of *Kali.* He shakes off (the evil effects of) *Kali* through the mere uttering of the name of the Lord Nārāyaṇa, who is the primeval *Puruṣa.*" Again Nārada asked Brahmā : "What is the name?" To which *Hiraṇyagarbha* (Brahmā) replied thus : (the words are :)" 1. *Harē*; 2. Rāma, 3. *Harē*, 4. Rāma 5. Rāma, 6. Rāma 7. *Harē*, 8. *Harē*; 9. *Harē*, 10. Kṛṣṇa] 11. *Harē*, 12. Kṛṣṇa, 13. Kṛṣṇa, 14. Kṛṣṇa 15. *Harē*, 16. *Harē*. These sixteen names) (words) are destructive of the evil effects of *Kali*. No better means than this is to be seen in all the Vedas. These (sixteen names) destory of *āvaraṇa* (or the centripetal force which produces the sense of individuality) of *jīva* surrounded by the sixteen *kalās* (rays). Then like the sphere of the sun which shines fully after the clouds (screening it) disperse, *Parabrahman* (alone) shines."

Nārada asked : "O Lord, what are the rules to be observed with reference to it. To which Brahmā replied that there were no rules for it. Whoever in a pure or an impure state, utters these always, attains the same world of, or proximity with, or the same form of, or obsorption into Brahmā.

Whoever utters three and a half kotis[4] (or thirty-five millions) times this *mantra* composed of sixteen names (or words) crosses the sin of the

---

1. This *Upaniṣad* treats of the means of crossing *Kali* completely: Nārada having asked the question in *Dvāpara yuga*— the third of the four *yugas*.
2. Nārada is called *Kali-Kāraka* or the generator of *kali* or strife and discord. If Nārada is himself the strife-maker, why should he go to Brahmā for the means of crossing *Kali*? Nārada being himself an adjuster of the laws of *karma*, this *Upaniṣad* gives the means of getting over strife, etc., in this *Kali*-age when the whole of nature is thrown off its balance by the depraved tendencies of men. The *jīva* has sixteen *kalās*, corresponding to which sixteen *mantras* or words are given.
3. The story is that he was cursed by Dakṣha to roam over the worlds with a lute in his hand (*viz.*, to adjust the laws of harmony).
4. This number can be reached by uttering the *mantra* completely within one year if uttered at the rate of a lakh per day : and within ten years if uttered at the rate of 10,000 per day; and within 100 years if uttered at the rate of 1,000 per diem.

murder of a *Brāhamaṇa*. He becomes purified from the sin of the theft of gold. He becomes purified from the sin of cohabitation with a woman of low caste. he is purified from the sin of wrong done to pitṛs, devas, and men. Having given up all dharmas, he becomes freed at once from all sins. He is at once released from all bondage. That he is at once released from bondage is the *Upaniṣad*.

Thus ends the Upaniṣad

Bhikṣuka[1]-Upaniṣad

OF

ŚUKLA-YAJURVEDA

Among *bhikṣus* (religious mendicants) who long for *mokṣa* (salvation), there are four[2] kinds, *viz,. Kutīchaka, Bahūdaka, Haṁsa*, and *Paramahaṁsa. Gautama, Bharadvāja, Yājñavalkya, Vaṣiṣṭha* and others belong to the first kind. They take eight mouthfuls (of food daily) and strive after *mokṣa* alone through the path of *yoga*. The second kind carry thee (bamboo) staves (tied together) amd a waterpot, and wear tuft of hair (*śikhā*), sacred thread (*yajñopavīta*) and red-colourd cloth. They take eight mouthfuls of food in the house of *Brahmaṛṣis*, abstain from flesh and alcohol and strive after emancipation alone through the path of *yoga*. Then The *Haṁas* should live not more than a night in a village, five nights in a town, and seven nights in a sacred place, partaking daily of cow's urine and cow's dung, observing *cāndrāyaṇa*[3] and striving after *mokṣa* alone through the path of *yoga*. *Paramahaṁsas* like *Samvartaka, Āruṇi, Svetaketu, Jadabharata, Dattātreya, Śuka, Vāmadeva, Hārītake* and others take eight mouthfuls and strive after *mikṣa* alone through the path of *yoga*. They live clothed or naked at the foot of trees, in ruined houses, or inburning grounds, With them, there are no dualities as *dharma* and *adharma*, gain and loss, and purity and impurity. They look upon gold and stone and clod of earth with the same eye (indifference), live on alms, begging from all without any distinction of caste and look upon everything as *Ātmā* alone. Being (naked) as nature made them, being free from the sense of duality and from covetousness, being engaged in pure contemplation (*śukladhyāna*), meditating on *Ātmā*, and begging at stated times, simply to keep the body and soul together, they reside in ruined houses, temples, straw-huts, ant-hills, the foot of trees, potteries, the places of *agnihotra*, the sand in the bed of rivers, mountain-caves,

---

1. One who lives on *bhikṣā* or alms. Hence a religious mendicant.
2. In Nāradaparivrājaka *Upaniṣad* there are state to be six kinds.
3. A religious expiatory ceremony regulated by the moon's age diminishing the daily consumption of food daily by one mouthful for the dark half of the month beginning with fifteen at the fullmoon until it is reduced to one at the new moon and then increasing it in like manner during the fortnight of the moon's increase.—Wilson.

cavities, the hollows of trees, waterfalls, and *sthaṇḍila* (the level square piece of ground prepared for sacrifice). Having advanced far in the path of *Brahman*, and being pure in mind, they quit this body through the methods prescribed for *Paramahṁsa Saṅnyāsins*. These are the *Paramahaṁsas*.

Thus ends the Upaniṣad

Nāradaparivrājaka-Upaniṣad

OF

ATHARVAVEDA

Upadeśa I

Om. One upon a time, Nārada, the ornament of *Parivrājakas* (roaming ascetics), after roaming over all worlds and cleansing, through merely by looking at the places of pilgrimage able to impart rare religious merits, observed, with a mind that had attained purity, without hate, quiescent and patient, and indifferent towards all (objects), the forest of *Naimiśa* (the modern *Nimsār*), filled with *Rusuis* that were engaged in the contemplation of Reality and had attained the greatness of the ordained bliss; (there) through the recitation of stories about Hari (Viṣṇu), associated with the musical motes of *Sa*, *Ri*, *Ga*, *Ma*, *Pa*, *Dha*, and *Ni* (of the gamut), able to impart indifference to objects and to make one look down upon the universe, and instilling divine devotion, fixed and movable (or mental and bodily), he entered (the forest, fascinating the crowds of beings human, animal, *Kimpuruṣas*[1], celestials, *Kinnaras*[2], *Apsaras* (Houris), and *Uragas*[3] (collected there). (Thereupon the) great *Ṛṣ is Śâunaka* and others who had been engaged for twelve years in *Sattra* sacrifice well-skilled in the recitation of Vedas, the knowers of all, and the good practisers of tapas, observed Nārada the son of Brahmā and the devotee of the Lord, and having risen up, paid due respect to him. Then having with due respect requested him to sit down, they also seated themselves and addressed him thus : "O Lord, son of Brahmā, what is the means of salvation for us? It is meet that it should be communicated (to us)." Thus addressed, Nārada replied to them thus : "One born in a good family and fit to go through the forty-four *saṁskāras, upanayana* and others, should, under a teacher to whom he is devoted, study, after the recitation of the Veda of his own *śākhā* (division), all the different branches of knowledge; then should fulfil, according to the rules ordained, for twelve years the observance of Brahmacharya (celibacy), such as the service of the *Guru*, etc.; then for twenty-five years the āśrama (order of life) of a *gṛhastha* (house-holder), and for twenty-five years the *āśrama* of a *vānaprastha* (forester). After thus practising well the fourfold

---

1. A higher being with the form of a horse but with a human head.
2. A higher being with a human form but with the head of a horse.
3. A semidivine serpent with a human face.

celibacy,[1] the sixfold[2] householder's life, and the fourfold[3] forester's life, and having performed all the duties thereof, he should acquire the fourfold[4] means of salvation; thus the *sannyāsin* who gives up the desires along with the *karmas* of mind, speech, and body in this *saṁsāra* as well as the vāsanā towards the threefold desire (of son, wife, and wealth), being without malice and endowed with quiescence and patience, undisturbed in the order of life of *Paramahaṁsa*, quits the body in the contemplation of Reality, is an emancipated person.Such is the *Upaniṣad*.

Upadeśa II

All the *Ṛṣis*, *Śaunaka* and others addressing Lord Nārada said thus : "O Lord, please tell us the rules of *sannyāsa*." At which, seeing them, Nārada replied : "It is but meet that we should know the whole truth from the mouth of Brahmā Himself." After the *sattra* sacrifice was completed, he took the *ṛṣis* along with him to *satyaloka*; an after duly making prostrations to and eulogising Brahmā engaged in meditation upon *Brahman*, he along with others was duly seated under the orders of Brahmā. Then Nārada addressed Brahmā thus : "Thou art *Guru*; thou art father; thou art the knower of the secret of all learning; thou art the knower of all; thou shalt therefore tell me one secret. Who else but thee is fit to tell the secret dear unto me. It is this. Please tell us the rules of the real *sannyāsa* (asceticism).

Thus prayed to by Nārada, Brahmā surveyed all in the four quarters; and after meditating for one muhūrta (48 minutes), and assuring himself that the inquiry was truly for the purpose of escaping from the pain of *saṁsāra*, Brahmā eyeing Nārada, said thus : "The mystery that was imparted before by *Virāṭ-Puruṣa* of illimitable form according to the *Puruṣa-Sūkta-Upaniṣad* is now being divulged to you. It is very mysterious. It is fit to be hearkened to with great attention. O Nārada, one born in a good family and obedient to his parents, should, after the performance of *upanayana* according to the rules, find a virtuous *Guru* that is other than his father, is of good custom and habits, of faith, born of good family, a knower of Vedas, a lover of *Śāstras*, of (good) qualities and free from duplicity. Having made prostrations and rendered useful service to him, he should respectfully acquaint him with his intention. Having studies all departments of knowledge and rendered service for twelve years, he should, under his (the *Guru*'s) orders, marry a girl fit for

---

1. The four Brahmacaryas are : (1) *Gāyatrī*; (2) *Prājāpatya*; (3) Vaidika; (4) Naiṣṭika.
2. The six *Gṛhasthas* are : (1) *Vārtāvṛtti*; *viz.*, Agriculture; (2) *Sālīnavṛtti*; (3) *Yāyāvara*; (4) *Ghorasannyāsin*; etc.
3. The four *Vānaprasthas* are : (1) ***Audumbara***; (2) ***Vaikhānasa***; (3) ***Samaprakṣāli***; (4) ***Pourṇama***.
4. They are *Viveka*, *Vairāgya*, etc.

his family and dear unto him. Then having performed for twenty-five years the *karmas* incidental to a householder and attained the status of a *Brāhmaṇa* that has performed sacrifices and the rest, he should beget a son with the only desire of perpetuating the family. After thus spending twenty-five years in the performance of household *dharma*, he should bathe thrice daily for twenty-five years and take only one meal in the fourth period; he should live alone in the forest, after giving up his previous wanderings in city and village; and without desire for fruit, should perform the *karmas* incidental to that (forester's) order of life, and be without desire for objects seen and heard. Being skilled in the forty *saṁskāras*, he should be devoid of desire for all, have a purified mind, have burnt up desire, jealousy, envy and egoism, and have developed the four means of salvation. Then he becomes fit for *sannyāsa*. Such is the *Upaniṣad*."

Upadeśa III

Then Nārada addressed the grandfather thus :

"O Lord, by whom, after attaining the qualifications of *sannyāsa*, is it fit to be taken ?" To which Brahmā replied : "After first expounding the qualifications of *sannyāsa*, the rules of *sannyāsa* will then be stated. Hearken carefully. A eunuch, the outcaste, the maimed, the lewd, the deaf, the youth, the dumb, the heretic, the discus-bearer, the Liṅga-wearer, the *vaikhānasa* (forester), the *Haradhvaja* (carrier of Śiva's flag), the reciter of Vedas for hire, the bald-headed, one without (sacrificial) fire— all these, even though they have attained *vairāgya* are unfit for *sannyāsa*. Even though they have become *sannyāsins*, they are unfit to be initiated into the mahāvākyas (sacred vedic sentences). The *Paramahaṁsa sannyāsin* stated before (as fit to take *sannyāsa*) is the one qualified. It is stated in the *smṛtis* that he is a *parivrāt* who is not afraid of others, as others are not afraid of him. The eunuch, the limbless, the blind, the youth, the sinful, the outcaste, the door-keeper, the *vaikhānasa*, the *Haradhvaja*, the *Cakrī* (discus-bearer), the *Liṅgī* (*Liṅga*-wearer), the heretic, the bald-headed, one without fire (sacrifice), one that had undergone *sannyāsa* twice or thrice, the reciter of Vedas for hire— all these are not fit for regular *sannyāsa* but only for *ātura-sannyāsa* (viz., *sannyāsa* taken while a person is afflicted, etc.). What is the opinion of āryas (Hindus) on the (fit) time for *ātura-sannyāsa* (being taken)? The time when *prāṇa* (life) is about to rise (out of the body) is called ātura. The time other than it is incapable of conferring (upon one) the path of salvation and is not ātura. Even in *ātura-sannyāsa*, the wise should according to rules, initiate themselves into *sannyāsa* after reciting the *mantras* again and again in the course of respective *mantras*. There is no difference between regular and *ātura*-sannyās in the *mantras* to be uttered at the time of taking *sannyāsa*. There is no *karma* without *mantras*; (hence) *karma* needs *mantras*. Anything done without *mantra* cannot be termed *karma*. Hence *mantras* should not be given up. Any *karma* done without *mantra* is like an offering made in ashes. Through the consciseness (of the performance) of the *karmas*, it is stated to be *ātura-sannyāsa*.

"Therefore, O *Muni*, the recitation of *mantras* is stated to be in ātura-*sannyāsa*. one who is always duly doing *agni-hotra* (fire-sacrifice) should, when he quits (the house) for foreign places through indifference, perform the *prājāpatya* sacrifice in water and then take up *sannyāsa*. After completing in water the observances of *karma* through the mind, or the recitation of *mantras*, the wise man should attain *sannyāsa*. Else he becomes a fallen man. When, in the mind, indifference to all objects arises, then men should long after *sannyāsa*, (that being the best time for it); otherwise they are fallen. One who attains *vairāgya* should taken *sannyāsa*. One who does not, should remain at home. That vile twice-born with desire, should he take *sannyāsa*, reaches hell. That *Brāhmaṇa* who is a celibate, who has under control his tongue, sexual organ, stomach, and hand may become a *sannyāsin* without undergoing the ceremony of marriage. Having known *saṁsāra* as one without *sāra* (or essence) and not having undergone any marriage on account of the desire to know the sāra (or essence of God), they become sannyāsins on account of the practice of the supreme *vairāgya*. The characteristic of *Pravṛtti* (path) is the performance of *karma*; that of *nivṛtti* of *jñāna*. Therefore placing *jñāna* in the forefront, the wise man should take up *sannyāsa*. When the reality of the eternal *Parabrahman* is understood, then he should take up one daṇḍa (staff) and abandon the holy thread and tuft of hair. then he becomes fit to eat the alms-food (of *sannyāsa*), having become devoted to *Paramātmā*, indifferent to those that are non-*Paramātmā* and freed from all desires. He becomes fit to be the eater of alms food who peserves the same countenance when he is beaten, as when he is worshipped or prostrated to. He becomes fit to be the eater of alms-food who is of the firm certitude that he his no other than the non-dual and indestructible *Brahman*, otherwise named *Vāsudeva*. He in whom are existent *śānti* (control of the organs), *śama* (control of mind), purity (of mind and body), *satya* (truth), *santoṣa* (contentment, *ārjava* (straight for wardness), poverty, and non-ostentatiousness should be in the order of life of *kaivalya* (*sannyāsa*). When one does not, through actions, mind, or speech, commit any sinful action to any being, then he becomes fit for eating alms-food. Having become quiescent (through the control of the mind), having practised the ten kinds of *dharmas*, having, according to rules, studied *vedānta*, and having paid the three debts (to devas, *ṛṣis*, and *pitṛs*), one should take up *sannyāsa*. Courage, fortitude, the control of the body, honesty, purity of (mind and body), control of the (inner) organs, shame, knowledge, truth, and absence of anger— these ten are the characteristics of *dharma*. One who does not look back (with pleasure) upon past enjoyments, nor forward into the future,and one who does not rejoice in the present, is fit to become a *sannyāsin*. One who is able to control within, the inner organs and without, the external organs, may be in the order of life of *kaivalya*. One who while in life is not affected by pleasures and pains, as the body is unaffected by them after death, may be in the order of life of *kaivalya*.

"An ascetic of the *Paramahaṁsa* (order) shall wear two loin-cloths, one ragged cloth, and one staff. Nothing more is ordained (in his case). Should he through desire wear more than these, he will fall into the hell or raurava and be born into the womb of an animal. Having stitched together old and clean cloths into one and having coloured it with red (ochre), he should wear it as his upper cloth. He may be with one cloth or even without it. He should roam about alone with the sole vision (of *Brahman*), devoid of desires; but he may be in one place alone in the rainy season. Having quite abandoned his family, including son and wife, *vedānta*, sacrifice, and the sacred thread, the ascetic should wander incognition. Having given up all faults, such as passion, anger, pride, desire, and delusion, he *parivrāt* (ascetic) should become one that owns nothing. He is a *muni* who is devoid of love and hate, who regards equally a clod of earth, stone, or gold, who does no injury to any living creature, and is freed from all. That ascetic reaches salvation who is associated with *Ātmajñāna*, who is freed from ostentation and egoism, from doing injury and tale-bearing. Through attraction to the senses, he becomes subject to fault, there is no doubt : through their control, he gains perfection. Lust when enjoyed is never gratified. Just as fire increases with the oblation (of ghee, etc., poured into it) so also lust waxes strong (with enjoyment). It should be known that that man who does not rejoice or grieve through hearing, touching, eating, seeing, or smelling is a *jitendriya* (conqueror of the organs). He whose speech and mind are well brought under control attains, completely and always, all the fruits of *vedānta*.

"That *Brāhmaṇa* who is always afraid of respect as poison and always longs after disrespect as nectar, sleeps soundly and rises happily even though he is treated with disrespect. He moves about happily in this world. The one who treats him with disrespect perishes. All cruel words should be endured. None should be treated with disrespect. On account of bodily relationship, none should be made inimical. No anger should be directed in turn towards one who is angry. Soft words (only) shold be spoken, even when (violently) pulled by another. No untrue words should be uttered, even should afflictions arise to the seven gates (of the body). One desirous of bliss should dwell in this universe through the aid of

Ātmā alone, intent upon *Ātmā*, free from desires, and without the desire of blessing (others). He becomes fit for salvation through the control of the organs, the destruction of love and hate and non-injury to beings. He should abandon (all identification with) this feeble, perishable, and impure body of five elements whereof the bones are the pillars, which is strung by the nerves, coated over with flesh and blood, covered up by the skin, is of bad odour, full of urine and faeces is ever haunted by dotage and miseries and is the seat of all ills. If an ignorant man be fond of this body firmly knit together with flesh, blood, pus, faeces, and urine, nerves, fat, and bones, he would, a *fortiori*, be fond of hell. That (identification of the body with the Self) is alone the seat of the *Kālasūtra* hell. That is alone the *Mahā-Vīchi-Vāgura* (hell). That is alone the *Asipatravanaśreṇi* (hell). Such an idea of the bodybeing the Self should be strenuously abandoned, though all should perish. That love of the body is not fit to be felt by one intent upon his welfare; just as a low-caste woman eating dog's flesh is unfit to be touched.

"One (fit to reach salvation), after leaving all meritorious actions to those dear to him and all sins to those not dear, attains the eternal *Brahman* through *dhyāna-yoga*. Such a man, through the ordinances, gives up little by little all associations, and being freed from all pairs of oposites, remains in *Brahman* alone. On account of the accomplishment (of salvation), he should be moving about alone and without any help. He who having understood the effect of being alone never derogates from it, is never left in want. The bowl, the foot of the tree, the tattered robe, the state of being without help, the equality of vision in all these are the characteristics of the emancipated one. One intent upon the welfare of all beings, with a quiescent mind, having the three-knotted staff and bowl, and ever devoted to the One (*Brahman*), after taking up *sannyāsa*, may enter a village. Such one is a *bhikṣu* (alms-taker). Should two unite, it is called *mithuna* (a pair or union); with three, it becomes a *grāma* (or village); with more it is a *nagara* (or city). No city or village, or *mithuna* should be made, and an ascetic who commits these three (offences) falls from his duty. Through such intercourse (or ascetics), all kinds of talks connected with the king and alms, friendship, tale-bearing, and malice occur between them. There is no doubt of it.

"He (the ascetic) should be alone and desireless. He should not converse with anybody. The ascetic should ever be uttering the word Nārāyaṇa in each sentence. Being alone, he should be meditating upon *Brahman* in all mental, spoken, and bodily actions. He should neither rejoice at dying or living. He should be anticipating the time when life will close. He should not be glad of dying; nor should he be glad of living. He should be biding his time like a hireling (for his pay). An ascetic who plays the Part of the dumb, the eununch, the lame, the blind, the deaf, and the idiot is emancipated though the (above six) means. There is no doubt of this. He who has not fondness for eating, saying that this is good and that is bad, who speaks only words that are beneficial, true, and moderate is said to be the dumb. He is a enunch who is no more affected by the sight of a sixteen years old girl than of a new-born female baby or a hundred-years old woman. He who does not move about for more than the distance of *yojana* for alms or for the calls of nature is a lame man. That *parivrāt* (ascetic) is said to be a blind man, who whether sitting or walking, has his vision extended to no more than four yokes distance on the ground. He is said to be deaf who, though hearing words, beneficial or non-beneficial, pleasant or painful to the mind, is as if he does not hear them. That clever ascetic is said to be an idiot who is ever in a state of sleep, as it were, having his organs non-agitated by objects, even though near. He should never observe the following six— the scenes of dancing, etc., gambling, lovely women, eatables, enjoyables, and women in their monthly course.

"The ascetic should never in thought even think of others with the six (*viz.,*) love, hate, pride, deceit, treachery, and the illusion (of confounding them). To the ascetics, the following six are sinful : cot, white cloth, the stories of women, love towards women, sleep during the day, and vehicles. He who is engaged in *Ātmic* contemplation should carefully avoid a long journey. He should ever practise the *upaniṣadic vidyā*-tending to salvation. The ascetic need not bathe daily. He need not observe *upavāsa* (fast). He need not be one that had studied Vedas. He need not be one that is able to produce a commentary (lecture). He should daily observe acts without sin, deceit, or falsehood. He who, having withdrawn the organs within, like a turtle its limbs (within its shell), is with the actions of the organs and the mind annihilated, without desires, without possessing any object as his own, without dualities, without prostrations, without the oblations to *pitṛ devatās* (they being with desires), without mine or I, without awaiting anything, without the desire to be happy, and living in places where men do not live— he alone is emancipated. There is no doubt of this.

"A celibate, or householder, or forester, who is (ever) vigilant, has *karma*, devotion, and knowledge and is independent, after understanding his peculiar tendency and having become indifferent (to his order of life), may become an householder after ending the celibate life, or may from the householder's life enter the life of a forester, and then the life of an ascetic; or from the life of a celibate, or householder, or forester may (directly) enter that of an ascetic. The moment *vairāgya* arises in him, he may become an ascetic that moment, whether he is with *vrata* (religious observance) or not, is *snātaka*[1] or not, or with discontinued fire-sacrifice

1. A celibate who has completed his first *Āśrama*.

or not. On account of that, some perform *Prājāpatya*-sacrifice alone; or *Āgneya*-sacrifice may be performed. Is not *agni*, *prāṇa*? Through this alone, one should perform that sacrifice only which is connected with the three *dhātus*. The three dhātus are *sattva, rajas*, and tamas alone. With the *mantra*, अयं ते योनिऋत्विजो यतो जातो अरोचथाः। तं जानन्नग्ना आरोह था नो वर्धया रयिं।।, *agni* (fire) should be taken in. Thus it is said (in the Śrutis) : एष वा अग्नेर्योनिर्यः प्राणः, प्राणं गच्छ स्वां योनिं गच्छ स्वाहा।। The *agni* from āhavanīya should be brought and taken in as before (with the *mantras* above mentioned). Should such an *agni* be not obtainable, the homa (oblation) should be done in water with the *mantras*, आपो वै सर्वा देवतास्सर्वाभ्यो देवताभ्यो जुहोमि स्वाहा। After performing homa, the water should be taken in and sipped. After uttering the *mantra*, (साज्यं हविरनामयं मोक्षदं) he abandons the tuft of hair in the head, the holy thread, father, son, wife, *karma*, vedic study and *mantra* and becomes an ascetic. The *Śrutis* say that a knower of *Ātmā* should be engaged in meditation upon *Brahman*, through the three *mantras* tending to salvation."

Then Nārada asked Brahmā thus : "How can one, without the holy thread, be a *Brāhmaṇa*?" To which Brahmā replied : "The wise should, after shaving (the head) together with the tuft of hair, cast off the holy thread. He should wear, as his *sūtra* (thread), the indestructible and supreme *Brahman*. On account of (*sācanāt*) its being an indication, it (thread) is called *sūtra*. *Sūtra* is the *Paramapada* (supreme seat). He by whom that *sūtra* is known is *Brāhmaṇ*. That *sūtra* (thread of *Brahman*) in which is strung the whole universe like beads on a *sūtra* (string), should be worn by the *yogin* that has known *yoga* and *tattva*. The wise man that is in supreme *yoga* should abandon the outer *sūtra* (thread). He who wears (in his heart) this *sūtra* of *Brāhmic* Reality is alone *Brāhmaṇa*. Through wearing this higher *sūtra*, it becomes not a rejected one, not an impure one. Those only whose *sūtra* is internal, having the holy thread as *jñāna* are the real knowers of the *sūtra*, they are said to possess the *yajñopavīta* (holy thread). To those whose *śikhā* (tuft of hair) is *jñāna*, whose holy thread is *jñāna*, and whose meditation is upon *jñāna*, *jñāna* alone is supreme. It is said that *jñāna* alone is able to purify. That wise man alone who possesses the *jñāna-śikhā* like the *śikhā* (flame) of *agni* (fire) is said to possess *śikhā* (tuft of hair). Those that have mere *śikhā* are no *śikhās*. The Brāhmaṇas and other that are entitled to perform the *vedic karmas* are allowed to wear the (external) thread, only as an auxiliary to the *karmas*. It is only vedic. The knowers of *Brahman* know that all *Brāhmaṇya* (the state of *Brahman*) accrues to him only that has the *jñānamaya śikhā* (knowledge-tuft of hair) and the *tanmaya* (that or *Brahmanful*) *upavīta* (holy thread).

"Having known it, a *Brāhmaṇa* should take up *sannyāsa*. Such a *sannyāsin*, should be, in order to bear the bodily afflictions, with one cloth, bald-headed and without having anything as being required (for his use); or according to rules, he may be (naked) as nature made his body, and should abandon his son, friend, wife, trustworthy relatives, etc., as well as all *karmas* and love for the universe, the loin-cloth, staff, and covering. Enduring all pairs of opposites without cold or heat, happiness or grief, fame or disgrace, without the six changes, I-ness, malice, pride, ostentation, jealousy, slander of others, love and hate, pleasure and pain, passion, anger, greed and delusion and regarding his body as a mere carcase, without thinking of all the things, internal and external; that are other than Self. Without Prostrations, without the worship of *devas* and *pitṛs* and without praise or condemnation, he should wander about of his own aceord. He should not receive gold and others. For him, these is no invocation or dismissal (of deities), *mantra* or non-*mantra*, meditation or worship, aim or non-aim, others or not-others without having another's or (his own) settled place of residence, and having a firm conviction, he should be in a desolate house or at the foot of trees, or in a temple, a plenteous turfed spot, a potter's place or that of *agnihotra* or sacrifice, river, tank, sand-heap, subterranean vault, cave, mountain-rill, the place prepared for sacrifice or forest; or like the asked personages, *Śveta-ketu, Ṛbhu, Nidāgha, Jadabharata, Ṛsabha, Durvāsas, Samvartaka, Sanatsujāta, Vaideha* (*Janaka*), *Vatasiddha, Śuka, Vāmadeva, Dattātreya, Raivataka*, and *Gorakṣa*, he should roam about as nature made him, without being recognised and without any means of discovery of his course of life, like a lad, or an insane man, or a ghost, with the action of a madman though not mad, after discarding in water the three-knotted staff, the stringed sling (bag), vessel, bowl, waist-strint, loin-cloth, stick and cloth. He should ever be engaged in *Ātmic* deliberation. Being in his natural state without being affected by the pairs, without receiving anything, being ever settled firmly in the *Brāhmic* path, having a pure mind, eating the food that is obtained without asking, in the palm as vessel, or in another's vessel in order to merely protect the body at the tim-required, being of equal mind whether the objet is gained or not, without having aught of his own, always meditating upon *Brahman*, being with *Ātma-nishṭhā*, having eradicated all actions, virtuous and sinful, and having given up all— that one who ever utters *Brahma-Praṇava*, that "I am *Brahman*" alone, with the blissful and non-dual *jñāna*, and after rising above the three bodies (to *Brahman*), like the analogy of the wasp and the worm,[1] gives up the body as a *sannyāsin*, is said to have done all his work (in this world). Such is the *Upaniṣad*."

1. Referring to the idea of the worm becoming the wasp, with the latter frequent stinging.

Upadeśa IV

"One who after giving up the world, the Vedas, the objects and the organs is in *Ātmā* alone, attains the supreme abode. A good ascetic should not make known his caste, name, gotra (clan), etc., his place and time, the Vedas, etc. studied by him, his family, age, history, observance, and conduct. He should neither converse with women nor remember the women he had seen. He should give up all stories conected with women. He should not even see the figure of a woman in a picture. The mind of an ascetic who through delusion adopts the above four things connected with women is necessarily affected and thereby perishes. The following are prohibited (in his case) : Thirst, malice, falsehood, deceit, greed, delusion, the pleasant and the unpleasant, manual work, lecture, *yoga*, *kāma* (passion), desire, begging, I-ness, mine-ness, the obstinacy of curing diseases, penance, pilgrimage and the accomplishment of fruits of *mantras*, and medicines. He who performs these interdicted things, goes into a debased state. A *muni* who has *mokṣa* as his supreme seat should address such respectful words as "Please come, please go, please stay, and welcome" to one, even though he be his intimate friend. He should neither receive presents, etc., nor ask for them to be given to others. Even in dream, an ascetic should never direct a person (to do work for him). Even shoud he witness or hear of the happiness or grief of his wife, brother, son, and other relatives, he should not be affected thereby. He should abandon all joy and sorrow.

"To the ascetics controlling their mind, the following are their svadharmas (own duties) : Harmlessness, truth, honesty, celibacy, non-coveting, humility, high-spiritedness, clearness of mind, steadiness of mind, straightforwardness, non-attachments ((to any), service to the *Guru*, faith, patience, bodily restraint, mental restraint, indifference, firm and sweet words, endurance, compassion, shame, *jñāna*, *vijñāna*, *yoga*, moderate food, and courage. That *paramahaṁsa* of an ascetic in the order of life of a *sannyāsin* who is without dualities, always follows the pure *sattvaguṇa* and sees all equally, is no other than the actual Nārāyaṇa Himself. He may live one day in a village and five days in a city, but five months in the wintry season. At other times he should live in other places (such as forest, etc.). He should not live in a village for two days (even); should he do so, desires and the rest will arise in him and thereby he becomes fit for hell. He should live like a (harmless) worm on the earth with his mind under control and with no settled place of residence, at the end of the village where there are no persons. He may live in the same place in the wintry season. He should roam about on the earth with one or no cloth, with the one vision (of *Brahman*) alone, with no desires (of objects), with no condemnation of the actions of the wise and with meditation. That *yogin* of an ascetic should go about, observing the duties of his order of life, and with the eyes cast on the earth, in pure places. He should not roam about in night, midday or the two twilight periods in which are places void or difficult to be waded through or likely to injure living creatures. He may live for one day in a village, for three days in a town, for two days in a hamlet and for five days in a city. He may live in the wintry season (longer) in one place surrounded fully by water. The ascetic should regard all creatures as Self and dwell upon earth like the blind, the hunch-back, the deaf, the insane, and the dumb. The *bahūdaka* and the forester should bathe thrice a day. In the case of *haṁsa*, one bath only is ordained; but none in the case of *paramahaṁsa*. In the case of the one having one staff, seven things are ordained, *viz.*, silence, *yoga*-posture, *yoga*, endurance, solitariness, desirelessness, and equal vision over all. Bathing being not prescribed for a *paramahaṁsa*, he should abandon all the modifications of the mind only; what is the difference between the worms and the men that rejoice over this ill-smelling body which is but a collection of skin, flesh, blood, nerves, fat, marrow, bone, offal and urine? What is the body but a collection of all, phlegm, etc.? And what are the qualities, the *vāsana* of the body, effulgence, beauty, etc.? (They are opposed to one another.) The ignorant man that is fond of this body, which is but a compound of flesh, blood, the ill-smelling urine and offal, nerve, fat and bone, will be fond of hell too. Though there is not difference between the women's secret parts that cannot be described by words and an (ever) oozing tubular wound, yet through the difference of the mind, (men are deluded). Such men are said to be without *prāṇa*, (*viz.*, dead) though alive. Prostrations to those that sport in that piece of flesh which is rent in twain and tainted with the breaking of the wind, etc. What more revolting thing is there than this?

"To the wise, there is nothing to do, no sign (of identification). The *muni* who is without 'mine' and fear, with quiescence, without duality and eating leaf (alone), should ever be in meditation with either loin-cloth or no cloth. A *yogin* who is thus in meditation becomes fit to be *Brahman*. Though he may have some signs (of identification to pass under this order of life or that), such signs are useless for gaining *mokṣa*. The cause of salvation is *jñāna* alone. He is a (true) *brāhmaṇa* who cannot be identified as *sat* (good person) or asat, knower of religious books or not, follower of good conduct or bad conduct. Therefore that learned man who is without signs, a knower of *dharma*, engaged in the actions of *Brahman* and a knower of the secret mysteries, should roam about, incognito. He should go about on this earth without any caste or order of life and without being (even) doubted (regarding his identity) by any beings, like the blind, the idiot, or the mute. Then (even) the angels become fond of him who has a quiescent mind. It is the dictate of the Vedas that the sign (of non-identification) itself is *Kaivalya*."

Then Nārada asked the Grandfather about the rules of *sannyāsa*. To which Brahmā assented and said : "Before either the ātura or regular *sannyāsa* is taken, *kṛchchhra* penance should be done and then the eight *śraddhas*. In each of the (eight) *śraddhas*, two *brāhmaṇas* should be fed, in lieu of *Viśvedevas* called *Satyavasu* and the (*Trimūrtis* called) Brahmā, Viṣṇu, and *Maheśvara*, in *Devaśrāddha* first; then in *Ṛṣiśrāddha* in lieu of *Devarṣī, Rājarṣi*, and *Manuṣyarṣi*; then in *Divyaśrāddha*, in lieu of *Vasu*, *Rudra*, and *Ādityas*; then in *manuṣyaśrāddha* in lieu of Sanaka, *Sanandana*, *Sanatkumāra*, and *Sanatsujāta*; then in *bhūtaśraddha*, in lieu of the five great elements, *pṛthivī*, etc., eye and other organs and the four kinds of collection of *bhūtas*; then in *Piṭṛśrāddha*, in lieu of father, grandfather and great-grandfather; then in *māṭṛśrāddha*, in lieu of mother, mother's father and mother's grandfather; and then in *Ātmaṣrāddha*, in lieu of himself, his father and grandfather or of himself, grandfather and great-grandfather, should his father be alive. He should perform the eight *śrāddhas* in one day, or eight days, with the *mantras* of his *śākhā* in one *yājñapakṣa* or eight *yājñpakṣas*. Then he should worship and feed the *brāhmaṇas* according to the rules contained in *piṭṛyajña*. Then offering the *piṇḍas* (balls of rice to the *piṭṛs*), he should gladden the *brāhmaṇas* with the *tāmbūla* (nut and betel, etc.,) presents and dismiss them. Then for the accomplishment of the remaining *karmas*, he should pluck off seven hairs; then again for finishing the rest of the *karmas*, he should hold seven or eight hairs and have the head shaved. Except his arm-pit and secret parts, he should have the hairs of his head, whiskers and mustache and nails shaved. Afer shaving, he should bathe and perform the evening *sandhyā*, uttering *Gāyatrī* a thousand times. Then performing *brahmayajña*, he should establish his own fire and acting up to his *śākhā*, should perform the oblation of ghee according to what is said therein till the *ājya* portion with those (*mantras* beginning with) *Ātmā*, etc.; should eat thrice the fried rice-powder, and then sipping the water, he should maintain the fire; then seated north of the fire on a deer-skin, he should be engaged in the study of *Purāṇas*; without sleeping, he should bathe at the end of the four *yāmas* and after cooking the oblation of (rice) in the fire, he should offer it to the fire in sixteen oblations according to (the *mantras* of) *Puruṣa-Sūkta*. Then having done *virajā-homa* and sipped water, he should close it with the gift (to *brāhmaṇas*) of cloth, golden vessel, and cows along with presents of money are then dismiss Brahmā (who had been invoked). With the prescribed *mantra*, he should attract *Agni* (fire) unto himself. After meditating upon and coming round and prostrating before the fire, he should dismiss it. Then in the morning performing *sandhyā* and uttering *Gāyatrī* a thousand times, he should make *upasthāna* (worship) to the sun. Then descending into water up to the navel, he should make arghya (water-offering) to the guardians of the eight quarters; then he should give leave to *Gāyatrī*, making *Sāvitrī* enter into *vyāhṛti*.

The *mantra* prescribed for this should be uttered through the mind and voice in high, middling, and low tones. With the *mantra*, अभयं सर्वभूतेभ्यो मत्तः सर्वं प्रवतते। the water should be sipped and having taken the water with the two hands, it should be dropped on east. Having uttered स्वाहा he should pluck his hair (yet left) and uttering the prescribed *mantra* and having torn off the sacred thread and taken it in the hand with water, should utter ओ भूः 'go to the ocean' and cast them down as oblation in water— ओं भूः संन्यस्तं मया। ओं भुवः संन्यस्तं मया। ओं स्वाः संन्यस्तं मया।। Having uttered thrice and saturated thrice (the water) with (the influence of) the *mantras*, he should sip the water; and then uttering the *mantras* ओं भूः, etc., he should cast aside in water the cloth and waist-cord. Having thought himself to be the abdicator of all *karmas*, he, being in the meditation of his own Reality as nature made him, should go as before northwards with hands upraised. Should he be a *sannyāsin* learned (in the Vedas, etc.), he should get himself initiated into *Praṇava* from his teacher and go about at his own free will with the thought of there being none other but his self, and feeding his body with fruits, leaves and water, live in mountains, forest and temples. That lover of salvation who after *sannyāsa* roams about nacked in all places with his heart full of the enjoyment of *Ātamic* bliss, with the fruit of avoidance of *karmas* and maintaining his life with fruits, juice, barks, leaves, roots and water should abandon his body mountain caves, uttering the *Praṇava*. But an aspirant after wisdom, should be become a *sannyāsin*, should, after walking a hundred steps, be addressed by the teacher and other *Brāhmaṇs* thus : "O *Mahābhāga* (very fortunate person), stay, stay, wear the staff, cloth and blow, come to the teacher in order to learn the meaning of *Praṇava mantra vākya*". He should then take up the waist-cord, loin-cloth, red-coloured cloth and bowl. A bamboo staff which is not injured from top to bottom, equal, beautiful, and not spotted with black, should be worn by him, after sipping the water and uttering *mantra* prescribed for the purpose. Then the bowl should be taken up, after uttering the *mantra* with the *Praṇava* preceding it : ओं जगज्जीवनं जीवनाधारभूतं मातेव मा मन्त्रयस्व सर्वदा सर्व सौम्य।। Then after first uttering (the *mantra*) गुह्याच्छादनं कौपीनं ओं। शीतवातोष्णत्राणकरं देहैकरक्षणं वस्त्रं ओं।। he should take up the waist cord, loin-cloth and cloth with the *ācamana* (sipping of water) preceding it.

"Thus consecreated with *yoga* and thinking that he had done all that should be done, he should be firm in the observances of his order of life. Thus is the *Upaniṣad*.

Upadeśa V

Then Nārada said to the Grandfather thus :

"You said that *sannyāsa* was the liberator of all *karmas*. Now you say again that the *sannyāsin* is one that should be in the observance of his *āśrama* (order of life). (How to reconcile the two?)" To which the

Grandfather replied thus : "To the *jīva* possessing the body, there are three *avasthās*— tha waking, the dreaming, and the dreamless sleeping with turya (the fourth). Those beings of *Puruṣas* that are subject to these *avasthās* follow the observances, incidental to them, of *karma*, *jñāna* and *vairāgya*." Nārada said: "O Lord, if so, what are the differences of different orders of *sannyāsa*? And what are the differences of their observances? Please tell us truly."

Therefore the differences of *sannyāsas*, and the differences of observances were related for the sake of Nārada by Brahmā, after assenting to his (Nārada's) question thus :

"Truly *sannyāsa* is of one kind only. On account of *ajñāna*, inability and non-performance of *karmas* of persons), it is divided into three and then into four, thus : *vairāgya-sannyāsa, jñāna-sannyāsa, jñānavairāgya-sannyāsa* and *karma-sannyāsa*. The *vairāgya-sannyāsin* is one who becomes an ascetic after being in a visious condition of lust, etc., and then, becomes disgusted with the objects through his former good *karmas*. A *jñāna-sannyāsin* is one who becomes an ascetic with the four means of salvation, after controlling the organs through book-wisdom, and becoming famliar with the experiences of the world of virtue and vice, after abandoning anger, jealousy, envy, *ahaṁkāra* and all *sannyāsa* productive of indentification, after giving up the three *vāsanās* of the body, books and world, which are of the form of desires for women, wealth and earth, and after thinking that the whole of the universe should be given up, like vomited food. A *jñānavairāgya-sannyāsin* is one who becomes an ascetic as nature made him, after practising and enjoying all, and having the body alon remaining, through *jñāna* and *vairāgya*, in the realisation of the Reality. A *karma-sannyāsin* is one who, though he has no *vairāgya*, becomes an ascetic by regularly passing from one *āśrama* to another, from the celibate, to the householder and then to the forester. A *vairāgya-sannyāsin* is one who becomes an ascetic from the celibate order (directly), being as nature made him.

"(There is another fourfold classification) The four kinds are : *vidvat-sannyāsa, vividiṣa-sannyāsa* and *karma-sannyāsa*. In *karma-sannyāsa*, there are two (sub-) divisions, *nimitta* (causal) and animitta (non-casual). *Ātura-sannyāsa* (on account of the cause of approaching death, disease, etc.), is *nimitta-sannyāsa*. The *karma* (regular) *sannyāsa* is *animitta*. *Ātura-sannyāsa* is on account of defective *karmas*. When *sannyāsa* is taken at the time of death, it is called *nimitta*, *Animitta* is that when one becomes duly a *sannyāsin* when the body is strong, (after being convinced) that all created things are subject to destruction, that body and others should be given up, that all *Ātmā* (souls)— each one shining in the pure *Ākāśa*, dwelling in all, moving in the *antarkṣa* (middle world) as of the form of *vāyu*, in the sacrificial pit as of the form of fire, in the moon, in all men, in the supreme angels, in the form of truth, in *ākāśa*, in the form of the conch, pearl, fish, etc., in water, in the form of grain, etc., in the form of the limbs of Vedas, in the form of the rivers form the mountains, in the form of truth and the great one— are no other than *brahman* and that others are but perishable.

"There are six classes of *sannyāsins— Kutīchaka, bahūdaka, haṁsa, paramahaṁsa, trīyātīta* and *adadhūta. Kutīchaka* is one who wears the tuft of hair, holy thread, staff, bowl, loin-cloth and tattered cloth, who worships mother, father, and teacher, who has potsherd and sling, who is uttering *mantras*, who takes food in one and the same place, who ears, varitically, the white earth (on the forehead as sect-mark) and who has a staff. *Buhūdaka* is one who, like *kutīchaka*, wears the tuft of hair, tattered cloth, etc., as well as the three (sect-) marks, but who eats eight morsels of food through getting alma. The *haṁsa* is one who wears matted hair and the three vetical sect-marks and eats the alms-food without any limit (as to the morsel) and wears the bare loin-cloth only. The *Paramahaṁsa* is he who is without tuft of hair and holy thread, begs food in one day from five houses, has one loin-cloth, wears one red cloth alone and sacred ashes and has given up all. The *trīyātīta* is one who either may take fruits, eating them with his mouth like cows, or if he is an eater of food, may beg food from three houses. The naked man having the body alone has the bodily actions (quiescent), like the dead body. Such an one is the *truīyātīta*. The avadhūta is he who is without any rules, gets his food (in his mouth), following the course of the boa constrictor,[1] from all persons except persons of ill-repute and outcastes, and is ever engaged in the realisation of the Real. Should the *Ātura-sannyāsin* be alive (after taking *sannyāsa*), he should take up regular *sannyāsa*. The rules to be observed in the case of the (three), *Kutīchaka, bahūdaka* and *haṁsa* are the same as for the orders of life from the celibate to the *sannyāsin*. For the three, *paramahaṁsa* upwards, they have no waist-cord, loin-cloth, cloth, bowl, and staff. they may get food from all castes and should be as nature made them. Such are the rules.

"At the time of the *sannyāsa*, the recitation of the Vedas should be made till the mind is cleared; and after casting aside in water the waist-cord, loin-cloth, staff, cloth, bowl, etc., he should roam about. He should be without even the slightest tattered cloth. He should neither utter anythig other than *Praṇava*, nor talk nor hear. he should not study logic or grammar. He should not talk many words; they will but pain his vocal organ. He should not converse with people through the vocal organ. He should not talk in other language (than Sanskrit). He has no worship of God and no witnessing of festivals; he should be free from pilgrimage.

1. The snake, or boa constrictor, is said to remain in one place only on account of its huge body, taking any food that may come to its mouth as it is lying there.

The other rules of ascetics are : The *kutīchaka* should beg alms in one house only; for the *bahūdaka*, eight morsels in eight houses; for the *haṁsa*, there is no limit; for *paramahaṁsa*, he should beg with his hand as the vessel in five houses; for the *turīyātīta*, he should eat fruits with his mouth like cows; (for *avadhūta*), he should take food like a boa constrictor in all castes. The ascetic should not dwell in one place for many days. He should not make prostrations to any one. among the *truīyātīta*, and *avadhūta* (ascetics), even though one in junior, he should not make prostrations to another, a senior who has known the Reality. He should not swim with his hands and cross the river. He should not climb up a tree, nor get into a carriage. Nothing should be purchased or sold (by him). No exchange should be made, no ostentation for him. There is nothing for the ascetic to do. If there is anything for him to do, he will perish. Therefore the only thing he is qualified to do is reflection, etc.

"To the *āturas* and *kutīcakas*, the world they attain is *bhūrloka* and *bhuvarloka*; to the *bāhūdakas*, *svargaloka*; to the hamsas, *tapoloka*; to the *paramahamsas*, *satyaloka*. To the *turīyātīta* and *avadhūta*, *Kaivalya* in *Ātmā* according to the analogy of wasp and the worm through the realisation of Reality. It is the command of the Vedas that whatever from one thinks of all the last (death) moment and before leaving the body is attained by him and no other. Knowing it thus, he should not be a practiser of anything but the realisation of Reality. Through the observance of any other, he goes to the world of that other. To one has attained *jñāna-varāgya*, his salvation is in the Self, as there is no other observance for him. The same one (*Ātmā*) alone is styled *Viśva* in the walking state, *Ṭaijasa* in the dreaming state and *Prājña* in the dreamless sleeping state. Through the difference of states, there is the difference of the agent presiding over them. To the fourteen organs (the ten organs of sense and fictions and the four organs of the mind in these states), the outer and inner *vṛttis*, (modifications) are the material cause. There are four *vṛttis viz., manas*, *buddhi, ahaṁkāra* and *Citta*. Through the differences of actions of the *vṛttis*, there arise the differences of separate functions. When (the presiding agent is) in the eyes, there is the waking state; in the throat, the dreaming state; in the heart, the dreamless sleeping state; and in the head, the turya (of fourth) state. Knowing these and that the turya is the indestructible, one should not hear or see anything in the waking state, as if he were in dreamless sleeping state. To such a one who does not apparently know them, even the dreaming state forms the same (dreamless sleeping) state. Such a one is termed *Jīvanmukta*. All the Vedas say that there is salvation to such a one.

"To the ascetic, there should be no desire of this world or the higher. Then he will be one that will practise accordingly. Through the practices of (the study of) books foreign to the realisation of Reality, he becomes a useless person like a camel bearing saffron paint. to him, there is no entry into *yoga* books, no study of *sāṁkhya* books, no practice of *mantra* or *tantra*. Should there be any entry into other books (than the one treating of Reality), then it will be like an ornament to a dead body. Like a cobbler, he should be beyond *karma* and knowledge and unfit for salutation and repeating the names of the Lord. He will duly get the benefit of the *karmas* (of his order of life). Having given up all like the foam (separating itself) from the castor oil, having the mental staff which controls the mind clinging to objects, having the hand as the vessel (for eating) and having the quarters alone as the cloth, the ascetic should go about like a lad, idiot, or ghost. He should neither desire to live nor die. Like a coolie abiding his appointed time (of pay), the ascetic should bide his time (of death). One who lives by taking alms without (the qualifications of) patience, wisdom, *vairāgya* and the qualifications beginning with *śama* (control of mind) is the spoiler of the order of life of an ascetic. There is no salvation obtained through the mere assumption of the staff or making the head bald or other disguise or through ostenstatious observances. That man who has *jñāna* as his staff is said to be the *ekaḍaṇḍī* (one having *Brahman* alone as the staff). An ascetic who, having merely a wooden staff without *jñāna*, eats all (indiscriminately) in all places, goes to the terrible hells called *Mahāraurava*. (The sense of) greatness in his case is likened by the *ṛṣis* to the pig's dung. Having given it up, he should move about like a worm. Food and cloth without being begged for by him should be obtained involuntarily through the will of others. A naked (ascetic) may bathe at the wish of another. A man who practises the meditation upon Self in the dreaming state as in the waking is said to be the foremost and first of *Brahmavādins*. he should neither grieve for things not obtained, nor rejoice at things obtained. With the organs not attached to objects, he should be engaged in the sole protection of life. he should always look down upon the gains obtained with much respect (shown to him). through the gains obtained with much respect, the ascetic though released becomes bound. What is meant by the protection of life, is this : When the fire (of the hearth in a house) had been extinguished and all have taken food, he may go to the houses of caste people that are fit for taking alms from : The *yogin* who has his hand only as his alms-bowl should not often take alms. He may take (food) standing or sitting; so in the middle (of taking food), he may sip water. Those who have pure mind should not over-step the limits like the ocean. The great ones do not give up their self-restraint like the sun. When the *muni* takes, like a cow, the food with the mouth only (without the use of the hand), he becomes of equal vision to all beings. Then he becomes fit for salvation. He may, for alms, go from a forbidden house to a non-forbidden one. He should go (for alms) to a house where the door is *ajav*, but not to a house where it is closed. The *muni* who has dusty body, an uninhabited house or the foot of a tree as his abode, without anything dear or not dear to him. sleeping where the sun sets, without any fire-worship, without any settled place and with patience and the organs under control, should live without any desire in any place obtained. He who after going to the forest dwells with *jñāna* as the sacrifice and the organs under his mastery and awaits his time (of death), is fit to be of the nature of *Brahman*. A *muni* who goes about with no cause for instilling fear into all beings need never have any fear from them. One without any *abhimāna* (identification with body) or egoism or dualities or doubt, never is angry, never hates, never lies through the vocal organ. That person who, having visited all sacred places does not do any injury to any living creature and gets alms at the proper time, is fit to be of the nature of *Brahman*. He should not associate with a forester or householder. he should conduct himself in such manner as not to be known to others. he should not be glad of anything. he should roam about on earth like a worm, according to the direction pointed out by the sun. He should not do or cause to do works tending to (his) fame or pains or people's benefit. He should not be inclined towards vicious books, He should not live dependent upon any. He should give up all over-disputatious reasoning. He should not join any party (fighting with another). He should not take any disciples. he should not study many books. He should not discourse. Neither should be commence any works. Without any distinguishing characteristics and without letting others know his opinions, that wise man, or *muni*, ever intent upon the *Brāhmic* vision, should exhibit himself to people like an idiot, or a lad, or a mute person. He should neither do nor talk anything. He should not think of a good or bad thing. Rejoicing in That within himself, the *muni* should go about like an idiot. He should roam about alone without associating with any, and with the senses under control. The clever *jñānī* sporting in *Ātmā*, ever delighting in *Ātmā*, looking upon all with equal vision like an *Ātmā-jñānī*, and playing like a child, should wander about like an idiot. That learned man versed in *Brahmavidyā* should talk like a madman. He should follow the observances of cows (by eating with the mouth, causing no trouble to anybody). A good *jñānī* whether pushed, disregarded, slighted, beaten, or hindered by the vicious, or burnt by their acts, or having urine and fæces thrown upon him by them, or afflicted in various other ways, should always think well of them, through pained, and thus make them lift themselves through their own Selves. A *yogin* whether praised or afflicted by others, never thinks of it in order to reach a superior state in *yoga*. A *yogin* who is slighted by people, attains a higher state in *yoga*. A *yogin* never goes against the actions of the virtuous. He is the same whether people slight him or do not desire his association. He should do all that is right through the actions of mind, speech and body to all beings born out of the embryo or the egg, etc. He should harbour no malice against any and give up all clinging to things. The ascetic after giving up passion, anger, pride, desire, delusion and other faults should be without fear. Eating alms-food preserving silence, tapas, special meditation, a good *jñāna*, and *vairāgya*— these are said, in the opinion (of the great), to be the *dharma* of the ascetic. Wearing the red cloth, and being ever in *dhyāna-yoga*, he should live either at the foot of a tree, outside the village, or in the temple Daily he should live upon begging. he should not eat one food alone (from one only). Till the mind becomes pure, the learned man should thus be moving about. Then when the mind is purified, he may be anywhere, as a *parivrājaka*. Seeing Janārdana in and out everywhere, preserving silence, being without stain like *vāyu*, roaming everywhere, being equal in happiness and pains, and with patience, eating whatever comes to hand, equally regarding without any hate *brāhmaṇa*, cow, horse, beasts and others, meditating through the mind upon Viṣṇu that is *Paramātmā* and *Īśvara*, thinking ever of Brāhmic bliss and thinking himself to be *Brahman* alone— such a one having known thus, regarding the staff to be no other than the certitude of the mind as above, having no desire, being naked and having abandoned all *saṁsāra* through the actions ever done through the mind, speech, and body, attains salvation, according to the analogy of the wasp and the worm, through the practice of the realisation of Reality without ever seeing the universe. Such is the *Upaniṣad*."

Upadeśa VI

Nārada addressing Brahmā asked : "O Lord ! You said of *abhyāsa* (practice) according to the analogy of wasp and the worm. What is that practice ?"

To which the Grandfather replied thus :

"One (*viz.*, an ascetic) should live with true speech and *jñāna-vairāgya* and with the body alone as the remaining (possession). Know *jñāna* alone as the body, *vairāgya* alone as *prāṇa*, *śānti* (mental control) and *dānti* (bodily control) as the eyes, *manas* alone as the face, *buddhi* alone as *kalā* (parts of effulgence), the twenty-five tattvas as the limbs, the *avasthās* as the five great elements, *karma*, *bhakti*, *jñāna*, and *vairāgya* as the branches (of parts) and that the waking, dreaming, dreamless sleeping, and *turya avasthās* and the fourteen organs as being of the nature of a pillar planted in the mud. Through such is the case, the man who masters these through his *buddhi* like a boatman regarding the boat immersed in the mire, or the elephant-driver regarding the elephant (under his control), and has known that all else besides Self is illusory and destructible and become indifferent, should ever utter : 'I am *Brahman* alone.' He should not know anything as other than Self. A *Jīvanmukta* who lives thus is a doer of that which should be done. he should not discourse that he is other than *Brahman*. But he should ever be discoursing : 'I am *Brahman*'. From the waking, dreaming and dreamless sleeping states, he should reach the turya state and then *turyātīta* (the state beyond *turya*). The waking state is in the day; the dreaming in the night and the dreamless sleeping in the midnight. Each *avasthā* (or state) has its sub-states. The functions of the fourteen organs, eye and others mutually dependent are the following : The eyes perceive forms; the ears, sounds;

the tongue perceives tastes; the nose, odours; the vocal organ speaks; the hand lifts; the leg walks; the anus excretes; the sexual organ enjoys; the skin feels; the *buddhi* perceives objects, being under the control of the organs; through *buddhi*, he understands; through *citta*, he thinks; through *ahaṁkāra*, be says 'I'. All these should be abandoned. Through the identification with the house (the body), he, like a householder, becomes a *jīva* thinking that the body is itself.

"The *jīva* is dwelling in this body. When he is in the eastern petal (of the heart), he is inclined to virtuous actions; in the south-eastern petal, to sleep and laziness; in the southern petal, to cruel actions; in the south-western petal, to sinful actions; in the western petal, to love of sport (of to flirt); in the north-weastern petal, to travelling; in the northern petal, to peace of mind; in the north-eastern petal, to *jñāna*; in (the middle of) the pericarp, to *vairāgya*; in the filament, to *Ātmā*-deliberation. Such are the different aspects to be understood (in the heart). The first living avasthā (of *jīva*) is the waking; the second is the dreaming; the third is the dreamless sleeping; the fourth *turya*; that which is not these four *turyātīta*. The one Lord alone that is witness and without qualities appears (as many) through the differences of *Viśva*. *Taijasa, Prājña*, the *Tatastha* (the neutral). One should (always) utter : 'I am *brahman* alone.' Else in the waking state, (he is) in the four states of the waking state and others:[1] in the dreaming state (he is) in the four states of the dreaming state and others; in the dreamless sleeping state, (he is) in the four states of the dreamless sleeping and others; in the turya, (he is) in the four states of turya and others; to the turyātīta that is *nirguṇa*, such states are not. There is only one witness in all the states of *Viśva*. *Taijasa* and *Prājña*, who is presiding over the gross, the subtle and the causal (bodies). Is *Tatastha* the seer ? or is he not? As (to *Tatastha*), there is the property of seeing; the *jīva* that is affected by the egoism, etc., of agency and enjoyment is not the seer. The one other than *jīva* (*viz., Tatastha*) is not concerned (with egoism, etc.). If it is said that the *jīva* is not so (concerned with egoism), then it is not a fact. Through the *abhimāna* of the *jīva*, there is the *abhimāna* of the body. And (conversely) through the *abhimāna* of the the body, there is the *abhimāna* of the *jīva*. The state of the *jīva* is as a screen (to screen *Brahman*) like (the pot and house in) the *pot-ākāsa* and the house-*ākāśa*. Through such a screen, he reaches self-realisation through the *mantra*— "*Haṁsa*-So '*aham*'[2] having the characteristics of inspiration and expiration. Having known thus, if he should give up the identification with the body, then he does not identification with the body, (*i.e.,* not attain the state of *jīva*). Such a one is stated to be *Brahman*.

---

1. Probably "others" refer to the subdivisions of the dreaming; so also of other states.
2. With *Haṁsa*, there is the inspiration, and with *So'ham*, there is the expiration.

Having given up *abhimāna* and anger, being content with moderate food, having conquered the organs and having controlled and avenues (of the organs), one should make the mind enter into meditation. The *yogin* who has always controlled (his mind and organs) should ever deligently commence his meditation in empty places, caves and forests. The knower of *yoga* who is bent upon accomplishing the end should never be engaged in giving feasts to *Brāhmaṇas*, in *śrāddha* sacrifices, etc., or in going to places of pilgrimages, festivals or crowds. The well-controlled *yogin* should go about as if people had treated him with disrespect. He should not go against the actions of the wise. That great ascetic is said to be a *tridaṇḍin* (or having a three-knotted staff) who holds firmly the three-*daṇḍa* (control) of mind, speech, and body. That ascetic is said to be supreme person who begs alms-food of worthy *brāhmaṇas*, when smoke has ceased and fire has been extinguished (in their houses). is he not a degraded ascetic who, though holding the staff and begging food, is without *vairāgya* and is not intent upon the observances of his order ? He is an ascetic— not any other-who does not go to the house where he expects to find special alms or which he already visited. he is said to transcend all castes and orders of life who realises the self-shinning supreme *Tattva* that is without body and organs, the all-witness, the real *vijñāna* that is of the form of bliss. To the *Ātmā* that is of the nature of *jñāna*, such an idea as : 'the order of life, etc., is mine', being generated out of *māyā* in this body, can never exist. He who knows thus through *vedānta* is beyond all castes and orders of life. He from whom all castes and orders of life slip away through *Ātmic* vision, transcends them all the remains in *Ātmā* alone. That person is said by knower of the meaning of the Vedas to be *ativarṇāśramī* (beyond caste and order of life) who after crossing all castes and orders of life abides in *Ātmā* alone. Therefore, O Nārada, the castes and orders of life which are foreign (to *Ātmā*) are attributed falsely, by the ignorant, to *Ātmā*. O Nārada, for those that are *brahma-jñānīs*, there are no rules ordained nor prohibited; there is nothing to be given up or not; similarly nothing else (for them). Having attained indifference to all objects even up to Brahmā's seat, haivng destroyed (or done away with) all fondness for everything, as for son, relatives, wife, etc., and having faith in the path of salvation, and through love of *vedānta-jñāna*, he should approach a *Guru* who is a knower of *Brahman* with gift (in his hand). Having an equilibrated mind, he should satisfy the *Guru* for a long time through service, etc., and learn with a steady firm mind the meaning of the sentences of Vedas. Then being devoid of 'I' and 'mine' and of all attractions, and having attained peace of mind, etc., he sees *Ātmā* in himself. Through observing the faults of *saṁsāra*, there arises indifference. There is no doubt that *sannyāsa* arises in one who becomes disgusted with *saṁsāra*. The aspirant after salvation who is called paramahaṁsa should, through the hearing, etc., of *vedānta*, practise *Brahma-jñāna*. which is the direct and chief means of salvation. In order to attain *Brahma-jñāna*, the one named paramahaṁsa should possess the qualities of the control of mind and body, etc. He should always be a practiser of *vedānta*, being master of the mind, the body and the organs, being without fear and egoism, with a firm mind, without the pairs (of opposites), without attaching himself to any, having a worn-out loin-cloth, and being bald-headed or naked. he should have the great intelligence of the knower of *vedānta*, a *yogin* without 'I' and 'mine' and being equal and friendly to friends and other beings. That *jñānī* alone and none else is able to cross *saṁsāra* who has his mind at peace. With the grace of the *Guru* towards him, he should live with him for year. He should be careful to observe *yama* (restraint) and *niyama* (religious observance). At the end of that (year), he should attain the supreme *jñāna-yoga*, and roam about on this earth without going against *dharma*; (or) at the end of one year, he should give up the three orders of life and attain the chief *āśrama* (of *sannyāsa*), as well as the supreme *jñāna-yoga*. Then, taking leave of the *Guru*, he should wander over the earth, having given up association (with wife, etc., as well as anger, and being content with moderate food and having controlled the senses. The householder who does not perform *karma*, and the ascetic who performs *karma*— both become fallen through their perverse doings. Each becomes intoxicated through seeing women. Each becomes intoxicated through drinking alcohol. Therefore, women, mere sight of whom is poison, should be shunned at a distance. Such things as conversation and proximity with, the sight of, women, dancing, singing, using violence against persons, and disputatious arguments should be given up. Therefore, O Nārada, to such a one, there is neither bath nor muttering of *mantras* nor worship nor homa, nor means of accomplishment, nor any *karma* of fire-sacrifice, etc., nor worshipping with flowers, etc., nor *karmas* to the pitṛs nor pilgrimages, nor religious observances, nor *dharmas*, nor adharmas, nor any rules of observance, nor any other worldly *karmas*. He should give up *karmas* and worldly observances. That *yogin* of an ascetic who is learned person, having his intelligence directed towards Reality, should never injure any worm or insect, birds or tree. O Nārada, roam through the world with vision ever directed inwards, with purity, with mind under control, with a mind that is full of *Brahman* and all attraction given up within. The *muni* that goes about alone, does (or should) not dwell in countries where there is no king. (In his case), there is neither praise nor prostration, nor the propitiation of devas or pitṛs. Thus the ascetic who has his abode changeful (in body), or changeless (in *Ātmā*), should be content with whatever he gets. Thus is the *Upaniṣad*.

Upadeśa VII

The Grandfather, after eulogizing Nārada who asked about the observance of ascetics, replied thus :—

"The ascetic that has attained indifference (to objects), should stay in one and the same place in the rainy season (for four months), and then for (the remaining) eight months should wander alone. Then also the ascetic should not stay in one and the same place for more than a day. Like a deer that does not stay in one place on account of fear, he should not stay in one place. he should not create an attraction (in his mind) that may serve as an obstacle to his going about. he should not cross a stream (by swimming) with his hand, nor ascend a tree, nor witness the festival of a God, nor partake or regal food, nor do the external worship of God. Having discarded all things other than the Self, he should be with his body emanciated by taking food (from each house) like the bees (from each flower). He should not increase that fat (in the body): he should discard ghee like blood. Regarding such royal food as flesh, sandal-coating, etc., as offal, the different tastes as the degraded caste, the cloth as a defiled vessel, the oil-bath as sexual union, the gladdening of a friend as urine, desires as cow's flesh, the country known to him as the outcastes place, gold and women as cobra or deadly poison, the place of assembly as the burning ground, the capital of the town as the hell called *Kumbhīpāka*, and royal food as balls of rice offered to the dead, he should be without any worship of God other than the Self; and having given up all the actions of the world and his own country, and ever thinking of the bliss of his Self like the bliss arising from the discovery of a lost object, forgetting his country and the fondness for his body, and knowing that his body should be slighted like a carcase, he should dwell away from son, relations and native place, like a thief released from prison. Taking whatever comes to him without effort, ever intent upon the relisation, through meditation, of *Brahma-Praṇava*, being freed from all *karmas*, having burnt up all passion, anger, greed, delusion, pride, malice, etc., having transcended the three *guṇas*, being without the six human infirmities,[1] without the six changes,[2] speaking the truth and being opposed to all savoury things, he should live for one day in a village, five days in a town, five days in a sacred place, and five days in sacred waters. With no settled place of residence and with a firm mind, he should dwell alone in mountain caves without uttering falsehood. Two persons should not join together. Should three join, there is created a village thereby; with four, is formed a city. Therefore he should live alone in a village. In

1. The six human infirmities are hunger, thirst, grief, delusion, dotage, and death.
2. The six changes are birth, existence, growth, transformation, decrease, and annihilation.

it, the ascetic should not give scope to his fourteen organs. Having attained wealth or *vairāgya* through the non-dissipated *jñāna*, and having deliberated within himself that there is none other than the Self, he should attain *Jīvanmukti*, having seen the Reality everywhere. Till *prārabdha karma* is over, he should understand the four kinds of svarūpa[1] (in *Tattvamasi*) and should live in the realisation of Reality, till his body falls (a prey to death).

"To the *kutīchaka* there is (prescribed) a bath three times daily; to the *bahūdaka*, twice; to the *haṁsa*, once; to the *paramahaṁsa* there is the mental bath; to the *turyātīta,* there is the holy-ashes bath; to the *avadhūta*, there is the wind as the bath. For the *kutīchaka*, there is the vertical sect-mark; for the *bahūdaka*, there is the three-lined (horizontal) sect-mark; for the *haṁsa*, both; for the *paramahaṁsa*, there is the holy-ashes sect-mark; for the *turyātīta*, there is the spot-sect-mark; for the *avadhūta* or for the *turyātīta* and *avadhūta*, there is none. For the *kutīcaka*, shaving takes place once in two months; for the *bahūdaka*, once in four months; for the hamsa and *paramahaṁsa*, none, or if wanted, once in a year; for the turyātīta and *avadhūta*, none at all. The *kutīchaka* should take the food in one (place only); the *bahūdaka* should take alms (in many places); for the *haṁsa* and *paramahaṁsa*, the hand is the vessel; the turyātīta, should take food with the mouth as the cow; for the *avadhūta*, it is like the action of the boa constrictor (opening the mouth and taking whatever comes into it). For the *kutīchaka*, there are two cloths; for the *bahūdaka*, there is one cloth; for the *haṁsa* there is a piece of cloth; and the *paramahaṁsa* should be naked or have only a loin-cloth; in the case of the *turyātīta* and *avadhūta*, they should be as nature made them. For the *haṁsa* and paramahaṁsa, there (prescribed) a deer-skin, and for no others. For the *kutīchaka* and *bahūdaka*, there is the worship of the divine (image); for the *haṁsa* and *paramahaṁsa*, there is mental worship; for the turyātīta and *avadhūta*, there is the idea that they alone are *Brahman*. The *Kutīchaka* and *bahūdaka* are entitled to *mantras* and japas; the *haṁsa* and *paramahaṁsa*, to *dhyāna* (editation); the *turyātīta* and *avadhūta* are entitled to none; but they are entitled to the initiation of the sacred sentences of the Vedas; so also the *paramahaṁsa*. The *kutīchaka* and *bahūdaka* are not entitled to initiate others; for them, there is (the uttering of) the mental *praṇava*; for the *haṁsa* and *paramahaṁsa*, there is the internal *pranva*; (in the heart); for the *turyātīta* and *avadhūta*, there is the *Brahma-praṇava* (always). For the *kutīchaka* and *bahūdaka*, there is *śravaṇa* (hearing and study): for the *haṁsa* and *paramahaṁsa*, there is *manana* (thinking and remembering); for the *turyātīta* and *avadhūta* there is *nididhyāsana* (profound meditation ever). For all these, there is necessarily the meditation upon *Ātmā*. Thus the aspirant after salvation

---

1. "Tat" has its two aspects of the word and its meaning which is *Nirguṇa*. In "Tvam" also there are two, *viz.*, the disciple and the *jīva*.

should ever be uttering the *Praṇava* which enables one to cross *samara*, and be living as a *Jīvanmukta*. Thus the ascetic, accroding to each one's capacity, should ever be seeking the means to attain *Kaivala*. Such the *Upaniṣad*."

Upadeśa VIII

Then Nārada asked *Parameṣṭhī* (Brahmā) to enlighten him, who had surrendered himself to Him, about *saṁsāra-tāraka* (or that *tāraka* or *Praṇava* which lifts one out of *saṁsāra*).

Assenting to which, Brahmā began thus : "*Omkāra* that is *Brahman* is the *vyaṣṭi* (individual) and the *samaṣṭi* (cosmic). What is the individual? What is the cosmic? *Brahma-praṇava* is of three kinds, *saṁhāra*-(destructive) *praṇava*, *sṛṣti*-(creative) *praṇava*, and *ubhayātmaka* (belonging to both) *praṇava*, as being of two forms, internal and external. (It is also eight:) *Antaḥpraṇava*, *Vyāvahārika-praṇava*, *bāhya-praṇava*, *ārṣa-praṇava*, *ubhayātmaka* or *virāṭ-praṇava*, *saṁhāra-praṇava*, *brahma-praṇava*, and *ardhamātrā praṇava*. *Om* is *Brahman*, Know that the *mantra* of the one-syllabled *Om* is *Praṇava*. It has the eight difference of *akāra, ukāra, makāra, ardhamātrā, nāda, bindu, kalā*, and *śakti*. Know it is not four (alone). *Akāra* is associated with ten thousand limbs; *ukāra* with one thousand limbs, *makāra* with one hundred limbs; *ardhamātrā* is of the nature of endless limbs. That which is *saguṇa* (associated with *guṇas*) is *virāṭ*-(preservation) *praṇava*; that which is *nirguṇa* (not associated with *guṇas*) is *saṁhāra*- (or destruction) *praṇava*; that which is associated with *guṇas* and is not so associated, is *utpatti*-(or origination) *praṇava*. *Pluta* (the elongated accent) is *virāṭ* : *plutapluta* is *samhāra*. The *virāt-praṇva* is of the form of sixteen *mātrās* and is above the thirty-six tattvas. The sixteen *mātrās* are thus : *Akāra* is the first *mātrā*; *ukāra* is the second; *makāra* is the third; *ardhamātra* is the fourth; *nāda* is the fifth; *bindu* is the sixth; *kalā* is the seventh; *kalātīta* is the eighth; *śānti* is the ninth; *śāntyatīta* is the tenth; *unmanī* is the eleventh; *manonmanī* is the twelfth; *purītati* is the thirteenth; *tanumadhyamā* is the fourteenth; pati is the fifteenth; *parā* is the sixteenth. Then (again) having sixty-four *mātrās* and their division into the two, *Prakṛti* and *Puruṣa* and resolving themselves into the one hundred and twenty-eight differences of *mātrās*, it becomes *saguṇa* and *nirguṇa*. Though *Brahma-praṇava* is one only, it is the substratum of all, the support of the whole universe, of the form of all *akṣaras* (letters), time, Vedas, and Śiva. this *Oṁkāra* should be sought after, that is mentioned in the Vedas of the nature of the *Upaniṣads*. Know that this *Oṁkāra* is the *Ātmā* that is indestructible during the three periods of time, past, present, and future, able to confer salvation and eulogized *Brahma*-sound (Vedas). Having experienced this one *Om* as immortal and ageless, and having brought about the *Brahma*-nature in this body, bcome convinced that your *Ātmā*, associated with the three bodies, is *Parabrahman*. Through *Viśva* and others (*viz., Taijasa, Prājña*, the

Turya) in order, the realisation of *parabrahman* should be attained since *Ātmā* is of four kinds through his identification with, and the enjoying of the gross as well as the enjoyer of the gross, the subtle as well as the enjoyer of the subtle, and through his identification (with the third body) enjoying bliss in the fourth. He has four feet. The one presiding over the waking state is gross; and since he is the enjoyer of *Viśva* (the universe), he becomes the *sthūla-prajñā* (gross consciousness). he has nineteen[1] facets and eight parts. He is pervading everywhere and Lord. he is the enjoyer of the gross and is the *caturātma* called *Viśva*. He alone is the *Puruṣa* called *Vaiśvānara*. He alone is *Viśvajit* (the conqueror of the universe). This is the first foot. When this Lord attains the dreaming condition, he is the *sūkṣma-prajñā* (subtle consciousness). O conqueror of all, he is the one having eight limbs, and there is none else. He is the enjoyer of the subtle and is *caturātma*, named *Taijasa* and the protector of elements. he alone is the *Hiraṇyagarbha*. presiding over the gross (or subtle matter rather). He is said to form the second foot. *Suśupti* (or the dreamless sleep) is that state where one sleeps without any desire and where one sees not any dreams. The one identified with this dreamless sleep is *Prajñāna-ghana*, is blissful, of the nature of eternal bliss and the *Ātmā* in all creatures; yet he is enjoyer of bliss, has cetas (consciousness) as his (one) foot, as all-pervading, indestructible *caturātma* and the Lord, and is named *Prājña*, the third foot. He alone is the Lord of all, the knower of all, the subtle-thoughted, the latent one, and the cause of all creation. He alone is the origin and the destruction. these three (states) are obstacles to all creatures obtaining (the final) peace. As is *svapna*, so is *suṣupti*, it (also) being said to be illusory. The *caturātmā*, the fourth, as he is *Sat*, *Cit* and *Ekarasa* (the one essence), ends as the fourth the follows (upon the heels of each of the above states), is the knower of the means of *vikalpa-jñāna* and is the *anujñātā* (the one following knower). Having known them, and known as *māyā* the three *vikalpa*s of *suṣupti*, *svapna* and *āntara* (the inner), even in this state, is he not (to be known as) *Sat-Cit-Ekarasa*? This shall be expressed as differentiated thus : It is not even the gross *prajñā*; nor is it the very subtle *prajña*; nor is it *prajñā* itself (of the causal body) : O *muni* neither is it the trifling *prajñā*; nor is it the non-*prajñā*; nor is it the dual *prajñā*; nor is it internal *prajñā*, though it is without *prajñā*; it is *Prajñāna-ghana*. It can never be known by the organs; nor it can be known by the reason; it cannot be grasped by the organs of action. it cannot be proved. It cannot be reached by thought. It cannot be proved by analogy. it can be realised by Self-realisation alone. It is with the waking state. etc. It is the auspicious, with changes, without a second. Such a one is thought to be *Turya*. this alone is *Brahman*, *Brahma-praṇava*. This should be known. There is no other turya. To the

1. The nineteen are the five organs of sense, the five organs of action, the five *prāṇas*, and the four of the mind.

aspirants after salvation, it is the support, like the sun everywhere; it is the Self-light. As it alone is *Brahman*, this *Brahma-Ākāśa* is shining always. Thus is the *Upaniṣad*."

Upadeśa IX

Nārada asked : "Who is *Brahma-svarūpa*?" To which Brahmā replied thus: "*Brahma-svarūpa* is thus : Those who know that 'he (*Brahman*) is one and I am another' are only *paśus* (animals). The real *paśus* (animals) are no animals. The wise man who knows *Brahman* thus (as himself, and himself as *Brahman*) escapes out of the mouth of death. There is no other path to salvation.

"Is time the cause[1] (of origination of universes)? or nature? or *karma*? or accident? or the (great) elements ? or *Puruṣa* ? This should be considered. It is not the union of them. (Then) there is the *Ātmā*, but (*jīva*) *Ātmā* is not the Lord, as it is subject to pleasrues and pains. Those (*Ṛṣis*) following *dhyāna-yoga* have beheld, as the cause, the *devātma-śakti* concealed by its own qualities of that One that presides over all the causes associated with time and *Ātmā*. Him (the Universal Soul), we consider as the wheel which has one circumference, which is covered by three (layers), which has sixteen end-parts, which has fifty spokes and twenty counter-spokes, which has six times eight (nails), which has one rope of various forms, which has the threefold path, and which has delusion arising from the twofold cause. Him (we worship as a river) which has (water) oozing out of the five currents (of organs), which is terrible and crooked through the five causes (of elements), whose *pranas* are the five waves, which has *buddhi*, etc., as the root cause, which has five whirlpools, which is impelled by the velocity of the five pains, which has fifty differents (or has the give miseries), and which has the five obstacles. In this wheel of *Brahman*, which is the support of life and the last abiding place of all beings, and and which is infinite, is whirling deluded the *jīva*, thinking that it is different from the one (Lord) Ordainer. Being blessed by Him, he gains salvation through such (a blessing). This is declared as *brahman*, as the supreme and the indestructible. In it, are the three (the enjoyer, the enjoyed and enjoyment). Hence it is the firm abode (of all). The knowers of *Brahman* having known *Brahman* within (the universe, etc.,) attain *samādhi* in *Brahman* and are absorbed in *Brahma*. Īśvara upholds this universe, closely associated with the destructible and indestructible, which are manifest and unmanifest; but the not-ruler of (*jīva-*) *Ātmā* is bound through the thought of its being the enjoyer; and having known the Lod is freed from all fetters. Both *Īśvara* and *jīva* are birthless; one (the former) is jñānī and the other (latter) is *ajñāni*. (The goddess of) *Brahmātma-śakti*, is birthless, is alone engaged

1. The *Svetāsvatara Upaniṣad* begins thus.

(in this world), on account of the enjoyment of the enjoyers. *Ātmā* is endless. The universe is Him from. He is not the agent. Whoever knows the *Brahman* that is threefold (as *jīva*, *Īśvara* and the universe) is released from bondage. It is *pradhāna* alone that is destructible. It is *Īśvara* that is immortal and indestructible. The one Lord (*Īśvara*) ordains *Pradhāna* and *Puruṣa*.

"The illusion of the universe disappears through meditation on union (of absorption) and *sattva-bhāva* of *Parameśvara* always. Through knowing the Lord, *avidyā* and the rest are destroyed. Through the removal of such pains, there is freedom from birth and death. Through the meditation of the *Parameśvara*, the third body is acquired after this (physical) body, all wealth is enjoyed, and he attains whatever should be attained. He should know with certitude that all the three things (*Viz.,*) the enjoyer, the enjoyed, and enjoyment are nothing but *Brahman*, and are of the nature of his own Self. There is none but It to be know. All *Ātmic* knowledge is through tapas (only). That, *Brahman* contains in itself all excellence. Having known thus, whoever meditates upon the (*Ātmā-*) *svarūpa*, to him were where then is grief? Where then is delusion ? Therefore the *Virāṭ* is the past, present, and future time, and is of indestructible nature.

"*Ātmā*, that is the atom of atoms and the greatest of the greatest, is in the cave of the heart of all creatures. One without the thought of objects and without grief, knows the *Ātmā* capable of neither increase nor decrease through the grace of *Īśvara* or through the non-attraction to the objects of the senses. he (*Ātmā*) walks speedily without legs, lifts objects without hands, sees without eyes and hears without ears. he knows all, but none knows Him. He is said to be the foremost *Mahā-Puruṣa*. Having known *Ātmā* that is bodiless in this fleeting body, the great, the all-pervading, the support of all, with incomprehensible power, fit to be known through the meaning, etc., of all the *Upaniṣads*, the supreme of the supreme, the supreme object fit to be known, the one remaining after all, the all-knowing, the eternal, the foremost of all foremost beings, the ordainer of all, the one fit to be worshipped by all angels, the one without beginning, end, and middle, without limit or destruction, the cause of Brahmā, Viṣṇu, and *Rudra*, the one that has all the universe latent in himself, of the nature of the five elements with the expansion of all the quintuplicated creation, without being enveloped by his own limbs of quintuplicated objects, superior to the supreme, greater than the greatest, of the nature of effulgence, the eternal and the auspicious, the undaunted personage never grieves. One who has neither given up vicious actions, nor controlled his organs, nor mastered his mind, nor given up longing after fruits of actions though the mind is undisturbed, nor brought his mind to one state (or point), will not attain this *Ātmā*.

"This (*Brahman*) is neither internal nor external consciousness; is neither gross, nor *jñāna*, nor *ajñāna*; nor is it the state between the waking and the dreaming states. It cannot be cognised by the organs; is not subject to proof; is within. He who knows that wich is by itself alone is emancipated person."

The Lord Brahmā said that he becomes an emancipated person. he who knows Reality is a *Parivrāt*. Such a *Parivrāt* roams about alone. Through fear, he is like a terrified deer. He will not be opposed to going anywhere. Having given up all but his body, he will live like a bee, and without considering others as foreign to himself; ever meditating upon Reality, he attains liberation in himself. Such a *Parivrāt* will be without delusion, without action or causing other to act, being absolved from teacher, disciple, books, etc., and having abandoned all *saṁsāra*. Such a *Parivrāṭ* roams about thus— without wealth, being happy, able to get wealth (if wanted), having crossed *jñāna* and *ajñāna* as well as happiness and grief, being Self-effulgence, being fit to be known by the Vedas, having known all, able to confer *siddhis* and remaining himself as *Brahman*, the Lord. such *Parivrāt* attains the supreme abode of Viṣṇu, from which a *yogin* that has gone to it does not return, and where the sun and moon do not shine. He does not return. Such is *Kaivalya*.

Thus ends the Upaniṣad

Śāṇḍilya-Upaniṣad

OF

ATHARVAṆAVEDA

Chapter I

Om. *Śāṇḍilya* questioned *Atharvan* thus : "Please tell me about the eight *aṅgas* (parts) of *Yoga* which is the means of attaining to *Ātmā*."

Atharvan replied : "The eight aṅgas of *yoga* are *yama*, *niyama*, *āsana*, *prāṇāyāma*, *pratyāhāra*, *dhāraṇa*, *dhyāna*, and *samādhi*. Of these, yame is of ten kinds : and so is *niyama*. There are eight *āsanas*. *Prāṇāyāma*, is of three kinds; *pratyāhāra* is of five kinds : so also is *dhāraṇā*. *Dhyāna* is of two kinds, and *samādhi*[1] is of one kind only.

"Under *yama* (forbearance) are ten: *ahiṁsā*, *satya*, *asteya*, brahmacarya, *dayā*, *ārjava*, *kṣamā*, *dhṛti*, *mitāhara*, and *śauca*. Of these, *ahiṁsā* is the not causing of any plan to any living being at any time through the actions of one's mind, speech, or body. *Satya* is the speaking of the truth that conduces to the well-being of creatures, through the actions of one's mind, speech, or body. Asteya is not coveting of another's property through the actions of one's mind, speech, or body. *Brahmacarya* is the refraining from sexual intercourse in all places and in all states in mind, speech or body. *Dayā* is kindliness towards all creatures in all places. *Ārjava* is the preserving of equanimity of mind, speech, or body in the performance or non-performance of the actions ordained or forbidden to be done. *Kṣamā* is the bearing patiently of all pleasant or unpleasant things, such as praise or blow. *Dhṛti* is the preserving of firmness of mind during the period of gain or loss of wealth or relatives. *Mitāhāra* is the taking of oily and sweet food, leaving one-fourth of the stomach empty. *Śauca* is of two kinds, external and internal. Of these, the external is the cleansing of the body by earth and water; the internal is the cleansing of the mind. This (the latter) is to be obtained by means of the *adhyātma-vidyā* (science of Self).

"Under *niyama* (religious observances), are ten, *viz.*, *tapas*, *santoṣa, āstikya, dāna, Īśvarapūjana, siddhānta-śravaṇa, hrīh, mati, japa*, and *vrata*, Of these tapas, is the emancipation of the body through the observances of such penances as *kṛcchra, cāndrāyaṇa*, etc., according to rules, *Santoṣa* is being satisfied with whatever comes to us of its own accord. *Āstikya* is the belief in the merits or demerits of actions as stated

1. Under yam and *niyama* patanjali has five kinds only.

in the vedas. *Dāna* is the giving with faith to deserving persons, money, grains, etc., earned lawfully. *Īśvarapūjana* is the worshipping of Viṣṇu, *Rudra*, etc., with pure mind according to one's power. *Siddhānta-śravaṇa* is the inquiry into the singificance of *Vedānta*. Hrīḥ is the shame felt in the performance of things contrary to the rules of the Vedas and of society. mati is the faith in the paths laid done by the Vedas. *Japa* is the practising of the *mantras* into which one is duly initiated by his spiritual instructor, and which is not against (the rules of) the Vedas. It is of two kinds— the spoken and the mental. The mental is associated with contemplation by the mind. The spoken is of two kinds— the loud and low. The loud pronunciation gives the reward as stated (in the Vedas) : (while) the low one (gives) a reward thousand times (that). The mental (gives) a reward a crores (of times that). *Vrata* is the regular observance of or the refraining from the actions enjoined or prohibited by the Vedas.

"*Āsanas* (the postures) are chiefly) eight. viz., *svastika, gomukha, padma*, *vīra*, *simha*, *bhadra*, *mukta*, and *mayūra*,

"*Svastika* is the sitting at ease with the body erect, placing each foot between the thighs and knees of the other. *Gomukha* is (the sitting at ease with the body erect,) placing the hollow of the left foot under the side of the right posteriors and the hollow of the right foot under the side of the left posteriors, resembling *Gomukha* (cow's face). *Padma* is (the sitting at ease with the body erect) placing the back of each foot in the thigh of the other, the right hand grasping the right toe and the left hand the left toe. This, O Śāṇḍilya, is praised by all. Vīra is the sitting at ease (with the body erect), placing one foot on the thigh of the other and the other foot underneath the corresponding (opposite thigh). *Siṁha* is (the sitting at ease with the body erect,) pressing the right side (of the thigh) with the hollow of left heel and *vice versa*. Rest your hands on the knees, spread out the fingers, open your mouth and carefully fix your gaze on the tip of your nose. This is always praised by the *yogins* *Siddha*[1] is (the siting at ease with the body erect), pressing the perineum with the left heel and placing the heel of the right foot above the genital rogan, concentrating the mind between the two eyebrows. *Bhadra* is (the sitting at ease with the body erect), pressing the two ankles of the two feet firmly together against the *Sīvinī (Viz.*, lower part of the seed) and the biding the knees firmly with the hands. This is the *bhadra* which destroys all diseases and poisons. *Mukta* is (the sitting at ease with the body erect), pressing with the left heel the right side of the tender part of the *Sīvinī*, and with the right heel the left side of the tender part of the *Sīvinī*. *Mayūri*— (lit., peacock). Rest your body upon the ground with both palms and place your elbows on the sides of the navel, lift up the head and feet and remain

1. In the explanation one more posture is introduced.

like a stick in the air, (like the plant balance in gymnastics). This is the *mayūra* posture which destroys all sins. By these, all the diseases within the body are destoryed; all the poisons are digested. Let the person who is unable to practise all these postures betake himself to any one (of these) which he may find easy and pleasant. He who conquers (or gets mastery over) the postures— he conquers the three worlds. A person who has the practice of *yama* and *niyama* should practise *prāṇāyāma*; by that the *nādis* become purified."

The Śāṇdilya questioned *Atharvan* thus : "By what means are the *nāḍīs* purified ? How many are they in number? How do they arise? What *vāyus* (vital airs) are located in them? What are their seats? What are their functions? Whatever is worthy of being known in the body, please tell me." To that *Atharvan* replied (thus): "This body is ninety-six digits in length. *Prāṇa* extends twelve digits beyond the body. He who through the practice of *yoga* reduces his *prāṇa* within his body to make it equal to or not less than the fire in it becomes the greatest of the *yogins*. In men, the region of fire which is triangular in form and brilliant as the molten gold is situated in the middle of the body. In four-footed animals. it (fire) is quadrangular. In birds, it is round. in its (the region of fire's) centre, the purifying, beneficial, and subtle flame is situate. Two digits above the anus and two digits below the sexual organ is the centre of the body for men. for four-footed animals, it is the middle of the heart. For birds, it is the middle of the body. Nine digits from (or above) the centre of the body and four digits in length and breadth is situated an oval form. In its midst in the navel. In it, is situated the cakra (*viz.*, (wheel) with twelve spokes. In the middle of the *cakra*, the *jīva* (*Ātmā*) wanders, driven by its good and bad deeds. As a spider flies to and fro within a web of fine threads. so *prāṇa* moves about here. In this body, the *jīva* rides upon *prāṇa*. Lying in the middle of the navel and above it, is the seat of *kuṇḍalinī*. The *kuṇḍalinī śakti* is of the form of eight *prakṛtis* (matter) and coils itself eight ways or (times). The movement of *vāyus* (vital airs) checks duly the food and drink all round by the side of *skandha*[1]. It closes by its head (the opening of) the *brahmarandhra*, and during the time of (the practice of) *yoga* is awakened by the fire (in the *apāna*): then it shines with great brilliancy in the *ākāśa* of the heart in the shape of wisdom. Depending upon *Kuṇḍalinī* which is situated in the centre, there are fourteen principal *nādis* (*viz.,*) *Iḍā, Piṅgalā, Suṣumnā, Sarasvatī, Vāruṇī, Pūṣā, Hastijihvā, Yaśasvinī, Yiśvodharī, Kuhūḥ, Śāṁkhinī, Payasvinī, Alambusā*, and *Gāndhārī*. Of them, *Suṣumnā* is said to be the sustainer of the universe and the path of salvation. Situated at the back of the anus, it is attached to the spinal column and extends to the *brahmarandhra* of the head and is invisible and subtle and is *vaiṣṇavī* (or has the *śakti* force of

1. In *varāha Upaniṣad* and later on, this is named "Kandha". Herein described the web of life.

Viṣṇu). On the left of *suṣumnā* is situated *Iḍā*, and on the right is *Piṅgalā*. The moon moves in *Iḍā* and the sun in *Piṅgalā*. The moon is of the nature of *tamas* and the sun of *rajas*. The poison share is of the sun and the nectar of the moon. They both direct (or indicate) time and *Suṣumnā* is the enjoyer (or consumer) of time. To the back and on the side of *Suṣ umnā* are situate *Sarasvatī* and *Kuhūḥ* respectively. Between *Yaśasvinī*[1] and *Kuhūḥ* stands *Vāruṇī*. Between *Pūṣā* and *Sarasvatī*[2] lies *Payasvinī*. Between *Gāndharī* and *Sarasvatī* is situated *Yaśasvinī*. In the centre of the navel is *Alambusā*. In front of *Suṣumnā* there is *Kuhūḥ*, which proceeds as far as the genital organ. Above and below *kuṇḍalinī* is situated *Vāruṇī*, which proceeds everywhere. *Yaśasvinī* which is beautiful (or belonging to the moon), proceeds to the great toes. *Piṅgalā* goes upwards to the right nostril. *Payasvinī* goes to right ear. *Sarasvatī* goes to the upper part or the tongue and *Śaṅkhinī* to the left ear, (while *Gāndhārī* goes from the back of *Iḍā* to the left eye. *Alambusā* goes upwards and downwards from the root of the anus. From these fourteen *nāḍīs*, other (minor) nādis spring; from them springing others, and from them springing others; so it should be known. As the leaf of the *aśvattha* three *(ficus religiosa)* etc., is covered with minute fibres so also is this body permeated with *nāḍīs*.

"*Prāṇa*. *Apāna*, *Samāna*, *Udāna*, *Vyāna*, *Nāga*, *Kūrma*, *Kṛkara*, *Devadatta*, and *Dhanañjaya*— these ten *vāyus* (vital airs) move in all the *nāḍīs*. *Prāṇa* moves in the nostrils, the throat, the navel, the two great toes and the lower and the upper parts of *kuṇḍalinī*. *Vyāna* moves in the ear, the eye, the loins, the ankles, the nose, the throat and the buttocks. *Apāna* moves in the anus, the genitals, the thighs, the knees. the stomach, the seeds, the loins, the calves, the navel, and the seat of the anus of fire. *Udāna* lives in all the joints and also in the hands and legs. *Samāna* lives, permeating in all parts of the body. Along with the fire in the body, it causes the food and drink taken in, to spread in the body. It moves in the seventy-two thousand *nāḍīs* and pervades all over the body along with the fire. The five *vāyus* beginning with *Nāga* go towards the skin, the bones, etc. The *prāṇa* which is in the navel separates the food[3] and drink which is there and brings about the rasas (juices) and others. Placing the water above the fire and the food above (or in) the water, it goes to the *Apāna* and along with it, fans up the fire in the centre of the body. The fire thus fanned up by the *Apāna* gradually increases in brightness in the middle of the body. Then it causes through its flames the water which is brought in the bowels by the *Prāṇa* to grow hot. The fire with the water causes the food and condiments, which are placed above, to be boiled to a proper degree. Then *Prāṇa* separates these into sweat, urine, water, blood,

---

1. This should be perhaps—between *Piṅgalā* and *Payasvainī* is *Pūṣā*.
2. *Yasasvinī* should be "*Sāṅkhinī*."
3. Here the process of digestion of food is described.

semen, the fæces,and the like. And along with the *Samāna*, it takes the juice (or essence) to all the *nāḍīs* and moves in the body in the shape of breath. The *vāyus* excrete the urine, the fæces, etc., through the nine openings in the body which are connected with the outside air. The functions of *Prāṇa* are inspiration, expiration, and cough. Those *Apāna* are excretion of the fæces and the urine. Those of *Vyāna* are (such actions as) giving and taking. Those of *Udāna* are keeping the body straight, etc. Those of *Samāna* are nourishing the body. Those of *Nāga* are vomiting, etc.; of *Kūrma*, the movement of the eyelids; the *Kṛkara*, the causing, of hunger, etc., of *Devadatta* idleness, etc., and *Dhanañjaya*, phlegm.

"Having thus acquired a through knowledge of the seat of the nādis and of the *vāyus* with their functions, one should begin with the purification of the *nāḍīs*. A person possessed of *yama* and *niyama*, avoiding all company, having finished his course of study, delighting in truth and virtue, having conquered (his) anger, being engaged in the service of his spiritual instructor and having been obedient to his parents and well instructed in all the religious practices and the knowledge of his order of life, should go to a sacred grove abounding in fruits, roots, and water. There he should select a pleasant spot always resouding with the chanting of the Vedas, frequented by the knowers of *Brahman* that persevere in the duties of their orders of life and filled with fruits, roots, flowers, and water. (Else) either in a temple or on the banks of a river or in a village or in a town, he should build a beautiful monastery. It should be neither too long nor too high, should have a small door, should be besmeared well with cow-dung and should have every sort of protection.[1] There listening to exposition of *Vedānta*, he should begin to practice *yoga*. In the beginning having worshipped *Vināyaka*[2] (Gaṇeśa), he should salute his *Īṣṭa-Devatā* (tutelary deity) and sitting in any of the above-mentioned postures of a soft seat, facing either the east or the north and having conquered them, the learned man keeping his head and neck erect and fixed his gaze on the tip of his nose, should see the sphere of the moon between his eyebrows and drink the nectar (flowing therefrom through his eyes. Inhaling the air through *Iḍā*[3] for the space of twelve *mātrās*,[4] he should contemplate on the sphere of fire[5] situated in the belly

---

1. Both by physical protection and that of *mantras* to scare away evil spirits.
2. He is the son of Śiva, having an elephant's face symbolical of wisdom. He is considered as the remover of all obstacles, and as such is he invoked and worshipped in tbe beginning of every religious rite.
3. *Iḍā* and *Piṅgalā* are the two *nāḍīs* upon which our breaths alternate from the left nostril to the right and *vice versa* and between which is *Suṣumnā*. Hence these two terms are applied to and mean the left and right nostrils.
4. According to *Yogatattva-Upaniṣad*, a *mātrā* is the time occupied in circling the knee once with the palm of the hand and filliping the fingers.
5. According to *Varāha-Upaniṣad*, the seat of fire is the *mūlādhāra* (sacral plexus).

as surrounded with flames and having as its seed र (ra); then he should exhale it through *Piṅgalā*. Again inhaling it through *Piṅgalā* and retaining it (within),[2] he should exhale it through *Iḍā*. For the period of twenty-eight months, he should practise six times at every sitting through the three *sandhyās* (morning, noon, and evening) and during the intervals. By this, the *nāḍīs* become purified. Then the body becomes light and bright, the (gastric) fire is increased (within) and there is the manifestation of *nāḍa* (internal sound).

"*Praṇāyāma* is said to be union of *Prāṇa* and *Apāna*. It is of three kinds— expiration, inspiration, and cessation.[3] They are associated with the letters of (Sanskrit) alphabet (for the right performance of *prāṇāyāma*). Therefore *Praṇava* (*Om*) only is said to be *Prāṇāyāma*. sitting in the *padma* posture,[4] the person should meditate that there is at the tip of his nose *Gāyatrī* , a girl of red complexion surrounded by the numberless rays of the image of the moon and mounted on a *haṁsa* (*svan*) and having a mace in hand. She is the visible[5] symbol of the latter A. The letter U has as its visible symbol *Sāvitrī* , a young woman of white colour having a disk in her hand and riding[6] on a garuda (eagle). The letter M has as its visible symbol *Sarasvatī*, an aged woman of black colour riding on a bull, having a trident in her hand. He should meditate that the single letter— the supreme light— the praṇava (*Om*)— is the origin or source of these three letters A, U. and M. Drawing up the air thorugh *Iḍā* for the space of sixteen *mātrās*, he should meditate on the letter A during that time; retaining the inspired air for the space of sixty-four *mātrās*, he should meditate on the letter U during the time; he should then exhale the inspired air for the space of thirty-two *mātrās*, meditating on the letter M during that time. he should practise this in the above order over and over again.

"Then having become firm in the posture and perserved perfect self-control, the *yogin* should, in order to clear away the impurities of the *Suṣ umnā*, sit in the *padmāsana* (*padma* posture), and having inhaled the air through the left nostril, should retain it as long as he can and should exhale it through the right. Then drawing it again through the right and having retained it, he should exhale it through the left in the order that he should draw it through the same nostril by which he exhaled it before and retained it. In this context, occur (to memory) the following verses : "In

---

1. See Foot-Note No. 1.
2. The original is not clear. It says, "For the space of 3, 4, 3, 4, 7, 3, and 4 months" which when added becomes 28.
3. Accoding to the *mantra Śāstra*, *Prāṇāyāma* is performed through the letters of *Saṁskṛti* alphabet, the vowels corresponding to inspiration etc.
4. These are the Goddess representing *Śakti* and being the wives of Brahmā, Viṣ ṇu, and *Rudra*.
5. See Foot-Note No. 7.
6. See Foot-Note No. 7.

the beginning having inhaled the breath (*Prāṇa*) through the left nostril, according to the rule, he should exhale it through the other; then having inhaled the air through the right nostril, should retain it and exhale it through the other." To those who practise according to these rules through the right and left nostrils, the nādis become purified within three months. He should practise cessation of breath at sunrise, in the midday, at sunset and at midnight slowly till eighty (times a day) for four weeks. In the early stages, perspiration is produced; in the middle stage the tremor of the body, and in the last stage levitation in the air. These (results) ensue out of the repression of the breath, while sitting in the *padma* posture. When perspiration arises with effort, he should rub his body well. By this, the body becomes firm and light. In the early course of his practice, food with milk and ghee is excellent. One sticking to this rule becomes firm in his practice and gets no *tāpa* (or burning sensation in the body). As lions, elephants and tigers are gradually tamed, so also the breath, when rightly managed (comes under control); else it kills the practitioner.[1]

"He should (as far as is consistent with his health and safety) properly exhale it, properly inhale it or retain it properly. Thus (only) will be attain success. By thus retaining the breath in an approved manner and by the purification of the *nāḍīs*, the brightening of the (gastric) fire, the hearing distincltly of (spiritual) sounds and (good) health result. When the nervous centres have become purified through the regular practice of *Prāṇāyāma*, the air easily forces its way up through the month of the *Sus umnā* which is in the middle. By the contraction of the muscles of the neck and by the contraction of the one below (*viz.,*) *Apāna* the *Prāṇa* (breath) goes into the *Suṣumnā* which is in the middle from the west *nāḍī*.[2] Drawing up the *Apāna* and forcing down the *Prāṇa* from the throat, the *yogin* free from old age becomes a youth of sixteen.

"Seated in pleasant posture and drawing up the air through the right nostril and retaining it inside from the top of the hair to the toe nails, he should exhale it through the same nostril. Through it, the brain becomes purified and the diseases in the air *nāḍīs*[3] are destroyed. Drawing up the air through the nostrils with noise (so as to fill the space) from the heart to

1. This passage clearly indicates the dreadful consequences of the performance of *Prāṇāyāma* rashly and without a *Guru*.
2. As already pointed out, the *Suṣumnā nāḍī* is between *Iḍā* and *Piṅgalā*. If *Prāṇa* which alternates ordinarily between *Iḍā* and *Piṅgalā* is restrained by long *kumbhaka*, then it along with the soul, it attendant will enter the *Suṣumnā* (central *nāḍi*) at one of the three places where it yields space for entrance through such restraint of breath and in the navel, from the *Sarasvatī nāḍī* on the west. After such entry it is that the *yogin* becomes dead to the world, being in the state called trance.
3. Through such and other methods of *Prāṇāyāma* prescribed in this passage and the subsequent ones, chronic diseases that defy European doctors will be rotted out.

the neck, and having retained it (within) as long as possible, he should exhale it through the nose. Through this, hunger, thirst, idleness and sleep do not arise.

"Taking in the air through the mouth (wide open) and having retained it as long as possible, he should expel it through the nose. Through this (such diseases as) *gulma, pleeha* (both being splentic diseases), bile and fever as also hunger, etc., are destroyed.

"Now we shall proceed to *kumbhaka* (restraint of breath). It is of two kinds— *sahita* and *kevala*. That which is coupled with expiration and inspiration is called *sahita*. That which is devoid of these is called *kevala* (alone). Until you become perfect in kevalas, practise *sahita*. To one who has mastered *kevala*, there is nothing unattainable in the three worlds. By *kevala*-restraint of breath, the knowledge of *kuṇḍalinī* arises. Then he becomes lean in body, serene in face and clear-eyed, hears the (spiritual) sounds distinctly,[1] becomes free from all diseases and conquers his (*bindu*) seminal fluid, his gastric fire being increased.

"Centring one's mind on an inward object whilst his eyes are looking outside without the shutting and opening of his eyelids, has been called *Vaiṣṇavīmudrā*. This is kept hidden in all the *tāntric* works. With his mind and breath absorbed in an internal object, the *yogin*, though he does not really see the objects outside and under him, still (appears to) see them with eyes in which the pupils are motionless. This is called Khecarīmudrā. It has as its sphere of extension one object and is very beneficial. (Then) the real seat of Viṣṇu, which is void and non-void, dawns on him. With eyes half closed and with a firm mind, fixing his eyes on the tip of his nose and becoming absorbed in the sun and moon, he after remaining thus unshaken (becomes conscious of) the thing which is of the form of light, which is free from all externals, which is resplendent, which is the supreme truth and which is beyond. O Śāṇḍilya, know this to be Tat (That). Merging the sound in the light and elevating the brows a little, this is of the way of (or is part of) the former practice. This brings about the state of *Unmanī* which causes the destruction of the mind. Therefore he should practise the *Khecarīmudrā*. Then he attains to the state of *Unmanī* and falls into the *yoga* sleep (trance). To one who obtains this *yoga* sleep, time does not exist. Placing the mind in the midst of *śakti* and *śakti*[2] in the midst of the mind and looking on the mind with the mind. O Śāṇḍilya be happy. Place the *Ātmā* in the midst of *ākāśa* and *ākāśa* in the midst of *Ātmā*, and having reduced everything to *ākāśa*, do not think anything else. You should not (then) entertain thoughts, either external or internal. Abandoning all thoughts, become abstract thought

---

1. He becomes an Ūrdhava-rētas—his vital energy goes up.
2. There are six centres of energy in the body (*mulādhāra*, sacr...etc.) which are presided over by six Śaktis (goddesses of energy).

itself. As comphor in fire and salt in water become absorbed, so also the mind becomes absorbed in the *Tattva* (Truth). What is termed *manas* (mind) is the knowledge of everything that is known and its clear apprehension. When the knowledge and the object cognised are lost alike, there is no second path (or that is the only path). By its giving up all cognition of objects, it (the mind) it absorbed and when the mind is absorbed, *kaivalya* (isolation) alone remains.

"For the destruction of the *citta*, there are two ways— *yoga* and *jñāna*. O prince of sages! *yoga* is the (forcible) repression of modifications of the mind, and *jñāna* is the through inquiry into them. When the modifications of the mind are repressed, it (the mind) verily obtains peace. Just as the actions of the people cease with the stopping of the fluctuations of the mind sun (*viz.*, with sunset), so when the fluctuations of the mind cease, the cycle of births and deaths comes to an end. (Then) the fluctuations of *prāṇa* are prevented, when one has no longing for this mundane existence or when he has gratified his desires therein-through the study of religious books, the company of good men, indifference (to enjoyments), practice and *yoga* or long contemplation with intentness on any desired (higher) object or through practising one truth firmly.

"By the repression of the breath through inhalation, etc., by continual practice therein which does not cause fatigue, and by meditating in a secluded place, the fluctuations of the mind are arrested. Through the right realisation of the true nature of the sound which is at the extreme end of the pronunciation of the syllable *Om* (*viz., Ardhamātrā*), and when suṣupti (dreamless sleeping state) is rightly cognised through consciousness, the fluctuations of *prāṇa* are repressed. When the passage at the root of the palate which is like the bell, *viz., uvula*, is closed by the tongue with effort and when the breath goes up through (the upper hole), then the fluctuations of *prāṇa* are stopped. When the consciousness (*smavit*) is merged in *prāṇa*, and when through practice the *prāṇa* goes through the upper hole intc the dvādaśānta[1] (the twelfth centre) above the palate, then the fluctuations of *prāṇa* are stopped. When the eye of consciousness (*viz.*, the spiritual or third eye) becomes calm and clear so as to be able to distinctly see in the transparent *ākāśa* at a distance of twelve digist from the tip of his nose, then the fluctuations of *prāṇa* are stopped. When the thoughts arising in the mind are bound up in the calm contemplation of the world of *tāraka* (star or eye) between one's eyebrows and are (thus) destroyed, then the fluctuations cease. when the knowledge which is of the form of the knowable, which is beneficent and which is untouched by any modifications arises in one and is known as

1. The twelfth centre is identified by some with the pituitary body in the head, there being sex centres in the brain besides the six below the brain.

Om only and no other, then the fluctuations of *prāṇa* cease. By the contemplation for a long time of the *ākāśa* which is in the heart, and by the contemplation of the mind free from *vāsanās*, then the fluctuations of *prāṇa* cease. By these methods and verious others suggested by (one's) thought and by means of the contact of the many (spiritual) guides, the fluctuations cease.

"Having by contraction opened the door of *kuṇḍalinī* one should force open the door of *mokṣa*. Closing with her mouth the doo through which one ought to go, the *kuṇḍalinī* sleeps spiral in form and coiled up like a serpent. he who causes this *kuṇḍalinī* to move— he is an emancipated person. If this *kuṇḍalinī* were to sleep in the upper part of the neck of any *yogin*, it goes towards his emancipation. (If it were to sleep) in the lower part (of the body), it is for the bondage of the ignorant. Leaving the two *nāḍīs*, *Iḍā* and the other (*Piṅgalā*), it (*prāṇa*) should move in the *Suṣumnā*. That is the supreme seat of Viṣṇu One should practise control of breath with the concentration of the mind. The mind should not be allowed by a clever man to rest on any other thing. One should not worship Viṣṇu during the day alone. One should not worship Viṣṇu during the night alone; but should always worship Him, and should not worship Him merely during day and night. the wisdom-producing opening (near uvula) has five passages. O Śāṇḍilya this is the *khecarīmudrā*, practise it. With one who sits in the *khecharīmudrā*, the *vāyu* which was flowing before through the left and right *nāḍīs* now flows through the middle one (*Suṣumna*). There is no doubt about it. You should swallow the air through the void (*Suṣumnā*) between *Iḍā Piṇgala*. In that place is *khecharīmudrā* situated, and that is the seat of Truth. Again that is *khecharīmudrā* which is situated in the and *ākāśa-cakra* (in the head) in the *nirālamba* (supportless) seat between the sun and moon (*viz.*, *Iḍā* and *Piṅgalā*). When the tongue has been lengthened to the length of a *kalā* (digit) by the incision (of the fraenum liṅgum) and by rubbing and milking it (*viz.*, the tongue), fix the gaze between the two eyebrows and close the hole in the skull with the tongue reversed. This is *khecarīmudrā*. When the tongue and the *citta* (mind) both move in the *ākāśa* (khecarī) then the person with his tongue raised up becomes immortal. Firmly pressing the yoni (perineum) by the left heel, stretching out the right leg, grasping the feet with hands and inhaling the air through the nostrils, practise *kaṇṭhabandha*,[1] retaining the air upwards. By that, all afflictions are destroyed; then poison is digested as if it were nectar. *Asthma*, splenetic disease, the turning up of the anus and the numbness of the skin are removed. This is the means of conquering *prāṇa* and destroying death. Pressing the youni by the left heel place the other foot

1. Lit., binding the air up the throat.

over the left thigh : inhale the air, rest the chin on the chest, contract the yoni and contemplate, (as far as possible), your *Ātmā* as situated within your mind.Thus is the direct perception (of truth) attained.

"Inhaling the *prāṇa* from outside and filling the stomach with it, centre the *prāṇa* with the mind in the middle of the navel, at the tip of the nose and at the toes during the *sandhyās* (sunset and sunrise) or at all times. (Thus) the *yogin* is freed from all diseases and fatigue. By centring his *prāṇa* at the tip of his nose, he obtains mastery over the elephant of air; by centring it at the middle of his navel, all diseases are destroyed; by centring it at the the toes, his body becomes light. He who drinks the air (drawn) through the tongue destroys fatigue, thirst and diseases. he who drinks the air with his mouth during the two sandhyās and the last two hours of the night, within three months the auspicious *Sarasvatī* (goddess of speech) is present in his *vāk* (speech) *viz.,* (he becomes eloquent and learned in his speech). In six months, he is free from all diseases. Drawing the air by the tongue, retain the air at the root of the tongue. The wise man thus drinking nectar enjoys all prosperity. Fixing the *Ātmā* in the *Ātmā* itself in the middle of the eyebrows, (having inhaled) through *Iḍā* and breaking through (centre) thirty times, even a sick man is freed from disease. He who draws the air through the *nādis* and retains it for twenty-four minutes in the navel and in sides of the stomach becomes freed from disease. he who for the space of a month during the three *sandhyās* (sunset), sunrise, and midnight or noon) draws the air through the tongue, pierces thirty times and retains his breath in the middle of his navel, becomes freed from all fevers and poisons. He who retains the *prāṇa* together with the mind at the tip of his nose even for space of a *muhūrta* (forty-eight minutes), destroys all sins that were committed by him during one hundred births.

"Through the samyama of *tāra* (*Om*), he known all things. By retaining the mind at the tip of his nose, he acquires a knowledge of Indra-world; below that, he acquires a knowledge of *Agni*-(fire) world, Through the *samyama* of *citta* in the eye, he gets a knowledge of all worlds : in the ear, a knowledge of *Yama*-(the god of death) world : in the sides of the ear, a knowledge of *Nṛṛti*-world: in the back of it (the ear), a knowledge of Varuṇa-world: left ear, a knowledge of *Vāyu*-world: in the throat, a knowledge of *Soma* (moon) world : in the left eye, a knowledge of Śiva-world : in the head, a knowledge of brahmā-world[1]: in the soles of the feet, a knowledge of *Atala*-world[2] : in the feet, a knowledge of *Vitala*-

1. These correspond severally to the several directions and the *devatās* presiding over them, corresponding respectively to east, south-east, south, south-west, west, north-west, north, and north-east.
2. The fourteen worlds, lokas and talas are referred to : the order in talas seems to be wrong, *Talātala* should be in the middle.

world : in the ankles, a knowledge of *Nitala* (rather *Sutala*) world : the calves, a knowledge of *Sutala* (rather *Talātāla* world) : in the knees, a knowledge of *Mahātala* world : in the thighs, a knowledge of *Rasātala* world : in the loins, a knowledge of *Talātala* (rather *Pātāla*) world : in the navel, a knowledge of *Bhūrloka* (earth world) : in the stomach, a knowledge of *Bhuvar* (world) : in the heart, a knowledge of *Suvar* (world) : in the place above the heart, a knowledge of *Mahar* world : in the throat, a knowledge of Jana world : in the middle of the brows, a knowledge of *Tapa* world : in the head, a knowledge of *Satya* world.

"By conquering *dharma* and *adharma*, one knows the past and the future. By centring it on the sound of every creature, a knowledge of the cry (or language) of the animal is produced. By centring it the sañcita-*karma* (past *karma* yet to be enjoyed), a knowledge of one's previous births arises in him. By centring it on the mind of another, a knowledge of the mind (or thoughts) of others is induced. By centring it on the *kāya-rūpa* (or form of the body), other forms are seen. By fixing it on the bala (strength), the strength of persons like Hanūmān is obtained. By fixing it on the sun, a knowledge of the worlds arises. By fixing it on the moon, a knowledge of the constellation is produced. By fixing it on the *Dhruva* (Polar star) a perception of its motion is induced. By fixing it on his own (Self), one acquires the knowledge of *Puruṣa*; on the navel, he attains a knowledge of the *kāya-vyūha* (mystical arrangement of all the particles of the body so as to enable a person to wear out his whole *karma* in one life): on the well of the throat, freedom from hunger and thirst arises : on the *Kūrma nāḍī* (which is situated in the well of the throat), a firmness (of concentration) takes place. By fixing it on the tārā (pupil of the eye), he obtains the sight of the *siddhas* (spiritual personages). By conquering the *ākāśa* in the body, he is able to soar in the *ākāśa* : (in short) by centring the mind in any place, he conquers the *siddhis* appertaining to that place.

"Then comes *pratyāhāra*, which is of five kinds. It is the drawing away of the organs from attaching themselves to the objects of senses. Contemplating upon everything that one sees as *Ātmā* is *pratyāhāra*. Renouncing the fruits of one's daily actions is *pratyāhāra*. Turning away from all objects of sense is *pratyāhāra*. *Dhāranā* in the eighteen important places (mentioned below is *pratyāhāra*, (*viz.,*) the feet, the toes, the ankles, the calves, the knees, the thighs, the anus, the penis, the navel, the heart, the well of the throat, the palate, the nose, the eyes, the middle of the brows, the forehead, and the head in asending and descending orders.

"Then (comes) *dhāraṇā*. It is of three kinds, (*viz.,*) fixing the mind in the *Ātmā*, bringing the external *ākāśa* into the *ākāśa* of the heart and contemplating the five *mūrtis* (froms of *devatās*) in the five elements—earth, *āpas*, fire, *vāyu*, and *ākāśa*.

"Then comes *dhyāna*. It is of two kinds, *saguṇa* (with *guṇas* or quality) and *nirguṇa* (without quality). *Saguṇa* is the meditation of a *mūrti*. *Nirguṇa* is on the reality of Self.

"*Samādhi* is the union of the *Jīvātmā* (individual self) and the *Paramātmā* (higher self) without the threefold state, (*viz.*, the knower, the known, and the knowledge). It is of the nature of extreme bliss and pure consciousness.

"Thus ends the first chapter of Śāṇḍilya *Upaniṣad*"

Chapter II

Then the *Brahmarṣi* Śāṇḍilya not obtaining the knowledge of *Brahman* in the four Vedas, approached the Lord Atharvan and asked him : "What is it? Teach me the science of *Brahman* by which I shall obtain that which is most excellent."

Atharvan replied : "O Śāṇḍilya, *Brahman* is *satya, vijñāna* and ananta in which all the (world) is interwoven, warp-wise and woof-wise, from which all originated and into which all are absorbed, and which being known makes everything else known. It is without hands and feet, without eyes and ears, without tongue or without body, and is unreachable and undefinable. From which, vāk (speech) and mind return, being unable to obtain (or reach) It. It is to be cognised by *jñāna* and *yoga*[1]. From which, *prajñā* of old sprang. That which is one and non-dual, that which pervades everything like *ākāśa*, which is extremely subtle, without a blemiresh, *sat* (be-ness) only, the essence of the bliss of consciousness, beneficent, calm and immortal and which is beyond. That is *Brahman*. Thou art that. Know That by wisdom. He who is the one, the shining, the giver of the power of *Ātmā*, the omniscient, the lord of all, and the inner soul of all beings, who lives in all beings, who is hidden in all beings and the sources of all beings, who is reachable only through *yoga* and who creates, supports and destroys everything— He is *Ātmā*. Know the several worlds in the *Ātmā*. Do not grieve, O knower of *Ātmā*, thou shalt reach the end of pains."

Chapter III

Then Śāṇḍilya questioned Atharvan thus : "From the *Brahman* that is *Om*, imperishable, actionless, beneficial, *sat* (be-ness) only and supreme, how did this universe arise? How does it exist in It? and how is it absorbed in It? Please solve me this doubt."

Atharvan replied : The Supreme *Brahman*, the Truth, is the imperishable and the actionless. then from the formless *Brahman*, three forms (or aspects) arose, (*viz.,*) *niṣkalā* (partless,) *sakalā* (with parts), and *sakalā-niṣkalā* (with and without parts). That which is *satya*, *vijñāna* and

---

1. Some texts leave the words "and *yoga*".

ānanda, That which is actionless, without any impurity, omnipresent, extermely subtle, having faces in every direction, undefinable and immortal— that is His *niṣkalā* aspect. *Maheśvara* (the great Lord) who is black and yellow rules with *avidyā*, mūlaprakṛti or *māyā* that is red, white, and black, and that is co-existent with Him. this is his *sakalā-niṣ kalā* aspect. Then the Lord desired (or willed) by his spiritual wisdom (thus) : May I become many"; may I bring forth? Then from this Person who was contemplating and[1] whose desires are fulfilled[2], three letters sprang up. Three *vyāhṛtis*, the three-footed *Gāyatrī* , the three Vedas, the three devas, the three varṇas (colours or castes) and the three fires sprang. That Supreme Lord who is endowed with all kinds of wealth, who is all pervading, who is situated the hearts of all beings, who is the Lord of *māyā* and whose from is *māyā*— he is Brahmā. He is Viṣṇu : He is *Rudra* : He is *Indra* : He is all the devas : He is all the bhūtas (elements or beings) : He only is before : He only is behind : He only is on our left : He only is on our right : He only is below[3] : He only is above : He only is the all. That form of him as *Dattātreya* , who sports with his *Śakti*, who is kind to his devotees, who is brilliant as fire, resembling the petals or a red lotus and is of four hands, who is mild and shines sinlessly— this is His *sakalā* from."

Then *Śāṇḍilya* questioned *Atharvan*, "O Lord, that which is *Sat* only and the essence of the bliss of consciousness— why is He called *Parabrahman* ?"

Atharvan replied : "Because He increases *bṛhati* and causes to increase everything (*bṛhanti*) so he is called *Prarabrahman*. Why is He called *Ātmā*? Since He obtains (*āpnoti*) everything, since He takes back everything and since He is everything, so he is called *Ātmā*. Why is He called *Maheśvara* (the great Lord) ? Since by the sound of the words *Mahat-Īśa* (the great Lord) and by His own power, the great Lord governs everything. Why is He called *Dattātreya* ? Because the Lord being extremely pleased with Atri (*Ṛṣi*) who was performing a most difficult penance and who had expressed his desire to see Him who is light itself, offered Himself (*datta*) as their son, and because the woman *Anasūyā* was his mother and Atri was his father. Therefore he who knows the (secret) meaning knows everything. He who always contemplates on the supreme that It is himself becomes a knower of *Brahman*. Here these *ślokas* (stanzas) occur (to memory). 'He who contemplates always the Lord of Lords and the ancient thus— as *Dattātreya*, the beneficent, the calm, of the colour of sapphire, one who delights in his own *māyā* and the Lord who has shaken off everything, as naked and as one whose whole body is besmeared with the holy ashes, who has matted hair, who is the Lord of

---

1. There relate to the *Gāyatrī mantras* depending upon sound.
2. Ibid.
3. According to *Bhāgavata*, he is one of the minor incarnations of Viṣṇu.

all, who has four arms, who is bliss in appearance, whose eyes are like full-blown lotus, who is the store of *jñāna* and *yoga*, who is the spiritual instructor of all the worlds and who is dear to all the *yogins*, and one who is merciful towards His devotees, who is the witness of all and who is worshipped by all the siddhas is freed from all sins and will attain (the Spirit).'

"O *Satyam* (thuth)."

Thus ends the Upanişad

Yogatattva-Upaniṣad

OF

KṚṢṆA-YAJURVEDA

I shall now describe *yoga-tattva* (*yoga*-truth) for the benefit of *yogins* who are freed from all sins through the hearing and the studying of it. The supreme *Puruṣa* called Viṣṇu, who is the great *yogin*, the great being the great tapasvin, is seen as a lamp in the path of the truth.The Grandfather (Brahmā) having saluted the Lord of the universe (Viṣṇu) and having paid Him due respects, asked Him (thus) : "Pray, explain to us the truth of *yoga* which includes in it the eight subservients." To which *Hṛṣīkeśa* (the Lord of the sence or Viṣṇu) replied thus : "Listen. I shall explain its truth. All souls are immersed in happiness and sorrow through the snare of *māyā*, *Kaivalya*, the supreme seat, is the path which gives them emancipation, which rends asunder the snare of *māyā*, which is the destroyer of birth, old age disease and which enables one to overcome death. There are no other paths to salvation. Those who go round the net of *Śāstras* are deluded by that knowledge. It is impossible even for the *Devas* to describe that indescribable state. How can that which is self-shining be illuminated by the *Śāstras* ? That only which is without parts and stains and which is quiescent beyond all the free from decay becomes the *jīva* (self) on account of the results of past virtues and sins. How did that which is the seat of *paramātmā*, is eternal, and above the state of all existing things and is of the form of wisdom and without stains attain the state of *jīva*? A bubble arose in it as in water and in this (bubble) arose *ahaṁkāra*. To it arose a ball (of body) made of the five (elements) and bound by *dhātus*. Know that to be *jīva* which is associated with happiness and misery and hence is the term *jīva* applied to *Paramātmā* which is pure. That *jīva* is considered to be the *kevala* (alone) which is freed from the stains of passion, anger, fear, delustion, greed, pride, lust, birth, death, miserliness, swoon, giddiness, hunger, thirst, ambition, shame fright, heart-burning, grief and gladness.

"So I shall tell you the means of destroying (these) sins. How could *jñāna* capable of giving *mokṣa* arise certainly without *yoga* ? And even *yoga* becomes powerless in (securing) *mokṣa* when it is devoid of *jñāna*. So the aspirant after emanicipation should practise (firmly) both *yoga* and *jñāna*. The cycle of births and deaths come only through ajñana and perishes only through *jñāna*. *Jñāna* along was originally. It should be known as the only means (of salvation). That is *jñāna* through which one cognises (in himself) the real nature of *kaivalya* as the supreme seat, the stainless, the partless, and of the nature of *Saccidānanda* without birth, existence and death and without birth, existence and death and without motion and *jñāna*.

"Now I shall proceed to describe *yoga* to you. *Yoga* is divided into many kinds on account of its actions : (*viz.,*) *Mantrayoga*, *Layayoga*, *Haṭ hayoga*, and *Rājayoga*. There are four states common to all these : (*viz.,*) *Ārambha*, *Ghata, Parichaya*, and *Niṣpatti*. O Brahmā, I shall describe these to you. Listen attentively. One should practise the *Mantra* along with its *mātrikās*. (proper intonations of the sounds) and others for a period of twelve years; then he gradually obtains wisdom along with the *siddhis*, (such as) *aṇimā* etc. Persons of weak intellect who are the least qualified for *yoga* practise this. The (second) Laya-*yoga* tends towards the absorption of the *citta* and is described inmyriads of ways; (one of which is)— one should contemplate upon the Lord who is without parts (even) while walking, sitting, sleeping, or eating. This is called *Laya-yoga*. Now hear (the description of) *Haṭha-yoga*. This *yoga* is said to possess (the following) eight subservients, *yama* (forbearance) *niyama* (religious observance), *āsana* (posture), *prāṇāyāma* (suppression of breath), *pratyāhāra* (sub-jugation of the senses), *dhāraṇā* (concentration), *dhyāna*, the contemplation on Hari in the middle of the eyebrows and *samādhi* that is the state of equality. *Mahāmudrā, Mahābandha* and *Khecarī, Jālandhara, Uddiyāṇa*, and *Mūla-bandha*, uttering without intermission *Praṇava* (*Om*) for a long time, and hearing the exposition of the supreme truths, *Vajrolī*, *Amarolī* and *Sahajolī*, which from a triad— all these separately I shall give a true description of. O four-faced one (Brahmā), among (the duties of) *yama* moderate eating— and not others— forms the principal factor; and non-injury is most important in *niyama*. (The chief postures are) four (*viz.,*) *Siddha*, *Padma*, *Simha*, and *Bhadra*. During the early stages of practice, the following obstacles take place, O four-faced one, (*viz.,*) laziness, idle talk, association with bad characters, acquisition of *mantras*, etc., playing with metals (alchemy) and woman, etc., the mirage. A wise man having found out these should abandon them by the force of his virtues. Then assuming *Padma* posture, he should practise *prāṇāyāma*. He should erect a beautiful monastery with a very small opering and with no crevices. It should be well pasted with cow-dung or with white coment. It should be carefully freed from dugs, mosquitoes and lice. It should be swept well every day with a broom. It should be perfumed with good odours; and fragrant resins should burn in it. Having taken his seat neither too high nor too low on a cloth, deerskin and *kuśa* grass spread, one over the other, the wise man should assume the *Padma* posture and keeping his body erect and his hands folded in respect, should salute his tuteary deity. Then closing the right nostril with his right thumb, he should gradually draw in the air through the left nostril. Having restrained it as long as possible, he should again expel it through the right nostril, he should retain it as long as he can and then expel it through the left nostril. drawing the air through the nostril by which he expels, he should continue this in uninterrupted succession. The time taken in making a round of the knee with the palm of the hand, neither very slowly nor very rapidly, and snapping the fingers once is called a *mātrā*. Drawing the air through the left nostril for about sixteen *mātrās* and having retained it (within) for about sixty-four *mātrās* one should expel it again through the right nostril for about thrity-two *mātrās*. Again fill the right nostril as before (and continue the rest). Practise cessation of breath four times daily (*viz.*,) at sunrise, noon, sunset and midnight, tilly eighty (times are reached). By a continual practice for about three months, the purification of the *nādis* takes place. When the nādis have become purified, certain external signs appear on the body of the *yogin*. I shall proceed to describe them. (They are) lightness of the body, brilliancy of complexion, increase of the gastric fire, leanness of the body, and along with these, absence of restlessness in the body. The proficient in *yoga* should abandon the food detriental to the practice of *yoga*. He should give up aslt, mustared, things sour, hot, pungent, or bitter, vegetables, asafoetida, etc., worship of fore, woman, walking, bathing at sunrise, emaciation of the body by fasts, etc. During he early stages of practice, food of milk and ghee is ordained; also food consisting of wheat, green pulse and red rice are said to favour the progress. Then he will be able to retain his breath as long as he like. By thus retaining the breath as long as he likes, *kevala kumbhaka* (cessation of breath without inspiration and expiration) is attained. When *kevala kumbhaka* is attained by one, and thus expiration and inspiration are dispensed with, there is nothing unattainable in the three worlds to him. In the commencement (of his practice), sweat is given out; he should wipe it off. Even after that, owing to the retaining of the breath, the person practising it gets phlegm. Then by increased practice of *dhāraṇā*. sweat arises. As a frog moves by leaps, so the *yogin* sitting in the *Padma* posture moves on the earth. With a (further) increased practice, he is able to rise from the ground. he, while seated in *Padma* posture, levitates. There arises to him the power to perform extraordinary feats. He does (or should) not disclose to others his feats of great powers (in the path). Any pain small great, does not affect the *yogin*. Then excretions and sleep are diminished, tears, reheum in the eye, salivary flow, sweat and bad smell in the mouth do not arise in him. With a still further practisce, he acquires great strenght by which he attains *Bhūcara siddhi*, which enables him to bring under his control all the creatures that tread this earth; tigers, *śarabhas*,[1] elephants, wild bulls or lions die on being struck by the palm of the *yogin*. He becomes as beautiful as the god of love himself. All females beings taken up with the beauty of his person will desire of/have intercourse with him. If he so keeps connection, his virility will be lost; so abandoning all copulation with women, he should continue his practice with gread sasiduity. By the

1. An animal said to have eight legs and to be stronger than lion.

preservation of the semen, a good odour pervades the body of the *yogin*. then sitting in a secluded place, he should repeat Praṇava (*Om*) with there pluta-*mātrās* (or prolonged intonation) for the destruction of his former sins. The *mantra*, *Praṇava* (*Om*) destroys all obstacles and all sins. By practising thus he attains the *ārambha* (beginning or first) state.

"Then follows the ghaṭa (second state)— one which is acquired by constantly practising suppresion of breath. When a perfect union takes place between *prāṇa* and *apāna*, *manas* and *buddhi*, or *jīvātmā* and *Paramātmā* without oposition, it is called the *ghaṭa* state. I shall describe its signs. He may now practice only for about one-fourth of the period prescribed for practice before. By day and evening let him practise only of a *yāma* (3 hours). Let him practise *kevala kumbhaka* once a day. Drawing away completely the organs from the objects of sense during cessation of breath is called *pratyāhāra*. Whatever he sees with his eyes, let him consider as *Ātmā*. Whatever he hears with his ears let him consider as *Ātmā*. Whatever he smells with his nose let him consider as *Ātmā*. Whatever he tastes with his tongue let him consider as *Ātmā*. Whatever the *yogin* touches with his skin let him consider as *Ātmā*. The *yogin* should thus unwearied gratify his organs of sense for a period of one *yāma* every day with great effort. then various wonderful powers are attained by the *yogin*, such as clairveyance, clairvoyance, clairaudience, ability to transport himself to great distances within a moment, great power of speech, ability to take any form, ability to become invisible, and the transmutation of iron into gold when the former is smearted over with his excretion.

"That *yogin* who is constantly practising *yoga* attains the power to levitate. Then should the wise *yogin* think that these powers are great obstacles to the attainment of *yoga*, and so he should never take delight in them. The king of *yogins* should not exercise his powers before any person whatsoever. he should live in the world as a fool, an idiot, or a deaf man, in order to keep his powers concealed. His disciples would, without doubt, request him to show his powers for the gratification of their own desires. One who is actively engaged in one's duties forgets to practise (*yoga*); so he should practise day and night *yoga* without forgetting the words of the *Guru*. Thus passes the ghata state to one who is constantly engaged in *yoga* practice. To one nothing is gained by useless company, since thereby he does not practise *yoga*. So one should with great effort practise *yoga*. Then by this constant practice is gained the paricaya state (the thrid state). *Vāyu*) (or breath) through arduous practice pierces along with *agni* the *Kuṇḍalinī* thought and enters the *Suṣ umnā* uninterrupted. When one's *citta* enters *Suṣumnā* aling with *prāṇa*, it reaches the high seat (of the head probebly) along with *prāṇa*.

"There are the five elements (*viz.,*) *Pṛthivī*, *āpas*, *agni*, *vāyu* and *ākāśa*. To the body of the five elements, there is the fivefold *dhāraṇā*.

From the feet to the knees is said to be the region *oftpṛthi*vī, is four-sided in shape, is yellow colour and has the *varṇa* (or letter) *La*. Carrying the breath with the latter *La* along the region of earth (*viz.,* from the foot to the knees) and contemplating upon Brahmā with four faces and four mouths and and of golden colour, one should perform *dhāraṇā* there for a period of two hours. he then attains mastery over the earth. Death does not trouble him, since he has obtained mastery over the earth element. The region of *āpas* is said to extend from the knees to the anus. *Āpas* is semi-lunar in shape and white in colour and has *Va* for its *bīja* (seed) letter. Carrying up the breath, with the letter *VA* along the region of *āpas*, he should contemplate on the God *nārāyaṇa* having four arms and a crowned head, as being of the colour of pure crystal, as dressed in orange clothes and as decayless; and practising *dhāraṇā* there for a period of two hours, he is freed from all sins. Then there is no fear for him from water, and he dọes not meet his death in water. From the anus to the heart is said to be the region of *agni*. *Agni* is triangular in shape, of red colour, and has the letter *Ra* for its (bīja) seed. Raising the breath made resplendent through the letter *Ra* along the region of fire, he should contemplate on *Rudra*, who has three eyes, who grants all wishes, who is of the colour of the midday sun, who is daubed all over with holy ashes and who is of a pleased contenance. Practising *dhāraṇa* there for a period of two hours, he is not burnt by fire even though his body enters the fire-pit. From the heart to the middle of the eyebrows is said to be the region of *vāyu*. *Vāyu* is hexangular in shape, black in colour and shines with the letter *Ya*. Carrying the breath along the region of *vāyu*, he should contemplate on *Īśvara*, the Omniscient, as possessing faces on all sides; and practising *dhārṇa* there for two hours, he entres *vāyu* and then *ākāśa*. The *yogin* does not meet his death through the fear of *vāyu*. From the centre of the eyebrows to the top of the head is said to be the region of *ākāśa*, is circular in shape, smoky in colour and shining with the letter *Ha*. Rising the breath along the region of *ākāśa*, he should contemplate on *Sadāśiva* in the following manner, as producing happiness, as of the shape of *bindu*, as the great deva, as have the shape of *ākāśa*, as shining like pure crystal, as wearing the rising crescent of moon on his head, as having five faces, ten heads and three eyes, as being of a pleased countenance, as armed with all weapons, as adorned with all ornaments, as having Umā (the goddess) in one-half of his body, as ready to grant favours, and as the cause of all the causes. By practising *dhāraṇā* in the region of *ākāśa*, he obtains certainly the power of levitating in the *ākāśa* (ether). Wherever he stays, he enjoys supreme bliss. The proficient in *yoga* should practise these five *dhāraṇās*. Then his body becomes strong and he does not know death. That great-minded man does not die even during the deluge of Brahmā.

"Then he should practise *dhāraṇā* for a period of six *ghatakās* (two hours, 24 minutes). Restraining the breath in (the region of) *ākāśa* and contemplating[1] on the deity who grants his wishes— this is said to be *saguṇa dhyāna* capable[2] of giving (the *siddhis*) *aṇimā*, etc. One who is engaged in *nirguṇa dhyāna* attains the stage of *samādhi*. Within twelve days at least, he attains the stage of *samādhi*. Restraining his breath, the wise one becomes an emanicipated person. *Samādhi* is that state in which the *jīvātmā* (lower self) and the *Paramātmā* (higher self) are differenceless (or of equal state). If he desires to lay aside his body, he can do so. He will become absorbed in *Parabrahman* and does not require *utkrānti* (going out or up). But if he does not so desire, and if his body is dear to him, he lives in all the worlds possessing the *siddhis* of *aṇimā*, etc. Sometimes he becomes a *deva* and lives honoured in svarga; or he becomes a man or an *yakṣa* through his will. He can also take the form of a lion, tiger, elephant, or horse through his own will. The *yogin* becoming the great Lord can live as long as he likes. There is difference only in the modes of procedure but the result is the same.

"Place the left heel pressed on the anus, stretch the right leg and hold it firmly with both hands, Place the head on the breast and inhale the air slowly. Restrain the breath as long as you can and then slowly breathe out. After practising it with the left foot, practise it with the right. Place the foot that was stretched before on the thigh. This is *mahābandha* and should be practised on both sides. The *yogin* sitting in *mahābandha* and having inhaled the air with intent mind, should stop the course of *vāyu* (inside) by means of the throat-*mudrā*, and occupying the two sides (of the throat) with speed. This is called *mahāvedha* and is frequently practised by the *siddhas*. With the tongue thrust into the interior cavity of the head (or throat) and with the eyes intent on the spot between the eyebrows, this is called *khecarīmudrā*. Contracting the muscles of the neck and placing the head with a firm will on the breast, this is called the *jālandhara* (*bandha*) and is a lion ot the elephant of death.That *bandha* by which *prāṇa* flies through *Suṣumnā* is called *uddiyāṇabandha* by the *yogins*. Pressing the heel firmly against the anus, contracting the anus and drawing up the *apāna*, this is said to be *yonibandha*. Through *mūlabandha*, *prāṇa* and *apāna* as well as *nāḍa* and *bindu* are united and gives success in *yoga* : there is no doubt about this. to one practising in a reversed manner (or on both sides) which destroyes all diseases, the gastric fie is increased. Therefore a practitioner should collect a large quantity of provisions, (for) if he takes a small quantity of food, the fire (within) will consume his body in a moment.

---

1. Lit., "with *guṇas*" and "without *guṇas*".
2. Ibid.

"On the first day, he should stand on his head with the feet raised up for a moment. He should increase this period gradually every day. Wrinkles and greyness of hair will disappear within three months. He who practises only for a period of a *yama* (twenty-four minutes) every day conquers time. he who practises *vajrolī* becomes a *yogin* and the respository of all *siddhis*. if the *yoga siddhis* are ever to be attained, he only has them within his reach. He knows the past and the future and certainly moves in the air. He who drinks of the nectar thus is rendered immortal day by day. He should daily practise *vajrolī*. Then it is called amarolī. Then he obtains the *rājayoga* and certainly he does not meet with obstacles. When a *yogin* fulfils his action by *rājayoga*, then he certainly obtain discrimination and indifference to objects. Viṣṇu, the great *yogin*, the grand one of great austerities and the most excellent *Puruṣa* is seen as a lamp in the path of truth.

"That breast from which one suckled before (in his previous birth) he now presses (in love) and obtains pleasure. He enjoys the same gential organ from which he was born before. She who was once his mother will now be wife and she who is now wife is (or will be) verily mother. he who is now father will be again son, and he who is now son will be again father. Thus are the egos of this world wandering in the womb of birth and death like a bucket in the wheel of a well and enjoying the worlds. There are the three worlds, three vadas, three *sandhyās*, (morning, noon and evening), three *svaras* (sounds), three *agnis*, and *guṇas*, and all these are placed in the three letters (*Om*). He who understands that which is indestructible and is the meaning of the three (*Om*)— by him are all these worlds strung. This is the Turth, the supreme seat. As the smell in the flower, as the ghee in the milk, as the oil in the gingelly seed and as the gold in the quartsz, so is he louts situated in the heart. Its face is downwards and its stem upwards. Its *bindu* is downwards and in its centre is situated *manas*. By the letter A, the lotus becomes expanded; by the letter U, it becomes spit (on opened), by the latter M, it obtains *nāda*; and the *ardhamātrā* (half-metre) is silence. The person engaged in *yoga* obtains the supreme seat, which is like a pure crystal, which is without parts and which destroys all sins. As a tortoise draws its hand and head within itself, so drawing in air thus and expelling it through the nine holes of the body, he breathes upwards and forwards, Like a lamp in an air-tight jar which is motionless, so that which is seen motionless through the process of *yoga* in the heart and which is free from turmoil, after having been drawn from the nine holes, is said to be *Ātmā* alone."

Thus ends the Upaniṣad

Dhyānabindu-Upaniṣad[1]

OF

SĀMAVEDA

Even if sin should accumulate to a mountain extending over many *yojanas* (distance), it is destroyed by *dhyānayoga*. At no time has been found a destroyer of sins like this. *Bījākṣara* (seed-letter) is the supreme bindu. *Nāda* (spiritual sound) is above it. When the *nāda* ceases along with letter, than the *nāda*-less is supreme state. That *yogins* who considers as the highest that which is above *nāda*, which is *anāhata*[2], has all his doubts destryoed. If the point of a hair be divided into one-hundred thousand parts, this (*nāda*) is one-half of that still further divided; and when (even) this is absorbed, the *yogin* attains to the stainless *Brahman*. One who is of a firm mind and without the delusion (of sensual pleasures) and ever resting in *Brahman*, should see like the string (in a rosary of beads) all creatures (as existing) in *Ātmā* like odour in flowers, ghee in milk, oil in gingelly seeds and gold in quartz. Again just as the oil depends for its manifestation upon gingelly seeds and odour upon flowers, so does the *Puruṣa* depend for its existence upon the body, both external and internal. The tree is with parts and its shadow is without parts but with and without parts, *Ātmā* exists everywhere.

The one *akṣara* (letter *Om*) should be contemplated upon as *Brahman* by all who aspire for emancipation. *Pṛthivī*, *agni*, *ṛgveda*, *bhūh* and Brahmā— all these (are absorbed) when *Akāra* (A), the first *aṁṣa* (part) of *Praṇava* (*Om*) becomes absorbed. *Antarikṣa*, *yajurveda*, *vāyu*, *bhuvah* and Viṣṇu, the *Janārdana*— all these (are absorbed) when *Ukāra* (U), the second *aṁṣa* of *praṇava* becomes absorbed. Dyur, sun, *sāmaveda*, *suvahu* and *Maheśvara*— all these (are absorbed) when *Makāra* (M), the third *aṁṣa* of *praṇava* becomes absorbed. *Akāra* is of (*pīta*) yellow colour and is said to be of *rajoguṇa*; *Ukāra* is of white colour and of *sattvaguṇa*; *Makāra* is of dark colour and of *tamoguṇa*. He who does not know *Omkāra* as having eight *aṅgas* (parts), four *pādas* (feet), three *sthānas* (seats) and five *devatās* (presiding deities) is not a *Brāhmaṇa*. *Praṇava* is the bow. *Ātmā* is the arrow and *Brahman* is said to be aim. One should aim at it with great care and then he, like the arrow, becomes one with It. When that Highest is cognised, all *karmas* return (from him, *viz.*, do not affect him). The Vedas have *Omkāra* as their cause. The *svaras* (sounds) have *Omkāra* as their cause. The three worlds with (all) the locomotive

1. The *Upaniṣad* of the seed of meditation.
2. Of the heart.

and the fixed (ones in them) have *Omkāra* as their cause. The short (accent of *Om*) burns all sins, the long one is decayless and the bestower of prosperity. United with *ardhamātrā* (half-metre of *Om*), the *praṇava* becomes the bestower of salvation. That man is the knower of the Vedas who knows that the end (*viz.*, *ardhamātrā*) of *praṇava* should be worshipped (or recited) as uninterrupted as the flow of oil and (resounding) as long as the sound of a bell. One should contemplate upon *Omkāra* as *Īśvara* resembling an unshaken light, as of the size of a thumb and as motionless in the middle of the pericarp of the lotus of the heart. Taking in *vāyu* through the left nostril and filling the stomach with it, one should contemplate upon *Omkāra* as being in the middle of the body and as surrounded by circling flames. Brahmā is said to be inspiration; Viṣṇu is said to be cessation (of breath), and *Rudra* is said to be expiration. These are the *devatās* of *Prāṇāyāma*. Having made *Ātmā* as the (lower) *araṇi* (sacrificial wood) and *praṇava* as the upper *araṇi*, one should see the God in secret through the practice of churning which is *dhyāna*. One should practise restraint of breath as much as it lies in his power along with (the uttering of) *Omkāra* sound, until it ceases completely. Those who look upon *Om* as of the form of *Haṁsa* staying in all, shining like crores of suns, being alone, staying in *gamāgama* (ever going and coming) and being devoid of motion— at last such persons are freed from sin. That *manas* which is the author of the actions (*viz.*,), creation, preservation and destruction of the three worlds, is (then) absorbed (in the supreme One). That is the highest state of Viṣṇu.

The lotus of the heart has eight petals and thirty-two filaments. The sun is in its midst : the moon is in the middle of the sun. *Agni* is in the middle of the moon : the *prabhā* (spiritual light) is in the middle of *agni*. *Pīṭha* (seat or centre) is in the midst of *prabhā*, being set in diverse gems. One should meditate upon the stainless Lord *Vāsudeva* as being (seated) upon the centre of *Pīṭha*, as having *Śrīvatsa*[1] (black mark) and *Kaustabha* (garland of gems) on his chest and as adorned with gems and pearls resembling pure crystal in lustre and as resembling crores of moons in brightness. He should meditate upon Mahā-Viṣṇu as above or in the following manner. (That is) he should meditate with inspiration (of breath) upon Mahā-Viṣṇu as resembling the atasī flower and as staying in the seat of navel with four hands; then with restraint of breath, he should meditate in the heart upon Brahmā, the Grandfather as being on the lotus with the *gaura* (pale-red) colour of gems and having four faces : then through expiration, he should meditate upon the three-eyed Śiva between the two eyebrows shining like the pure crystal, being stainless, destroying all sins, being in that which is like the lotus facing down with its flower (or face) below and the stalk above or like the flower of a plantain tree,

1. The black mark on the breast standing for *mūlaprakṛti* and the garland for the five elements.

being of the form of all Vedas, containing one hundred petals and one hundred leaves and having the pericarp full-expanded. There he should meditate upon the sun, the moon and the *agni*, one above another. Passing above through the lotus which has the brightness of the sun, moon and *agni*, and taking its Hrīm *bīja* (letter), one leads his *Ātmā* firmly. He is the knower of Vedas who knows the three seats, the three *mātrās*, the three Brahmās, the three *akṣaras* (letters) and the three *mātrās* associated with the *ardhamātrā*. He who knows that which is above bindu, *nāḍa* and *kalā* as uninterrupted as the flow of oil and (resounding) as long as the sound of a bell— that man is a knower of the Vedas. Just as a man would draw up (with his mouth) the water through the (pores of the) lotus-stalk, so the *yogin* treading the path of *yoga* should draw up the breath. Having made the lotus-sheath of the form of *ardhamātrā*, one should draw up the breath through the stalk (of the *nādis Suṣumnā*, *Iḍā* and *Piṅgalā*) and absorb it in the middle of the eyebrows. He should know that the middle of the eyebrows in the forehead which is also the root of the nose is the seat of nectar. That is the great place of *Brahman*.

Postures, restraint of breath, subjugation of the senses *dhāraṇā*, *dhyāna* and *samādhi* are the six parts of *yoga*. There are as many postures as there are living creatures; and *Maheśvara* (the great Lord) knows their distinguishing features. *Siddha*, *bhadra*, *siṁha* and *padma* are the four chief postures. *Mūlādhāra* is the first *chakra*. *Śvādhishthāna* is the second. Between these two is said to be the seat of yoni (perineum), having the form of *Kāma* (God of love). In tha *Ādhāra* of the anus, there is the lotus of four petals. In its midst is said to be the yoni called *Kāma* and worshipped by the *siddhas*. In the midst of the yoni is the *Liṅga* facing the west and split at its head like the gem. He who knows this, is a knower of the Vedas. A four-sided figure is situated above *agni* and below the genital organ, of the form of molten gold and shining like streaks of lightning. *Prāṇa* is with its *sva* (own) sound, having *Svādhishthāna* (seat), (or since *sva* of *prāṇa* arise from it). The *chakra Svādhishthāna* is spoken of as the genital organ itself. The *chakra* in the sphere of the navel is called *Maṇipūraka*, since the body is pierced through by *vāyu* like manuis (gems) by string. The *jīva* (ego) urged to actions by its past virtuous and sinful *karmas* whirls about in this great *chakra* of twleve[1] spokes, so long as it does not grasp the truth. Above the genital organ and below the navel is *kaṇda* of the shape of a bird's egg. There arise (from it) *nādis* seventy-two thousand in number. Of these seventy-two are generally known. Of these, the chief ones are ten and carry the *prāṇas*. *Iḍā*, *Piṅgalā*, *Sushumnā*, *Gāndhārī*, *Hastijihvā*, *Pūsā*, *Yaśasvinī*, *Alambusā*, *Kuhūh* and *Śāṅkhinā* are said tobe the ten. This *chakra* of the *nādis* should ever be known by the *yogins*. The three *nādis*

1. In other places, it is ten.

Iḍā, *Piṅgalā* and *Sushumnā* are said to carry *prāṇa* always and have as their *devatās*, moon, sun, and *agni*. *Iḍā* is on the left side and *Piṅgalā* on the right side, while the *Sushumnā* is in the middle. These three are known to be the paths of *prāṇa*. *Prāṇa*, *Apāna*, *Samāna*, *Udāna*, and *Vyāna*; *Nāga*, *Kūrma*, *Kṛkara*, *Devadatta* and *Dhanañjaya*; of these, the first five are called *prāṇas*, etc., and last five *Nāga*, etc. are called *vāyus* (or sub-*prāṇas*). All these are situated (or run along) the one thousand *nādis*, (being) in the form of (or producing) life. *Jīva* which is under the influence of *prāṇa* and *apāna* goes up and down. *Jīva* on account of its ever moving by the left and right paths is not visible. Just as a ball struck down (on the earth) with the bat of the hand springs up, so *jīva* ever tossed by *prāṇa* and *apāna* is never at rest. He is knower of *yoga* who knows that *prāṇa* always draws itself from *apāna* and *apāna* draws itself from *prāṇa*, like a bird (drawing itself from and yet not freeing itself) from the string (to which it is tied).

The *jīva* comes out with the letter Ha and gets in again with the letter Sa. Thus *jīva* always utters the *mantra* *'Haṁsa'*, *'Haṁsa'*. The *jīva* always utters the *mantra* twenty-one thousand and six hundred times in one day and night. This is called *Ajapā Gāyatrī* and is ever the bestower of *nirvāṇa* to the *yogins*. Through its very thought, man is freed froms ins. Neither in the past nor in the future is there a science equal to this, a japa equal to this or a meritorious action equal to this. *Parameśvarī* (*viz.*, *kuṇdalinī śakti*) sleeps shutting with her mouth that door which leads to the decayless *Brahma*-hole. Being aroused by the contact of *agni* with *manas* and *prāṇa*, she takes the form of a needle and pierces up through *Sushumnā*. The *yogin* should open with great effort this door which is shut. Then he will pierce the door to salvation by means of *kuṅdalinī*. Folding firmly the fingers of the hands, assuming firmly the *Padma* posture, placing the chin firmly onthe breast and fixing the mind in *dhyāna*, one should frequently raise up the *apāna*, fill up with air and then leave the *prāṇa*. Then the wise man gets matchless wisdom through (this) *śakti*. That *yogins* who assuming *Padma* posture worships (*i.e.*, conrols) *vāyu* at the door of the *nādis* and then performs restraint of breath is released without doubt. Rubbing off the limbs the sweat arising from fatigue, abandoning all acid, bitter and saltish (food), taking delight in the drinking of milk and *rasa*, practising celibacy, being moderate in eating and ever bent on *yoga*, the *yogin* becomes a *siddha* in little more than a year. No inquiry need be made concerning the result. *Kuṇdalinī śakti*, when it is up in the throat, makes the yogi get *siddhi*. The union of *prāṇa* and *apāna* has the extinction of urine and fæces.

One becomes young even when old through performing *mūlabandha* always. Pressing the yoni by means of the heels and contracting the anus and drawing up the *apāna*— this is called *mūlabandha*. *Uddiyāna bandha* is so called because it is (like) a great bird that flies up always without rest. One should bring the western part of the stomach above the navel. This *Uddiyāna bandha* is a lion to the elephant of death, since it binds the water (or nectar) of the *ākāśa* which arises in the head and flows down. The *Jālandhara bandha* is the destroyer of all the pains of the throat. When this *Jālandhara bandha* which is destroyer of the pains of the throat is performed, then nectar does not fall on *agni* nor does the *vāyu* move. When the tongue enters backwards into the hole of the skull, then there is the mudrā of vision latent in the eyebrow called *khecharī*. He who knows the mudrā, khecharī has not disease, death, sleep, hunger, thirst, or swoon. He who practises this *mudrā* is not affected by illness or *karma*; nor is he bound by the limitations of time. Since chitta moves in the kha (*ākāśa*) and since the tongue has entered (in the *mudrā*) *kha* (*viz.*, the hole in the mouth), therefore the *mudrā* is called *khecharī* and worshipped by the *siddhas*. He whose hole (or passage) above the uvula is closed (with the tongue backwards) be means of khecharīmudrā never loses his virility, even when embraced by a lovely woman. Where is the fear of death, so long as the bindu (virility) stays in the body. Bindu does not go out of the body, so long as the *khecharīmudrā* is practised. (Even) when bindu comes down to the sphere of the perineum, it goes up, being prevented and forced up by violent effort through *yonimudrā*. This bindu is twofold, white and red. The white one is called *śukla* and red one is said to contain much *rajas*. The *rajas* which stays in yoni is like the colour of a coral. The bindu stays in the seat of the genital organs. The union of these two moon and *rajas* is the sun. Through the union of these two is attained the highest body; when *rajas* is roused up by agitating the *śakti* through *vāyu* which unites with the sun, thence is produced the divine form. *Śukla* being united with the moon and *rajas* with the sun, he is a knower of *yoga* who knows the proper mixture of these two. The cleansing of the accumulated refuse, the unification of the sun and the moon and the complete drying of the rasas (essences), this is called *mahāmudrā*. Placing the chin of the breast, pressing the anus by means of the left heel, and seizing (the toe) of the extended right leg by the two hands, one should fill his belly (with air) and should slowly exhale. This is called *mahāmudrā*, the destroyer of the sins of men.

Now I shall give a description of *Ātmā*. In the seat of the heart is a lotus of eight petals. In its centre is *jīvātmā* of the form of *jyotiṣ* and atomic in size, moving in a circular line. In it is located everything. It knows everything. It does everything. It does all these actions attributing everything to its own power, (thinking) I do, I enjoy, I am happy, I am miserable, I am blind, I am lame, I am deaf, I am mute, I am lean, I am stout, etc. When it rests on the eastern petal which is of śveta (white) colour, then it has a mind (or is inclined) to *dharma* with bhakti (devotion). When it rests on the south-eastern petal, which is of *rakta* (blood colour), then it is inclined to sleep and laziness. When it rests on the southern petal, which is of *kṛṣṇa* (black) colour, then it is inclined to hate and ager. When it rests on the south-western petal which is of nīla (blue) colour, then it gets desire for sinful or harmful actions. When it rests on the western petal which is of crystal colour, then it is inclined to flirt and amuse. when it rests on the north-western petal which is of ruby colour, then it has a mind to walk, rove and have *vairāgya* (or be indifferent). When it rests on the northern petal which is *pīta* (yellow) colour, then it is inclined to be happy and to be loving. When it rests on the north-eastern petal which is of *vaidūrya* (lapis lazuli) colour, then it is inclined to amassing money, charity and passion. When it stays in the interspace between any two petals, then it gets the wrath arising from diesases generated through (the disturbance) of the equilibrium of) *vāyu*, bile and phlegm (in the body). When it stays in the middle, then it knows everything, sings, dances, speaks and is blissful. When the eye is pained (after a day's work), then in order to remove (its) pain, it makes first a circular line and sinks in the middle. The first line is of the colour of *bandhūka* flower (*Bassia*). Then is the state of sleep. In the mddle of the state of sleep is the state of dream,. In the middle of the state of dream, it experiences the ideas of perception, Vedas, inference, possibility, (sacred) words, etc. Then there arises much fatigue. In order to remove this fatigue, it circles the second line and sinks in the middle. the second is of the colour of (the insect) Indragopa (of red or white colour). Then comes the state of dreamless sleep.

During the dreamless sleep, it has only the thought connected with *Parameśvara* (the highest Lord) alone. This state is of the nature of eternal wisdom. Afterwards it attains the nature of the highest Lord (*Parameśvara*). Then it makes a round of the third circle and sinks in the middle. The third circle is of the colour of *padmarāga* (ruby). Then comes the state of turya (the fourth). In *turya*, there is only the connection of *Paramātmā*. It attains the nature of eternal wisdom. Then one should gradually attain the quiescence of *buddhi* with self-control. Placing the *manas* in *Ātmā*, one should think of nothing else. Then causing the union of *prāṇa* and *apāna*, he concentrates his aim upon the whole universe being of the nature of *Ātmā*. Then comes the state of *turyātīta* (*viz.*, that state beyond the fourth). Then everythig appears as bliss. He is beyond the pairs (of happiness and pains, etc.). He stays here as long as he should wear his body. Then he attans the nature of *Paramātmā* and attains emancipation through this means. this alone is the means of knowing *Ātmā*.

When *vāyu* (breath) which enters the great hole associated with a hall where four roads meet gets into the halp of the well-placed triangle[1], then is *Achyuta* (the indestructible) seen. Above the aforesaid triangle, one should meditate on the five *bīja* (seed) letters of (the elements) *pṛthivī*,

1. Probably it refers to the triangle of the initiates.

etc., as also on the five *prāṇas*, the colour of the bījas and their position. The letter य[1] is the *bīja* of *prāṇa* and resembles the blue cloud. The letter र is the *bīja* of *agni*, is of *apāna* and resembles the sun. The letter ल is the *bīja* of *pṛthivī*, is of *vyāna* and rsembless *bandhūka* flower. The letter व is the *bīja* of *jīva* (vīyu), is of *udāna* and is of the colour of the conch. The letter ह is the *bīja* of *ākāśa*, is of *samāna*, and is of the colour of crystal. *Prāṇa* stays in the heart, navel, nose, ear, foot, finger, and other places, travels through the seventy-two thousand *nādis*, stays in the twenty-eight crores of hair-pores and is yet the same everywhere. It is that which is called *jīva*. One should perform the three, expiration, etc., with a firm will and great control : and drawing in everything (with the breath) in slow degress, he should bind *prāṇa* and *apāna* in the cave of the lotus of the heart and utter *praṇava*, having contracted his throat and the genital organ. From the *Mūlādhāra* (to the head) is the *Sushumnā* resembliing the shining thread of the lotus. The *nāda* is located in the *Vīṇādanda* (spinal colum); that sound from its middle resembles (that of) the conch, etc. When it goes to the hole the *ākāśa*, it resembles that of the peacock. In the middle of cave of the skull between the four doors shines *Ātmā*, like the sun in the sky. Between the two bows in the Brahma-hole, one should see *Puruṣa* with *śakti* as his own *Ātmā*. Then his *manas* is absorbed there. That man attains *kaivalya* who understands the gems, moonlight, *nāda*, *bindu*, and the seat of *Maheśvara* (the great Lord).

Thus ends the Upaniṣad

1. There seems to be some mistake in the original.

Haṁsa[1]-Upaniṣad

OF

ŚUKLA-YAJURVEDA

Gautama addressed *Sanatkumāra* thus : "O Lord, thou art the knower of all *dharmas* and art well versed in all *Śāstras*, pray tell me the means by which I may obtain a knowledge of *Brahma-vidyā*. *Sanatkumāra* replied thus :

"Hear, O *Gautama*, that *Tattva* as expounded by *Pārvatī* after inquiring into all *dharmas* and ascertaining Śiva's opinion. This treatise on the nature of *Haṁsa* which gives the fruit of bliss and salvation and which is like a treasure to the *yogin*, is (a) very mystic (science) and should not be revealed (to the public).

"Now we shall explain the true nature of *Haṁsa* and *paramahaṁsa* for the benefit of a *brahmachārin* (a seeker after *Brahman* or celibate), who has his desires under control, is devoted to his *Guru* and always contemplates (as) *Haṁsa*, and realises thus : It (*Haṁsa*) is permeating all bodies like fire (or heat) in all kinds of wood or oil in all kinds of gingelly seeds. Having known (It) thus, one does not meet with death.

"Having contracted the anus (with the heels pressed against it), having raised the *vāyu* (breath) from (*Mūla*)[2] *Ādhāra* (*chakra*), having made circuit thrice round *Svādhishthāna*, having gone to *Maṇipūraka*, having crossed Anāhata, having controlled *Prāṇa* in *Viśuddhi* and then having reached *Ājñyā*, one contemplates in *Brahmarandhra* (in the head), and having meditated there always 'I am of three *mātrās*', cognises (his Self) and becomes formless. The *Śisna*[3] (penis) has two sides (left and right from head to foot). This is that *Paramahaṁsa* (Supreme *Haṁsa* or Higher Self) having the resplendence of crores of suns and bywhom all this world is pervaded.

---

1. This word "*Haṁsa*" is very mysterious and has manifold meanings according to different standpoints. It is composed of Ham (or Aham) and Sa (ha), which mean `I' (am) `that'. In its highest sense, it is *Kālahaṁsa* (or *Parabrahman*). It is also Brahmā when he has *Haṁsa* (or swan) as the vehicle of *Haṁsa-Vāhana*. When *Haṁsa* which is the manifestation of *Prāṇa* is applied to the human breath, we are said to exhale with Ha and to inhale with Sa. It is also called *Ajapā-Gāyatrī*.
2. The different chakras of those that are above the anus, inthe genitals; navel, heart, and throat, between the eyebrows and in the head.
3. This is omitted in the Calcutta edition and seemingly makes no sense here.

"It (this *Haṁsa* which has *buddhi* as vehicle)[1] has eight-fold *vṛtti*. (When it is) in the eastern[2] petal, there is the inclination (in a person) to virtuous actions; in the south-eastern petal, there arise sleep, laziness, etc.; in the southern, there is the inclination to cruelty; in the south-western, there is the inclation to sins; in the western, there is the inclination to sensual sport; in the north-western, there arise the desire of walking, and others; in the northern, there arises the desire of lust; in the north-eastern, there arises the desire of amassing money; in the middle (or the interpaces between the petals), there is the indifference to material pleasures. In the filament (of the lotus), there arises the waking state; in the pericarp, there arises the *svapna* (dreaming state); in the *bīja* (seed of pericarp), there arises the *suṣupti* (dreamless sleeping state); when leaving the lotus, there is the turya (fourth state). When *Haṁsa* is absorbed in *Nāda* (spiritual sound), the state beyond the fourth is reached. *Nāda* (which is at the end of sound and beyond speech and mind) is like a pure crystal extending from (*Mūla*) *Ādhāra* to *Brahmarandhra*. It is that which is spoken of as Brahmā *Paramātmā*.

"(Here the performance of *Ajapā Gāyatrī* is given).

"Now *Haṁsa* is the rusui; the metre is *Avyaktā Gāyatrī*; *Paramahaṁsa* is the *devatā* (or presiding deity) 'Ham' is the *bīja*; '*Sa*' is the *śaktī*' So'ham is the *kilaka*[3]. Thus there are six. There are 21,600 *Haṁsas* (or breaths)[4] in a day and night. (Salutation[5] to) *Surya*, *Soma*, *Nirañjana* (the stainless) and *Nirābhāsa* (the universeless). *Ajapā-mantra*. (May) the bodiless and subtle one guide[6] (or illuminate my understanding). *Vaushat* to *Agni-Soma*. Then *Aṅganyāsas* and *Karanyāsas* occur (or should be performed after the *mantras* as they are

1. This is how a commentator explains.
2. This refers to the different petals in the heart. vide the same in *Nārada-Parivrājaka* and *Dhyānabindu Upaniṣads*.
3. *Kīlaka* means wedge. In the *Ajapā mantra* `*Haṁsa-so'ham*', *So'ham* is the wedge to which the whole *mantra* is fastened.
4. One commentator gives the table for 21,600 thus : 60 breaths make one *Prāṇa*; 6 *Prāṇas*, one *nāḍī*; and 60 *nādis*, one day and night.
5. The words are : *Sūryāya*, *Somāya*, *Nirañjanāya*, *Nirabhāsāya*. It is with the pronunciation of these words that the different places in the body are touched, *viz.*, *Aṅganyāsas* and *Karanyāsas* are performed. The first word is pointed to the heart with the thumb; the second, to the head, and the third, to the hair of the head. Witht he last, a kavacha (armour) is made by circling the fingers round the head and then circling one hand over another. This process is carried on again after the pronunciation of *Ajapā mantra* which follows. Here *Soma* (moon) is that which is united with Umā or the emblem of the union of the lower and higher Selves. Sūrya or Sun is the causer of the state of one-ness.
6. As it stands, it means "the bodiless, the subtle and the guide. The original is *Atanu Sukṣmam Prachodayāt*.

performed before the *mantras*) in the heart and other (seats). Having done so, one should contemplate upon *Haṁsa* as the *Ātmā* in his heart. *Agni* and *Soma* are its wings (right and left sides); *Omkāra* is its head; *Ukāra* and bindu are the three eyes[1] and face rspectively; *Rudra* and *Rudrāṇī* (or *Rudra*'s wife) are the feet *kanthata* (or the realisation of the oneness of *jīvātmā* or *Haṁsa*, the lower self with *Paramātmā* or *Paramahaṁsa*, the Higher Self) is done in two ways, (*samprajñāta*[2] and *asamprajñāta)*.

"After that, *Unmanī*[3] is the end of the *Ajapā* (*Mantra*). Having thus reflected upon *manas* by means of this (*Haṁsa*), one hears *Nāda* after the uttering of this japa (*mantra*) a crore of times. It (*Nāda*) is (begun to heard as) of ten kinds. The first is chini (like the sound of that word); the second is chini-chini; the third is the sound of bell; the fourth is that of conch; the fifth is that of *tantri* (lute); the sixth is that sound of *tāla* (cymbals); the seventh is that of flute; the eighth is that of bheri (drum); the ninth is that of mṛdaṅga (double drum); and the tenth is that of clouds (*viz.*, thunder). He may experience the tenth without the first nine sounds (through the initiation of a *Guru*). In the first stage, his body becomes chini-chini; in the second, there is the (*bhañjana*) breaking (or affecting) in the body; in the third, there is the (bhedana) piercing; in the fourth, the head shakes; in the fifth, the palate produces saliva; in the sixth, nectar is attained; in the seventh, the knowledge of the hidden (things in the world) arises; in the eighth, *Parāvāk* is heard; in the ninth, the body becomes invisible and the pure divine eye is developed; in the tenth, he attains *Parabrahman* in the presence of (or with) *Ātmā* which is *Brahman*. After that, when *manas* is destroyed, when it which is the source of *saṅkalpa* and *vikalpa* disappears, owing to the destruction of these two, and when virtues and sins are burnt away, then he shines as *Sadāśiva* of the nature of *Śakti* pervading everywhere, being effulgence in its very essence, the immaculate, the eternal, the stainless and the most quiescent *Om*. Thus is the teaching of the Vedas."

Thus ends the Upaniṣad

---

1. The three eyes are the two eyes commonly now in use with the Divine eye.
2. Contemplation with an object as seed and the seedless one.
3. A state above *manas* or when *manas* is transcended.

Amṛtanāda-Upaniṣad[1]

OF

KṚṢṆA-YAJURVEDA

The wise having studied the *Śāstras* and reflected on them again and again and having come to know *Brahman*, should abandon them all like a firebrand. Having ascended the car of *Om* with Viṣṇu (the Higher Self) as the charioteer, one wishing to go to the seat of *Brahmaloka* intent on the worship of *Rudra*, should go in the chariot so long as he can go. Then abandoning the car, he reaches the place of the Lord of the car. Having given up *mātrās*, *linga*[2], and *pada*[3], he attains the subtle pada (seat or word) without vowels or consonants by means of the letter M without the *svara* (accent). That is called *pratyāhāra* when one merely thinks of the five objects of sense, such as sound, etc., as also the very unsteady mind as the reins of *Ātmā*. *Pratyāhāra* (subjugation of the senses), *dhyāna* (contemplation), *prāṇāyāma* (control of breath), *dhāraṇā* (concentration), *tārka*[4] and *samādhī* are said to be the six parts of *yoga*. Just as the impurities of mountain-minerals are burnt by the blower, so the stains committed by the organs are burned by checking *prāṇa*. Through *prāṇāyāmas* should be burnt the stains; through *dhāraṇā*, the sins; through *pratyāhāra*, the (bad) association; and through *dhyāna*, the godless qualities. Having destroyed the sins, one should think of *Ruchira* (the shining). *Ruchira* (cessation), expiration and inspiration— these three are *prāṇāyāma* of (*rechaka*, *pūraka* and *kumbhaka*) expiration, inspiration and cessation of breath. That is called (one) *prāṇāyāma* when one repeats with a prolonged (or elongated) breath three times the *Gāyatrī* with its vyāhrutis[5] and *Praṇava* (before it) along with the śiras (the head) joining after it. Raising up the *vāyu* from the *ākāśa* (region, *viz.*, the heart) and making the body void (of *vāyu*) and empty and uniting (the soul) to the state of void, is called *rechaka* (expiration). That is called *pūraka* (inspiration) when one takes in *vāyu*, as a man would take water into his mouth through the lotus-stalk. That is called *kumbhaka* (cessation of

1. The *upaniṣad* treating of *Nāda* (spiritual sound) which is *Amṛta* (nectar). Here *Prāṇas* are spoken of, as they produce *nāda* within and without.
2. It is said to be the subtle, gross and other microcosmic bodies. It also means sign.
3. It is said to be the macrocosmic bodies of *Virāṭ*, etc. it means a word or letter.
4. In this classification, *tāraka* is introduced newly. It means : the examination of the mind being attracted to objects and knowing that siddhis are impediments to progress.
5. The *vyāhṛtis* are *Bhūḥ*, *Bhuvaḥ*, etc., and the head of *Om*, *Āpo*, etc.

breath) when there is no expiration or inspiration and the body is motionless, remaining still in one state. Then he sees forms like the blind, hears sounds like the deaf and sees the body like wood. This is the characteristic of one that has attained much quiescence. That is called *dhāraṇā* when the wise man regards the mind as *saṅkalpa* and merging *saṅkalpa* into *Ātmā*, contemplates upon his *Ātmā* (alone). That is called *tāraka* when one makes inference which does not conflict with the Vedas. That is called *samādhi* in which one, on attaining it, thinks (all) equal.

Seating himself on the ground on a seat of *kuśa* grass which is pleasant and devoid of all evils, having protected himself mentally (from all evil influences), uttering *ratha-maṇḍala*[1], assuming either *padma*, *svastika*, or *bhadra* posture or any other which can be practised esily, facing the north and closing the nostril with the thumb, one should inspire through the other nostril and retain breath inside inside and preserve the *Agni* (fire). Then he should think of the sound (*Om*) alone. *Om*, the one letter is *Brahman*; *Om* should not be breathed out. Through this divine *mantra* (*Om*), it shoud be done many times to rid himself of impurity. Then as said before, the *mantra*-knowing wise should regularly meditate, beginning with the navel upwards in the gross, the primary (or less) gross and subtle (states). The greatly wise should give up all (sight) seeing across, up or down, and should practise *yoga* always being motionless and without tremor. The union as stated (done) by remaining without tremor in the hollow stalk (*viz.*, *Sushumnā*) alone is *dhāraṇā*. The *yoga* with the ordained duration of twelve *manrās* is called (*dhāraṇā*). That which never decays is *Akṣara* (*Om*) which is without *ghosha* (third, fourth, and fifth letters from K), consonant, vowel, palatal, guttural, nasal, letter R and sibilants. *Prāṇa* travels through (or goes by) that path through which this *Akṣara* (*Om*) goes. Therefore it should be practised daily, in order to pass along that (course). It is through the opening (or hole) of the heart, through the opening of *vāyu* (probably navel), through the opening of the head and through the opening of *mokṣa*. They call it bila (cave), sushira (hole), or *maṇḍala* (wheel)[2].

(Then about the obstacles of *yoga*). A *yogin* should always avoid fear, anger, laziness, too much sleep or waking and too much food or fasting. If the above rule be well and strictly practised each day, spiritual wisdom will arise of itself in three months without doubt. In four months, he sees the devas; in five months, he knows (or becomes) *Brahmaniṣṭha*; and truly in six months he attains *kaivalya* at-will. There is no doubt.

---

1. Lit., car-circle which is a mystical cakra or diagram for invoking the *devatā*; but some commentators make ratha mean *Om* : and maṇḍala, the circle of Śiva.
2. There are four openings in the body; three from which the astral, the lower mental and the higher mental bodies escape : the last being of turya.

That which is of the earth is of five *mātrās* (or it takes five *mātrās* to pronounce *Pārthiva-Praṇava*) That which is of water of four *mātrās*; of *agni*, three *mātrās*; of *vāyu*, two; and of *ākāśa*, one. But he should think of that which is with no *mātrās*. Having united *Ātmā* with *manas*, one should contemplate upon *Ātmā* by means of *ātmā*. *Prāṇā* is thirty[1] digits. long. Such is the position (ro range) of *prāṇas*. This is called *Prāṇa* which is the seat of the external *prāṇas*. The breaths by day and night are numbered as 1, 13, 180[2]. (Of the *prāṇas*) the firse (*viz.,*) *Prāṇa* is pervading the heart; *Apāna*, the anus; *samāna*, the navel; *Udāna*, the throat; and *Vyāna*, all parts of the body. Then come the colours of the five *prāṇas* in order. *Prāṇa* is said to be of the colour of a blood-red gem or coral); *Apāna* which is in the middle is of the colour of *Indra-gopa* (in insect of white or red colour); *Samāna* is between he colour of pure milk and crystal (or oily and shining), between both (*Prāṇa* and *Apāna*: *Udāna* is *apāṇdara* (pale white); and *Vyāna* resembles the colour of archis (or ray of light). That man is never reborn wherever he may die, whose breath goes out of the head after piercing through this *maṇḍala* (of the pineal gland). That man is never reborn.

Thus ends the Upaniṣad

---

1. As measured by the width of the middle finger : Yājñavalkya says, *Prāṇa* is 12 digits beyond the body.
2. One commentator makes it thus : Takin 21,600 for each of the five *Prāṇas*, we get 1,08,000 : for the five sub-*prāṇas*, 5 X 1036 is 5,180. Hence the total is 1,13.180. Another commentator makes it 21,600 alone.

Varāha[1]-Upaniṣad

OF

KṚṢṆA-YAJURVEDA

Chapter I

The great sage *Rubhu* performed penance for twelve deva (divine) years. At the end of the time, the Lord appeared before him in the form of a boar. He said : "Rise, rise and choose your boon." The sage got up and having prostrated himself before him said : "O Lord, I will not, in my dream, wish of thee those things that are desired by the worldy. All the Vedas, *Śāstras*, Itihāsa[2] and all the hosts of the other sciences, as well as Brahmā and all the other *Devas*, speak of emancipation as resulting from a knowledge of thy nature. So Impart to me that science of *Brahman* which treats of thy nature."

Then the boar-shaped *Bhagavān* Lord) said : "Some disputants hold that there are twenty-four tattvas (principles) and some thirty-six, whilst other maintain that there are ninety-six. I shall relate them in their order. Listen with an attentive mind. The organs of sense are five, *viz.*, ear, skin, eye and others, The organs of action are five, *viz.*, mouth[3], hand, leg and others, *Prāṇas* (vital airs) are five ; sound and other (*viz.*, rudimentary[5] principles) are five[4]. *Manas*, *buddhi*, *citta* and *ahaṁkāra* are four ; thus those that know *Brahman* know these to be the twenty-four tattvas. Besides these, the wise hold the quintuplicated elements to be five, *viz.* : earth, water, fire, *vāyu* and *ākāśa*; the bodies to be three, *viz.*, : the gross, the subtle and the *kāraṇa* or causal; the states of consciousness to be three *viz.*, : the waking, the dreaming and the dreamless sleeping. The munis know the total collection of *tattvas* to be thirty-six (coupled with *jīva*).

"With these *tattvas*, there are six changes, *viz.* : existence, birth, growth, transformation, decay and destruction. Hunger, thirst, grief, delusion, old age and death are said to be the six infirmities. Skin, blood, flesh, fat, marrow and bones are said to be the six sheaths. Passion, anger, avarice, delusion, pride and malice are the six kinds of foes. *Viśva,*

---

1. This means boar refers to the incarnation of Viṣṇu as a boar.
2. Books such as *Mahābhāra* and *Rāmāyaṇa.*
3. *Prāṇa*, *Apāna*, *Udāna*, *Vyāna* and *Samāna*, having their respective places and functions in the body.
4. Sound, touch, form, taste and odour.
5. Producing respectively uncertainty, certain knowledge, fluctuation of thought, and egoism and having certain centres in the body.

Taijasa and *prājña*[1] are the three aspects of the *jīva*. *Sattva*, *rajas* and *tamas* are the three *guṇas* (qualities). *Prārabdha*[2], *sañcita* and *āgāmin* are the three *karmas*. Talking, lifting, walking, excerting and enjoying the five actions (of the organs of action); and there are also thought, certainly, egoism, compassion, memory (funtions of *manas*, etc.,), complacency, sympathy and indifference : dik (the quarters, *Vāyu*, Sun, Varuṇa[3], *Aśvini* devas[4], *Agni*, *Indra*, *Upendra*[5], and *Mṛtyu* (death) : and then the moon, the fourfaced Brahmā *Rudra*, *Kṣetrajña*[6], and *Īśvara*. Thus these are the ninety-six *tattvas*. Those that worship, with devotion, me of the form of boar, who am other than the aggregate of these tattvas and am without decay are released from *ajñāna* and its effects and becoms *jīvanmuktas*. Those that know these ninety-six tattvas will attain salvation in whatever order of life they may be, whether they have[7] matted hair of are of shaven head or have (only) their tuft of hair on . There is no doubt of this. Thus ends the first chapter."

Chapter II

The great *Ṛbhu* (again) addressed the Lord of *Lakśmī* of the from of boar thus : "O Lord, place initiate me into the supreme *Brahmavidyā* (or science)." Then the Lord who removes the miseries of his devotees being thus questioned, answered thus : "Through (the right observance of) the duties of one's own caste and orders of life, through religious austerities and through the pleasing of the *Guru* (by serving him rightly), arise to persons the four, *vairāgya*, etc. They are the discrimination of the eternal from the non-external; indifference to the enjoyments of this and the other worlds: acquisition of the six virtues, *sama*[8], etc., and the longing after liberation. These should be practised. Having subdued the sensual organs and having given up the conception of 'mine' in all objects, you should place your consciousness of 'I' in (or identify yourself with) me, who am the witness caitanya (consciousness). To be born as a human being is difficult— more difficult it is to be born as a male being— and more so is it to be born as a *Brāhman*. Even then, if the fool does not cognise

1. In the states of waking, dreamless sleeping.
2. Being past *karmas* now being enjoyed, past *karmas* being in store to be enjoyed hereafter and the *karmas* now produced to be enjoyed hereafter.
3. Presiding over water or tongue.
4. Presiding over odour or nose.
5. Presiding over leg or nether world.
6. *Vide* the translation of *Sarvasātra Upaniṣad.*
7. This refers to the several class of persons in different modes of life who wear their hair in different ways as *yogins*, ascetics and so on.
8. Meaning respectively mental restraint, bodily restraint, the renunciation or practising of works without reference to their fruits, endurance of heart and soul, etc. faith and settled peace of mind.

through the hearing[1], etc., of *vedānta*, the ture nature of the *Sacicidānanda* (of *Brahman*) that is all-prevading, and that is beyond all caste and orders of life, when will he obtain *mokṣa*? I alone am happiness. There is none other. If there is said to be another, then it is not happiness. There is no such things as love, except on my account. The love that is on account of me is not natural to me. As I am the seat of supreme love, that 'I am not' is not. He who is sought after by all, saying "I should become such", is myself, the all-pervading. How can non-light affect *Ātmā*, the self-shining which is no other than the light whence originates the words 'I am not light'. My firm conviction is, whoever knows for certain that (*Ātmā*) which is self-shining and has itself no basis (to rest upon), is one of *vijñāna*.

"The universe, *jīva*, *Īśvara*, *māyā* and others do not really exist, except, my full *Ātmā*. I have not their characteristics. *Karma* which has *dhāraṇa* and other attributes and is of the form of darkness and *ajñāna* is not fit to touch (or effect) me, who am *Ātmā*, the self-resplendent. That man who sees (his) *Ātmā* which is all-witness and is beyond all caste and orders of life as of the nature of *Brahman*, becomes himself *Brahman*. Whoever sees, through the evidence of *Vedānta*, this visible universe as the Supreme Seat which is of the form of light, attains *mokṣa* at once. When that knowledge which dispels the idea that this body (alone) is *Ātmā*, arises firmly in one's mind as was before the knowledge that this body (alone) is *Ātmā*, then that person, even though he does not desire *mokṣa*, gets it. Therefore how will a person be bound by *karma*, who always enjoys the bliss of *Brahman* which has the characteristics of *Saccidānanda*, and which is other than *ajñāna*? Persons with spiritual eyes see *Brahman*, that is the witness of the three states that has the characteristics of be-ness, wisdom and bliss, that is the underlying meaning of the words 'Thou' (*Tvam*) and 'I' (*Aham*), and that is untouched by all the stains. As a blind man does not see the sun that is shining, so an ignorant person does not see (*brahman*). *Prajñāna* alone is *Brahman*. It has truth and *prajñāna* as its characteristics. By thus cognising *Brahman* well, a person becomes immortal. One who knows his own *Ātmā* as *Brahman*, that is bliss, and without duality and guṇas (qualities), and that is truth and absolute consciousness is not afraid of anything. That which is consciousness alone which is all-pervading, which is eternal, which is all-full, which is of the form of bliss, and which is indestructible, is the only true *Brahman*. It is the settled determination of *Brahmajñanīs* that there is naught else but that. As the world appears dark to the blind and bright to those having good eyes, so this world full of manifold miseries to the ignorant is full of happiness of the wise. In

1. Meaning meditation and reflection there.

me, of the form of boar, who am infinite and the Bliss of absolute Consciousness, if there is the conception of non-dualism, where then is bondage? And who is the one to be emancipated? The real nature of all embodied objects is ever the absolute Consciousness. Like the pot seen by the eyes, the body and its aggregates are not (*viz.,* do not really exist). Knowing, as *Ātmā*, all the locomotive and fixed worlds that appear as other than *Ātmā*, meditate upon them as 'It I am'. Such a person then enjoy his real nature. There is no other to be enjoyed than one-Self. If there is anything that is then *Brahman* alone has that attribute. One who is perfect in *Brahmajñāna*, though he always sees this established universe, does not see it other than his *Ātmā*. By cognising clearly my form, one is not trammelled by *karma*. He is an undaunted person who by his own experience cognises as his own real nature all (the universe and *Brahman*) that is without the body and the organs of sense— that is the all-witness— that is the one noumenal *vijñāna*, that is the blissful *Ātmā* (as contrasted with *jīvātmā* or the lower self) and that is self-resplendent. He is one that should be known as . . . (myself). O *Ṛbhu*, may you become He. After this, there will be never any experience of world. Thereafter there will always be the experience of wisdom of one's own true nature. One who has thus known fully *Ātmā* has neither emancipation nor bondage. Whoever meditates, even for the *muhūrta* (48 minutes) through the cognition of one's own real form, upon Him who is dancing as the all-witness, is released from all bondage. Prostrations— prostrations to me who am in all the elements, who am the *Cidātmā* (*viz., Ātmā* of the nature of wisdom) that is eternal and free and who am the *Pratyagātmā*. O *Devtā*, you are I. I am you. Prostrations on account of myself and yourself who are infinite and who are *Cidātmā*, myself being the supreme *Īśa* (Lord) and yourself being Śiva (of a beneficent nature). What should I do ? Where should I go? What should I reject? (Nothing, because) the universe is filled by me as with the waters of the universal deluge. Whoever gives up (fond) love of the external, love of the internal and love of the body and thus gives up all associations, is merged in me. There is no doubt about it. That *Parmahaṁsa* (ascetic) who, though living in the world, keeps aloof frim human congregation as from serpent, who regards a beautiful woman as a (living) corpse and the endless sensual objects as position, and who has abandoned all passion and is indifferent towards all objects is no other than *Vāsudeva,*[1] (*viz.,*) myself. This is *satya* (truth). This is nothing but truth. It is turth alone that is now said. I am *Brahman*, the turth. There is naught else but I.

"(The world) '*Upavāsa*' (lit., dwelling near) signifies the dwelling near (or union) of *jīvātmā* and *Paramātmā* and not (the religious

1. *Viz.,* Viṣṇu, the Lord of all persons.

observance as accepted by the worldy of) emanciating the body through fasts. To the ignorant, what is the use of the mere drying up of the body? By beating about the hole of a snake, can we be said to have killed the big snake within. A man is said to attain *parokṣa* (indirect) wisdom when he knows (theoreticaly) that there is *Brhaman*; but he is said to attain *sākṣ ātkāra* (direct cognition) when he knows (or realises) that he is himself *Brahman*. When a *yogin* knows his *Ātmā* to be the absoulte, then he becomes a *jīvanmukta*. To *mahātmās*, to be always in the state 'I am *Brahman*' conduces to their salvation. There are two words for bondage and *mokṣa*. They are 'mine' and 'not mine'. Man is bound by 'mine', but he is relased by 'not time'. He should abandon all the thoughts relating to externals and so also with reference to internals. O *Ṛbhu* haivng given up all thoughts, you should rest content (in your *Ātmā*) ever.

"The whole of the universe is caused through *saṅkalpa* alone. It is only through *saṅkalpa* that the universe manifests. Having abandoned the universe, which is of the form of *saṅkalpa* and having fixed our mind upon the *nirvikalpa* (one which is changeless), meditate upon my abode in your heart. O most intelligent being, pass your time in meditating upon me, glorifying me in songs, talking about me to one another and thus devoting yourself entirely to me as the Supreme. Whatever is *cit* (consciousness) in the universe in only *Cinmātra*. This universe is *Cinmaya* only. You are *Cit*. I am *Cit* : contemplate upon the worlds also as *Cit*. Make the desire *nil*. Always be without any stain. How then can the bright lamp of *Ātmic vijñāna* arising through the Vedas be affected by the *karma* arising from the ignorance of the actor and the agent? Having given up not-*Ātmā* and being in the world unaffected by it, delight only in the *Cnimātra* within, ever intent on the One. As the *ākāśa* of the pot and that of the house are both located in all-pervading *ākāśa*, so the jīvas and *Īśvara* are only evolved out of me, the *cidākāśa* (the one *ākāśa* of universal consciousness). So that which did not exist before the evolution of *Ātmās* (*jīvas* and *Īśvara*) and that which is rejected at the end (*viz.*, universal deluge) is called *māyā* and its effects (the universe) be annihilated, there is no state of *Īśvara*, there is no state of *jīva*. Therefore like the *ākāśa* without its vehicle, I am the immaculate and *Cit*.

"The creation, sentient as well as non-sentient from *īkṣaṇā* (thinking) to *praveśa* (entry) (as stated in *Chāndogya-Upaniṣad*, *Prapāthaka* VI, *Khaṇḍas* II and III) of those having the forms of *jīvas* and *Īśvara* is due to the creation (or illusion) of *Īśvara*; while the saṁsāra (worldly existence) from the waking state to salvation is due to the creation of *jīva*. So the *karmas* ordained in the sacrifice (called) *Triṇācaka* (so called after *Naciketas* of *Kaṭhaupaniṣad*) to *yoga* are dependent upon the illusion of *Īśvara*; while (the systems form) *Lokāyata* (atheistical system) to *sāṁkhya* rest on the illusion of *jīva*. Therefore aspirants after salvation should never make their heads enter into the field of controversy regarding *jīva* and *Īśvara*. But with an undistrubed mind, the tattvas of *Brahman* should be investigated. Those who do not cognise the *tattva* of the secondless *Brahman* are all deluded person only. Whence (then) is salvation of them? Whence then is happiness (to them) in this universe? What if they have the thoughts of superiority and inferiority (of *Īśvara* and *jīva*)? Will soveregnty and mendicancy (experienced by a person) in the dreaming state affect him in his waking state? When *buddhi* is absorbed in *ajñāna*, then it is termed, by the wise, sleep. Whence then is sleep to me who have not *ajñāna* and its effects? When *buddhi* is in full bloom, then it is said to be the jāgrat (waking state). As I have no changes, etc., there is no waking state to me). The moving about of *buddhi* in the subtle *nādis* constitutes the dreaming state. In me without the act of moving about, there is no dreaming. Then at the time of *suṣupti* when all things are absorbed, enveloped by tamas, he then enjoys the highest bliss of his own nature in an invisible state. If he sees everything as *Cit* without any differnce, he alone is an actual *vijñānī*, He alone is Śiva. He alone is Hari. He alone is Bahmā. This mundane existence which is an ocean of sorrow, is nothing but a long-lived dream, or an illusion of the mind or a long-lived reign of the mind. From the rising from sleep till going to bed, the one *Brahman* alone should be contemplated upon. By causing to be absorbed this universe which is but a super-imposition, the *citta* partakes of my nature. Having annihilated all the six powerful enemies, through their destruction become the non-dual. One like the scent-elephant. Whether the body perishes now or lasts the age of moon and stars, what matters it to me having *Cit* alone as my body? What matters it to the *ākāśa* in the pot, whether it (the pot) is destroyed now or exists for a long time. While the slough of a serpent lies cast off lifeless in its hole, it (the serpent) does not evince any affection towards it. Likewise the wise do not identify themselves with their gross and subtle bodies. If the delusive knowledge (that the universe is real) with its cause should be destroyed by the fire of *ātmajñāna*, the wise man becomes bodiless, through the idea 'It (*Brahman*) is not this; It is not this.' Through the stduy of *Śāstras*, the knowledge of reality (of the universe) perishes. Through direct perception of truth, one's fitness for action (in this universe) ceases. With the cessation of prārabdha (the portion of the past *karma* which is being enjoyed in this life), the destruction of the manifestation (of the universe) takes place. *Māyā* is thus destroyed in a threefold manner. If within himself no identification (of *jīva*) with *Brahman* takes place, the state (of the separateness) of *jīva* does not perish. If the non-dual one is truly discerned, then all affinities (for objects) cases. With the cessation of prārabdha (arising from the cessation of affinities), there is that of the body. Therefore it is certain that *māyā* perishes thus entirely.

"If it is said that all the universe is, that *Brahman* alone is that is of the nature of Sat. If it is said that the universe shines, then it is *Brahman* alone that shines. (The mirage of) all the water in an oasis is really no other than the oasis itself. Through inquiry of one's Self, the three worlds (above, below and middle) are only of the nature of *Cit*. In *Brahman*, which is one and alone, the essence of whose nature is absolute Consciousness and which is remote from the differences of *jīva*, *Īśvara* and *Guru*, there is no *ajñāna*. Such being the case, where then is the occasion for the universe there ? I am that *Brahman* which is all full. While the full moon of wisdom is robbed of its lustre[1] by the rāhu (one of the two nodes of the moon) of delusion, all actions such as the rites of bathing, alms-giving and sacrifice performed during the time of eclipse are all fruitless. As salt dissolved in water becomes one, so if *Ātmā* and *manas* become indentified, it is termed *samādhi*. Without the grace of a good (perfect) *Guru*, the abandonment of sensual objects is very difficult of attainment; so also the perception of (divine) truth and the attainment of one's true state. Then the state of being in one's own self shines of its own accord in a *yogin* in whom jñanaśakti[2] has dawned and who has abandoned all *karmas*. The (property of) fluctuation is natural to mercury and mind. If either mercury is bound (or consolidated) or mind is bound (or controlled),[3] what then on this earth cannot be accomplished? He who obtains *mūrcchā* cures all diseases. The dead are brought to life again. He who has bound (his mind or mercury) is able to move in the air. Therefore mercury and mind confer upon one the state of *Brahman*. The master of indryas (the organs) is *manas* (mind). The master of *manas* is *prāṇa*. The master of *prāṇa* is laya (absorption *yoga*). Therefore laya-*yoga* should be practised. To the *yogins*, laya (-*yoga*) is said to be without actions and changes. This laya (absorption) of mind which is above speech and in which one has to abandon all *saṅkalpas* and to give up completely all actions, should be known through one's own (experience). As an actress, though subject (or dancing in harmony) to music, cymbals and other musical instruments of time, has her mind intent upon the protection of the pot on her head, so the *yogin*, though intent for the time being upon the hosts of objects, never leaves off the mind contemplating on *Brahman*. The person who desires all the wealth of *yoga* should, after having given up all thoughts, practise with a subdued mind concentration on *nāda* (spiritual sound) alone."

---

1. During the solar and lunar eclipses, these rites are done by the Hindus.
2. Of the saktis, she is one that gives wisdom.
3. Either controlling the breath through *prāṇāyāma* or the consolidation of mercury through some means, leading in both cases to siddhis, etc.

Chapter III

"The One Principle cannot at any time become of manifold forms. As I am the partless, there is none else but myself. Whatever is seen and whatever is heard is no other than *Brahman*. I am that *Parabrahman*, which is the eternal, the immaculate, the free, the one, the undivided bliss, the non-dual, the truth, the wisdom, and the endless. I am of the nature of bliss; I am of undivided wisdom; I am the supreme of the supreme; I am the resplendent absolute Consciousness. As the clouds do not touch the *ākāśa*, so the miseries attendant of mundane existence do not affect me. Know all to be happiness through the annihilation of sorrow and all to be of the nature of sat (be-ness) through the annihilation of asat (not be-ness). It is only the nature of *Cit* (Consciousness) that is associated with this visible universe. Therefore my form is partless. To an exalted *yogin*, there is neither birth nor death, nor going (to other spheres), nor returning (to earth); there is no stain or purity or knowledge but (the universe) shines to him as absolute Consciousness. Practise always silence 'I am (*viz.*, that you yourself are) *Parabrahman*' which is truth and absolute Consciousness, which is undivided and non-dual, which is invisible, which is stainless, which is pure, which is secondless, and which is beneficent. It (*Brahman*) is not subject to birth and death, happiness and misery. It is not subject to caste, law, family and gotra (clan). Practice silence— I am *Cit* which is the *vivarta-upādāna*[1] (*viz.*, the illusory cause) of the universe. Always practice silence— I am (*viz.*, you are) the *Brahman*, that is the full, the secondless, the undivided consciousness which has neither the relationship nor the diferences existing in the universe and which partakes of the essence of the non-dual and the supreme Sat and *Cit*.

"That which always is and that which preserves the same nature during the three periods of time, unaffected by anything, is my eternal from Sat. Even the state of happiness which is eternal without upādhis (vehicles) and which is superior to all the happiness derivable from *suśupti* is of my bliss only. As by the rays the sun, thick gloom is soon destroyed, so darkness, the cause of rebirth is destroyed by Hari (Viṣṇu) *viz.*, the sun's lustre. Through the contemplation and worship of my (Hari's) feet, every person is delivered from his ignorance. The *manas* of destroying deaths and births is only through the contemplation of my feet. As a lover of wealth praises a wealthy man, so if with earnestness a

---

1. Of the two causes of the universe, Spirit in the nimitta (instrumental) causes while matter is the *upādāna* (material) cause. This material cause is again subdivided into three : *viz., ārambha* (initial), *pariṇāma* (changed) and vivarta (illusory). The first or material cause may be exemplified by the cotton or woollen threat being the without changing the threads; the second by milk which becomes curd; the thrid by a serpent being the illusory cause of a rope, for here through illusion we mistake the rope for the serpent.

person praises the Cause of the universe, who will not be delivered from bondage?

"As in presence of the sun the world of its own accord begins to perform its actions, so in my presence all the worlds are animated to action. As to the mother-of-pearl, the illusory conception of silver is falsely attributed, so to me is falsely attributed through *māyā* this universe which is composed of mahat, etc. I amnot with those differences that are (observable) in the body of low caste men, the body of cow, etc., the fixed ones, bodies of *brāhmaṇas* and others. As to a person, even after being relieved from the misconception of the directions, the (same misconception of) direction continues (as before) just so is to me the universe through destroyed by *vijñana*. Therefore the universe is not. I am neither the body nor the organs of sense and action, nor *prāṇas*, nor *manas*, nor *buddhi*, nor *ahaṁkāra*, nor *citta*, nor *māyā*, nor the universe including *ākāśa* and others. Neither am I the actor, the enjoyer, nor he who causes the enjoyment. I am *Brahman* that is *Cit*, *Sat* and *Ānanada* alone and that is *Janārdana* (Viṣṇu).

"As, through the fluctuation of water, the sun (reflected therein) is moved, so *Ātmā* arises in this mundane existence through its mere connection with *ahaṁkāra*. This mundane existence has *citta* as its root. This (*citta*) should be cleansed by repeated effort. How is it you have your confidence in the greatness of *citta*? Alas, where is all the wealth of the kings ! Where are the Brahmās? Where are all the worlds ? All old ones are gone. Many fresh evolutions have occurred. Many crores of Brahmās have passed away. Many kings have fitted away like particles of dust. Even to a *jñānī*, the love of the body may arise through the asure (demoniacal) nature. If the asura nature should arise in a wise man, his knowledge of truth becomes fruitless. Should *rajas* and other generated in us be burnt by the fire of discriminative (divine) wisdom, how can they germinate again? Just as a very intelligent person delights in the shortcomings of another, so if one finds out his own faults (and corrects them) who will not be relived from bondage? O Lord of munis, only he who has not *ātmajñāna* and who is not an emancipated person, longs after siddhis. he attains such *siddhis* through medicine , (or wealth), *mantras*, religious works, time and skill. In the eyes of an *ātmajñanī*, these siddhis are of no importance. One who has become an *ātmajñānī*, one who has his sight solely on *ātmā*, and one who is content with *Ātmā* (the higher self) through (his) *ātmā* (or the lower self), never follows (the dictates of) *avidyā*. Whatever eixsts in this world, he knows to be of the nature of *avidyā*. How then will an *ātmajñānī* who has relinquished *avidyā* be immersed in (or affected by) it. Through medicine. *mantras*, religious work, time and skill (or mystical expressions) lead to the development of

1. The mystic Hindu Tamil books teem with works on medicine through which the higher siddhis can be developed.

siddhis, yet they cannot in any way help one to attain the seat of *Paramātmā*. How then can who is *ātmājñānī* and who is without his mind be said to long after *siddhis*, while all the actions of his desires are controlled?

Chapter IV

On another occasion *Nidāgha* asked Lord *Ṛbhu* to enlighten him as to the characteristics of *jīvanmukti*.[1] To which *Ṛbhu* replied in the affirmative and said the following :

"In the seven *bhūmikās* (states of development of wisdom) there are four kinds of *jīvanmuktas*[2]. Of these the first stage[3] is *śubhecchā* (good) desire); the second is *vicāraṇā* (inquiry); the third is *tanumānasī* (or attainment of *śattva*); the fifth is *asamsakti* (non-attachment); the sixth is the *padārthabhāvanā* (analysis of objects) and the seventh is the *turya* (fourth or final stage). The *bhūmikā* which is of the form of *praṇava* (*Om*) is formed of (or is divided into) *akāra*— A, *ukāra*— U, *makāra*— M, and *ardhamātrā*. *Akāra* and other are of four kinds on account of the differnce of *sthūla* (gross), *sūkṣma* (subtle,) *bīja* (seed or causal), and *sākṣī* (witness.) Their *avasthās* are four : waking, dreaming, dreamless sleeping and turya (fourth). He who is in (or the entity that identifies itself with) the waking state in the gross *amśa* (essence or part) of *akāra* is named *Viśva*; in the subtle essence, he is termed *Taijasa*; in the *bīja* essence, he is termed *Prājña*; and in the sākṣī essence, he is termed *Turya*.

"He who is in the dreaming state (or the entity which identifies itself with the dreaming state) in the gross essence of *ukāra* is *Viśva*; in the subtle essence, he is termed *Taijasa*; in the *bīja* essence, is termed *Prājñā*; and in the *sākṣī* essence, he is termed *Turya*.

"He who is in the *suṣupti* state in the gross essence of *makāra* is termed *Viśva*; in the subtle essence. *Taijasa*; in the *bīja* essence, he is termed *Prājña*; and to the sākṣī essence, he is termed *Turya*.

"He who is in *turya* state in the gross essence of *ardhamātrā* is termed *Turya-viśva*. In the subtle, he is termed *Taijasa*; in the *bīja* essence, he is termed *Prājña*; and in the *sākṣī* essence, he is termed *Turya-turya*.

"The *turya* essence of *akāra* is (or embraces) the first, second and third (bhūmikās or stages of the seven). The turya essence of *ukāra* embraces the fourth *bhūmikā*. The turya essence of *makāra* embraces the fifth *bhūmikā*. The turya essence of *ardhamātrā* is the sixth stage. Beyond this, is the seventh stage.

---

1. *Jīvanmukti* is emancipation. *Jīvanmuktas* are those that have attained emancipation.
2. Ibid.
3. This word and others are explained in full later on in the text.

"One who functions in the (first) three *bhūmikā* is called *mumukṣu*; one who functions in the fourth *bhūmikā* is called *brahmavit*; one who functions in the sixth *bhūmikā* is called a *brahmavidvara*; one who functions in the sixth *bhūmikā* is called a *brahmavidvarīya*; and one in the seventh *bhūmikā* is called a *brahmavidvariṣṭha*. With reference to this, there are *ślokas*. They are :

"*Śubhecchā* is said to be the first *jñanabhūmi*) or stage of wisdom); *vichāraṇā*, the second; *tanumānasī*, the third; *sattvāpatti*, the fourth; then come *asaṃsakti* as the fifth, *padārthabhāvanā* as the sixth and *turya* as the seventh.'

"The desire that arises in one through sheer *vairāgya* (after resolving) 'Shall I be ignorant ? I will be seen by the *Śāstras* and the wise (or I will study the books and be with the wise)' is termed by the wise as *Śubhecchā*. The association with the wise and *Śāstras* and the following of the right path preceding the practice of indifference is termed *vicāraṇā*. That stage wherein the hankering after sensual objects is thinned through the first and second stages is said to be *tanumānasī*. That stage wherein having become indifferent to all sensual objects through the exercise in the (above) three stages, the purified *citta* rests on *Ātmā* which is of the nature of sat is called *sattvāpatti*. The light (or manifestation) of *sattvaguṇa* that is firmly rooted (in one) without any desire for the fruits of actions through the practice in the above four stages is termed *asamsakti*. That stage wherein through the practice in the (above) five stages one, having found delight in *Ātmā*, has no conception of the internals or externals (through before him) and engages in actions only when impelled to do so by others is termed *padārthabhāvanā*, the sixth state. The states wherein after exceedinlgy long practice in the (above) stages one is (immovably) fixed in the contemplation of *Ātmā* alone without the difference (of the universe) is the seventh stage called turya. The three stages beginning with *Śubhecchā* are said to be attained with (or amidst) differences and non-differences. (Because) the universe one sees in the waking state he thinks to be really existent. when the mind is firmly fixed on the non-dual. One and the conception of duality is put down, then he sees this universe as a dream through his union with the fourth stage. As the autumnal cloud being dispersed vanishes, so this universe perishes. O *Nidāgha*, be convinced that such a person has only *sattva* remaining. Then having ascended the fifth stage called *suśuptipada* (dreamless sleeping seat), he remains simply in the non-dual state, being freed from all the various differences. Having always introvision though ever participating in external actions, those that are engaged in the practice of this (sixth stage) are seen like one sleeping when fatigued (*viz*., being freed from all affinities). (Lastly) the seventh stage which is the ancient and which is called *gūdhasupti*[1] is generally attained. Then one

1. Lit., secret sleep.

remains in that secondless state without fear and with his consciousness almost annihilated where there is neither sat nor asat, neither self nor not-self. Like an empty pot in the *ākāśa*, there is void both within and, without; like a filled vessel in the midst of an ocean, he is full both within in without. Do not become either the knower or the known. May you become the Reality which remains after all thoughts are given up. Having discarded (all the distinctions of) the seer, the sight and the seen with their affinities, meditate solely upon *Ātmā* which shines as the supreme Light.

"He is said to be a *jīvanmukta* (emancipated person) in whom, thought participating in the material concerns of the world, the universe is not seen to exist like the invisible *ākāśa*. He is said to be a *jīvanmukta*, the light of whose mind never sets or rises in misery or happiness, and who does not seek to change what happens to him (*viz.*, either to diminish his misery or increase his happiness). He is said to be a *jīvanmukta* who thought in his *suṣupti* is awake and to whom the waking state is unknown and whose wisdom is free from the affinities (of objects).

"He is said to be a *jīvanmukta* whose heart is pure like *ākāśa*, though acting (as if) in consonance to love, hatred, fear and others. He is said to be a *jīvanmukta*, who has not the conception of his being the actor and whose *buddhi* is not attached to material objects, whether he performs actions or not. He is said to be a *jīvanmukta*, of whom people are not affraid, who is not afraid of people and who has given up joy, anger and fear. He is said to be a *jīvanmukta* who, though participating in all the illusory objects, is cool amidst them and is a full *Ātmā*, (being) as if they belonged to other. O muni, he is called a *jīvanmukta* who, having eradicated all the desires of his *citta*, is (fully) content with me who am the *Ātmā* of all. He is said to be a *jīvanmukta* who rests with an unshaken mind in that all pure abode which is *Cinmātrā* and free from all the modifications of *citta*. he is said to be a *jīvanmukta* in whose *citta* do not dawn (the distinctions of) the universe, I, he, thou and others that are visible and unreal. Through the path of the *Guru* and *Śāstras*, enter soon Sat— the *Brahman* that is immutable, great, full and without objects— and be firmly seated there. Śiva alone is *Guru*; Śiva alone is Vedas; Śiva alone is Lord; Śiva alone is I; Śiva alone is all. There is none other than Śiva. The undaunted *Brāhmaṇa* having known Him (Śiva) should attain wisdom. One need not utter many words as they but injure the organs of speech.

"The *Ṛṣi*) *Śuka*[1] is mukta (emancipated person). (The *Ṛṣi*) *Vāmadeva* is a mukta. There are no others (who have attained emancipation) than through these (*viz.*, the two paths of these two *Ṛṣis*). Those brave men who follow the path of *Śuka* in this world become *sadyomuktas* (*viz.*, emancipated) immediately after (the body were away); while those who

1. Śuka is a *Ṛṣi*, the son of the present Vyāsa and the narrator of *Bhāgavata Purāṇa*. Vāmadeva is also a *Ṛṣi*.

always follow the path of *vedānta* in this world are subject again and again to rebirths and attain *krama* (gradual) emancipation, through *yoga, sāṁkhya* and *karmas* associated with *Sattva (guṇa)*. Thus there are two paths laid down by the Lord of *Devas (viz.,)* the *Śuka* and *Vāmadeva* paths. The *Śuka* path[1] is called the bird's path : while the *Vāmadeva* path is called the ant's path. Those persons that have cognised the true nature of their *Ātmā* through the mandatory and prohibitory injunctions (of the Vedas), the inquiry into (the true meaning of) *mahāvākyas* (The sacred sentences of the Vedas), the *samādhi* of *sāṁkhya yoga* or *assamprajñāta samādhi*[2] and that have thereby purified themselves, attain the supreme seat through the *Śuka* path. Having, through haṭhayoga[3] practice with the pain caused by *yama*, postures, etc., become liable to the ever recurring obstacles caused by *aṇimā* and other (siddhis) and having not obtained good results, one is born again in a great family and practises *yoga* through his previous (*kārmic*) affinities. Then through the practice of *yoga* during many lives, he attains salvation (*viz.,*) the supreme seat of Viṣ ṇu through the Vāmadeva path. Thus there are two paths that lead to the attainment of *Brahman* and that are beneficent. The one confers instantaneous salvation and the other confers gradual salvation.

"To one that sees (all) as the one (*Braham*), where is delusion? Where is sorrow? Those that are under the eyes of those whose bulddhi is solely occupied with the truth (of *Brahman*) that is the end of all experience are released from all heinous sins. All beings inhabiting heaven and earth that fall under the vision of *Brahmavits* are at once emancipated from the sins committed during many crores of births."

Chapter V

Then *Nidāgha* asked Lord *Ṛbhu* to enlighten him as to the rules (to be observed) in the practice of *Yoga*. Accrodingly He (the Lord) said thus:

"The body is composed of the five elements. It is filled with five maṇḍalas (spheres)[4]. That which is hard is Pṛthivī (earth), one of them; that which is liquid is *Apas*; that which is bright is Tejas (fire); motion is the property of *vāyu*; that which pervades everywhere in *Ākāśa*. All these

---

1. Bird's path like birds which fly at once to the place they intend to go; ant's path, like ants which move slowly.
2. It is that of intense self-absorption when one loses his consciousness of individuality.
3. *Hathayoga*, as stated in Patañjali's *Yoga* philosophy.
4. There are either the five elements or *Mūlādhāra* (sacral plexus), *Svādhiṣthāna* (epigastric or prostatic plexus), *maṇipūraka* (solar plexus), *Anāhata* (cardiac plexus) and *visuddhi* (laryngeal or pharyngeal plexus). There are situated respectively in the anus, the geneital organs, navel, heart and throat. The last or the sixth plexus is omitted here, as the five plexuses mentioned above correspond to the five elements. This chapter treating of *yoga* is very mystical.

should be known by an aspirant after *Yoga*. Through the blowing of *Vāyumaṇḍala* in this body, (there are caused) 21,600 breahts every day and night. If there is a diminution in the *Pṛthivīmiṇḍala*, there arise folds in the body; if there is diminution in the essence of *Āpas*, there arises gradually greyness of hair; if there is diminution in the essence of *Tejas*, there is loss of hunger and lustre; if there is diminution in the essence of *Vāyu*, there is incessant tremor; if there is diminution in the essence of *Ākāśa*, one dies. The *jīvita* (*viz., Prāṇa*) which possesses these elements havings no place to rest (in the body) owing to the diminution of the elements, rises up like birds flying up in the air. It is for this reason that it is called *Udyāna* (lit., flying up). With reference to this, there is said to be a *bandha* (binding, also meaning a posture called *Uddiyāṇabandha*, by which this flight can be arrested). This *Uddiyānabandha*[1] is to (or does away with) death, as alion to an elephant. Its experiene is in the body, as also the *bandha*. Its binding (in the body) is hurtful. If there is agitation of *Agni* (fire) within the belly, then there will be caused much of pain. Therefore this (*Uddiyānabandha*) should not be practised by one who is hungry or who has urgency to make water or void excrement. He should take many times in small quantities proper and moderate food. He should practise *Mantrayoga*[2], Layayoga and Haṭhayoga, through mild, middling and transcendental methods (or periods) respectively. *Laya*, *Mantra*, and Haṭhayogas have each (the same) eight subservients. They are *yama*, *niyama*, *āsana*, *prāṇāyāma*, *pratyāhāra*, *dhāraṇā*, *dhyāna*, and *samādhi*[3]. (Of these), *yama* is of ten kinds. They are non-injury, truth, non-coveting continence, compassion, straight forwardness, patience, courage, moderate eating, and purity (bodily and mental). *Niyama* is of ten kinds. They are tapas (religious austerities), contentment, belief in the existence of God or Vedas, charity, worship of *Īśvara* (or God), listening to the exposition of religious doctrines, modesty, a (good) intellect, japa (muttering or Prayers), and vrata (religious observances). There are eleven postures beginning with cakra. *Cakra*, *padma*, *kūrma*, *mayūra*, *kukkuta*, *vīra*, svastika, *bhadra*, *siṁha*, *mukta*, and *gomukha*, are the postures enumerated by the knowers of *yoga*. Placing the left ankle on the right thigh and the right ankle is the posture "*Cakra*". *Prāṇāyāma* should practised again and again in the following order, *viz.*, inspiration, restraint of breath and expiration. The *prāṇāyāma* is done through the *nādis* (nerves). Hence it is called the *nādis* themselves.

---

1. This is one of the postures treated of in *Śiva saṁhitā* and other books.
2. There are four kinds of *yoga*—the fourth being *Rājayoga*. Mantrayoga is that is which perfection is obtained through the pronunciation of *mantras*. Layayoga is that in which perfection is obtained through laya (absorption).
3. They mean respectively forebearance, religious restraint, posture, restraint of breath subjugation of the senses, contemplation, meditation, and intense self-absorption.

"The body of every sentient being is ninety-six digits long. In the middle of the body, two digits above the anus and two digits below the sexual organ, is the centre of the body (called *Mūlādhāra* or sacral plexus). Nine digits above the genitals, there is kanda of *nādis* which revolves oval-shaped, four digits high and four digits broad. It is surrounded by fat, flesh, bone, and blood. In it, is situate a *nādi-cakra* (wheel of nerves) having twelve spokes. *Kuṇḍalī* by which this body is supported is there. It is covering by its face the *Brahmarandhra* (*viz.*, Brahmā's hole) of *Suṣumnā*. (By the side) of *Suṣumnā* dwell the *nādis* *Alambusā* and Kuhūḥ. In the next two (spokes) are *Vāruṇā* and *Yaśaśvinī*. On the spoke south of *Suśumnā* is, in regular course *piṅgalā*. On the next two spokes, are *Pūṣa* and *Payaśvinī*, On the spoken west of *Suśumnā* is the nādi called Payaśvinī. On the spoke west of *Suśumnā* is the nāḍi called *Sarasvatī*. On the next two spokes are *Śaṁkhinī* and *Gāndhārī*. To the north of *Suśumnā* dwells *Iḍā*; in the next is *Hastijihvā*; in the next is *Viśvodarā*. In these spokes of the wheel, the twelve *nādis* carry the twelve *vāyus* from left to right (to the different parts of the body). The *nādis* are like (*i.e.*, woven like the warp and woof of) cloth. They are said to have different colours. The central portion of the cloth (here the collection of the *nādis*) is called the *nābhicakra* (navel plexus). *Jvalantī, Nādarūpinī, Pararandhrā*, and *Suśumnā* are called the (basic) supports of *nāda* (spiritual sound). These four *nādis* are of ruby colour. The central portion of *Brahmarandhra* is again and again covered by *Kuṇḍalī*. Thus ten *vāyus* move in these *nādis*. A wise man who has understood the course of *nādis* and *vāyus* should, after keeping his neck and body erect with his mouth closed, contemplate immovably upon turyaka (*Ātmā*) at the tip of his nose, in the centre of his heart and in the middle of *bindu* . and should see, with a tranquil mind through the (mental) eyes, the nectar flowing from there. Having closed the anus and drawn up the *vāyu* and caused it to rise through (the repetition of) *praṇava* (*Om*), he should complete with *Śrī bīja*. he should contemplate upon his *Ātmā* as Śrī (or Parāśakti) and as being bathed by nectar. This is *Kālavañcana* (lit., time illusion). It is said to be the most important of all. Whatever is thought of by the mind is accomplished by the mind itself. (Then) *agni* (fire) will flame in *jala* (water) and in the flame (of *agni*) will arise the branches and blossoms. Then the words uttered and the actions done regarding the universe are not in vain. By checking the bindu in the path, by making the fire flame up in the water and by causing the water to dry up, the body is made firm. Having contracted simultaneously the anus and yoni (the womb) united together, he should draw up *Apāna* and unite with it *Samāna*. He should contemplate upon his *Ātmā* as Śiva and then as being bathed on nectar. In

1. Lit., germ.

the central part of each spoke, the *yogin* should commence to concentrate bala (will or strength). He should try to go up by the union of *Prāṇa* and *Apāna*. This most important *yoga* brightens up in the body the path of *siddhis*. As a dam across the water serves as an obstacle to the floods, so it should ever be known by the *yogins* that the *chayā* of the body is (to *jīva*). This *bandha* is said of all *nādīs*. Through the grace of this *bandha*, *Devatā* (goddess) becomes visible. This *bandha* of four feet serves as a check to the three paths. This brightens up the path through which the *siddhas* obtained (their *siddhis*). If with *Prāṇa* is made to rise up soon *Udāna*, this *bandha* checking all *nādis* goes up. This is called *Samputayoga* or *Mūlabandha*. Through the practising of this *yoga*, the three band has are mastered. By practising day and night intermittingly or at any convenient time, the *vāyu* will come under his control. With the control of *vāyu*, *agni* (the gastric fire) in the body will increase daily. With the increase of *agni*, food, etc., will be easily digested. Should food be properly digested, there is increase of *rasa* (essence of food). With the daily increase of rasa, there is the increase of *dhātus* (spiritual substances). With the increase of *dhātus*, there is the increase of wisdom in the body. Thus all the sings collected together during many crores of births are burnt up.

"In the centre of the anus and the genitals, there is the triangular *Mūlādhāra*. It illumines the seat of Śiva of the from of bindu. There is located the Parāśakti named *kuṇḍalinī*. From the seat, *vāyu* arises. From the seat, *agni* becomes increased. From that seat, *bindu* originates and *nāda* becomes increased. From that seat, *Haṁsa* is born. From that seat, *manas* is born. The six cakras beginning with *Mūlādhāra* are said to be the seat of *Śakti* (Goddess). From the neck to the top of the head is said to the seat of *Śambhu* (Śiva). To the *nādis*, the body is the support (or vehicle); to *Prāṇa*, the *nādis* are the support; to *jīva*, *Prāṇa*, is the dwelling place; to *Haṁsa*, *jīva* is the support; to *Śakti Haṁsa* is the seat and the locomotive and fixed universe.

"Being without distraction and of a calm mind, one should practise *prāṇāyāma*. Even a person who is well-skilled in the practice of the three bandhas should try always to cognise with a true heart that Principle which should be known and is the cause of all objects and their attributes. Both expiration and inspiration should (be stopped and made to) rest in restraint of breath (alone). He should depend solely on *Brahman* which is the highest aim of all visibles. (The giving out of) all external objects is said to be recaka (expiration). The (taking in of the) spiritual knowledge of the *Śāstras* is said to be *pūraka* (Inspiration) and (the keeping to oneself of) such knowledge is said to be kumbhaka (or restraint of breath). He is an emancipated person who practises thus such a *citta*. There is no doubt about it. Through *kumbhaka*, it (the mind) should be always taken up, and through kumbhaka alone it should be filled up within. It is only through kumbhaka that *kumbhaka* should be firmly mastered. Within it is *Paramaśiva*. That (*vāyu*) which is non-motionless should be shaken again through *kaṇṭha-mudrā* (throat-posture). Having checked the course of *vāyu*, having become perfect in the practice of expiration and restraint of breath and having planted evenly on the ground the two hands and the two feet, one should pierce the four seats through *vāyu* through the three yogas. He should shake *Mahāmeru* with the (aid of) prakotis (forces)[1] at the mouth of *vāyu*. The two *putas* (cavities) being drawn, *vāyu* throbs quickly. The union of moon, sun and *agni* should be known on account of nectar. Through the motion of Meru, the *devatās* who stay in the centre of *Meru* move. At first in his *Brahmagranthi*, there is produced soon a hole (or passage). Then having pierced *Brahmagranthi*, he pierces Viṣṇu-granthi : then he pierces *Rudra-granthi*. Then to the *yogin* comes *vedha*[2] (piercing) through his liberation from the impurities of delusion, through the religious ceremonies (performed) in various births, through the grace of *Gurus* and *devatās* and through the practice of *yoga*.

"In the *maṇḍala* (sphere or region) of *Suśumnā* (situated between *Iḍā* and *Piṅgalā*, *vāyu* should be made to rise up through the feature known as *Mudrā-bandha*. The short pronunciation[3] (of *Praṇava*) frees (one) from sins : its long pronunciation confers (on one) *mokṣa*. So also its pronunciation in *āpyāyana* or pluta *svara* (tone). He is a knower of Veda, who through the above-mentioned three ways or pronunciation knows the end of *Praṇava* which is beyond the power of speech, like the never-ceasing flow of oil or the long-drawn bell-sound. The short svara goes to bindu. The long svara goes to *brahmarandhara* : the pluta to *dvādaśānta* (twelfth centre). The *mantras* should be uttered on account of getting *mantra siddhis*. This *Praṇva* (*Om*) will remove all obstacles. It will remove all sins. Of this, are four *bhūmikās* (states) predicated, *viz.*, *ārambha, ghata, paricaya*, and *niṣpatti*. *Ārambha* is that state in which one having abandoned external *karmas* performed by the three organs (mind, speech and body), is always engaged in mental *karma* only. It is said by the wise that the *ghata* state is that in which *vāyu* having forced an opening on the western side and being full, is firmly fixed there. *Paricaya* state is that in which *vāyu* is firmly fixed to *ākāśa*, neither associated with *jīva* nor not, while the body is immovable. It is said that niṣpatti state is that in which there take place creation and dissolution through *Ātmā* or

---

1. It is mystic here and later on.
2. He has pierced all the granthis and hence becomes a master of vedha.
3. There are the three kinds of pronunciation with 1. *mātrā*, 2. *mātrā* and 3. *mātras*. They are respectively hrasva, *dīrgha* and *pluta* which may be translated as short, long and very long.

that state in which a *yogin* having become a *jīvanmukta* performs *yoga* without effort.

"Whoever recites this *Upaniṣad* becomes immaculate like *agni*. Like *vāyu*, be becomes pure. He becomes freed from the sin of drinking alcohol. He becomes freed from the sins of the theft of gold. He becomes a *Jīvanmukta*. This is what is said by the *Ṛgveda*. Like the eye pervading the *ākāśa* (seeing without effort everything above), a wise man sees (always) the supreme seat of Viṣṇu. The *brāhmaṇas* who have always their spiritual eyes wide open praise and illuminate in diverse ways the spritiual seat of Viṣṇu.

Thus ends the Upaniṣad

Maṇḍalabrāhmaṇa-Upaniṣad[1]

OF

ŚUKLA-YAJURVEDA

Brāhmaṇa I

Om. The great Muni *Yājñavalkya* went to *Ādityaloka* (the sun's world) and saluting him (the *Puruṣa* of the sun) said: "O reverened sir, describe to me the *Ātmā-tattva* (the *tattva* or truth of *Ātmā*)."

(To which), Nārāyaṇa (*viz.,* the *Puruṣa* of the sun) replied : "I shall describe the eightfold *yoga* together with *Jñāna*. The conquering of cold and heat as well as hunger and sleep, the preserving of (sweet) patience and unruffledness ever and the restraining of the organs (from sensual objects)— all these come under (or are) *yama*. Devotion to one's *Guru*, love of the true path, enjoyment of objects producing happiness, internal satisfaction, freedom from association, living in a retired place, the controlling of the *manas* and the not longing after the fruits of actions and a state of *vairāgya*— all these consitute *niyama*. The sitting in any posture pleasant to one and clothed in tatters (or bark) is prescribed for *āsana* (posture). Inspiration, restraint of breath and expiration, which have respectively 16, 64 and 32 (*mātrās*) constitute *prāṇāyāma* (restraint of breath). The restraining of the mind from the object of senses is *pratyāhāra* (subjugation of the senses). The contemplation of the oneness of consciousness in all objects is *dhyāna*. The mind having been drawn away from the objects of the senses, the fixing of the caitanya (consciousness) (on one alone) is *dhāraṇā*. The forgetting of oneself in *dhyāna* is *samādhi*. He who thus knows the eight subtle parts of *yoga* attains salvation.

"The body has five stains (*viz.,*) passion, anger, outbreathing, fear, and sleep. The removal of these can be effected respectively by absence of *saṅkalpa*, forgiveness, moderate food, carefulness, and a spiritual sight of tattvas. In order to cross the ocean of *saṁsāra* where sleep and fear are the serpents, injury, etc., are thewaves, *tṛṣṇā* (thirst) is whirlpool, and wife is the mire, one should adhere to the subtle path and overstepping

---

1. *Maṇḍala* means sphere. As the *Puruṣa* in the maṇḍala or sphere of the sun gives out this *Upaniṣad* to Yājñavalkya, hence it is called *Maṇḍala-Brāhmaṇa*. It is very mystic. There is a book called *Rājayoga Bhāṣya* which is a commentary thereon; in the light of it which is by some attributed to Śrī Saṅkarācārya, notes are given herein.

tattva[1] and other *guṇas* should look out for *Tāraka*[2]. *Tāraka* is *brahman* which being in the middle of the two eyebrows, is of the nature of of the spiritual effulgence of *Saccidānanda*. The (spritual) seeing through the three *lakṣyas* (or the three kinds of introvision) is the means to It (*Brahman*). *Suṣumnā* which is from the *mūlādhāra* to *brahma- randhra* has the radiance of the sun. In the centre of it, is *kuṇḍalinī* shining like crores of lightning and subtle as the thread in the lotus-stalk. Tamas is destroyed there. Through seeing it, all sins are destroyed. When the two ears are closed by the tips of the forefingers, a *phūtkāra* (or booming) sound is heard. When the mind is fixed on it, it sees a blue light between the eyes as also in the heart. (This is *antarlakṣya* or internal introvision). In the *bahirlakṣya* (or internal introvision) one sees in order before his nose at distance of 4, 6, 8, 10, and 12 digits,the space of blue colour, then a colour resembling *Śyāma* (indigo-black) and then shining as *rakta* (red) wave and then with the two *pīta* (yellow and orange red) colours. Then he is a *yogin*. When one looks at the external space, moving the eyes and sees streaks of light at the corners of his eyes, then his vision can be made steady. When one sees jyotis (spiritual light) above his head 12 digits in length, then he attains the state of nectar. In the *madhyalakṣya* (or the middle one), one sees the variegated colours of the morning as if the sun, the moon and the fire had joined together in the *ākāśa* that is without them. Then he comes to have their nature (or light). Through practice, he becomes one with *ākāśa*. devoid of all *guṇas* and peculiarities. As first *ākāśa* with its shining starts becomes to him *Parākāśa* as dark as *tamas* itself, and he becomes one with *Parākāśa* shining with stars and sleep as tamas. (Then) he becomes one with *Mahā-ākāśa* resplendent (as) with the fire of the deluge. Then he becomes one with *Tattva-ākāśa*, lighted with the brightness which is the highest and the best of all. Then he becomes one with *Sūrya-ākāśa* (sun-*ākāśa*) brightened by a crore of suns. By practising thus, he becomes one with them. He who knows them becomes thus.

"Know that *yoga* is twofold through its division into the *pūrva* (earlier) and the *uttara* (latter). The earlier is tāraka and the later is *amanaska* (the mindless). *Tāraka* is divided into *mūrti* (with limitation) and *amūrti* (without limitation. That is *mūrti tāraka* which goes to the end of the sence (or eixsts till the sense are conquered). That is *amūrti tāraka* which goes beyond the two eyebrows (above the senses). Both these

1. Comm.: Rising above the seven *Prāṇas*, one should with introvision cognise in the region of *Ākāśa*, Tamas and should then make Tamas get into *Rajas*, *Rajas* into *Sattva*, *Sattva* into Nārāyaṇa and Nārāyaṇa, into the Supreme One.
2. *Taraka* is from *tṛ.*, cross, as it enables one to cross saṁsara. The higher vision is here said to take place in a centre between the eyebrows—probably in the brain.

should be performed through *manas*. *Antaridṛṣṭi* (internal vision) associated with *manas* comes to aid *tāraka*. Tejas (spiritual light) appears in the hole between the two eyebrows. This *tāraka* is the earlier one. The later is *amanaska*. The great jyotis (light) is above the root of the palate. By seeing it, one gets the *siddhis aṇimā*. etc. *Śāmbhavī-mudrā* occurs when the *lakṣya* (spiritual vision) is internal while the (physical) eyes are seeing externally without winking. This is the great science which is concealed in all the tantras. When this is known, one does not stay in *saṁsāra*. Its worship (or practice) gives salvation. *Antarlakṣya* is of the nature of Jalajyotis (or waterjyotis). It is known by the great *Ṛṣis* and is invisible both to the internal and external sences.

"Sahasrāra[2] (*viz.,* the thousand-petalled lotus of the pineal gland) Jalajyotis is the *antarlakṣya*. Some say the form of *Puruṣa* in the cave of *buddhi* beautiful in all its parts is *antarlakṣya*. some again say that the all-quiescent *Nīlakaṇṭha* accompanied by *Umā* (his wife) and having five mouths and later in the midst of the sphere in the brain is *antarlakṣya*. Whilst others say that the *Puruṣa* of the dimension of a thumb is *antarlakṣya*. A few again say *antarlakṣya* is the One Self made supreme through introvision in the state of *jīvanmukta*. all the differents statements above made pertain to *Ātmā* alone. He alone is a *Brahmaniṣṭha* who sees that the above *lakṣya* is the pure *Ātmā*. The *jīva* which in the twenty-fifth *tattva*, having abandoned the twenty-four *tattvas*, becomes a *jīvanmukta* through the conviction that the twenty-sixth *tattva* (*viz.,*) *Paramātmā* is 'I' alone. Becoming one with *antarlakṣya* (*brahman*) in the emancipated state by means of *antarlakṣya* (introvision), *jīva* becomes one with the partless sphere of *Paramākāśa*.

"Thus ends the first *Brāhmaṇa*."

Brāhmaṇa II

Then *Yāñavalkya* asked the *Puruṣa* in the sphere of the sun : "O Lord, *antarlakṣya* has been described many times, but it has never has understood by me (clearly). Pray describe it to me. "He replied : "It is the source of the five elemnts, has the lustre of many (streaks of) lightning, and has four seats having (or rising from) 'That' (*Brahman*). In its midst, there arises the manifestation of *tattva*. It is very hidden and unmanifested. It can be known (only) by who has go into the boat of *jñāna*. It is the object of both bahir and antar (external and internal) *lakṣ yas*. In its midst is absorbed the whole world. It is the vast partless

1. The commentator puts it as 12 digits above the root of the palate—perhaps the *Dvādaśānta* or twelfth centre corresponding to the pituitary body.
2. The commentator to support the above that *antarlakṣya, viz., Brahman* is jala, or water-*jyotis* quotes the *Prāṇāyāma-Gāyatrī* which says : "*Om Āpo jyotī-raso'amṛtam-brahma,* etc."—*Āpo-jyotis* or water-*jyotis* is *Brahman*.

universe beyond *Nāda*, Bindu and *Kalā*. Above it (*viz.,* the sphere of *agni*) is the sphere of the sun; in its midst is the sphere of the nectary moon; in its midst is the sphere of the partless *Brahma-tejas* (or the spiritual effulgence of *Brahman*). It has the brightness of *Śukla* (white light)[1] like the ray of lightning. It alone has the characteristic of *Śāmbhavī*. In seeing this, there are three kinds of dṛṣṭi (sight) *viz., amā* (the new moon), pratipat (the first day of lunar fortnight), and *pūrṇimā* (the full moon). The sight of *amā* is the one (seen) with closed eyes. That with half opened eyes is pratipat; while that with fully opened eyes is *pūrṇimā*. Of these, the practice of *pūrṇimā* should be resorted to. Its lakṣ ya (or aim) is the tip of the nose. Then is seen a deep darkness at the root of the palate. By practising thus, a jyotis (light) of the form of an endless sphere is seen. This alone is *Brahman*, the *Saccidānanda*. When the mind is absorbed in bliss thus naturally produced, then does *Śāmbhavī* take place. She (*Śāmbhavī*) alone is called *Khecarī*. By practising it (*viz.,* the *mudrā*), a man obtains firmness of mind. Through it, he obtain firmness of *vāyu*. The following are the signs : first it is seen like a star; then a reflecting (or dazzling) diamond[2]; then the sphere of full moon; then the sphere of the brightness of nine gems; then the sphere of the midday sun; then the sphere of the flame of *agni* (fire); all these are seen in order.

"(Thus much for the light in pūrva or first stage.) Then there is the light in the weastern direction (in the uttara or second stage). Then the lustres of crystal, smoke, bindu, *nāda*, *kalā*, star, firefly, lamp, eye, gold, and nine gems, etc. are seen. This alone is the form of *Praṇava*. Having united *Prāṇa* and *Apāna* and holding the breath in *kumbhaka*, one should fix his concentration at the tip of his nose and making *śaṇmukhi*[3] with the fingers of both his hands, one hears the sound of Pranva (*Om*) in which *manas* becomes absorbed. Such a man has not even the touch of *karma*. The *karma* of (*Sandhyāvandana* or the daily prayers) is verily performed at the rising or setting of the sun. As there is no rising or setting (but only the ever shining) of the sun of *Cit* (the higher consciousness) in the heart of a man who knows thus, he has no *karma* to perform. Rising above (the conception of) day and night through the annihilation of sound and time, he becomes one with *Brahman* through the all-full *jñāna* and the attaining of the state of *unmanī* (the state above *manas*). Through the state of *unmanī*, he becomes *amanaska* (or without *manas*).

---

1. Comm. : *Śukla* is *Brahman*.
2. The original is, 'Vajra-Darpaṇam'.
3. Ṣaṇmukhi is said to be the porcess of hearing the internal sound by closing the two ears with the two thumbs, the two eyes with the two forefingers, the two notrils with the two middle fingers, and the mouth with the remaining two fingers of both hands.

"Not being troubled by any throughts (of the world) then constitutes of *dhyāna*[1]. The abandoning of all *karmas* constitutes *āvāhana* (invocation of god). Being firm in the unshaken (spiritual) wisdomconstitutes *āsana* (posture). Being in the state of *unmanī* constitutes the *pādya* (offering of water for washing the feet of god). Preserving the state of *amanaska* (when *manas* is offered as sacrifice) constitutes the *arghya* (offering of water as ablation generally). Being in state of eternal brightness and shoreless nectar constitutes *snāna* (bathing). The contemplation of *Ātmā* as present in all constitutes (the application to the idol of) *sandal*. The remaining in the real state of ḍṛk (spiritual eye) is (the worshipping with) *akṣata* (non-broken rice). The attaining of *Cit* (consciousness) is (the worshipping with) flower. The real state of *agni* (fire) of *Cit* is the dhūpa (burning of incense). The state of the sun of *Cit* is the dīpa (light waved before the image). The union of oneself with the nectar of full moon is the naivēdya (offering of food, etc.)[2]. The immobility in that state (of the ego being one with all) is *pradakṣiṇa* (going round the image). The conception of 'I am He' is *namaskāra* (prostration). The silence (then is the stuti (praise). The all-contentment (or serenity then) is the *visarjana* (giving leave to god or finishing worship). (This is the worship of *Ātmā* by all *Rāja-yogins*). He who knows this knows all.

"When the triputi[3] are thus dispelled, he becomes the *kaivalya* jyotis without *bhāva* (existence) or *abhāva* (non-existence), full and motionless, like the ocean without tides or like the lamp wihtout wind. He becomes a *brahmavit* (knower of *brahman*) by cognising the end of the sleeping state, even while in the waking state. Thought the (sam) mind is absorbed in *suṣupti* as also is *samādhi*, there is much difference between them. (In the former case) as the mind is absorbed in tamas, it does not become the means of salvation, (but) in *samādhi* as the modifications of tamas in him are rotted away, the mind raises itself to the nature of the Partless. All that is no other than *Sākṣī-Caitanya* (witness-consciousness or the Higher Self) into which the absorption of the whole universe takes place, inasmuch as the universe is but a dulusion (or creation) of the mind and is therefore not different from it. Though the universe appears perhaps as outside of the mind, still it is unreal. He who knows *Brahman* and who is the sole enjoyer of brāhmic bliss which is eternal and has dawned once

1. In this paragraph, the higher or secret meaning is given of all actions done in the *pūjā* or whrship of God in the Hindu houses as well as temples. Regarding the clothing of the idol which is left out here, the commentator explains it as *āvaraṇa* or screen.
2. Here also the commentator brings in *nīrājanā* or the waving of the light before the image. That is according to him, the idea, "I am the self-shining."
3. The Triputi are the there, the knower, the known and the knowledge. Commom. : *Dhyāna* and others stated before wherein the three distinctions are made.

(for all in him)— that man becomes one with *Brahman*. He in whom *saṅkalpa* perishes has got mukti in his hand. therefore one becomes an emancipated person through the contemplation of *Paramātmā*. Having given up both *bhāva* and *abhāva*, one becomes *jīvanmukta* by leaving off again and again in all states *jñāna* (wisdom) and *jñāna* (object of wisdom), *dhyāna* (meditation) and *dhyeya* (object of meditation), *lakṣya* (the aim) and *alakṣya* (non-aim), *ḍṛsya* (the visible) and *aḍṛsya* (the non-visible and ūha (reasoning) the apoha (negative reasoning).[1] He who knows this knows all.

"There are five *avasthās* (states), *viz.*, *jāgarat* (waking), *svapna* (dreaming), *suṣupti* (dreamless sleeping), the *turya* (fourth) and *turyātīta* (that beyond the fourth). The *jīva* (ego) that is engaged in the waking state becomes attached to the pravrtti (worldly) path and is the participator or *naraka* (hell) as the fruit of sins. he desires *svarga* (heaven) as the fruit of his virtuous actions. This very same person becomes (afterwards) indifferent to all these saying, "Enough of the births tending to actions, the fruits of which tend to bondage till the end of this mundane existence." Then he pursues the nivṛṭṭi (return) path with a view to attain emancipation. And this person then takes refuge in a spiritual instructor in order to cross this mundane existence. Giving up passion and others, he does only those he is asked to do. Then having acquired the four *sādhanas* (means to salvation), he attains, in the middle of the lotus of his heart, the Reality of *antarlakṣya* that is but the Sat of Lord and begins to recognise (or recollect) the bliss *Brahman* which he had left (or enjoyed) in the *suṣupti* state. At last he attains this state of discrimination (thus) : 'I think I am the non duel One only. I was in *ajñāna* for some time (in the waking state and called therefore *Viśva*). I became shomehow (or involuntarily) a *Taijasa* (in the dreaming state) through the reflection (in that state) of the affinities of the forgotton waking state; and now I am a *Prājña* through the disappearance of those two states. Therefore I am one only. I (appear) as more than one though the difference of state and place. And there is nothing of differentiation of class besides me.' Having expelled even the smack of the difference (of conception) between 'I' and 'That' through the thought 'I am the pure and secondless Brahman', and having attained the path of salvation which is of the nature of *parabrahman*, after having become one with It through the *dhyāna* of the sun's sphere as shining with himself, he becomes fully ripened forgetting salvation. *Saṅkalpa* and others are the causes of the bondage of the mind; and the mind devoid of these becomes fit for salvation. Possessing such a mind free from all (*saṅkalpa*, etc.,) and withdrawing himself out of the odour of the universe, he looks upon all the worlds as *Ātmā*, abandons the conception of 'I', thinks 'I am Brahman' and considers all these as *Ātmā*. Through these, he becomes one who had done his duty.

---

1. Ūha and apoha—the consideration of the prots and cons.

"The *yogin* is one that has realised *Brahman* that is all full beyond turya. They (the people) extol him as *Brahman*; and becoming the object of the praise of the whole world, he wanders over different countries. Placing the bindu in the *ākāśa* of *Paramātmā* and pursuing the path of the partless bliss produced by the pure, secondless, stainless, and innate *yoga* sleep of *amanaska*, he becomes an emancipated person. Then the *yogin* becomes immersed in the ocean of bliss. when compared to it, the bliss of *Indra* and others is very little. he who gets this bliss is the supreme *yogin*.

"Thus ends the second *Brāhmaṇa*."

Brāhmaṇa III

The great sage *Yājñavalkya* then asked the *Puruṣa* in the sphere (of the sun) : "O Lord, though the nature of *amanaska* has been defined (by you), yet I forget it (or do not understand it clearly). Therefore pray explain it again to me." Accordingly the *Puruṣa* said : "This *amanaska* is a great secret. By knowing this, one becomes a person who has done his duty. One should look upon it as *Paramātmā*, associated with *Śāmbhavī-mudrā* and should know also all those that can be known through a (through) cognition of them. Then seeing *Parabrahman* is his own *Ātmā* as the Lord of all, the immeasurable, the birthless, the auspicious, the supreme *ākāśa*, the supportless, the secondless the only goal of Brahmā, Viṣṇu and *Rudra* and the cause of all and assuring himself that he who plays in the cave (of the heart) is a such a one, he should raise himself above the dualities of existence and non-existence; and knowing the experience of the *unmanī* of his *manas*, he then attains the state of *Parabrahman* which is motionless as a lamp in a windless place, having reached the ocean of *brāhmic* bliss by means of the river of *amanaskayoga* through the destruction of all his sense. Then he resembles a dry tree, Having lost all (idea of) the universe through the disappearance of growth, sleep, disease, expiration and inspiration, his body being always steady, he comes to have a supreme quiescence, being devoid of the movements of his *manas* and becomes absorbed in *Paramātmā*. The destruction of *manas* takes place after the destruction of the collective senses, like cow's udder (that shrivels up) after the milk has been drawn. It is this that is *amanaska*. By following this, one becomes always pure and becomes one that has done his duty, having been filled with the partless bliss by means of the path of *tāraka-yoga* through the initiation into the sacred sentences 'I am *Paramātmā*', 'That art thous', 'I am thou alone', 'Thou art I alone', etc.

"When his *manas* is immersed in the *ākāśa* and he becomes all-full, and when he attains the *unmanī* state, having abandoned all his collective senses, he conquers all sorrows and impurities through the partless bliss, having attained the fruits of *kaivalya*, ripened through the collective merits gathered in all his pervious lives and thinking always 'I am *Brahman*', becomes one that has done his duty. 'I am thou alone'. There is no difference between thee and me owing to the fullness of *Paramātmā*. Saying thus, he (the *Puruṣa* of the sun) embraced his pupil and made him understand it.[1]

"Thus ends the third *Brāhmaṇa*."

Brāhmaṇa IV

The *Yājñavaklya* addressed the *Puruṣa* in the sphere (of the sun) thus : "Pray explain to me in detail the nature of the fivefold division of *ākāśa*." He replied : "there are five (*viz.,*) : *ākāśa, parākāśa, mahākāśa, sūryākāśa* and *paramākāśa*. That which is of the nature of darkness, both in and out is the first *ākāśa*. That which has the fire of the deluge, both in and out if truly *mahākāśa*, That which has the brightness of the sun, both in and out is *sūryākāśa*. That brightness which is indescribable, all-pervading and of the nature of unrivallled bliss is *paramākāśa*, By cognising these according to this description, one becomes of their nature. He is *yogin* only in name, who does not cognise well the nine cakras, the six *ādhāras*, the thee *lakṣyas* and the five *ākāśa*. Thus ends the fourth *Brāhmaṇa*."

Brāhmaṇa V

"The *manas* influenced by worldly objects is liable to bondage; and that (*manas*) which is not so influenced by these is fit for salvation. Hence all the world becomes an object of *citta*; whereas the same *citta* when it is supportless and well-ripe in the state of *unmanī*, becomes worthy of laya (absorption in *Brahman*). This absorption you should learn from me who am the all-full. I alone am the cause of the absorption of *manas*. The *manas* is within the jyotis (spiritual light) which again is latent in the spiritual sound which pertains to the *anāhaṭa* (heart) sound. That *manas* which is the agent of cretion, perservation, and destruction of the three worlds— that same *manas* becomes absorbed in that which is the highest seat of Viṣṇu; through such an absorption, one gets the pure and secondless state, owing to the absence of difference then. This alone is the highest truth. He who knows this, will wander in the world like a lad or an idiot or a demon or a simpleton. By practising this a*manas*ka, one is ever contented, his urine and faeces become diminished, his food becomes lessened : he becomes strong in body and his limbs are free from disease and sleep. Then his breath and eyes being motionless, he realises *Brahman* and attains the nature of bliss.

"That ascetic who is intent on drinking the nectar of *Brahman* produced by the long practice of this kind of *samādhi*, becomes a *paramahaṁsa* (ascetic) or an avadhūta (naked asetic). By seeing him, all

1. This ia a reference to the secret way of imparting higher truth.

the world becomes pure, and even an illiterate person who serves him is freed from bondage. He (the ascetic) enables the member of his family for one hundred and one generations to cross the ocean of *saṁsāra*; and his mother, father, wife, and childern— all these are similarly freed. Thus ends the fifth *Brāhmaṇa*."

Thus ends the Upaniṣad

Nādabindu[1]-Upaniṣad

OF

ṚGVEDA

This syllable A is considered to be its (the bird Om's) right wing, U, its left : m[2], its tail; and the *ardhamātrā* (half-metre) is said to be its head.

The (*rājasic* and *tāmasic*[3]) qualities, its feet upwards (to the loins); *sattva*, its (main) body; *dharma* is considered to be its right eye, and *adharma*, its left.

The *Bhūroloka* is situtated in its feet; the *Bhuvarloka*, in its knees; the *Suvarloka*, in its loins; and the *Maharloka*, in its navel.

In its heart is situate the *janoloka*; the *tapoloka* in its throat, and the *satyaloka* in the centre of the forehead between the eyebrows.

The the *mātrā* (or *mantra*) beyond the *Sahasrāra* (thousand-rayed) is explained (*viz.,)* should be explained.

An adept in *yoga* who bestrides the *Hamsa* (bird) thus (*viz.,* cotemplates of[4] *Om*) is not affected by *kārmic* influences or by tens of crores of sins.

The first *mātrā* has *agni*, as its *devatā* (presiding deity); the second, *vāyu* as its *devatā*; the next *mātrā* is respledent like this shpere of the sun and the last, the *Ardhamātrā* the wise know as belonging to Varuṇa (the presiding deity of water).

Each of these *mātrās* has indeed three *kalās* (parts). This is called *Omkāra*. Know it by means of the *dhāraṇās*, *viz.,* concentration on each of the twelve *kalās*, or the variations of the *mātrās* produced by the difference of svaras or intonation). The first *mātra* is called *ghoṣiṇī*; the second, *vidyumāli* (or *vidyunmātrā*); the third, *pataṅginī*; the fourth *vāyuveginī*; the fifth, *nāmadheya*; the sixth, *aindrī*; the seventh, *viṣṇavī*;

---

1. Lit., Sound-seed.
2. The commentator says that M is the last letter and hence tail and *ardhamātrā* is the head, as it enables one to attain to higher worlds.
3. Another reading is : The qualities are its feet, etc., and *Tattva* is its body.
4. Comm. : Since this *mantra* has laready occurred in the preceeding khaṇḍa to the same *sākhā*, it is simply referred in the text. The *Mantra* is :
"सहस्त्राण्यंवियतां वस्यपक्षोहरैहस्यपतत: स्वर्गंसदेवानुस्यपदध्यसाक्षी संपश्यन् भवनानिविश्वा"
The Meaning seems to be—the letters A and U are the two wings of the *Hamsa* (*Om*) of the from of Viṣṇu which goes to *svarga*, the abode of *Sūrya*, the thousand-rayed God; that syllable, '*Om*' bearing in its heart all the devas (of *sattvaguṇa*). He goes up to *Sahasrānha* seeing the worlds personally : *Sahasrānha* being the seat of the spiritual sun.

the eighth, *śaṅkarī*; the ninth, *mahatī*; the tenth, *dhṛti* (*dhruva*, Calcutta ed.); the eleventh, *nārī* (*mauni*, Calcutta ed.); and the twelfth, *brāhmī*.[1]

If a person happens to die in the first *mātrā* (while contemplating on it), he is born again as a great emperor in *Bhāratavarṣa*.

If in the second *mātrā*, he becomes an illustrious *yakṣa*; if in the third *mātrā*, a *vidyādhara*; if in the fourth, a *gandharva* (these three beings the celestial hosts). If happens to die in the fifth, *viz., ardhamātrā*, he lives in the world of the moon, with the rank of a deva greatly florified there.

If in the sixth, he merges into *Indra*; if in the seventh, he reaches the seat of Viṣṇu; if in the eighth, *Rudra*, the Lord of all creatures.

If in the ninth, in *Maharloka*; if in the tenth, in *Janoloka* (*Dhruvaloka*, Calcutta ed.; if in the eleventh, *Tapoloka*, and if in the twelfth, he attains the eternal[2] state of Brahmā.

That which is beyond these (*viz.,*) *Parabrahman* which is beyond (the above *mātrās*), the pure, the all-pervading, beyond *kalās*, the ver resplendent and the source of all *joytis* (light) should be known.

When3 the mind goes beyond the organs and the *guṇās* and is absorbed, having no separate existence and no mental action, then (the *Guru*) should instruct him (as to his further course of development).

That person always engaged in its contemplation and always absorbed in it should gradually leave off his body (or family) following the course or *yoga* and avoiding all intercourse with society.

Then he, being freed from the bonds of *karma* and the existence as a *jīva* and being pure, enjoys the supreme bliss by his attaining of the state of Brahmā.[4]

O intelligent man, spend your life always in the knowing of the supreme bliss, enjoying the whole of your *prārabdha* (that portion of past *karma* now being enjoyed) without making any complaint (of it).

Even after *ātmajñāna* (knowledge of *Ātmā* of Self) has awakened (in one), *prārabdha* does ot leave (him); but he does not feel *prārabdha* after

---

1. Comm : The four *mātrās* are subdivided into twelve by their having each three *svaras*, *Udātta*, *Anudātta*, and *Svarīta*. Here the author goes on to give the names of the twelve *kalās* and shows the method of practising *Dhārana* on each. *Ghoṣiṇī* is that which gives Pranjña : *Vidyunmālī* is that which secures entrance into the loka of *Vidyumālī,* the king of the *yakṣas* : *pataṅginī* is that which confers the power of movement through air like the bird *Pataṅginī*, *Vāyuveginī* is that which gives the power of moving very rapidly : *Nāmadheya* means that which confers existence in *Piṭrloka* : *Aindrī Indraloka* : *Vaiṣṇavī* and *Saṅkarī* Viṣṇu and Śiva lokas respectively " Mauni to the loka of Munis or *jñānaloka* and *Brāhmī* to *Brahmaloka*.
2. Eternal here means the lifetime of Brahmā.
3. Another edition says : he should enter through *yoga* the incomparable and quiescent Śiva.
4. Here the Calcutta edition stops.

the dawning of *tattvajñāna*[1] (knowledge of *tattva* or truth) because the body and other things are asat (unreal). like the things seen in a dream to one on awaking from it.

That (portion of the) *karma* which is done in former births, and called *prārabdha* does not at all affect the person (*tattvajñānī*), as there is no rebirth to him.

As the body that exists in the dreaming state is untrue, so is this body. Where then is rebirth to a thing that is illusory? How can a thing have any existence, when there is no birth (to it)?

As the clay is the material cause of the pot, so one learns from *Vedānta* that *ajñāna* is the material cause of the universe : and when *ajñāna* ceases to exist, where then is the cosmos?

As a person through illusion mistakes a rope for a serpent, so the fool not knowing *Satya* (the eternal truth) sees the world (to be true).

When he knows it to be a piece of rope, the illusory idea of a serpent vanishes.

So when he knows the eternal substratum of everything and all the universe bcomes (therefore) void (to him), where then is *prārabdha* to him, the body being a part of the world? Therefore the word *prārabdha* is accepted to enlighten the ignorant (only).

Then as *prārabdha* has, in course fo time, worn, out he who is the sound resulting from the union of *Praṇava* with *brahman* who is the absolute effulgence itself, and who is the bestower of all good, shines himself like the sun at the dispersion of the clouds.

The *yogin* being in the *siddhāsana* (posture) and practising the *vaiṣ ṇavīmudrā*, should always hear the internal sound through the right ear.

The sound which he thus practises makes him deaf to all external sounds. Having overcome all obstacles, he enters the turya state within fifteen days.

In the beginning of his practice, he hears many loud sounds. They gradually increase in pitch and are head more and more subtly.

At first, the sounds are like those proceeding from the ocean, clouds, kettle-drum, and cataracts : in the middle (stage) those proceeding from *mardala* (a musical instrument), bell, and horn.

At the last stage, those proceeding from tinkling bless, flute, vīṇā (a musical instrument), and bells. Thus he hears many such sounds more and more subtle.

When he comes to that stage when the sound of the great kettle-drum is being heard, he should try to distinguish only sounds more and more subtle.

---

1. *Tattvajñāna* is the discrimination of the *tattvas* of this universe and man. *Ātmajñāna*—the discrimination of *Ātmā* or the Self in man.

He may change his concentration from the gross sound to the subtle, of from the subtle to the gross, but he should not allow his mind to be diverted from them towards others.

The mind having at first concentrated itself on any one sound fixes firmly to that and is absorbed in it.

It (the mind) becoming insensible to the external impressions, becomes one with the sound as milk water, and then becomes rapidly absorbed in *cidākāśa* (the *ākāśa* where *Cit* prevails).

Being indifferent towards all objects, the *yogin* having controlled his passions, should by continual practice concentrate his attention upon the sound which destroys the mind.

Having abandoned all thoughts and being freed from all actions, he should always concentrate his attention on the sound, and (then) his *citta* becomes absorbed in it.

Just as the bee drinking the honey (alone) does not care for the odour, so the *citta* which is always absorbed in sound, does not long for sensual objects as it is bound by the sweet smell of *nāda* and has abandoned its fitting nature.

The serpent *citta* through listening to the *nāda* is entirely absorbed in it, and becoming unconscious of everything concentrates itself on the sound.

The sound serves the purpose of a sharp good to control the maddened elephant— *citta* which roves in the pleasure-garden of the sensual objects.

It serves the purpose of a snare for binding the deer— *citta*. It also serves the purpose of a shore to the ocean waves of *citta*.

The sound proceeding from *Praṇava* which is *Brahman* is of the nature of effulgence; the mind becomes absorbed in it; that is the supreme seat of Viṣṇu.

The sound exists till there is the *ākāśic* conception (*ākāśa-saṅkalpa*). Beyond this, is the (aśabda) soundless *Parabrahman* which is *Pramātmā*.

The mind exists so long as there is sound, but with its (sound's) cessation, there is the state called *unmanī manas* (*viz.*, the state of being above the mind).

This sound is absorbed in the *Akṣara* (indestructible) and the soundless state is the supreme seat.

The mind which along with *Prāṇa* (*Vāyu*) has (its) *kārmic* affinities destroyed by the constant concetration upon *nāda* is absorbed in the unstained One. There is no doubt of it.

Many myriads of *nāḍas* and many more of bindus-(all) become absorbed in the *Brahma-Praṇava* sound.

Being freed from all states and all thoughts whatever, the *yogin* remains like one dead. He is a *mukta*. There is no doubt about this.

After that, he does not any time hear the sounds of conch or *dundubhi* (large kettle-drum).

The body in the state of *unmanī* is certainly like a log and does not feel heat or cold, joy or sorrow.

The yogin's *citta* having given up fame or disgrace is in *samādhi* above the three states.

Being freed from the waking and the sleeping states, he attains to his true state.

When the (spiritual) sight becomes fixed without any object to be seen, when the *vāyu* (*prāṇa*) becomes still without any effort, and when the *citta* becomes firm without any support, he becomes of the form of the internal sound of *Brahma-Praṇava*.

Thus ends the Upaniṣad

Yogakuṇḍalī[1]-Upaniṣad

OF

KṚṢṆA-YAJURVEDA

Chapter I

Citta[2] has two causes, *vāsanās* and (*prāṇa*) *vāyu*. if one of them is controlled, then both are contolled. Of these two, a person should control (*prāṇa*) *vāyu* always through moderate food, postures, and thirdly *śakti-cāla*.[3] I shall explain the nature of these. Listen to it, O *Gautama*. One should take a sweet and nutritious food[4], leaving a fourth (of his stomach) unfilled in roder to please Śiva (the patron of *yogin*). This is called moderate food. Posture herein required is of two kinds, *padma* and *vajra*. Placing the two heels over the two opposite thighs (respectively) is the *padma* (posture) which is the destroyer of all sins. Placing one heel below the *mūlakanda*[5] and the other over it and sitting with the neck, body had head erect is the vajra posture. The *śakti* (mentioned above) is only *kuṇḍalinī*. A wise man should take it up from its place (*viz.*, the navel, upwards) to the middle of the eyebrows. This is called *śakti-cāla*.[6] In practising it, two things are necessary, *Sarasvatīcāla* and the restraint of *prāṇa* (breath). Then through practice, *kuṇḍalinī* (which is spiral) becomes straightened. Of these two, I shall explain to you first *Sarasvatī-cālana*. It is said by the wise of old that *Sarasvatī* is no other than *Arundhatī*[7]. It is only by rousing her up that *kuṇḍalinī* is roused. When *prāṇa* (breath) is passing through (one's) *Iḍā* (left nostril), he should assume firmly *padma*-posture and should lengthen (inwards) 4 digits the

1. In this *Upaniṣad* are stated the ways by which the *Kuṇḍalinī* power is roused from the navel upwards to the middle of the eyebrows and then up to *sahasrāra* in the head : this being one of the important works of an adept to master the forces of nature.
2. *Citta* is the flitting aspect of *Antaḥakaraṇa*.
3. Lit., the moving of *śakti* which is *kundalinī*.
4. Regarding the quantity to be taken, one should take of solid food half of his stomach : of liquid food, one quarter, leaving the remaining quarter empty for the air to percolate.
5. *Mūlakaṇḍa* is the root of *khaṇḍa*, the genital organ.
6. The moving of *sarasvatī nāḍī* situated on the west of the navel among the 14 *nādis* (*vide Varāha* and other *Upaniṣad*).
7. Sarasvatī is called also Arundhatī who is literally one that helps good actions being done and the wife of Ṛṣi Vasiṣtha—also the star that is shown to the bride on marriage occasions.

ākāśa of 12 digits[1]. Then the wise man should bind the (*saravatī*) *nādi* by means of this lengthened (breath) and holding firmly together (both his ribs near the navel) by means of the forefingers and thumbs of both hands, (one hand on each side) should stir up *kuṇḍalinī* with all his might from right to left often and often; for a period of two *muhūrtas* (48 minutes), he should be stirring it up fearlessly. Then he should draw up a little when *kuṇḍalinī* enters *suṣumnā*. By this means, *kuṇḍalinī* enters the mouth of *suśumnā*. *Prāṇa* (also) having left (that place) enters of itself the *suṣumnā* (along with *kuṇḍalinī*. By compressing the neck, one should also expand the navel. Then by shaking *sarasvatī*, *prāṇa* goes above (to) the chest. Through the contraction of the neck, *prāṇa* goes above from the chest. *Sarasvatī* who has sound in her womb should be shaken (or thrown into vibration) each day. Therefore by merely shaking it, one is cured of diseases. *Gulma* (a splenetic disease), *jalodara* (dropsy), *plīha* (a splenetic disease) and all other diseases arising within the belly, are undoubtedly destroyed by shaking this *Śakti*.

I shall now briefly de describe to you *prāṇāyāma*. *Prāṇa* is the *vāyu* that move in the body and its restraint within is known as *kumbhaka*. It is of two kinds, *sahita* and *kevala*[2]. One should practise *sahita* till he gets *kevala*. There are four bhedas (lit., piercings or divisions) *viz.*, *sūrya*, *ujjāyī*, *śītalī*, and bhastrī. The *kumbhaka* associated with these four is called *sahita-kumbhaka*.

Being seated in the *padma* posture upon a pure and pleasant seat which gives ease end is neither too high nor too low, and in a place which is pure, lovely and free from pebbles, etc., and which for the length of a bow is free from cold, fire, and water, one should shake (or throw into vibration) *Sarasvatī*; slowly inhaling the breath from outside, as long as he desires, through the right nostril, he should exhale it through the left nostril. He should exhale it after purifying his skull (by forcing the breath up). This destroyes the four kinds of evils caused by *vāyu* as also by intestinal worms. This should be done often and it is this which is spoken of as *sūryabheda*.

Closing the mouth and drawing up slowly the breath as before with the nose through both the *nādis* (or nostrils) and retaining it in the space between the heart and the neck, one should exhale it through the left nostril. This destroys the heat caused in the head as well as the phlegm in the throat. It removes all diseases, purifies his body and increases the (gastric) fire within. It removes also the evils arising in the *nādis*, *jalodara* (water-belly or dropsy) and *dhātus*. This *kumbhaka* is called *ujjāyī* and may be practised (even) when walking or standing.

1. In exhalation, *prāṇa* goes out 16 digits and in inhalation, goes in only for 12, thus losing 4. But if inhaled for 16, then the power is aroused.
2. Lit., associated with and alone. *Vide Śāṇḍilya-Upaniṣad.*

Drawing up the breath as before through the gongue with (the hissing sound of) स and retaining it as before, the wise man should slowly exhale it through (both) the nostrils. This is called śītalī *kumbhaka* and destroys diseases, such as *gulma*, *plīha*, consumption, bile, fever, thirst, and poison.

Seated in the *padma* posture with belly and neck erect, the wise man should close the mouth and exhale with care through the nostrils. then he should inhale a little with speed up to the heart, so that the breath may fill the space with noise between the neck and skull. Then he should exhale in the same way and inhale often and often. Just as th bellows of a smith are moved (*viz.,* stuffed with air within and then the air is let out), so he should move the air within his body. If the body gets tired, then he should inhale through the right nostril. If his belly is full of *vāyu*, then he should press well his nostrils with all his fingers except his forefinger, and peforming *kumbhaka* as before, should exhale through the left nostril. This frees one from diseases of fire in (or inflammation of) the throat, increases the gastric fire within, enables one to know the *kuṇḍalinī*, produces purity removing sins, gives happiness and pleasure and destroys phlegm which the bolt (or obstacle) to the door at the mouth of *brahmanāḍi* (*viz., suṣumnā*). It pierces also the three granthis[1] (or knots) differentiated through the three guṇas. This *kumbhaka* is known as *bhastrī* and should especially be performed.

Through these four ways when *kumbhaka* is near (or is about to be performed), the sinless *yogin* should practise the three *bandhas*[2]. The first is called *mūlabandha*. The second is called *uddiyāna*, and the third is *jālandhara*. Their nature will be thus described. *Apāna* (breath) which has a downward tendency is forced up by one bending down. This process is called *mūlabandha*. When *apāna* is raised up and reaches the sphere of *agni* (fire), then the flame of *agni* grows long, being blown about by *vāyu*. Then *agni* and *apāna* come to (or commingle with) *prāṇa* in a heated state. Through this *agni* which is very fiery, there airses in the body the flamming (or the fire) which rouses the sleeping *kuṇḍalinī* through its heat. Then this *kuṇḍalinī* makes a hissing noise, becomes erect like a serpent beaten with stick and enters the hole of *brahmanāḍi* (*suṣ umnā*). Therefore *yogin* should daily practise *mūlabandha* often. *Uddiyāna* should be performed at the end of *kumbhaka* and at the beginning of expiration. Because *prāṇa uddīyatē* (*viz.,* goes up) the *suṣ umnā* in this *bandha*, therefore it called *uddiyāna* by the *yogins*. Being seated in the *vajra* posture and holding firmly the two toes by the two hands, he should press at the *kaṇḍa* and at the place near the two ankles. Then he should gradually upbear the *tāna*[3] (thread or nāḍi) which is on

---

1. They are *Brahmagranthi*, *viṣṇugranthi*, and *rudragranthi*.
2. *Bandhas* are certain kinds of position of the body.
3. This probably refers to *Sarasvatī nāḍī*.

the western side first to udara (the upper part of the abdomen above the navel), then to the heart and then to the neck. When *prāṇa* reaches the *saṅdhi* (junction) of navel, slowly it removes the impurities (or diseases) in the navel. Therefore this should be frequently practised. The *bandha* called *jālandhara* should be practised at the end of *kumbhaka*. This *jālandhara* is of the form of contraction of the neck and is an impediment to the passage of *vāyu* (upwards). When the neck is contracted at once by bending downwards (so that the chin may touch the breast), *prāṇa* goes through *brahmanādi* on the western *tāna* in the middle. Assuming the seat as mentioned before, one should stir up *sarasvatī* and control *prāṇa*. On the first day *kumbhaka* should be done four times; on the second day it should be done ten times, and then five times separately; on the third day, twenty times will do, and afterwards *kumbhaka* should be performed with three *bandhas* and with an increase of five times each day.

Diseases are generated in one's body through the following causes, *viz.,* sleeping in daytime, late vigils over night, excess of sexual intercourse, moving in crowd, the checking of the discharge of urine and faeces. the evil of unwholesome food and laborious mental operation with *prāṇa*. If *yogin* is afraid of such diseases (when attacked by them), he says, "My disease hae arisen from my practice of *yoga*." Then he will discontinue this practice. This is said to be the first obstacle to *yoga*. The second (obstacle) is doubt; the third is carelessness; the fourth, laziness; the fifth, sleep; the sixth, the not leaving of objects (of sense); the seventh, erroneous perception; the eighth, sensual object; the ninth, want of faith[1]; and the tenth, the failure to attain the truth of *yoga*. A wise man should abandon these ten obstacles after great deliberation. The practice of *prāṇāyāma* should be performed daily with the mind firmly fixed on Truth. Then *citta* is absorbed in *suṣumnā*, and *prāṇa* (therefore) never moves. When the impurities (of *citta*) are thus removed and *prāṇa* is absorbed in *suṣumnā*, he becomes a (true) *yogin*. *Apāna*, which has a downward tendency should be raised up with effoort by the contraction (of the anus), and this is spoken of as *mūlabandhā*. *Apāna* thus raised up mixes with *agni* and then they go up quickly to the seat of *prāṇa*. Then *prāṇa* and *apāna* uniting with one another go to *kuṇḍalinī*, which is coiled up and sleep. *Kuṇḍalinī* being heated by *agni* and stirred up by *vāyu*, extends her body in the mouth of *suṣumnā*, pierces the *brahmagranthi* formed of *rajas*, and flashes at once like lightning at the mouth of *suṣumnā*. Then it goes up at once through *viṣṇugranthi* to the heart. Then it goes up through *rudragranthi* and above it to the middle of the eyebrows; having pierced this place, it goes up to the *maṇḍala* (sphere) of the moon. It dries up the moisture produced by the moon in

1. The text is *Anākhiam* which has no sense. It has been translated as *Anāsthā*.

the *anāhatacakra* having sixteen petals[1]. When the blood is agitated through the speed of *prāṇa*, it becomes bile from its contact with the sun, after which it goes to the sphere of the moon where it becomes of the nature of the flow of pure phlegm. How does it (blood) which is very cold become hot when it flows there? (Since) at the same time the intence white form of moon is speedily heated[2]. Then being agitated, it goes up. Through taking in this, *citta* which was moving amidst sensual objects externally, it restrained there. The novice enjoying this high state attains peace and becomes devoted to *Ātmā*. *Kuṇḍalinī* assumes the eight[3] forms of prakṛti (matter) and attain Śiva by encircling him and dissolves itself in Śiva. Thus *rajas-śukla*[4] (seminal fluid) which rises up goes to Śiva alone with marut (*vāyu*): *prāṇas* and *apāna* which are always produced become equal. *Prāṇas* flow in all things, great and small, describable or indescribable, as fire in gold. Then this body which is *ādhibhautika* (composed of elements) becomes *ādhidaivata* (relating to a tutelar deity) and is thus purified. Then it attains the stage of *ativāhika*[5]. Then the body being freed from the inert state becomes stainless and of the nature of *Cit*. In it, the *ativāhika* become the chief of all, being of the nature of That. Like the conception of the snake in a rope, so the idea of the release from wife and *saṁsāra* is the delusion of time. Whatever appears is unreal. Whatever is absorbed is unreal. Like the illusory conception of silver in the mother-of-pearl, so is the idea of man and woman. The microcosm and the microcosm are one and the same; so also the *liṅga* and *sūtrātma*, *svabhāva* (substance) and from and the self-resplendent light and *Cidātmā*.

The *Śakti* named *kuṇḍalinī*, which is like a thread in the the lotus and is resplendent, is biting with the upper end of its hood (namely, mouth) at the root of the lotus the *mūlakanda*. Taking hold of its tail with it mouth, it is in contact with the hole of *brahmarandra* (or *suṣumnā*). If a person seated in the *padma* posture and having accustomed himself of the contraction of his anus makes his *vāyu* go upward with the mind intent on *kumbhaka*, then *agni* comes to *svādhiṣṭhāna* flamming, owing to the

---

1. Twelve seems to be the right number of petals in the *anāhata-cakra* of the heart; but the moon is probably means having sixteen rays.
2. The passages here are obscure.
3. They are *Mūlaprakṛti*, *Mahat*, *Anaṁkāra* and the five elements.
4. Here it is the astral seminal fluid which, in the case of a neophyte, not having descended to a gross fluid through the absence of sexual desire, rises up being conserved as spiritual energy.
5. A stage of being able to convey to other bodies the deity appointed by God to help in the conveying of *sūkṣma* (subtle) body to other bodies at the expiry of good actions which contribute to the enjoyment of materials pleasures (*vide* Apte's Dictionary).

blowing of *vāyu*. From the blowing of *vāyu* and *agni*, the chief (*kuṇḍalinī*) pierces open the *brahmagranthi* and then *viṣṇugranthi*. Then it pierces *rudragranthi*, after that, (all) the six lotuses (or plexuses). Then *Śakti* in happy with Śiva in *sahasrāra kamala* (1,000 lotuses seat or pineal gland). This should be known as the highest *avasthā* (state) and it alone is the giver of final beatitude. Thus ends the first chapther.

Chapter II

I shall hereafter describe the science called *khecarī* which is such that one who knows it is freed from old age and death in this world. One who is subject to the pains of death, disease and old age should, O stage, on knowing this science make his mind firm and practise *khecarī*. One should regard that person as his *Guru* on earth who knows *kehecharī*, the destroyer of old age and death, both from knowing the meaning of books and practice, and should perform it with all his heart. The science of *khecarī* is not easily attainable, as also its practice. Its practice and *melana*[1] are not accomplished simultaneously. Those that are bent upon practice alone do not get *melana*. Only some get the practice, O *Brāhman*, after several births, but *melana* is not obtained even after a hundred births. Having undergone the practice after several births, some (solitary) *yogin* gets the melana in some future bitrth as the result of his practice. When a *yogin* gets this *melana* from the mouth of his *Guru*, then he obtains the siddhis mentioned in the several books. When a man gets this melana through books and the significance, then he attains the state of Śiva freed from all rebirth. Even *Guru* may not be able to know this without books. Therefore this science is very difficult to master. An ascetic should wander over the earth so long as he fails to get this science, and when this science is obtained, then he has got the siddhi in his hand (*viz.*, mastered the psychical powers). Therefore one should regard as *Acyuta* (Viṣṇu) the person who imparts the *melana*, as also him who gives out the science. He should regard as Śiva him who teaches the practice. Having got this science from me, you should not reveal it to others. Therefore one who knows this should protect it with all his efforts (*viz.*, should never give it out except to persons who deserve it). O *Brāhman*, one should go to the place where lives the *Guru*, who is able to teach the divine *yoga* and there learn from him the science *khecarī*, and being then teach the divine *yoga* and there learn from him the science khecarī, and being then thought well by him, should at first practise it carefully. By means of this science, a person will attain the siddh of khecarī, Joining with khecarī *śakti* (*viz.*, kuṇḍalinī *śakti*) by means of the (science) of

1. Melana is lit., joining. This is the key to this science which seems to be kept profoundly secret and revealed by adepts only in initiation, as will appear from the subsequent passages in this *Upaniṣad*.

khecharī which contains the *bīja* (seed of letter) of *khecharī*, one becomes the lord of the *khecharas* (*Devas*) and lives always amongst them. *Khecharī bījā* (seed-letter) is spoken of as *agni* encircles with water and as the abode of *khecaras* (*Devas*). Through this *yoga*, siddhi is mastered. The ninth (*bīja*) letter of *somāṁṣa* (*soma* or moon part) should also be pronounced in the reverse order. Then a letter composed of three *aṁṣas* of the form of moon has been described; and after that, the eighth letter should be pronounced in the reverse order; then consider it as the supreme and its beginning as the fifth, and this is said to the *kūṭa* (horns) of the several bhinnas (or parts) of the moon. This which tends to the accomplishment of all *yogas*, should be learnt through the initiation of a *Guru*. He who recites this twelve times every day, will not get even in sleep that *māyā* (illusion) which is born in his body and which is the source of all vicious deeds. He who recites this five lakhs of times with every great care— to him the science of khecarī will reveal itself. All obstacles vanish and the devas are pleased. The destruction of *valīpalita* (*viz.,* wrinkle and grayness of hair) will take place without doubt. Having acquired this great science, one should practise it afterwards. if not, O *Brāhman*, he will suffer without getting any *siddhi* in the path of *khecarī*. If one does not get this nectarlike science in this practice, he should get it in the beginning of melana and recite it always; (else) one who is without is never gets *siddhi*. As soon as he gets this science, he should practise it; and then the sage will soon get the siddhi. Having drawn out the tongue from the root of palate, a knower of *Ātmā* should clear the impurity (of the tongue) for seven days according to the advice of his *Guru*. He should take a sharp knife which is oiled and cleaned and which resembles the leaf of the plant snuhī ("Euphorbia antiquorum") and should cut for the space of a hair (the fraenum Lingui). Having powdered saindhave (rock-salt) and pathya (sea-salt), he should apply it to the place. On the seventh day, he should again cut for the space of a hair. Thus for the space of six months, he should continue it always gradually with great care. In six months, *Śiro-bandha* (*bandha* at the head)[2]. which is at the root of the tongue is destroyed. Then the *yogin* who knows timely action should encircle with *Śiro-vastra* (lit., the cloth of he head) the *Vāk-Īśvarī* (the deity presiding over speech) and should draw (it) up. Again by daily drawing it up for six months, it comes, O sage, as far as the middle of the dyebrows and obliquely up to the opening of the ears; having gradually practised, it goes to the root of the chin. Then in three years, it goes up[3] easily to the end of the hair (of the head) It goes up obliquely to *Śākha*

1. All these are very first.
2. Ibid.
3. Probably it here means some part below the skull.

and downwards to the well of the throat. In antoher three years, it occupies *brahmarandhra* and stops there without doubt. Crosswise it goes up to the top of the head and downwards to the well of the throat. Gradually it opens the great adamantine door in the head. The rare science (of *khecarī*) *bīja* has been explained before. One should perform the six *aṅgas* (parts) of this *mantra* by pronouncing it in six different intonations. One should do this in order to attain all the *siddhis*; and this *karanyāsam*[1] should be done gradually and not all at a time, since the body of one who does it all at once will soon decay. Therefore it should be practised, O best of sages, little by little. When the tongue goes to the *brahmarandhra* through the outer path, then one should place the tongue after moving the bolt of Brahmā which cannot be mastered by the devas. On doing this for three years with the point of the finger, he should make the tongue enter within : then it enters *brahmadvāra* (or hole). On entering the *brahmadvāra*, one should practise mathana (churning) well. Some intelligent men attain *siddhi* even without *mathana*. One who is versed in khecharī *Mantra* accomplishes it wihout *mathana*. By doing the *japa* and *mathana*, one reaps the fruits soon. By connecting a wire made of gold, silver or iron with the nostrils by means of a thread soaked in milk, one should restrain his breath in his heart and seated a convenient posture with his eyes concentrated between his eyebrows, he should perform *mathana* slowly. In six months, the state of *mathana* becomes natural like sleep in children. And it is not advisable to do *mathana* always. it should be done (once) only in every month. A *yogin* should not reolve his tongue in the path. After doing this for twelve years, siddhis is surely obtained. Then he sees the whole universe in his body as not being different from *Ātmā*. This path of the *ūrdhvakuṇḍalinī* (higher *kuṇḍalinī*), O chief of kings conquers the macrocosm. Thus ends the second chapter.

Chapter III

Melanamantra.— ह्रीं (*Hrīm*), भं (*bham*), सं (*sham*), फं (*pham*), सं (*sam*), and क्षं (*kṣam*).

The lotus-born (Brahmā) said :

O *Śṅkara*, (among) new moon (the first day of the lunar fortnight) and full moon, which is spoken of as its *mantra*'s) sign ? In the first day of lunar fortnight and during new moon and full moon (days), It should be made firm and there is no other way (or time). A man longs for an object through passion and is infatuated with passion for objects.One should always leave these two and seek the *Nirañjana* (stainless). He should abandon everything else which he thinks is favourable to himself. Keeping the *manas* in the midst of *śakti*, and *śakti* in the midst of *manas*, one should look into *manas* by means of *manas*. Then he leaves even the

---

1. Certain motions of the fingers and hands in the pronunciation of *mantras*.

highest stage. *Manas* alone is the bindu, the cause of creation and preservation. It is only through *manas* that bindu is produced, like the curd from milk. The organs of *manas* is not that which is situated in the middle of *bandhana*. *Bandhana* is there where *Śakti* is between the sun and moon, Having known *suṣumnā* and its bheda (piercing) and making the *vāyu* go in the middle, one should stand in the seat of bindu, and close the nostrils, Having known *vāu*, the above-mentioned *bindu* and the *sattva-prakṛti* as well as the six *cakras*, one should enter the *sukha-maṇḍala* (*viz.,* the *sahasrāra* or pineal gland, the sphere of happinss). There are six cakras. *Mūlādhāra* is in the anus; *svādhiṣṭhana* is near the genital organ; *maṇipūraka* is in the navel; *anāhata* is in the heart; *viśuddhi* is at the root of the neck and *ajñā* is in the head (between the two eyebrows). Having known these six *maṇḍalas* (spheres), one should enter the *sukhamaṇḍala* (pineal gland), drawing up the *vāyu* and should sent it (*vāyu*) upwards. He who practises thus (the control of) *vāyu*) becomes one with *brahmāṇḍa* (the macrocosm). He should practise (or master) *vāyu*, bindu, *citta*, and *cakra*.

Yogins attain the nectar of equality through *samādhi* alone. Just as the fire latent in (sacrificail) wood does not appear without churning, so the lamp of wisdom does not arise without the *abhyāsa yoga* (or practice of *yoga*). The fire pleaced in a vessel does not give light outside. When the vessel is broken, its light appears without. One's body is spoken of as the vessel, and the seat of 'That' is the fire (or light) within; and when (the body) is broken through the words of a *Guru*, the light of *brahmajñāna* becomes resplendent. With the *Guru* as the helmsman, one crosses the subtle body and the ocean of *saṁsāra* through the affinities of practice. That *vāk*[1] (power of speech) which sprouts in *parā*, gives fourth two leaves in *paśyantī*, buds forth in *madhyamā* and blossoms in *vaikharī*—that *vāk* which has before been described, reaches the state of the absorption of sound, reversing the above order (*viz.*, beginning with *vaikharī*, etc). Whoever thinks that He who is great lord of that *vāk*, who is the undifferentiated and who is the illuminator of that *vāk* is Self; whoever thinks over thus, is never affected by words, high or low (or good or bad). The three (aspects[2] of consciousness), *viśva*, *taijasa*, and *prāṇa* (in man), the three *Virāṭ*, *Hiraṇyagarbha*, and *Īśvara* in the

---

1. *Vāk* is of four kinds (as said here) *parā*, *paśyanti*, *madhyamā*, and *vaikharī*. *Vaikharī* being the lowest and the grossest of sounds, and *parā* being the highest. In evolution *vāk* beings from the highest to the lowest and in involution it takes a reverse order, to merge into the highest subtle sound (*Parā*).
2. The first three aspects of consciousness refer to the gross, subtle, and *kāraṇa* bodies of men, while the second three aspects refer to the three bodies of the universe. this is from the standpoint of the three bodies.

universe, the egg of the universe, the egg of man[1] and the seven worlds—all these in turn are absorbed in *Pratyagātma* through the absorption of their respective *upādhis* (vehicles). The egg being heated by the fire of *jñāna* is absorbed with its *kāraṇa* (cause) into *Paramātmā* (Universal Self). Then it becomes one with *Parabrahman*. It is then neither steadiness nor depth, neither light nor darkness, neither describable nor distinguishable. Sat (Be-ness) alone remains. One should think of *Ātmā* as being within the body like a light in a vessel. *Ātmā* is of the dimensions of a thumb, is a light without smoke and without form, is shining within (the body) and is undifferentiated and immutable.

The *Vijñana Ātmā* that dwells in this body is deluded by *māyā* during the states of waking, dreaming, and dreamless sleep; but after many births, owing to the effect of good *karma*, it wishes to attain its own state. Who am I? How has this stain of mundane existence accrued to me? What becomes in the dreamless sleep of me who am engaged in business in waking and dreaming states? Just as a bale of cotton is burnt by fire, so the *Cidābhāsa*[2] which is the result of non-wisdom, is burnt by the (wise) thoughts like the above and by its own supreme illuminations. The outer burning (of body as done in world) is no burning at all. When the worldly wisdom is destroyed, *Pratyagātma* that is in the *dahara* (*ākāśa* or either of the heart) obtains *vijñāna*, diffusing itself everywhere and burns in an instant *jñānamaya* and *manomaya* (sheaths). After this, He himself shines always within, like a light within a vessel.

That muni who contemplates thus till sleep and till death is to be known as a *jīvanmukta*. Having done what ought to be done, he is a fortunate person. And having given up (even) the state of a *jīvanmukta*, he attains *videhamukti* (emancipation in a disemobodied state), after his body wears off. He attains the state, as if of moving in the air, Then That alone remain which is soundless, touchless, formless, and deathless, which is the rasa (essence), eternal and odourless, which had neither beginning nor end, which is greater than the great, and which is permanent, stainless, and decayless.

Thus ends the Upaniṣad

1. The egg of man—this shows that man in his formation is and appears as an egg, just as universe is, and appears as an egg.
2. It is the consciousness that becomes distorted and is unable to cognise itself through the bodies.

१. मुक्तिकोपनिषत्

ईशाद्यष्टोत्तरशतवेदान्तपटलाशयम्।
मुक्तिकोपनिषद्वेद्यं रामचन्द्रपदं भजे ॥१॥

हरिः ॐ पूर्णमद इति शान्तिः ॥

ॐ अयोध्यानगरे रम्ये रत्नमण्डपमध्यमे। सीताभरतसौमित्रिशत्रुघ्नाद्यैः समन्वितम् ॥१॥ सनकाद्यैर्मुनिगणैर्वसिष्ठाद्यैः शुकादिभिः अन्यैर्भागवतैश्चापि। स्तूयमानमहर्निशम् ॥२॥ धीविक्रियासहस्राणां साक्षिणं निर्विकारिणम्। स्वरूपध्याननिरतं समाधिविरमे हरिम् ॥३॥ भक्त्या शुश्रूषया रामं स्तुवन्पप्रच्छ मारुतिः। राम त्वं परमात्मासि सच्चिदानन्दविग्रहः ॥४॥

इदानीं त्वां रघुश्रेष्ठ प्रणमामि मुहुर्मुहुः। त्वद्रूपं ज्ञातुमिच्छामि तत्त्वतो राम मुक्तये ॥५॥ अनायासेन येनाहं मुच्येयं भवबन्धनात्। कृपया वद मे राम येन मुक्तो भवाम्यहम् ॥६॥ साधु पृष्टं महाबाहो वदामि शृणु तत्त्वतः। वेदान्ते सुप्रतिष्ठोऽहं वेदान्तं समुपाश्रय ॥७॥ वेदान्ताः के रघुश्रेष्ठ वर्तन्ते कुत्र ते वद। हनूमञ्छृणु वक्ष्यामि वेदान्तस्थितिमञ्जसा ॥८॥ निश्वासभूता मे विष्णोर्वेदा जाताः सुविस्तराः। तिलेषु तैलवद्वेदे वेदान्तः सुप्रतिष्ठितः ॥९॥

राम वेदाः कतिविधास्तेषां शाखाश्च राघव। तासूपनिषदः काः स्युः कृपया वद तत्त्वतः ॥१०॥ श्रीराम उवाच। ऋग्वेदादिविभागेन वेदाश्चत्वार ईरिताः। तेषां शाखा ह्यनेकाः स्युस्तासूपनिषद-स्तथा ॥११॥ ऋग्वेदस्य तु शाखाः स्युरेकविंशतिसंख्यकाः। नवाधिकशतं शाखा यजुषो मारुतात्मज ॥१२॥ सहस्रसंख्यया जाताः शाखाः साम्नः परन्तप। अथर्वणस्य शाखाः स्युः पञ्चाशद्भेदतो हरे ॥१३॥

एकैकस्यास्तु शाखाया एकैकोपनिषन्मता। तासामेकामृचं यश्च पठते भक्तितो मयि ॥१४॥ स मत्सायुज्यपदवीं प्राप्नोति मुनिदुर्लभाम्। राम केचिन्मुनिश्रेष्ठा मुक्तिरेकेति चक्षिरे ॥१५॥ केचित्त्वन्नामभजनात्काश्यां तारोपदेशतः। अन्येतु सांख्ययोगेन भक्तियोगेन चापरे ॥१६॥ अन्ये वेदान्तवाक्यार्थविचारात्परमर्षयः। सालोक्यादिविभागेन चतुर्धा मुक्तिरीरिता ॥१७॥

सहोवाच श्रीरामः। कैवल्यमुक्तिरेकैव पारमार्थिकरूपिणी। दुराचाररतो वापि मन्नामभजनात्कपे ॥१८॥ सालोक्यमुक्तिमाप्नोति न तु लोकान्तरादिकम्। काश्यां तु ब्रह्मनालेऽस्मिन्मृतो मत्तारमाप्नुयात् ॥१९॥ पुनरावृत्तिरहितां मुक्तिं प्राप्नोति मानवः। यत्र कुत्रापि वा काश्यां मरणे च महेश्वरः ॥२०॥ जन्तोर्दक्षिणकर्णे तु मत्तारं समुपादिशेत्। निर्धूताशेषपापौघो मत्सारूप्यं भजत्ययम् ॥२१॥

सैव सालोक्यसारूप्यमुक्तिरित्यभिधीयते। सदाचाररतो भूत्वा द्विजो नित्यमनन्यधीः ॥२२॥ मयि सर्वात्मके भावो मत्सामीप्यं भजत्ययम्। सैव सालोक्यसारूप्यसामीप्या मुक्तिरिष्यते ॥२३॥ गुरूपदिष्टमार्गेण ध्यायन्मद्गुणमव्ययम्। मत्सायुज्यं द्विजः सम्यग्भजेद्भ्रमरकीटवत् ॥२४॥ सैव सायुज्यमुक्तिः स्याद्ब्रह्मानन्दकरी शिवा। चतुर्विधा तु या मुक्तिर्मदुपासनया भवेत् ॥२५॥

इयं कैवल्यमुक्तिस्तु केनोपायेन सिध्यति। माण्डूक्यमेकमेवालं मुमुक्षूणां विमुक्तये ॥२६ ॥ तथाप्यसिद्धं चेज्ज्ञानं दसोपनिषदं पठ। ज्ञानं लब्ध्वाचिरादेव मामकं धाम यास्यसि ॥२७॥ तथापि दृढता नो चेद्विज्ञानस्याञ्जनासुत। द्वात्रिंशाख्योपनिषदं समभ्यस्य निवर्तय ॥२८॥ विदेहमुक्ताविच्छा चेदष्टोत्तरशतं पठ। तासां क्रमं सशान्तिं च शृणु वक्ष्यामि तत्त्वतः ॥२९॥ ईशकेनकठप्रश्नमुण्डमाण्डूक्यतित्तिरिः। ऐतरेयं च छान्दोग्यं बृहदारण्यकं तथा ॥३०॥

ब्रह्मकैवल्यजाबालश्वेताश्वो हंस आरुणिः। गर्भो नारायणो हंसो बिन्दुर्नादशिरः शिखा ॥३१ मैत्रायणी कौषीतकी बृहज्जाबालतापनी। कालाग्निरुद्रमैत्रेयी सुबालक्षुरिमन्त्रिका ॥३२॥ सर्वसारं निरालम्बं रहस्यं वज्रसूचिकम्। तेजोनादध्यानविद्यायोगतत्त्वात्मबोधकम् ॥३३॥

परिव्राट् त्रिशिखी सीता चूडा निर्वाणमण्डलम्। दक्षिणा शरभं स्कन्दं महानारायणाह्वयम् ॥३४॥ रहस्यं रामतपनं वासुदेवं च मुद्गलम्। शाण्डिल्यं पैङ्गलं भिक्षुमहच्छारीरकं शिखा ॥३५॥ तुरीयातीतसंन्यासपरिव्राजाक्षमालिका। अव्यक्तैकाक्षरं पूर्णा सूर्याक्ष्यध्यात्मकुण्डिका ॥३६॥ सावित्र्यात्मा पाशुपतं परं ब्रह्मावधूतकम्। त्रिपुरा-तपनं देवीत्रिपुरा कठभावना। हृदयं कुण्डली भस्म रुद्राक्षगणदर्शनम् ॥३७॥

तारसारमहावाक्यपञ्चब्रह्माग्निहोत्रकम्। गोपालतपनं कृष्णं याज्ञवल्क्यं वराहकम् ॥३८॥ शाट्यायनी हयग्रीवं दत्तात्रेयं च गारुडम्। कलिजाबालिसौभाग्यरहस्यऋचमुक्तिका ॥३९॥ एवमष्टोत्तरशतं भावनात्रयनाशनम्। ज्ञानवैराग्यदं पुंसां वासनात्रयनाशनम् ॥४०॥ पूर्वोत्तरेषु विहिततत्तच्छान्तिपुरःसरम्। वेदविद्याव्रतस्नातदेशिकस्य मुखात्स्वयम् ॥४१॥

गृहीत्वाष्टोत्तरशतं ये पठन्ति द्विजोत्तमाः। प्रारब्धक्षयपर्यन्तं जीवन्मुक्ता भवन्ति ते ॥४२॥ ततः कालवशादेव प्रारब्धे तु क्षयं गते। वैदेहीं मामकीं मुक्तिं यान्ति नास्त्यत्र संशयः ॥४३॥ सर्वोपनिषदां मध्ये सारमष्टोत्तरं शतम्। सकृच्छ्रवणमात्रेण सर्वाघौघ-निकृन्तनम् ॥४४॥ मयोपदिष्टं शिष्याय तुभ्यं पवननन्दन। इदं शास्त्रं मयादिष्टं गुह्यमष्टोत्तरं शतम् ॥४५॥

ज्ञानतोऽज्ञानतो वापि पठतां बन्धमोचकम्। राज्यं देयं धनं देयं याचतः कामपूरणम् ॥४६॥ इदमष्टोत्तरशतं न देयं यस्य कस्यचित्। नास्तिकाय कृतघ्नाय दुराचाररताय वै ॥४७॥ मद्भक्तिविमुखायापि शास्त्रगर्तेषु मुह्यते। गुरुभक्तिविहीनाय दातव्यं न कदाचन ॥४८॥ सेवापराय शिष्याय हितपुत्राय मारुते। मद्भक्ताय सुशीलाय कुलीनाय सुमेधसे ॥४९॥ सम्यक् परीक्ष्य दातव्यमेवमष्टोत्तरं शतम्। यः पठेच्छृणुयाद्वापि स मामेति न संशयः। तदेतदृचाभ्युक्तम्। विद्या ह वै ब्राह्मणमाजगाम गोपाय मा शेवधिष्टेऽहमस्मि। असूयकायानृजवे शठाय मा मा ब्रूया वीर्यवती तथा स्याम्।

यमेव विद्याश्रुतमप्रमत्तं मेधाविनं ब्रह्मचर्योपपन्नम्। तस्मा इमामुपसन्नाय सम्यक् परीक्ष्य दद्याद्वैष्णवीमात्मनिष्ठाम् ॥१॥ इति॥ अथ हैनं श्रीरामचन्द्रं मारुतिः पप्रच्छ ऋग्वेदादिविभागेन पृथक् शान्तिमनुब्रूहीति। स होवाच श्रीरामः। ऐतरेय-कौपीतकीनादबिन्द्वात्मप्रबोधनिर्वाणमुद्गलाक्षमालिकात्रिपुरासौभाग्यबह्वृचानामृग्वेदगतानां दशसंख्याकानामुपनिषदां वाङ्मे मनसीति शान्तिः ॥१॥

ईशावास्यबृहदारण्यजाबालहंसपरमहंससुबालमन्त्रिकानिरालम्बत्रिशिखीब्राह्मण-मण्डलब्राह्मणाद्वयतारकपैङ्गलभिक्षुतुरीयातीताध्यात्मतारसारयाज्ञवल्क्यशाठ्यायनीमुक्तिकानां शुक्लयजुर्वेदगतानामेकोनविंशतिसंख्याकानामुपनिषदां पूर्णमद इति शान्तिः ॥२ ॥

कठवल्लीतैत्तिरीयकब्रह्मकैवल्यश्वेताश्वतरगर्भनारायणामृतबिन्द्वमृतनादकालाग्निरुद्रक्षुरिकासर्वसारशुकरहस्यतेजोबिन्दुध्यानबिन्दुब्रह्मविद्यायोगतत्त्वदक्षिणामूर्तिस्कन्दशारीरकयोगशिखैकाक्षराक्ष्यवधूतकठरुद्रहृदययोगकुण्डलिनीपञ्चब्रह्मप्राणाग्निहोत्रवराहकलिसंतरणसरस्वतीरहस्यानां कृष्णयजुर्वेदगतानां द्वात्रिंशत्संख्याकानामुपनिषदां सह नाववत्विति शान्तिः ॥३ ॥

केनच्छान्दोग्यारुणिमैत्रायणिमैत्रेयीवज्रसूचिकायोगचूडामणिवासुदेवमत्संन्यासाव्यक्तकुण्डिकासावित्रीरुद्राक्षजाबालदर्शनजाबालीनां सामवेदगतानां षोडशसंख्याकानामुपनिपदामाप्यायन्त्विति शान्तिः ॥४ ॥

प्रश्नमुण्डकमाण्डूक्याथर्वशिरोऽथर्वशिखाबृहज्जाबालनृसिंहतापनीनारदपरिव्राजकसीताशरभमहानारायणरामरहस्यरामतापनीशाण्डिल्यपरमहंसपरिव्राजकान्नपूर्णासूर्यात्मपाशुपतपरब्रह्मत्रिपुरातपनदेवीभावनाब्रह्मजाबालगणपतिमहावाक्यगोपालतपनकृष्णहयग्रीवदत्तात्रेयगारुडानामथर्ववेदगतानामेकत्रिंशत्संख्याकानामुपनिषदां भद्रं कर्णेभिरिति शान्तिः ॥५ ॥

मुमुक्षवः पुरुषाः साधनचतुष्टयसंपन्नाः श्रद्धावन्तः सुकुलभवं श्रोत्रियं शास्त्रवात्सल्यगुणवन्तमकुटिलं सर्वभूतहिते रतं दयासमुद्रं सद्गुरुं विधिवदुपसंगम्योपहारपाण्योऽष्टोत्तरशतोपनिषदं विधिवदधीत्य श्रवणमनननिदिध्यासनानि नैरन्तर्येण कृत्वा प्रारब्धक्षयाद्देहत्रयभङ्गं प्राप्योपाधिविनिर्मुक्तघटाकाशवत्परिपूर्णता विदेहमुक्तिः ।

सैव कैवल्यमुक्तिरिति । अतएव ब्रह्मलोकस्था अपि ब्रह्ममुखाद्वेदान्तश्रवणादि कृत्वा तेन सह कैवल्यं लभन्ते । अतः सर्वेषां कैवल्यमुक्तिर्ज्ञानमात्रेणोक्ता । न कर्मसांख्ययोगोपासनादिभिरित्युपनिषत् । इति प्रथमोऽध्यायः ॥१ ॥

तथा हैनं श्रीरामचन्द्रं मारुतिः पप्रच्छ । केयं वा तत्सिद्धिः सिद्ध्या वा किं प्रयोजनमिति । सहोवाच श्रीरामः । पुरुषस्य कर्तृत्वभोक्तृत्वसुखदुःखादिलक्षणश्चित्तधर्मः क्लेशरूपत्वाद्बन्धो भवति । तन्निरोधनं जीवन्मुक्तिः । उपाधिविनिमुक्तघटाकाशवत्प्रारब्धक्षयाद्विदेहमुक्तिः ।

जीवन्मुक्तिविदेहमुक्त्योरष्टोत्तरशतोपनिषदः प्रमाणम् । कर्तृत्वादिदुःखनिवृत्तिद्वारा नित्यानन्दावाप्तिः प्रयोजनं भवति । तत्पुरुषप्रयत्नसाध्यं भवति । यथा पुत्रकामेष्टिना पुत्रं वाणिज्यादिना वित्तं ज्योतिष्टोमेन स्वर्गं तथा पुरुषप्रयत्नसाध्यवेदान्तश्रवणादिजनितसमाधिना जीवन्मुक्त्यादिलाभो भवति ।

सर्ववासनाक्षयात्तल्लाभः । अत्र श्लोका भवन्ति ॥ उच्छास्त्रं शास्त्रितं चेति पौरुषं द्विविधं मतम् । तत्रोच्छास्त्रमनर्थाय परमार्थाय शास्त्रितम् ॥१ ॥ लोकवासनया जन्तोः शास्त्रवासनयापि च । देहवासनया ज्ञानं यथावन्नैव जायते ॥२ ॥ द्विविधो वासनाव्यूहः शुभश्चैवाशुभश्च तौ । वासनौघेन शुद्धेन तत्र चेदनुनीयसे ॥३ ॥ तत्क्रमेणाशु तेनैव मामकं

पदमाप्नुहि । अथ चेदशुभो भावस्त्वां योजयति संकटे ॥४ ॥ प्राक्तनस्तदसौ यत्नाज्जेतव्यो भवता कपे । शुभाशुभाभ्यां मार्गाभ्यां वहन्ती वासनासरित् ॥५ ॥

पौरुषेण प्रयत्नेन योजनीया शुभे पथि । अशुभेषु समाविष्टं शुभेष्वेवावतारयेत् ॥६ ॥ अशुभाच्चालितं याति शुभं तस्मादपीतरत् । पौरुषेण प्रयत्नेन लालयेच्चित्तबालकम् ॥७ ॥ द्रागभ्यासवशाद्याति यदा ते वासनोदयम् । तदाभ्यासस्य साफल्यं विद्धि त्वममरिमर्दन ॥८ ॥ संदिग्धायामपि भृशं शुभामेव समाचर । शुभायां वासनावृद्धौ न दोषाय मरुत्सुत ॥९ ॥

वासनाक्षयविज्ञानमनोनाशा महामते । समकालं चिराभ्यस्ता भवन्ति फलदा मताः ॥१० ॥ त्रय एवं समं यावन्नाभ्यस्ताश्च पुनः पुनः । तावन्न पदसंप्राप्तिर्भवत्यपि समाशतैः ॥११ ॥ एकैकशो निषेव्यन्ते यद्येते चिरमप्यलम् । तन्न सिद्धिं प्रयच्छन्ति मन्त्राः संकीर्तिता इव ॥१२ ॥ त्रिभिरेतैश्चिराभ्यस्तैर्हृदयग्रन्थयो दृढाः । निःशङ्कमेव त्रुठ्यन्ति बिसच्छेदाद्गुणा इव ॥१३ ॥

जन्मान्तरशताभ्यस्ता मिथ्या संसारवासना । सा चिराभ्यासयोगेन विना न क्षीयते क्वचित् ॥१४ ॥तस्मात्सौम्य प्रयत्नेन पौरुषेण विवेकिना । भोगेच्छां दूरतस्त्यक्त्वा त्रयमेव समाश्रय ॥१५ ॥ तस्माद्वासनया युक्तं मनो बद्धं विदुर्बुधाः । सम्यग्वासनया त्यक्तं मुक्तमित्यभिधीयते । मनोनिर्वासनीभावमाचराशु महाकपे ॥१६ ॥ सम्यगालोचनात्सत्याद्वासना प्रविलीयते । वासनाविलये चेतः शममायाति दीपवत् ॥१७ ॥

वासनां संपरित्यज्य मयि चिन्मात्रविग्रहे । यस्तिष्ठति गतव्यग्रः सोऽहं सच्चित्सुखात्मकः ॥१८ ॥ समाधिमथ कार्याणि मा करोतु करोतु वा । हृदयेनात्तसर्वेहो मुक्त एवोत्तमाशयः ॥१९ ॥ नैष्कर्म्येण न तस्यार्थस्तस्यार्थोऽस्ति न कर्मभिः । न ससाधानजाप्याभ्यां यस्य निर्वासनं मनः ॥२० ॥ संत्यक्तवासनान्मौनादृते नास्त्युत्तमं पदम् ॥२१ ॥

वासनाहीनमप्येतच्चक्षुरादीन्द्रियं स्वतः । प्रवर्तते बहिः स्वाऽर्थे वासनामात्रकारणम् ॥२२ ॥ अयत्नोपनतेष्वक्षि दृग्द्रव्येषु यथा पुनः । नीरागमेव पतति तद्वत्कार्येषु धीरधीः ॥२३ ॥ भावसंवित्प्रकटितामनुरूपा च मारुते । चित्तस्योत्पत्त्युपरमा वासनां मुनयो विदुः ॥२४ ॥ दृढाभ्यस्तपदार्थैकभावनादतिचञ्चलम् । चित्तं संजायते जन्मजरामरणकारणम् ॥२५ ॥

वासनावशतः प्राणस्पन्दस्तेन च वासना । क्रियते चित्तबीजस्य तेन बीजाङ्कुरक्रमः ॥२६ ॥ द्वे बीजे चित्तवृक्षस्य प्राणस्पन्दनवासने । एकस्मिंश्च तयोः क्षीणे क्षिप्रं द्वे अपि नश्यतः ॥२७ ॥ असङ्गव्यवहारत्वाद्भवभावनवर्जनात् । शरीरनाशदर्शित्वाद्वासनां न प्रवर्तते । वासनासंपरित्यागाच्चित्तं गच्छत्यचित्तताम् ॥२८ ॥ अवासनत्वात्सततं यदा न मनुते मनः । अमनस्ता तदोदेति परमोपशमप्रदा ॥२९ ॥

अव्युत्पन्नमना यावद्भवानज्ञाततत्पदः । गुरुशास्त्रप्रमाणैस्तु निर्णितं तावदाचार ॥३० ॥ ततः पक्वकषायेण नूनं विज्ञात वस्तुना । शुभोऽप्यसौ त्वया त्याज्यो वासनौघो निराधिना ॥३१ ॥ द्विविधश्चित्तनाशोऽस्ति सरूपोऽरूप एव च । जीवन्मुक्तः सरूपः स्यादरूपो देहमुक्तिगः ॥३२ ॥

अस्य नाशमिदानीं त्वं पावने शृणु सादरम् ॥३३ ॥ चित्तनाशाभिधानं हि यदा ते विद्यते पुनः। मैत्र्यादिभिर्गुणैर्युक्तं शान्तिमेति न संशयः। भूयोजन्मविनिर्मुक्तं जीवन्मुक्तस्य तन्मनः ॥३४ ॥ सरूपोऽसौ मनोनाशो जीवन्मुक्तस्य विद्यते। अरूपस्तु मनोनाशो वैदेहीमुक्तिगो भवेत् ॥३५ ॥ सहस्राङ्कुरशाखात्मफलपल्लवशालिनः ॥३६ ॥

अस्य संसारवृक्षस्य मनोमूलमिदं स्थितम्। संकल्प एव तन्मन्ये संकल्पोपशमेन तत् ॥३७ ॥ शोषयाशु यथा शोषमेति संसारपादपः। उपाय एक एवास्ति मनसः स्वस्य निग्रहे ॥३८ ॥ मनसोऽभ्युदयो नाशो मनोनाशो महोदयः। ज्ञमनो नाशमभ्येति मनो ज्ञस्य हि शृङ्खला ॥३९ ॥ तावन्निशीव वेताला वल्गन्ति हृदि वासनाः। एकतत्त्वदृढाभ्यासाद्यावन्न विजितं मनः ॥४० ॥

प्रक्षीणचित्तदर्पस्य. निगृहीतेन्द्रियद्विषः। पद्मिन्य इव हेमन्ते क्षीयन्ते भोगवासनाः ॥४१ ॥ हस्तं हस्तेन संपीड्य दन्तैर्दन्तान्विचूर्ण्य च। अङ्गान्यङ्गैः समाक्रम्य जयेदादौ स्वकं मनः ॥४२ ॥ उपविश्योपविश्यैकां चिन्तकेन मुहुर्मुहुः। न शक्यते मनो जेतुं विना युक्तिमनिन्दिताम् ॥४३ ॥ अङ्कुशेन विना मत्तो यथा दुष्टमतङ्गजः। अध्यात्मविद्याधिगमः साधुसंगतिरेव च ॥४४ ॥

वासनासंपरित्यागः प्राणस्पन्दनिरोधनम्। एतास्ता युक्तयः पुष्टाः सन्ति चित्तजयेकिल ॥४५ ॥ सतीषु युक्तिष्वेतासु हठान्नियमयन्ति ये। चेतसो दीपमुत्सृज्य विचिन्वन्ति तमोऽञ्जनैः ॥४६ ॥ विमूढाः कर्तुमुद्युक्ता ये हठाच्चेतसो जयम्। ते निवध्नन्ति नागेन्द्रमुन्मत्तं बिसतन्तुभिः ॥४७ ॥ द्वे बीजे चित्तवृक्षस्य वृत्तिव्रततिधारिणः। एकं प्राणपरिस्पन्दो द्वितीयं दृढभावना ॥४८ ॥

सा हि सर्वगता संवित्प्राणास्पन्देन चाल्यते। चित्तैकाग्र्याद्यतो ज्ञानमुक्तं समुपजायते ॥४९ ॥ तत्साधनमथो ध्यानं यथावदुपदिश्यते। विनाप्यविकृतिं कृत्स्नां संभवव्यत्ययक्रमात्। यशोऽरिष्टं च चिन्मात्रं चिदानन्दं विचिन्तय ॥५० ॥ अपानेऽस्तंगते प्राणो यावन्नाभ्युदितो हृदि। तावत्सा कुम्भकावस्था योगिभिर्यानुभूयते ॥५१ ॥

बहिरस्तंगते प्राणे यावन्नापान उद्गतः। तावत्पूर्णां समावस्थां बहिष्ठं कुम्भकं विदुः ॥५२ ॥ ब्रह्माकारमनोवृत्तिप्रवाहोऽहंकृतिं विना। संप्रज्ञातसमाधिः स्याद्ध्यानाभ्यासप्रकर्षतः ॥५३ ॥ प्रशान्तवृत्तिकं चित्तं परमानन्ददायकम्। असंप्रज्ञातनामायं समाधिर्योगिनां प्रियः ॥५४ ॥

प्रभाशून्यं मनःशून्यं बुद्धिशून्यं चिदात्मकम्। अतद्व्यावृत्तिरूपोऽसौ समाधिर्मुनि-भावितः ॥५५ ॥ ऊर्ध्वपूर्णमधःपूर्णं मध्यपूर्णं शिवात्मकम्। साक्षाद्विधिमुखो ह्येष समाधिः पारमार्थिकः ॥५६ ॥ दृढभावनया त्यक्तपूर्वापरविचारणम्। यदादानं पदार्थस्य वासना सा प्रकीर्तिता ॥५७ ॥

भावितं तीव्रसंवेगादात्मना यत्तदेव सुः। भवत्याशु कपिश्रेष्ठ विगतेतरवासनः ॥५८ ॥ तादृग्रूपो हि पुरुषो वासनाविवशीकृतः। संपश्यति यदैवैतत्सद्वस्त्विति विमुह्यति ॥५९ ॥ वासनावेगवैचित्र्यात्स्वरूपं न जहाति तत्। भ्रान्तं पश्यति दुर्दृष्टिः सर्वं मदवशादिव ॥६० ॥ वासना द्विविधा प्रोक्ता शुद्धा च मलिना तथा। मलिना जन्महेतुः स्याच्छुद्धा जन्मविनाशिनी ॥६१ ॥

अज्ञानसुधनाकारा घनाहंकारशालिनी । पुनर्जन्मकरी प्रोक्ता मलिना वासना बुधैः । पुनर्जन्माङ्कुरं त्यक्त्वा स्थितिः संभृष्टबीजवत् ॥६२॥ बहुशास्त्रकथाकन्थारोमन्थेन वृथैव किम् । अन्वेष्टव्यं प्रयत्नेन मारुते ज्योतिरान्तरम् ॥६३॥ दर्शनादर्शने हित्वा स्वयं केवलरूपतः । य आस्ते कपिशार्दूल ब्रह्म स ब्रह्मवित्स्वयम् ॥६४॥

अधीत्य चतुरो वेदान्सर्वशास्त्राण्यनेकशः । ब्रह्मतत्त्वं न जानाति दर्वी पाकरसं यथा ॥६५॥ स्वदेहाशुचिगन्धेन न विरज्येत यः पुमान् । विरागकारणं तस्य किमन्यदुपदिश्यते ॥६६॥ अत्यन्तमलिनो देहो देही चात्यन्तनिर्मलः । उभयोरन्तरं ज्ञात्वा कस्य शौचं विधीयते ॥६७॥ बद्धो हि वासनाबद्धो मोक्षः स्याद्वासनाक्षयः । वासनां संपरित्यज्य मोक्षार्थित्वमपि त्यज ॥६८॥ मानसीर्वासनाः पूर्वं त्यक्त्वा विषयवासनाः । मैत्र्यादिवासनानाम्नीर्गृहाणामलवासनाः ॥६९॥

ता अप्यतः परित्यज्य ताभिर्व्यवहरन्नपि । अन्तःशान्तः समस्नेहो भव चिन्मात्रवासनः ॥७०॥ तामप्यथ परित्यज्य मनोबुद्धिसमन्विताम् । शेषस्थिरसमाधानो मयि त्वं भव मारुते ॥७१॥ अशब्दमस्पर्शमरूपमव्ययं तथाऽरसं नित्यमगन्धवच्च यत् । अनामगोत्रं मम रूपमीदृशं भजस्व नित्यं पवनात्मजार्तिहन् ॥७२॥ दृशिस्वरूपं गगनोपमं परं सकृद्विभातं त्वजमेकमक्षरम् । अलेपकं सर्वगतं यदद्वयं तदेव चाहं सकलं विमुक्तॐ ॥७३॥ दृशिस्तु शुद्धोऽहमविक्रियात्मको न मेऽस्ति कश्चिद्विषयः स्वभावतः । पुरस्तिरश्चोर्ध्वमधश्च सर्वतः सुपूर्णभूमाहमितीह भावय ॥७४॥

अजोऽमरश्चैव तथाजरोऽमृतः स्वयंप्रभः सर्वगतोऽहमव्ययः । न कारणं कार्यमतीत्य निर्मलः सदैव तृप्तोऽहमितीह भावय ॥७५॥ जीवन्मुक्तपदं त्यक्त्वा स्वदेहे कालसात्कृते । विशत्यदेहमुक्तत्वं पवनोऽस्पन्दतामिव ॥७६॥ तदेतदृचाभ्युक्तम् । तद्विष्णोः परमं पदं सदा पश्यन्ति सूरयः । दिवीव चक्षुराततम् ॥

तद्विप्रासो विपन्यवो जागृवांसः समिन्धते । विष्णोर्यत्परमं पदम् । ॐ सत्यमितयुपनिषत् । ॐ पूर्णमदः पूर्णमिदं पूर्णात्पूर्णमुदच्यते । पूर्णस्य पूर्णमादाय पूर्णमेवावशिष्यते ॥ ॐ शान्तिः शान्तिः शान्तिः ॥ हरिः ॐ तत्सत् ॥

इति शुक्लयजुर्वेदगता मुक्तिकोपनिषत्समाप्ता ॥

२. सर्वसारोपनिषत्

समस्तवेदान्तसारसिद्धान्तार्थकलेवरम् ।
विकलेवरकैवल्यं रामचन्द्रपदं भजे ।
सर्वसारं निरालम्बं रहस्य वज्रसूचिकम् ।
तेजोनादध्यानविद्यायोगतत्त्वात्मबोधकम् ॥

ॐ सह नाववत्विति शान्तिः ॥

कथं बन्धः कथं मोक्षः का विद्या काऽविद्येति । जाग्नत्स्वग्नसुषुप्तितुरीयं च कथम् । अन्नमयप्राणमयमनोमयविज्ञानमयानन्दमयकोशाः कथम् । कर्ता जीवः पञ्चवर्गः क्षेत्रज्ञः साक्षी कूटस्थोऽन्तर्यामी कथम् । प्रत्यगात्मा परात्मा माया चेति कथम् । आत्मेश्वरजीवः

अनात्मनां देहादीनामात्मत्वेनाभिमन्यते सोऽभिमान आत्मनो बन्धः। तन्निवृत्तिर्मोक्षः। या तदभिमानं कारयति सा अविद्या। सोऽभिमानो यया निवर्तते सा विद्या। मनआदिचतुर्दशकरणैः पुष्कलैरादित्याद्यनुगृहीतैः शब्दादीन्विषयान्स्थूलान्यदोपलभते तदात्मनो जागरणम्। तद्वासनासहितैश्चतुर्दशकरणैः शब्दाद्यभावेऽपि वासनामयाञ्छब्दादीन्यदोपलभते तदात्मनः स्वप्नम्।

चतुर्दशकरणोपरमाद्विशेपविज्ञानाभावाद्यदा शब्दादीन्नोपलभते तदात्मनः सुपुप्तम्। अवस्थात्रयभावाभावसाक्षी स्वयंभावरहितं नैरन्तर्यं चैतन्यं यदा तदा तुरीयं चैतन्यमित्युच्यते। अन्नकार्याणां कोशानां समूहोऽन्नमयः कोश इत्युच्यते। प्राणादिचतुर्दशवायुभेदा अन्नमयकोशे यदा वर्तन्ते तदा प्राणमयः कोश इत्युच्यते। एतत्कोशद्वयसंसक्तं मनआदिचतुर्दशकरणैरात्मा शब्दादिविषयसंकल्पादीन्धर्मान्यदा करोति तदा मनोमयः कोश इत्युच्यते। एतत्कोशत्रयसंसक्तं तद्गतविशेषज्ञो यदा भासते तदा विज्ञानमयः कोश इत्युच्यते। एतत्कोशचतुष्टयं संसक्तं स्वकारणाज्ञाने वटकणिकायामिव वृक्षो यदा वर्तते तदानन्दमयः कोश इत्युच्यते। सुखदुःखबुद्ध्या श्रेयोऽन्तः कर्ता यदा तदा इष्टविषये बुद्धिः सुखबुद्धिरनिष्टविषये बुद्धिर्दुःखबुद्धिः। शब्दस्पर्शरूपरसगन्धाः सुखदुःखहेतवः। पुण्यपापकर्मानुसारी भूत्वा प्राप्तशरीरसंयोगमप्राप्तशरीरसंयोगमिव कुर्वाणो यदा दृश्यते तदोपहितजीव इत्युच्यते। मनआदिश्च प्राणादिश्चेच्छादिश्च सत्त्वादिश्च पुण्यादिश्चैते पञ्चवर्गा इत्येतेषां पञ्चवर्गाणां धर्मीभूतात्मा ज्ञानादृते न विनश्यत्यात्मसन्निधौ नित्यत्वेन, प्रतीयमान आत्मोपाधिर्यस्तल्लिङ्गशरीरं हृद्ग्रन्थिरित्युच्यते तत्र यत्प्रकाशते चैतन्यं स क्षेत्रज्ञ इत्युच्यते। ज्ञातृज्ञानज्ञेयानामाविर्भावतिरोभावज्ञाता स्वयमाविर्भावतिरोभावरहितः स्वयंज्योतिः साक्षीत्युच्यते।

ब्रह्मादिपिपीलिकापर्यन्तं सर्वप्राणिबुद्धिष्ववशिष्टतयोपलभ्यमानः सर्वप्राणिबुद्धिस्थो यदा तदा कूटस्थ इत्युच्यते। कूटस्थोपहित भेदानां स्वरूपलाभहेतुर्भूत्वा मणिगणे सूत्रमिव सर्वक्षेत्रेष्वनुस्यूतत्वेन यदा काश्यते आत्मा तदान्तर्यामीत्युच्यते। सत्यं ज्ञानमनन्तमानन्दं सर्वोपाधिविनिर्मुक्तं कटकमुकुटाद्युपाधिरहितसुवर्णघनवद्विज्ञानचिन्मात्रस्वभावात्मा यदा भासते तदा त्वंपदार्थः। सत्यं ज्ञानमनन्तं ब्रह्म। सत्यमविनाशि। अविनाशि नाम देशकालवस्तु निमित्तेषु विनश्यत्सु यन्न विनश्यति तदविनाशि। ज्ञानं नामोत्पत्तिविनाशरहितं नैरन्तर्यं चैतन्यं ज्ञानमित्युच्यते। अनन्तं नाम मृद्विकारेषु मृदिव स्वर्णविकारेषु स्वर्णमिव तन्तुविकारेषु तन्तुरिवाव्यक्तादिसृष्टिप्रपञ्चेषु पूर्णं व्यापकं चैतन्यमनन्तमित्युच्यते।

आनन्दं नाम सुखचैतन्यस्वरूपोऽपरिमितानन्दसमुद्रोऽवशिष्टसुखस्वरूपश्चानन्द इत्युच्यते। एतद्वस्तुचतुष्टयं यस्य लक्षणं देशकालवस्तुनिमित्तेष्वव्यभिचारी तत्पदार्थः परमात्मेत्युच्यते। त्वंपदार्थादौपाधिकात्तत्पदार्थादौपाधिकभेदाद्विलक्षणमाकाशवत्सूक्ष्मं केवलसत्तामात्रस्वभावं परं ब्रह्मेत्युच्यते। माया नाम अनादिरन्तवती प्रमाणाप्रमाणसाधारणा न सती नासती न सदसती स्वयमधिका विकाररहिता निरूप्यमाणा सतीतरलक्षणशून्या सा मायेत्युच्यते। अज्ञानं तुच्छाप्यसती कालत्रयेऽपि पामराणां वास्तवी च सत्त्वबुद्धिर्लौकिकानामिदमित्थमित्यनिर्वचनिया वक्तुं न शक्यते। नाहं भवाम्यहं देवो नेन्द्रियाणि दशैव तु। न बुद्धिर्न मनः शश्वन्नाहंकारस्थैव च ॥१॥

अप्राणो ह्यमनाः शुभ्रो बुद्ध्यादीनां हि सर्वदा। साक्ष्यहं सर्वदा नित्यश्चिन्मात्रोऽहं न संशयः ॥२ ॥ नाहं कर्ता नैव भोक्ता प्रकृतेः साक्षिरूपकः। मत्सान्निध्यात्प्रवर्तन्ते देहाद्या अजडा इव ॥३ ॥ स्थाणुर्नित्यः सदानन्दः शुद्धो ज्ञानमयोऽमलः। आत्माहं सर्वभूतानां विभुः साक्षी न संशयः ॥४ ॥ ब्रह्मैवाहं सर्ववेदान्तवेद्यं नाहं वेद्यं व्योमवातादिरूपम्। रूपं नाहं नाम नाहं न कर्म ब्रह्मैवाहं सच्चिदानन्दरूपम् ॥५ ॥ नाहं देहो जन्ममृत्यू कुतो मे नाहं प्राणः क्षुत्पिपासे कुतो मे। नाहं चेतः शोकमोहौ कुतो मे नाहं कर्ता बन्धमोक्षौ कुतो म इत्युपनिषत् ॥ ॐ सह नाववत्विति शान्तिः ॥

इति सर्वसारोपनिषत्समाप्ता ॥

३. निरालम्बोपनिषत्

यत्रालम्बालम्बिभावो विद्यते न कदाचन।

ज्ञविज्ञसम्यग्ज्ञालम्बं निरालम्बं हरिं भजे ॥

ॐ पूर्णमद इति शान्तिः ॥

ॐ नमः शिवाय गुरवे सच्चिदानन्दमूर्तये। निष्प्रपञ्चाय शान्ताय निरालम्बाय तेजसे ॥ निरालम्बं समाश्रित्य सालम्बं विजहाति यः। संन्यासी च योगी च कैवल्यं पदमश्नुते। एषामज्ञानजन्तूनां समस्तारिष्टशान्तये। यद्यद्बोद्धव्यमखिलं तदाशङ्क्य ब्रवीम्यहम् ॥ किं ब्रह्म। क ईश्वरः। को जीवः। का प्रकृतिः। कः परमात्मा। को ब्रह्मा। को विष्णुः। को रुद्रः। क इन्द्रः। कः शमनः। कः सूर्यः। कश्चन्द्रः। के सुराः। के असुराः। के पिशाचाः। के मनुष्याः। काः स्त्रियः। के मश्वादयः। किं स्थावरम्। के ब्राह्मणादयः। का जातिः। किं कर्म। किमकर्म। किं ज्ञानम्। किमज्ञानम्। किं सुखम्। किं दुःखम्। कः स्वर्गः। को नरकः। को बन्धः। को मोक्षः। क उपास्यः। कः शिष्यः। को विद्वान्। को मूढः। किमासुरम्। किं तपः। किं परमं पदम्। किं ग्राह्यम्। किमग्राह्यम्। कः संन्यासीत्याशङ्क्याह ब्रह्मेति। स होवाच महदहंकारपृथिव्यप्तेजोवाय्वाकाशत्वेन बृहद्रूपेणाण्डकोशेन कर्मज्ञानार्थरूपतया भासमानमद्वितीयमखिलोपाधिविनिर्मुक्तं तत्सकलशक्त्युपबृंहितमनाद्यनन्तं शुद्धं शिव शान्तं निर्गुणमित्यादिवाच्यमनिर्वाच्यं चैतन्यं ब्रह्म ॥ ईश्वर इति च ॥

ब्रह्मैव स्वशक्तिं प्रकृत्यभिधेयामाश्रित्य लोकान्सृष्ट्वा प्रवि३यान्तर्यामित्वेन ब्रह्मादीनां बुद्धीन्द्रियनियन्तृत्वादीश्वरः ॥ जीव इति च ब्रह्मविष्ण्वीशानेन्द्रादीनां नामरूपद्वारा स्थूलोऽहमिति मिथ्याध्यासवशाज्जीवः। सोऽहमेकोऽपि देहारम्भकभेदवशाद्बहुजीवः। प्रकृतिरिति च ब्रह्मणः सकाशान्नानाविचित्रजगन्निर्माणसामार्थ्यबुद्धिरूपा ब्रह्मशक्तिरेव प्रकृतिः। परमात्मेति च देहादेः परतरत्वद्ब्राह्मैव परमात्मा स ब्रह्मा स विष्णुः स इन्द्रः स शमनः स सूर्यः स चन्द्रस्ते सुरास्ते असुरास्ते पिशाचास्ते मनुष्यास्ताः स्त्रियस्ते पश्वादयस्तत्स्थावरं ते ब्राह्मणादयः। सर्वं खल्विदं ब्रह्म नेह नानास्ति किंचन। जातिरिति च। न चर्मणो न रक्तस्य न मांसस्य न चास्थिनः। न जातिरात्मनो जातिर्व्यवहारप्रकल्पिता। कर्मेति च क्रियमाणेन्द्रियैः कर्माण्यहं करोमीत्यध्यात्मनिष्ठतया

कृतं कर्मैव कर्म । अकर्मेति च कर्तृत्वभोक्तृत्वाद्यहंकारतया बन्धरूपं जन्मादि कारणं नित्यनैमित्तिकयागव्रततपोदानादिषु फलाभिसंधानं यत्तदकर्म ।

ज्ञानमिति च देहेन्द्रियनिग्रहसद्गुरूपासनश्रवणमनननिदिध्यासनैर्यद्यद्दृग्दृश्यस्वरूपं सर्वान्तरस्थं सर्वसमं घटपटादिपदार्थमिवाविकारं विकारेषु चैतन्यं विना किंचिन्नास्तीति साक्षात्कारानुभवो ज्ञानम् । अज्ञानमिति च रज्जौ सर्पभ्रान्तिरिवाद्वितीये सर्वानुस्यूते सर्वमये ब्रह्मणि देवतिर्यङ्नरस्थावरस्त्रीपुरुषवर्णाश्रमबन्धमोक्षोपाधिनानात्मभेदकल्पित ज्ञानमज्ञानम् । सुखमिति च सच्चिदानन्दस्वरूपं ज्ञात्वानन्दरूपा या स्थितिः सैव सुखम् । दुःखमिति अनात्मरूपः विषयसंकल्प एव दुःखम् । स्वर्ग इति च सत्संसर्गः स्वर्गः । नरक इति च असत्संसारविषयजनसंसग एव नरकः ।

बन्ध इति च अनाद्यविद्यावासनया जातोऽहमित्यादिसंकल्पो बन्धः । पितृमातृसहोदरदारापत्यगृहारामक्षेत्रममता संसारावरणसंकल्पो बन्धः । कर्तृत्वाद्यहंकारसंकल्पो बन्धः । अणिमाद्यष्टैश्वर्याशासिद्धसंकल्पो बन्धः । देवमनुष्याद्युपासनाकामसंकल्पो बन्धः । यमाद्यष्टाङ्गयोगसंकल्पो बन्धः । वर्णाश्रमधर्मकर्मसंकल्पो बन्धः । आज्ञाभयसंशयात्मगुणसंकल्पो बन्धः । यागव्रततपोदानविधिविधानज्ञानसंभवो बन्धः । केवलमोक्षापेक्षासंकल्पो बन्धः । संकल्पमात्रसंभवो बन्धः । मोक्ष इति च नित्यानित्यवस्तुविचारादनित्यसंसारसुखदुःखविषयसमस्तक्षेत्रममताबन्धक्षयो मोक्षः । उपास्य इति च सर्वशरीरस्थचैतन्यब्रह्मप्रापको गुरुरुपास्यः । शिष्य इति च विद्याध्वस्तप्रपञ्चावगाहितज्ञानावशिष्टं ब्रह्मैव शिष्यः । विद्वानिति च सर्वान्तरस्थस्वसंविद्रूपविद्विद्वान् । मूढ इति च कर्तृत्वाद्यहंकारभावारूढो मूढः । आसुरमिति च ब्रह्मविष्ण्वीशानेन्द्रादीनामैश्वर्यकामनया निरशनजपाग्निहोत्रादिष्वन्तरात्मानं संतापयति चात्युग्ररागद्वेषविहिंसादम्भाद्यपेक्षितं तप आसुरम् ।

तप इति च ब्रह्म सत्यं जगन्मिथ्येत्यपरोक्षज्ञानाग्निना ब्रह्माद्यैश्वर्याशासिद्धसंकल्पबीजसंतापं तपः । परमं पदमिति च प्राणेन्द्रियाद्यन्तःकरणगुणादेः परतरं सच्चिदानन्दमयं नित्यमुक्तब्रह्मस्थानं परमं पदम् । ग्राह्यमिति च देशकालवस्तुपरिच्छेदराहित्यचिन्मात्रस्वरूपं ग्राह्यम् । अग्राह्यमिति च स्वस्वरूपव्यतिरिक्तमायामयबुद्धीन्द्रियगोचरजगत्सत्यत्वचिन्तनमग्राह्यम् । संन्यासीति च सर्वधर्मान्परित्यज्य निर्ममो निरहंकारो भूत्वा ब्रह्मेष्टं शरणमुपगम्य तत्त्वमसि अहं ब्रह्मास्मि सर्वं खल्विदं ब्रह्म नेह नानास्ति किंचनेत्यादिमहावाक्यार्थानुभवज्ञानाद्ब्रह्मैवाहमस्मीति निश्चित्य निर्विकल्पसमाधिना स्वतन्त्रो यतिश्चरति स संन्यासी स मुक्तः स पूज्यः स योगी स परमहंसः सोऽवधूतः स ब्राह्मण इति । इदं निरालम्बोपनिषदं योऽधीते गुर्वनुग्रहतः सोऽग्निपूतो भवति स वायुपूतो भवति न स पुनरावर्तते न स पुनरावर्तते पुनर्नाभिजायते पुनर्नाभिजायत इत्युपनिषत् । ॐ पूर्णमद इति शान्तिः ॥

इति निरालम्बोपनिषत्समाप्ता ॥

४. मैत्रेय्युपनिषत्

श्रुत्याचार्योपदेशेन मुनयो यत्पदं ययुः।
तत्स्वानुभूतिसंसिद्धं स्वमात्रं ब्रह्म भावये॥
ॐ आप्यायन्त्विति शान्तिः॥

ॐ बृहद्रथो वै नाम राजा राज्ये ज्येष्ठं पुत्रं निधापयित्वेदमशाश्वतं मन्यमानः शरीरं वैराग्यमुपेतोऽरण्यं निर्जगाम। स तत्र परमं तप आस्थायादित्यमीक्षमाण ऊर्ध्वबाहुस्तिष्ठत्यन्ते सहस्रस्य मुनिरन्तिकमाजगामाग्निरिवाधूमकस्तेजसा निर्दहन्निवात्मविद्भगवाञ्छाकायन्य उत्तिष्ठोत्तिष्ठ वरं वृणीष्वेतिराजानमब्रवीत्स तस्मै नमस्कृत्योवाच भगवन्नाहमात्मवित्त्वं तत्त्वविच्छृणुमो वयं स त्वं नो ब्रूहीत्येतद्वृत्तं पुरस्तादशक्यं मा पृच्छ प्रश्नमैक्ष्वाकान्यान्कामान्वृणीष्वेति शाकायन्यस्य चरणावभिमृश्यमानो राजेमां गाथां जगाद॥१॥ अथ किमेतैर्वान्यानां शोषणं महार्णवानां शिखरिणां प्रपतनं ध्रुवस्य प्रचलनं स्थानं वा तरूणां निमज्जनं पृथिव्याः स्थानादपसरणं सुराणां सोऽहमित्येतद्विधेऽस्मिन्संसारे किं कामोपभोगैर्यैरेवाश्रितस्यासकृदुपावर्तनं दृश्यत इत्युद्धर्तुमर्हसीत्यन्धोदपानस्थो भेक इवाहमस्मिन्संसारे भगवंस्त्वं नो गतिरिति॥२॥

भगवञ्शरीरमिदं मैथुनादेवोद्भूतं संविदपेतं निरय एव मूत्रद्वारेण निष्क्रान्तमस्थिभिश्चितं मांसेनानुलिप्तं चर्मणावबद्धं विण्मूत्रवातपित्तकफमज्जामेदोवसाभिरन्यैश्च मलैर्बहुभिः परिपूर्णमेतादृशे शरीरे वर्तमानस्य भगवंस्त्वं नो गतिरिति॥३॥ अथ भगवाञ्छाकायन्यः सुप्रीतोऽब्रवीद्राजानं महाराज बृहद्रथेक्ष्वाकुवंशध्वजशीर्षात्मज्ञः कृतकृत्यस्त्वं मरुन्नाम्नो विश्रुतोऽसीत्ययं खल्वात्मा ते कतमो भगवान्वर्ण्य इति तं होवाच॥ शब्दस्पर्शमया येऽर्था अनर्था इव ते स्थिताः। येषां सक्तस्तु भूतात्मा न स्मरेच्च परं पदम्॥१॥ तपसा प्राप्यते सत्त्वं सत्त्वात्संप्राप्यते मनः। मनसा प्राप्यते ह्यात्मा ह्यात्मापत्त्या निवर्तते॥२॥ यथा निरिन्धनो वह्निः स्वयोनावुपशाम्यति। तथा वृत्तिक्षयाच्चित्तं स्वयोनावुपशाम्यति॥३॥ स्वयोनावुपशान्तस्य मनसः सत्यगामिनः। इन्द्रियार्थविमूढस्यानृताः कर्मवशानुगाः॥४॥ चित्तमेव हि संसारस्तत्प्रयत्नेन शोधयेत्। यच्चित्तस्तन्मयो भवति गुह्यमेतत्सनातनम्॥५॥ चित्तस्य हि प्रसादेन हन्ति कर्म शुभाशुभम्। प्रसन्नात्मात्मनि स्थित्वा सुखमक्षयमश्नुते॥६॥ समासक्तं यदा चित्तं जन्तोर्विषयगोचरम्॥ यद्येवं ब्रह्मणि स्यात्तत्को न मुच्येत बन्धनात्॥७॥ हृत्पुण्डरीकमध्ये तु भावयेत्परमेश्वरम्। साक्षिणं बुद्धिवृत्तस्य परमप्रेमगोचरम्॥८॥ अगोचरं मनोवचामवधूतादिसंप्लवम्। सत्तामात्रप्रकाशैकप्रकाशं भावनातिगम्॥९॥ अहेयमनुपादेयमसामान्यविशेषणम्। ध्रुवं स्तिमितगम्भीरं न तेजो न तमस्ततम्। निर्विकल्पं निराभासं निर्वाणमयसंविदम्॥१०॥

नित्यः शुद्धो बुद्धमुक्तस्वभावः सत्यः सूक्ष्मः संविभुश्चाद्वितीयः। आनन्दाब्धिर्यः परः सोऽहमस्मि प्रत्यग्धातुर्नात्र संशीतिरस्ति॥११॥

आनन्दमन्तर्निजमाश्रयं तमाशापिशाचीमवमानयन्तम्। आलोकयन्तं जगदिन्द्रजालमापत्कथं मां प्रविशेदसङ्गम्॥१२॥ वर्णाश्रमाचारयुता विमूढाः कर्मानुसारेण फलं लभन्ते। वर्णादिधर्मं हि परित्यजन्तः स्वानन्दतृप्ताः पुरुषा भवन्ति॥१३॥ वर्णाश्रमं

सावयवं स्वरूपमाद्यन्तयुक्तं ह्यतिकृच्छ्रमात्रम्। पुत्रादिदेहेष्वभिमानशून्यं भूत्वा वसेत्सौख्यतमे ह्यनन्त इति ॥ १४ ॥४ ॥ प्रथमोऽध्यायः ॥१ ॥

अथ भगवान्मैत्रेयः कैलासं जगाम तं गत्वोवाच भो भगवन्परमतत्त्वरहस्यमनुब्रूहीति ॥ स होवाच महादेवः ॥ देहो देवालयः प्रोक्तः स जीवः केवलः शिवः। त्यजेदज्ञाननिर्माल्यं सोऽहंभावेन पूजयेत् ॥१ ॥ अभेददर्शनं ज्ञानं ध्यानं निर्विषयं मनः। स्नानं मनोमलत्यागः शौचमिन्द्रियनिग्रहः ॥२ ॥ ब्रह्मामृतं पिबेद्भैक्षमाचरेद्देहरक्षणे। वसेदेकान्तिको भूत्वा चैकान्ते द्वैतवर्जिते। इत्येवमाचरेद्धीमान्स एवं मुक्तिमाप्नुयात् ॥३ ॥ जातं मृतमिदं देहं मातापितृमलात्मकम्। सुखदुःखालयामेध्यं स्पृष्ट्वा स्नानं विधीयते ॥५ ॥ नवद्वारमलस्रावं सदा काले स्वभावजम्। दुर्गन्धं दुर्मलोपेतंस्पृष्ट्वा स्नानं विधीयते ॥६ ॥ मातृसूतकसंबन्धं सूतके सह जायते। मृतसूतकजं देहं स्पृष्ट्वा स्नानं विधीयते ॥७ ॥ अहंममेति विण्मूत्रलेपगन्धादिमोचनम्। शुद्धशौचमिति प्रोक्तं मृज्जलाभ्यां तु लौकिकम् ॥८ ॥ चित्तशुद्धिकरं शौचं वासनात्रयनाशनम्। ज्ञानवैराग्यमृत्तोयैः क्षालनाच्छौचमुच्यते ॥९ ॥ अद्वैतभावनाभैक्षमभक्ष्यं द्वैतभावनम्। गुरुशास्त्रोक्तभावेन भिक्षोर्भैक्षं विधीयते ॥१० ॥

विद्वान्स्वदेशमुत्सृज्य संन्यासानन्तरं स्वतः। कारागारविनिर्मुक्तचोरवद्दूरतो वसेत् ॥११ ॥ अहंकारसुतं वित्तभ्रातरं मोहमन्दिरम्। आशापत्नी त्यजेद्यावत्तावन्मुक्तो न संशयः ॥१२ ॥ मृता मोहमयी माता जातो बोधमयः सुतः। सूतकद्वयसंप्राप्तौ कथं संध्यामुपास्महे ॥१३ ॥ हृदाकाशे चिदादित्यः सदा भासति भासति। नास्तमेति न चोदेति कथं संध्यामुपास्महे ॥१४ ॥ एकमेवाद्वितीयं यद्गुरोर्वाक्येन निश्चितम्। एतदेकान्तमित्युक्तं न मठो न वनान्तरम् ॥१५ ॥ असंशयवतां मुक्तिः संशयाविष्टचेतसाम्। न मुक्तिर्जन्मजन्मान्ते तस्माद्विश्वासमाप्नुयात् ॥१६ ॥ कर्मत्यागान्न संन्यासो न प्रेषोच्चारणेन तु। संधौ जीवात्मनोरैक्यं संन्यासः परिकीर्तितः ॥१७ ॥ वमनाहारवद्यस्य भाति सर्वेषणादिषु। तस्याधिकारः संन्यासे त्यक्तदेहाभिमानिनः ॥१८ ॥

यदा मनसि वैराग्यं जातं सर्वेषु वस्तुषु। तदैव संन्यसेद्विद्वानन्यथा पतितो भवेत् ॥१९ ॥ द्रव्यार्थमन्नवस्त्रार्थं यः प्रतिष्ठार्थमेव वा। संन्यसेदुभयभ्रष्टः स मुक्तिं नाप्तुमर्हति ॥२० ॥ उत्तमा तत्त्वचिन्तैव मध्यमं शास्त्रचिन्तनम्। अधमा मन्त्रचिन्ता च तीर्थभ्रान्त्यधमाधमा ॥२१ ॥ अनुभूतिं विना मूढो वृथा ब्रह्मणि मोदते। प्रतिबिम्बितशाखाग्रफलास्वादनमोदवत् ॥२२ ॥ न त्यजेच्चेद्यतिर्मुक्तो यो माधुकरमातरम्। वैराग्यजनकं श्रद्धाकलत्रं ज्ञाननन्दनम् ॥२३ ॥ धनवृद्धा वयोवृद्धा विद्यावृद्धास्तथैव च। ते सर्वे ज्ञानवृद्धस्य किंकराः शिष्यकिंकराः ॥२४ ॥ यन्मायया मोहितचेतसो मामात्मानमापूर्णमलब्धवन्तः। परं विदग्धोदरपूरणाय भ्रमन्ति काका इव सूरयोऽपि ॥२५ ॥ पाषाणलोहमणिमृण्मयविग्रहेषु पूजा पुनर्जननभोगकरी मुमुक्षोः। तस्माद्यतिः स्वहृदयार्चनमेव कुर्याद्बाह्यार्चनं परिहरेदपुनर्भवाय ॥२६ ॥ अन्तःपूर्णो बहिःपूर्णः पूर्णकुम्भ इवार्णवे। अन्तःशून्यो बहिःशून्यः शून्यकुम्भ इवाम्बरे ॥२७ ॥ मा भव ग्राह्यभावात्मा ग्राहकात्मा च मा भव। भावनामखिलां त्यक्त्वा यच्छिष्टं तन्मयो भव ॥२८ ॥ द्रष्टृदर्शनदृश्यानि त्यक्त्वा वासनया सह। दर्शनप्रथमाभासमात्मानं केवलं भज ॥२९ ॥

संशान्तसर्वसंकल्पा या शिलावदवस्थितिः। जाग्रन्निद्राविनिर्मुक्ता सा स्वरूपस्थितिः परा ॥३०॥ इति द्वितीयोऽध्यायः ॥२॥

अहमस्मि परश्चास्मि ब्रह्मास्मि प्रभवोऽस्म्यहम्। सर्वलोकगुरुश्चास्मि सर्वलोकेऽस्मि सोऽस्म्यहम् ॥१॥ अहमेवास्मि सिद्धोऽस्मि शुद्धोस्मि परमोऽस्म्यहम्। अहमस्मि सदा सोऽस्मि नित्योऽस्मि विमलोऽस्म्यहम् ॥२॥ विज्ञानोऽस्मि विशेषोऽस्मि समोऽस्म्यहम्। शुभोऽस्मि शोकहीनोऽस्मि चैतन्योऽस्मि समोऽस्म्यहम् ॥३॥ मानावमानहीनोऽस्मि निर्गुणोऽसस्म शिवोऽस्म्यहम्। द्वैताद्वैतविहीनोऽस्मि द्वन्द्वहीनोऽस्मि सोऽस्म्यहम् ॥४॥ भावाभावविहीनोऽस्मि भासाहीनोऽस्मि भास्म्यहम्। शून्याशून्यप्रभावोऽस्मि शोभनाशोभनोऽस्म्यहम् ॥५॥ तुल्यातुल्यविहीनोऽस्मि नित्यः शुद्धः सदाशिवः। सर्वासर्वविहीनोऽस्मि सात्त्विकोऽस्मि सदास्म्यहम् ॥६॥ एकसंख्याविहीनोऽस्मि द्विसंख्यावानहं न च। सदसद्भेदहीनोस्मि संकल्परहितोऽस्म्यहम् ॥७॥ नानात्मभेदहीनोऽस्मि ह्यखण्डानन्दविग्रहः। नाहमस्मि न चान्योऽस्मि देहादिरहितोऽस्म्यहम् ॥८॥ आश्रयाश्रयहीनोऽस्मि आधाररहितोऽस्म्यहम्। बन्धमोक्षादिहीनोऽस्मि शुद्धब्रह्मास्मि सोऽस्म्यहम् ॥९॥ चित्तादिसर्वहीनोऽस्मि परमोऽस्मि परात्परः। सदा विचाररूपोऽस्मि निर्विचारोऽस्मि सोऽस्म्यहम् ॥१०॥ आकारोकाररूपोऽस्मि मकारोऽस्मि सनातनः। ध्यातृध्यानविहीनोऽस्मि ध्येयहीनोस्मि सोऽस्म्यहम् ॥११॥ सर्वपूर्णस्वरूपोऽस्मि सच्चिदानन्दलक्षणः। सर्वतीर्थस्वरूपोऽस्मि परमात्मास्म्यहं शिवः ॥१२॥ लक्ष्यालक्ष्यविहीनोऽस्मि लयहीनरसोऽस्म्यहम्। मातृमानविहीनोऽस्मि मेयहीनः शिवोऽस्म्यहम् ॥१३॥ न जगत्सर्वद्रष्टास्मि नेत्रादिरहितोऽस्म्यहम्। प्रवृद्धोऽस्मि प्रबुद्धोऽस्मि प्रसन्नोऽस्मि परोऽस्म्यहम् ॥१४॥ सर्वेन्द्रियविहनोऽस्मि सर्वकर्मकृदप्यहम्। सर्ववेदान्ततृप्तोऽस्मि सर्वदा सुलभोऽस्म्यहम् ॥१५॥

मुदितामुदिताख्योऽस्मि सर्वमौनफलोऽस्म्यहम्। नित्यचिन्मात्ररूपोऽस्मि सदा सच्चिन्मयोऽस्म्यहम् ॥१६॥ यत्किंचिदपि हीनोऽस्मि स्वल्पमप्यति नास्म्यहम्। हृदयग्रन्थिहीनोऽस्मि हृदयाम्भोजमध्यगः ॥१७॥ पड्विकारविहीनोऽस्मि षट्कोशरहितोऽस्म्यहम्। अरिषड्वर्गमुक्तोऽस्मि अन्तरादन्तरोऽस्म्यहम् ॥१८॥ देशकालविमुक्तोऽस्मि दिगम्बरसुखोऽस्म्यहम्। नास्ति नास्ति विमुक्तोऽस्मि नकाररहितोऽस्म्यहम् ॥१९॥ अखण्डाकाशरूपोऽस्मि ह्यखण्डाकारमस्म्यहम्। प्रपञ्चमुक्तचित्तोस्मि प्रपञ्चरहितोऽस्म्यहम् ॥२०॥ सर्वप्रकाशरूपोस्मि चिन्मात्रज्योतिरस्म्यहम्। कालत्रयविमुक्तोऽस्मि कामादिरहितोऽस्म्यहम् ॥२१॥ कायिकादिविमुक्तोऽस्मि निर्गुणः केवलोऽस्म्यहम्। मुक्तिहीनोऽस्मि मुक्तोऽस्मि मोक्षहीनोऽस्म्यहं सदा ॥२२॥ सत्यासत्यादिहीनोऽस्मि सन्मात्रान्नास्म्यहं सदा। गन्तव्यदेशहीनोऽस्मि गमनादिविवर्जितः ॥२३॥ सर्वदा समरूपोऽस्मि शान्तोऽस्मि पुरुषोत्तमः। एवं स्वानुभवो यस्य सोऽहमस्मि न संशयः ॥२४॥ यः शृणोति सकृद्वापि ब्रह्मैव भवति स्वयमित्युपनिषत् ॥ ॐ आप्यायन्त्विति शान्तिः ॥

इति मैत्रेय्युपनिषत्समाप्ता ॥

५. कैवल्योपनिषत्

कैवल्योपनिषद्वेद्यं कैवल्यानन्दतुन्दिलम्।
कैवल्यगिरिजारामं स्वमात्रं कलयेऽन्वहम्।
ॐ सह नाववत्विति शान्तिः ॥

ॐ यथाश्वलायनो भगवन्तं परमेष्ठिनमुपसमेत्योवाच। अधीहि भगवन्ब्रह्मविद्यां वरिष्ठां, सदा सद्भिः सेव्यमानां निगूढाम्। यथाऽचिरात्सर्वपापं व्यपोह्य परात्परं पुरुषं याति विद्वान् ॥१॥ तस्मै स होवाच पितामहश्च श्रद्धाभक्तिध्यानयोगादवैहि ॥२॥ न कर्मणा न प्रजया धनेन, त्यागेनैके अमृतत्वमानशुः। परेण नाकं वेदान्तविज्ञानसुनिश्चितार्थाः, संन्यासयोगाद्यतयः शुद्धसत्त्वाः। ते ब्रह्मलोकेषु परान्तकाले, परामृताः परिमुच्यन्ति सर्वे ॥४॥ विविक्तदेशे च सुखासनस्थः, शुचिः समग्रीवशिरः शरीरः। अन्त्याश्रमस्थः सकलेन्द्रियाणि निरुध्य भक्त्या स्वगुरुं प्रणम्य ॥५॥ हृत्पुण्डरीकं विरजं विशुद्धं, विचिन्त्य मध्ये विशदं विशोकम्। अचिन्त्यमव्यक्तमनन्तरूपं, शिवं प्रशान्तममृतं ब्रह्मयोनिम् ॥६॥ तमादिमध्यान्तविहीनमेकं, विभुं चिदानन्दमरूपमद्भुतम्। उमासहायं परमेश्वरं प्रभुं त्रिलोचनं नीलकण्ठं प्रशान्तम्। ध्यात्वा मुनिर्गच्छति भूतयोनिं, समस्तसाक्षिं तमसः परस्तात् ॥७॥ स ब्रह्मा स शिवः सेन्द्रः सोऽक्षरः परमः स्वराट्। स एव विष्णुः स प्राणः स कलोऽग्निः स चन्द्रमाः ॥८॥

स एव सर्वं यद्भूतं, यच्च भव्यं सनातनम्। ज्ञात्वा तं मृत्युमत्येति नान्यः पन्था विमुक्तये ॥९॥ सर्वभूतस्थमात्मानं सर्वभूतानि चात्मनि। संपश्यन्ब्रह्म परमं, याति नान्येन हेतुना ॥१०॥ आत्मानमरणिं कृत्वा, प्रणवं चोत्तरारणिम्। ज्ञाननिर्मथनाभ्यासात्पापं दहति पण्डितः ॥११॥

स एव मायापरिमोहितात्मा, शरीरमास्थाय करोति सर्वम्। स्त्रियन्नपानादिविचित्रभोगैः स एव जाग्रत्परितृप्तिमेति ॥१२॥ स्वप्ने स जीवः सुखदुःखभोक्ता, स्वमायया कल्पितजीवलोके। सुषुप्तिकाले सकले विलीने तमोऽभिभूत-सुखरूपमेति ॥१३॥ पुनश्च जन्मान्तरकर्मयोगात्स एव जीवः स्वपति प्रबुद्धः। पुरत्रये क्रीडति यश्च जीवस्ततः सुजातं सकलं विचित्रम् ॥ आधारमानन्दमखण्डबोधं, यस्मिँल्लयं याति पुरत्रयं च ॥१४॥ एतस्माज्जायते प्राणो, मनः सर्वेन्द्रियाणि च। खं वायुर्ज्योतिरापश्च पृथ्वी विश्वस्य धारिणी ॥१५॥ यत्परं ब्रह्म सर्वात्मा विश्वस्यायतनं महत्। सूक्ष्मात्सूक्ष्मतरं नित्यं स त्वमेव त्वमेव तत् ॥१६॥ जाग्रत्स्वप्नसुषुप्त्यादिप्रपञ्चं यत्प्रकाशते। तद्ब्रह्माहमिति ज्ञात्वा, सर्वबन्धैः प्रमुच्यते ॥१७॥ त्रिषु धामसु यद्भोग्यं, भोक्ता भोगश्च यद्भवेत्। तेभ्यो विलक्षणः साक्षी चिन्मात्रोऽहं सदाशिवः ॥१८॥ मय्येव सकलं जातं मयि सर्वं प्रतिष्ठितम्। मयि सर्वं लयं याति, तद्ब्रह्माद्वयमस्म्यहम् ॥१९॥ प्रथमः खण्डः ॥१॥

अणोरणीयानहमेव तद्वन्महानहं विश्वमहं विचित्रम्। पुरातनोऽहं पुरुषोऽहमीशो, हिरण्मयोऽहं शिवरूपमस्मि ॥२०॥ अपाणिपादोऽहमचिन्त्यशक्तिः पश्याम्यचक्षुः स शृणोम्यकर्णः। अहं विजानामि विविक्तरूपो, न चास्ति वेत्ता मम चित्सदाहम् ॥२१॥ वेदैरनेकैरहमेव वेद्यो, वेदान्तकृद्वेदविदेव चाहम्। न पुण्यपापे मम नास्ति नाशो, न जन्म

देहेन्द्रियबुद्धिरस्ति ॥२२॥ न भूमिरापो न च वह्निरस्ति न चानिलो मेऽस्ति न चाम्बरं च। एवं विदित्वा परमात्मरूपं गुहाशयं निष्कलमद्वितीयम् ॥२३॥

समस्तसाक्षिं सदसद्विहीनं प्रयाति शुद्धं परमात्मरूपम्॥ यः शतरुद्रियमधीते, सोऽग्निपूतो भवति स वायुपूतो भवति स आत्मपूतो भवति स सुरापानात्पूतो भवति स ब्रह्महत्यायाः पूतो भवति स सुवर्णस्तेयात्पूतो भवति स कृत्याकृत्यात्पूतो भवति तस्मादविमुक्तमाश्रितो भवत्वित्याश्रमी सर्वदा सकृद्वा जपेत्॥ अनेन ज्ञानमाप्नोति, संसारार्णवनाशनम्। तस्मादेवं विदित्वैनं कैवल्यं पदमश्नुते कैवल्यं पदमश्नुत इति ॥२४॥ द्वितीयः खण्डः ॥२॥ ॐ सहनाववत्विति शान्तिः॥

इत्यथर्ववेदीया कैवल्योपनिषत्समाप्ता ॥१३॥

६. अमृतबिन्दूपनिषत्

अमृतबिन्दूपनिषद्वेद्यं यत्परमाक्षरम्।

तद्देव हि त्रिपाद्रामचन्द्राख्यं नः परा गतिः॥

ॐ सह नाववत्विति शान्तिः॥ ॐ मनो हि द्विविधं प्रोक्तं शुद्धं चाशुद्धमेव च। अशुद्धं कामसंकल्पं शुद्धं कामविवर्जितम् ॥१॥ मन एव मनुष्याणां कारणं वन्धमोक्षयोः। बन्धाय विषयासक्तं मुक्त्यै निर्विषयं स्मृतम् ॥२॥

यतो निर्विषयस्यास्य मनसो मुक्तिरिष्यते। तस्मान्निर्विषयं नित्यं मनः कार्यं मुमुक्षुणा ॥३॥ निरस्तविषयासङ्गं संनिरुद्धं मनो हृदि। यदा यात्युन्मनीभावं तदा तत्परमं पदम् ॥४॥ तावदेव निरोद्धव्यं यावद्धृदि गतं क्षयम्। एतज्ज्ञानं च मोक्षं च अतोऽन्यो ग्रन्थविस्तरः ॥५॥१॥

नैव चिन्त्यं न चाचिन्त्यमचिन्त्यं चिन्त्यमेव च। पक्षपातविनिर्मुक्तं ब्रह्म संपद्यते तदा ॥६॥ स्वरेण संधयेद्योगमस्वरं भावयेत्परम्। अस्वरेण हि भावेन भावो नाभाव इष्यते ॥७॥ तदेव निष्कलं ब्रह्म निर्विकल्पं निरञ्जनम्। तद्ब्रह्माहमिति ज्ञात्वा ब्रह्म संपद्यते ध्रुवम् ॥८॥

निर्विकल्पमनन्तं च हेतुदृष्टान्तवर्जितम्। अप्रमेयमनाद्यं च ज्ञात्वा च परमं शिवम् ॥९॥ न निरोधो न चोत्पत्तिर्न वन्द्यो न च शासनम्। न मुमुक्षा न मुक्तिश्च इत्येषा परमार्थता ॥१०॥२॥

एक एवात्मा मन्तव्यो जाग्रत्स्वप्नसुषुप्तिषु। स्थानत्रयाद्यतीतस्य पुनर्जन्म न विद्यते ॥११॥ एक एव हि भूतात्मा भूते भूते व्यवस्थितः। एकधा बहुधा चैव दृश्यते जलचन्द्रवत् ॥१२॥ घटसंभृतमाकाशं लीयमाने घटे यथा। घटो लीयेत नाकाशं तद्वज्जीवो घटोपमः ॥१३॥

घटवद्विविधाकारं भिद्यमानं पुनः पुनः। तद्भग्नं न च जानाति स जानाति च नित्यशः ॥१४॥ शब्दमायावृतो यावत्तावत्तिष्ठति पुष्करे। भिन्ने तमसि चैकत्वमेकमेवानुपस्यति ॥१५॥३॥

शब्दाक्षरं परं ब्रह्म यस्मिन्क्षीणे यदक्षरम्। तद्विद्वानक्षरं ध्यायेद्यदीच्छेच्छान्तिमात्मनः ॥१६॥ द्वे विद्ये वेदितव्ये तु शब्दब्रह्म परं च यत्।

शब्दब्रह्मणि निष्णातः परं ब्रह्माधिगच्छति ॥१७॥ ग्रन्थमभ्यस्य मेधावी ज्ञान-विज्ञानतत्त्वतः। पलालमिव धान्यार्थी त्यजेद्ग्रन्थमशेषतः ॥१८॥

गवामनेकवर्णानां क्षीरस्याप्येकवर्णता। क्षीरवत्पश्यते ज्ञानं लिङ्गिनस्तु गवां यथा ॥१९॥ घृतमिव पयसि निगूढं भूते भूते च वसति विज्ञानम्। सततं मन्थयितव्यं मनसा मन्थानभूतेन ॥२०॥

ज्ञाननेत्रं समादाय चरेद्वह्निमतः परम्। निष्कलं शान्तं तद्ब्रह्माहमिति स्मृतम् ॥२१॥ सर्वभूताधिवासं च यद्भूतेषु वसत्यधि। सर्वानुग्राहकत्वेन तदस्म्यहं वासुदेवः तदस्म्यहं वासुदेव इति ॥२२॥४॥ सहेति शान्तिः॥

इत्यथर्ववेदीया ब्रह्मबिन्दूपनिषत्समाप्ता ॥१२॥

७. आत्मप्रबोधोपनिषत्

श्रीमन्नारायणाकारमष्टाक्षरमहाशयम्।
स्वमात्रानुभवात्सिद्धमात्मबोधं हरिं भजे ॥१॥

ॐ वाङ्मे मनसीति शान्तिः॥

ॐ प्रत्यगानन्दं ब्रह्मपुरुषं प्रणवस्वरूपं अकार उकारो मकार इति त्र्यक्षरं प्रणवं तदेतदोमिति। यमुक्त्वा मुच्यते योगी जन्मसंसारबन्धनात्। ॐ नमो नारायणाय शङ्खचक्रगदाधराय तस्मात् ॐ नमो नारायणायेति मन्त्रोपासको वैकुण्ठभवनं गमिष्यति। अथ यदिदं ब्रह्मपुरं पुण्डरीकं तस्मात्तडिदाभमात्रं दीपवत्प्रकाशं।

ब्रह्मण्यो देवकीपुत्रो ब्रह्मण्यो मधुसूदनः। ब्रह्मण्यः पुण्डरीकाक्षो ब्रह्मण्यो विष्णुरच्युतः॥ सर्वभूतस्थमेकं नारायणं कारणपुरुषमकारणं परं ब्रह्मों। शोकमोहविनिर्मुक्तो विष्णुं ध्यायन्न सीदति। द्वैताद्वैतमभयं भवति। मृत्योः स मृत्युमाप्नोति य इह नानेव पश्यति। हृत्पद्ममध्ये सर्वं यत्तत्प्रज्ञाने प्रतिष्ठितम्।

प्रज्ञानेत्रो लोकः प्रज्ञा प्रतिष्ठा प्रज्ञानं ब्रह्म। स एतेन प्रज्ञेनात्मनास्माल्लोकादुत्क्रम्यामुष्मिन्स्वर्गे लोके सर्वान्कामानाप्त्वाऽमृतः समभवदमृतः समभवत्। यत्र ज्योतिरजस्रं यस्मिल्लोकेऽभ्यर्हितम्। तस्मिन्मां देहि स्वमानमृते लोके अक्षते अच्युते लोके अक्षते अमृतत्वं च गच्छत्यों नमः ॥१॥

प्रगलितनिजमायोऽहं निस्तुलदृशिरूपवस्तुमात्रोऽहम्। अस्तमिताहंतोऽहं प्रगलितजगदीशजीवभेदोऽहम् ॥१॥ प्रत्यगभिन्नपरोऽहं विध्वस्ताशेषविधिनिषेधोऽहम्। समुदास्ताश्रमितोऽहं प्रविततसुखपूर्णसंविदेवाहम् ॥२॥ साक्ष्यनपेक्षोऽहं निजमहिम्नि संस्थोऽहमचलोऽहम्। अजरोऽहमव्ययोऽहं पक्षविपक्षादिभेदविधुरोऽहम् ॥३॥

अवबोधैकरसोऽहं मोक्षानन्दैकसिन्धुरेवाहम्। सूक्ष्मोऽहमक्षरोऽहं विगलितगुणजालकेवलात्माहम् ॥४॥ निस्त्रैगुण्यपदोऽहं कुक्षिस्थानेकलोककलनोऽहम्। कूटस्थ चेतनोऽहं निष्क्रियधामाहमप्रतर्क्योऽहम् ॥५॥

एकोऽहमविकलोऽहं निर्मलनिर्वाणमूर्तिरेवाहम्। निरवयवोऽहमजोऽहं केवलसन्मात्रसारभूतोऽहम् ॥६॥ निरवधिनिजबोधोऽहं शुभतरभावोऽहमप्रभेद्योऽहम्। विभुरहमनवद्योऽहं निरवधिनिःसीमतत्त्वमात्रोऽहम् ॥७॥

वेद्योऽहमागमान्तैराराध्यः सकलभुवनहृद्योऽहम्। परमानन्दघनोऽहं परमानन्दैकभूमरूपोऽहम् ॥८॥ शुद्धोऽहमद्वयोऽहं संततभावोऽहमादिशून्योऽहम्। शमितान्तत्रितयोऽहं बद्धो मुक्तोऽहमद्भुतात्माहम् ॥९॥

शुद्धोऽहमान्तरोऽहं शाश्वतविज्ञानसमरसात्माहम्। शोधितपरतत्त्वोऽहं बोधानन्दैकमूर्तिरिवाहम् ॥१०॥ विवेकयुक्तिबुद्ध्याहं जानाम्यात्मानमद्वयम्। तथापि बन्धमोक्षादिव्यवहारः प्रतीयते ॥११॥

निवृत्तोऽपि प्रपञ्चो मे सत्यवद्भाति सर्वदा। सर्पादौ रज्जुसत्तेव ब्रह्मसत्तैव केवलम्। प्रपञ्चाधाररूपेण वर्ततेऽतो जगन्नहि ॥१२॥ यथेक्षुरससंव्याप्ता शर्करा वर्तते तथा। अद्वयब्रह्मरूपेण व्याप्तोऽहं वै जगन्त्रयम् ॥१३॥

ब्रह्मादिकीटपर्यन्ताः प्राणिनो मयि कल्पिताः। बुद्बुदादिविकारान्तस्तरङ्गः सागरे यथा ॥१४॥ तरङ्गस्थं द्रवं सिन्धुर्न वाञ्छति यथा तथा। विषयानन्दवाञ्छा मे माभूदानन्दरूपतः ॥१५॥ दारिद्र्याशा यथा नास्ति संपन्नस्य तथा मम। ब्रह्मानन्दे निमग्नस्य विषयाशा न तद्भवेत् ॥१६॥

विषं दृष्ट्वाऽमृतं दृष्ट्वा विषं त्यजति बुद्धिमान्। आत्मानमपि दृष्ट्वाहमनात्मानं त्यजाम्यहम् ॥१७॥ घटावभासको भानुर्घटनाशे न नश्यति। देहावभासकः साक्षी देहनाशे न नश्यति।.१८॥ न मे बन्धो न मे मुक्तिर्न मे शास्त्रं न मे गुरुः। मायामात्रविकासत्वान्मायातीतोऽहमद्वयः ॥१९॥

प्राणाश्चलन्तु तद्धर्मैः कामैर्वा हन्यतां मनः। आनन्दबुद्धिपूर्णस्य मम दुःखं कथं भवेत् ॥२०॥ आत्मानमञ्जसा वेद्मि क्वाप्यज्ञानं पलायितम्। कर्तृत्वमद्य मे नष्टं कर्तव्यं वापि न क्वचित् ॥२१॥

ब्राह्मण्यं कुलगोत्रे च नामसौन्दर्यजातयः। स्थूलदेहगता एते स्थूलाद्भिन्नस्य मे नहि ॥२२॥ क्षुत्पिपासान्ध्यबाधिर्यकामक्रोधादयोऽखिलाः। लिङ्गदेहगता एते ह्यलिङ्गस्य न सन्ति हि ॥२३॥

जडत्वप्रियमोदत्वधर्माः कारणदेहगाः। न सन्ति मम नित्यस्य निर्विकारस्वरूपिणः ॥२४॥ उलूकस्य यथा भानुरन्धकारः प्रतीयते। स्वप्रकाशे परानन्दे तमो मूढस्य जायते ॥२५॥ चतुर्दृष्टिनिरोधेऽभ्रैः सूर्यो नास्तीति मन्यते। तथाज्ञानावृतो देही ब्रह्म नास्तीति मन्यते ॥२६॥

यथामृतं विषाद्भिन्नं विषदोषैर्न लिप्यते। न स्पृशामि जडाद्भिनो जडदोषाप्रकाशतः ॥२७॥ स्वल्पापि दीपकणिका बहुलं नाशयेत्तमः। स्वल्पोऽपि बोध निबिडं बहुलं नाशयेत्तमः ॥२८॥ कालत्रये यथा सर्पो रज्जौ नास्ति तथा मयि। अहंकारादिदेहान्तं जगन्नास्त्यहमद्वयः ॥२९॥

चिद्रूपत्वान्न मे जाड्यं सत्यत्वान्नानृतं मम। आनन्दत्वान्न मे दुःखमज्ञानाद्भाति सत्यवत् ॥३०॥ आत्मप्रबोधोपनिषन्मुहूर्तमुपासित्वा न स पुनरावर्तते न स पुनरावर्तत इत्युपनिषत् ॥ ॐ वाङ्मे मनसीति शान्तिः ॥

इत्यात्मप्रबोधोपनिषत्समाप्ता ॥

८. स्कन्दोपनिषत्

यत्रासंभिन्नतां याति स्वातिरिक्तभिदाततिः ।
संविन्मात्रं परं ब्रह्म तत्स्वमात्रं विजृम्भते ॥

ॐ सहनाववत्विति शान्तिः ॥

अच्युतोऽस्मि महादेव तव कारुण्यलेशतः । विज्ञानघन एवास्मि शिवोस्मि किमतः परम् ॥१ ॥ न निजं निजवद्भात्यन्तःकरणजृम्भणात् । अन्तःकरणनाशेन संविन्मात्रस्थितो हरिः ॥२ ॥ संविन्मात्रस्थितश्चाहमजोऽस्मि किमतः परम् । व्यतिरिक्तं जडं सर्वं स्वप्नवच्च विनश्यति ॥३ ॥

चिज्जडानां तु यो द्रष्टा सोऽच्युतो ज्ञानविग्रहः । स एव हि महादेवः स एव हि महाहरिः ॥४ ॥ स एव ज्योतिषां ज्योतिः स एव परमेश्वरः । स एव हि परब्रह्म तद्ब्रह्माहं न संशयः ॥५ ॥ जीवः शिवः शिवो जीवः स जीवः केवलः शिवः । तुषेण बद्धो व्रीहिः स्यात्तुषाभावेन तण्डुलः ॥६ ॥

एवं बद्धस्तथा जीवः कर्मनाशे सदाशिवः । पाशबद्धस्तथा जीवः पाशमुक्तः सदाशिवः ॥७ ॥ शिवाय विष्णुरूपाय शिवरूपाय विष्णवे । शिवस्य हृदयं विष्णुर्विष्णोश्च हृदयं शिवः ॥८ ॥ यथा शिवमयो विष्णुरेवं विष्णुमयः शिवः । यथान्तरं न पश्यामि तथा मे स्वस्तिरायुषि ॥९ ॥ यथान्तरं न भेदाः स्युः शिवकेशवयोस्तथा । देहो देवालयः प्रोक्तः स जीवः केवलः शिवः । त्यजेदज्ञाननिर्माल्यं सोऽहंभावेन पूजयेत् ॥१० ॥

अभेददर्शनं ज्ञानं ध्यानं निर्विषयं मनः । स्नानं मनोमलत्यागः शौचमिन्द्रियनिग्रहः ॥११ ॥ ब्रह्मामृतं पिबेद्भैक्षमाचरेद्देहरक्षणे । वसेदेकान्तिको भूत्वा चैकान्ते द्वैतवर्जिते । इत्येवमाचरेद्धीमान्स एवं मुक्तिमाप्नुयात् ॥१२ ॥ श्रीपरमधाम्ने स्वस्ति चिरायुष्योन्नम इति । विरिञ्चिनारायणशंकरात्मकं नृसिंह देवेश तव प्रसादतः । अचिन्त्यमव्यक्तमनन्तमव्ययं वेदात्मकं ब्रह्म निजं विजानते ॥१३ ॥

तद्विष्णोः परमं पदं सदा पश्यन्ति सूरयः । दिवीव चक्षुराततम् ॥१४ ॥ तद्विप्रासो विपन्यवो जागृवांसः समिन्धते । विष्णोर्यत्परमं पदमित्येतन्निर्वाणानुशासनमिति वेदानुशासनमिति वेदानुशासनमित्युपनिषत् ॥१५ ॥ ॐ सहनाववत्विति शान्तिः ॥

इति स्कन्दोपनिषत्समाप्ता ॥

९. पैङ्गलोपनिषत्

पैङ्गलोपनिषद्वेद्यं परमानन्दविग्रहम् ।
परितः कलये राम परमाक्षरवैभवम् ॥

ॐ पूर्णमद इति शान्तिः ॥

अथ ह पैङ्गलो याज्ञवल्क्यमुपसमेत्य द्वादशवर्षशुश्रूषापूर्वकं परमरहस्यकैवल्यमनुब्रूहीति पप्रच्छ । स होवाच याज्ञवल्क्यः सदेव सोम्येदमग्र आसीत् । तन्नित्यमुक्तमविक्रियं सत्यज्ञानानन्दं परिपूर्णं सनातनमेकमेवाद्वितीयं ब्रह्म ।

तस्मिन्मरुशुक्तिकास्थाणुस्फटिकादौ जलरौप्यपुरुषरेखादिवल्लोहितशुक्लकृष्णगुणमयी गुणसाम्यानिर्वाच्या मूलप्रकृतिरासीत्।

तत्प्रतिबिम्बितं यत्तत्साक्षिचैतन्यमासीत्। सा पुनर्विकृतिं प्राप्य सत्त्वोद्रिक्ताऽव्यक्ताख्यावरणशक्तिरासीत्। तत्प्रतिबिम्बितं यत्तदीश्वरचैतन्यमासीत्। स स्वाधीनमायः सर्वज्ञः सृष्टिस्थितिलयानामादिकर्ता जगदङ्कुररूपो भवति। स्वस्मिन्विलीनं सकलं जगदाविर्भावयति। प्राणिकर्मवशादेष पटो यद्वत्प्रसारितः प्राणिकर्मक्षयात्पुनस्तिरोभावयति।

तस्मिन्नेवाखिलं विश्वं संकोचितपटवद्वर्तते। ईशाधिष्ठितावरणशक्तितो रजोद्रिक्ता महदाख्या विक्षेपशक्तिरासीत्। तत्प्रतिबिम्बितं यत्तद्धिरण्यगर्भचैतन्यमासीत्। स महत्तत्त्वाभिमानी स्पष्टास्पष्टवपुर्भवति। हिरण्यगर्भाधिष्ठितविक्षेपशक्तितस्तमोद्रिक्ताहंकाराभिधा स्थूलशक्तिरासीत्।

तत्प्रतिबिम्बितं यत्तद्विराट्चैतन्यमासीत्। स तदभिमानी स्पष्टवपुः सर्वस्थूलपालको विष्णुः प्रधानपुरुषो भवति। तस्मादात्मन आकाशः संभूतः। आकाशाद्वायुः। वायोरग्निः। अग्नेरापः। अद्भ्यः पृथिवी। तानि पञ्च तन्मात्राणि त्रिगुणानि भवन्ति। स्रष्टुकामो जगद्योनिस्तमोगुणमधिष्ठाय सूक्ष्मतन्मात्राणि भूतानि स्थूलीकर्तुं सोऽकामयत्।

सृष्टेः परिमितानि भूतान्येकमेकं द्विधा विधाय पुनश्चतुर्धा कृत्वा स्वस्वेतरद्वितीयांशैः पञ्चधा संयोज्य पञ्चीकृतभूतैरनन्तकोटिब्रह्माण्डानि तत्तदण्डोचितचतुर्दशभुवनानि तत्तद्भुवनोचितगोलकस्थूलशरीराण्यसृजत्। स पञ्चभूतानां रजोंशांश्चतुर्धा कृत्वा भागत्रयात्पञ्चवृत्त्यात्मकं प्राणमसृजत्।

स तेषां तुर्यभागेन कर्मेन्द्रियाण्यसृजत्। स तेषां सत्त्वांशं चतुर्धा कृत्वा भागत्रयसमष्टितः पञ्चक्रियावृत्त्यात्मकमन्तःकरणमसृजत्। त तेषां सत्त्वतुरीयभागेन ज्ञानेन्द्रियाण्यसृजत्। तत्त्वसमष्टित इन्द्रियापालकानसृजत्। तानि सृष्टान्यण्डे प्राचिक्षिपत्।

तदाज्ञया समष्ट्यण्डं व्याप्य तान्यतिष्ठन्। तदाज्ञयाहंकारसमन्वितो विराट् स्थूलान्यरक्षत्। हरिण्यगर्भस्तदाज्ञया सूक्ष्माण्यपालयत्। अण्डस्थानि तानि तेन विना स्पन्दितुं चेष्टितुं वा न शेकुः। तानि चेतनीकर्तुं सोऽकामयत ब्रह्माण्डब्रह्मरन्ध्राणि समस्तव्यष्टिमस्तकान्विदार्थ तदेवानुप्राविशत्। तदा जडान्यपि तानि तानि चेतनवत्स्वकर्माणि चक्रिरे। सर्वज्ञेशो मायालेशसमन्वितो व्यष्टिदेहं प्रविश्य तया मोहितो जीवत्वमगमत्।

शरीरत्रयतादात्म्यात्कर्तृत्वभोक्तृत्वतामगमत्। जाग्रत्स्वप्नसुषुप्तिमूर्च्छामरणधर्मयुक्तो घटीयन्त्रवदुद्विग्नो जातो मृत इव कुलालचक्रन्यायेन परिभ्रमतीति॥ इति प्रथमोऽध्यायः॥१॥

अथ पैङ्गलो याज्ञवल्क्यमुवाच सर्वलोकानां सृष्टिस्थित्यन्तकृद्विभुरीशः कथं जीवत्वमगमदिति। स होवाच याज्ञवल्क्यः स्थूलमूक्ष्मकारणदेहोद्भवपूर्वकं जीवेश्वरस्वरूपं विविच्य कथयामीति सावधानेनैकाग्रतया श्रूयताम्। ईशः पञ्चीकृतमहाभूतलेशानादाय व्यष्टिसमष्ट्यात्मकस्थूलशरीराणि यथाक्रममकरोत्।

कपालचर्मान्त्रास्थिमांसनखानि पृथिव्यंशाः। रक्तमूत्रलालस्वेदादिकमवंशाः। क्षुत्तृष्णोष्णमोहमैथुनाद्या अग्नयंशाः। प्रचारणोत्तारणश्वासादिका वाय्वंशाः। कामक्रोधादयो

व्योमांशाः। एतत्संघातं कर्मणि संचितं त्वगादियुक्तं बाल्याद्यवस्थाभिमानास्पदं बहुदोषाश्रयं स्थूलशरीरं भवति ॥

अथापञ्चीकृतमहाभूतरजोंशभागत्रयसमष्टितः प्राणमसृजत्। प्राणापानव्यानोदानसमानाः प्राणवृत्तयः। नागकूर्मवृक्करदेवदत्तधनंजया उपप्राणाः। हृदासननाभिकण्ठसर्वाङ्गानि स्थानानि। आकाशादिरजोगुणतुरीयभागेन कर्मेन्द्रियमसृजत्। वाक्पाणिपादपायूपस्थास्तद्वृत्तयः। वचनादानगमनविसर्गानन्दास्तद्विषयाः ॥

एवं भूतसत्त्वांशभागत्रयसमष्टितोऽन्तः करणमसृजत्। अन्तःकरणमनोबुद्धिचित्ताहंकारास्तद्वृत्तयः। संकल्पनिश्चयस्मरणाभिमानानुसंधानास्तद्विषयाः। गलवदननाभिहृदयभ्रूमध्यं स्थानम्। भूतसत्वतुरीयभागेन ज्ञानेन्द्रियमसृजत्। श्रोत्रत्वक्चक्षुर्जिह्वाघ्राणास्तद्वृत्तयः। शब्दस्पर्शरूपरसगन्धास्तद्विपयाः।

दिग्वातार्कप्रचेतोऽश्विवह्नीन्द्रोपेन्द्रमृत्युकाः। चन्द्रो विष्णुश्चतुर्वक्त्रः। शंभुश्च कारणाधिपाः ॥ अथान्नमयप्राणमयमनोमयविज्ञानमयानन्दमयाः पञ्च कोशाः। अन्नरसेनैव भूत्वान्नरसेनाभिवृद्धिं प्राप्यान्नरसमयपृथिव्यां यद्विलीयते सोऽन्नमयकोशः। तदेव स्थूलशरीरम्। कर्मेन्द्रियैः सह प्राणादिपञ्चकं प्राणमयकोशः। ज्ञानेन्द्रियैः सह मनो मनोमयकोशः।

ज्ञानेन्द्रियैः सह बुद्धिर्विज्ञानमयकोशः। एतत्कोशत्रयं लिङ्गशरीरम्। स्वरूपाज्ञानमानन्दमयकोशः। तत्कारणशरीरम् ॥ अथ ज्ञानेन्द्रियपञ्चकं कर्मेन्द्रियपञ्चकं प्राणादिपञ्चकं वियदादिपञ्चकमन्तः करणचतुष्टयं कामकर्मतमांस्यष्टपुरम् ॥ ईशाज्ञयाविराजो व्यष्टिदेहं प्रविश्य बुद्धिमधिष्टाय विश्वत्वमगमत्। विज्ञानात्मा चिदाभासो विश्वो व्यावहारिको जाग्रत्स्थूलदेहाभिमानी कर्मभूरिति च विश्वस्य नाम भवति।

ईशाज्ञया सूत्रात्मा व्यष्टिसूक्ष्मशरीरं प्रविश्य मन अधिष्ठाय तैजसत्वमगमत्। तैजसः प्रातिभासिकः स्वप्नकल्पित इति तैजसत्य नाम भवति। ईशाज्ञया मायोपाधिरव्यक्तसमन्वितो व्यष्टिकारणशरीरं प्रविश्य प्राज्ञत्वमगमत्। प्राज्ञोऽविच्छिन्नः पारमार्थिकः सुषुप्त्यभिमानीति प्राज्ञस्य नाम भवति। अव्यक्तलेशाज्ञानाच्छादितपारमार्थिकजीवस्य तत्त्वमस्यादिवाक्यानि ब्रह्मणैकतां जगुः नेतरयोर्व्यावहारिकप्रातिभासिकयोः

अन्तः करणप्रतिबिम्बितचैतन्यं यत्तदेवावस्थात्रयभाग्भवति। स जाग्रत्स्वप्नसुषुप्त्यवस्थाः प्राप्य घटीयन्त्रवदुद्विग्नो जातो मृत इव स्थितो भवति। अथ जाग्रत्स्वप्नसुषुप्तिमूर्च्छामरणाद्यवस्थाः पञ्च भवन्ति ॥ तत्तद्देवताग्रहान्वितैः श्रोत्रादिज्ञानेन्द्रियैः शब्दाद्यर्थविषयग्रहणज्ञानं जाग्रदवस्था भवति।

तत्र भ्रूमध्यं गतो जीव आपादमस्तकं व्याप्य कृषिश्रवणाद्यखिलक्रियाकर्ता भवति। तत्तत्फलभुक् च भवति। लोकान्तरगतः कर्मार्जितफलं स एव भुङ्क्ते। स सार्वभौमवद्व्यवहाराच्छ्रान्त अन्तर्भवनं प्रवेष्टुं मार्गमाश्रित्य तिष्ठति। करणोपरमे जाग्रत्संस्कारोत्थप्रबोधवद्ग्राह्यग्राहकरूपस्फुरणं स्वप्नावस्था भवति। तत्र विश्व एव जाग्रद्व्यवहारलोपानाडीमध्यं चरंस्तैजसत्वमवाप्य वासनारूपकं जगद्वैचित्र्यं स्वभासा भासयन्यथेप्सितं स्वयं भुङ्क्ते ॥

चित्तैकक्करणा सुषुप्त्यवस्था भवति। भ्रमविश्रान्तशकुनिः पक्षौ संहृत्य नीडाभिमुखं यथा गच्छति तथा जीवोऽपि जाग्रत्स्वप्नप्रपञ्चे व्यवहृत्य श्रान्तोऽज्ञानं प्रविश्य स्वानन्दं भुङ्क्ते॥ अकस्मान्मुद्गरदण्डाद्यैस्ताडितवद्भयाज्ञानाभ्यामिन्द्रियसंघातैः कम्पन्निव मृततुल्या मूर्छा भवति।

जाग्रत्स्वप्नसुषुप्तिमूर्च्छावस्थानामन्या ब्रह्मादिस्तम्बपर्यन्तं सर्वजीवभयप्रदा स्थूलदेहविसर्जनी मरणावस्था भवति। कर्मेन्द्रियाणि ज्ञानेन्द्रियाणि तत्तद्विषयान्प्राणान्संहृत्य कामकर्मान्वित अविद्याभूतवेष्टितो जीवो देहान्तरं प्राप्य लोकान्तरं गच्छति। प्राक्कर्मफलपाकेनावर्तान्तरकीटवद्विश्रान्ति नैव गच्छति। सत्कर्मपरिपाकतो बहूनां जन्मनामन्ते नृणां मोक्षेच्छा जायते। तदा सद्गुरुमाश्रित्य चिरकालसेवया बन्धं मोक्षं कश्चित्प्रयाति।

अविचारकृतो बन्धो विचारान्मोक्षो भवति। तस्मात्सदा विचारयेत्। अध्यारोपापवादतः स्वरूपं निश्चयीकर्तुं शक्यते। तस्मात्सदा विचारयेज्जगज्जीवपरमात्मनो जीवभावजगद्भावबाधे प्रत्यगभिन्नं ब्रह्मैवावशिष्यत इति॥ इति द्वितीयोऽध्यायः॥२॥

अथ हैनं पैङ्गलः प्रपच्छ याज्ञवल्क्यं महावाक्यविवरणनुब्रूहीति। स होवाच याज्ञवल्क्यस्तत्त्वमसि त्वं तदसि त्वं ब्रह्मास्यहं ब्रह्मास्मीत्यनुसंधानं कुर्यात्। तत्र पारोक्ष्यशबलः सर्वज्ञत्वादिलक्षणो मायोपाधिः सच्चिदानन्दलक्षणो जगद्योनिस्तत्पदवाच्यो भवति।

स एवान्तःकरणसंभिन्नबोधोऽस्मत्प्रत्ययावलम्बनस्त्वंपदवाच्यो भवति। परजीवोपाधिमायाविद्ये विहाव तत्त्वंपतलक्ष्यं प्रत्यगभिन्नं ब्रह्म। तत्त्वमसीत्यहं ब्रह्मास्मीति वाक्यार्थविचारः श्रवणं भवति। एकान्तेन श्रवणार्थानुसंधानं मननं भवति। श्रवणमनननिर्विचिकित्सेऽर्थे वस्तुन्येकतानवत्तया चेतःस्थापनं निदिध्यासनं भवति।

ध्यातृध्याने विहाय निवातस्थितदीपवद्ध्येयैकगोचरं चित्तं समाधिर्भवति। तदानीमात्मगोचरा वृत्तयः समुत्थिता अज्ञाता भवन्ति। ताः स्मरणादनुमीयन्ते। इहानादिसंसारे संचिताः कर्मकोटयोऽनेनैव विलयं यान्ति। ततोभ्यासपाटवात्सहस्रशः सदामृतधारा वर्षति। ततो योगवित्तमाः समाधि धर्ममेघं प्राहुः। वासनाजाले निःशेषममुना प्रविलापिते कर्मसंचये पुण्यपापे समूलोन्मूलिते प्राक्परोक्षमपि करतलामलकवद्वाक्यमप्रतिबद्धापरोक्षसाक्षात्कारं प्रसूयते।

तदा जीवन्मुक्तो भवति॥ ईशः पञ्चीकृतभूतानामपञ्चीकरणं कर्तुं सोऽकामयत्। ब्रह्माण्डतद्गतलोकान्कार्यरूपांश्च कारणत्वं प्रापयित्वा ततः सूक्ष्माङ्गं कर्मेन्द्रियाणि प्राणांश्च ज्ञानेन्द्रियाण्यन्तःकरणचतुष्टयं चैकीकृत्य सर्वाणि भौतिकानि कारणे भूतपञ्चके संयोज्य भूमिं जले जलं वह्नौ वह्निं वायौ वायुमाकाशे चाकाशमहंकारे चाहंकारं महति महदव्यक्तेऽव्यक्तं पुरुषे क्रमेण विलीयते।

विराड्ढिरण्यगर्भेश्वरा उपाधिविलयात्परमात्मनि लीयन्ते। पञ्चीकृतमहाभूतसंभवकर्मसंचितस्थूलदेहः कर्मक्षयात्सत्कर्मपरिपाकतोऽपञ्चीकरणं प्राप्य सूक्ष्मेणैकीभूत्वा कारणरूपत्वमासाद्य तत्कारणं कूटस्थे प्रत्यगात्मनि विलीयते। विश्वतैजसप्राज्ञाः स्वस्वोपाधिलयात्प्रत्यगात्मनि लीयन्ते। अण्डं ज्ञनाग्निना दग्धं कारणैः सह परमात्मनि लीनं भवति।

ततो ब्राह्मणः समाहितो भूत्वा तत्त्वंपदैक्यमेव सदा कुर्यात्। ततो मेघापायेंऽशुमानिवात्माविर्भवति। ध्यात्वा मध्यस्थमात्मानं कलशान्तरदीपवत्। अङ्गुष्ठमात्रमात्मानमधूमज्योतिरूपकम् ॥१ ॥ प्रकाशयन्तमन्तःस्थंध्यायेत्कूटस्थमव्ययम्।

ध्यायन्नास्ते मुनिश्चैव चासुप्तेरामृतेस्तु यः ॥२ ॥ जीवन्मुक्तः स विज्ञेयः स धन्यः कृतकृत्यवान्। जीवन्मुक्तपदं त्यक्त्वा स्वदेहे कालसात्कृते। विशत्यदेहमुक्तत्वं पवनोऽस्पन्दतामिव ॥३ ॥ अशब्दमस्पर्शमरूपमव्ययं तथा रसं नित्यमगन्धवच्च यत्। अनाद्यनन्तं महतः परं ध्रुवं तदेव शिष्यत्यमलं निरामयम् ॥४ ॥ इति ॥ इति तृतीयोऽध्यायः ॥३ ॥

अथ हैनं पैङ्गलः प्रपच्छ याज्ञवल्क्यं ज्ञानिनः किं कर्म का च स्थितिरिति। स होवाच याज्ञवल्क्यः। अमानित्वादिसंपन्नो मुमुक्षुरेकविंशतिकुलं तारयति। ब्रह्मविन्मात्रेण कुलनेकोत्तरशतं तारयति। आत्मानं रथिनं विद्धि शरीरं रथमेव च। बुद्धिं तु सारथिं विद्धि मनः प्रग्रहमे व च ॥१ ॥ इन्द्रियाणि हयानाहुर्विषयांस्तेषु गोचरान्। जङ्गमानि विमानानि हृदयानि भनीषिणः ॥२ ॥

आत्मेन्द्रियमनोयुक्तं भोक्तेत्याहुर्महर्षयः। ततो नारायणः साक्षाद्धृदये सुप्रतिष्ठितः ॥३ ॥ प्रारब्धकर्मपर्यन्तमहिनिर्मोकवद्व्यवहरति। चन्द्रवच्चरते देही स मुक्तश्चानिकेतनः ॥४ ॥ तीर्थे श्वपचंगृहे वा तनुं विहाय याति कैवल्यम्। प्राणानवकीर्य याति कैवल्यत् ॥ तं पश्चाद्दिग्बलिं कुर्यादथवा खननं चरेत्। पुंसः प्रव्रजनं प्रोक्तं नेतराय कदाचन ॥५ ॥

नाशौचं नाग्निकार्यं च न पिण्डं नोदकक्रिया। न कुर्यात्पार्वणादिति ब्रह्मभूताय भिक्षवे ॥६ ॥ दग्धस्य दहनं नास्ति पक्वस्य पचनं यथा। ज्ञानाग्निदग्धदेहस्य न च श्राद्धं न च क्रिया ॥७ ॥ यावच्चोपाधिपर्यन्तं तावच्छुश्रूषयेद्गुरुम्। गुरुवद्गुरुभार्यायां तत्पुत्रेषु च वर्तनम् ॥८ ॥ शुद्धमानसः शुद्धचिद्रूपः सहिष्णुः सोऽहमस्मि सहिष्णुः सोऽहमस्मीति प्राप्ते ज्ञानेन विज्ञाने ज्ञेये परमात्मनि हृदि संस्थिते देहे लब्धशान्तिपदं गते तदा प्रभामनोबुद्धिशून्यं भवति। अमृतेन तृप्तस्य पयसा किं प्रयोजनम्।

एतं स्वात्मानं ज्ञात्वा वेदैः प्रयोजनं किं भवति। ज्ञानामृततृप्तयोगिनो न किंचित्कर्तव्यमस्ति तदस्ति चेन्न स तत्त्वविद्भवति। दूरस्थोऽपि न दूरस्थः पिम्डवर्जितः पिण्डस्थोऽपि प्रत्यगात्मा सर्वव्यापी भवति। हृदयं निर्मलं कृत्वा चिन्तयित्वाप्यनामयम्। अहमेव परं सर्वमिति पश्येत्परं सुखम् ॥९ ॥

यथा जले जलं क्षिप्तं क्षिरे घृते घृतम्। अविशेषो भवेत्तद्वज्जीवात्मपरमात्मनोः ॥१० ॥ देहे ज्ञानेन दीपिते बुद्धिरखण्डाकाररुपा यदा भवति तदा विद्वान्ब्रह्मज्ञानाग्निना कर्मबन्धं निर्दहेत्। ततः पवित्रं परमेश्वराख्यमद्वैतरूपं विमलाम्बराभम्। यथोदके तोयमनुप्रविष्टं तथात्मरुपो निरूपाधिसंस्थितः ॥११ ॥ आकाशवत्सूक्ष्मशरीर आत्मा न दृश्यते वायुवदन्तरात्मा। स ब्राह्यमभ्यन्तरनिश्चलात्मा ज्ञानोल्कया पश्यति चान्तरात्मा ॥१२ ॥

यत्रयत्र मृतो ज्ञानी येन वा केन मृत्युना। यथा सर्वगतं व्योम तत्रतत्र लयं गतः ॥१३ ॥ घटाकाशमिवात्मानं विलयं वेत्ति तत्त्वतः। स गच्छति निरालम्बं ज्ञानालोकं

समन्ततः ॥१४ ॥ तपेद्वर्षसहस्राणि एकपादस्थितो नरः । एतस्य ध्यानयोगस्य कलां नार्हति षोडशीम् ॥१५ ॥

इदं ज्ञानमिदं ज्ञेयं तत्सर्वं ज्ञातुमिच्छति। अपि वर्षसहस्रायुः शास्त्रान्तं नाधिगच्छति ॥१६ ॥विज्ञेयोऽक्षरतन्मात्रो जीवितं वापि पञ्चलम् । विहाय शास्त्रजालानि यत्सत्यं तदुपास्यताम् ॥१७ ॥ अनन्तकर्मशौचं च जपो यज्ञस्तथैव च । तीर्थयात्राभिगमनं यावत्तत्त्वं न विन्दति ॥१८ ॥

अहं ब्रह्मेति नियतं मोक्षहेतुर्महात्मनाम् । द्वे पदे बन्धमोक्षाय न ममेति ममेति च ॥१९ ॥ ममेति बध्यते जन्तुर्निर्ममेति विमुच्यते। मनसो ह्युन्मनीभावे द्वैतं नैवोपलभ्यते ॥२० ॥ यदा यात्युन्मनीभावस्तदा तत्परमं पदम् । यत्रयत्र मनो याति तत्रतत्र परं पदम् ॥२१ ॥ तत्रतत्र परं ब्रह्म सर्वत्र समवस्थितम् । हन्यान्मुष्टिभिराकाशं क्षुधार्तः खण्डयेत्तुषम् ॥२२ ॥

नाहं ब्रह्मेति जानाति तस्य मुक्तिर्न जायते । य एतदुपनिषदं नित्यमधीते सोऽग्निपूतो भवति । स वायुपूतो भवति । स आदित्यपूतो भवति । स ब्रह्मपूतो भवति । स विष्णुपूतो भवति । स रुद्रपूतो भवति । स सर्वेषु तीर्थेषु स्नातो भवति । स सर्वेषु वेदेष्वधीतो भवति । स सर्ववेदव्रतचर्यासु चरितो भवति । तेनेतिहासपुराणानां रुद्राणां शतसहस्राणि जप्तानि फलानि भवन्ति ।

प्रणवानामयुतं जप्तं भवति । दश पूर्वान्दशोत्तरान्पुनाति । स पङ्क्तिपावनो भवति । स महान्भवति । ब्रह्महत्यासुरापानस्वर्णस्तेयगुरुतल्पगमनतत्संयोगिपातकेभ्यः पूतो भवति । तद्विष्णोः परमं पदं सदा पश्यन्ति सूरयः । दिवीव चक्षुराततम् ॥ तद्विप्रासो विपन्यवो जागृवांसः समिन्धते । विष्णोर्यत्परमं पदम् ॥ ॐ सत्यमित्युपनिषत् । । ॐ पूर्णमद इति शान्तिः ॥

इति पैङ्गलोपनिषत्समाप्ता ॥

१०. अध्यात्मोपनिषत्

यत्रान्तर्याम्यादिभेदस्तत्त्वतो न हि युज्यते ।
निर्भेदं परमाद्वैतं स्वमात्रमवशिष्यते ॥

ॐ पूर्णमद इति शान्तिः ॥

हरिः ॐ ॥ अन्तःशरीरे निहितो गुहायामज एको नित्यमस्य पृथिवी शरीरं यः पृथिवीमन्तरे संचरन्यं पृथिवी न वेद । यस्यापःशरीरं यो अपोऽन्तरे संचरन्यमापो न विदुः । यस्य तेजः शरीरं यस्तेजोऽन्तरे संचरन्यं तेजो न वेद ।

यस्य वायुः शरीरं यो वायुमन्तरे संचरन्यं वायुर्न वेद। यस्याकाशः शरीरं य आकाशमन्तरे संचरन्यभाकाशो न वेद । यस्य मनः शरीरं यो मनोऽन्तरे संचरन्यं मनो न वेद। यस्य बुद्धिः शरीरं यो बुद्धिमन्तरे संचरन्यं बुद्धिर्न वेद। यस्याहंकारः शरीरं योऽहंकारमन्तरे संचरन्यमहंकारो न वेद ।

यस्य चित्तं शरीरं यश्चित्तमन्तरे संचरन्यं चित्तं न वेद। यस्याव्यक्तं शरीरं योऽव्यक्तमन्तरे संचरन्यमव्यक्तं न वेद । यस्याक्षरं शरीरं योऽक्षरमन्तरे संचरन्यमक्षरं न

वेद । यस्य मृत्युः शरीरं यो मृत्युमन्तरे संचरन्यं मृत्युर्न वेद । स एष सर्वभूतान्तरात्मापहतपाप्मा दिव्यो देव एको नारायणः । अहं ममेति यो भावो देहाक्षादावनात्मनि । अध्यासोऽयं निरस्तव्यो विदुषा ब्रह्मनिष्ठया ॥१ ॥

ज्ञात्वा स्वं प्रत्यगात्मानं बुद्धितद्वृत्तिसाक्षिणम्। सोऽहमित्येव तद्वृत्त्या स्वान्यत्रात्ममतिं त्यजेत् ॥२ ॥ लोकानुवर्तनं त्यक्त्वा त्यक्त्वा देहानुवर्तनम् । शास्त्रानुवर्तनं त्यक्त्वा स्वाध्यासापनयं कुरु ॥३ ॥ स्वात्मन्येव सदा स्थित्या मनो नश्यति योगिनः । युक्त्या श्रुत्या स्वानुभूत्या ज्ञात्वा सार्वात्म्यमात्मनः ॥४ ॥

निद्राया लोकवार्तायाः शब्दादेरात्मविस्मृतेः। क्वचिन्नावसरं दत्त्वा चिन्तयात्मानमात्मनि ॥५ ॥ मातापित्रोर्मलोद्भूतं मलमांसमयं वपुः । त्यक्त्वा चण्डालवद्दूरं ब्रह्मभूय कृती भव ॥६ ॥ घटाकाशं महाकाश इवात्मानं परात्मनि । विलाप्याखण्डभावेन तूष्णीं भव सदा मुने ॥७ ॥ स्वप्रकाशमधिष्ठानं स्वयंभूय सदात्मना। ब्रह्माण्डमपि पिण्डाण्डं त्यज्यतां मलभाण्डवत् ॥८ ॥

चिदात्मनि सदानन्दे देहरूढामहंधियम्। निवेश्य लिङ्गमुत्सृज्य केवलो भव सर्वदा ॥८ ॥ यत्रैष जगदाभासो दर्पणान्तःपुरं यथा । तद्ब्रह्माहमिति ज्ञात्वा कृतकृत्यो भवानघ ॥१० ॥ अहंकारग्रहान्मुक्तः स्वरूपमुपपद्यते। चन्द्रवद्विमलः पूर्णः सदानन्दः स्वयंप्रभः ॥११ ॥ क्रियानाशाद्भवेच्चिन्तानाशोऽस्माद्वासनाक्षयः । वासनाप्रक्षयो मोक्षः सा जीवन्मुक्तिरिष्यते ॥१२ ॥

सर्वत्र सर्वतः सर्वब्रह्ममात्रावलोकनम्। सद्भावभावनादाढ्यद्वासनालयमश्नुते ॥१३ ॥ प्रमादो ब्रह्मनिष्ठायां न कर्तव्यः कदाचन। प्रमादो मृत्युरित्याहुर्विद्यायां ब्रह्मवादिनः ॥१४ ॥ यथापकृष्टं शैवालं क्षणमात्रं न तिष्ठति । आवृणोति तथा माया प्राज्ञं वापि पराङ्मुखम् ॥१५ ॥ जीवतो यस्य कैवल्यं विदेहोऽपि स केवलः। समाधिनिष्ठतामेत्य निर्विकल्पो भवानघ ॥१६ ॥

अज्ञानहृदयग्रन्थेर्निःशेषविलयस्तदा। समाधिना विकल्पेन यदाद्वैतात्मदर्शनम् ॥१७ ॥ अत्रात्मत्वं दृढीकुर्वन्नहमादिषु संत्यजन्। उदासीनतया तेषु तिष्ठेद्घटपटादिवत् ॥१८ ॥ ब्रह्मादिस्तम्बपर्यन्तं मृषामात्रा उपाधयः । ततः पूर्णं स्वमात्मानं पश्येदेकात्मना स्थितम् ॥१९ ॥

स्वयं ब्रह्मा स्वयं विष्णुः स्वयमिन्द्रः स्वयं शिवः । स्वयं विश्वमिदं सर्वं स्वस्मादन्यन्न किंचन ॥२० ॥ स्वात्मन्यारोपिताशेषाभासवस्तुनिरासतः। स्वयमेव परंब्रह्म पूर्णमद्वयमक्रियम् ॥२१ ॥ असत्कल्पो विकल्पोऽयं विश्वमित्येकवस्तुनि। निर्विकारे निराकारे निर्विशेषे भिदा कुतः ॥२२ ॥

द्रष्टृदर्शनदृश्यादिभावशून्ये निरामये। कल्पार्णव इवात्यन्तं परिपूर्णे चिदात्मनि ॥२३ ॥ तेजसीव तमो यत्र विलीनं भ्रान्तिकारणम्। अद्वितीये परे तत्त्वे निर्विशेषे भिदा कुतः ॥२४ ॥ एकात्मके परे तत्त्वे भेदकर्ता कथं वसेत् । सुषुप्तौ सुखमात्रायां भेदः केनावलोकितः ॥२५ ॥ चित्तमूलो विकल्पोऽयं चित्ताभावे न कश्चन । अतश्चित्तं समाधेहि प्रत्यग्रूपे परात्मनि ॥२६ ॥

अखण्डानन्दमात्मानं विज्ञाय स्वस्वरूपतः। बहिरन्तः सदानन्दरसास्वादनमात्मनि ॥२७ ॥ वैराग्यस्य फलं बोधो बोधस्योपरतिः फलम्।

स्वानन्दानुभवाच्छान्तिरेषैवोपरतेः फलम् ॥२८ ॥ यद्युत्तरोत्तराभावे पूर्वरूपं तु निष्फलम्। निवृत्तिः परमा तृप्तिरानन्दोऽनुपमः स्वतः ॥२९ ॥ मायोपाधिर्जगद्योनिः सर्वज्ञत्वादि-लक्षणः। पारोक्ष्यशबलः सत्याद्यात्मकस्तत्पदाभिधः ॥३० ॥

आलम्बनतया भाति योऽस्मत्प्रत्यशब्दयोः। अन्तःकरणसंभिन्नबोधः स त्वंपदाभिधः ॥३१ ॥ मायाविद्ये विहायैव उपाधी परजीवयोः। अखण्डं सच्चिदानन्दं परं ब्रह्म विलक्ष्यते ॥३२ ॥ इत्थं वाक्यैस्तथार्थानुसंधानं श्रवणं भवेत्। युक्त्या संभावितत्वानुसंधानं मननं तु तत् ॥३३ ॥

ताभ्यां निर्विचिकित्सेऽर्थे चेतसः स्थापितस्य यत्। एकतानत्वमेतद्धि निदिध्यासनमुच्यते ॥३४ ॥ ध्यातृध्याने परित्यज्य क्रमाद्ध्येयैकगोचरम्। निवातदीपवच्चित्तं समाधिरभिधीयते ॥३५ ॥ वृत्तयस्तु तदानीमप्यज्ञाता आत्मगोचराः। स्मरणादनुमीयन्ते व्युत्थितस्य समुत्थिताः ॥३६ ॥ अनादाविह संसारे संचिताः कर्मकोटयः। अनेन विलयं यान्ति शुद्धो धर्मो विवर्धते ॥३७ ॥

धर्ममेघमिमं प्राहुः समाधिं योगवित्तमाः। वर्षत्येष यथा धर्मामृतधाराः सहस्रशः ॥३८ ॥ अमुना वासनाजाले निःशेषं प्रविलापिते। समूलोन्मूलिते पुण्यपापाख्ये कर्मसंचये ॥३९ ॥ वाक्यमप्रतिबद्धं सत्प्राक्परोक्षावभासिते। करामलकमद्बोधमपरोक्षं प्रसूयते ॥४० ॥ वासनानुदयो भोग्ये वैराग्यस्य तदावधिः। अहंभावोदयाभावो बोधस्य परमावधिः ॥४१ ॥

लीनवृत्तेरनुत्पत्तिर्मर्यादोपरतेस्तु सा। स्थितप्रज्ञो यतिरयं यः सदानन्दमश्नुते ॥४२ ॥ ब्रह्मण्येव विलीनात्मा निर्विकारो विनिष्क्रियः। ब्रह्मात्मनोः शोधितयो-रेकभावावगाहिनि ॥४३ ॥ निर्विकल्पा च चिन्मात्रा वृत्तिः प्रज्ञेति कथ्यते। सा सर्वदा भवेद्यस्य स जीवन्मुक्त इष्यते ॥४४ ॥

देहेन्द्रियेष्वहंभाव इदंभावस्तदन्यके। यस्य नो भवतः क्वापि स जीवन्मुक्त इष्यते ॥४५ ॥ न प्रत्यग्ब्रह्मणोर्भेदं कदापि ब्रह्मसर्गयोः। प्रज्ञया यो विजानाति स जीवन्मुक्त इष्यते ॥४६ ॥ साधुभिः पूज्यमानेऽस्मिन्पीड्यमानेऽपि दुर्जनैः। समभावो भवेद्यस्य स जीवन्मुक्त इष्यते ॥४७ ॥ विज्ञातब्रह्मतत्त्वस्य यथापूर्वं न संसृतिः। अस्ति चेन्न स विज्ञातब्रह्मभावो बहिर्मुखः ॥४८ ॥

सुखाद्यनुभवो यावत्तावत्प्रारब्धमिष्यते। फलोदयः क्रियापूर्वो निष्क्रियो नहि कुत्रचित् ॥४९ ॥ अहं ब्रह्मेति विज्ञानात्कल्पकोटिशतार्जितम्। संचितं विलयं याति प्रबोधात्स्वप्नकर्मवत् ॥५० ॥ स्वमसङ्गमुदासीनं परिज्ञाय नभो यथा। न श्लिष्यते यतिः किंचित्कदाचिद्भाविकर्मभिः ॥५१ ॥ न नभो घटयोगेन सुरागन्धेन लिप्यते। तथात्मोपाधियोगेन तद्धर्मै नैव लिप्यते ॥५२ ॥

ज्ञानोदयात्पुरारब्धं कर्म ज्ञानान्न नश्यति। अदत्त्वा स्वफलं लक्ष्यमुद्दिश्योत्सृष्ट-बाणवत् ॥५६ ॥ व्याघ्रबुद्ध्या विनिर्मुक्तो बाणः पश्चात्तु गोमतौ। न तिष्ठति भिनत्त्येव लक्ष्यं वेगेन निर्भरम् ॥५४ ॥ अजरोऽस्म्यमरोऽस्मीति य आत्मानं प्रपद्यते। तदात्मना तिष्ठतोऽस्य कुतः प्रारब्धकल्पना ॥५५ ॥

प्रारब्धं सिद्ध्यति तदा यदा देहात्मना स्थितिः। दैहात्मभावो नैवेष्टः प्रारब्धं त्यज्यतामतः ॥५६ ॥ प्रारब्धकल्पनाप्यस्य देहस्य भ्रान्तिरेव हि ॥५७ ॥ **अध्यस्तस्य**

कुतस्तत्त्वमसत्यस्य कुतो जनिः । अजातस्य कुतो नाशः प्रारब्धमसतः कुतः ॥५८ ॥ ज्ञानेनाज्ञानकार्यस्य समूलस्य लयो यदि । तिष्ठत्ययं कथं देह इति शङ्कावतो जडान् । समाधातुं बाह्यदृष्ट्या प्रारब्धं वदति श्रुतिः ॥५९ ॥

न तु देहादिसत्यत्वबोधनाय विपश्चिताम् । परिपूर्णमनाद्यन्तमप्रमेयमविक्रियम् ॥६० ॥ सद्घनं चिद्घनं नित्यमानन्दघनमव्ययम् । प्रत्यगेकरसं पूर्णमनन्तं सर्वतोमुखम् ॥६१ ॥ अहेयमनुपादेयमनाधेयमनाश्रयम् । निर्गुणं निष्क्रियं सूक्ष्मं निर्विकल्पं निरञ्जनम् ॥६२ ॥

अनिरूप्यस्वरूपं यन्मनोवाचामगोचरम् । सत्समृद्धं स्वतःसिद्धं शुद्धं बुद्धमनोदृशम् । एकमेवाद्वयं ब्रह्म नेह नानास्ति किंचन ॥६३ ॥ स्वानुभूत्या स्वयं ज्ञात्वा स्वमात्मानमखण्डितम् । स सिद्धः सुसुखं तिष्ठ निर्विकल्पात्मनात्मनि ॥६४ ॥ क्व गतं केन वा नीतं कुत्र लीनमिदं जगत् । अधुनैव मया दृष्टं नास्ति किं महदद्भुतम् ॥६५ ॥

किं हेयं किमुपादेयं किमन्यत्किं विलक्षणम् । अखण्डानन्दपीयूषपूर्णब्रह्ममहार्णवे ॥६६ ॥ न किंचिदत्र पश्यामि न शृणोमि न वेद्म्यहम् । स्वात्मनैव सदानन्दरूपेणास्मि स्वलक्षणः ॥६७ ॥ असङ्गोऽहमनङ्गोऽहमलिङ्गोऽहमहं हरिः । प्रशान्तोऽहमनन्तोऽहं परिपूर्णश्चिरन्तनः ॥६८ ॥

अकर्ताहमभोक्ताहमविकारोऽहमव्ययः । शुद्धो बोधस्वरूपोऽहं केवलोऽहं सदाशिवः ॥६९ ॥ एतां विद्यामपान्तरतमाय ददौ । अपान्तरतमो ब्रह्मणे ददौ । ब्रह्मा घोराङ्गिरसे ददौ । घोराङ्गिरा रैक्वाय ददौ । रैक्वो रामाय ददौ । रामः सर्वेभ्यो भूतेभ्यो ददावित्येतन्निर्वाणानुशासनं वेदानुशासनं वेदानुशासनमित्युपनिषत् ॥ ॐ पूर्णमद इति शान्तिः ॥ हरिः ॐ तत्सत् ॥

इति अध्यात्मोपनिषत्समाप्ता ॥

११. सुबालोपनिषत्

बीजाज्ञानमहामोहापह्नवाद्यद्विशिष्यते ।
निर्बीजं त्रैपदं तत्त्वं तदस्मीति विचिन्तये ॥
ॐ पूर्णमद इति शान्तिः ॥

ॐ तदाहुः किं तदासीत्तस्मै स होवाच न सन्नासन्न सदसदिति तस्मात्तमः संजायते तमसो भूतादिर्भूतादेराकाशमाकाशाद्वायुर्वायोरग्निरग्नेरापोऽद्भ्यः पृथिवी तदण्डं समभवत्तत्संवत्सरमात्रमुषित्वा द्विधाकरोदधस्ताद्भूमिमुपरिष्टादाकाशं मध्ये पुरुषो दिव्यः सहस्रशीर्षा पुरुषः सहस्राक्षः सहस्रपात् । सहस्रबाहुरिति सोऽग्रे भूतानां मृत्युमसृजत्त्र्यक्षरं त्रिशिरस्कं त्रिपादं खण्डपरशुं तस्य ब्रह्माभिधेति स ब्रह्माणमेव विवेश समानसान्सप्त पुत्रानसृजत्तेह विराजः सत्यमानसानसृजन्तेह प्रजापतयो ब्राह्मणोऽस्य मुखमासीद्बाहू राजन्यः कृतः । ऊरू तदस्य यद्वैश्यः पद्भ्यां शूद्रो अजायत ॥ चन्द्रमा मनसो जातश्चक्षोः सूर्यो अजायत । श्रोत्राद्वायुश्च प्राणश्च हृदयात्सर्वमिदं जायते ॥ इति प्रथमः खण्डः ॥१ ॥

अपानान्निषादा यक्षराक्षसगन्धर्वाश्चास्थिभ्यः पर्वता लोमभ्य ओषधिवनस्पतयो ललाटात्क्रोधजो रुद्रो जायते तस्यैतस्य महतो भूतस्य निःश्वसितमेवैतद्यदृग्वेदो यजुर्वेद

सामवेदोऽथर्ववेदः शिक्षा कल्पो व्याकरणं निरुक्तं छन्दो ज्योतिषामयनं न्यायो मीमांसा धर्मशास्त्राणि व्याख्यानान्युपव्याख्यानानि च सर्वाणि च भूतानि हिरण्यज्योतिर्यस्मिन्नयमात्माधिक्षियन्ति भुवनानि विश्वा ॥ आत्मानं द्विधाकरोदर्धेन स्त्री अर्धेन पुरुषो देवो भूत्वा देवानसृजदृषिर्भूत्वा ऋषीन्यक्षराक्षसगन्धर्वान्ग्राम्यानारण्यांश्च पशूनसृजदितरा गौरितरोऽनड्वानितरो वडवेतरोऽश्व इतरा गर्दभीतरो गर्दभ इतरा विश्वभरीतरो विश्वंभरः सोऽन्ते वैश्वानरो भूत्वा संदग्ध्वा सर्वाणि भूतानि पृथिव्यप्सु प्रलीयत आपस्तेजसि प्रलीयन्ते तेजो वायौ विलीयते विलीयते वायुराकाशे विलीयत आकाशमिन्द्रियेष्विन्द्रियाणि तन्मात्रेषु तन्मात्राणि भूतादौ विलीयन्ते भूतादिर्महति विलीयते महानव्यक्ते विलीयतेऽव्यक्तमक्षरे विलीयते अक्षरं तमसि विलीयते तमः परे देव एकीभवति परस्तान्न सन्नासन्नासदसदित्येतन्निर्वाणानुशासनमिति वेदानुशासनमिति वेदानुशासनम् ॥ इति द्वितीयः खण्डः ॥२ ॥

असद्वा इदमग्र आसीदजातमभूतमप्रतिष्ठितमशब्दमस्पर्शमरूपमरसमगन्धमव्ययममहान्तमबृहन्तमजमात्मानं मत्वा धीरो शोचति ॥ अप्राणममुखमश्रोत्रमवागमनोऽतेजस्कमचक्षुष्कमनामगोत्रमशिरस्कमपाणिपादमस्निग्धमलोहितमप्रमेयमह्रस्वमदीर्घमस्थूलमनण्वनल्पमपारमनिर्देश्यमनपावृतमप्रतर्क्यमप्रकाश्यमसंवृतमनन्तरमबाह्यं न तदश्नाति किंचन न तदश्नाति कश्चनैतद्वै सत्येन दानेन तपसाऽनाशकेन ब्रह्मचर्येण निर्वेदनेनानाशकेन षडङ्गेनैव साधयेदेतत्त्रयं वीक्षेत दमं दानं दयामिति न तस्य प्राणा उत्क्रामन्त्यत्रैव समवलीयन्ते ब्रह्मैव सन्ब्रह्माप्येति य एवं वेद ॥ इति तृतीयः खण्डः । ।३ ॥

हृदयस्य मध्ये लोहितं मांसपिण्डं यस्मिंस्तद्दहरं पुण्डरीकं कुमुदमिवानेकधा विकसितं हृदयस्य दश छिद्राणि भवन्ति येषु प्राणाः प्रतिष्ठिताः स यदा प्राणेन सह संयुज्यते तदा पश्यति नद्यो नगराणि बहूनि विविधानि च यदा व्यानेन सह संयुज्यते तदा पश्यति देवांश्च ऋषींश्च यदापानेन सह संयुज्यते तदा पश्यति यक्षराक्षसगन्धर्वान्यदा दानेन सह संयुज्यते तदा पश्यति देवलोकान्देवान्स्कन्दं जयन्तं चेति यदा समानेन सह संयुज्यते तदा पश्यति देवलोकान्धनानि च यदा वैरम्भेण सह संयुज्यते तदा पश्यति दृष्टं च श्रुतं च भुक्तं चाभुक्तं च सच्चासच्च सर्वं पश्यति अथेमा दश दश नाड्यो भवन्ति तासामेकैकस्य द्वासप्ततिर्द्वासप्ततिः शाखा नाडीसहस्राणि भवन्ति यस्मिन्नयमात्मा स्वपिति शब्दानां च करोत्यथ यद्द्वितीये संकोशे स्वपिति तदेमं च लोकं परं च लोकं पश्यति सर्वाञ्छब्दान्विजानाति स संप्रसाद इत्याचक्षते प्राणः शरीरं परिरक्षति हरितस्य नीलस्य पीतस्य लोहितस्य श्वेतस्य नाड्यो रुधिरस्य पूर्णा अथात्रैतद्दहरं पुण्डरीकं कुमुदमिवानेकधा विकसितं यथा केशः सहस्रधा भिन्नस्तथा हिता नाम नाड्यो भवन्ति हृद्याकाशे परे कोशे दिव्योऽयमात्मा स्वपिति यत्र सुप्तो न कंचन कामं कामयते न कंचन स्वप्नं पश्यति न तत्र देवा न देवलोका यज्ञा न यज्ञा वा न माता न पिता न बन्धुर्न बान्धवो न स्तेनो न ब्रह्महा तेजस्कायममृतं सलिलं एवेदं सलिलं वनं भूयस्तेनैव मार्गेण जाग्राय धावति सम्राडिति होवाच ॥ इति चतुर्थः खण्डः ॥४ ॥

स्थानानि स्थानिभ्यो यच्छति नाडी तेषां निबन्धनं चक्षुरध्यात्मं द्रष्टव्यमधिभूतमादित्यस्तत्राधिदैवतं नाडी तेषां निबन्धनं यश्चक्षुषि यो द्रष्टव्ये य आदित्ये यो नाड्यां यः प्राणे यो विज्ञाने य आनन्दे यो हृद्याकाशे य एतस्मिन्सर्वस्मिन्नन्तरे संचरति

सोऽयमात्मा तमात्मानमुपासीताजरममृतमभयमशोकमनन्तम्। श्रोत्रमध्यात्मं श्रोतव्यमधिभूतं दिशस्तत्राधिदैवतं नाडी तेषां निबन्धनं यः श्रोत्रे यः श्रोतव्ये यो दिक्षु यो नाड्यां यः प्राणे यो विज्ञाने य आनन्दे यो हृद्याकाशे य एतस्मिन्सर्वस्मिन्नन्तरे संचरति सोऽयमात्मा तमात्मानमुपासीताजरममृतमभयमशोकमनन्तम्॥ नासाध्यात्मं घ्रातव्यमधिभूतं पृथिवी तत्राधिदैवतं नाडी तेषां निबन्धनं यो नासायां यो घ्रातव्ये यः पृथिव्यां यो नाड्यां॰ नन्तम्॥ जिह्वाध्यात्मं रसयितव्यमधिभूतं वरुणस्तत्राधिदैवतं नाडी तेषां निबन्धनं यो जिह्वायां यो रसयितव्ये यो वरुणे यो नाड्यां॰ नन्तम्॥

त्वगध्यात्मं स्पर्शयितव्यमधिभूतं वायुस्तत्राधिदैवतं नाडी तेषां निबन्धनं यस्त्वचि यः स्पर्शयितव्ये यो वायौ यो नाड्यां॰ नन्तम्॥ मनोऽध्यात्मं मन्तव्यमधिभूतं चन्द्रस्तत्राधिदैवतं नाडी तेषां निबन्धनं यो मनसि यो मन्तव्ये यश्चन्द्रे यो नाड्यां॰ नन्तम्।। बुद्धिरध्यात्मं बोद्धव्यमधिभूतं ब्रह्मा तत्राधिदैवतं नाडी तेषां निबन्धनं यो बुद्धौ यो बौद्धव्ये यो ब्रह्मणि यो नाड्यां॰ नन्तम्॥ अहंकारोऽध्यात्ममहंकर्तव्यमधिभूतं रुद्रस्तत्राधिदैवतं नाडी तेषां निबन्धनं योऽहंकारे योऽहंकर्तव्ये यो रुद्रे यो नाड्यां॰ नन्तम्॥ चित्तमध्यात्मं चेतयितव्यमधिभूतं क्षेत्रज्ञस्तत्राधिदैवतं नाडी तेषां निबन्धनं यश्चित्ते यश्चेतयितव्ये यः क्षेत्रज्ञे यो नाड्यां॰ नन्तम्॥ वागध्यात्मं वक्तव्यमधिभूतमग्निस्तत्राधिदैवतं नाडी तेषां निबन्धनं यो वाचि यो वक्तव्य योऽग्नौ यो नाड्यां॰ नन्तम्॥

हस्तावध्यात्ममादातव्यमधिभूतमिन्द्रस्तत्राधिदैवतं नाडी तेषां निबन्धनं यो हस्ते य आदातव्ये य इन्द्रे यो नाड्यां॰ नन्तम्॥ पादावध्यात्मं गन्तव्यमधिभूतं विष्णुस्त्राधिदैवतं नाडी तेषां निबन्धनं यः पादे यो गन्तव्ये यो विष्णौ यो नाड्यां॰ नन्तम्॥ पायुरध्यात्मं विसर्जयितव्यमधिभूतं मृत्युस्तत्राधिदैवतं नाडी तेषां निबन्धनं यः पायौ यो विसर्जयितव्ये यो मृत्यौ यो नाड्यां॰ नन्तम्॥ उपस्थोऽध्यात्ममानन्दयितव्यमधिभूतं प्रजापतिस्तत्राधिदैवतं नाडी तेषां निबन्धनं य उपस्थे य आनन्दयितव्ये यः प्रजापतौ यो नाड्यां यः प्राणे यो विज्ञाने य आनन्दे यो हृद्याकाशे य एतस्मिन्सर्वस्मिन्नन्तरे संचरति सोऽयमात्मा तमात्मानमुपासीताजरममृतमभयमशोकमनन्तम्॥

एष सर्वज्ञ एष सर्वेश्वर एष सर्वाधिपतिरेषोऽन्तर्यामियेष योनिः सर्वस्य सर्वसौख्यैरुपास्यमानो न च सर्वसौख्यान्युपास्यति वेदशास्त्रैरुपास्यमानो न च वेदशास्त्राण्युपास्यति यस्यान्नमिदं सर्वं न च योऽन्नं भवत्यतः परं सर्वनयनः प्रशास्तान्नमयो भूतात्मा प्राणमय इन्द्रियात्मा मनोमयः संकल्पात्मा विज्ञानमयः कालात्मानन्दमयो लयात्मैकत्वं नास्ति द्वैतं कुतो मर्त्यं नास्त्यमृतं कुतो नान्तःप्रज्ञो बहिःप्रज्ञो नोभयतःप्रज्ञो न प्रज्ञानघनो न प्रज्ञो नाप्रज्ञोऽपि नो विदितं वेद्यं नास्तीत्येतन्निर्वाणानुशासनमिति वेदानुशासनमिति वेदानुशासनम्॥ इति पञ्चमः खण्डः॥५॥

नैवेह किंचनाग्र आसीदमूलमनाधारमिमाः प्रजाः प्रजायन्ते दिव्यो देव एको नारायणश्चक्षुश्च द्रष्टव्यं च नारायणः श्रोत्रं च श्रोतव्यं च नारायणो घ्राणं च घ्रातव्यं च नारायणो जिह्वा च रसयितव्यं च नारायणस्त्वक् च स्पर्शयितव्यं च नारायणो मतश्च मन्तव्यं च नारायणो बुद्धिश्च बोद्धव्यं च नारायणोऽहंकारश्चाहंकर्तव्यं च नारायणश्चित्तं च चेतयितव्यं च नारायणो वाक् च वक्तव्यं च नारायणो हस्तौ चादातवां च नारायणः पादौ च गन्तव्यं च नारायणः पायुश्च विसर्जयितव्यं च नारायण उपस्थश्चानन्दयितव्यं च नारायणो धाता विधाता

कर्ता विकर्ता दिव्यो देव एको नारायण आदित्या रुद्रा मरुतो वसवोऽश्विनवृचो यजूंषि सामानि मन्त्रोऽग्निराजाहुतिर्नारायण उद्भवः संभवो दिव्यो देव देव एको नारायणो माता पिता भ्राता निवासः शरणं सुहृद्गतिर्नारायणो विराजा सुदर्शनाजितासोम्या-मोधाकुमारामृतासत्यामध्यमानासीराशिशुरासूरासूर्यास्वराविज्ञयानि नाडीनामानि दिव्यानि गर्जति गायति वाति वर्षति वरुणोऽयेमा चन्द्रमाः कला कलिर्धाता ब्रह्मा प्रजापतिर्मघवा दिवसाश्चार्धदिवसाश्च कलाः कल्पाश्चोर्ध्वं च दिशश्च सर्वं नारायणः ॥

पुरुष एवेदं सर्वं यद्भूतं यच्च भव्यम् । उतामृतत्वस्येशानो यदन्नेनातिरोहति ॥ तद्विष्णोः परमं सदा पश्यन्ति सूरयः । दिवीच चक्षुराततम् ॥ तद्विप्रासो विपन्यवो जागृवांसः समिन्धते । विष्णोर्यत्परमं पदम् ॥ तदेतन्निर्वाणानुशासनमिति वेदानुशासनमिति वेदानु-सासनम् ॥ इति षष्ठः खण्डः ॥६ ॥

अन्तः शरीरे निहितो गुहायामज एको नित्यो यस्य पृथिवी शरीरं यः पृथिवीमन्तरे संचरन् यं पृथिवी न वेदः ॥ यस्यापः शरीरं योऽपोन्तरे संचरन्यमापो न विदुः । । यस्य तेजः शरीरं यस्तेजोन्तरे संचरन् यं तेजो न वेद । यस्य वायुः शरीरं यो वायुमन्तरे संचरन् यं वायुर्न वेद ॥ यस्याकाशः शरीरं य आकाशमन्तरे संचरन् यमाकाशो न वेद ॥ यस्ये मनः शरीरं यो मनोन्तरे संचरन् यं मनो न वेद ॥ यस्य वुद्धिः शरीरं यो बुद्धिमन्तरे संचरन् यं बुद्धिर्न वेद ॥ यस्याहंकारः शरीरं योऽहंकारमन्तरे संचरन् यमहंकारो न वेद ॥ यस्य चित्त शरीरं यश्चित्तमन्तरे संचरन् यं चित्तं न वेद ॥ यस्याव्यक्तं शरीरं योऽव्यक्तमन्तरे संचरन् यमव्यक्त न वेद ॥ यस्याक्षरं शरीरं योऽक्षरमन्तरे संचरन् यमक्षरं न वेद ॥ यस्य मृत्युः शरीरं यो मृत्युमन्तरे संचरन् यं मृत्युर्न वेद ॥

स एष सर्वभूतान्तरात्म, पहतपाप्मा दिव्यो देव एको नारायणः ॥ एतां विद्यामपान्तरतमाय ददावपान्तरतमो ब्रह्मणे ददौ ब्रह्मा घोराङ्गिरसे ददौ घोराङ्गिरा रैक्वाय ददौ रैक्वो रामाय ददौ रामः सर्वेभ्यो भूतेभ्यो ददावित्येवं निर्वाणानुशासनमिति वेदानु-शासनमिति वेदानुशासनम् ॥ इति सप्तमः खण्डः ॥७ ॥

अन्तः शरीरे निहितो गुहायां शुद्धः सोऽयमात्मा सर्वस्य मेदोमांसक्लेदावकीर्णे शरीरमध्येऽत्यन्तोपहते चित्रभित्तिप्रतीकाशे गन्धर्वनगरोपमे कदलीगर्भवन्निःसारे जलबुद्बुदवच्चञ्चले निःसृतमात्मानमचिन्त्यरूपं दिव्यं देवमसङ्गं शुद्धं तेजस्कायमरूपं सर्वेश्वरमचिन्त्यमशरीरं निहितं गुहायाममृतं विभ्राजसानमानन्दं तं पश्यन्ति विद्वांसस्तेन लये न पश्यन्ति ॥ इत्यष्टमः खण्डः ॥८ ॥

अथ हैनं रैक्वः पप्रच्छ भगवन्कस्मिसन्सर्वेऽस्तं गच्छन्तीति ॥ तस्मै स होवाच चक्षुरेवाप्येति यच्चक्षुरेवास्तमेति द्रष्टव्यमेवाप्येति यो द्रष्टव्यमेवास्तमेत्यादित्यमेवाप्येति य आदित्यमेवास्तमेति विराजमेवाप्येति यो विराजमेवास्तमेति प्राणमेवाप्येति यः प्राणमेवास्तमेति विज्ञानमेवाप्येति यो विज्ञानमेवाप्येति यो विज्ञानमेवास्तमेत्यानन्दमेवाप्येति य आनन्दमेवास्तमेति तुरीयमेवाप्येति यस्तुरीयमेवास्तमेति तदमृतमभयमशोकमनन्तनिर्बीजमेवाप्येतीति होवाच ॥ श्रोत्रमेवाप्येति यः श्रोत्रमेवास्तमेति श्रोतव्यमेवाप्येति यः श्रोतव्यमेवास्तमेति दिशमेवाप्येति यो दिशमेवास्मेति सुदर्शनामेवाप्येति यः सुदर्शनामेवतमेत्यपानमेवाप्येति योऽपानमेवास्तमेति विज्ञानमेवाप्येति यो विज्ञानमेवास्तमेति

तदमृतमभयमशोकमनन्तनिर्बीजमेवाप्येतीति होवाच ॥ नासामेवाप्येति यो नासामेवास्मेति घ्रातव्यमेवाप्येति यो घ्रातव्यमेवास्तमेति पृथिवीमेवाप्येति यः पृथिवी मेवास्तमेति जितामेवाप्येति यो जितामेवास्तमेति व्यानमेवाप्येति यो व्यानमेवास्तमेति विज्ञानमेवाप्येति तदमृत० होवाच ॥

जिह्वामेवाप्येति यो जिह्वामेवास्तमेति रसयितव्यमेवाप्येति यो रसयितव्यमेवास्तमेति वरुणमेवाप्येति यो वरुणमेवास्तमेति सौम्यामेवाप्येति यः सौम्यामेवास्तमेत्युदानमेवाप्येति य उदानमेवास्तमेति विज्ञानमेवाप्येति तदमृत० होवाच ॥ त्वचमेवाप्येति यस्त्वचमेवास्तमेति स्पर्शयितव्यमेवाप्येति यः स्पर्शयितव्यमेवास्तमेति वायुमेवाप्येति यो वायुमेवास्तमेति मोधामेवाप्येति यो मोधामेवास्मेति समानमेवाप्येति यः समानमेवास्तमेति विज्ञानमेवाप्येति तद० होवाच ॥ वाचमेवाप्येति यो वाचमेवास्तमेति वक्तव्यमेवाप्येति यो वक्तव्यमेवास्तमेत्यग्निमेवाप्येति योऽग्निमेवास्तमेति कुमारामेवाप्येति यः कुमारामेवास्तमेति वैरम्भमेवाप्येति यो वैरम्भमेवास्तमेति विज्ञानमेवाप्येति तद० होवाच ॥

हस्तमेवाप्येति यो हस्तमेवास्तमेत्यादातव्यमेवाप्येति य आदातव्यमेवास्तमेतीन्द्रमेवाप्येति य इन्द्रमेवास्तमेत्यमृतामेवाप्येति योऽमृतामेवास्तमेति मुख्यमेवाप्येति यो मुख्यमेवास्तमेति विज्ञानमेवाप्येति तद० होवाच ॥ पादमेवाप्येति यः पादमेवास्तमेति गन्तव्यमेवाप्येति यो गन्तव्यमेवास्तमेति विष्णुमेवाप्येति यो विष्णुमेवास्तमेति सत्यामेवाप्येति यः सत्यामेवास्तमेत्यन्तर्याममेवाप्येति योऽन्तर्याममेवास्तमेति विज्ञानमेवाप्येति तद० होवाच ॥ पायुमेवाप्येति यः पायुमेवास्तमेति विसर्जयितव्यमेवाप्येति यो विसर्जयितव्यमेवास्तमेति मृत्युमेवाप्येति यो मृत्युमेवास्तमेति मध्यमामेवाप्येति यो मध्यमामेवास्तमेति प्रभञ्जनमेवाप्येति यः प्रभञ्जनमेवास्तमेति विज्ञानमेवाप्येति तद० होवाच ॥ उपस्थमेवाप्येति य उपस्थमेवास्तमेत्यानन्दयितव्यमेवाप्येति य आनन्दयितव्यमेवास्तमेति प्रजापतिमेवाप्येति यः प्रजापतिमेवास्तमेति नासीरामेवाप्येति यो नासीरामेवास्तमेति कुमारमेवाप्येति यः कुमारमेवास्तमेति विज्ञानमेवाप्येति तदमृत० होवाच ॥

मन एवाप्येति यो मन एवास्तमेति मन्तव्यमेवाप्येति यो मन्तव्यमेवास्तमेति चन्द्रमेवाप्येति यश्चन्द्रमेवास्तमेति शिशुमेवाप्येति यः शिशुमेवास्तमेति श्येनमेवाप्येति यः श्येनमेवास्तमेति विज्ञानमेवाप्येति तदमृत० होवाच ॥ बुद्धिमेवाप्येति यो बुद्धिमेवास्तमेति बोद्धव्यमेवाप्येति यो बोद्धव्यमेवास्तमेति ब्रह्माणमेवाप्येति यो ब्रह्माणमेवास्तमेति सूर्यामेवास्तमेति यः सूर्यामेवास्तमेति कृष्णमेवाप्येति यः कृष्णमेवास्तमेति विज्ञानमेवाप्येति तदमृतः होवाच ॥

अहंकारमेवाप्येति योऽहंकारमेवास्तमेत्यहंकर्तव्यमेवाप्येति योऽहंकर्तव्यमेवास्तमेति रुद्रमेवाप्येति यो रुद्रमेवास्तमेत्यसुरामेवाप्येति योऽसुरामेवास्तमेति श्वेतमेवाप्येति यः श्वेतमेवास्तमेति विज्ञानमेवाप्येति तदमृत० होवाच ॥ चित्तमेवाप्येति यश्चित्तमेवास्तमेतिचेतयितव्यमेवाप्येति यश्चेतयितव्यमेवास्तमेति क्षेत्रज्ञमेवाप्येति यः क्षेत्रज्ञमेवास्तमेति भास्वतीमेवाप्येति यो भास्वतीमेवास्तमेति नागमेवाप्येति यो नागमेवास्तमेति विज्ञानमेवाप्येति यो विज्ञानमेवास्तमेत्यानन्दमेवाप्येति य आनन्दमेवास्तमेति तुरीयमेवाप्येति यस्तुरीयमेवास्तमेति तदमृतमभयमशोकमनन्तं निर्बीजमेवाप्येति तद०

होवाच ॥ य एवं निर्बीजं वेद निर्बीज एव स भवति न जायते न म्रियते न मुह्यते न भिद्यते न दह्यते न छिद्यते न कम्पते न कुप्यते सर्वदहनोऽयमात्मेत्याचक्षते नैवमात्मा प्रवचनशतेनापि लभ्यते न बहुश्रुतेन न बुद्धिज्ञानाश्रितेन न मेधया न वेदैर्न यज्ञैर्न तपोभिरुग्रैर्न सांख्यैर्न योगैर्नाश्रमैर्नान्यैरात्मानमुपलभन्ते प्रवचनेन प्रशंसया व्युत्थानेन तमेतं ब्राह्मणा शुश्रुवांसोऽनूचाना उपलभन्ते शान्तो दान्त उपरतस्तितिक्षुः समाहितो भूत्वात्मन्येवात्मानं पश्यति सर्वस्यात्मा भवति य एवं वेद ॥ इति नवमः खण्डः ॥९ ॥

अथ हैनं रैक्वः पप्रच्छ भगवन्कस्मिन्सर्वे संप्रतिष्ठिता भवन्तीति रसातललोकेष्विति होवाच कस्मिन्रसातललोका ओताश्च प्रोताश्चेति भूर्लोकेष्विति होवाच कस्मिन्भूर्लोका ओताश्च प्रोताश्चेति भुवर्लोकेष्विति होवाच कस्मिन्भुवर्लोका ओताश्च प्रोताश्चेति सुवर्लोकेष्विति होवाच कस्मिन्सुवर्लोका ओताश्च प्रोताश्चेति महर्लोकेष्विति होवाच कस्मिन्महर्लोका ओताश्च प्रोताश्चेति जनोलोकेष्विति होवाच कस्मिन् जनोलोका ओताश्च प्रोताश्चेति तपोलोकेष्विति होवाच कस्मिंस्तपोलोका ओताश्च प्रोताश्चेति सत्यलोकेष्विति होवाच कस्मिन्सत्यलोका ओताश्च प्रोताश्चेति प्रजापतिलोकेष्विति होवाच कस्मिन्प्रजापतिलोका ओताश्च प्रोताश्चेति ब्रह्मलोकेष्विति होवाच कस्मिन्ब्रह्मलोका ओताश्च प्रोताश्चेति सर्वलोका आत्मनि ब्रह्मणि मणय इवौताश्च प्रोताश्चेति स होवाचैवमेतान् लोकानात्मनि प्रतिष्ठितान्वेदात्मैव स भवतीत्येतन्निर्वाणानुशासनमिति वेदानुशासनमिति वेदानुशासनम् ॥ इति दशमः खण्डः ॥१० ॥

अथ हैनं रैक्वः पप्रच्छ भगवन्योऽयं विज्ञानधन उत्क्रामन्स केन कतरद्वाव स्थानमुत्सृज्यापक्रामतीति तस्मै स होवाच हृदयस्थ मध्ये लोहितं मांसपिण्डं यस्मिंतद्दहरं पुण्डरीकं कुमुदमिवानेकधा विकसितं तस्य मध्ये समुद्रः समुद्रस्य मध्ये कोशस्तस्मिन्नाड्यश्चतस्रो भवन्ति रमारमेच्छाऽपुनर्भवेति तत्र रमा पुण्येन पुण्यं लोकं नयत्यरमा पापेन पापमिच्छया यत्स्मरति तदभिसंपद्यते अपुनर्भवया कोशं भिनत्ति कोशं भित्त्वा शीर्षकपालं भिनत्ति शीर्षकपालं भित्त्वा पृथिवीं भिनत्ति पृथिवीं भित्त्वापो भिनत्त्यापो भित्तवा तेजो भिनत्ति तेजो भित्त्वा वायुं भिनत्ति वायुं भित्त्वाकाशं भिनत्त्याकाशं भित्त्वा मनो भिनत्ति मनो भित्त्वा भूतादिं भिनत्ति भूतादिं भित्त्वा महान्तं भिनत्ति महान्तं भित्त्वाव्यक्तं भिनत्त्यव्यक्तं भित्त्वाक्षरं भिनत्त्यक्षरं भित्त्वा मृत्युं भिनत्ति मृत्युर्वै परे देव एकीभवतीति परस्तान्न सन्नासन्न सदसदित्येतन्निर्वाणानुशासनमिति वेदानुशासनमिति वेदानशासनम् ॥ इत्येकादशः खण्डः ॥११ ॥

ॐ नारायणाद्वा अन्नमागतं पक्वं ब्रह्मलोके महासंवर्तके पुनः पक्वमादित्ये पुनः पक्वं क्रव्यादि पुनः पक्वं जालकिलक्लिन्नं पर्युषितं पूतमन्नमयाचितमसंक्लृप्तमश्नीयान्न कंचन याचेत ॥ इति द्वादशः खण्डः ॥१२ ॥

बाल्येन तिष्ठासेद्वालस्वभावोऽसङ्गो निरवद्यो मौनेन पाण्डित्येन निरवधिकारतयोपलभ्येत कैवल्यमुक्तं निगमनं प्रजापतिरुवाच महत्पदं ज्ञात्वा वृक्षमूले वसेत कुचेलोऽसहाय एकाकी समाधिस्थ आत्मकाम आप्तकामो निष्कामो जीर्णकामो हस्तिनि सिंहे दंशे मशके नकुले सर्पराक्षसगन्धर्वे मृत्यो रूपाणि विदित्वा न बिभेति कुतश्चनेति वृक्षमिव तिष्ठासेच्छिद्यमानोऽपि न कुप्येत न कम्पेतोत्पलमिव तिष्ठासेच्छिद्यमानोऽपि न कुप्येत न कम्पेताकाशमिव तिष्ठासेच्छिद्यमानोऽपि न कुप्येत न

कम्पेत सत्येन तिष्ठासेत्यत्योऽयमात्मा सर्वेषामेव गन्धानां पृथिवी हृदयं सर्वेषामेव रसानामापो हृदयं सर्वेषामेव रूपाणां तेजो हृदयं सर्वेषामेव स्पर्शानां वायुर्हृदयं सर्वेषामेव शब्दानामाकाशं हृदयं सर्वेषामेव गतीनामव्यक्तं हृदयं सर्वेषामेव सत्त्वानां मृत्युर्हृदयं मृत्युर्वै परे देव एकीभवतीति परस्तान्न सन्नासन्न सदसदित्येतन्निर्वाणानुशासनमिति वेदानुशासनमिति वेदानुशासनम् ॥ इति त्रयोदशः खण्डः ॥१३ ॥

ॐ पृथिवी वान्नमापोऽन्नादा आपो वान्नं ज्योतिरन्नादं ज्योतिर्वान्नं वायुरन्नादो वायुर्वान्नमाकाशोऽन्नाद आकाशो वान्नमिन्द्रियाण्यन्नादानीन्द्रियाणि वान्नं मनोऽन्नादं मनो वान्नं बुद्धिरन्नादा बुद्धिर्वान्नमव्यक्तमन्नादमव्यक्तं वान्नमक्षरमन्नादमक्षरं वान्नं मृत्युरन्नादो मृत्युर्वै परे देव एकीभवतीति परस्तान्न सन्नासन्न सदसदित्येतन्निर्वाणानुशासनमिति वेदानुशासनमिति वेदानशासनम् ॥ इति चतुर्दशः खण्डः ॥१४ ॥

अथ हैनं रैक्वः पप्रच्छ भगवन्योऽयं विज्ञानघन उत्क्रामन्स केन कतरद्वाव स्थानं दहतीति तस्मै स होवाच योऽयं विज्ञानघन उत्क्रामन्प्राणं दहत्यपानं व्यानमुदानं समानं वैरम्भं मुख्यमन्तर्यामं प्रभञ्जनं कुमारं श्येनं श्वेतं कृष्णं नागं दहति पृथिव्यापस्तेजोवाय्वाकाशं दहति जागरितं स्वप्नं सुषुप्तं तुरीयं च महतां च लोकं परं च लोकं दहति लोकालोकं दहति धर्माधर्मं दहत्यभास्करममर्यादं निरालोकमतः परं दहति महान्तं दहत्यव्यक्तं दहत्यक्षरं दहति मृत्यु दहति मृत्युर्वै परे देव एकीभवतीति परस्तान्न संन्नासन्न सदसदित्येतन्निर्वाणानुशासनमिति वेदानुशासनमिति वेदानुशासनम् ॥ इति पञ्चदशः खण्डः ॥१५ ॥

सौबालबीजब्रह्मोपनिपन्नाप्रशान्ताय दातव्या नापुत्राय नाशिष्याय नासंवत्सररोषिताय नापरिज्ञातकुलशीलाय दातव्या नैव च प्रवक्तव्या । यस्य देवे परा भक्तिर्यथा देवे तथा गुरौ । तस्यैते कथिता ह्यर्थाः प्रकाशन्ते महात्मन इत्येतन्निर्वाणानुशासनमिति वेदानुशासनमिति वेदानुशासनम् ॥ इति षोडशः खण्डः ॥१६ ॥ ॐ पूर्णमद इति शान्तिः ॥

इति सुबालोपनिषत्समाप्ता ॥

१२. तेजोबिन्दूपनिषत्

यत्र चिन्मात्रकलना यात्यपह्नवमञ्जसा ।
तच्चिन्मात्रमखण्डैकरसं ब्रह्म भवाम्यहम् ॥

ॐ सह नाववत्विति शान्तिः ॥

ॐ तेजोबिन्दूः परं ध्यानं विश्वात्महृदि संस्थितम् ।

ॐ तेजोबिन्दुः परं ध्यानं विश्वात्महृद्दि संस्थितम् । आणवं शांभवं शान्त स्थूलं सूक्ष्म परं च यत् ॥१ ॥ दुःखाढ्यं च दुराराध्यं दुष्प्रेक्ष्यं मुक्तमव्ययम् । दुर्लभं तत्स्वयं ध्यानं मुनीनां च मनीषिणाम् ॥२ ॥ यताहारो जितक्रोधो जितसङ्गो जितेन्द्रियः । निर्द्वन्द्वो निरहंकारो निराशीरपरिग्रहः ॥३ ॥ अगम्यागमकर्ता यो गम्याऽगमनमानसः । मुखे त्रीणि च विन्दन्ति त्रिधामा हंस उच्यते ॥४ ॥ परं गुह्यतमं विद्धि ह्यस्ततन्द्रो निराश्रयः । सोमरूपकला सूक्ष्मा विष्णोस्तत्परमं पदम् ॥५ ॥ त्रिवक्त्रं त्रिगुणं स्थानं त्रिधातुं रूपवर्जितम् । निश्चलं निर्विकल्पं च निराकारं निराश्रयम् ॥६ ॥ उपाधिरहितं स्थानं वाङ्मनोऽतीतगोचरम् । स्वभावं

भावसंग्राह्यमसंघातं पदाच्युतम् ॥७॥ अनानानन्दनातीतं दुष्प्रेक्ष्यं मुक्तमव्ययम्। चिन्त्यमेवं विनिर्मुक्तं शाश्वतं ध्रुवमच्युतम् ॥८॥ तद्ब्रह्मणस्तदध्यात्मं तद्विष्णोस्तत्परायणम्। अचिन्त्यं चिन्मयात्मानं यद्व्योम परमं स्थितम् ॥९॥

अशून्यं शून्यभावं तु शून्यातीतं हृदि स्थितम्। न ध्यानं च न च ध्याता न ध्येयो ध्येय एव च ॥१०॥ सर्वं च न परं शून्यं न परं नापरात्परम्। अचिन्त्यमप्रबुद्धं च न सत्यं न परं विदुः ॥११॥ मुनीनां संप्रयुक्तं च न देवा न परं विदुः। लोभं मोहं भयं दर्पं कामं क्रोधं च किल्बिषम् ॥१२॥ शीतोष्णे क्षुत्पिपासे च संकल्पकविकल्पकम्। न ब्रह्मकुलदर्पं च न मुक्तिग्रन्थिसंचयम् ॥१३॥ न भयं न सुखं दुःखं तथा मानावमानयोः। एतद्भावविनिर्मुक्तं तद्ग्राह्यं ब्रह्म तत्परम् ॥१४॥ यमो हि नियमस्त्यागो मौनं देशश्च कालतः। आसनं मूलबन्धश्च देहसाम्यं च दृक्स्थितिः ॥१५॥ प्राणसंयमनं चैव प्रत्याहारश्च धारणा। आत्मध्यानं समाधिश्च प्रोक्तान्यङ्गानि वै क्रमात् ॥१६॥ सर्वं ब्रह्मेति वै ज्ञानादिन्द्रियग्रामसंयमः। यमोऽयमिति संप्रोक्तोऽभ्यसनीयो मुहुर्मुहुः ॥१७॥

सजातीयप्रवाहश्च विजातीयतिरस्कृतिः। नियमो हि परानन्दो नियमात्क्रियते बुधैः ॥१८॥ त्यागो हि महता पूज्यः सद्यो मोक्षप्रदायकः ॥१९॥ यस्माद्वाचो निवर्तन्ते अप्राप्य मनसा सह। यन्मौनं योगिभिर्गम्यं तद्भजेत्सर्वदा बुधः ॥२०॥ वाचो यस्मान्निवर्तन्ते तद्वक्तुं केन शक्यते। प्रपञ्चो यदि वक्तव्यः सोऽपि शब्दविवर्जितः ॥२१॥ इति वा तद्भवेन्मौनं सर्वं सहजसंज्ञितम्। गिरां मौनं तु बालानामयुक्तं ब्रह्मवादिनाम् ॥२२॥ आदावन्ते च मध्ये च जनो यस्मिन्न विद्यते। येनेदं सततं व्याप्तं स देशो विजनः स्मृतः ॥२३॥ कल्पना सर्वभूतानां ब्रह्मादीनां निमेषतः। कालशब्देन निर्दिष्टं ह्यखण्डानन्दमद्वयम् ॥२४॥

सुखेनैव भवेद्यस्मिन्नजस्रं ब्रह्मचिन्तनम्। आसनं तद्विजानीयादन्यत्सुखविनाशनम् ॥२५॥ सिद्धये सर्वभूतादि विश्वाधिष्ठानमद्वयम्। यस्मिन्सिद्धिं गताः सिद्धास्तत्सिद्धासनमुच्यते ॥२६॥ यन्मूलं सर्वलोकानां यन्मूलं चित्तबन्धनम्। मूलबन्धः सदा सेव्यो योग्योऽसौ ब्रह्मवादिनाम् ॥२७॥ अङ्गानां समतां विद्यात्समे ब्रह्मणि लीयते। नो चेन्नैव समानत्वमृजुत्वं शुष्कवृक्षवत् ॥२८॥ दृष्टिं ज्ञानमयीं कृत्वा पश्येद्ब्रह्ममयं जगत्। सा दृष्टिः परमोदारा न नासाग्रावलोकिनी ॥२९॥ द्रष्टृदर्शनदृश्यानां विरामो यत्र वा भवेत्। दृष्टिस्तत्रैव कर्तव्या न नासाग्रावलोकिनी ॥३०॥ चित्तादिसर्वभावेषु ब्रह्मत्वेनैव भावनात्। निरोधः सर्ववृत्तीनां प्राणायामः स उच्यते ॥३१॥ निषेधनं प्रपञ्चस्य रेचकाख्यः समीरितः। ब्रह्मैवास्मीति या वृत्तिः पूरको वायुरुच्यते ॥३२॥

ततस्तद्वृत्तिनैश्चल्यं कुम्भकः प्राणसंयमः। अयं चापि प्रबुद्धानामज्ञानां घ्राणपीडनम् ॥३३॥ विषयेष्वात्मतां दृष्ट्वा मनसश्चित्तरञ्जकम्। प्रत्याहारः स विज्ञेयोऽभ्यसनीयो मुहुर्मुहुः ॥३४॥ यत्र यत्र मनो याति ब्रह्मणस्तत्र दर्शनात्। मनसा धारणं चैव धारणा सा परा मता ॥३५॥ ब्रह्मैवास्मीति सद्वृत्त्या निरालम्बतया स्थितिः। ध्यानशब्देन विख्यातः परमानन्ददायकः ॥३६॥ निर्विकारतया वृत्त्या ब्रह्माकारतया पुनः। वृत्तिविस्मरणं सम्यक्समाधिरभिधीयते ॥३७॥ इमं चाकृत्रिमानन्दं तावत्साधु समभ्यसेत्। लक्ष्यो यावत्क्षणात्पुंसः प्रत्यक्त्वं संभवेत्स्वयम् ॥३८॥

ततः साधननिर्मुक्तः सिद्धो भवति योगिराट्। तत्स्वं रूपं भवेत्तस्य विषयो मनसो गिराम् ॥३९ ॥ समाधौ क्रियमाणे तु विघ्नान्यायान्ति वै बलात्। अनुसंधानराहित्यमालस्यं भोगलालसम् ॥४० ॥ लयस्तमश्च विक्षेपस्तेजः स्वेदश्च शून्यता। एवं हि विघ्नबाहुल्यं त्याज्यं ब्रह्मविशारदैः ॥४१ ॥ भाववृत्त्या हि भावत्वं शून्यवृत्त्या हि शून्यता। ब्रह्मवृत्त्या हि पूर्णत्वं तया पूर्णत्वमभ्यसेत् ॥४२ ॥ ये हि वृत्तिं विहायैनां ब्रह्माख्यां पावनीं पराम्। वृथैव ते तु जीवन्ति पशुभिश्च समा नराः ॥४३ ॥

ये तु वृत्तिं विजानन्ति ज्ञात्वा वै वर्धयन्ति ये। ते वै सत्पुरुषा धन्या वन्द्यास्ते भुवनत्रये ॥४४ ॥ येषां वृत्तिः समा वृद्धा परिपक्वा च सा पुनः। ते वै सद्ब्रह्मतां प्राप्ता नेतरे शब्दवादिनः ॥४५ ॥ कुशला ब्रह्मवार्तायां वृत्तिहीनाः सुरागिणः। तेऽप्यज्ञानतया नूनं पुनरायान्ति यान्ति च ॥४६ ॥ निमिषार्धं न तिष्ठन्ति वृत्तिं ब्रह्ममयीं विना। यथा तिष्ठन्ति ब्रह्मद्याः सनकाद्याः शुकादयः ॥४७ ॥ कारणं यस्य वै कार्यं कारणं तस्य जायते। कारणं तत्त्वतो नश्येत्कार्याभावे विचारतः ॥४८ ॥ अथ शुद्धं भवेद्वस्तु यद्वै वाचामगोचरम्। उदेति शुद्धचित्तानां वृत्तिज्ञानं ततः परम् ॥४९ ॥ भावितं तीव्रवेगेन यद्वस्तु निश्चयात्मकम्। दृश्यं ह्यदृश्यतां नीत्वा ब्रह्माकारेण चिन्तयेत् ॥५० ॥ विद्वान्नित्यं सुखे तिष्ठेद्धिया चिद्रसपूर्णया ॥

इति प्रथमोऽध्यायः ॥१ ॥

अथ ह कुमारः शिवं पप्रच्छाऽखण्डैकरसचिन्मात्रस्वरूपमनुब्रूहीति। स होवाच परमः शिवः। अखण्डैकरसं दृश्यमखण्डैकरसं जगत्। अखण्डैकरसं भावमखण्डैकरसं स्वयम् ॥१ ॥ अखण्डैकरसो मन्त्र अखण्डैकरसा क्रिया। अखण्डैकरसं ज्ञानमखण्डैकरसं जलम् ।२ ॥ अखण्डैकरसा भूमिरखण्डैकरसं वियत्। अखण्डैकरसं शास्त्रमखण्डैकरसा त्रयी ॥३ ॥ अखण्डैकरसं ब्रह्म चाखण्डैकरसं व्रतम्। अखण्डैकरसो जीव अखण्डैकरसो ह्यजः ॥४ ॥

अखण्डैकरसो ब्रह्म अखण्डैकरसो हरिः। अखण्डैकरसो रुद्र अखण्डैकरसोऽस्म्यहम् ॥५ ॥ अखण्डैकरसो ह्यात्मा ह्यखण्डैकरसो गुरुः। अखण्डैकरसं लक्ष्यमखण्डैकरसं महः ॥६ ॥ अखण्डैकरसो देह अखण्डैकरसं मनः। अखण्डैकरसं चित्तमखण्डैकरसं सुखम् ॥७ ॥ अखण्डैकरसा विद्या अखण्डैकरसोऽव्ययः। अखण्डैकरसं नित्यमखण्डैकरसं परम् ॥८ ॥ अखण्डैकरसं किंचिदखण्डैकरसं परम्। अखण्डैकरसादन्यन्नास्ति अखण्डैकरसान्न हि। अखण्डैकरसात्किंचिदखण्डैकरसादहम् ॥१० ॥

अखण्डैकरसं स्थूलं सूक्ष्मं चाखण्डरूपकम्। अखण्डैकरसं वेद्यमखण्डैकरसो भवान् ॥११। अखण्डैकरसं गुह्यमखण्डैकरसादिकम्। अखण्डैकरसो ज्ञाता ह्यखण्डैकरसा स्थितिः ॥१२ ॥ अखण्डैकरसा माता अखण्डैकरसः पिता। अखण्डैकरसो भ्राता अखण्डैकरसः पतिः ॥१३ ॥ अखण्डैकरसं सूत्रमखण्डैकरसो विराट्। अखण्डैकरसं गात्रमखण्डैकरसं शिरः ॥१४ ॥ अखण्डैकरसं चान्तरखण्डैकरसं वहिः। अखण्डैकरसं पूर्णमखण्डैकरसामृतम् ॥१५ ॥ अखण्डैकरसं गोत्रमखण्डैकरसं गृहम्। अखण्डैकरसं गोप्यमखण्डैकरसशशशी ॥१६ ॥ अखण्डैकरसास्तारा अखण्डैकरसो रविः। अखण्डैकरसं क्षेत्रमखण्डैकरसा क्षमा ॥१७ ॥ अखण्डैकरसः शान्त अखण्डैकरसोऽगुणः।

अखण्डैकरसः साक्षी अखण्डैकरसः सुहृत् ॥१८ ॥ अखण्डक्रसो बन्धुरखण्डैकरसः सखा । अखण्डैकरसो राजा अखण्डैकरसं पुरम् ॥१९ ॥

अखण्डैकरसं राज्यमखण्डैकरसाः प्रजाः । अखण्डैकरसं तारमखण्डैकरसो जपः ॥२० ॥ अखण्डैकरसं ध्यानमखण्डैकरसं पदम् । अखण्डैकरसं ग्राह्यमखण्डैकरसं महत् ॥२१ ॥ अखण्डैकरसं ज्योतिरखण्डैकरसं धनम् । अखण्डैकरसं भोज्यमखण्डैकरसं हविः ॥२२ ॥ अखण्डैकरसो होम अखण्डैकरसोः जपः । अखण्डैकरसं स्वर्गमखण्डैकरसः स्वयम् ॥२३ ॥ अखण्डैकरसं सर्वं चिन्मात्रमिति भावयेत् । चिन्मात्रमेव चिन्मात्रमखण्डैकरसं परम् ॥२४ ॥

भववर्जितचिन्मात्रं सर्वं चिन्मात्रमेव हि । दिं च सर्वं चिन्मात्रमयं चिन्मयमेव हि ॥२५ ॥ आत्मभावं च चिन्मात्रमखण्डैकरसं विदुः । सर्वलोकं च चिन्मात्रं वत्ता मत्ता च चिन्मयम् ॥२६ ॥ आकाशो भूर्जलं वायुरग्निर्ब्रह्मा हरिः शिवः । यत्किंचिद्यन्न किंचिच्च सर्वं चिन्मात्रमेव हि ॥२७ ॥ अखण्डैकरसं सर्वं यद्यच्चिन्मात्रमेव हि । भूतं भव्यं भविष्यच्च सर्वं चिन्मात्रमेव हि ॥२८ ॥ द्रव्यं कालं च चिन्मात्रं ज्ञानं ज्ञेयं चिदेव हि । ज्ञाता चिन्मात्ररूपश्च सर्वं चिन्मयमेव हि ॥२९ ॥ संभाषणं च चिन्मात्रं यद्यच्चिन्मात्रमेव हि । असच्च सच्च चिन्मात्रमाद्यन्तं चिन्मयं सदा ॥३० ॥ आदिरन्तश्च चिन्मात्रं गुरुशिष्यादि चिन्मयम् । दृगदृष्यं यदि चिन्मात्रमस्ति चेच्चिन्मयं सदा ॥३१ ॥ सर्वाश्चर्यं हि चिन्मात्रं देहं चिन्मात्रमेव हि । लिङ्गं च कारणं चैव चिन्मात्रान्न हि विद्यते ॥३२ ॥

अहं त्वं चैव चिन्मात्रं मूर्तामूर्तादिचिन्मयम् । पुण्यं पापं च चिन्मात्रं जीवश्चिन्मात्रविग्रहः ॥३३ ॥ चिन्मात्रान्नास्ति संकल्पश्चिन्मात्रान्नास्ति वेदनम् । चिन्मात्रान्नास्ति मन्त्रादि चिन्मात्रान्नास्ति देवता ॥३४ ॥ चिन्मात्रान्नास्ति दिक्पालाश्चिन्मात्राद्व्यवहारिकम् । चिन्मात्रात्परमं ब्रह्म चिन्मात्रान्नास्ति कोऽपि हि ॥३५ ॥ चिन्मात्रान्नास्ति माया च चिन्मात्रान्नास्ति पूजनम् । चिन्मात्रान्नास्ति मन्तव्यं चिन्मात्रान्नास्ति सत्यकम् ॥३६ ॥ चिन्मात्रान्नास्ति कोशादि चिन्मात्रान्नास्ति वै वसु । चिन्मात्रान्नास्ति मौनं च चिन्मात्रान्नास्त्यमौनकम् ॥३७ ॥ चिन्मात्रान्नास्ति वैराग्यं सर्वं चिन्मात्रमेव हि । यच्च यावच्च चिन्मात्रं यच्च यावच्च दृश्यते ॥३८ ॥ यच्च यावच्च दूरस्थं सर्वं चिन्मात्रमेव हि । यच्च यावच्च भूतादि यच्च यावच्च लक्ष्यते ॥३९ ॥ यच्च यावच्च वेदान्ताः सर्वं चिन्मात्रमेव हि । चिन्मात्रान्नास्ति गमनं चिन्मात्रान्नास्ति मोक्षकम् ॥४० ॥

चिनात्रान्नास्ति लक्ष्यं च सर्वं चिन्मात्रमेव हि । अखण्डैकरसं ब्रह्म चिन्मात्रान्न हि विद्यते ॥४१ ॥ शास्त्रे मयि त्वयीशे च ह्यखण्डैकरसो भवान् । इत्येकरूपकतया यो वा जानात्यहं त्विति ॥४२ ॥ सकृज्ज्ञानेन मुक्तिः स्यात्सम्यग्ज्ञाने स्वयं गुरुः ॥४३ ॥ इति द्वितीयोऽध्यायः ॥२ ॥

कुमारः पितरमात्मानुभवमनुब्रूहीति पप्रच्छ । स होवाच परः शिवः । परब्रह्मस्वरूपोऽहं परमानन्दमस्म्यहम् । केवलं ज्ञानरूपोऽहं केवलं परमोऽस्म्यहम् ॥१ ॥ केवलं शान्तरूपोऽहं केवलं चिन्मयोऽस्म्यहम् । केवलं नित्यरूपोऽहं केवलं शाश्वतोऽस्म्यहम् ॥२ ॥ केवलं सत्त्वरूपोऽहमहं त्यक्त्वाहमस्म्यहम् । सर्वहीनस्वरूपोऽहं चिदाकाशमयोऽस्म्यहम् ॥३ ॥ केवलं तुर्यरूपोऽस्मि तुर्यातीतोऽस्मि केवलः । सदा चैतन्यरूपोऽस्मि चिदानन्दमयोऽस्म्यहम् ॥४ ॥ केवलाकाररूपोऽस्मि शुद्धरूपोऽस्म्यहं

सदा। केवलं ज्ञानरूपोऽस्मि केवलं प्रियमस्म्यहम् ॥५॥ निर्विकल्पस्वरूपोऽस्मि निरीहोऽस्मि निरामयः। सदाऽसङ्गस्वरूपोऽस्मि निर्विकारोऽहमव्ययः ॥६॥ सदैकरसरूपोऽस्मि सदा चिन्मात्रविग्रहः। अपरिच्छिन्नरूपोऽस्मि ह्यखण्डानन्दरूपवान् ॥७॥ सत्परानन्दरूपोऽस्मि चित्परानन्दमस्म्यहम्। अन्तरान्तररूपोऽहमवाङ्मनसगोचरः ॥८॥

आत्मानन्दस्वरूपोऽहं सत्यानन्दोऽस्म्यहं सदा। आत्मारामस्वरूपोऽस्मि ह्यहमात्मा सदाशिवः ॥९॥ आत्मप्रकाशरूपोऽस्मि ह्यात्मज्योती रसोऽस्म्यहम्। आदिमध्यान्तहीनोऽस्मि ह्याकाशसदृशोऽस्म्यहम् ॥१०॥ नित्यशुद्धचिदानन्दसत्तामात्रोऽहमव्ययः। नित्यबुद्धविशुद्धैकसच्चिदानन्दमस्म्यहम् ॥११॥ नित्यशेषस्वरूपोऽस्मि सर्वातीतोऽस्म्यहं सदा। रूपातीतस्वरूपोऽस्मि परमाकाशविग्रहः ॥१२॥ भूमानन्दस्वरूपोऽस्मि भाषाहीनोऽस्म्यहं सदा। सर्वाधिष्ठानरूपोऽस्मि सर्वदा चिद्घनोऽस्म्यहम् ॥१३॥ देहभावविहीनोऽस्मि चिन्ताहीनोऽस्मि सर्वदा। चित्तवृत्तिविहीनोऽहं चिदात्मैकरसोऽस्म्यहम् ॥१४॥

सर्वदृश्यविहीनोऽहं दृग्रूपोऽस्म्यहमेव हि। सर्वदा पूर्णरूपोऽस्मि नित्यतृप्तोऽस्म्यहं सदा ॥१५॥ अहं ब्रह्मैव सर्वं स्यादहं चैतन्यमेव हि। अहमेवाहमेवास्मि भूमाकाशस्वरूपवान् ॥१६॥ अहमेव महानात्मा ह्यहमेव परात्परः। अहमन्यवदाभामि ह्यहमेव शरीरवत् ॥१७॥ अहं शिष्यवदाभामि ह्ययं लोकत्रयाश्रयः। अहं कालत्रयातीत अहं वेदैरुपासितः ॥१८॥ अहं शास्त्रेण निर्णीत अहं चित्ते व्यवस्थितः। मत्त्यक्तं नास्ति किंचिद्वा मत्त्यक्तं पृथिवी च वा ॥१९॥ मयातिरिक्तं यद्यद्वा तत्तन्नास्तीति निश्चिनु। अहं ब्रह्मास्मि सिद्धोऽस्मि नित्यशुद्धोऽस्म्यहं सदा ॥२०॥ निर्गुणः केवलात्मास्मि निराकारोऽस्म्यहं सदा। केवलं ब्रह्ममात्रोऽस्मि ह्यजरोऽस्म्यमरोऽस्म्यहम् ॥२१॥

स्वयमेव स्वयं भामि स्वयमेव सदात्मकः। स्वयमेवात्मनि स्वस्थः स्वयमेव परा गतिः ॥२२॥ स्वयमेव स्वयं भञ्जे स्वयमेव रमे। स्वयमेव स्वयं ज्योतिः स्वयमेव स्वयं महः ॥२३॥ स्वस्यात्मनि स्वयं स्वात्मन्येव विलोकये। स्वात्मन्येव सुखासीनः स्वात्ममात्रावशेषकः ॥२४॥ स्वचैतन्ये स्वयं स्थास्ये स्वात्मराज्ये सुखे रमे। स्वात्मसिंहासने स्थित्वा स्वात्मनोऽन्यत्र चिन्तये ॥२५॥ चिद्रूपमात्रं ब्रह्मैव सच्चिदानन्दमद्वयम्। आनन्दघन एवाहमहं ब्रह्मास्मि केवलम् ॥२६॥ सर्वदा सर्वसून्योऽहं सर्वात्मानन्दवानहम्। नित्यानन्दस्वरूपोऽहमात्माकाशोऽस्मि नित्यदा ॥२७॥ अहमेव हृदाकाशश्चिदादित्यस्वरूपवान्। आत्मनात्मनि तृप्तोऽस्मि ह्यरूपोऽस्म्यहमव्ययः ॥२८॥

एकसंख्याविहीनोऽस्मि नित्यमुक्तस्वरूपवान्। आकाशादपि सूक्ष्मोऽहमाद्यन्ताभाववानहम् ॥२९॥ सर्वप्रकाशरूपोऽहं परावरसुखोऽस्म्यहम्। सत्तामात्रस्वरूपोऽहं शुद्धमोक्षस्वरूपवान् ॥३०॥ सत्यानन्दस्वरूपोऽहं ज्ञानानन्दघनोऽस्म्यहम्। विज्ञानमात्ररूपोऽहं सच्चिदानन्दलक्षणः ॥३१॥ ब्रह्ममात्रमिदं सर्वं ब्रह्मणोऽन्यत्र किंचन। तदेवाहं सदानन्दं ब्रह्मैवाहं सनातनम् ॥३२॥ त्वमित्येतत्तदित्येतन्मत्तोऽन्यन्नास्ति किंचन। चिच्चैतन्यस्वरूपोऽहमहमेव परः शिवः ॥३३॥ अतिभावस्वरूपोऽहमहमेव सुखात्मकः। साक्षिवस्तुविहीनत्वात्साक्षित्वं नास्ति मे सदा ॥३४॥ केवलं ब्रह्ममात्रत्वादहमात्मा सनातनः। अहमेवादिशेषोऽहमहं

शेषोऽहमेव हि ॥३५ ॥ नामरूपविमुक्तोऽहमहमानन्दविग्रहः । इन्द्रियाभावरूपोऽहं सर्वभावस्वरूपकः ॥३६ ॥ बन्धमुक्तिविहीनोऽहं शाश्वतानन्दविग्रहः । आदिचैतन्यमात्रोऽहमखण्डैकरसोऽस्म्यहम् ॥३७ ॥ वाङ्मनोऽगोचरश्चाहं सर्वत्र सुखवानहम् । सर्वत्र पूर्णरूपोऽहं भूमानन्दमयोऽस्म्यहम् ॥३८ ॥ सर्वत्र तृप्तिरूपोऽहं परामृतरसोऽस्म्यहम् । एकमेवाद्वितीयं सद्ब्रह्मैवाहं न संशयः ॥३९ ॥

सर्वशून्यस्वरूपोऽहं सकलागमगोचरः । मुक्तोऽहं मोक्षरूपोऽहं निर्वाणसुखरूपवान् ॥४० ॥ सत्यविज्ञानमात्रोऽहं सन्मात्रानन्दवानहम् । तुरीयातीतरूपोऽहं निर्विकल्पस्वरूपवान् ॥४१ ॥ सर्वदा ह्यजरूपोऽहं नीरागोऽस्मि निरञ्जनः । अहं शुद्धोऽस्मि बुद्धोऽस्मि नित्योऽस्मि प्रभुरस्म्यहम् ॥४२ ॥ ओङ्कारार्थस्वरूपोऽस्मि निष्कलङ्कमयोऽस्म्यहम् । चिदाकारस्वरूपोऽस्मि नाहमस्मि न सोऽस्म्यहम् ॥४३ ॥ न हि किंचित्स्वरूपोऽस्मि निर्व्यापारस्वरूपवान् । निरंशोऽस्मि निराभासो न मनो नेन्द्रियोऽस्म्यहम् ॥४४ ॥

न बुद्धिर्नविकल्पोऽहं न देहादित्रयोऽस्म्यहम् ॥ न जाग्रत्स्वप्नरूपोऽहं सुषुप्तिस्वरूवान् ॥४५ ॥ तापत्रयरूपोऽहं नेषणात्रयवानहम् । श्रवणं नास्ति मे सिद्धेर्मननं च चिदात्मनि ॥४६ ॥ सजातीयं न मे किंचिद्विजातीयं न मे क्वचित् । स्वगतं च न मे किंचिन्न मे भेदत्रयं क्वचित् ॥४७ ॥ असत्यं हि मनोरूपमसत्यं बुद्धिरूपकम् । अहंकारमसद्धीति नित्योऽहं शाश्वतो ह्यजः ॥४८ ॥ देहत्रयमसद्विद्धि कालत्रयमसत्सदा । गुणत्रयमसद्विद्धि ह्यहं सत्यात्मकः शुचिः ॥४९ ॥ श्रुतं सर्वमसद्विद्धि वेदं सर्वमसत्सदा । शास्त्रं सर्वमसद्विद्धि ह्यहं सत्यचिदात्मकः ॥५० ॥ मूर्तित्रयमसद्विद्धि सर्वभूतमसत्सदा । सर्वतत्त्वमसद्विद्धि ह्यहं भूमा सदाशिवः ॥५१ ॥ गुरुशिष्यमसद्विद्धि गुरोर्मन्त्रमसत्ततः । यदृश्यं तदसद्विद्धि न मां विद्धि तथाविधम् ॥५२ ॥

यच्चिन्त्यं तदसद्विद्धि यन्नयाय्य तदसत्सदा । यद्धितं तदसद्विद्धि न मां विद्धितथाविधम् ॥५३ ॥ सर्वान्प्राणानसद्विद्धि सर्वान्भोगानसत्त्विति । दृष्टं श्रुतमसद्विद्धि ओतं प्रोतसमन्मयम् ॥५४ ॥ कार्याकार्यमसद्विद्धि नष्टं प्राप्तमसन्मयम् । दुःखादुःखमसद्विद्धि सर्वासर्वमसन्मयम् ॥५५ ॥ पूर्णापूर्णमसद्विद्धि धर्माधर्ममसन्मयम् । लाभालाभावसद्विद्धि जयाजयमसन्मयम् ॥५६ ॥ शब्दं सर्वमसद्विद्धि स्पर्शं सर्वमसत्सदा । रूपं सर्वमसद्विद्धि रसं सर्वमसन्मयम् ॥५७ ॥ गन्धं सर्वमसद्विद्धि सर्वाज्ञानमसन्मयम् । असदेव सदा सर्वमसदेव भवोद्भवम् ॥५८ ॥ असदेव गुण सर्वं सन्मात्रमहमेव हि । स्वात्ममन्त्रं सदा पश्येत्स्वात्ममन्त्रं सदाभ्यसेत् ॥५९ ॥

अहं ब्रह्मास्मिमन्त्रोऽयं दृश्यपापं विनाशयेत् । अहं ब्रह्मास्मि मन्त्रोऽयमन्यमन्त्रं विनाशयेत् ॥६० ॥ अहं ब्रह्मास्मि मन्त्रोऽयं देहदोषं विनाशयेत् । अहं ब्रह्मास्मि मन्त्रोऽयं जन्मपापं विनाशयेत् ॥६१ ॥ अहं ब्रह्मास्मि मन्त्रोऽयं मृत्युपाशं विनाशयेत् । अहं ब्रह्मास्मि मन्त्रोऽयं द्वैतदुःखं विनाशयेत् ॥६२ ॥ अहं ब्रह्मास्मि मन्त्रोऽयं भेदबुद्धिं विनाशयेत् । अहं ब्रह्मास्मि मन्त्रोऽयं चिन्तादुःखं विनाशयेत् ॥६३ ॥ अहं ब्राह्मास्मि मन्त्रोऽयं बुद्धिव्याधिं विनाशयेत् । अहं ब्रह्मास्मि मन्त्रोऽयं चित्तबन्धं विनाशयेत् ॥६४ ॥

अहं ब्रह्मास्मि मन्त्रोऽयं सर्वव्याधीन्विनाशयेत् । अहं ब्रह्मास्मि मन्त्रोऽयं सर्वशोकं विनाशयेत् ॥६५ ॥ अहं ब्रह्मास्मि मन्त्रोऽयं कामादीन्नाशयेत्क्षणात् । अहं ब्रह्मास्मि

मन्त्रोऽयं क्रोधशक्तिं विनाशयेत् ॥६६ ॥ अहं ब्रह्मास्मि मन्त्रोऽयं चित्तवृत्ति विनाशयेत् । अहं ब्रह्मास्मि मन्त्रोऽयं संकल्पादीन्विनाशयेत् ॥६७ ॥ अहं ब्रह्मास्मि मन्त्रोऽयं कोटिदोषं विनाशयेत् । अहं ब्रह्मास्मि मन्त्रोऽयं सर्वतन्त्रं विनाशयेत् ॥६८ ॥ अहं ब्रह्मास्मि मन्त्रोऽयमात्माज्ञानं विनाशयेत् । अहं ब्रह्मास्मि मन्त्रोऽयमात्मलोकजयप्रदः ॥६९ ॥ अहं ब्रह्मास्मि मन्त्रोऽयमप्रतर्क्यसुखप्रदः । अहं ब्रह्मास्मि मन्त्रोऽयमजडत्वं प्रयच्छति ॥७० ॥

अहं ब्रह्मास्मि मन्त्रोऽयमनात्मासुरमर्दनः । अहं ब्रह्मास्मि वज्रोऽयमनात्माख्यगिरीन्हरेत् ॥७१ ॥ अहं ब्रह्मास्मि मन्त्रोऽयमनात्माख्यासुरान्हरेत् । अहं ब्रह्मास्मि मन्त्रोऽयं सर्वांस्तान्मोक्षयिष्यति ॥७२ ॥ अहं ब्रह्मास्मि मन्त्रोऽयं ज्ञानानन्दं प्रयच्छति । सप्तकोटिमहामन्त्रं जन्मकोटिशतप्रदम् ॥७३ ॥ सर्वमन्त्रान्समुत्सृज्य एतं मन्त्रं समभ्यसेत् । सद्यो मोक्षमवाप्नोति नात्र संदेहमण्वपि ॥७४ ॥ इति तृतीयोऽध्यायः ॥३ ॥

कुमारः परमेश्वरं पप्रच्छ जीवन्मुक्तविदेहमुक्तयोः स्थितिमनुब्रूहीति । स होवाच परः शिवः । चिदात्माहं परात्माहं निर्गुणोऽहं परात्परः । आत्ममात्रेण यस्तिष्ठेत्स जीवन्मुक्त उच्यते ॥१ ॥ देहत्रयातिरिक्तोऽहं शुद्धचैतन्यमस्म्यहम् । ब्रह्माहमिति यस्यान्तः स जीवन्मुक्त उच्यते ॥२ ॥ आनन्दघनरूपोऽस्मि परानन्दघनोऽस्म्यहम् । यस्य देहादिकं नास्ति यस्य ब्रह्मेति निश्चयः । परमानन्दपूर्णो यः स जीवन्मुक्त उच्यते ॥३ ॥ यस्य किंचिदहं नास्ति चिन्मात्रेणावतिष्ठते । चैतन्यमात्रो यस्यान्तश्चिन्मात्रैकस्वरूपवान् ॥४ ॥ सर्वत्र पूर्णरूपात्मा सर्वत्रात्मावशेषकः । आनन्दरतिरव्यक्तः परिपूर्णश्चिदात्मकः ॥५ ॥ शुद्धचैतन्यरूपात्मा सर्वसङ्गविवर्जितः । नित्यानन्दः प्रसन्नात्मा ह्यन्यचिन्ताविवर्जितः । ।६ ॥ किं चिदस्तित्वहीनो यः स जीवन्मुक्त उच्यते । न मे चित्तं न मे बुद्धिर्नाहंकारो न चेन्द्रियम् ॥७ ॥

न मे देहः कदाचिद्वा न मे प्राणादयः क्वचित् । न मे माया न मे कामो न मे क्रोधः परोऽस्म्यहम् ॥८ ॥ न मे किंचिदिदं वापि न मे किंचित्क्वचिज्जगत् । न मे दोषो न मे लिङ्गं न मे चक्षुर्न मे मनः ॥९ ॥ न मे श्रोत्रं न मे नासा न मे जिह्वा न मे करः । न मे जाग्रन्न मे स्वप्नं न मे कारणमण्वपि ॥१० ॥ न मे तुरीयमिति यः स जीवन्मुक्त उच्यते । इदं सर्वं न मे किंचिदयं सर्वं न मे क्वचित् ॥११ ॥ न मे कालो न मे देशो न मे वस्तु न मे मतिः । न मे स्नानं न मे संध्या न मे दैवं न मे स्थलम् ॥१२ ॥ न मे तीर्थं न मे सेवा न मे ज्ञानं न मे पदम् । न मे बन्धो न मे जन्म न मे वाक्यं न मे रविः ॥१३ ॥

न मे पुण्यं न मे पापं न मे कार्यं न मे शुभम् । न मे जीव इति स्वात्मा न मे किंचिज्जगत्त्रयम् ॥१४ ॥ न मे मोक्षो न मे द्वैतं न मे वेदो न मे विधिः । न मेऽन्तिकं न मे दूरं न मे बोधो न मे रहः ॥१५ ॥ न मे गुरुर्न मे शिष्यो न मे हीनो न चाधिकः । न मे ब्रह्म न मे विष्णुर्न मे रुद्रो न चन्द्रमाः ॥१६ ॥ न मे पृथ्वी न मे तोयं न मे वायुर्न मे वियत् । न मे वह्निर्न मे गोत्रं न मे लक्ष्यं न मे भवः ॥१७ ॥

न मे ध्याता न मे ध्येयं न मे ध्यानं न मे मनुः । न मे शीतं न मे चोष्णं न मे तृष्णा न मे क्षुधा ॥१८ ॥ न मे मित्रं न मे शत्रुर्न मे मोहो न मे जयः । न मे पूर्वं न मे पश्चान्न मे चोर्ध्वं न मे दिशः ॥१९ ॥ न मे वक्तव्यमल्पं वा न मे श्रोतव्यमण्डवपि । न मे गन्तव्यमीषद्वा न मे ध्यातव्यमण्वपि ॥२० ॥ न मे भोक्तव्यमीषद्वा न मे स्मर्तव्यमण्वपि । न मे भोगो न मे रागो न मे यागो न मे लयः ॥२१ ॥ न मे मौर्ख्यं न मे शान्तं न मे बन्धो न मे प्रियम् । न मे मोदः

प्रमोदो वा न मे स्थूलं न मे कृशम् ॥२२॥ न मे दीर्घं न मे ह्रस्वं न मे वृद्धिर्न मे क्षयः । अध्यारोपोऽपवादो वा न मे चैकं न मे बहु ॥२३॥ न मे आन्ध्यं न मे मान्द्यं न मे पट्विदमण्वपि । न मे मांसं न मे रक्तं न मे मेदो न मे ह्यसृक् ॥२४॥

न मे मज्जा न मेऽस्थिर्वा न मे त्वग्धातुसप्तकम् । न मे शुक्लं न मे रक्तं न मे नीलं न मे पृथक् ॥२५॥ न मे तापो न मे लाभो मुख्यं गौणं न मे क्वचित् । न मे भ्रान्तिर्न मे स्थैर्यं न मे गुह्यं न मे कुलम् ॥२६॥ न मे त्याज्यं न मे ग्राह्यं न मे हास्यं न मे नयः । न मे वृत्तं न मे ग्लानिर्न मे शोष्यं न मे सुखम् ॥२७॥ न मे ज्ञाता न मे ज्ञानं न मे ज्ञेयं न मे स्वयम् । न मे तुभ्यं न मे मह्यं न मे त्वं च न मे त्वहम् ॥२८॥ न मे जरा न मे बाल्यं न मे यौवनमण्वपि । अहं ब्रह्मास्म्यहं ब्रह्मास्म्यहं ब्रह्मेति निश्चयः ॥२९॥ चिदहं चिदहं चेति स जीवन्मुक्त उच्यते । ब्रह्मैवाहं चिदेवाहं परो वाहं न संशयः ॥३०॥ स्वयमेव स्वयं हंसः स्वयमेव स्वयं स्थितः । स्वयमेव स्वयं पश्येत्स्वात्मराज्ये सुखं वसेत् ॥३१॥

स्वात्मानन्दं स्वयं भोक्ष्येत्स जीवन्मुक्त उच्यते । स्वयमेवैकवीरोऽग्रे स्वयमेव प्रभुः स्मृतः । स्वस्वरूपे स्वयं स्वप्स्येत्स जीवन्मुक्त उच्यते ॥३२॥ ब्रह्मभूतः प्रशान्तात्मा ब्रह्मानन्दमयः सुखी । स्वच्छरूपो महामौनी वैदेही मुक्त एव सः ॥३३। सर्वात्मा समरूपात्मा शुद्धात्मा त्वहमुत्थितः । एकवर्जित एकात्मा सर्वात्मा स्वात्ममात्रकः ॥३४॥ अजात्मा चामृतात्माहं स्वयमात्माहमव्ययः । लक्ष्यात्मा ललितात्माहं तूष्णीमात्मस्वभाववान् ॥३५॥ आनन्दात्मा प्रियो ह्यात्मा मोक्षात्मा बन्धवर्जितः । ब्रह्मैवाहं चिदेवाहमेवं वापि न चिन्त्यते ॥३६॥

चिन्मात्रेणैव यस्तिष्ठैद्वैदेही मुक्त एव सः ॥३७॥ निश्चयं च परित्यज्य अहं ब्रह्मेति निश्चयम् । आनन्दभरितस्वान्तो वैदेही मुक्त एव सः ॥३८॥ सर्वमस्तीति नास्तीति निश्चयं त्यज्य तिष्ठति । अहं ब्रह्मास्मि नास्मीति सच्चिदानन्दमात्रकः ॥३९॥ किंचित्क्वचित्कदाचिच्च आत्मानं न स्पृशत्यसौ । तूष्णीमेव स्थितस्तूष्णीं तूष्णीं सत्यं न किंचन ॥४०॥ परमात्मा गुणातीतः सर्वात्मा भूतभावनः । कालभेदं वस्तुभेदं देशभेदं स्वभेदकम् ॥४१॥ किंचिद्भेदं न तस्यास्ति किंचिद्वापि न विद्यते । अहं त्वं तदिदं सोऽयं कालात्मा कालहीनकः ॥४२॥

शून्यासा सूक्ष्मरूपात्मा विश्वात्मा विश्वहीनकः । देवात्मा देवहीनात्मा मेयात्मा मेयवर्जितः ॥४३॥ सर्वत्र जडहीनात्मा सर्वेषामन्तरात्मकः । सर्वसंकल्पहीनात्मा चिन्मात्रोऽस्मीति सर्वदा ॥४४॥ केवलः परमात्माहं केवलो ज्ञानविग्रहः । सत्तामात्रस्वरूपात्मा नान्यत्किंचिज्जगद्भयम् ॥४५॥ जीवेश्वरेति वाक् क्वेति वेदशास्त्राद्यहं त्विति । इदं चैतन्यमेवेति अहं चैतन्यमित्यपि ॥४६॥ इति निश्चयशून्यो यो वैदेही मुक्त एव सः । चैतन्यमात्रसंसिद्धः स्वात्मारामः सुखासनः ॥४७॥ अपरिच्छिन्नरूपात्मा अणुस्थूलादिवर्जितः । तुर्यतुर्यः परानन्दो वैदेही मुक्त एव सः ॥४८॥ नामरूपविहीनात्मा परसंवित्सुखात्मकः । तुरीयातीतरूपात्मा सुभाशुभविवर्जितः ॥४९॥

योगात्मा योगयुक्तात्मा बन्धमोक्षविवर्जितः । गुणागुणविहीनात्मा देशकालादिवर्जितः ॥५०॥ साक्ष्यसाक्षित्वहीनात्मा किंचित्किंचित्र किंचन । यस्य पप्रञ्चमानं न ब्रह्माकारमपीह न ॥५१॥ स्वस्वरूपे स्वयंज्योतिः स्वस्वरूपे स्वयंरतिः ।

वाचामगोचरानन्दो वाङ्मनोगोचरः स्वयम् ॥५२ ॥ अतीतातीतभावो यो वैदेही मुक्त एव सः । चित्तवृत्तेरतीतो यश्चित्तवृत्त्यवभासकः ॥५३ ॥ सर्ववृत्तिविहीनात्मा वैदेही मुक्त एव सः । तस्मिन्काले विदेहीति देहस्मरणवर्जितः ॥५४ ॥ ईषन्मात्रं स्मृतं चेद्यस्तदा सर्वसमन्वितः । परैरदृष्टबाह्यात्मा परमानन्दचिद्घनः ॥५५ ॥

परैरदृष्टबाह्यात्मा सर्ववेदान्तगोचरः । ब्रह्मामृतरसास्वादो ब्रह्मामृतरसायनः ॥५६ ॥ ब्रह्मामृतरसासक्तो ब्रह्मामृतरसः स्वयम् । ब्रह्मामृतरसे मग्नो ब्रह्मानन्दशिवार्चनः ॥५७ ॥ ब्रह्मामृतरसे तृप्तो ब्रह्मानन्दानुभावकः । ब्रह्मानन्दशिवानन्दो ब्रह्मानन्दरसप्रभः ॥५८ ॥ ब्रह्मानन्दपरं ज्योतिर्ब्रह्मानन्दनिरन्तरः । ब्रह्मानन्दरसान्नादो ब्रह्मानन्दकुटुम्बकः ॥५९ ॥ ब्राह्मानन्दरसारूढो ब्रह्मानन्दैकचिद्घनः । ब्रह्मानन्दरसोद्वाहो ब्रह्मानन्दरसंभरः ॥६० ॥ ब्रह्मानन्दजनैर्युक्तो ब्रह्मानन्दात्मनि स्थितः । आत्मरूपमिदं सर्वमात्मनोऽन्यत्र किंचन ॥६१ ॥ सर्वमात्माहमात्मास्मि परमात्मा परात्मकः । नित्यानन्दस्वरूपात्मा वैदेही मुक्त एव सः ॥६२ ॥

पूर्णरूपो महानात्मा प्रीतात्मा शाश्वतात्मकः । सर्वान्तर्यामिरूपात्मा निर्मलात्मा निरात्मकः ॥६३ ॥ निर्विकारस्वरूपात्मा शुद्धात्मा शान्तरूपकः । शान्ताशान्तस्वरूपात्मा नैकात्मत्वविवर्जितः ॥६४ ॥ जीवात्मपरमात्मेति चिन्तासर्वस्ववर्जितः । मुक्तामुक्तस्वरूपात्मा मुक्तामुक्तविवर्जितः ॥६५ ॥ बन्धमोक्षस्वरूपात्मा बन्धमोक्षविवर्जितः । द्वैताद्वैतस्वरूपात्मा द्वैताद्वैतविवर्जितः ॥६६ ॥ सर्वासर्वस्वरूपात्मा सर्वासर्वविवर्जितः । मोदप्रमोदरूपात्मा मोदादिविनिवर्जितः ॥६७ ॥ सर्वसंकल्पहीनात्मा वैदेही मुक्त एव सः । निष्कलात्मा निर्मलात्मा बुद्धात्मा पुरुषात्मकः ॥६८ ॥ आनन्दादिविहीनात्मा अमृतात्मामृतात्मकः । कालत्रयस्वरूपात्मा कालत्रयविवर्जितः ॥६९ ॥

अखिलात्मा ह्यमेयात्मा मानात्मा मानवर्जितः । नित्यप्रत्यक्षरूपात्मा नित्यप्रत्यक्षनिर्णयः ॥७० ॥ अन्यहीनस्वभावात्मा अन्यहीनस्वयंप्रभः । विद्याविद्यादिमेयात्मा विद्याविद्यादिवर्जितः ॥७१ ॥ नित्यानित्यविहीनात्मा इहामुत्रविवर्जितः । शमादिषट्कशून्यात्मा मुमुक्षुत्वादिवर्जितः ॥७२ ॥ स्थूलदेहविहीनात्मा सूक्ष्मदेहविवर्जितः । कारणादिविहीनात्मा तुरीयादिविवर्जितः ॥७३ ॥ अन्नकोशविहीनात्मा प्राणकोशविवर्जितः । मनःकोशविहीनात्मा विज्ञानादिविवर्जितः ॥७४ ॥ आनन्दकोशहीन्त्मा पञ्चकोशविवर्जितः । निर्विकल्पस्वरूपात्मा सविकल्पविवर्जितः ॥७५ ॥ दृश्यानुविद्धहीनात्मा शब्दविद्धविवर्जितः । सदा समाधिशून्यात्मा आदिमध्यान्तवर्जितः ॥७६ ॥ प्रज्ञानवाक्यहीनात्मा अहंब्रह्मास्मिवर्जितः । तत्त्वमस्यादिहीनात्मा अयमात्मेत्यभावकः ॥७७ ॥ ओंकारवाच्यहीनात्मा सर्ववाच्यविवर्जितः । अवस्थात्रयहीनात्मा अक्षरात्मा चिदात्मकः ॥७८ ॥

आत्मज्ञेयादिहीनात्मा यत्किंचिदिदमात्मकः । भानाभानविहीनात्मा वैदेही मुक्त एव सः ॥७९ ॥ आत्मानमेव वीक्षस्व आत्मानं बोधय स्वकम् । स्वमात्मानं स्वयं भुङ्क्ष्व स्वस्थो भव षडानन ॥८० ॥ स्वमात्मनि स्वयं तृप्तः स्वमात्मानं स्वयं चर । आत्मानमेव मोदस्व वैदेही मुक्तिको भवेत्युपनिषत् ॥ इति चतुर्थोऽध्यायः ॥४ ॥

निदाघो नाम वै मुनिः पप्रच्छ ऋभुं भगवन्तमात्मानात्मविवेकमनुब्रूहीति । स होवाच ऋभुः । सर्ववाचोऽवधिर्ब्रह्म सर्वचिन्तावधिर्गुरुः । सर्वकारणकार्यात्मा कार्यकारणवर्जितः ॥१ ॥ सर्वसंकल्परहितः सर्वनादमयः शिवः । सर्ववर्जितचिन्मात्रः सर्वानन्दमयः परः ॥२ ॥ सर्वतेजःप्रकाशात्मा नादानन्दमयात्मकः । सर्वानुभवनिर्मुक्तः सर्वध्यानविवर्जितः ॥३ ॥ सर्वनादकलातीत एष आत्माहमव्ययः । आत्मानात्मविवेकादि-भेदाभेदविवर्जितः ॥४ ॥ शान्ताशान्तादिहीनात्मा नादान्तर्ज्योतिरूपकः । महावाक्यार्थतो दूरो ब्रह्मास्मीत्यतिदूरतः ॥५ ॥ तच्छब्दवर्ज्यस्त्वंशब्दहीनो वाक्यार्थवर्जितः । क्षराक्षर-विहीनो यो नादान्तर्ज्योतिरेव सः ॥६ ॥ अखण्डैकरसो वाहमानन्दोऽस्मीति वर्जितः । सर्वातीतस्वभावात्मा नादान्तर्ज्योतिरेव सः ॥७ ॥

आत्मेति शब्दहीनो य आत्मशब्दार्थवर्जितः । सच्चिदानन्दहीनो य एषैवात्मा सनातनः ॥८ ॥ स निर्देष्टुमशक्यो यो वेदवाक्यैरगम्यतः । यस्य किंचिद्बहिर्नास्ति किंचिदन्तः कियन्न च ॥९ ॥ यस्य लिङ्गं प्रपञ्चं वा ब्रह्मैवात्मा न संशयः । नास्ति यस्य शरीरं वा जीवो वा भूतभौतिकः ॥१० ॥ नामरूपादिकं नास्ति भोज्यं वा भोगभुक्च वा । सद्वाऽसद्वा स्थितिर्वापि यस्य नास्ति क्षराक्षरम् ॥११ ॥ गुणं वा विगुणं वापि सम आत्मा न संशयः । यस्य वाच्यं वाचकं वा श्रवणं मननं च वा ॥१२ ॥ गुरुशिष्यादिभेदं वा देवलोकाः सुरासुराः । यत्र धर्ममधर्मं वा शुद्धं वाशुद्धमण्वपि ॥१३ ॥ यत्र कालमकालं वा निश्चयः संशयो न हि । यत्र मन्त्रममन्त्रं वा विद्याविद्ये न विद्यते ॥१४ ॥

द्रष्टृदर्शनदृश्यं वा ईषन्मात्रं कलात्मकम् । अनात्मेति प्रसङ्गो वा ह्यनात्मेति मनोऽपि वा ॥१५ ॥ अनात्मेति जगद्वापि नास्ति नास्तीति निश्चिनु । सर्वसंकल्पशून्यत्वात्सर्वकार्य-विवर्जनात् ॥१६ ॥ केवलं ब्रह्ममात्रत्वान्नास्त्यनात्मेति निश्चिनु । देहत्रयविहीनत्वात्कालत्रयविवर्जनात् ॥१७ ॥ जीवत्रयगुणाभावात्तापत्रयविवर्जनात् । लोकत्रयविहीनत्वात्सर्वमात्मेति शासनात् ॥१८ ॥ चित्ताभावाच्चिन्तनीयं देहाभावाज्जरा न च । पादाभावाद्गतिर्नास्ति हस्ताभावात्क्रिया न च ॥१९ ॥

मृत्युर्नास्ति जनाभावाद्बुद्ध्यभावात्सुखादिकम् । धर्मो नास्ति शुचिर्नास्ति सत्यं नास्ति भयं न च ॥२० ॥ अक्षरोच्चारणं नास्ति गुरुशिष्यादि नास्त्यपि । एकाभावे द्वितीयं न न द्वितीये न चैकता ॥२१ ॥ सत्यत्वमस्ति चेत्किंचिदसत्यं न च संभवेत् । असत्यत्वं यदि भवेत्सत्यत्वं न घटिष्यति ॥२२ ॥ शुभं यद्यशुभं विद्धि अशुभाच्छुभमिष्यते । भयं यद्यभयं विद्धि अभयाद्भयमापतेत् ॥२३ ॥

बन्धत्वमपि चेन्मोक्षो बन्धाभावे क्व मोक्षता । मरणं यदि चेज्जन्म जन्माभावे मृतिर्न च ॥२४ ॥ त्वमित्यपि भवेच्चाहं त्वं नो चेदहमेव न । इदं यदि तदेवास्ति तदभावादिदं न च ॥२५ ॥ अस्तीति चेन्नास्ति तदा नास्ति चेदस्ति किंचन । कार्यं चेत्कारणं किंचित्कार्या-भावे न कारणम् ॥२६ ॥ द्वैतं यदि तदाऽद्वैतं द्वैताभावे द्वयं न च । दृश्यं यदि दृगप्यस्ति दृश्याभावे दृगेव न ॥२७ ॥ अन्तर्यदि बहिः सत्यमन्ताभावे बहिर्न च । पूर्णत्वमस्ति चेत्किंचिदपूर्णत्वं प्रसज्यते ॥२८ ॥ तस्मादेतत्त्वचिन्नास्ति त्वं चाहं वा इमे इदम् । नास्ति दृष्टान्तिकं सत्ये नास्ति दार्ष्टान्तिकं ह्यजे ॥२९ ॥ परंब्रह्माहमस्मीति स्मरणस्य मनो न हि । ब्रह्ममात्रं जगदिदं ब्रह्ममात्रं त्वमप्यहम् ॥३० ॥ चिन्मात्रं केवलं चाहं नास्त्यनात्म्येति निश्चिनु । इदं प्रपञ्चं नास्त्येव नोत्पन्नं नो स्थितं क्वचित् ॥३१ ॥

चित्तं प्रपञ्चमित्याहुर्नास्ति नास्त्येव सर्वदा। न प्रपञ्चं न चित्तादि नाहंकारो न जीवकः ॥३२॥ मायाकार्यादिकं नास्ति माया नास्ति भयं नहि। कर्ता नास्ति क्रिया नास्ति श्रवणं मननं नहि ॥३३। समाधिद्वितयं नास्ति मातृमानादि नास्ति हि। अज्ञानं चापि नास्त्येव ह्यविवेकं कदाचन ॥३४॥ अनुबन्धचतुष्कं न संबन्धत्रयमेव न। न गङ्गा न गया सेतुर्न भूतं नान्यदस्ति हि ॥३५॥ न भूमिर्न जलं नाग्निर्न वायुर्न च खं क्वचित्। न देवा न च दिक्पाला न वेदा न गुरुः क्वचित् ॥३६॥

न दूरं नान्तिकं नालं न मध्यं न क्वचित्स्थितम्। नाद्वैतं द्वैतसत्यं वा ह्यसत्यं वा इदं न च ॥३७॥ बन्धमोक्षादिकं नास्ति सद्वाऽसद्वा सुखादि वा। जातिर्नास्ति गतिर्नास्ति वर्णो नास्ति न लौकिकम् ॥३८॥ सर्वं ब्रह्मेति नास्त्येव ब्रह्म इत्यपि नास्ति हि। चिदित्येवेति नास्त्येव चिदहंभाषणं नहि ॥३९॥ अहं ब्रह्मास्मि नास्त्येव नित्यशुद्धोऽस्मि न क्वचित्। वाचा यदुच्यते किंचिन्मनसा मनुते क्वचित् ॥४०॥ बुद्धया निश्चिनुते नास्ति चित्तेन ज्ञायते नहि। योगी योगादिकं नास्ति सदा सर्वं सदा न च ॥४१॥ अहोरात्रादिकं नास्ति स्नानध्यानादिकं नहि। भ्रान्तिरभ्रान्तिर्नास्त्येव नास्त्यनात्मेति न निश्चिनु ॥४२॥ वेदशास्त्रं पुराणं च कार्यं कारणमीश्वरः। लोको भूतं जनस्त्वैक्यं सर्वं मिथ्या न संशयः ॥४३॥ बन्धो मोक्षः सुखः दुःखं ध्यानं चित्तं सुरासुराः। गौणं मुख्यं परं चान्यत्सर्वं मिथ्या न संशयः ॥४४॥

वाचा वदति यत्किंचित्संकल्पैः कल्प्यते च यत्। मनसा चिन्त्यते यद्यत्सर्वं मिथ्या न संशयः ॥४५॥ बुद्ध्या निश्चीयते किंचिच्चित्ते निश्चीयते क्वचित्। शास्त्रैः प्रपञ्चयते यद्यन्नेत्रेणैव निरीक्ष्यते ॥४६॥ श्रोत्राभ्यां श्रूयते यद्यदन्यत्सद्भावमेव च। नेत्रं श्रोत्र गात्रमेव मिथ्येति च सुनिश्चितम् ॥४७॥

इदमित्येव निर्दिष्टमयमित्येव कल्प्यते। त्वमहं तदिदं सोऽहमन्यत्सद्भावमेव च ॥४८॥ यद्यत्संभाव्यते लोके सर्वसंकल्पसंभ्रमः। सर्वाध्यासं सर्वगोप्यं सर्वभोगप्रभेदकम् ॥४९॥ सर्वदोषप्रभेदाच्च नास्त्यनात्मेति निश्चिनु। मदीयं च त्वदीयं च ममेति च तवेति च ॥५०॥

मह्यं तुभ्यं मयेत्यादि तत्सर्वं वितथं भवेत्। रक्षको विष्णुरित्यादि ब्रह्मा सृष्टेस्तु कारणम् ॥५१॥ संहारे रुद्र इत्येवं सर्वं मिथ्येति निश्चिनु। स्नानं जपस्तपो होमः स्वाध्यायो देवपूजनम् ॥५२॥

मन्त्रं तन्त्रं च सत्सङ्गो गुणदोषविजृम्भणम्। अन्तःकरणसद्भाव अविद्यायाश्च संभवः ॥५३॥ अनेककोटिब्रह्माण्डं सर्वं मिथ्येति निश्चिनु। सर्वदेशिकवाक्योक्तिर्येन केनापि निश्चितम् ॥५४॥ दृश्यते जगति यद्यद्यज्जगति वीक्ष्यते। वर्तते जगति यद्यत्सर्वं मिथ्येति निश्चिनु ॥५५॥

येन केनाक्षरेणोक्तं येन केन विनिश्चितम्। येन केनापि गदितं येन केनापि मोदितम् ॥५६॥ येन केनापि यद्दत्तं येन केनापि यत्कृतम्। यत्र यत्र शुभं कर्म यत्र यत्र च दुष्कृतम् ॥५७॥ यद्यत्करोषि सत्येन सर्वं मिथ्येति निश्चिनु। त्वमेव परमात्मासि त्वमेव परमो गुरुः ॥५८॥ त्वमेवाकाशरूपोऽसि साक्षिहीनोऽसि सर्वदा। त्वमेव सर्वभावोऽसि त्वं ब्रह्मासि न संशयः ॥५९॥

कालहीनोऽसि कालोऽसि सदा ब्रह्मासि चिद्घनः। सर्वतः स्वस्वरूपोसि चैतन्यघनवानसि ॥६०॥ सत्योऽसि सिद्धोऽसि सनातनोऽसि मुक्तोऽसि मोक्षोऽसि मुदामृतोऽसि। देवोऽसि शान्तोऽसि नारामयोऽसि ब्रह्मासि पूर्णोऽसि परात्परोऽसि ॥६१॥

समोऽसि सच्चापि सनातनोऽसि सत्यादिवाक्यैः प्रतिबोधितोऽसि। सर्वाङ्गहीनोऽसि सदा स्थितोऽसि ब्रह्मेन्द्ररुद्रादिविभावितोऽसि ॥६२॥ सर्वप्रपञ्चभ्रमवर्जितोऽसि सर्वेषु भूतेषु च भासितोऽसि। सर्वत्र संकल्पविवर्जितोऽसि सर्वागमान्तार्थ-विभावितोऽसि ॥६३॥ सर्वत्र संतोषसुखासनोऽसि सर्वत्र गत्यादिविवर्जितोऽसि। सर्वत्र लक्ष्यादिविवर्जितोऽसि ध्यातोऽसि विष्ण्वादिसुरैरजस्त्रम् ॥६४॥

चिदाकारस्वरूपोऽसि चिन्मात्रोऽसि निरङ्कुशः। आत्मन्येव स्थितोऽसि त्वं सर्वशून्योऽसि निर्गुणः ॥६५॥ आनन्दोऽसि परोऽसि त्वमेक एवाद्वितीयकः। चिद्घनानन्दरूपोऽसि परिपूर्णस्वरूपकः ॥६६। सदसि त्वमसि ज्ञोऽसि सोऽसि जानासि वीक्षसि। सच्चिदानन्दरूपोऽसि वासुदेवोऽसि वै प्रभुः ॥६७॥

अमृतोऽसि विभुश्चासि चञ्चलो ह्यचलो ह्यसि। सर्वोऽसि सर्वहीनोऽसि शान्ताशान्तविवर्जितः ॥६८॥ सत्तामात्रप्रकाशोऽसि सत्तासामान्यको ह्यसि। नित्यसिद्धिस्वरूपोऽसि सर्वसिद्धिविवर्जितः ॥६९॥ ईषन्मात्रविशून्योऽसि अणुमात्रविवर्जितः। अस्तित्ववर्जितोऽसि त्वं नास्तित्वादिविवर्जितः ॥७०॥

लक्ष्यलक्षणहीनोऽसि निर्विकारो निरामयः। सर्वनादान्तरोऽसि त्वं कलाकाष्ठाविवर्जितः ॥७१॥ ब्रह्मविष्णवीशहीनोऽसि स्वस्वरूपं प्रपश्यसि। स्वस्वरूपावशेषोऽसि स्वानन्दाब्धौ निमज्जसि ॥७२॥ स्वात्मराज्ये स्वमेवासि स्वयंभावविवर्जितः। शिष्टपूर्णस्वरूपोऽसि स्वस्मात्किंचिन्न पश्यसि ॥७३॥ स्वस्वरूपान्न चलसि स्वस्वरूपेण जृम्भसि। स्वस्वरूपादनन्योऽसि ह्यहमेवासि निश्चिनु ॥७४॥

इदं प्रपञ्चं यत्किंचिद्यद्यज्जगति विद्यते। दृश्यरूपं च दृग्रुपं सर्वं शशविषाणवत् ॥७५॥ भूमिरापोऽजलो वायुः खं मनो बुद्धिरेव च। अहंकारश्च तेजश्च लोकं भुवनमण्डलम् ॥७६॥ नाशो जन्म च सत्यं च पुण्यपापजयादिकम्। रागः कामः क्रोधलोभौ ध्यानं ध्येयं गुणं परम् ॥७७॥

गुरुशिष्योपदेशादिरादिरन्तं शमं शुभम्। भूतं भव्यं वर्तमानं लक्ष्यं लक्षणमद्वयम् ॥७८॥ शमो विचारः संतोषो भोक्तृभोज्यादिरूपकम्। यमाद्यष्टाङ्गयोगं च गमनागमनात्मकम् ॥७९॥ आदिमध्यान्तरङ्गं च ग्राह्यं त्याज्यं हरिः शिवः। इन्द्रियाणि मनश्चैव अवस्थात्रितयं तथा ॥८०॥

चतुर्विंशतितत्त्वं च साधनानां चतुष्टयम्। सजातीयं विजातीयं लोका भूरादयः क्रमात् ॥८१॥ सर्ववर्णाश्रमाचारं मन्त्रतन्त्रादिसंग्रहम्। विद्याविद्यादिरूपं च सर्ववेदं जडाजडम् ॥८२॥ बन्धमोक्षविभागं च ज्ञानविज्ञानरूपकम्। बोधाबोधस्वरूपं वा द्वैताद्वैतादिभाषणम् ॥८३॥

सर्ववेदान्तसिद्धान्तं सर्वशास्त्रार्थनिर्णयम्। अनेक जीवसद्भावमेकजीवादिनिर्णयम् ॥८४॥ यद्यद्ध्यायति चित्तेन यद्यत्संकल्पते क्वचित्। युद्ध्या निश्चीयते यद्यद्गुरुणा

संशृणोति यत् ॥८५॥ यद्यद्वाचा व्याकरोति यद्यदाचार्यभाषणम्। यद्यत्स्वरेन्द्रियैर्भाव्यं यद्यन्मीमांस्यते पृथक् ॥८६॥

यद्यन्न्यायेन निर्णीतं महद्भिर्वेदपारगैः। शिवः क्षरति लोकान्वै विष्णुः पाति जगत्त्रयम् ॥८७॥ ब्रह्मा सृजति लोकान्वै एवमादिक्रियादिकम्। यद्यदस्ति पुराणेषु यद्यद्वेदेषु निर्णयम् ॥८८॥ सर्वोपनिषदां भावं सर्वं शशविषाणवत्। देहोऽहमिति संकल्पं तदन्तःकरणं स्मृतम् ॥८९॥

देहोऽहमिति संकल्पो महत्संसार उच्यते। देहोऽहमिति संकल्पस्तद्बन्धमिति चोच्यते ॥९०॥ देहोऽहमिति संकल्पस्तद्दुःखमिति चोच्यते। देहोऽहमिति यद्भानं तदेव नरकं स्मृतम् ॥९१॥ देहोऽहमिति संकल्पो जगत्सर्वमितीर्यते। देहोऽहमिति संकल्पो हृदयग्रन्थिरीरितिः ॥९२॥

देहोऽहमिति यज्ज्ञानं तदेवाज्ञानमुच्यते। देहोऽहमिति यज्ज्ञानं तदसद्भावमेव च ॥९३॥ देहोऽहमिति या बुद्धिः सा चाविद्येति भण्यते। देहोऽहमिति यज्ज्ञानं तदेव द्वैतमुच्यते ॥९४॥ देहोऽहमिति संकल्पः सत्यजीवः स एव हि। देहोऽहमिति यज्ज्ञानं परिच्छिन्नमितीरितम् ॥९५॥

देहोऽहमिति संकल्पो महापापमिति स्फुटम्। देहोऽहमिति या बुद्धिस्तृष्णा दोषामयः किल ॥९६॥ यत्किंचिदपि संकल्पस्तापत्रयमितीरितम्। कामं क्रोधं बन्धनं सर्वदुःखं विश्वं दोषं कालनानास्वरूपम्। यत्किंचेदं सर्वसंकल्पजालं तत्किंचेदं मानसं सोम्य विद्धि ॥९७॥

मन एव जगत्सर्वं मन एव महारिपुः। मन एव हि संसारो मन एव जगत्त्रयम् ॥९८॥ मन एव महदुःखं मन एव जरादिकम्। मन एव हि कालश्च मन एव मलं तथा ॥९९॥ मन एव हि संकल्पो मन एव हि जीवकः। मन एव हि चित्तं च मनोऽहंकार एव च ॥१००॥

मन एव महद्बन्धं मनोऽन्तःकरणं च तत्। मन एव हि भूमिश्च मन एव हि तोयकम् ॥१०१॥ मन एव हि तेजश्च मन एव मरुन्महान्। मन एव हि चाकाशं मन एव हि शब्दकम् ॥१०२॥ स्पर्शं रूपं रसं गन्धं कोशाः पञ्च मनोभवाः। जाग्रत्स्वप्नसुषुप्त्यादि मनोमयमितीरितम् ॥१०३॥

दिक्पाला वसवो रुद्रा आदित्याश्च मनोमयाः। दृश्यं जडं द्वन्द्वजातमज्ञानं मानसं स्मृतम् ॥१०४॥ संकल्पमेव यत्किंचित्तत्तन्नास्तीति निश्चिनु। नास्ति नास्ति जगत्सर्वं गुरुशिष्यादिकं नहीत्युपनिषत् ॥१०५॥ इति पञ्चमोऽध्यायः ॥५॥

ऋभुः ॥ सर्वं सच्चिन्मयं विद्धि सर्वं सच्चिन्मयं ततम्। सच्चिदानन्दमद्वैतं सच्चिदानन्दमद्वयम् ॥१॥ सच्चिदानन्दमात्रं हि सच्चिदानन्दमन्यकम्। सच्चिदानन्दरूपोऽहं सच्चिदानन्दमेव खम् ॥२॥

सच्चिदानन्दमेव त्वं सच्चिदानन्दकोऽस्म्यहम्। मनोबुद्धिरहंकारचित्तसंघातका अमी ॥३॥ न त्वं नाहं न चान्यद्वा सर्वं ब्रह्मैव केवलम्। न वाक्यं न पदं वेदं नाक्षरं न जडं क्वचित् ॥४॥ न मध्यं नादि नान्तं वा न सत्यं न निबन्धनम्। न दुखं न सुःखं भावं न माया प्रकृतिस्तथा ॥५॥

न देहं न मुखं घ्राणं न जिह्वा न च तालुनी। न दन्तोष्ठौ ललाटं च निश्वासोच्छ्वास एव च ॥६॥ न स्वेदमस्थि मांसं च न रक्तं न च मूत्रकम्। न दूरं नान्तिकं नाङ्गं नोदरं न

किरीटकम् ॥७ ॥ न हस्तपादचलनं न शास्त्रं न च शासनम्। न वेत्ता वेदनं वेद्यं न जाग्रत्स्वप्नसुप्तयः ॥८ ॥

तुर्यातीतं न मे किंचित्सर्वं सच्चिन्मयं ततम्। नाध्यात्मिकं नाधिभूतं नाधिदैवं न मायिकम् ॥९ ॥ न विश्वस्तैजसः प्राज्ञो विराट्सूत्रात्मकेश्वराः। न गमागमचेष्टा च न नष्टं न प्रयोजनम् ॥१० ॥ त्याज्यं ग्राह्यं न दूष्यं वा ह्यमेध्यामेध्यकं तथा। न पीनं न कृशं क्लेदं न कालं देशभाषणम् ॥११ ॥

न सर्वं न भयं द्वैतं न वृक्षतृणपर्वताः। न ध्यानं योगसंसिद्धिर्न ब्रह्मक्षत्रवैश्यकम् ॥१२ ॥ न पक्षी न मृगो नाङ्गी न लोभो मोह एव च। न मदो न च मात्सर्यं कामक्रोधादयस्तथा ॥१३ ॥ न स्त्रीशूद्रबिडालादि भक्ष्यभोज्यादिकं च यत्। न प्रौढहीनो नास्तिक्यं न वार्तावसरोऽस्ति हि ॥१४ ॥

न लौकिको न लोको वा न व्यापारो न मूढता। न भोक्ता भोजनं भोज्यं न पात्रं पानपेयकम् ॥१५ ॥ न शत्रुमित्रपुत्रादिर्न माता न पिता स्वसा। न जन्म न मृतिर्वृद्धिर्न देहोऽहमिति भ्रमः ॥१६ ॥ न शून्यं नापि चाशून्यं नान्तःकरणसंसृति। न रात्रिर्न दिवा नक्तं न ब्रह्मा न हरिः शिवः ॥१७ ॥

न वारपक्षमासादि वत्सरं न च चञ्चलम्। न ब्रह्मलोको वैकुण्ठो न कैलासो न चान्यकः ॥१८ ॥ न स्वर्गो न च देवेन्द्रो नाग्निलोको न चाग्निकः। न यमो यमलोको वा न लोका लोकपालकाः ॥१९ ॥ न भूर्भुवःस्वस्त्रैलोक्यं न पातालं न भूतलम्। नाविद्या न च विद्या च न माया प्रकृतिर्जडा ॥२० ॥

न स्थिरं क्षणिकं नाशं न गतिर्न च धावनम्। न ध्यातव्यं न मे ध्यानं न मन्त्रो न जपः क्वचित् ॥२१ ॥ न पदार्था न पूजार्हं नाभिषेको न चार्चनम्। न पुष्पं न फलं पत्रं गन्ध-पुष्पादिधूपकम् ॥२२ ॥ न स्तोत्रं न नमस्कारो न प्रदक्षिणमण्वपि। न प्रार्थना पृथग्भावो न हविर्नाग्निवन्दनम् ॥२३ ॥

न होमो न च कर्माणि न दुर्वाक्यं सुभाषणम्। न गायत्री न वा संधिर्न मनस्यं न दुःस्थितिः ॥२४ ॥ न दुराशा न दुष्टात्मा न चाण्डालो न पौल्कसः। न दुःसहं दुरालापं न किरातो न कैतवम् ॥२५ ॥

न पक्षपातं पक्षं वा न विभूषणतस्करौ न च दम्भो दाम्भिको वा न हीनो नाधिको नरः ॥२६ ॥ नैकं द्वयं त्रयं तुर्यं न महत्वं न चाल्पता। न पूर्णं न परिच्छिन्नं न काशी न व्रतं तपः ॥२७ ॥ न गोत्रं न कुलं सूत्रं न विभूत्वं न शून्यता। न स्त्री न योषिन्नो वृद्धा न कन्या न वितन्तुता ॥२८ ॥

न सूतकं न जातं वा नान्तर्मुखसुविभ्रमः। न महावाक्यमैक्यं वा नाणिमादिविभूतयः ॥२९ ॥ सर्वचैतन्यमात्रत्वात्सर्वदोषः सदा न हि। सर्वं सन्मात्र-रूपत्वात्सच्चिदानन्दमात्रकम् ॥३० ॥ ब्रह्मैव सर्वं नान्योऽस्ति तदहं तदहं तथा। तदेवाहं तदेवाहं ब्रह्मैवाहं सनातनम् ॥३१ ॥ ब्रह्मैवाहं न संसारी ब्रह्मैवाहं न मे मनः। ब्रह्मैवाहं न मे बुद्धिर्ब्रह्मैवाहं न चेन्द्रियः ॥३२ ॥

ब्रह्मैवाहं न देहोऽहं ब्रह्मैवाहं न गोचरः। ब्रह्मैवाहं न जीवोऽहं ब्रह्मैवाहं न भेदभूः ॥३३ ॥ ब्रह्मैवाहं जडो नाहमहं ब्रह्म न मे मृतिः। ब्रह्मैवाहं न च प्राणो ब्रह्मैवाहं

परात्परः ॥३४ ॥ इदं ब्रह्म परं ब्रह्म सत्यं ब्रह्म प्रभुर्हि सः । कालो ब्रह्म कला ब्रह्म सुखं ब्रह्म स्वयंप्रभम् ॥३५ ॥

एकं ब्रह्म द्वयं ब्रह्म मोहो ब्रह्म शमादिकम् । दोषो ब्रह्म गुणो ब्रह्म दमः शान्तं विभुः प्रभुः ॥३६ ॥ लोका ब्रह्म गुरुर्ब्रह्म शिष्यो ब्रह्म सदाशिवः । पूर्वं ब्रह्म परं ब्रह्म शुद्धं ब्रह्म शुभाशुभम् ॥३७ ॥ जीव एव सदा ब्रह्म सच्चिदानन्दमस्म्यहम् । सर्वं ब्रह्ममयं प्रोक्तं सर्वं ब्रह्ममयं जगत् ॥३८ ॥

स्वयं ब्रह्म न संदेहः स्वस्मादन्यन्न किंचन। सर्वमात्मैव शुद्धात्मा सर्वं चिन्मात्रमद्वयम् ॥३९ ॥ नित्यनिर्मलरूपात्मा ह्यात्मनोऽन्यन्न किंचन। अणुमात्रलसद्रूपमणुमात्रमिदं जगत् ॥४० ॥ अमुमात्रं शरीरं वा ह्यणुमात्रमसत्यकम् । अणुमात्रमचिन्त्यं वा चिन्त्यं वा ह्यणुमात्रकम् ॥४१ ॥

ब्रह्मैव सर्वं चिन्मात्रं ब्रह्ममात्रं जगत्त्रयम्। आनन्दं परमानन्दमन्यत्किंचिन्न किंचन ॥४२ ॥ चैतन्यमात्रमोंकारं ब्रह्मैव सकलं स्वयम् । अहमेव जगत्सर्वमहमेव परं पदम् ॥४३ ॥ अहमेव गुणातीत अहमेव परात्परः। अहमेव परं ब्रह्म अहमेव गुरोर्गुरुः ॥४४ ॥

अहमेवाखिलाधार अहमेव सुखात्सुखम्। आत्मनोऽन्यज्जगन्नास्ति आत्मनोऽन्यत्सुखं न च ॥४५ ॥ आत्मनोऽन्या गतिर्नास्ति सर्वमात्ममयं जगत्। आत्मनोऽन्यन्नहि क्वापि आत्मनोऽन्यत्तृणं नहि ॥४६ ॥ आत्मनोऽन्यत्तुषं नास्ति सर्वमात्ममयं जगत् । ब्रह्ममात्रमिदं सर्वं ब्रह्ममात्रमसन्न हि ॥४७ ॥

ब्रह्ममात्रं श्रुतं सर्वं स्वयं ब्रह्मैव केवलम् । ब्रह्ममात्रं वृतं सर्वं ब्रह्ममात्रं रसं सुखम् ॥४८ ॥ ब्रह्ममात्रं चिदाकाशं सच्चिदानन्दमव्ययम्। ब्रह्मणोऽन्यतरन्नास्ति ब्रह्मणोऽन्यज्जगन्न च ॥४९ ॥ ब्रह्मणोऽन्यदह नास्ति ब्रह्मणोऽन्यत्फलं नहि। ब्रह्मणोऽन्यत्तृणं नास्ति ब्रह्मणोऽन्यत्पदं नहि ॥५० ॥

ब्रह्मणोऽन्यद्गुरुर्नास्ति ब्रह्मणोऽन्यमसद्वपुः । ब्रह्मणोऽन्यन्न चाहंता त्वत्तेदन्ते नहि क्वचित् ॥५१ ॥ स्वयं ब्रह्मात्मकं विद्धि स्वस्मादन्यन्न किंचन । यत्किंचिद्दृश्यते लोके यत्किंचिद्भाष्यते जनैः ॥५२ ॥ यत्किंचिद्भुज्यते क्वापि तत्सर्वमसदेव हि। कर्तृभेदं क्रियाभेदं गुणभेदं रसादिकम् ॥५३ ॥

लिङ्गभेदमिदं सर्वमसदेव सदा सुखम्। कालभेद देशभेदं वस्तुभेदं जयाजयम् ॥५४ ॥ यद्यद्भेदं च तत्सर्वमसदेव हि केवलम्। असदन्तःकरणकमसदेवेन्द्रियादिकम् ॥५५ ॥ असत्प्राणादिकं सर्वं संघातमसदात्मकम् । असत्यं पञ्चकोशाख्यमसत्यं पञ्च देवताः ॥५६ ॥ असत्यं षड्विकारादि असत्यमरिवर्गकम् । असत्यं षड्टतुश्चैव असत्यं षड्टसस्तथा ॥५७ ॥

सच्चिदानन्दमात्रोऽहमनुत्पन्नमिदं जगत्। आत्मैवाहं परं सत्यं नान्याः संसारदृष्टयः ॥५८ ॥ सत्यमानन्दरूपोऽहं चिद्घनानन्दविग्रहः । अहमेव परानन्द अहमेव परात्परः ॥५९ ॥ ज्ञानाकारमिदं सर्वं ज्ञानानन्दोऽहमद्वयः । सर्वप्रकाशरूपोऽहं सर्वाभावस्वरूपकम् ॥६० ॥

अहमेव सदा भामीत्येवं रूपं कुतोऽप्यसत् । त्वमित्येवं परं ब्रह्म चिन्मयानन्दरूपवान् ॥६१ ॥ चिदाकारं चिदाकाशं चिदेव परमं सुखम् । आत्मैवाहमसन्नाहं कूटस्थोऽहं गुरुः परः ॥६२ ॥

सच्चिदानन्दमात्रोऽहमनुत्पन्नमिदं जगत्। कालो नास्ति जगन्नास्ति मायाप्रकृतिरेव न ॥६३ ॥ अहमेव हरिः साक्षादहमेव सदाशिवः। शुद्धचैतन्यभावोऽहं शुद्धसत्त्वानुभावनः ॥६४ ॥ अद्वयानन्दमात्रोऽहं चिद्घनैकरसोऽस्म्यहम्। सर्वं ब्रह्मैव सततं सर्वं ब्रह्मैव केवलम् ॥६५ ॥

सर्वं ब्रह्मैव सततं सर्वं ब्रह्मैव चेतनम्। सर्वान्तर्यामिरूपोऽहं सर्वसाक्षित्वलक्षणः ॥६६ ॥ परमात्मा परं ज्योतिः परं धाम परा गतिः। सर्ववेदान्तसारोऽहं सर्वशास्त्रसुनिश्चितः ॥६७ ॥ योगानन्दस्वरूपोऽहं मुख्यानन्दमहोदयः। सर्वज्ञानप्रकाशोऽस्मि मुख्यविज्ञानविग्रहः ॥६८ ॥ तुर्यातुर्यप्रकाशोऽस्मि तुर्यातुर्यादिवर्जितः। चिदक्षरोऽहं सत्योऽहं वासुदेवोऽजरोऽमरः ॥६९ ॥

अहं ब्रह्म चिदाकाशं नित्यं ब्रह्म निरञ्जनम्। शुद्धं बुद्धं सदामुक्तमनामकमरूपकम् ॥७० ॥ सच्चिदानन्दरूपोऽहमनुत्पन्नमिदं जगत्। सत्यासत्यं जगन्नास्ति संकल्पकलनादिकम् ॥७१ ॥ नित्यानन्दमयं ब्रह्म केवलं सर्वदा स्वयम्। अनन्तमव्ययं शान्तमेकरूपमनामयम् ॥७२ ॥ मत्तोऽन्यदस्ति चेन्मिथ्या यथा मरुमरीचिका। वन्ध्याकुमारवचने भीतिश्चेदस्ति किंचन ॥७३ ॥

शशशृङ्गेण नागेन्द्रो मृतश्चेज्जगदस्ति तत्। मृगतृष्णाजलं पीत्वा तृप्तश्चेदस्त्विदं जगत् ॥७४ ॥ नरशृङ्गेण नष्टश्चेत्कश्चिदस्त्विदमेव हि। गन्धर्वनगरे सत्ये जगद्भवति सर्वदा ॥७५ ॥ गगने नीलिमासत्ये जगत्सत्यं भविष्यति। शुक्तिकारजतं सत्यं भूषणं चेज्जगद्भवेत् ॥७६ ॥ रज्जुसर्पेण दष्टश्चेन्नरो भवतु संसृतिः। जातरूपेण बाणेन ज्वालाग्नौ नाशिते जगत् ॥७७ ॥

विन्ध्याटव्यां पायसान्नमस्ति चेज्जगदुद्भवः। रम्भास्तम्भेन काष्ठेन पाकसिद्धौ जगद्भवेत् ॥७८ ॥ सद्यः कुमारिकारूपैः पाके सिद्धे जगद्भवेत्। चित्रस्थदीपैस्तमसो नाशश्चेदस्त्विदं जगत् ॥७९ ॥ मासात्पूर्वं मृतो ह्यागतश्चेज्जगद्भवेत्। तक्रं क्षीरस्वरूपं चेतक्वचिन्नत्यं जगद्भवेत् ॥८० ॥ गोस्तनादुद्भवं क्षीरं पुनरारोपणे जगत्। भूरजोऽब्धौ समुत्पन्ने जगद्भवतु सर्वदा ॥८१ ॥ कूर्मरोम्णा गजे बद्धे जगदस्तु मदोत्कटे। नालस्थतन्तुना मेरुश्चालितश्चेज्जगद्भवेत् ॥८२ ॥

तरङ्गमालया सिन्धुर्बद्धश्चेदस्त्विदं जगत्। अग्नेरधश्चेज्ज्वलनं जगद्भवतु सर्वदा ॥८३ ॥ ज्वालावह्निः शीतलश्चेदस्तिरूपमिदं जगत्। ज्वालाग्निमण्डले पद्मवृद्धिश्चेज्जगदस्त्विदम् ॥८४ ॥ महच्छैलेन्द्रनीलं वा संभवच्चेदिदं जगत्। मेरुरागत्य पद्माक्षे स्थितश्चेदस्त्विदं जगत् ॥८५ ॥ निगिरेच्चेद्भृङ्गसूनुर्मेरुं चलवदस्त्विदम्। मशकेन हते सिंहे जगत्सत्यं तदास्तु ते ॥८६ ॥

अणुकोटरविस्तीर्णे त्रैलोक्यं चेज्जगद्भवेत्। तृणानलश्च नित्यश्चेत्क्षणिकं तज्जगद्भवेत् ॥८७ ॥ स्वप्नदृष्टं च यद्वस्तु जागरे चेज्जगद्भवः। नदीवेगो निश्चलश्चेतत्केनापीदं भवेज्जगत् ॥८८ ॥

क्षुधितस्याग्निर्भोज्यश्चेन्निमिषं कल्पितं भवेत्। जात्यन्धै रत्नविषयः सुज्ञातश्चेज्जगत्सदा ॥८९ ॥ नपुंसककुमारस्य स्त्रीसुखं चेद्भवेज्जगत्। निर्मितः शशशृङ्गेण रथश्चेज्जगदस्ति तत् ॥९० ॥ सद्योजाता तु या कन्या भोगयोग्या भवेज्जगत्। वन्ध्या गर्भापतत्सौख्यं ज्ञाता चेदस्त्विदं जगत् ॥९१ ॥ काको वा हंसवद्गच्छेज्जगद्भवतु

निश्चलम्। महाखरो वा सिंहेन युध्यते चेज्जगत्स्थितिः ॥९२॥ महाखरो गजगतिं गतश्चेज्जगदस्तु तत्। संपूर्णचन्द्रसूर्यश्चेज्जगद्भातु स्वयं जडम् ॥९३॥

चन्द्रसूर्यादिकं त्यक्त्वा राहुश्चेद्दृश्यते जगत्। भृष्टबीजसमुत्पन्नवृद्धिश्चेज्जगदस्तु सत् ॥९४॥ दरिद्रो धनिकानां च सुखं भुङ्क्ते तदा जगत्। शुना वीर्येण सिंहस्तु जितो यदि जगत्तदा ॥९५॥ ज्ञानिनो हृदयं मूढैर्ज्ञातं चेत्कल्पनं तदा। श्वानेन सागरे पीते निःशेषेण मनो भवेत् ॥९६॥ शुद्धाकाशो मनुष्येषु पतितश्चेत्तदा जगत्। भूमौ वा पतितं व्योम व्योमपुष्पं सुगन्धकम् ॥९७॥

शुद्धाकाशे वने जाते चलिते तु तदा जगत्। केवले दर्पणे नास्ति प्रतिबिम्बं तदा जगत् ॥९८॥ अजकुक्षौ जगन्नास्ति ह्यात्मकुक्षौ जगन्नहि। सर्वथा भेदकलनं द्वैताद्वैतं न विद्यते ॥९९॥ मायाकार्यमिदं भेदमस्ति चेद्ब्रह्मभावनम्। देहोऽहमिति दुःखं चेद्ब्रह्माहमिति निश्चयः ॥१००॥

हृदयग्रन्थिरस्तित्वे छिद्यते ब्रह्मचक्रकम्। संशये समनुप्राप्ते ब्रह्मनिश्चयमाश्रयेत् ॥१०१॥ अनात्मरूपचोरश्चेदात्मरत्नस्य रक्षणम्। नित्यानन्दमयं ब्रह्म केवलं सर्वदा स्वयम् ॥१०२॥ एवमादिसुदृष्टान्तैः साधितं ब्रह्ममात्रकम्। ब्रह्मैव सर्वभवनं भुवनं नाम संत्यज ॥१०३॥

अहं ब्रह्मेति निश्चित्य अहंभावं परित्यज। सवमेव लयं याति सुप्तहस्तस्थपुष्प-वत् ॥१०४॥ न देहो न च कर्माणि सर्वं ब्रह्मैव केवलम्। न भूतं न च कार्यं च न चावस्थाचतुष्टयम् ॥१०५॥ लक्षणात्रयविज्ञानं सर्वं ब्रह्मैव केवलम्। सर्वव्यापारमुत्सृज्य ह्यहं ब्रह्मेति भावय ॥१०६॥

अहं ब्रह्म न संदेहो ह्यहं ब्रह्म चिदात्मकम्। सच्चिदानन्दमात्रोऽहमिति निश्चित्य तत्त्यज ॥१०७॥ शांकरीयं महाशास्त्रं न देयं यस्य कस्यचित्त। नास्तिकाय कृतघ्नाय दुर्वृत्ताय दुरात्मने ॥१०८॥ गुरुभक्तिविशुद्धान्तःकरणाय महात्मने। सम्यक् परीक्ष्य दातव्यं मासं षाण्मासवत्सरम् ॥१०९॥

सर्वोपनिषदभ्यासं दूरतस्त्यज्य सादरम्। तेजोबिन्दूपनिषदमभ्यसेत्यर्स्वदा मुदा ॥११०॥ सकृदभ्यासमात्रैण ब्रह्मैव भवति स्वयं ब्रह्मैव भवति स्वयमित्युपनिषत् ॥
ॐ सह नाववत्विति शान्तिः ॥

इति तेजोबिन्दूपनिषत्समाप्ता ॥

१३. ब्रह्मोपनिषत्

ॐ सह नाववत्विति शान्तिः ॥

ब्रह्मकैवल्यजाबालः श्वेताश्वो हंस आरुणिः।
गर्भो नारायणो हंसो विन्दुनादशिरः शिखा ॥१॥

एतास्त्रयोदश ॐ ॥ अथास्य पुरुषस्य चत्वारि स्थानानि भवन्ति। नाभिर्हृदयं कण्ठं मूर्धा च। तत्र चतुष्पादं ब्रह्म विभाति। जागरिते ब्रह्म स्वप्ने विष्णुः सुषुप्तौ रुद्रस्तुरीयमक्षरम्। स आदित्यो विष्णुश्चेश्वरश्च। स्वयममनस्कमश्रोत्रमपाणिपादं ज्योतिर्विदितम्। यत्र लोका न लोका देवा न देवा वेदा न वेदा यज्ञा न यज्ञा माता न माता

पिता न पिता स्नुषा न स्नुषा चाण्डालो न चाण्डालः पौष्कसो न पौष्कसः श्रमणो न श्रमणस्तापसो न तापस एकभेव तत्परं ब्रह्म विभाति निर्वाणम्। न तत्र देवा ऋषयः पितरं ईशते प्रतिबुध्यः सर्वविद्येति। हृदिस्था देवताः सर्वा हृदि प्राणाः प्रतिष्ठिताः। हृदि प्राणाश्च ज्योतिश्च त्रिवृत्सूत्रं च तद्विदुरिति। हृदि चैतन्ये तिष्ठति यज्ञोपवीतं परमं पवित्रं प्रजायतेर्यत्सहजं पुरस्तात्। आयुषयमग्र्यं प्रतिमुञ्च शुभ्रं यज्ञोपवितं बलमस्तु तेजः। सशिखं वपनं कृत्वा बहिः सूत्रं त्यजेद्बुधः। यदक्षरं परं ब्रह्म तत्सूत्रमिति धारयेत्। सूचनात्सूत्रमित्याहुः सूत्रं नाम परं पदम्। तत्सूत्रं विदितं येन स विप्रो वेदपारगः येन सर्वमिदं प्रोतं सूत्रे मणिगणा इव। तत्सूत्रं धारयेद्योगी योगवित्तत्त्वदर्शिवान्। बहिःसूत्रं त्यजेद्विद्वान्योगमुत्तममास्थितः। ब्रह्मभावमिदं सूत्रं धारयेद्यः स चेतनः। धारणात्तस्य सूत्रस्य नोच्छिष्टो नाशुचिर्भवेत्॥ सूत्रमन्तर्गतं येषां ज्ञानयज्ञोपवीतिनाम्। ते वै सूत्रविदो लेके ते च यज्ञोपवीतिनः॥ ज्ञानशिखिनो ज्ञाननिष्ठा ज्ञानयज्ञोपवीतिनः। ज्ञानमेव परं तेषां पवित्रं ज्ञानमुच्यते॥ अग्नेरिव शिखा नान्या यस्य ज्ञानमयी शिखा। स शिखीत्युच्यते विद्वान्नेतरे केशधारिणः॥ कर्मण्यधिकृता ये तु वैदिके ब्राह्मणादयः तेभिर्धार्यमिदं सूत्रं क्रियाङ्गं तद्धि वै स्मृतम्॥ शिखा ज्ञानमयी यस्य उपवीतं च तन्मयम्। ब्राह्मण्यं सकलं तस्य इति ब्रह्मविदो विदुः॥

इदं यज्ञोपवीतं तु परमं यत्परायणम्। स विद्वान्यज्ञोपवीति स्यात्स यज्ञस्तं यज्वानं विदुः॥ एको देवः सर्वभूतेषु गूढः सर्वव्यापी सर्वभूतान्तरात्मा। कर्माध्यक्षः सर्वभूताधिवासः साक्षी चेता केवलो निर्गुणश्च॥ एको वशी सर्वभूतान्तरात्मैकं रूपं बहुधा यः करोति। तमात्मस्थं येनु पश्यन्ति धीरास्तेषां सुखं शाश्वतं नेतरेषाम्॥ आत्मानमरणिं कृत्वा प्रणवं चोत्तरारणिम्। ध्याननिर्मयनाभ्यासादेवं पश्येन्निगूढवत्॥ तिलेषु तैलं दधनीव सर्पिरापः स्रोतःस्वरणीषु चाग्निः। एवमात्मात्मनि जायतेऽसौ सत्येन तपसा योऽनुपश्यति॥ ऊर्णनाभिर्यथा तन्तून्सृजते संहरत्यपि। जाग्रत्स्वप्ने तथा जीवो गच्छत्यागच्छते पुनः॥ नेत्रस्थं जागरितं विद्यात्कण्ठे स्वप्नं समाविशेत्। सुषुप्तं हृदयस्थं तु तुरीयं मूर्ध्नि संस्थितम्॥ यतो वाचो निवर्तन्ते अप्राप्य मनसा सह। आनन्दमेतज्जीवस्य यज्ज्ञात्वा मुच्यते बुधः॥ सर्वव्यापिनमात्मानं क्षीरे सर्पिरिवार्पितम्। आत्मविद्यातपोमूलं तद्ब्रह्मोपनिषत्पदं तद्ब्रह्मोपनिषत्पदमिति॥ सह नाववत्विति शान्तिः॥

इति ब्रह्मोपनिषत्समाप्ता॥

१४. वज्रसूचिकोपनिषत्

यज्ज्ञानाद्यान्ति मुनयो ब्राह्मण्यं परमाद्भुतम्।
तन्त्रैपदब्रह्मतत्त्वमहमस्मीति चिन्तये॥
ॐ आप्यायन्त्विति शान्तिः॥
चित्सदानन्दरूपाय सर्वधीवृत्तिसाक्षिणे।
नमो वेदान्तवेद्याय ब्रह्मणेऽनन्तरूपिणे॥

ॐ वज्रसूचीं प्रवक्ष्यामि शास्त्रमज्ञानभेदनम्। दूषणं ज्ञानहीनानां भूषणं ज्ञानचक्षुषाम्॥१॥ ब्रह्मक्षत्रियवैश्यशूद्रा इति चत्वारो वर्णास्तेषां वर्णानां ब्राह्मण एव प्रधान

इति वेदवचनानुरूपं स्मृतिभिरप्युक्तम् । तत्र चोद्यमस्ति को वा ब्राह्मणो नाम किं जीवः किं देहः किं जातिः किं ज्ञानम् किं कर्म किं धार्मिक इति । तत्र प्रथमो जीवो ब्राह्मण इति चेत्तन्न । अतीतानागतानेकदेहानां जीवस्यैकरूपत्वात् एकस्यापि कर्मवशादनेकदेहसंभवात् सर्वशरीराणां जीवस्यैकरूपत्वाच्च । तस्मान्न जीवो ब्राह्मण इति । तर्हि देहो ब्राह्मण इति चेत्तन्न । आचाण्डालादिपर्यन्तानां मनुष्याणां पाञ्चभौतिकत्वेन देहस्यैकरूपत्वाज्जरामरण-धर्माधर्मादिसाम्यदर्शनाद्ब्राह्मणः श्वेतवर्णः क्षत्रियो रक्तवर्णो वैश्यः पीतवर्णः शूद्रः कृष्णवर्ण इति नियमाभावात् । पित्रादिशरीरदहने पुत्रादीनां ब्रह्महत्यादिदोषसंभवाच्च । तस्मान्न देहो ब्राह्मण इति ॥ तर्हि जातिब्राह्मण इति चेत्तन्न । तत्र जात्यन्तरजन्तुष्वनेकजातिसंभवा महर्षयो बहवः सन्ति । ऋष्यशृङ्गो मृग्या, कौशिकः कुशात्, जाम्बूको जम्बूकात्, वाल्मीको वल्मीकात्, व्यासः कैवर्तकन्यकायाम्, शशपृष्ठात् गौतमः, वसिष्ठ उर्वश्याम्, अगस्त्यः कलशे जात इति श्रुतत्वात् । एतेषां जात्या विनाप्यग्रे ज्ञानप्रतिपादिता ऋषयो बहवः सन्ति । तस्मान्न जातिर्ब्राह्मण इति । तर्हि ज्ञानं ब्राह्मण इति चेत्तन्न । क्षत्रियादयोऽपि परमार्थदर्शिनोऽभिज्ञा बहवः सन्ति । तस्मान्न ज्ञानं ब्राह्मण इति ॥

तर्हि कर्म ब्राह्मण इति चेत्तन्न । सर्वेषां प्राणिनां प्रारब्धसंचितागामिकर्मसाधर्म्यदर्शनात्कर्माभिप्रेरिताः सन्तो जनाः क्रियाः कुर्वन्तीति । तस्मान्न कर्म ब्राह्मण इति ॥ तर्हि धार्मिको ब्राह्मण इति चेत्तन्न । क्षत्रियादयो हिरण्यदातारो बहवः सन्ति । तस्मान्न धार्मिको ब्राह्मण इति ॥ तर्हि को वा ब्राह्मणो नाम । यः कश्चिदात्मानमद्वितीयं जातिगुणक्रियाहीनं षडूर्मिषड्भावेत्यादिसर्वदोषरहितं सत्यज्ञाना-नन्दानन्तस्वरूपं स्वयं निर्विकल्पमशेषकल्पाधारमशेषभूतान्तर्यामित्वेन वर्तमानमन्त-र्बहिश्चाकाशवदनुस्यूतमखण्डानन्दस्वभावमप्रमेयमनुभवैकवेद्यमपरोक्षतया भासमानं करतलामलकवत्साक्षादपरोक्षीकृत्य कृतार्थतया कामरागादिदोषरहितः शमदमादिसंपन्नो भावमात्सर्यतृष्णाशामोहादिरहितो दम्भाहंकारादिभिरसंस्पृष्टचेता वर्तत एवमुक्तलक्षणो यः स एव ब्राह्मण इति श्रुतिस्मृतिपुराणेतिहासानामभिप्रायः । अन्यथा हि ब्राह्मणत्वसिद्धिर्नास्त्येव । सच्चिदानन्दमात्मानमद्वितीयं ब्रह्म भावयेदात्मानं सच्चिदानन्दं ब्रह्म भावयेदित्युपनिषत् ॥ ॐ आप्यायन्त्विति शान्तिः ॥

इति वज्रसूच्युपनिषत्समाप्ता ॥

१५. शारीरकोपनिषत्

तत्त्वग्रामोपायसिद्ध परतत्त्वस्वरूपकम् ।
शरीरोपनिषद्वेद्यं श्रीरामब्रह्म मे गतिः ॥

ॐ सह नाववत्विति शान्तिः ॥

ॐ अथातः पृथिव्यादिमहाभूतानां समवायं शरीरम् । यत्कठिनं सा पृथिवी यद्द्रवं तदापो यदुष्णं तत्तेजो यत्संचरति स वायुर्यत्सुषिरं तदाकाशम् । श्रोत्रादीनि ज्ञानेन्द्रियाणि । श्रोत्रमाकाशे वायौ त्वगग्नौ चक्षुरप्सु जिह्वा पृथिव्यां घ्राणमिति ।

एवमिन्द्रियाणां यथाक्रमेण शब्दस्पर्शरूपरसगन्धाश्चैति विषयाः पृथिव्यादिमहाभूतेषु क्रमेणोत्पन्नाः । वाक्पाणिपादपायूपस्थाख्यानि कर्मेन्द्रियाणि । तेषां क्रमेण

वचनादानगमनविसर्गानन्दाश्चैते विषयाः पृथिव्यादिमहाभूतेषु क्रमेणोत्पन्नाः। मनोबुद्धिरहंकारश्चित्तमित्यन्तः करणचतुष्टयम्।

तेषां क्रमेण संकल्पविकल्पाध्यवसायाभिमानावधारणास्वरूपाश्चैते विषयाः। मनःस्थानं गलान्तं बुद्धेर्वदनमहंकारस्य हृदयं चित्तस्य नाभिरिति। अस्थिचर्मनाडीरोममांसाश्चेति पृथिव्यंशाः। मूत्रश्लेष्मरक्तशुक्रस्वेदा अबंशाः। क्षुत्तृष्णालस्यमोहमैथुनान्यग्नेः।

प्रचारणविलेखनस्थूलाद्युन्मेषनिमेषादि वायोः। कामक्रोधलोभमोहभयान्याकाशस्य। शब्दस्पर्शरूपरसगन्धाः पृथिवीगुणाः। शब्दस्पर्शरूपरसाश्चापां गुणाः। शब्दस्पर्शरूपाण्यग्निगुणाः। शब्दस्पर्शाविति वायुगुणौ। शब्द एक आकाशस्य। सात्त्विकराजसतामसलक्षणानि त्रयो गुणाः॥ अहिंसासत्यमस्तेयब्रह्मचर्यापरिग्रहाः। अक्रोधो गुरुशुश्रूषा शौचं संतोष आर्जवम्॥१॥

अमानित्वमदम्भित्वमास्तिकत्वमहिंस्रता। एते सर्वे गुणा ज्ञेयाः सात्त्विकस्य विशेषतः॥२॥ अहं कर्तास्म्यहं भोक्तास्म्यहं वक्ताभिमानवान्। एते गुणा राजसस्य प्रोच्यन्ते ब्रह्मवित्तमैः॥३॥ निद्रालस्ये मोहरागौ मैथुनं चौर्यमेव च। एते गुणास्तामसस्य प्रोच्यन्ते ब्रह्मवादिभिः॥४॥ ऊर्ध्वे सात्त्विको मध्ये राजसोऽधस्तामस इति। सत्यज्ञानं सात्त्विकम्।

धर्मज्ञानं राजसम्। तिमिरान्धं तामसमिति। जाग्रत्स्वप्नसुषुप्तितुरीयमिति चतुर्विधा अवस्थाः। ज्ञानेन्द्रियकर्मेन्द्रियान्तःकरणचतुष्टयं चतुर्दशकरणयुक्तं जाग्रत्। अन्तःकरणचतुष्टयैरेव संयुक्तः स्वप्नः। चित्तैककरणा सुषुप्तिः। केवलजीवयुक्तमेव तुरीयमिति। उन्मीलितनिमीलितमध्यस्थजीवपरमात्मनोर्मध्ये जीवात्मा क्षेत्रज्ञ इति विज्ञायते।

बुद्धिकर्मेन्द्रियप्राणपञ्चकैर्मनसा धिया। शरीरं सप्तदशभिः सुसूक्ष्मं लिङ्गमुच्यते॥५॥ मनो बुद्धिरहंकारः खानिलाग्निजलानि भूः। एताः प्रकृतयस्त्वष्टौ विकाराः षोडशापरे॥६॥ श्रोत्रं त्वक्चक्षुषी जिह्वा घ्राणं चैव तु पञ्चमम्। पायूपस्थौ करौ पादौ वाक्चैव दशमी मता॥७॥

शब्दः स्पर्शश्च रूपं च रसो गन्धस्तथैव च। त्रयोविंशतिरेतानि तत्त्वानि प्रकृतानि तु॥८॥ चतुर्विंशतिरव्यक्तं प्रधानं पुरुषः परः॥९॥ इत्युपनिषत्॥ ॐ सह नाववत्विति शान्तिः॥ ॐ तत्सत्॥

इति शारीरकोपनिषत्समाप्ता॥

१६. गर्भोपनिषत्

यद्गर्भोपनिषद्वेद्यं गर्भस्य स्वात्मबोधकम्।
शरीरापह्नवात्सिद्धं स्वमात्रं कलये हरिम्॥
ॐ सह नाववत्विति शान्तिः॥

ॐ पञ्चात्मकं पञ्चसु वर्तमानं षडाश्रयं षड्गुणयोगयुक्तम्। तं सप्तधातुं त्रिमलं द्वियोनिं चतुर्विधाहारमयं शरीरं भवति। पञ्चात्मकमिति कस्मात् पृथिव्यापस्तेजो वायुराकाशमित्यस्मिन्पञ्चात्मके शरीरे का पृथिवी का आपः किं तेजः को वायुः

किमाकाशमित्यस्मिन्पञ्चात्मके शरीरे तत्र यत्कठिनं सा पृथिवी यद्द्रवं ता आपः यदुष्णं तत्तेजः यत्संचरति स वायुः यत्सुषिरं तदाकाशमित्युच्यते। तत्र पृथिवी धारणे आपः पिण्डीकरणे तेजः प्रकाशने वायुर्व्यूहने आकाशमवकाशप्रदाने। पृथक्श्रोत्रे शब्दोपलब्धौ त्वक् स्पर्शे चक्षुषी रूपे जिह्वा रसने नासिका घ्राणे उपस्थ आनन्दने अपान उत्सर्गे बुद्ध्या बुध्यति मनसा संकल्पयति वाचा वदति। षडाश्रयमिति कस्मात्। मधुराम्ललवणतिक्तकटुकषायरसान्विन्दतीति। षड्जऋषभगान्धारमध्यमपञ्चमधैवत-निषादाश्चेतीष्टानिष्टशब्दसंज्ञा प्रणिधानाद्दशविधा भवन्ति ॥१ ॥

शुक्लो रक्तः कृष्णो धूम्रः पीतः कपिलः पाण्डर इति ॥ सप्तधातुकमिति कस्मात् यदा देवदत्तस्य द्रव्यादिविषया जायन्ते। परस्परं सौम्यगुणत्वात् षड्विधो रसो रसाच्छोणितं शोणितान्मांसं मांसान्मेदो मेदसः स्नायवः स्नायुभ्योऽस्थीनि अस्थिभ्यो मज्जा मज्जातः शुक्रं शुक्रशोणितसंयोगादावर्तते गर्भो हृदि व्यवस्थां नयति हृदयेन्तराग्निः अग्निस्थाने पित्तं पित्तस्थाने वायुः वायुतो हृदयं प्राजापत्यात्क्रमात् ॥२ ॥ ऋतुकाले संप्रयोगादेकरात्रोषितं कललं भवति सप्तरात्रोषितं बुद्बुदं भवति अर्धमासाभ्यन्तरे पिण्डो भवति। मासाभ्यन्तरे कठिनो भवति मासद्वयेन शिरः संपद्यते। मासत्रयेण पादप्रदेशो भवति। अथ चतुर्थे मासे गुल्फजठरकटिप्रदेशा भवन्ति।

पञ्चमे मासे पृष्ठवंशो भवति। षष्ठे मासे मुखनासिकाक्षिश्रोत्राणि भवन्ति। सप्तमे मासे जीवेन संयुक्तो भवति। अष्टमे मासे सर्वलक्षणसंपूर्णो भवति। पितू रेतोऽतिरेकात्पुरुषो मातू रेतोऽतिरेकात्स्त्री उभयोर्बीजतुल्यत्वान्नपुंसको भवति। व्याकुलितमनसोऽन्धाः खञ्जाः कुब्जा वामना भवन्ति। अन्योन्यवायुपरिपीडितशुक्रद्वैविध्यात्तनु स्यात्ततो युग्माः प्रजायन्ते। पञ्चात्मकः समर्थः पञ्चात्मिका चेतसा बुद्धिर्गन्धरसादिज्ञानाक्षराक्षरमोंकारं चिन्तयतीति तदेतदेकाक्षरं ज्ञात्वाष्टौ प्रकृतयः षोडश विकाराः शरीरे तस्यैव देहिनः अथ मात्राशितपीतनाडीसूत्रगतेन प्राण आप्यायते। अथ नवमे मासि सर्वलक्षणज्ञानकरणसंपूर्णो भवति। पूर्वजातिं स्मरति। शुभाशुभं च कर्म विन्दति ॥३ ॥

पूर्वयोनिसहस्राणि दृष्ट्वा चैव ततो मया। आहारा विविधा भुक्ताः पीता नानाविधाः स्तनाः ॥ जातश्चैव मृतश्चैव जन्म चैव पुनः पुनः। यन्मया परिजनस्यार्थे कृतं कर्म शुभा-शुभम् ॥ एकाकी तेन दह्येऽहं गतास्ते फलभोगिनः। अहो दुःखोदधौ मग्नो न पश्यामि प्रतिक्रियाम् ॥ यदि योन्याः प्रमुच्येऽहं तत्प्रपद्ये महेश्वरम्। अशुभक्षयकर्तारं फलमुक्तिप्रदायकम्। यदि योन्याः प्रमुच्येऽहं तत्प्रपद्ये नारायणम्। अशुभक्षयकर्तारं फलमुक्तिप्रदायकम्। यदि योन्याः प्रमुच्येऽहं तत्सांख्यं योगमभ्यसे। अशुभक्षयकर्तारं फलमुक्तिप्रदायकम्। यदि योन्याः प्रमुच्येऽहं ध्याये ब्रह्म सनातनम्। अथ योनिद्वारं संप्राप्तो यन्त्रेणापीड्यमानो महता दुःखेन जातमात्रस्तु वैष्णवेन वायुना संस्पृष्टस्तदा न स्मरति जन्ममरणानि न च कर्म शुभाशुभं विन्दति ॥४ ॥

शरीरमिति कस्मात्। अग्नयो ह्यत्र श्रियन्ते ज्ञानाग्निर्दर्शनाग्निः कोष्ठाग्निरिति। तत्र कोष्ठाग्निर्नामाशितपीतलेह्यचोष्यं पचति। दर्शनाग्नी रूपाणां दर्शनं करोति। ज्ञानाग्निः शुभाशुभं च कर्म विन्दति। त्रीणि स्थानानि भवन्ति मुखे आहवनीय उदरे गार्हपत्यो हृदि दक्षिणाग्निः आत्मा यजमानो मनो ब्रह्म लोभादयः पशवो धृतिर्दीक्षा संतोषश्च बुद्धीन्द्रियाणि

यज्ञपात्राणि हर्वींषि कर्मेन्द्रियाणि शिरः कपालं केशा दर्भा मुखमन्तर्वेदिः चतुष्कपालं शिरः षोडश पार्श्वदन्तपटलानि सप्तोत्तरं मर्मशतं साशीतिकं संधिशतं सनवकं स्नायुशतं सप्त शिराशतानि पञ्च मज्जाशतानि अस्थीनि च ह वै त्रीणि शतानि षष्टीः सार्धचतस्रो रोमाणि कोट्यो हृदयं पलान्यष्टौ द्वादश पला जिह्वा पित्तप्रस्थं कफस्याढकं शुक्रकुडवं मेदः प्रस्थौ द्वावनियतं मूत्रपुरीषमाहारपरिमाणात्। पैप्पलादं भोक्षशास्त्रं पैप्पलादं मोक्षशास्त्रमिति॥
ॐ सहनाववत्विति शान्तिः॥

इति गर्भोपनिषत्समाप्ता॥१७॥

१७. तारसारोपनिषत्

यन्नारायणतारार्थसत्यज्ञानसुखाकृति।
त्रिपान्नारायणाकारं तद्ब्रह्मैवास्मि केवलम्॥१॥

ॐ पूर्णमद इति शान्तिः॥

हरिः ॐ॥ बृहस्पतिरुवाच याज्ञवल्क्यं यदनु कुरुक्षेत्रं देवानां देवयजनं सर्वेषां भूतानां ब्रह्मसदनं तस्माद्यत्र क्वचन गच्छेत्तदेव मन्येतेति। इदं वै कुरुक्षेत्रं देवानां देवयजनं सर्वेषां भूतानां ब्रह्मसदनमविमुक्तं वै कुरुक्षेत्रं देवानां देवयजनं सर्वेषां भूतानां ब्रह्मसदनम्। अत्र हि जन्तोः प्राणेषूत्क्रममाणेषु रुद्रस्तारकं ब्रह्म व्याचष्टे येनासावमृतीभूत्वा मोक्षी भवति। तस्मादविमुक्तमेव निषेवेत। अविमुक्तं न विमुञ्चेत्। एवमेवैष भगवन्निति वै याज्ञवल्क्यः॥१॥

अथ हैनं भारद्वाजः पप्रच्छ याज्ञल्क्यं किं तारकम्। किं तारयतीति। स होवाच याज्ञवल्क्यः। ॐ नमो नारायणायेति तारकं चिदात्मकमित्युषासितव्यम्। ओमित्येकाक्षरमात्मस्वरूपम्। नम इति द्व्यक्षरं प्रकृतिस्वरूपम्। नारायणायेति पञ्चाक्षरं परंब्रह्मस्वरूपम्। इति य एवं वेद। सोऽमृतो भवति। ओमिति ब्रह्मा भवति। नकारो विष्णुर्भवति। मकारो रुद्रो भवति। नकार ईश्वरो भवति। रकारोऽण्डं विराड् भवति। यकारः पुरुषो भवति। णकारो भगवान्भवति। यकारः परमात्मा भवति। एतद्वै नारायणस्याष्टाक्षरं वेद परमपुरुषो भवति। अयमृग्वेदः प्रथमः पादः॥१॥

ॐमित्येतदक्षरं परं ब्रह्म। तदेवोपासितव्यम्। एतदेव सूक्ष्माष्टाक्षरं भवति। तदेतदष्टात्मकोऽष्टधा भवति। अकारः प्रथमाक्षरो भवति। उकारो द्वितीयाक्षरो भवति। मकारास्तृतीयाक्षरो भवति। बिन्दूस्तुरीयाक्षरो भवति। नादः पञ्चमाक्षरो भवति। कला षष्ठाक्षरो भवति। कलातीता सप्तमाक्षरो भवति। तत्परश्चाष्टमाक्षरो भवति। तारकत्वात्तारको भवति। तदेव तारकं ब्रह्म त्वं विद्धि। तदेवोपासितव्यम्। अत्रैते श्लोका भवन्ति॥ अकारादाभवद्ब्रह्मा जाम्बवानितिसंज्ञकः। उराकाक्षरसंभूत उपेन्द्रो हरिनायकः॥१॥

मकाराक्षरसंभूतः शिवस्तु हनुमान्समृतः। बिन्दुरीश्वरसंज्ञस्तु शत्रुघ्नश्चक्रराट् खयम्॥२॥ नादो महाप्रभुर्ज्ञेयो भरतः शङ्खनामकः। कलायाः पुरुषः साक्षाल्लक्ष्मणो धरणीधरः॥३॥ कलातीता भगवती स्वय सीतेति संज्ञिता। तत्परः परमात्मा च श्रीरामः पुरुषोत्तमः॥४॥ ओमित्येतदक्षरमिदं सर्वम्। तस्योपव्याख्यानं भूतं भव्यं भविष्य-

द्यच्चान्यत्तत्त्वमन्त्रवर्णदेवताछन्दोऋक्कलाशक्तिसृष्ट्यात्मकमिति । य एवं वेद । यजुर्वेदो द्वितीयः पादः ॥२ ॥

अथ हैनं भारद्वाजो याज्ञवल्क्यमुवाचाथ कैर्मन्त्रैः परमात्मा प्रीतो भवति स्वात्मानं दर्शयति तन्नो ब्रूहि भगव इति । स होवाच याज्ञवल्क्यः । ॐ या ह वै श्रीपरमात्मा नारायणः स भगवानकारवाच्यो जाम्बवान्भूर्भुवः सुवस्तस्मै वै नमोनमः ॥१ ॥ ॐ यो ह वै श्रीपरमात्मा नारायणः स भगवानुकारवाच्य उपेन्द्रस्वरूपो हरिनायको भुर्भुवः सुवस्तस्मै वै नमोनमः ॥२ ॥

ॐ यो ह वै परमात्मा नारायणः स भगवान्मकारवाच्यः शिवस्वरूपो हनूमान्भूर्भुवः सुवस्तस्मै वै नमोनमः ॥३ ॥ ॐ यो ह वै श्रीपरमात्मा नारायणः स भगवान्बिन्दुस्वरूपः शत्रुघ्नो भूर्भवः सुवस्तस्मै वै नमोनमः ॥४ ॥ ॐ यो ह वै श्रीपरमात्मा नारायणः स भगवान्नादस्वरूपो भरतो भूर्भुवः सुवस्तस्मै वै नमोनमः ॥५ ॥ ॐ यो ह वै श्रीपरमात्मा नारायणः स भगवान्कलास्वरूपो लक्ष्मणो भूर्भुवः सुवस्तस्मै वै नमोनमः ॥६ ॥ ॐ यो ह वै श्रीपरमात्मा नारायणः स भगवान्कलातीता भगवती सीता चित्स्वरूपा भूर्भुवः सुवस्तस्मै वै नमोनमः ॥७ ॥

यथा प्रथमन्त्रोक्तावाद्यन्तौ तथा सर्वमन्त्रेषु द्रष्टव्यम् । उकारवाच्य उपेन्द्रस्वरूपो हरिनायकः २ मकारवाच्यः शिवस्वरूपो हनुमान् ३ बिन्दुस्वरूपः शत्रुघ्नः ४ नादस्वरूपो भरतः ५ कलास्वरूपो लक्ष्मणः ६ कलातीता भगवती सीता चित्स्वरूपा ७ ॐ यो ह वै श्रीपरमात्मा नारायणः स भगवांस्तत्परः परमपुरुषः पुराणपुरुषोत्तमो नित्यशुद्धबुद्धमुक्तसत्यपरमानन्ताद्वयपरिपूर्णः परमात्मा ब्रह्मैवाहं रामोऽस्मि भूर्भुवः सुवस्तमै नमोनमः ॥८ ॥

एतदष्टविधमन्त्रं योऽधीते सोऽग्निपूतो भवति । स वायुपूतो भवति । स आदित्यपूतो भवति । स स्थाणुपूतो भवति । स सर्वैर्देवैर्ज्ञातो भवति । तेनेतिहासपुराणानां रुद्राणां शतसहस्राणि जप्तानि फलानि भवन्ति । श्रीमन्नारायणाष्टाक्षरानुस्मरणेन गायत्र्याः शतसहस्रं जप्तं भवति । प्रणवानामयुतं जप्तं भवति । दशपूर्वान्दशोत्तरान्पुनाति । नारायणपदमवाप्नोति य एवं वेद । तद्विष्णोः परमं पदं सदा पश्यन्ति सूरयः दिवीव चक्षुराततम् । तद्विप्रासो विपन्यवो जागृवांसः समिन्धते । विष्णोर्यत्परमं पदम् ॥ इत्युपनिषत् ॥ सामवेदस्तृतीयः पादः ॥३ ॥ ॐ पुराणमद इति शान्तिः हरिः ॐ तत्सत् । ।

इति तारसारोपनिषत्समाप्ता ॥

१८. नारायणोपनिषत्

मायातत्कार्यमखिलं यद्बोधाद्यात्यपह्नवम् ।
त्रिपान्नारायणाख्यं तत्कलये स्वात्ममात्रतः ॥

ॐ सहनाववत्विति शान्तिः ॥

ॐ अथ पुरुषो ह वै नारायणोऽकामयत प्रजाः सृजेयेति । नारायणात्प्राणो जायते । मनः सर्वेन्द्रियाणि च । खं वायुर्ज्योतिरापः पृथिवी विश्वस्य धारिणी । नारायणाद्ब्रह्मा जायते । नारायणाद्रुद्रो जायते । नारायणादिन्द्रो जायते । नारायणात्प्रजापतिः प्रजायते ।

नारायणाद्द्वादशादित्या रुद्रा वसवः सर्वाणि छन्दासि नारायणादेव समुत्पद्यन्ते। नारायणात्प्रवर्तन्ते। नारायणे प्रलीयन्ते। एतदृग्वेदशिरोऽधीते ॥१ ॥ अथ नित्यो नारायणः। ब्रह्मा नारायणः। शिवश्च नारायणः। शक्रश्च नारायणः। कालश्च नारायणः। दिशश्च नारायणः। विदिशश्च नारायणः। ऊर्ध्वं च नारायणः। अधश्च नारायणः। अन्तर्बहिश्च नारायणः। नारायण एवेदं सर्वं यद्भूतं यच्च भव्यम्। निष्कलङ्को निरञ्जनो निर्विकल्पो निराख्यातः शुद्धो देव एको नारायणो न द्वितीयोऽस्ति कश्चित्। य एवं वेद स विष्णुरेव भवति स विष्णुरेव भवति। एतद्यजुर्वेदशिरोऽधोते ॥२ ॥

ॐमित्यग्रे व्याहरेत्। नम इति पश्चात्। नारायणायेत्युपरिष्टात्। ॐ मित्येकारक्षरम्। नम इति द्वे अक्षरे। नारायणायति पञ्चाक्षराणि। एतद्वै नारायणस्याष्टाक्षरं पदम्। यो ह वै नारायणस्याष्टाक्षरं मदमध्येति। अनपब्रुवः सर्वमायुरेति। विन्दते प्राजापत्यं रायस्पोषं गौपत्यं ततोऽमृतत्वमश्नुत इति। एतत्सामवेदशिरोऽधीते ॥३ ॥ प्रत्यगानन्दं ब्रह्मपुरुषं प्रणवस्वरूपम्। अकार उकारो मकार इति। ता अनेकधा समभवत्तदेतदोमिति। यमुक्त्वा मुच्यते योगी जन्मसंसारबन्धनात्। ॐ नमो नारायणायेति मन्त्रोपासको वैकुण्ठभुवनं गमिष्यति। तदिदं पुण्डरीकं विज्ञानघनं तस्मात्तडिदाभमात्रम्। ब्रह्मण्यो देवकीपुत्रो ब्रह्मण्यो मधुसूदनः। ब्रह्मण्यः पुण्डरीकाक्षो ब्रह्मण्यो विष्णुरच्युत इति। सर्वभूतस्थमेकं वै नारायणं कारणपुरुषमकारणं परं ब्रह्मोम्। एतदथर्वशिरोऽधीते ॥४ ॥

प्रातरधीयानो रात्रिकृतं पापं नाशयति। सायमधीयानो दिवसकृतं पापं नाशयति। तत्सायं प्रातरधीयानो पापोऽपापो भवति। मध्यंदिनमादित्याभिमुखोऽधीयानः पञ्चमहापातकोपपातकात्प्रमुच्यते। सर्ववेदपारायणपुण्यं लभते। नारायणसायुज्यमवाप्नोति श्रीमन्नारायणसायुज्यमवाप्नोति य एवं वेद। ॐ सहनाववत्-वति शान्तिः ॥

इति नारायणोपनिषत्समाप्ता ॥

१९. कलिसंतरणोपनिषत्

यद्दिव्यनाम स्मरतां संसारो गोष्पदायते।
स्वा नव्यभक्तिर्भवति तद्रामपदमाश्रये ॥१ ॥
ॐ सह नाववत्विति शान्तिः ॥

हरिः ॐ ॥ द्वापरान्ते नारदो ब्रह्माणं जगाम कथं भगवन् गां पर्यटन्कलिं संतरेयमिति। स होवाच ब्रह्मा साधु पृष्टोऽस्मि सर्वश्रुतिरहस्य गोप्यं तच्छृणु येन कलिसंसारं तरिष्यसि। भगवत आदिपुरुषस्य नारायणस्य नामोच्चारण मात्रेण निर्धूतकलिर्भवति। नारदः पुनः पप्रच्छ तन्नाम किमिति। स होवाच हरिण्यगर्भः। हरे राम हरे राम राम राम हरे हरे। हरे कृष्ण हरे कृष्ण कृष्ण कृष्ण हरे हरे ॥१ ॥

इति षोडशकं नाम्नां कलिकल्मपनाशनम्। नातः परतरोपायः सर्ववेदेषु दृश्यते ॥१ ॥ इति षोडशकलावृतस्य जीवस्यावरणविनाशनम्। ततः प्रकाशते परं ब्रह्म मेघापाये रविरश्मिमण्डलीवेति। पुनर्नारदः पप्रच्छ भगवन्कोऽस्य विधिरिति। तं होवाच नास्य विधिरिति। सर्वदा शुचिरशुचिर्वा पठन्ब्राह्मणः सलोकतां समीपतां सरूपतां सायुज्यतामेति।

यदास्य षोडशीकस्य सार्धत्रिकोटीर्जपित तदा ब्रह्महत्यां तरति। तरति वीरहत्याम्। स्वर्णस्तेयात्पूतो भवति। पितृदेवमनुष्याणामपकारात्पूतो भवति। सर्वधर्मपरित्यागपापात्सद्यः शुचितामाप्नुयात्। सद्यो मुच्यते सद्यो मुच्यते इत्युपनिषत्॥ ॐ सह नाववत्विति शान्तिः॥ हरिः ॐ तत्सत्॥

इति श्रीकलिसंतरणोपनिषत्समाप्ता॥

२०. भिक्षुकोपनिषत्

भिक्षूणां पटलं यत्र विश्रान्तिमगमत्सदा।
तन्त्रैपदं ब्रह्मतत्त्वं ब्रह्ममात्रं करोतु माम्॥
ॐ पूर्णमद इति शान्तिः॥

ॐ अथ भिक्षूणां मोक्षार्थिनां कुटीचकबहूदकहंसपरमहंसाश्चेति चत्वारः। कुटीचका नाम गौतमभरद्वाजयाज्ञवल्क्यवसिष्ठप्रभृतयोऽष्टौ ग्रासांश्चरन्तो योगमार्गे मोक्षमेव प्रार्थयन्ते। अथ बहूदका नाम त्रिदण्डकमण्डलुशिखायज्ञोपवीतकाषायवस्त्रधारिणो ब्रह्मर्षिगृहे मधुमांसं वर्जयित्वाष्टौ ग्रासान्भैक्षाचरणं कृत्वा योगमार्गे मोक्षमेव प्रार्तयन्ते।

अथ हंसा नाम ग्राम एकरात्रं नगरे पञ्चरात्रं क्षेत्रे सप्तरात्रं तदुपरि न वसेयुः। गोमूत्रगोमयाहारिणो नित्यं चान्द्रायणपरायणा योगमार्गे मोक्षमेव प्रार्थयन्ते। अथ परमहंसा नाम संवर्तकारुणिश्वेतकेतुजडभरतदत्तात्रेयशुकवामदेवहारितकप्रभृतयोऽष्टौ ग्रासांश्चरन्तो योगमार्गे मोक्षमेव प्रार्थयन्ते। वृक्षमूले शून्यगृहे श्मशानवासिनो वा साम्बरा वा दिगम्बरावा।

न तेषां धर्माधर्मौ लाभालाभौ शुद्धाशुद्धौ द्वैतवर्जिता समलोष्टाश्मकाञ्चनाः सर्ववर्णेषु भैक्षाचरणं कृत्वा सर्वत्रात्मैवेति पश्यन्ति। अथ जातरूपधरा निर्द्वन्द्वा निष्परिग्रहाः शुक्लध्यानपरायणा आत्मनिष्ठाः प्राणसंधारणार्थं यथोक्तकाले भैक्षमाचरन्तः शून्यागारदेवगृहतृणकूटवल्मीकवृक्षमूलकुलालशालाग्निहोत्रशालानदीपुलिनगिरिकन्दरकुहरकोटरनिर्झरस्थण्डिले तत्र ब्रह्ममार्गे सम्बक्संपन्नाः शुद्धमानसाः परमहंसाचरणेन संन्यासेन देहत्यागं कुर्वन्ति ते परमहंसा नामेत्युपनिषत्॥ ॐ पूर्णमद इति शान्तिः॥

इति भिक्षुकोपनिषत्समाप्ता॥

२१. नारदपरिव्राजकोपनिषत्

पारिव्राज्यधर्मपूगालङ्कारा यत्प्रबोधतः।
दशप्रणवलक्ष्यार्थं यान्ति तं राममाश्रये ॥१ ॥
ॐ भद्रं कर्णेभिरिति शान्तिः ॥

परिव्राटत्रिशिखी सीताचूडानिर्वाणमण्डलम्। दक्षिणा शरभं स्कन्दं महानारायणाद्वयम् ॥ अथ कदाचित्परिव्राजकाभरणो नारदः सर्वलोकसंचारं कुर्वन्नपूर्वपुण्यस्थलानि पुण्यतीर्थानि तीर्थीकुर्वन्नवलोक्य चित्तशुद्धिं प्राप्य निर्वैरः शान्तो दान्तः सर्वतो निर्वेदमासाद्य स्वरूपानुसंधानमनुसंधय नियमानन्दविशेषगण्यं मुनिजनैरुपसंकीर्णं-नैमिषारण्यं पुण्यस्थलमवलोक्य सरिगमपधनिससंज्ञैर्वैराग्यबोधकरैः स्वरविशेषैः प्रापञ्चिकपराङ्मुखैर्हरिकथालापैः स्थावरजङ्गमनामकैर्भगवद्भक्तिविशेषैर्नरमृगकिंपुरुषामर-किंनराप्सरोगणान्संमोहयन्नागतं ब्रह्मात्मजं भगवद्भक्तं नारदमवलोक्य द्वादशवर्षसत्रयागोपस्थिताः श्रुताध्ययनसंपन्नाः सर्वज्ञास्तपोनिष्ठापराश्च ज्ञानवैराग्यसंपन्नाः शौनकादिमहर्षयः प्रत्युत्थानं कृत्वा नत्वा यथोचितातिथ्यपूर्वकमुपवेशयित्वा स्वयं सर्वेऽप्युपविष्टा भो भगवन् ब्रह्मपुत्र कथं मुक्त्युपायोऽस्माकं वक्तव्य इत्युक्तस्तान् स होवाच नारदः सत्कुलभवोपनीतः सम्यगुपनयनपूर्वकं चतुश्चत्वारिंशत्संस्कारसंपन्नः स्वाभिमतैकगुरुसमीपे स्वशाखाध्ययनपूर्वकं सर्वविद्याभ्यासं कृत्वा द्वादशवर्षशुश्रूषापूर्वकं ब्रह्मचर्यं पञ्चविंशतिवत्सरं गार्हस्थ्यं पञ्चविंशतिवत्सरं वानप्रस्थाश्रमं तद्विधिवत्क्रमान्निर्वर्त्य चतुर्विधब्रह्मचर्यं षड्विधं गार्हस्थ्यं चतुर्विधं वानप्रस्थधर्मं सम्यगभ्यस्य तदुचितं कर्म सर्वं निर्वर्त्य साधनचतुष्टयसंपन्नः सर्वसंसारोपरि मनोवाक्कायकर्मभिर्यथाशानिवृत्तस्तथा वासनैषणोपर्यपि निर्वैरः शान्तो दान्तः संन्यासी परमहंसाश्रमेणास्खलितस्वस्वरूपध्यानेन देहत्यागं करोति स मुक्तो भवति स मुक्तो भवतीत्युपनिषत् ॥ प्रथमोपदेशः ॥१ ॥

अथ हैनं भगवन्तं नारदं सर्वे शौनकादयः पप्रच्छुर्भो भगवन्संन्यासविधिं नो ब्रूहीति तानवलोक्य नारदस्तत्स्वरूपं सर्वं पितामहमुखेनैव ज्ञातुमुचितमित्युक्त्वा सत्रयागपूर्त्य-नन्तरं तैः सह सत्यलोकं गत्वा विधिवद्ब्रह्मनिष्ठापरं परमेष्ठिनं नत्वा स्तुत्वा यथोचितं तदाज्ञया तैः सहोपविश्य नारदः पितामहमुवाच गुरुस्त्वं जनकस्त्वं सर्वविद्यारहस्यज्ञः सर्वज्ञस्त्वमतो मत्तो मदिष्टं रहस्यमेकं वक्तव्यं त्वद्विना मदभिमतरहस्यं वक्तुं कः समर्थः।

किमितिचेत् पारिव्राज्यस्वरूपक्रमं नो ब्रूहीति नारदेन प्रार्थितः परमेष्ठी सर्वतः सर्वानवलोक्य मुहूर्तमात्रं समाधिनिष्ठो भूत्वा संसारार्तिनिवृत्त्यन्वेषण इति निश्चित्य नारदमवलोक्य तमाह पितामहः।

पुरा मत्पुत्र पुरुषसूक्तोपनिषद्रहस्यप्रकारं निरतिशयाकारावलम्बिना विराट्पुरुषेणो-पदिष्टं रहस्यं ते विविच्योच्यते तत्क्रममतिरहस्यं बाढमवहितो भूत्वा श्रूयतां भो नारद विधिवदादावनुपनीतोपनयनानन्तरं तत्सत्कुलप्रसूतः पितृमातृविधेयः पितृसमीपादन्यत्र सत्संप्रदायस्थं श्रद्धावन्तं सत्कुलभवं श्रोत्रियं शास्त्रवात्सल्यं गुणवन्तमकुटिलं सद्गुरुमासाद्य नत्वा यथोपयोगशुश्रूषापूर्वकं स्वाभिमतं विज्ञाप्य द्वादशवर्षसेवापुरः सरं सर्वविद्याभ्यासं कृत्वा तदनुज्ञया स्वकुलानुरूपामभिमत कन्यां विवाह्य पञ्चविंशतिवत्सरं गुरुकुलवासं

कृत्वाथ गुर्वनुज्ञया गृहस्थोचितकर्म कुर्वन्दौर्ब्राह्मण्यनिवृत्तिमेत्य स्ववंशवृद्धिकामः पुत्रमेकमासाद्य गार्हस्थ्योचितपञ्चविंशतिवत्सरं तीर्त्वा ततः पञ्चविंशतिवत्सरपर्यन्तं त्रिषवणमुदकस्पर्शनपूर्वकं चतुर्थकालमेकवारमाहारमाहरन्नयमेक एव वनस्थो भूत्वा पुरग्रामप्राक्तनसंचारं विहाय निकिर (?) विरहिततदाश्रितकर्मोचितकृत्यं निर्वर्त्य दृष्टश्रवण-विषयवैतृष्ण्यमेत्य चत्वारिंशत्संस्कारसंपन्नः सर्वतो विरक्तश्चित्तशुद्धिमेत्याशासूयेर्ष्याहंकारं दग्ध्वा साधनचतुष्टयसंपन्नः संन्यस्तुमर्हतीत्युपनिषत् ॥ द्वितीयोपदेशः ॥२ ॥

अथ हैनं नारदः पितामहं पप्रच्छ भगवन् केन संन्यासाधिकारी वेत्येवमादौ संन्यासाधिकारिणं निरूप्य पश्चात्संन्यासविधिरुच्यते अवहितः शृणु। अथ षण्डः पतितोऽङ्गविकलः स्त्रैणो बधिरोऽर्भको मूकः पाषण्डश्चक्री लिङ्गी वैखानसहरद्विजौ भृतकाध्यापकः शिपिविष्टोऽनग्निको वैराग्यवन्तोऽप्येते न संन्यासार्हाः संन्यस्ता यद्यपि महावाक्योपदेशेनाधिकारिणः। पूर्वसंन्यासी परमहंसाधिकारी ॥—परेणैवात्मनश्चापि परस्यैवात्मना तथा। अभयं समवाप्नोति स परिव्राडिति स्मृतिः ॥१ ॥ षण्ढोऽथ विकलोऽप्यन्धो बालकश्चापि पातकी। पतितश्च परद्वारी वैखानसहरद्विजौ ॥२ ॥ चक्री लिङ्गी च पाषण्डी शिपिविष्टोऽप्यनग्निकः। द्वित्रिवारेण संन्यस्तो भृतकाध्यापकोऽपि च। एते नार्हन्ति संन्यासमातुरेण विना क्रमम् ॥३ ॥

आतुरकालः कथमार्यसंमतः ॥—प्राणस्योत्क्रमणासन्नकालस्त्वातुरसंज्ञकः। नेतरस्त्वातुरः कालो मुक्तिमार्गप्रवर्तकः ॥४ ॥ आतुरेऽपि च संन्यासे तत्तन्मन्त्रपुरः सरम्। मन्त्रावृत्तिं च कृत्वैव संन्यसेद्विधिवद्बुधः ॥५ ॥

आतुरेऽपि क्रमे वापि प्रैषभेदो न कुत्रचित्। न मन्त्रं कर्मरहितं कर्म मन्त्रमपेक्षते ॥६ ॥ अकर्म मन्त्ररहितं नातो मन्त्रं परित्यजेत्। मन्त्रं विना कर्म कुर्याद्भस्मन्याहुतिवद्भवेत् ॥७ ॥ विध्युक्तकर्मसंक्षेपात्संन्यासस्त्वातुरः स्मृतः। तस्मादातुरसंन्यासे मन्त्रावृत्तिविधिर्मुने ॥८ ॥

आहिताग्निर्विरक्तश्चेद्देशान्तरगतो यदि। प्राजापत्येष्टिमप्स्वेव निर्वृत्यैवाथ संन्यसेत् ॥९ ॥ मनसा वाथ विध्युक्तमन्त्रावृत्त्याथवा जले। श्रुत्यनुष्ठानमार्गेण कर्मानुष्ठानमेव वा ॥१० ॥ समाप्य संन्यसेद्विद्वान्नो चेत्पातित्यमाप्नुयात् ॥११ ॥

यदा मनसि संजातं वैतृष्ण्यं सर्ववस्तुषु। तदा संन्यासमिच्छेत पतितः स्याद्विपर्यये ॥१२ ॥ विरक्तः प्रव्रजेद्धीमान्सरक्तस्तु गृहे वसेत्। सरागो नरकं याति प्रव्रजन्हि द्विजाधमः ॥१३ ॥ यस्यैतानि सुगुप्तानि जिह्वोपस्थोदरं करः। संन्यसेदकृतोद्वाहो ब्राह्मणो ब्रह्मचर्यवान् ॥१४ ॥

संसारमेव निःसारं दृष्ट्वा सारदिदृक्षया। प्रव्रजन्त्यकृतोद्वाहाः परं वैराग्यमाश्रिताः ॥१५ ॥ प्रवृत्तिलक्षणं कर्म ज्ञानं संन्यासलक्षणम्। तस्माज्ज्ञानं पुरस्कृत्य संन्यसेदिह बुद्धिमान् ॥१६ ॥ यदा तु विदितं तत्त्वं परं ब्रह्म सनातनम्। तदैकदण्डं संगृह्य सोपवीतां शिखां त्यजेत् ॥१७ ॥

परमात्मनि यो रक्तो विरक्तोऽपरमात्मनि। सर्वैषणाविनिर्मुक्तः स भैक्षं भोक्तुमर्हति ॥१८ ॥ पूजितो वन्दितश्चैव सुप्रसन्नो यथा भवेत्। तथा चेत्ताड्यमानस्तु तदा भवति भैक्षभुक् ॥१९ ॥ अहमेवाक्षरं ब्रह्म वासुदेवाख्यमद्वयम्। इति भावो ध्रुवो यस्य तदा भवति भैक्षभुक् ॥२० ॥

यस्मिञ्शान्तिः शमः शौचं सत्यं संतोष आर्जवम् । अकिंचनमदम्भश्च स कैवल्याश्रमे वसेत् ॥२१ ॥ यदा न कुरुते भावं सर्वभूतेषु पापकम् । कर्मणा मनसा वाचा तदा भवति भैक्षभुक् ॥२२ ॥ दशलक्षणकं धर्ममनुतिष्ठन्समाहितः । वेदान्तान्विधिवच्छ्रुत्वा संन्यसेदनृणो द्विजः ॥२३ ॥

धृतिः क्षमा दमोऽस्तेयं शौचमिन्द्रियनिग्रहः । धीर्विद्या सत्यमक्रोधो दशकं धर्मलक्षणम् ॥२४ ॥ अतीतान्न स्मरेद्भोगान्न तथानागतानपि । प्राप्तांश्च नामिनन्देद्यः स कैवल्याश्रमे वसेत् ॥२५ ॥ अन्तस्थानीन्द्रियाण्यन्तर्बहिष्ठान्विषयान्बहिः । शक्नोति यः सदा कर्तुं स कैवल्याश्रमे वसेत् ॥२६ ॥

प्राणे गते यथा देहः सुखं दुःखं न विन्दति । तथा चेत्प्राणयुक्तोऽपि स कैवल्याश्रमे वसेत् ॥२७ ॥ कौपीनयुगलं कन्था दण्ड एकः परिग्रहः । यतेः परमहंसस्य नाधिकं तु विधीयते ॥२८ ॥ यदि वा कुरुते रागादधिकस्य परिग्रहम् । रौरवं नरकं गत्वा तिर्यग्योनिषु जायते ॥२९ ॥ विशीर्णान्यमलान्येव चेलानि ग्रथितानि तु । कृत्वा कन्थां बहिर्वासो धारयेद्धातुरञ्जितम् ॥३० ॥ एकवासा अवासा वा एकदृष्टिरलोलुपः । एक एव चरेन्नित्यं वर्षास्वेकत्र संवसेत् ॥३१ ॥

कुटुम्बं पुत्रदारांश्च वेदाङ्गानि च सर्वशः । यज्ञं यज्ञोपवीतं च त्यक्त्वा गूढश्चरेद्यतिः ॥३२ ॥ कामः क्रोधस्तथा दर्पो लोभमोहादयश्च ये । तांस्तु दोषान्परित्यज्य परिव्राण्निर्ममो भवेत् ॥३३ ॥ रागद्वेषवियुक्तात्मा समलोष्टाश्मकाञ्चनः । प्राणिहिंसानिवृत्तश्च मुनिः स्यात्सर्वनिःस्पृहः ॥३४ ॥ दम्भाहंकारनिर्मुक्तो हिंसापैशून्यवर्जितः । आत्मज्ञानगुणोपेतो यतिर्मोक्षमवाप्नुयात् ॥३५ ॥

इन्द्रियाणां प्रसङ्गेन दोषमृच्छत्यसंशयः । संनियम्य तु तान्येव ततः सिद्धिं निगच्छति ॥३६ ॥ न जातु कामः कामानामुपभोगेन शाम्यति । हविषा कृष्णवर्त्मेव भूय एवाभिवर्धते ॥३७ ॥ श्रुत्वा स्पृष्ट्वा च भुक्त्वा च दृष्ट्वा घ्रात्वा च यो नरः । न हृष्यति ग्लायति वा स विज्ञेयो जितेन्द्रियः ॥३८ ॥ यस्य वाङ्मनसी शुद्धे सम्यग्गुप्ते च सर्वदा । स वै सर्वमवाप्नोति वेदान्तोपगतं फलम् ॥३९ ॥

संमानाद्ब्राह्मणो नित्यमुद्विजेत विषादिव । अमृतस्येव चाकाङ्क्षेदवमानस्य सर्वदा ॥४० ॥ सुखं ह्यवमतः शेते सुखं च प्रतिबुध्यते । सुखं चरति लोकेऽस्मिन्नवमन्ता विनश्यति ॥४१ ॥ अतिवादांस्तितिक्षेत नावमन्येत कंचन । न चेमं देहमाश्रित्य वैरं कुर्वीत केनचित् ॥४२ ॥ क्रुध्यन्तं न प्रतिक्रुध्येदाक्रुष्टः कुशलं वदेत् । सप्तद्वारावकीर्णां च न वाचमनृतां वदेत् ॥४३ ॥

अध्यात्मरतिरासीनो निरपेक्षो निराशिषः । आत्मनैव सहायेन सुखार्थी विचरेदिह ॥४४ । इन्द्रियाणां निरोधेन रागद्वेषक्षयेण च । अहिंसया च भूतानाममृतत्वाय कल्पते ॥४५ ॥ अस्थिस्थूणं स्नायुबद्धं मांसशोणितलेपितम् । चर्मावबद्धं दुर्गन्धि पूर्णं मूत्रपुरीषयोः ॥४६ ॥

जराशोकसमाविष्टं रोगायतनमातुरम् । रजस्वलमनित्यं च भूतावासमिमं त्यजेत् ॥४७ ॥ मांसासृक्पूयविण्मूत्रस्नायुमज्जास्थिसंहतौ । देहे चेत्प्रीतिमान्मूढो भविता नरकेऽपि सः ॥४८ ॥

सा कालपुत्रपदवी सा महावीचिवागुरा । सासिपत्रवनश्रेणी या देहेऽहमिति स्थितिः ॥४९ ॥ सा त्याज्या सर्वयत्नेन सर्वनाशेऽप्युपस्थिते । स्प्रष्टव्या सा न भव्येन

शश्वमांसेव पुल्कसी ॥५० ॥ प्रियेषु स्वेषु सुकृतमप्रियेषु च दुष्कृतम् । विसृज्य ध्यानयोगेन ब्रह्माप्येति सनातनम् ॥५१ ॥

अनेन विधिना सर्वांस्त्यक्त्वा सङ्गाञ्शनैः शनैः । सर्वद्वन्द्वैर्विनिर्मुक्तो ब्रह्मण्येवावतिष्ठते ॥५२ ॥ एक एव चरेन्नित्यं सिद्ध्यर्थमसहायकः । सिद्धिमेकस्य पश्यन्हि न जहाति न हीयते ॥५३ ॥ कपालं वृक्षमूलानि कुचेलान्यसहायता । समता चैव सर्वस्मिन्नैतन्मुक्तस्य लक्षणम् ॥५४ ॥ सर्वभूतहितः शान्तस्त्रिदण्डी सकमण्डलुः । एकारामः परिव्रज्य भिक्षार्थं ग्राममाविशेत् ॥५५ ॥

एको भिक्षुर्यथोक्तः स्याद्द्वावेव मिथुनं स्मृतम् । त्रयो ग्रामः समाख्यात ऊर्ध्वं तु नगरायते ॥५६ ॥ नगरं नहि कर्तव्यं ग्रामो वा मिथुनं तथा । एतत्त्रयं प्रकुर्वाणः स्व-धर्माच्च्यवते यतिः ॥५७ ॥ राजवार्तादि तेषां स्याद्भिक्षावार्ता परस्परम् । स्नेहपैशून्यमात्सर्यं संनिकर्षान्न संशयः ॥५८ ॥

एकाकी निःस्पृहस्तिष्ठेन्न हि केन सहालपेत् । दद्यान्नारायणेत्येव प्रतिवाक्यं सदा यतिः ॥५९ ॥ एकाकी चिन्तयेद्ब्रह्म मनोवाक्कायकर्मभिः । मृत्युं च नाभिनन्देत जीवितं वा कथंचन ॥६० ॥ कालमेव प्रतीक्षेत यावदायुः समाप्यते । नाभिनन्देत मरणं नाभिनन्देत जीवितम् । कालमेव प्रतीक्षेत निर्देशं भृतको यथा ॥६१ ॥ अजिह्वः षण्डकः पङ्गुरन्धो बधिर एव च । मुग्धश्च मुच्यते भिक्षुः षड्भिरेतैर्न संशयः ॥६२ ॥

इदमिष्टमिदं नेति योऽश्नन्नपि न सज्जति । हितं सत्यं मितं वक्ति तमजिह्वं प्रचक्षते ॥६३ ॥अद्यजातां यथा नारीं तथा षोडशवार्षिकीम् । शतवर्षां च यो दृष्ट्वा निर्विकारः स षण्डकः ॥६४ ॥ भिक्षार्थमटनं यस्य विण्मुत्रकरणाय च । योजनान्न परं याति सर्वथा पङ्गुरेव सः ॥६५ ॥

तिष्ठतो व्रजतो वापि यस्य चक्षुर्न दूरगम् । चतुर्युगां भुवं मुक्त्वा परिव्राट् सोऽन्ध उच्यते ॥६६ ॥ हिताहितं मनोरामं वचः शोकावहं तु यत् । श्रुत्वापि न शृणोतीव बधिरः स प्रकीर्तितः ॥६७ ॥ सान्निध्ये विषयाणां यः समर्थो विकलेन्द्रियः । सुप्तवद्वर्तते नित्यं स भिक्षुर्मुग्ध उच्यते ॥३८ ॥ नटादिप्रेक्षणं द्यूतं प्रमदासुहृदं तथा । भक्ष्यं भोज्यमुदक्यां च षण्न पश्येत्कदाचन ॥६९ ॥

रागं द्वेषं मदं मायां द्रोहं मोहं परात्मसु । षडेतानि यतिर्नित्यं मनसापि न चिन्तयेत् ॥७० ॥ मञ्चकं शुक्लवस्त्रं च स्त्रीकथालौल्यमेव च । दिवा स्वापं च यानं च यतीनां पातकानि षट् ॥७१ ॥ दूरयात्रां प्रयत्नेन वर्जयेदात्मचिन्तकः । सदोपनिषदं विद्यामभ्यसेन्मुक्तिहैतुकीम् ॥७२ ॥

न तीर्थसेवी नित्यं स्यान्नोपवासपरो यतिः । न चाध्ययनशीलः स्यान्न व्याख्यानपरो भवेत् ॥७३ ॥ अपापमशठं वृत्तमजिह्मं नित्यमाचरेत् । इन्द्रियाणि समाहृत्य कूर्मोऽङ्गानीव सर्वशः ॥७४ ॥ क्षीणेन्द्रियमनोवृत्तिर्निराशीर्निष्परिग्रहः । निर्द्वन्द्वो निर्नमस्कारो निःस्वधाकार एव च ॥७५ ॥

निर्ममो निरहंकारो निरपेक्षो निराशिषः । विविक्तदेशसंसक्तो मुच्यते नात्र संशय इति ॥७६ ॥—अप्रमत्तः कर्मभक्तिज्ञानसंपन्नः स्वतन्त्रो वैराग्यमेत्य ब्रह्मचारी गृही वानप्रस्थो वा मुख्यवृत्तिका चेद्ब्रह्मचर्यं समाप्य गृही भवेद्गृहाद्वनी भूत्वा प्रव्रजेद्यदिवेतरथा ब्रह्मचर्यादेव प्रव्रजेद्गृहाद्वा वनाद्वाथ पुनरव्रती वा व्रती वा स्नातको वाऽस्नातको

वोत्सन्नाग्निरनग्निको वा यदहरेव विरजेत्तदहरेव प्रव्रजेत्तद्धैके प्राजापत्यामेवेष्टिं कुर्वन्त्यथवा न कुर्यादाग्नेय्यामेव कुर्यादग्निर्हिप्राणः प्राणमेवैतया करोति तस्मान्त्रैधातवीयामेव कुर्यादेतयैव त्रयो धातवो यदुत सत्त्वं रजस्तम् इति ॥

अयं ते योनिर्ऋत्वियो यतो जातो अरोचथाः । तं जानन्नग्न आरोहाथानो वर्धया रयिमित्यनेन मन्त्रेणाग्निमाजिघ्रेदेष वा अग्नेर्योनिर्यः प्राणः प्राणं गच्छ स्वां योनिं गच्छ स्वाहेत्येवमेवैतदाहवनीयादग्निमाहृत्य पूर्ववदग्निमाजिघ्रेद्यदग्निं न विन्देदप्सु जुहुयादापो वै सर्वा देवताः सर्वाभ्यो देवताभ्यो जुहोमि स्वाहेति हुत्वोद्धृत्य तदुदकं प्राश्नीयात्साज्यं हविरनामयं मोदमिति शिखां यज्ञोपवीतं पितरं पुत्रं कलत्रं कर्म चाध्ययनं मन्त्रान्तरं विसृज्यैव परिव्रजत्यात्मविन्मोक्षमन्त्रैस्त्रैधातवीयैर्विधेस्तद्ब्रह्म तदुपासितव्यमेवैतदिति ॥

पितामहं पुनः पप्रच्छ नारदः कथमयज्ञोपवीती ब्राह्मण इति ॥ तमाह पितामहः ॥ सशिखं वपनं कृत्वा बहिःसूत्रं त्यजेद्बुधः । यदक्षरं परं ब्रह्म तत्सूत्रमिति धारयेत् ॥७७ ॥ सूचनात्सूत्रमित्याहुः सूत्रं नाम परं पदम् । तत्सूत्रं विदितं येन स विप्रो वेदपारगः ॥७८ ॥ येन सर्वमिदं प्रोतं सूत्रे मणिगणा इव । तत्सूत्रं धारयेद्योगी योगवित्तत्त्वदर्शनः ॥७९ ॥

बहिःसूत्रं त्यजेद्विद्वान्योगमुत्तममास्थितः । ब्रह्मभावमिदं सूत्रं धारयेद्यः सचेतनः । धारणात्तस्य सूत्रस्य नोच्छिष्टो नाशुचिर्भवेत् ॥८० ॥ सूत्रमन्तर्गतं येषां ज्ञानयज्ञोपवीतिनाम् । ते वै सूत्रविदो लोके ते च यज्ञोपवीतिनः ॥८१ ॥ ज्ञानशिखिनो ज्ञाननिष्ठा ज्ञानयज्ञोपवीतिनः । ज्ञानमेव परं तेषां पवित्रं ज्ञानमुच्यते ॥८२ ॥

अग्नेरिव शिखा नान्या यस्य ज्ञानमयी शिखा । स शिखीत्युच्यते विद्वान्नेतरे केशधारिणः ॥८३ ॥ कर्मण्यधिकृता ये तु वैदिके ब्राह्मणादयः । तेभिर्धार्यमिदं सूत्रं क्रियाङ्गं तद्धि वै स्मृतम् ॥८४ ॥ शिखा ज्ञानमयी यस्य उपवीतं च तन्मयम् । ब्राह्मण्यं सकलं तस्य इति ब्रह्मविदो विदुरिति ॥८५ ॥—

तदेतद्विज्ञाय ब्राह्मणः परिव्रज्य परिव्राडेकशाटी मुण्डोऽपरिग्रहः शरीरक्लेशासहिष्णुश्चेदथवा यथाविधिश्चेज्जातरूपधरो भूत्वा सपुत्रमित्रकलत्राप्तबन्ध्वादीनि स्वाध्यायं सर्वकर्माणि संन्यस्यायं ब्रह्माण्डं च सर्वं कौपीनं दण्डमाच्छादनं च त्यक्त्वा द्वन्द्वसहिष्णुर्न शीतं न चोष्णं न सुखं न दुःखं न निद्रा न मानावमाने च षडूर्मिवर्जितो निन्दाहंकारमत्सरगर्वदम्भेर्ष्यासूयेच्छाद्वेषसुखदुःखकामक्रोधलोभमोहादीन्विसृज्य स्ववपुः शवाकारमिव स्मृत्वा स्वव्यतिरिक्तं सर्वमन्तर्बहिरमन्यमानः कस्यापि वन्दनमकृत्वा न नमस्कारो न स्वाहाकारो न स्वधाकारो न निन्दास्तुतिर्यादृच्छिको भवेद्यदृच्छालाभसंतुष्टः सुवर्णादीन्न परिग्रहेन्नावाहनं न विसर्जनं न मन्त्रं नामन्त्रं न ध्यानं नोपासनं न लक्ष्यं नालक्ष्यं न पृथक् नापृथक् न त्वन्यत्र सर्वत्रानिकेतः स्थिरमतिः शून्यागारवृक्षमूलदेवगृहतृणकूटकूलालशालाग्निहोत्रशालाग्निदिगन्तरनदीतटपुलिनभूगृहकन्दरनिर्झरस्थण्डिलेषु वने वा श्वेतकेतुऋभुनिदाघऋषभदुर्वासः संवर्तकदत्तात्रेयरैवतकवदव्यक्तलिङ्गोऽव्यक्ताचारो

बालोन्मत्तपिशाचवदनुन्मत्तोन्मत्तवदाचरंस्त्रिदण्डं शिक्यं पात्रं कमण्डलुं कटिसूत्रं कौपीनं न तत्सर्वं भूः स्वाहेत्यप्सु परित्यज्य कटिसूत्रं च कोपीनं दण्डं वस्त्रं कमण्डलुं सर्वमप्सु विसृज्याथ जातरूपधरश्चरेदात्मानमन्विच्छेद्यथा जातरूपधरो निर्द्वन्द्वो निष्परिग्रहस्तत्त्वब्रह्ममार्गे सम्यक् संपन्नः शुद्धमानसः प्राणसंधारणार्थं यथोक्तकाले

करपात्रेणान्येन वा याचिताहारमाहरन् लाभालाभे समो भूत्वा निर्ममः शुक्लध्यानपरायणोऽध्यात्मनिष्ठः शुभाशुभकर्मनिर्मूलनपरः संन्यस्य पूर्णानन्दैकबोधस्तद्ब्रह्माहमस्मीति ब्रह्मप्रणवमनुस्मरन्भ्रमरकीटन्यायेन शरीरत्रयमुत्सृज्य संन्यासेनैव देहत्यागं करोति स कृतकृत्यो भवतीत्युपनिषत् ॥ तृतीयोपदेशः ॥३ ॥

त्यक्त्वा लोकांश्च वेदांश्च विषयानिन्द्रियाणि च । आत्मन्येव स्थितो यस्तु स याति परमां गतिम् ॥१ ॥ नामगोत्रादिवरणं देशं कालं श्रुतं कुलम् । वयो वृत्तं व्रतं शीलं ख्यापयेन्नैव सद्यतिः ॥२ ॥ न संभाषेत्स्त्रियं कांचित्पूर्वदृष्टां च न स्मरेत् । कथां च वर्जयेत्तासां न पश्येल्लिखितामपि ॥३ ॥ एतच्चतुष्टयं मोहात्स्त्रीणामाचरतो यतेः । चित्तं विक्रियतेऽवश्यं तद्विकारात्प्रणश्यति ॥४ ॥

तृष्णा क्रोधोऽनृत माया लोभमोहौ प्रियाप्रिये । शिल्पं व्याख्यानयोगश्च कामो रागपरिग्रहः ॥५ ॥ अहंकारो ममत्वं च चिकित्सा धर्मसाहसम् । प्रायश्चित्तं प्रवासश्च मन्त्रौषधगराशिषः ॥६ ॥ प्रतिषिद्धानि चैतानि सेवमानो व्रजेदधः । आगच्छ गच्छ तिष्ठेति स्वागतं सुहृदोऽपि वा ॥७ ॥

सन्माननं च न ब्रूयान्मुनिर्मोक्षपरायणः । प्रतिग्रहं न गृह्णीयान्नैव चान्यं प्रदापयेत् ॥८ ॥ प्रेरयेद्वा तया भिक्षुः स्वप्नेऽपि न कदाचन । जायाभ्रातृसुतादीनां बन्धूनां च शुभाशुभम् ॥९ ॥ श्रुत्वा दृष्ट्वा न कम्पेत शोकहर्षौ त्यजेद्यतिः । अहिंसा सत्यमस्तेयब्रह्मचर्यापरिग्रहाः ॥१० ॥ अनौद्धत्यमदीनत्वं प्रसादः स्थैर्यमार्जवम् । अस्नेहो गुरुशुश्रूषा श्रद्धा क्षान्तिर्दमः शमः ॥११ ॥

उपेक्षा धैर्यमाधुर्ये तितिक्षा करुणा तथा । ह्रीस्तथा ज्ञानविज्ञाने योगो लध्वशनं धृतिः ॥१२ ॥ एष स्वधर्मो विख्यातो यतीनां नियतात्मनाम् । निर्द्वन्द्वो नित्यसत्वस्थः सर्वत्र समदर्शनः ॥१३ ॥ तुरीयः परमो हंसः साक्षान्नारायणो यतिः । एकरात्रं वसेद्ग्रामे नगरे पञ्चरात्रकम् ॥१४ ॥ वर्षाभ्योऽन्यत्र वर्षासु मासांश्च चतुरो वसेत् । द्विरात्रं व वसेद्ग्रामे भिक्षुर्यदि वसेत्तदा ॥१५ ॥

रागादयः प्रसज्येरंस्तेनासौ नारकी भवेत् । ग्रामान्ते निर्जने देशे नियतात्माऽनिकेतनः ॥१६ ॥ पर्यटेत्कीटवद्भूमौ वर्षास्वेकत्र संवसेत् । एकवासा अवासा एकदृष्टिरलोलुपः ॥१७ ॥ अदूषयन्सतां मार्गं ध्यानयुक्तो महीं चरेत् । शुचौ देशे सदा भिक्षुः स्वधर्ममनुपालयन् ॥१८ ॥ पर्यटेत सदा योगी वीक्षयन्वसुधातलम् । न रात्रौ न च मध्याह्ने संध्ययोर्नैव पर्यटन् ॥१९ ॥

न शून्ये न च दुर्गे वा प्राणिबाधाकरे न च । एकरात्रं वसेद्ग्रामे पत्तने तु दिनत्रयम् ॥२० ॥ पुरे दिनद्वयं भिक्षुर्नगरे पञ्चरात्रकम् । वर्षास्वेकत्र तिष्ठेत स्थाने पुण्यजलावृते ॥२१ ॥ आत्मवत्सर्वभूतानि पश्यन्भिक्षुश्चरेन्महीम् । अन्धवत्कुब्जवच्चैव बधिरोन्मत्तमूकवत् ॥२२ ॥ स्नानं त्रिषवणं प्रोक्तं बहूदकवनस्थयोः । हंसे तु सकृदेव स्यात्परहंसे न विद्यते ॥२३ ॥

मौनं योगासनं योगस्तितिक्षैकान्तशीलता । निःस्पृहत्वं समत्वं च सप्तैतान्यैकदण्डिनाम् ॥२४ ॥ परहंसाश्रमस्थो हि स्नानादेरविधानतः । अशेषचित्तवृत्तीनां त्यागं केवलमाचरेत् ॥२५ ॥ त्वङ्मांसरुधिरस्नायुमज्जामेदोस्थिसंहतौ । विण्मूत्रपूये रमतां क्रिमीणां कियदन्तरम् ॥२६ ॥

क्व शरीरमशेषाणां श्लेष्मादीनां महाचयः। क्व चाङ्गशोभा सौभाग्यकमनीयादयो गुणाः ॥२७॥ मांसासृक्पूयविण्मूत्रस्नायुमज्जास्थिसंहतौ। देहे चेत्प्रीतिमान्मूढो भविता नरकेऽपि सः ॥२८॥ स्त्रीणामवाच्यदेशस्य क्लिन्ननाडीव्रणस्य च। अभेदेऽपि मनोभेदाज्जनः प्रायेण वञ्च्यते ॥२९॥ चर्मखण्डं द्विधा भिन्नमपानोद्गारधूपितम्। ये रमन्ति मनस्तेभ्यः साहसं किमतः परम् ॥३०॥

न तस्य विद्यते कार्यं न लिङ्गं वा विपश्चितः। निर्ममो निर्भयः शान्तो निर्द्वन्द्वोऽवर्णभोजनः ॥३१॥ मुनिः कौपीनवासाः स्यान्नग्नो वा ध्यानतत्परः। एवं ज्ञानपरो योगी ब्रह्मभूयाय कल्पते ॥३२॥

लिङ्गे सत्यपि खल्वस्मिञ्ज्ञानमेव हि कारणम्। निर्मोक्षायेह भूतानां लिङ्गग्रामो निरर्थकः ॥३३॥ यन्न सन्तं न चासन्तं नाश्रुतं न बहुश्रुतम्। न सुवृत्तं न दुर्वृत्तं वेद कश्चित्स ब्राह्मणः ॥३४॥ तस्मादलिङ्गो धर्मज्ञो ब्रह्मवृत्तमनुव्रतम्। गूढधर्माश्रितो विद्वानज्ञातचरितं चरेत् ॥३५॥ संदिग्धः सर्वभूतानां वर्णाश्रमविवर्जितः। अन्धवज्जडवच्चापि मूकवच्च महीं चरेत् ॥३६॥ तं दृष्ट्वा शान्तमनसं स्पृहयन्ति दिवौकसः। लिङ्गाभावात्तु कैवल्यमिति ब्रह्मानुशासनमिति ॥३७॥

अथ नारदः पितामहं संन्यासविधिं नो ब्रूहीति पप्रच्छ। पितामहस्तथेत्यङ्गीकृत्यातुरे वा क्रमे वापि तुरीयाश्रमस्वीकारार्थं कृच्छ्र-प्रायश्चित्तपूर्वकमष्टश्राद्धं कुर्याद्देवर्षिदिव्यमनुष्यभूतपितृमात्रात्मेत्यष्टश्राद्धानि कुर्यात्। प्रथमं सत्यवसु-संज्ञकान्विश्वान्देवान्देवश्राद्धे ब्रह्मविष्णुमहेश्वरानृषिश्राद्धे देवर्षिक्षत्रियर्षिमनुष्यर्षीन् दिव्यश्राद्धे वसुरुद्रादित्यरूपान्मनुष्यश्राद्धे सनकसनन्दन-सनत्कुमारसनत्सुजातान्भूतश्राद्धे पृथिव्यादिपञ्चमहाभूतानि चक्षुरादिकरणानि चतुर्विधभूतग्रामान्पितृश्राद्धे पितृपितामह-प्रपितामहान्मातृश्राद्धे मातृपितामहीप्रपितामहीरात्मश्राद्धे आत्मपितृपितामहा-ञ्जीवत्पितृकश्चेत्पितरं त्यक्त्वा आत्मपितामहप्रपितामहानिति सर्वत्र युग्मक्लृप्त्या ब्राह्मणानर्चयेदेकाध्वरपक्षेऽष्टाध्वपक्षे वा स्वशाखानुगत-मन्त्रैरष्टश्राद्धान्यष्टदिनेषु वा एकदिने वा पितृयागोक्तविधानेन ब्राह्मणानभ्यर्च्य भुक्त्यन्तं यताविधि निर्वर्त्य पिण्डप्रदानानि निर्वर्त्य दक्षिणाताम्बूलैस्तोषयित्वा ब्राह्मणान्प्रेषयित्वा शेषकर्मसिद्ध्यर्थं सप्तकेशान्विसृज्य— 'शेषकर्मप्रसिद्ध्यर्थं केशान्सप्ताष्ट वा द्विजः। संक्षिप्य वापयेत्पूर्वं केशश्मश्रुनखानि चे' ति सप्तकेशान्संरक्ष्य कक्षोपस्थवर्जं क्षौरपूर्वकं स्नात्वा सायंसंध्यावन्दनं निर्वर्त्य सहस्रगायत्रीं जप्त्वा ब्रह्मयज्ञं निर्वर्त्य स्वाधीनाग्निमुपस्थाप्य स्वशाखोपसंहरणं कृत्वा तदुक्तप्रकारेणाज्याहुतिमाज्यभागान्तं हुत्वाहुतिविधिं समाप्यात्मादिभिस्त्रिवारं स्क्तुप्राशनं कृत्वाचमनपूर्वकमाग्निं संरक्ष्य स्वयमेग्नेरुत्तरतः कृष्णाजिनोपरि स्थित्वा पुराणश्रवणपूर्वकं जागरणं कृत्वा चतुर्थयामान्ते स्नात्वा तदग्नौ चरुं श्रपयित्वा पुरुषसूक्तेनान्नस्य षोडशाहुतीर्हुत्वा विरजाहोमं कृत्वा अथाचम्य सदक्षिणं वस्त्रं सुवर्णपात्रं धेनुं दत्वा समाप्य ब्रह्मोद्वासनं कृत्वा। संमासिञ्चन्तु मरुतः समिन्द्रः संवृहस्पतिः। संमायमग्निः सिञ्चत्वायुषा च धनेन च बलेन चायुष्मन्तः करोतु मेति। या ते अग्ने यज्ञिया तनूस्तयेह्यारोहात्मात्मानम्। अच्छा वसूनि कृण्वन्नस्मे नर्या पुरूणि। यज्ञो भूत्वा यज्ञमासीद स्वां योनिं जातवेदो भुव आजायमानः स क्षय एधीत्यनेनाग्निमात्मन्यारोप्य ध्यात्वाग्निं प्रदक्षिण-नमस्कारपूर्वकमुद्वास्य प्रातःसंध्यामुपास्य सहस्रगायत्रीपूर्वकं सूर्योपस्थानं कृत्वा

नाभिदघ्नोदकमुपविश्याष्टदिक्पालकार्घ्यपूर्वकं गायत्र्युद्वासनं कृत्वा सावित्रीं व्याहृतिषु प्रवेशयित्वा।

अहं वृक्षस्य रेरिव। कीर्तिः पृष्ठं गिरेरिव। ऊर्ध्वपवित्रो वाजिनीवस्वमृतमस्मि। द्रविणं मे सवर्चसं सुमेधा अमृतोक्षितः। इति त्रिशङ्कोर्वेदानुवचनम्। यश्छन्दसामृषभो विश्वरूपः। छन्दोभ्योध्यमृतात्संबभूव। स मेन्द्रो मेधया स्पृणोतु। अमृतस्य देवधारणो भूयासं। शरीरं मे विचर्षणं। जिह्वा मे मधुमत्तमा। कर्णाभ्यां भूरि विश्रवं। ब्रह्मणः कोशोऽसि मेधयापिहितः।

श्रुतं मे गोपाय। दारेषणायाश्च वित्तेष्णायाश्च लोकेषणायाश्च व्युत्थितोऽहं ॐ भूः संन्यस्तं मया ॐ भुवः संन्यस्तं मया ॐ सुवः संन्यस्तं मया ॐ भूर्भुवःसुवः संन्यस्तं मयेति मन्द्रमध्यमतालजध्वनिभिर्मनसा वाचोच्चार्याभयं सर्वभूतेभ्यो मत्तः सर्व प्रवर्तते स्वाहेत्यनेन जलं प्राश्य प्राच्यां दिशि पूर्णाञ्जलिं प्रक्षिप्योंस्वाहेति शिखामुत्पाठ्य। यज्ञोपवीतं परमं पवित्रं प्रजापतेर्यत्सहजं पुरस्तात्। आयुष्यमग्र्यं प्रतिमुञ्च शुभ्रं यज्ञोपवीतं बलमस्तु तेजः। यज्ञोपवीत बहिर्न निवसेत्त्वमन्तः प्रविश्य मध्ये ह्यजस्रं परमं पवित्रं यशो बलं ज्ञानवैराग्यं मेधां प्रयच्छेति यज्ञोपवीतं छित्त्वा उदकाञ्जलिना सह ॐ भूः समुद्रं गच्छ स्वाहेत्यप्सु जुहुयादो भूः संन्यस्तं मया ॐ भुवः संन्यस्तं मया ॐ सुवः संन्यस्तं मयेति त्रिरुक्त्वा त्रिवारमभिमन्त्र्य तज्जलं प्राश्याचम्य ॐ भूः स्वाहेत्यप्सु वस्त्रं कटिसूत्रमपि विसृज्य सर्वकर्मनिर्वर्तकोऽहमिति स्मृत्वा जातरूपधरो भूत्वा स्वरूपानुसंधानपूर्वकमूर्ध्वबाहुरुदीचीं गच्छेत्पूर्ववद्विद्वत्संन्यासी चेद्गुरोः सकाशात्प्रणवमहावाक्योपदेशं प्राप्य यथासुखं विहरन्मत्तः कश्चिन्नान्यो व्यतिरिक्त इति फलपत्रोदकाहारः पर्वतवनदेवालयेषु संचरेत्संन्यस्याथ दिगम्बरः सकलसंचारकः सर्वदानन्दस्वानुभवैकपूर्णहृदयः कर्मातिदूरलाभः प्राणायामपरायणः फलरसत्वक्पत्रमूलोदकैर्मोक्षार्थी गिरिकन्दरेषु विसृजेद्देहं स्मरंस्तारकम्।

विविदिषासंन्यासी चेच्छतपथं गत्वाचार्यादिभिर्विप्रैस्तिष्ठ तिष्ठ महाभाग दण्डं वस्त्रं कमण्डलुं गृहाण प्रणवमहावाक्यग्रहणार्थं गुरुनिकटमागच्छेत्याचार्यैर्दण्डकटिसूत्रकौपीनं शाटीमेकां कमण्डलुं पादादिमस्तकप्रमाणमव्रणं समं सौम्यमकाकपृष्ठं सलक्षणं वैणवं दण्डमेकमाचमनपूर्वकं सखा मा गोपायौजः सखायोऽसीन्द्रस्य वज्रोऽसि वार्त्रघ्नः शर्म मे भव यत्पापं तन्निवारयेति दण्डं परिग्रहेज्जगज्जीवनं जीवनाधारभूतं मा ते मा मन्त्रयस्व सर्वदा सर्वसौम्येति प्रणवपूर्वकं कमण्डलुं परिगृह्य कौपीनाधारं कटिसूत्रमोमिति गुह्याच्छादकं कौपीनमोमिति शीतवातोष्णत्राणकरं देहैकरक्षणमोमिति कटिसूत्रकौपीनवस्त्रमाचमनपूर्वकं योगपट्टाभिषिक्तो भूत्वा कृतार्थोऽहभिति मत्त्वा स्वाश्रमाचारपरो भवेदित्युपनिषत्॥ चतुर्थोपदेशः॥४॥

अथ हैनं वितामहं नारदः पप्रच्छ भगवन्सर्वकर्मनिवर्तकः संन्यास इति त्वयैवोक्तः पुनः स्वाश्रमाचारपरो भयेदित्युच्यते। ततः पितामह उवाच। शरीरस्य देहिनो जाग्रत्स्वप्न-सुषुप्तितुरीयावस्थाः सन्ति तदधीनाः कर्मज्ञानवैराग्यप्रवर्तकाः पुरुषा जन्तवस्तदनुकूलाचाराः सन्ति तथैव चेद्भगवन्संन्यासाः कतिभेदास्तदनुष्ठानभेदाः कीदृशास्तत्त्वतोऽस्माकं वक्तुमर्हसीति।

तथेत्यङ्गीकृत्य तु वितामहेन संन्यासभेदैराचारभेदः कथमिति चेत्तत्त्वतस्त्वेक एव संन्यासः अज्ञानेनाशक्तिवशात्कर्मलोपश्च त्रैविध्यमेत्य वैराग्यसंन्यासो ज्ञानसंन्यासो

ज्ञानवैराग्यसंन्यासः कर्मसंन्यासश्चेति चातुर्विध्यमुपागतस्तद्यथेति दुष्टमदनाभावाच्चेति विषयवैतृष्ण्यमेत्य प्राक्पुण्यकर्मवशात्संन्यस्तः स वैराग्यसंन्यासी शास्त्रज्ञानात्पापपुण्यलोकानुभवश्रवणात्प्रपञ्चोपरतः क्रोधेर्ष्यासूयाहंकाराभिमानात्मकसर्वसंसारं निर्वृत्य दारेषणाधनेषणालोकेषणात्मकदेहवासनां शास्त्रवासनां लोकवासनां त्यक्त्वा वमनान्नमिव प्रकृतीयं सर्वमिदं हेयं मत्वा साधनचतुष्टयसंपन्नो यः संन्यस्यति स एव ज्ञानसंन्यासी।

क्रमेण सर्वमभ्यस्य सर्वमनुभूय ज्ञानवैराग्याभ्यां स्वरूपानुसंधानेन देहमात्रावशिष्टः संन्यस्य जातरूपधरो भवति स ज्ञानवैराग्यसंन्यासी। ब्रह्मचर्यं समाप्य गृही भूत्वा वानप्रस्थाश्रममेत्य वैराग्यभावेऽप्याश्रमक्रमानुसारेण यः संन्यस्यति स कर्मसंन्यासी। ब्रह्मचर्येण संन्यस्य संन्यासाज्जातरूपधरो वैराग्यसंन्यासी। विद्वत्संन्यासी ज्ञानसंन्यासी विविदिषासंन्यासी कर्मसंन्यासी। कर्मसंन्यासोऽपि द्विविधः निमित्तसंन्यासोऽनिमित्तसंन्यासश्चेति। निमित्तस्त्वातुरः। अनिमित्तः कर्मसंन्यासः। आतुरः सर्वकर्मलोपः प्राणस्योत्क्रमणकालसंन्यासः स निमित्तसंन्यासः। दृढाङ्गो भूत्वा सर्वं कृतकं नश्वरमिति देहादिकं सर्वं हेयं प्राप्य। हंसः शुचिषद्वसुरन्तरिक्षसद्धोता वेदिषदतिथिर्दुरोणसत्। नृषद्वरसदृतसद्व्योमसदब्जा गोजा ऋतजा अद्रिजा ऋतं बृहत्। ब्रह्मव्यतिरिक्तं सर्वं नश्वरमिति निश्चित्याथो क्रमेण यः संन्यस्यति स संन्यासोऽनिमित्तसंन्यासः।

संन्यासः षड्विधो भवति। कुटीचको बहूदको हंसः परमहंसः तुरीयातीतोऽवधूतश्चेति। कुटीचकः शिखायज्ञोपवीती दण्डकमण्डलुधरः कौपीनकन्थाधरः पितृमातृगुर्वा-राधनपरः पिठरखनित्रशिक्यादिमन्त्रसाधनपर एकत्रान्नादनपरः श्वेतोर्ध्वपुण्ड्रधारी त्रिदण्डः। बहूदकः शिखादिकन्थाधरस्त्रिपुण्ड्रधारी कुटीचकवत्सर्वसमो मधुकरवृत्त्याष्टकवलाशी हंसो जटाधारी त्रिपुण्ड्रोर्ध्वपुण्ड्रधारी असंक्लृप्तमाधुकरान्नाशी कौपीनखण्डतुण्डधारी। परमहंसः शिखायज्ञोपवीतरहितः पञ्चगृहेष्वेकरात्रान्नादनपरः करपात्री एककौपीनधारी शाटीमेकामेकं वैणवं दण्डमेकशाटीधरो वा भस्मोद्धूलनपरः सर्वत्यागी। तुरीयातीतो गोमुखः फलाहारी-अन्नाहारी चेद्गृहत्रये देहमात्रावशिष्टो दिगम्बरः कुणपवच्छरीरवृत्तिकः। अवधूतस्त्वनियमोऽभिशस्तपतितवर्जनपूर्वकं सर्ववर्णेष्वजगरवृत्त्याहारपरः स्वरूपानुसंधानपरः।

आतुरो जीवति चेत्क्रमसंन्यासः कर्तव्यः कुटीचकबहूदकहंसानां ब्रह्मचर्याश्रमादितुरीयाश्रमवत् कुटीचकादीनां संन्यासविधिः। परमहंसादित्रयाणां न कटिसूत्रं न कौपीनं न वस्त्रं न कमण्डलुर्न दण्डः सार्ववर्णैकभैक्षाटनपरत्वं जातरूपधरत्वं विधिः। संन्यासकालेऽप्यलंबुद्धिपर्यन्तमधीत्य तदनन्तरं कटिसूत्रं कौपीनं दण्डं वस्त्रं कमण्डलुं सर्वमप्सु विसृज्याथ जातरूपधरश्चरेन्न कन्थावेशो नाध्येतव्यो न श्रोतव्यमन्यत्किंचित्प्रणवादन्यं न तर्कं पठेन्न शब्दमपि बृहच्छब्दान्नाध्यापयेन्न महद्वाचोविग्लापनं गिरा पाण्यादिना संभाषणं नान्यस्माद्वा विशेषेण न शूद्रस्त्रीपतितोदक्यासंभाषणं न यतेर्देवपूजा नोत्सवदर्शनं तीर्थयात्रावृत्तिः।

पुनर्यतिविशेषः। कुटीचस्यैकत्र भिक्षा बहूदकस्यासंक्लृप्तं माधुकरं हंसस्याष्टगृहेष्वष्टकवलं परमहंसस्य पञ्चगृहेषु करपात्रं फलाहारो गोमुखं तुरीयातीतस्यावधूतस्याजगरवृत्तिः सार्ववर्णिकेषु यतिर्नैकरात्रं वसेन्न कस्यापि नमेत्तुरीयातीतावधूतयोर्न ज्येष्ठो यो न स्वरूपज्ञः स ज्येष्ठोऽपि कनिष्ठो हस्ताभ्यां नद्युत्तरणं

न कुर्यान्न वृक्षमारोहेन्न यानादिरूढो न क्रयविक्रयपरो न किं चिद्विनिमयपरो न दाम्भिको नानृतवादी न यतेः किंचित्कर्तव्यमस्त्यस्तिचेत्सांकर्यम्।

तस्मान्मननादौ संन्यासिनामधिकारः। आतुरकुटीचकयोर्भूर्लोको बहूदकस्य स्वर्गलोको हंसस्य तपोलोकः परमहंसस्य सत्यलोकस्तुरीयातीतावधूतयोः स्वात्मन्येव कैवल्यं स्वरूपानुसन्धानेन भ्रमरकीटन्यायवत्। यं यं वापि स्मरन्भावं त्यजत्यन्ते कलेवरम्। तं तमेव समाप्नोति नान्यथा श्रुतिशासनम्। तदेवं ज्ञात्वा स्वरूपानुसंधानं विनान्यथाचारपरो न भवे तदाचारवशात्तत्तल्लोकप्राप्तिर्ज्ञानवैराग्यसंपन्नस्य स्वस्मिन्नेव मुक्तिरिति न सर्वत्राचारप्रसक्तिस्तदाचारः। जाग्रत्स्वप्नसुषुप्तिष्वेकशरीरस्य जाग्रत्काले विश्वः स्वप्नकाले तैजसः सुषुप्तिकाले प्राज्ञः अवस्थाभेदादवस्थेश्वरभेदः कार्यभेदात्कारणभेदस्तासु चतुर्दशकारणानां बाह्यवृत्तयोऽन्तर्वृत्तयस्तेषामुपादानकारणम्। वृत्तयश्चत्वारः मनोबुद्धिरहंकारश्चित्तं चेति।

तत्तद्वृत्तिव्यापारभेदेन पृथगाचारभेदः। नेत्रस्थं जागरितं विद्यात्कण्ठे स्वप्नं समाविशत्। सुषुप्तं हृदयस्थं तु तुरीयं मूर्ध्नि संस्थितम्। तुरीयमक्षरमिति ज्ञात्वा जागरिते सुषुप्त्यवस्थापन्न इव यद्यच्छ्रुतं यद्यदृष्टं तत्तत्सर्वमविज्ञातमिव यो वसेत्तस्य स्वप्नावस्थायामपि तादृगवस्था भवति। स जीवन्मुक्त इति वदन्ति। सर्वश्रुत्यर्थप्रतिपादनमपि तस्यैव मुक्तिरिति। भिक्षुर्नैहिकामुष्मिकापेक्षः। यद्यपेक्षास्ति तदनुरूपो भवति। स्वरूपानुसन्धान-व्यतिरिक्तान्यशास्त्राभ्यासैरुष्ट्रकुङ्कुमभारवद्व्यर्थो न योगशास्त्रप्रवृत्तिर्न सांख्यशास्त्राभ्यासो न मन्त्रतन्त्रव्यापारः। इतरशास्त्रप्रवृत्तिर्यतेरस्ति चेच्छवालंकारवच्चर्मकारवदतिविदूरकर्माचारविद्यादूरो न प्रणवकीर्तनपरो यद्यत्कर्म करोति तत्तत्फलमनुभवति एरण्डतैलफेनवदतः सर्वं परित्यज्य तत्प्रसक्तं मनोदण्डं करपात्रं दिगम्बरं दृष्ट्वा परिव्रजेद्भिक्षुः। बालोन्मत्तपिशाचवन्मरणं जीवितं वा न काङ्क्षेत कालमेव प्रतीक्षेत निर्देशभृतकन्यायेन परिव्राडिति। तितिक्षाज्ञानवैराग्यशमादिगुणवर्जितः। भिक्षामात्रेण जीवि स्यात्स यतिर्यतिवृत्तिहा ॥१॥

न दण्डधारणेन न मुण्डनेन न वेषेण न दम्भाचारेण मुक्तिः। ज्ञानदण्डो धृतो येन एकदण्डी स उच्यते। काष्ठदण्डो धृतो येन सर्वाशी ज्ञानवर्जितः। स याति नरकान्घोरान्महारौरवसंज्ञितान् ॥२॥

प्रतिष्ठा सूकरीविष्ठासमा गीता महर्षिभिः। तस्मादेनां परित्यज्य कीटवत्पर्यटेद्यतिः ॥३॥ अयाचितं यथालाभं भोजनाच्छादनं भवेत्। परेच्छया च दिग्वासाः स्नानं कुर्यात्परेच्छया ॥४॥ स्वप्नेऽपि यो हि युक्तः स्याज्जाग्रतीव विशेषतः। ईदृक्चेष्टः स्मृतः श्रेष्ठो वरिष्ठो ब्रह्मवादिनाम् ॥५॥ अलाभे न विषादी स्याल्लाभे चैव न हर्षयेत्। प्राणयात्रिकमात्रः स्यान्मात्रासङ्गाद्विनिर्गतः ॥६॥

अभिपूजितलाभांश्च जुगुप्सेतैव सर्वशः। अभिपूजितलाभैस्तु यतिर्मुक्तोऽपि बध्यते ॥७॥ प्राणयात्रानिमित्तं च व्यङ्गारे भुक्तवज्जने। काले प्रशस्ते वर्णानां भिक्षार्थं पर्यटेद्गृहान् ॥८॥ पाणिपात्रश्चरन्योगी नामकृद्भैक्षमाचरेत्। तिष्ठन्भुञ्ज्याच्चरन् भुञ्ज्यान्मध्येनाचमनं तथा ॥९॥ अब्धिवद्धृतमर्यादा भवन्ति विशदाशयाः। नियतिं न विमुञ्चन्ति महान्तो भास्करा एव ॥१०॥

आस्येन तु यदाहारं गोवन्मृगयते मुनिः तदा समः स्यात्सर्वेषु सोऽमृतत्वाय कल्पते ॥११ ॥ अनिन्द्यं वै व्रजन्गेहं निन्द्यं गेहं तु वर्जयेत् । अनावृते विशेद्द्वारि गेहे नैवावृते व्रजेत् ॥१२ ॥ पांसुना च प्रतिच्छन्नशून्यागारप्रतिश्रयः । वृक्षमूलनिकेतो वा त्यक्तसर्वप्रियाप्रियः ॥१३ ॥ यत्रास्तमितशायी स्यान्निरग्निरनिकेतनः । यथालब्धोपजीवी स्यान्मुनिर्दान्तो जितेन्द्रियः ॥१४ ॥ निष्क्रम्य वनमास्थाय ज्ञानयज्ञो जितेन्द्रियः । कालकाङ्क्षी चरन्नेव ब्रह्मभूयाय कल्पते ॥१५ ॥ अभयं सर्वभूतेभ्यो दत्त्वा चरति यो मुनिः । न तस्य सर्वभूतेभ्यो भयमुत्पद्यते क्वचित् ॥१६ ॥ निर्मानश्चानहंकारो निर्द्वन्द्वश्छिन्नसंशयः । नैव क्रुध्यति न द्वेष्टि नानृतं भाषते गिरा ॥१७ ॥

पुण्यायतनचारी च भूतानामविहिंसकः । काले प्राप्ते भवन्भैक्षं कल्प्यते ब्रह्मभूयसे ॥१८ ॥ वानप्रस्थगृहस्थाभ्यां न संसृज्येत कर्हिचित् । अज्ञातचर्यां लिप्सेत न चैनं हर्ष आविशेत् ॥१९ ॥ अध्वा सूर्येण निर्दिष्टः कीटवद्विचरेन्महीम् । आशीर्युक्तानि कर्माणि हिंसायुक्तानि यानि च ॥२० ॥ लोकसंग्रहयुक्तानि नैव कुर्यान्न कारयेत् । नासच्छास्त्रेषु सज्जेत नोपजीवेत जीविकाम् । अतिवादांस्त्यजेत्तर्कान्पक्षं कंचन नाश्रयेत् ॥२१ ॥ न शिष्याननुबध्नीत ग्रन्थान्नैवाभ्यसेद्बहून् । न व्याख्यामुपयुञ्जीत नारम्भानारबेत्क्वचित् ॥२२ ॥ अव्यक्तलिङ्गोऽव्यक्तार्थो मुनिरुन्मत्तबालवत् । कविर्मूकवदात्मानं तद्दृष्ट्या दर्शयेन्नृणाम् ॥२३ ॥ न कुर्यान्न वदेत्किंचिन्न ध्यायेत्साध्वसाधु वा । आत्मारामोऽनया वृत्त्या विचरेज्जडवन्मुनिः ॥२४ ॥ एकश्चरेन्महीमेतां निःसङ्गः संयतेन्द्रियः । आत्मक्रीड आत्मरतिरात्मवान्समदर्शनः ॥२५ ॥ बुधो बालकवत्क्रीडेत्कुशलो जडवच्चरेत् । वदेदुन्मत्तवद्विद्वान् गोचर्यां नैगमश्चरेत् ॥२६ ॥

क्षिप्तोऽवमानितोऽसद्भिः प्रलब्धोऽसूयितोऽपि वा । ताडितः संनिरुद्धो वा वृत्त्या वा परिहापितः ॥२७ ॥ विष्ठितो मूत्रितो वाज्ञैर्बहुधैवं प्रकम्पितः । श्रेयस्कामः कृच्छ्रगत आत्मनात्मानमुद्धरेत् ॥२८ ॥ संमाननं परां हानिं योगर्द्धेः कुरुते यतः । जनेनावमतो योगी योगसिद्धिं च विन्दति ॥२९ ॥ तथा चरेत वै योगी सतां धर्ममदूषयन् । जना यथावमन्येरन्गच्छेयुर्नैव सङ्गतिम् ॥३० ॥

जरायुजाण्डजादीनां वाङ्मनःकायकर्मभिः युक्तः कुर्वीत न द्रोहं सर्वसङ्गांश्च वर्जयेत् ॥३१ ॥ कामक्रोधौ तथा दर्पलोभमोहादयश्च ये । वांस्तु दोषान्परित्यज्य परिव्राड् भयवर्जितः ॥३२ ॥ भैक्षाशनं च मौनित्वं तपो ध्यानं विशेषतः । सम्यग्ज्ञानं च वैराग्यं धर्मोऽयं भिक्षुके मतः ॥३३ ॥ काषायवासाः सततं ध्यानयोगपरायणः । ग्रामान्ते वृक्षमूले वा वसेद्देवालयेऽपि वा ॥३४ ॥

भैक्षेण वर्तयेन्नित्यं नैकान्नाशी भवेत्क्वचित् । चित्तशुद्धिर्भवेद्यावत्तावन्नित्यं चरेत्सुधीः ॥३५ ॥ ततः प्रव्रज्य शुद्धात्मा संचरेद्यत्र कुत्रचित् । बहिरन्तश्च सर्वत्र संपश्यन्हि जनार्दनम् ॥३६ ॥ सर्वत्र विचरेन्मौनी वायुवद्वीतकल्मषः । समदुःखसुखः क्षान्तो हस्तप्राप्तं च भक्षयेत् ॥३७ ॥ निर्वैरेण समं पश्यन्द्विजगोश्वमृगादिषु । भावयन्मनसा विष्णुं परमात्मानमीश्वरम् ॥३८ ॥

चिन्मयं परमानन्दं ब्रह्मैवाहमिति स्मरन् । ज्ञात्वैवं मनोदण्डं धृत्वा आशानिवृतो भूत्वा आशाम्बरधरो भूत्वा सर्वदा मनोवाक्कायकर्मभिः सर्वसंसारमुत्सृज्य प्रपञ्चावाङ्मुखः स्वरूपानुसन्धानेन भ्रमरकीटन्यायेन मुक्तो भवतीत्युपनिषत् ॥ पञ्चमोपदेशः ॥५ ॥

अथ नारदः पितामहमुवाच ॥ भगवन् तदभ्यासवशात् भ्रमरकीटन्यायवत्तदभ्यासः कथमिति । तमाह पितामहः । सत्यवाग्ज्ञानवैराग्याभ्यां विशिष्टदेहावशिष्टो वसेत् । ज्ञानं शरीरं वैराग्यं जीवनं विद्धि शान्तिदान्ती नेत्रे मनो मुखं बुद्धिः कला पञ्चविंशतितत्त्वान्यवयव अवस्था पञ्चमहाभूतानि कर्म भक्तिज्ञानवैराग्यं शाखा जाग्रत्स्वप्नसुषुप्तितुरीयाश्चतुर्दशकरणानि पङ्कस्तम्भाकाराणीति । एवमपि नावमतिपङ्कं कर्णधार इव यन्तेव गजं स्वबुद्ध्या वशीकृत्य स्वव्यतिरिक्तं सर्वं कृतकं नश्वरमिति मत्वा विरक्तः पुरुषः सर्वदा ब्रह्माहमिति व्यवहरेन्नान्यत्किंचिद्वेदितव्यं स्वव्यतिरेकेण । जीवन्मुक्तो वसेत्कृतकृत्यो भवति । न नाहं ब्रह्मेति व्यवहरेत्किंतु ब्रह्माहमस्मीत्यजस्रं जाग्रत्स्वप्नसुषुप्तिषु ।

तुरीयावस्थां प्राप्य तुरीयातीतत्वं व्रजेद्दिवा जाग्रन्नक्तं स्वप्नं सुषुप्तमर्धरात्रं गतमित्येकावस्थायां चतस्रोऽवस्थास्त्वेकैककरणाधीनानां चतुर्दशकरणानां व्यापारश्चक्षुरादीनां । चक्षुषो रूपग्रहणं श्रोत्रयोः शब्दग्रहणं जिह्वाया रसास्वादनं घ्राणस्य गन्धग्रहणं वचसो वाग्व्यापारः पाणेरादानं पादयोः संचारः पायोरुत्सर्ग उपस्थस्यानन्दग्रहणं त्वचः स्पर्शग्रहणम् ।

तदधीना च विषयग्रहणबुद्धिः बुद्ध्या बुद्ध्यति चित्तेन चेतयत्यहंकारेणाहंकरोति । विसृज्य जीव एतान्देहाभिमानेन जीवो भवति । गृहाभिमानेन गृहस्थ इव शरीरे जीवः संचरति । प्राग्दले पुण्यावृत्तिराग्नेय्यां निद्रालस्यौ दक्षिणायां क्रौर्यबुद्धिर्नैर्ऋत्यां पापबुद्धिः पश्चिमे क्रीडारतिर्वायव्यां गमने बुद्धिरुत्तरे शान्तिरीशान्ये ज्ञानं कर्णिकायां वैराग्यं केसरेष्वात्मचिन्ता इत्येवं वक्त्रं ज्ञात्वा जीवदवस्थां प्रथमं जाग्रद्द्वितीयं स्वप्नं तृतीयं सुषुप्तं चतुर्थं तुरीयं चतुर्भिर्विरहितं तुरीयातीतम् । विश्वतैजसप्राज्ञतटस्थभेदैरेक एव एको देवः साक्षी निर्गुणश्च तद्ब्रह्माहमिति व्याहरेत् । नो चेज्जाग्रदवस्थायां जाग्रदादिचतस्रोऽवस्थाः स्वप्ने स्वप्नादिचतस्रोऽवस्थाः सुषुप्ते सुषुप्त्यादिचतस्रोऽवस्थाः तुरीये तुरीयादिचतस्रोऽवस्थाः नत्वेवं तुरीयातीतस्य निर्गुणस्य । स्थूलसूक्ष्मकारणरूपैर्विश्वतैजसप्राज्ञेश्वरैः सर्वावस्थासु साक्षी त्वेक एवावतिष्ठते । उत तटस्थो द्रष्टा तटस्थो न द्रष्टा द्रष्टृत्वान्न द्रष्टैव कर्तृत्वभोक्तृत्वाहंकारादिभिः स्पृष्टो जीवः जीवेतरो न स्पृष्टः ।

जीवोऽपि न स्पृष्ट इति चेन्न । जीवाभिमानेन क्षेत्राभिमानः । शरीराभिमानेन जीवत्वम् । जीवत्वं घटाकाशमहाकाशवद्व्यवधानेऽस्ति । व्यवधानवशादेव हंसः सोऽहमिति मन्त्रेणोच्छ्वासनिःश्वासव्यपदेशेनानुसन्धानं करोति । एवं विज्ञाय शरीराभिमानं त्यजेन्न शरीराभिमानी भवति । स एव ब्रह्मेत्युच्यते । त्यक्तसङ्गो जितक्रोधो लघ्वाहारो जितेन्द्रियः । पिधाय बुद्ध्या द्वाराणि मनो ध्याने निवेशयेत् ॥१ ॥

शून्येष्वेवावकाशेषु गुहासु च वनेषु च । नित्ययुक्तः सदा योगी ध्यानं सम्यगुपक्रमेत् ॥२ ॥ आतिथ्यश्राद्धयज्ञेषु देवयात्रोत्सवेषु च । महाजनेषु सिद्ध्यर्थी न गच्छेद्योगवित्क्वचित् ॥३ ॥ यथैनमवमन्यन्ते जनाः परिभवन्ति च । तथा युक्तश्चरेद्योगी सतां वर्त्म न दूषयेत् ॥४ ॥ वाग्दण्डः कर्मदण्डश्च मनोदण्डश्च ते त्रयः । यस्यैते नियता दण्डाः स त्रिदण्डी महायतिः ॥५ ॥ विधूमे च प्रशान्ताग्नौ यस्तु माधुकरीं चरेत् । गृहे च विप्रमुख्यानां यतिः सर्वोत्तमः स्मृतः ॥६ ॥ दण्डभिक्षां च यः कुर्यात्स्वधर्मे व्यसनं विना ।

यस्तिष्ठति न वैराग्यं याति नीचयतिर्हि सः ॥७ ॥ यस्मिन् गृहे विशेषेण लभेद्भिक्षां च वासनात्। तत्र नो याति यो भूयः स यतिर्नेतरः स्मृतः ॥८ ॥

यः शरीरेन्द्रियादिभ्यो विहीनं सर्वसाक्षिणम्। पारमार्थिकविज्ञानं सुखात्मानं स्वयंप्रभम् ॥९ ॥ परतत्त्वं विजानाति सोऽतिवर्णाश्रमी भवेत्। वर्णाश्रमादयो देहे मायया परिकल्पिताः ॥१० ॥ नात्मनो बोधरूपस्य मम ते सन्ति सर्वदा। इति यो वेद वेदान्तैः सोऽतिवर्णाश्रमी भवेत् ॥११ ॥ यस्य वर्णाश्रमाचारो गलितः स्वात्मदर्शनात्। स वर्णानाश्रमान्सर्वानतीत्य स्वात्मनि स्थितः ॥१२ ॥

योऽतीत्य स्वाश्रमान्वर्णानात्मन्येव स्थितः पुमान्। सोऽतिवर्णाश्रमी प्रोक्तः सर्ववेदार्थवेदिभिः ॥१३ ॥ तस्मादन्यगता वर्णा आश्रमा अपि नारद। आत्मन्यारोपिताः सर्वे भ्रान्त्या तेनात्मवेदिना ॥१४ ॥ न विधिर्न निषेधश्च न वर्ज्यावर्ज्यकल्पना। ब्रह्मविज्ञानिनामस्ति तथा नान्यच्च नारद ॥१५ ॥

विरज्य सर्वभूतेभ्य आविरिञ्चिपदादपि। घृणां विपाट्य सर्वस्मिन्पुत्रमित्रादिकेष्वपि ॥१६ ॥ श्रद्धालुर्मुक्तिमार्गेषु वेदान्तज्ञानलिप्सया। उपायनकरो भूत्वा ब्रह्मविदं व्रजेत् ॥१७ ॥ सेवाभिः परितोष्यैनं चिरकालं समाहितः। सदा वेदान्तवाक्यार्थं शृणुयात्सुसमाहितः ॥१८ ॥ निर्ममो निरहंकारः सर्वसङ्गविवर्जितः। सदा शान्त्यादियुक्तः सन्नात्मन्यात्मानमीक्षते ॥१९ ॥

संसारदोषदृष्ट्यैव विरक्तिर्जायते सदा। विरक्तस्य तु संसारात्संन्यासः स्यान्न संशयः ॥२० ॥ मुमुक्षुः परहंसाख्यः साक्षान्मोक्षैकसाधनम्। अभ्यसेद्ब्रह्मविज्ञानं वेदान्तश्रवणादिना ॥२१ ॥ ब्रह्मविज्ञानलाभाय परहंससमाह्वयः। शान्तिदान्त्यादिभिः सर्वैः साधनैः सहितो भवेत् ॥२२ ॥

वेदान्ताभ्यासनिरतः शान्तो दान्तो जितेन्द्रियः। निर्भयो निर्ममो नित्यो निर्द्वन्द्वो निष्परिग्रहः ॥२३ ॥ जीर्णकौपीनवासाः स्यान्मुण्डी नग्नोऽथवा भवेत्। प्राज्ञो वेदान्तविद्योगी निर्ममो निरहंकृतिः ॥२४ ॥ मित्रादिषु समो मैत्रः समस्तेष्वेव जन्तुषु। एको ज्ञानी प्राशान्तात्मा स संतरति नेतरः ॥२५ ॥

गुरूणां च हिते युक्तस्त्र संवत्सरं वसेत्। नियमेष्वप्रमत्तस्तु यमेषु च सदा भवेत् ॥२६ ॥ प्राप्य चान्ते ततश्चैव ज्ञानयोगमनुत्तमम्। अविरोधेन धर्मस्य संचरेत्पृथिवीमिमाम् ॥२७ ॥ ततः संवत्सरस्यान्ते ज्ञानयोगमनुत्तसम्। आश्रमत्रयमुत्सृज्य प्राप्तश्च परमाश्रमम् ॥२८ ॥

अमुज्ञाप्य गुरूंश्चैव चरेद्धि पृथिवीमिमाम्। त्यक्तसङ्गो जितक्रोधो लघ्वाहारो जितेन्द्रियः ॥२९ ॥ द्वाविमौ न विरज्यते विपरीतेन कर्मणा। निरारम्भो गृहस्थश्च कार्यवांश्चैव भिषुकः ॥३० ॥ माद्यति प्रमदां दृष्ट्वा सुरां पीत्वा च माद्यति। तस्माद्दृष्टिविषां नारीं दूरतः परिवर्जयेत् ॥३१ ॥

संभाषणं सह स्त्रीभिरालापः प्रेक्षणं तथा। नृत्तं गानं सहासं च परिवादांश्च वर्जयेत् ॥३२ ॥ न स्नानं न जपः पूजा न होमो नैव साधनम्। नाग्निकार्यादिकार्यं च नैतस्यास्तीह नारद ॥३३ ॥ नार्चनं पितृकार्यं च तीर्थयात्रा व्रतानि च। धर्माधर्मादिकं नास्ति न विधिर्लौकिकी क्रिया ॥३४ ॥ संत्यजेत्सर्वकर्माणि लोकाचारं च सर्वशः। कृमिकीटपतङ्गांश्च तथा योगी वनस्पतीन् ॥३५ ॥ न नाशयेद्बुधो जीवन्परमार्थमतिर्यतिः।

नित्यमन्तर्मुखः स्वच्छः प्रशान्तात्मा स्वपूर्णधीः ॥३६॥ अन्तःसङ्गपरित्यागी लोके विहर नारद। नाराजके जनपदे चरत्येकचरो मुनिः ॥३७॥ निःस्तुतिर्निर्नमस्कारो निःस्वधाकार एव च। चलाचल-निकेतश्चयतिर्यादृच्छिको भवेदित्युपनिषत्। षष्ठोपदेशः ॥६॥

अथ यतेर्नियमः कथमिति पृष्टं नारदं पितामहः पुरस्कृत्य विरक्तः सन्यो वर्षासु ध्रुवशीलोऽष्टौ मास्येकाकी चरन्नेकत्र निवसेद्भिक्षुर्भयात्सारङ्गवदेकत्र न तिष्ठेत्स्वगमन-निरोधग्रहणं न कुर्याद्धस्ताभ्यां नद्युत्तरणं न कुर्यान्न वृक्षारोहणमपि न देवोत्सवदर्शनं कुर्यान्नैकत्राशी न बाह्यदेवार्चनं कुर्यात्स्वव्यतिरिक्तं सर्वं त्यक्त्वा मधु-करवृत्त्याहारमाहरन्कृशो भूत्वा मेदोवृद्धिमकुर्वन्नाज्यं रुधिरमिव त्यजेदेकत्रान्नं पललमिव गन्धलेपनमशुद्धिलेपनमिव क्षारमन्त्यजमिव वस्त्रमुच्छिष्टपात्रमिवाभ्यङ्गं स्त्रीसङ्गमिव मित्राह्लादकं मूत्रमिव स्पृहां गोमांसमिव ज्ञातचरदेशं चण्डालवाटिकामिव स्त्रियमहिमिव सुवर्णं कालकूटमिव सभास्थलं स्मशानस्थलमिव राजधानीं कुम्भीपाकमिव शवपि-ण्डवदेकत्रान्नं न देहान्तरदर्शनं प्रपञ्चवृत्तिं परित्यज्य स्वदेशमुत्सृज्य ज्ञातचरदेशं विहाय विस्मृतपदार्थं पुनः प्राप्तहर्ष इव स्वमानन्दमनुस्मरन्स्वशरीराभिमानदेशविस्मरणं मत्वा स्वशरीरं शवमिव हेयमुपगम्य कारागृह- विनिर्मुक्तचोरवत्पुत्राप्त बन्धुभवस्थलं विहाय दूरतो वसेत्।

अयत्नेन प्राप्तमाहरन्ब्रह्मप्रणवध्यानानुसन्धानपरो भूत्वा सर्वकर्मनिर्मुक्तः कामक्रोधलोभमोहमदमात्सर्यादिकं दग्ध्वा त्रिगुणातीतः षडूर्मिरहितः षड्भावविकारशून्यः। सत्यवाक्छुचिरद्रोही ग्राम एकरात्रं पत्तने पञ्चरात्रं क्षेत्रे पञ्चरात्रं तीर्थे पञ्चरात्रमनिकेतः स्थिरमतिर्नानृतवादी गिरिकन्दरेषु वसेदेक एव द्वौ वा चरेत् ग्राम त्रिभिर्नगरं चतुर्भिर्ग्राममित्येकश्चरेत्।

भिक्षुश्चतुर्दशकरणानां न तत्रावकाशं दद्यादविच्छिन्नज्ञानाद्वैराग्यसंपत्तिमनुभूय मत्तो न कश्चिन्नान्यो व्यतिरिक्त इत्यात्मन्यालोच्य सर्वतः स्वरूपमेव पश्यञ्जीवन्मुक्तिमवाप्य प्रारब्धप्रतिभासनाशपर्यन्तं चतुर्विधं स्वरूपं ज्ञात्वा देहपतनपर्यन्तं स्वरूपानुसंधानेन वसेत्। त्रिषवणस्नानं कुटीचकस्य बहूदकस्य द्विवारं हंसस्यैकवारं परमहंसस्य मानसस्नानं तुरीयातीतस्य भस्मस्नानमवधूतस्य वायव्यस्नानम् ऊर्ध्वपुण्ड्रं कुटीचकस्य त्रिपुण्ड्रं बहूदकस्य ऊर्ध्वपुण्ड्रं त्रिपुण्ड्रं हंसस्य भस्मोद्धूलनं परमहंसस्य तुरीयातीतस्य तिलकपुण्ड्रमवधूतस्य न किंचित्।

तुरीयातीतावधूतयोः ऋतुक्षौरं कुटीचकस्य ऋतुद्वयक्षौरं बहूदकस्य न क्षौरं हंसस्य परमहंसस्य च न क्षौरम्। अस्तिचेदयनक्षौरम्। तुरीयातीतावधूतयोः न क्षौरम्। कुटीचकस्यैकान्नं माधुकरं बहूदकस्य हंसपरमहंसयोः करपात्रं तुरीयातीतस्य गोमुखं अवधूतस्याजगरवृत्तिः। शाटीद्वयं कुटीचकस्य बहूदकस्यैकशाटी हंसस्य खण्डं दिगम्बरं परमहंसस्य एककौपीनं वा तुरीयातीतावधूतयोर्जातरूपधरत्वं हंसपरमहंसयोरजिनं न त्वन्येषाम्।

कुटीचकबहूदकयोर्देवार्चनं हंसपरमहंसयोर्मानसार्चनं तुरीयातीतावधूतयोः सोहं-भावना। कुटीचकबहूदकयोर्मन्त्रजपाधिकारो हंसपरमहंसयोर्ध्यानाधिकारस्तुरीयातीता-वधूतयोर्न त्वन्याधिकारस्तुरीयातीतावधूतयोर्महावाक्योपदेशाधिकारः परमहंसस्यापि। कुटीचकबहूदकहंसानां नान्धस्योपदेशाधिकारः।

कुटीचकबहूकयोर्मानुषप्रणवः हंसपरमहंसयोरान्तरप्रणवः तुरीयातीतावधूतयोर्ब्रह्मप्रणवः। कुटीचकहूदकयोः श्रवणं हंसपरमहंसयोर्मननं तुरीयातीतावधूतयोर्निदिध्यासः। सर्वेषामात्मानुसन्धानं विधिरित्येव मुमुक्षुः सर्वदा संसारतारकं तारकमनुस्मरञ्जीवन्मुक्तो वसेदधिकारविशेषेण कैवल्यप्राप्त्युपायमन्विष्येद्यतिरित्युपनिषत्॥ सप्तमोपदेशः॥७॥

अथ हैनं भगवन्तं परमेष्ठिनं नारदः पप्रच्छ संसारतारकं प्रसन्नो ब्रूहीति। तथेति परमेष्ठी वक्तुमुपचक्रमे ओमिति ब्रह्मेति व्यष्टिसमष्टिप्रकारेण। का व्यष्टिः का समष्टिः संहारप्रणवः सृष्टिप्रणवश्चान्तर्बहिश्चोभयात्मकत्वात्त्रिविधो ब्रह्मप्रणवः। अन्तःप्रणवो व्यावहारिकप्रणवः बाह्यप्रणव आर्षप्रणवः। उभयात्मको विराट्प्रणवः। संहारप्रणवो ब्रह्मप्रणव अर्धमात्राप्रणवः। ओमितिब्रह्म। ओमित्येकाक्षरमन्तःप्रणवं विद्धि। सचाष्टधा भिद्यते। अकारोकारमकारार्धमात्रानादबिन्दुकलाशक्तिश्चेति। तत्र चत्वार अकारश्चायुतावयवान्वित उकारः सहस्रावयवान्वितो मकारः शतावयवोपेतोऽर्धमात्राप्रणवोऽनन्तावयवाकारः।

सगुणो विराट्प्रणवः संहारो निर्गुणप्रणव उभयात्मकोत्पत्तिप्रणवो यथाप्लुतो विराट्प्लुतः प्लुतसंहारो विराट्प्रणवः षोडशमात्रात्मकः षट्त्रिंशत्तत्त्वातीतः। षोडशमात्रात्मकत्वं कथमित्युच्यते। अकारः प्रथमोकारो द्वितीया मकारस्तृतीयार्धमात्रा चतुर्थी नादः पञ्चमी बिन्दुः षष्ठी कला सप्तमी कलातीताष्टमी शान्तिर्नवमी शान्त्यतीता दशमी उन्मन्येकादशी मनोन्मनी द्वादशी पुरी त्रयोदशी मध्यमा चतुर्दशी पश्यन्ती पञ्चदशी परा। षोडशी पुनश्चतुः षष्टिमात्रा प्रकृतिपुरुषद्वैविध्यमासाद्याष्टाविंशत्युत्तरभेदमात्रास्वरूपमासाद्य सगुणनिर्गुणत्वमुपैत्यैकोऽपि ब्रह्मप्रणवः सर्वाधारः परंज्योतिरेष सर्वेश्वरो विभुः। सर्वदेवमयः सर्वप्रपञ्चाधारगर्भितः॥१॥

सर्वाक्षरमयः कालः सर्वागममयः शिवः। सर्वश्रुत्युत्तमो मृग्यः सकलोपनिषन्मयः॥२॥ भूतं भव्यं भविष्यद्यन्त्रिकालोदितमव्ययम्। तदप्योंकारमेवायं विद्धि मोक्षप्रदायकम्॥३॥ तमेवात्मानमित्येतद्ब्रह्मशब्देन वर्णितम्। तदेकममृतमजरमनुभूय तथोमिति॥४॥ सशरीरं समारोप्य तन्मयत्वं तथोमिति। त्रिशरीरं तमात्मानं परंब्रह्म विनिश्चिनु॥५॥

परंब्रह्मानुसंदध्याद्विश्वादीनां क्रमः क्रमात्। स्थूलत्वात्स्थूलभुक्त्वाच्च सूक्ष्मत्वात्सूक्ष्मभुक् परम्॥६॥ ऐक्यत्वानन्दभोगाच्चसोऽयमात्मा चतुर्विधः। चतुष्पाज्जागरितः स्थूलः स्थूलप्रज्ञो हि विश्वभुक्॥७॥ एकोनविंशतिमुखः साष्टाङ्गः सर्वगः प्रभुः। स्थूलभुक् चतुरात्माथ विश्वो वैश्वानरः पुमान्॥८॥

विश्वजित्प्रथमः पादः स्वप्नस्थानगतः प्रभुः। सूक्ष्मप्रज्ञः स्वतोऽष्टाङ्ग एको नान्यः परंतप॥९॥ सूक्ष्मभुक् चतुरात्माथ तैजसो भूतराडयम्। हिरण्यगर्भः स्थूलोऽन्तर्द्वितीयः पाद उच्यते॥१०॥ कामं कामयते यावद्यत्र सुप्तो न कंचन। स्वप्नं पश्यति नैवात्र तत्सुषुप्तमपि स्फुटम्॥११॥

एकीभूतः सुषुप्तस्थः प्रज्ञानघनवान्सुखी। नित्यानन्दमयोऽप्यात्मा सर्वजीवान्तरस्थितः॥१२॥ तथाप्यानन्दभुक् चेतोमुखः सर्वघतोऽव्ययः। चतुरात्मेश्वरः। प्राज्ञस्तृतीयः पादसंज्ञितः॥१३॥ एष सर्वेश्वरश्चैष सर्वज्ञः सूक्ष्मभावनः। एषोऽन्तर्याम्येष

योनिः सर्वस्य प्रभवाप्ययौ ॥१४॥ भूतानां त्रयमप्येतत्सर्वोपरमबाधकम्। तत्सुषुप्तं हि यत्स्वप्नं मायामात्रं प्रकीर्तितम् ॥१५॥

चतुर्थश्चतुरात्मापि सच्चिदेकरसो ह्ययम्। तुरीयावसितत्वाच्च एकैकत्वानुसारतः ॥१६॥ ज्ञातानुज्ञात्रननुज्ञातृविकल्पज्ञानसाधनम्। विकल्पत्रयमत्रापि सुषुप्तं स्वप्नमान्तरम् ॥१७॥ मायामात्रं विदित्वैवं सच्चिदेकरसो ह्ययम्। विभक्तो ह्ययमादेशो न स्थूलप्रज्ञमन्वहम् ॥१८॥ न सूक्ष्मप्रज्ञमत्यन्तं न प्रज्ञं न क्वचिन्मुने। नैवाप्रज्ञं नोभयतःप्रज्ञं न प्रज्ञ- मान्तरम् ॥१९॥ नाप्रज्ञमपि न प्रज्ञाघनं चादृष्टमेव च। तदलक्षणमग्राह्यं यद्व्यवहार्यमचिन्त्यमव्यपदेश्यमेकात्मप्रत्ययसारं प्रपञ्चोपशमं शिवं शान्तमद्वैतं चतुर्थं मन्यन्ते स ब्रह्म प्रणवः स विज्ञेयो नापरस्तुरीयः सर्वत्र भानुवन्मुमुक्षूणामाधारः स्वयंज्योतिर्ब्रह्माकाशः सर्वदा विराजते परंब्रह्मत्वादित्युपनिषत् ॥ अष्टमोपदेशः ॥८॥

अथ ब्रह्मस्वरूपं कथमिति नारदः पप्रच्छ। तं होवाच पितामहः किं ब्रह्मस्वरूपमिति। अन्योसावन्योहमस्मीति ये विदुस्ते पशवो न स्वभावपशवस्तमेवं ज्ञात्वा विद्वान्मृत्युमुखात्प्रमुच्यते नान्यः यन्था विद्यतेऽयनाय। कालः स्वभावो नियतिर्यदृच्छा भूतानि योनिः पुरुष इति चिन्त्यम्। संयोग एषां नत्वात्मभावादात्मा ह्यनीशः सुखदुःखहेतोः ॥१॥

ते ध्यानयोगानुगता अपश्यन्देवात्मशक्तिं स्वगुणैर्निगूढाम्। यः कारणानि निखिलानि तानि कालात्मयुक्तान्यधितिष्ठत्येकः ॥२॥ तमेकस्मिंस्त्रिवृतं षोडशान्तं शतार्धारं विंशप्रतित्यराभिः अष्टकैः षड्भिर्विश्वरूपैकपाशं त्रिमार्गभेदं द्विनिमित्तैकमोहम् ॥३॥

पञ्चस्रोतोम्बुं पञ्चयोन्युग्रवक्रां पञ्चपाणोर्मिं पञ्चवुद्ध्यादिमूलाम्। पञ्चावर्तां पञ्चदुःखौघवेगां पञ्चाशद्भेदां पञ्चपर्वामधीमः ॥४॥ सर्वाजीवे सर्वसंस्थे बृहन्ते तस्मिन्हंसो भ्राम्यते ब्रह्मचक्रे। पृथगात्मानं प्रेरितारं त मत्वा जुष्टस्ततस्तेनामृतत्वमेति ॥५॥ उद्गीथमेतत्परमं तु ब्रह्म तस्मिंस्त्रयं स्वप्रतिष्ठाक्षरं च। अत्रान्तरं वेदविदो विदित्वा लीनाः परे ब्रह्मणि तत्परायणाः ॥६॥

संयुक्तमेतत्क्षरमक्षरं च व्यक्ताव्यक्तं भरते विश्वमीशः। अनीशश्चात्मा बध्यते भोक्तृभावाज्ज्ञात्वा देवं मुच्यते सर्वपाशैः ॥७॥ ज्ञाज्ञौ द्वावजावीशानीशावजा ह्येका भोक्तृभोगार्थयुक्ता। अनन्तश्चात्मा विश्वरूपो ह्यकर्ता त्रयं यदा विन्दते ब्रह्ममेतत् ॥८॥ क्षरं प्रधानममृताक्षरं हरः क्षरात्मानावीशते देव एकः। तस्याभिध्यानाद्योजनात्तत्वभावाद्भूयश्चान्ते विश्वमायानिवृत्तिः ॥९॥

ज्ञात्वा देवं मुच्यते सर्वपाशैः क्षीणैः क्लेशैर्जन्ममृत्युप्रहाणिः तस्याभिध्यानात्तृतयं देहभेदे विश्वैश्वर्यं केवल आत्मकामः ॥१०॥ एतज्ज्ञेयं नित्यमेवामसंस्थं नातः परं वेदितव्यं हि किंचित्। भोक्ता भोग्यं प्रेरितारं च मत्वा सर्वं प्रोक्तं त्रिविधं ब्रह्ममेतत् ॥११॥

आत्मविद्यातपोमूलं तद्ब्रह्मोपनिपत्परम्। य एवं विदित्वा स्वरूपमेवानुचिन्तयंस्तत्र को मोहः कः शोक एकत्वमनुपश्यतः ॥१२॥ तस्माद्विराड्भूतं भव्यं भविष्यद्भवत्यनश्वरस्वरूपम्। अणोरणीयान्महतो महीयानात्मास्य जन्तोर्निहितो गुहायाम्। तमक्रतुं पश्यति वीतशोको धातुः प्रसादान्महिमानमीशम् ॥१३॥

अपाणिपादो जवनो ग्रहीता पश्यत्यचक्षुः स शृणोत्यकर्णः। स वेत्ति वेद्यं न च तस्यास्ति वेत्ता तमाहुरग्र्यं पुरुषं महान्तम् ॥१४॥ अशरीरं शरीरेष्वनवस्थेष्ववस्थितम्। महान्तं विभुमात्मानं मत्वा धीरो न शोचति ॥१५॥ सर्वस्य धातारमचिन्त्यशक्तिं सर्वागमान्तार्थविशेषवेद्यम्। परात्परं परमं वेदितव्यं सर्वावसाने सकृद्वेदितव्यम् ॥१६॥

कविं पुराणं पुरुषोत्तमोत्तमं सर्वेश्वरं सर्वदेवैरुपास्यम्। अनादिमध्यान्तमनन्तमव्ययं शिवाच्युताम्भोरुहगर्भभूधरम् ॥१७॥ स्वेनावृतं सर्वमिदं प्रपञ्चं पञ्चात्मकं पञ्चसु वर्तमानम्। पञ्चीकृतानन्तभवप्रपञ्चं पञ्चीकृतस्यावयवैरसंवृतम्। परात्परं यन्महतो महान्तं स्वरूपतेजोमयशाश्वतं शिवम् ॥१८॥

नाविरतो दुश्चरितान्नाशान्तो नासमाहितः। नाशान्तमनसो वापि प्रज्ञानेनैनमाप्नुयात् ॥१९॥ नान्तःप्रज्ञं न बहिःप्रज्ञं न स्थूलं नास्थूलं न ज्ञानं नाज्ञानं नोभयतः प्रज्ञमग्राह्यमव्यवहार्यं स्वान्तःस्थितः स्वयमेवेति य एवं वेद स मुक्तो भवति स मुक्तो भवतीत्याह भगवान्पितामहः। स्वस्वरूपज्ञः परिव्राट् परिव्राडेकाकी चरति भयत्रस्तसारङ्गवत्तिष्ठति। गमनविरोधं न करोति।स्वशरीरव्यतिरिक्तं सर्वं त्यक्त्वा षट्पदवृत्त्या स्थित्वा स्वरूपानुसन्धानं कुर्वन्सर्वमनन्यबुद्ध्या स्वस्मिन्नेव मुक्तो भवति। स परिव्राट् सर्वक्रियाकारकनिवर्तको गुरुशिष्यशास्त्रादिविनिर्मुक्तः सर्वसंसारं विसृज्य चामोहितः परिव्राट् कथं निर्धनिकः सुखी धनवाञ्ज्ञानाज्ञानोभयातीतः सुखदुःखातीतः स्वयंज्योतिःप्रकाशः सर्ववेद्यः सर्वज्ञः सर्वसिद्धिदः सर्वेश्वरः सोऽहमिति।

तद्विष्णोः परमं पदं यत्र गत्वा न निवर्तन्ते योगिनः। सूर्यो न तत्र भाति न शशाङ्कोऽपि न स पुनरावर्तते न स पुनरावर्तते तत्कैवल्यमित्युपनिषत्। नवमोपदेशः॥ ॐ भद्रंकर्णेभिरितिशान्तिः॥

इति नारदपरिव्राजकोपनिषत्समाप्ता॥

२२. शाण्डिल्योपनिषत्

शाण्डिल्योपनिषत्प्रोक्तयमाद्यष्टाङ्गयोगिनः।
यद्बोधाद्यान्ति कैवल्यं स रामो मे परा गतिः॥
ॐ भद्रं कर्णेभिरिति शान्तिः॥

शाण्डिल्यो ह वा अथर्वाणं पप्रच्छात्मलाभोपायभूतमष्टाङ्गयोगमनुब्रूहीति। स होवाचाथर्वा यमनियमासनप्राणायामप्रत्याहारधारणाध्यानसमाधयोऽष्टाङ्गानि। तत्र दश यमाः। तथा नियमाः। आसनान्यष्टौ। त्रयः प्राणायामाः। पञ्च प्रत्याहाराः। तथा धारणा।

द्विप्रकारं ध्यानम्। समाधिस्त्वेकरूपः। तत्राहिंसासत्यास्तेयब्रह्मचर्यदयाजपक्षमाधृतिमिताहारशौचानि चेति यमा दश। तत्र हिंसा नाम मनोवाक्कायवर्मभिः सर्वभूतेषु सर्वदा क्लेशजननम्। सत्यं नाम मनोवाक्कायकर्मभिर्भूतहितयथार्थाभिभाषणम्। अस्तेयं नाम मनोवाक्कायवर्मभिः परद्रव्येषु निःस्पृहा। ब्रह्मचर्यं नाम सर्वावस्थासु मनोवाक्कायवर्मभिः सर्वत्र मैथुनत्यागः। दया नाम सर्वभूतेषु सर्वत्रानुग्रहः। आर्जवं नाम

मनोवाक्कायकर्मणां विहिताविहितेषु जनेषु प्रवृत्तौ निवृत्तौ वा एकरूपत्वम्। क्षमा नाम प्रियाप्रियेषु सर्वेषु ताडनपूजनेषु सहनम्। धृतिर्नामार्थहानौ स्वेष्टबन्धुवियोगे तत्प्राप्तौ सर्वत्र चेतःस्थापनम्। मिताहारो नाम चतुर्थांशावशेषकसुस्निग्धमधुराहारः। शौचं नाम द्विविधं बाह्यमान्तरं चेति। तत्र मृज्जलाभ्यां बाह्यम्। मनःशुद्धिरान्तरम्। तदध्यात्मविद्यया लभ्यम् ॥१ ॥

तपः सन्तो-षास्तिक्यदानेश्वरपूजनसिद्धान्तश्रवणह्रीमतिजपो व्रतानि दश नियमाः। तत्र तपो नाम विध्युक्तकृच्छ्रचान्द्रायणादिभिः शरीरशोषणन्। संतोषो नाम यदृच्छालाभसंतुष्टिः। आस्तिक्यं नाम वेदोक्तधर्माधर्मेषु विश्वासः। दानं नाम न्यायार्जितस्य धनधान्यादेः श्रद्धयार्थिभ्यः प्रदानम्। ईश्वरपूजनं नाम प्रसन्नस्वभावेन यथाशक्ति विष्णुरुद्रादिपूजनम्। सिद्धान्तश्रवणं नाम वेदान्तार्थविचारः। ह्रीर्नाम वेदलौकिकमार्गकुत्सितकर्मणि लज्जा। मतिर्नाम वेदविहितकर्ममार्गेषु श्रद्धा। जपो नाम विधिवद्गुरूपदिष्टवेदाविरुद्ध-मन्त्राभ्यासः। तद्द्विविधं वाचिकं मानसं चेति। मानसं तु मनसा ध्यानयुक्तम्। वाचिकं द्विविधमुच्चैरुपांशुभेदेन। उच्चैरुच्चारणं यथोक्तफलम्। उपांशु सहस्रगुणम्। मानसं कोटिगुणम्। व्रतं नाम वेदोक्तविधिनिषेधानुष्ठाननैयत्यम् ॥२ ॥

स्वस्तिकगोमुखपद्मवीरसिंहभद्रमुक्तमयूराख्यान्यासनान्यष्टौ। स्वस्तिकं नाम— जानूर्वोरन्तरे सम्यक्कृत्वा पादतले उभे। ऋजुकायः समासीनः स्वस्तिकं तत्प्रचक्षते ॥१ ॥

सव्ये दक्षिणगुल्फं तु पृष्ठपार्श्वे नियोजयेत्। दक्षिणेऽपि तथा सव्यं गोमुखं गोमुखं यथा ॥२ ॥ अङ्गुष्ठेन निबध्नीयाद्धस्ताभ्यां व्युत्क्रमेण च। ऊर्वोरुपरि शाण्डिल्य कृत्वा पादतले उभे। पद्मासनं भवेदेतत्सर्वेषामपि पूजितम् ॥३ ॥ एकं पादमथैकस्मिन्विन्यस्योरुणि संस्थितः। इतरस्मिंस्तथा चोरुं वीरासनमुदीरितम् ॥४ ॥ दक्षिणं सव्यगुल्फेन दक्षिणेन तथेतरम्। हस्तौ च जान्वोः संस्थाप्य स्वाङ्गुलीश्च प्रसार्य च ॥५ ॥ व्यक्तवक्त्रो निरीक्षेत नासाग्रं सुसमाहितः। सिंहासनं भवेदेतत्पूजितं योगिभिः सदा ॥६ ॥ योनिं वामेन संपीड्य मेढ्रादुपरि दक्षिणम्। भ्रूमध्ये च मनोलक्ष्यं सिद्धासनमिदं भवेत् ॥७ ॥

गुल्फौ तु वृषणस्याधः सीवन्याः पार्श्वयोः क्षिपेत्। पादपार्श्वे तु पाणिभ्यां दृढं बध्वा सुनिश्चलम्। भद्रासनं भवेदेतत्सर्वव्याधिविषापहम् ॥८ ॥ संपीड्य सीविनीं सूक्ष्मां गुल्फेनैव तु सव्यतः। सव्यं दक्षिणगुल्फेन मुक्तासनमुदीरितम् ॥९ ॥अवष्टभ्य धरां सम्यक्तलाभ्यां तु करद्वयोः। हस्तयोः कूर्परौ चापि स्थापयेन्नाभिपार्श्वयोः ॥१० ॥

समुन्नतशिरःपादो दण्डवद्व्योम्नि संस्थितः। मयूरासनमेतत्तु सर्वपापप्रणाशनम् ॥११ ॥ शरीरान्तर्गताः सर्वे रोगा विनश्यन्ति। विषाणि जीर्यन्ते। येन केनासनेन सुखधारणं भवत्यशक्तस्तत्समाचरेत्। येनासनं विजितं जगत्त्रयं तेन विजितं भवति। यमनियमाभ्यां संयुक्तः पुरुषः प्राणायामं चरेत्। तेन नाड्यः शुद्धा भवन्ति ॥३ ॥

अथ हैनमथर्वाणं शाण्डिल्यः पप्रच्छ कनोपायेन नाड्यः शुद्धाः स्युः। नाड्यः कतिसंख्याकाः। तासामुत्पत्तिः कीदृशी। तासु कति वायवस्तिष्ठन्ति। तेषां कानि स्थानानि। तत्कर्माणि कानि। देहे यानि यानि विज्ञातव्यानि तत्सर्वं मे ब्रूहीति। स होवाचाथर्वा अथेदं शरीरं षण्णवत्यङ्गुलात्मकं भवति। शरीरात्प्राणो द्वादशाङ्गुलाधिको भवति।

शरीरस्थं प्राणमग्निना सह योगाभ्यासेन समं न्यूनं वा यः परोत स योगिपुङ्गवो भवति। देहमध्ये शिखिस्थानं त्रिकोणं तप्तजाम्बूनदप्रभं मनुष्याणाम्। चतुष्पदां चतुरस्रम्। विहङ्गानां वृत्ताकारम्। तन्मध्ये शुभा तन्वी पावकी शिखा तिष्ठति। गुदाद्द्व्यङ्गुलादूर्ध्वं मेढ्राद्द्व्यङ्गुलादधो देहमध्यं मनुष्याणां भवति। चतुष्पदां हृन्मध्यम्। विहगानां तुन्दमध्यम्। देहमध्यं नवाङ्गुलं चतुरङ्गुलमुत्सेधायतमण्डाकृति। तन्मध्ये नाभिः। तत्र द्वादशारयुतं चक्रम्।

तच्चक्रमध्ये पुण्यापापप्रचोदितो जीवो भ्रमति। तन्तुपञ्जरमध्यस्थलूतिका यथा भ्रमति तता चासौ तत्र प्राणश्चरति। देहेऽस्मिञ्जीवः प्राणारूढो भवेत्। नाभेस्तिर्यगधऊर्ध्वं कुण्डलिनीस्थानम्। अष्टप्रकृतिरूपाष्टधा कुम्डलीकृता कुण्डलिनी शक्तिर्भवति।

यथावद्वायुसंचारं जलान्नादीनि परितः स्कन्धः पार्श्वेषु निरुध्यैनं मुखेनैव समावेष्ट्य ब्रह्मरन्ध्रं योगकाले चापानेनाग्निना च स्फुरति। हृदयाकाशे महोज्ज्वला ज्ञानरूपा भवति। मध्यस्थकुम्डलिनीमाश्रित्य मुख्या नाड्यश्चतुर्दश भवन्ति। इडा पिङ्गला सुषुम्ना सरस्वती वारुणी पूषा हस्तिजिह्वा यशस्विनी विश्वोदरी कुहूः शङ्खिनी पयस्विनी अलम्बुसा गान्धारीति नाड्यश्चतुर्दश भवन्ति।

तत्र सुषुम्ना विश्वधारिणी मोक्षमार्गेति चाचक्षते। गुदस्य पृष्ठभागे वीणादण्डाश्रिता मूर्धपर्यन्तं ब्रह्मरन्ध्रे विज्ञेया व्यक्ता सूक्ष्मा वैष्णवी भवति। सुषुम्नायाः सव्यभागे इडा तिष्ठति। दक्षिणभागे पिङ्गला इडायां चन्द्रश्चरति। पिङ्गलायां रविः।

तमोरूपश्चन्द्रः। रजोरूपो रविः। विषभागो रविः। अमृतभागश्चन्द्रमाः। तावेव सर्वकालं धत्ते। सुषुम्ना कालभोक्त्री भवति। सुषुम्ना पृष्टपार्श्वयोः सरस्वतीकुहू भवतः। यशस्विनीकुहूमध्ये वारुणी प्रतिष्ठिता भवति। पूषासरस्वतीमध्ये पयस्विनी भवति। गान्धारीसरस्वतीमध्ये यशस्विनी भवति। कन्दमयेऽलम्बुसा भवति। सुषुम्नापूर्वभागे मेढ्रान्तं कुहूर्भवति।

कुण्डलिन्या अधश्चोर्ध्वं वारुणी सर्वगामिनी भवति। यशस्विनी सौम्या च पादाङ्गुष्ठान्तमिष्यते। पिङ्गला चोर्ध्वगा याम्यनासान्तं भवति। पिङ्गलायाः पृष्ठतो याम्यनेत्रान्तं पूषा भवति। याम्यकर्णान्तं यशस्विनी भवति। जिह्वाया ऊर्ध्वान्तं सरस्वती भवति। आसव्यकर्णान्तमूर्ध्वगा शङ्खिनी भवति। इडापृष्ठभागात्सव्यनेत्रान्तगा गान्धारी भवति। पायुमूलादधोर्ध्वगालम्बुसा भवति। एताश्च चतुर्दशसु नाडीष्वन्या नाड्यः संभवन्ति। तास्वन्यास्तास्वन्या भवन्तीति विज्ञेयाः॥ यथाश्वत्थादिपत्रं शिराभिर्व्याप्तमेवं शरीरं नाडीभिर्व्याप्तम्। प्राणापानसमानोदानव्याना नागकूर्मकृकरदेवदत्तधनञ्जया एते दश वायवः सर्वासु नाडीषु चरन्ति।

आस्यनासिकाकण्ठनाभिपादाङ्गुष्ठद्वयकुण्डल्यधश्चोर्ध्वभागेषु प्राणः संचरति। श्रोत्राक्षिकटिगुल्फघ्राणगलस्फिग्देशेषु व्यानः संचरति। गुदमेढ्रोरुजानूदरवृषणकटिजङ्घानाभिगुदाग्न्यगारेष्वपानः संचरति। सर्वसंधिस्थ उदानः। पादहस्तयोरपि सर्वगात्रेषु सर्वव्यापी समानः। भुक्तान्नरसादिकं गात्रेग्निना सह व्यापयन्द्विसप्ततिसहस्रेषु नाडीमार्गेषु चरन्समानवायुरग्निना सहसाङ्गोपाङ्गकलेवरं व्याप्नोति। नागादिवायवः पञ्चत्वगस्थ्यादिसंभवाः।

तुन्दस्थं जलमन्नं च रसादिषु समीरितं तुन्दमद्यगतः प्रागस्तानि पृथक्कुर्यात्। अग्नेरुपरि जलं स्थाप्य जलोपर्यन्नादीनि संस्थाप्य स्वयमपानं संप्राप्य तेनैव सह मारुतः प्रयाति देहमध्यगतं ज्वलनग्। वायुना पालितो वह्निरपानेन शनैर्देहमध्ये ज्वलति। ज्वलनो ज्वालाभिः प्राणेन कोष्ठमव्यगतं जलमत्युष्णमकरोत्।

जलोपरि समर्पितव्यञ्जनसंयुक्तमन्नं वह्निसंयुक्तवारिणा पक्वमकरोत्। तेन स्वेद-मूत्रजलरक्तवीर्यरूपरसपुरीषादिकं प्राणः पृथक्कुर्यात्। समानवायुना सह सर्वासु नाडीषु रसं व्यापयञ्छ्वासरूपेण देहे वायुश्चरति। नवभिर्व्योमरन्ध्रैः शरीरस्य वायवः कुर्वन्ति विण्मूत्रादिविसर्जनम्। निश्वासोच्छ्वासकासश्च प्राणकर्मोच्यते।

विण्मूत्रादिविसर्जनमपानवायुकर्म। हानोपादानचेष्टादि व्यानकर्म। देहस्योन्नयनादिकमुदानकर्म। शरीरपोषणादिकं समानकर्म। उद्गारादि नागकर्म। निमील-नादि कूर्मकर्म। क्षुत्करणं कृकरकर्म। तन्द्रा देवदत्तकर्म। श्लेष्मादि धनञ्जयकर्म। एवं नाडीस्थानं वायुस्थानं तत्कर्म च सम्यग्ज्ञात्वा नाडीसंशोधनं कुर्यात् ॥४॥

यमनियमयुतः पुरुषः सर्वसङ्गविवर्जितः कृतविद्यः सत्यधर्मरतो जितक्रोधो गुरुशुश्रूपानिरतः पितृमातृविधेयः स्वाश्रमोक्तसदाचारविद्वच्छिक्षितः फलमूलोदकान्वितं तपोवनं प्राप्य रम्यदेशे ब्रह्मघोषसमन्विते स्वधर्मनिरतब्रह्मवित्समावृते फलमूलपुष्पवारिभिः सुसंपूर्णे देवायतने नदीतीरे ग्रामे नगरे वापि सुशोभनमठं नात्युच्चनीचायतमल्पद्वारं गोमयादिलिप्तं सर्वरक्षासमन्वितं कृत्वा तत्र वेदान्तश्रवणं कुर्वन्योगं समारभेत्।

आदौ विनायकं संपूज्य स्वेष्टदेवतां नत्वा पूर्वोक्तासने स्थित्वा प्राङ्मुख उदङ्मुखो वापि मृद्वासनेषु जितासनगतो विद्वान्समग्रीवशिरोनासाग्रदृग्भ्रूमध्ये शशभृद्बिम्बं पश्यन्नेत्राभ्याममृतं पिबेत्। द्वादशमात्रया इडया वायुमापूर्योदरे स्थितं ज्वालावलीयुतं रेफबिन्दुयुक्तमग्निमण्डलयुतं ध्यायेद्रेचयेत्पिङ्गलया। पुनः पिङ्गलयापूर्य कुम्भित्वा रेचयेदिडया। त्रिचतुस्त्रिचतुः सप्तत्रिचतुर्मासपर्यन्तं त्रिसंधिषु तदन्तरालेषु च षट्कृत्व आचरेन्नाडीशुद्धिर्भवति। ततः शरीरे लघुदीप्तिवह्निवृद्धिनादाभिव्यक्तिर्भवति ॥५॥

प्राणापानसमायोगः प्राणायामो भवति। रेचकपूरककुम्भकभेदेन स त्रिविधः। ते वर्णात्मकाः। तस्मात्प्रणव एव प्राणायामः पद्माद्यासनस्थः पुमान्नासाग्रे शश-भृद्बिम्बज्योत्स्नाजालवितानिताकारमूर्ती रक्ताङ्गी हंसवाहिनी दण्डहस्ता बाला गायत्री भ-वति। उकारमूर्तिः श्वेताङ्गी तार्क्ष्यवाहिनी युवती चक्रहस्ता सावित्री भवति। मकारमूर्तिः कृष्णाङ्गी वृषभवाहिनी वृद्धा त्रिशूलधारिणी सरस्वती भवति। अकारादित्रयाणां सर्वकारणमेकाक्षरं परंज्योतिः प्रणवं भवतीति ध्यायेत्। इडया बाह्याद्वायुमापूर्य षोडशमात्राभिरकारं चिन्तयन्पूरितं वायुं चतुःषष्टिमात्राभिः कुम्भयित्वोकारं ध्यायन्पूरितं पिङ्गलया द्वात्रिंशन्मात्रया मकारमूर्तिध्यानेनैवं क्रमेण पुनः पुनः कुर्यात् ॥६॥ अथासनदृढो योगी वशी मितहिताशनः सुषुम्नानाडीस्थमलशोषार्थं योगी बद्धपद्मासनो वायुं चन्द्रेणापूर्य यथाशक्ति कुम्भयित्वा सूर्येण रेचयित्वा पुनः सूर्येणापूर्य कुम्भयित्वा चन्द्रेण विरेच्य यया त्यजेत्तया संपूर्य धारयेत्।

तदेते श्लोका भवन्ति। प्राणं प्रागिडया पिबेन्नियमितं भूयोऽन्यया रेचयेत्पीत्वा पिङ्गलया समीरणमथो बध्वा त्यजेद्वामया। सूर्याचन्द्रमसोरनेन विधिनाऽभ्यासं सदा तन्वतां शुद्धा नाडिगणा भवन्ति यमिनां मासत्रयादूर्ध्वतः ॥१॥ प्रातर्मध्यन्दिने सायमर्धरात्रे तु कुम्भकान्। शनैरशीतिपर्यन्तं चतुर्वारं समभ्यसेत् ॥२॥

कनीयसि भरेत्स्वेदः कम्पो भवति मध्यमे। उत्तिष्ठत्युत्तमे प्राणरोधे पद्मासनं महत् ॥३॥ जलेन श्रमजातेन गात्रमर्दनमाचरेत्। दृढता लघुता चापि तस्य गात्रस्य जायते ॥४॥ अभ्यासकाले प्रथमं शस्तं क्षीराज्यभोजनम्। ततोऽभ्यासे स्थिरीभूते न तावन्नियमग्रहः ॥५॥ यथा सिंहो गजो व्याघ्रो भवेद्वश्यः शनैः शनैः। तथैव सेवितो वायुरन्यथा हन्ति साधकम् ॥६॥

युक्तंयुक्तं त्यजेद्वायुं युक्तंयुक्तं च पूरयेत्। युक्तंयुक्तं च बध्नीयादेवं सिद्धिमवाप्नुयात् ॥७॥ यथेष्टधारणाद्वायोरनलस्य प्रदीपनम्। नादाभिव्यक्तिरारोग्यं जायते नाडिशोधनात् ॥८॥ विधिवत्प्राणसंयामैर्नाडीचक्रे विशोधिते। सुषुम्नावदनं भित्त्वा सुखाद्विशति मारुतः ॥९॥ मारुते मध्यसंचारे मनःस्थैर्यं प्रजायते। यो मनःसुस्थिरो भावः सैवावस्था मनोन्मनी ॥१०॥

पूरकान्ते तु कर्तव्यो बन्धो जालन्धराभिधः। कुम्भकान्ते रेचकादौ कर्तव्यस्तूड्डियाणकः ॥११॥ अधस्तात्कुञ्चनेनाशु कण्ठसंकोचने कृते। मध्ये पश्चिमतानेन स्यात्प्राणो ब्रह्मनाडिगः ॥१२॥ अपानमूर्ध्वमुत्थाप्य प्राणं कण्ठादधो नयन्। योगी जराविनिर्मुक्तः षोडशो वयसा भवेत् ॥१३॥

सुखासनस्थो दक्षनाड्या बहिःस्थं पवनं समाकृष्याकेशमानखाग्रं कुम्भयित्वा सव्यनाड्या रेचयेत्। तेन कपालशोधनं वातनाडीगतसर्वरोगसर्वविनाशनं भवति। हृदयादिकण्ठपर्यन्तं सस्वनं नासाभ्यां शनैः पवनामाकृष्य यथाशक्ति कुम्भयित्वा इडया विरेच्य गच्छंस्तिष्ठन्कुर्यात्। तेन श्लेष्महरं जठराग्निवर्धनं भवति। वक्त्रेण सीत्कारपूर्वक वायुं गृहीत्वा यथाशक्ति कुम्भयित्वा नासाभ्यां रेचयेत्। तेन क्षुत्तृष्णालस्यनिद्रा न जायते। जिह्वया वायुं गृहीत्वा यथाशक्ति कुम्भयित्वा नासाभ्यां रेवयेत्।

तेन गुल्मप्लीहज्वरपित्तक्षुधादीनि नश्यन्ति॥ अथ कुम्भकः। स द्विविधा सहितः केवलश्चेति। रेचकपूरकयुक्तः सहितः तद्विवर्जितः केवलः। केवलसिद्धिपर्यन्तं सहितमभ्यसेत्। केवलकुम्भके सिद्धे त्रिषु लोकेषु न तस्य दुर्लभं भवति। केवलकुम्भकात्कुण्डलिनीबोधो जायते। ततः कृशवपुः प्रसन्नवदनो निर्मललोचनोऽभिव्यक्तनादो निर्मुक्तरोगजालो जितबिन्दुः पट्वग्निर्भवति। अन्तर्लक्ष्यं बहिर्दृष्टिर्निमेषोन्मेषवर्जिता। एषा सा वैष्णवी मुद्रा सर्वतन्त्रेषु गोपिता ॥१४॥ अन्तर्लक्ष्यविलीनचित्तपवनो योगी सदा वर्तते दृष्ट्या निश्चलतारया बहिरधः पश्यन्नपश्यन्नपि। मुद्रेयं खलु खेचरी भवति सा लक्ष्यैकताना शिवा शून्याशून्यविवर्जितं स्फुरति सा तत्त्वं पदं वैष्णवी ॥१५॥ अर्धोन्मीलितलोचनः स्थिरमना नासाग्रदत्तेक्षणश्चन्द्रार्कावपि लीनतामुपनयन्निष्पन्दभावोत्तरम्। ज्योतीरूपमशेषबाह्यरहितं देदीप्यमानं परं तत्त्वं तत्परमस्ति वस्तुविषयं शाण्डिल्य विद्धीह तत् ॥१६॥

तारं ज्योतिषि संयोज्य किंचिदुन्नमयन्भ्रुवौ। पूर्वाभ्यासस्य मार्गोऽयमुन्मनीकारकः क्षणात् ॥१७॥ तस्मात्खेचरीमुद्रामभ्यसेत्। तत उन्मनी भवति। ततो योगनिद्रा भवति। लब्धयोगनिद्रस्य योगिनः कालो नास्ति। शक्तिमध्ये मनः कृत्वा शक्तिं मानसमध्यगाम्। मनसा मन आलोक्य शाण्डिल्य त्वं सुखी भव ॥१८॥ खमध्ये कुरु चात्मानमात्ममध्ये च खं कुरुः। सर्वं च खमयं कृत्वा न किंचिदपि चिन्तय ॥१९॥ बाह्यचिन्ता न कर्तव्या तथैवान्तरचिन्तिका। सर्वचिन्तां परित्यज्य चिन्मात्रपरमो भव ॥२०॥

कर्पूरमनले यद्वत्सैन्धवं सलिले यथा। तथा च लीयमानं स मनस्तत्त्वे विलीयते ॥२१ ॥ ज्ञेयं सर्वप्रतीतं च तज्ज्ञानं मन उच्यते। ज्ञानं ज्ञेयं सम नष्टं नान्यः पन्था द्वितीयकः ॥२२ ॥ ज्ञेयवस्तुपरित्यागाद्विलयं याति मानसम्। मानसे विलयं याते कैवल्यमवशिष्यते ॥२३ ॥ द्वौ क्रमौ चित्तनाशस्य योगी ज्ञानं मुनीश्वर। योगस्तूद्बृत्तिरोधो हि ज्ञानं सम्यगवेक्षणम् ॥२४ ॥

तस्मिन्निरोधिते नूनमुपसान्तं मनो भयेत्। मनःस्पन्दोपशान्त्यायं संसारः प्रविलीयते ॥२५ ॥ सूर्यालोकपरिस्पन्दशान्तौ व्यवहृतिर्यथा। शास्त्रासज्जनसंपर्क-वैराग्याभ्यासयोगतः ॥२६ ॥ अनास्थायां वृत्तास्थायां पूर्वं संसारवृत्तिषु। यथाभिवाञ्छितध्यानाच्चिरमेकतयोहितात् ॥२७ ॥ एकतत्त्वदृढाभ्यासाप्राणस्पन्दो निरुध्यते। पूरकाद्यनिलायामाद्दृढाभ्यासादखेदजात् ॥२८ ॥ एकान्तध्यानयोगाच्च मनःस्पन्दो निरुध्यते। ओङ्कारोच्चारणप्रान्तशब्दतत्त्वानुभावनात्। सुषुप्ते संविदा ज्ञाते प्राणस्पन्दो निरुध्यते ॥२९ ॥

तालुमूलगतां यत्नाज्जिह्वयाक्रम्य घण्टिकाम्। ऊर्ध्वरन्ध्रं गते प्राणे प्राणस्पन्दो निरुध्यते ॥३० ॥ प्राणे गलितसंवित्तौ तालूर्ध्वं द्वादशान्तगे। अभ्यासादूर्ध्वरन्ध्रेण प्राणस्पन्दो निरुध्यते ॥३१ ॥ द्वादशाङ्गुलपर्यन्ते नासाग्रे विमलेऽम्बरे। संविद्दृशि प्रशाम्यन्त्यां प्राणस्पन्दो निरुध्यते ॥३२ ॥ भ्रूमध्ये तारकालोकशान्तावन्तमुपागते। चेतनैकतने बद्धे प्राणस्पन्दो निरुध्यते ॥३३ ॥

ओमित्येव यदुद्भूतं ज्ञानं ज्ञेयात्मकं शिवम्। असंस्पृष्टविकल्पांशं प्राणस्पन्दो निरुध्यते ॥३४ ॥ चिरकालं हृदेकान्तव्योमसंवेदनान्मुने। अवासनमनोध्यानात्प्राणस्पदो निरुध्यते ॥३५ ॥ एभिःक्रमैस्तथान्यैश्च नानासंकल्पकल्पितैः। नानादेशिकवक्त्रस्थैः प्राणस्पन्दो निरुध्यते ॥३६ ॥

आकुञ्चनेन कुण्डलिन्याः कवाटमुद्घाट्य मोक्षद्वारं विभेदयेत्। येन मार्गेण गन्तव्यं तद्द्वारं मुखेनाच्छाद्य प्रसुप्ता कुण्डलिनी कुटिलाकारा सर्पवद्वेष्टिता भवति। सा शक्तिर्येन चालिता स्यात्स तु मुक्तो भवति। सा कुण्डलिनी कण्ठोर्ध्वभागे सुप्ता चेद्योगिनां मुक्तये भवति। बन्धनायाधो मूढानाम। इडादिगार्गाद्वयं विहाय सुषुम्नामार्गेणागच्छेत्तद्विष्णोः परमं पदम्। मरुदभ्यसनं सर्वं मनोयुक्तं समभ्यसेत्। इतरत्र न कर्तव्या मनो-वृत्तिर्मनीषिणा ॥३७ ॥ दिवा न पूजयेद्विष्णु रात्रौ नैव प्रपूजयेत्। सततं पूजयेद्विष्णुं दिवारात्रं न पूजयेत् ॥३८ ॥ सुषिरो ज्ञानजनकः पञ्चस्रोतःसमन्वितः। तिष्ठते खेचरी मुद्रा त्वं हि शाण्डिल्य तां भज ॥३९ ॥ सव्यदक्षिणनाडीस्थो मध्ये चरति मारुतः। तिष्ठतः खेचरी मुद्रा तस्मिन्स्थाने न संशयः ॥४० ॥

इडापिङ्गलयोर्मध्ये शून्यं चैवानिलं ग्रसेत्। तिष्ठन्ती खेचरी मुद्रा तत्र सत्यं प्रतिष्ठितम् ॥४१ ॥ सोमसूर्यद्वयोर्मध्ये निरालम्बतले पुनः। संस्थिता व्योमचक्रे सा मुद्रा नाम्ना च खेचरी ॥४२ ॥

छेदनचालनदाहैः फलां परां जिह्वां वृत्वा दृष्टिं भ्रूमध्ये स्थाप्य कपालकुहरे जिह्वा विपरीतगा यदा भवति तदा खेचरी मुद्रा जायते। जिह्वा चित्तं च खे चरति तेनोर्ध्वजिह्वः पुमानमृतो भवति। वामपादमूलेन योनिं संपीड्य दक्षिणपादं प्रसार्य तं कराभ्यां धृत्वा

नासाभ्यां वायुमापूर्य कण्ठबन्धं समारोप्योर्णतो (?) वायुं धारयेत्। तेन सर्वक्लेशहानिः। ततः पीयूषमिव विषं जीर्यते। क्षयगुल्मगुदावर्तजीर्णत्वगादिदोषा नश्यन्ति। एष प्राणजयोपायः सर्वमृत्यूपघातकः। वामपादपार्ष्णिं योनिस्थाने नियोज्य दक्षिणचरणं वामोरूपरि संस्थाप्य वायुमापूर्य हृदये चुबुकं निधाय योनिमाकुञ्च्य मनोमध्ये यथाशक्ति धारयित्वा स्वात्मानं भावयेत्। तेनापरोक्षसिद्धिः।

बाह्यात्प्राणं समाकृष्य पूरयित्वोदरे स्थितम्। नाभिमध्ये च नासाग्रे पादाङ्गुष्ठे च यत्नतः ॥४३॥ धारयेन्मनसा प्राणं सन्ध्याकालेषु वा सदा। सर्वदोगविनिर्मुक्तो भवेद्योगी गतक्लमः ॥४४॥ नासाग्रे वायुविजयं भवति। नाभिमध्ये सर्वरोगविनाशः। पादाङ्गुष्ठधारणाच्छरीरलघुता भवति। रसनाद्वायुमाकृष्य यः पिबेत्सततं नरः। श्रमदाहौ तु न स्यातां नश्यन्ति व्याधयस्तथा ॥४५॥ सन्ध्ययोर्ब्राह्मणः काले वायुमाकृष्य यः पिबेत्। त्रिमासात्तस्य कल्याणी जायते वाक् सरस्वती ॥४६॥

एवं षण्मासाभ्यासात्सर्वरोगनिवृत्तिः। जिह्वया वायुमानीय जिह्वामूले निरोधयेत्। यः पिबेदमृतं विद्वान्सकलं भद्रमश्नुते ॥४७॥ आत्मन्यात्मानमिडया धारयित्वा भ्रुवोन्तरे। विभेद्य त्रिदशाहारं व्याधिस्थोऽपि विमुच्यते ॥४८॥ नाडीभ्यां वायुमारोप्य नाभो तुन्दस्य पार्श्वयोः। घटिकैकां वहेद्यस्तु व्याधिभिः स विमुच्यते ॥४९॥ मासमेकं त्रिसन्ध्यं तु जिह्वयारोप्य मारुतम्। विभेद्य त्रिदशाहारं धारयेत्तुन्दमध्यमे ॥५०॥ ज्वराः सर्वेऽपि नश्यन्ति विषाणि विविधानि च। मुहूर्तमपि यो नित्यं नासाग्रे मनसा सह ॥५१॥

सर्वं तरति पाप्मानं तस्य जन्मशतार्जितम्। तारसंयमात्सकलविषयज्ञानं भवति। नासाग्रे चित्तसंयमादिन्द्रलोकज्ञानम्। तदधश्चित्त-संयमादग्निलोकज्ञानम्। चक्षुषि चित्तसंयमात्सर्वलोकज्ञानम्। श्रोत्रे चित्तस्य संयमाद्यमलोकज्ञानम्। तत्पार्श्वे संयमान्निर्ऋतिलोकज्ञानम्। पृष्ठभागे संयमाद्वरुणलोकज्ञानम्। वामकर्णे संयमाद्वायुलोकज्ञानम्। कण्ठे संयमात्सोम-लोकज्ञानम्। वामचक्षुपि संयमाच्छिवलोकज्ञानम्। मूर्ध्नि संयमाद्ब्रह्मलोकज्ञानम्। पादाधोभागे संयमादतललोकज्ञानम्। पादे संयमाद्वितललोकज्ञानम्। पादसन्धौ संयमान्नितललोकज्ञानम्। जङ्घे संयमात्सुतललोकज्ञानम्। जानौ संयमान्महातललोकज्ञानम्। ऊरौ चित्तसंयमाद्रसातललोकज्ञानम्। कटौ चित्तसंयमात्तलातललोकज्ञानम्। नाभौ चित्त-संयमाद्भूलोकज्ञानम्। कुक्षौ संयमाद्भुवर्लोकज्ञानम्। हृदि चित्तस्य संयमात्स्वर्लोकज्ञानम्। हृदयोर्ध्वभागे चित्तसंयमान्महर्लोकज्ञानम्। कण्ठे चित्तसंयमाज्जनोलोकज्ञानम्। भ्रूमध्ये चित्त-संयमात्तपोलोकज्ञानम्। मूर्ध्नि चित्तसंयमात्सत्यलोकज्ञानम्। धर्माधर्म-संयमादतीतानागतज्ञानम्। तत्तज्जन्तुध्वनौ चित्तसंयमात्सर्वजन्तुरुतज्ञानम्। संचितकर्मणि चित्त-संयमात्पूर्वजातिज्ञानम्। परचित्ते चित्तसंयमात्परचित्तज्ञानम्। कायरूपे चित्त-संयमादन्यादृश्यरूपम्। बले चित्तसंयमाद्धनुमदादिवलम्। सूर्ये चित्तसंयमाद्भुवनज्ञानम्। चन्द्रे चित्तसंयमात्ताराव्यूहज्ञानम्। ध्रुवे तद्गतिदर्शनम्। स्वार्थसंयमात्पुरुषज्ञानम्। नाभिचक्रे कायव्यूहज्ञानम्। कण्टकूपे क्षुत्पिपासानिवृत्तिः। कूर्मनाड्यां स्थैर्यम्। तारे सिद्धदर्शनम्। कायाकाशसंयमादाकाशगमनम्। तत्तत्स्थाने संयमात्तत्तत्सिद्धयो भवन्ति ॥७॥

अथ प्रत्याहारः। स पञ्चविधः विषयेषु विचरतामिन्द्रियाणां बलादाहरणं प्रत्याहारः। यद्यत्पश्यति तत्सर्वमात्मेति प्रत्याहारः। नित्याविहितकर्मफलत्यागः प्रत्याहारः सर्वविषयपराङ्मुखत्वं प्रताहारः अष्टादशसु मर्मस्थानेषु क्रमाद्धारणं प्रत्याहारः। पादाङ्गुष्ठगुल्फजङ्घाजानूरुपायुमेढ्रनाभिहृदयकण्ठकूपतालुनासाक्षिभ्रूमध्यललाटमूर्ध्नि स्थानानि। तेषु क्रमादारोहावरोहक्रमेण प्रत्याहरेत् ॥८॥ अथ धारणा। सा त्रिविधा। आत्मनि मनोधारणं दहराकाशे बाह्याकाशधारणं पृथिव्यप्तेजोवाय्वाकाशेषु पञ्चमूर्तिधारणं चेति ॥९॥

अथ ध्यानम्। तद्द्विविधं सगुणं निर्गुणं चेति। सगुणं मूर्तिध्यानम्। निर्गुणमात्मयाथात्म्यम् ॥१०॥ अथ समाधिः। जीवात्मपरामात्मैक्यावस्थात्रिपुटीरहिता परमानन्दस्वरूपा शुद्धचैतन्यात्मिका भवति ॥११॥ इति प्रथमोऽध्यायः ॥१॥

अथ ह शाण्डिल्यो ह वै ब्रह्मऋषिश्चतुर्षु वेदेषु ब्रह्मविद्यामलभमानः किं नामेत्यथर्वाणं भगवन्तमुपसन्नः पप्रच्छाधीहि भगवन् ब्रह्मविद्या येन श्रेयोऽवाप्स्यामीति। स होवाचाथर्वा शाण्डिल्य सत्यं विज्ञानमनन्तं ब्रह्म यस्मिन्निदमोतं च प्रोतं च। यस्मिन्निदं सं च विचैति सर्वं यस्मिन्विज्ञाते सर्वमिदं विज्ञातं भवति।

तदपाणिपादमचक्षुः श्रोत्रमजिह्वमशरीरमग्राह्यमनिर्देश्यम्। यतो वाचो निवर्तन्ते। आप्राप्य मनसा सह। यत्केवलं ज्ञानगम्यम्। प्रज्ञा च यस्मात्प्रसृता पुराणी। यदेकमद्वितीयम्। आकाशवत्सर्वगतं सुसूक्ष्मं निरञ्जनं निष्क्रियं सन्मात्रं चिदानन्दैकरसं शिवं प्रशान्तममृतं तत्परं च ब्रह्म।

तत्त्वमसि। तज्ज्ञानेन हि विजानीहि य एको देव आत्मशक्तिप्रधानः सर्वज्ञः सर्वेश्वरः सर्वभूतान्तरात्मा सर्वभूताधिवासः सर्वभूतनिगूढो भूतयोनिर्योगै कगम्यः। यश्च विश्वं सृजति विश्वं विभर्ति विश्वं भुङ्क्ते स आत्मा। आत्मनि तं तं लोकं विजानीहि। मा शोचीरात्मविज्ञानी शोकस्यान्तं गमिष्यति॥ इति द्वितीयोऽध्यायः ॥२॥

अथैनं शाण्डिल्योऽथर्वाणं पप्रच्छ यदेकमक्षरं निष्क्रियं शिवं सन्मात्रं परंब्रह्म। तस्मात्कथमिदं विश्वं जायते कथं स्थीयते कथमस्मिंल्लीयते। तन्मे संशयं छेत्तुमर्हसीति। स होवाचाथर्वा सत्यं शाण्डिल्य परंब्रह्म निष्क्रियमक्षरमिति। अथाप्यस्यारूपस्य ब्रह्मणस्त्रीणि रूपाणि भवन्ति सकले निष्कलं सकलनिष्कलं चेति। यत्सत्यं विज्ञानमानन्दं निष्क्रियं निरञ्जनं सर्वगतं सुसूक्ष्मं सर्वतोसुखमनिर्देश्यममृतमस्ति तदिदं निष्कले रूपम्। अथास्य या सहजास्त्यविद्या मूलप्रकृतिर्माया लोहितशुक्लकृष्णा। तया सहायवान् देवः कृष्णपिङ्गलो ममेश्वर ईष्टे। तदिदमस्य सकलनिष्कलं रूपम्॥ अथैप ज्ञानमयेन तपसा जीयमानोऽकामयत् बहु स्यां प्रजायेयेति। अथैतरमात्तप्यमानात्सत्यकामान्त्रीण्यक्षराण्यजायन्त।

तिस्रो व्याहृतयस्त्रिपदा गायत्री त्रयो वेदास्त्रयो देवास्त्रयो वर्णास्त्रयोऽग्नयश्च जायन्ते। योऽसौ देवो भगवान्सर्वैश्वर्यसंपन्नः सर्वव्यापी सर्वभूतानां हृदये संनिविष्टो मायावी मायया क्रीडति स ब्रह्मा स विष्णुः स रुद्रः स इन्द्रः स सर्वे देवाः सर्वाणि भूतानि स एव पुरस्तात्स एव पश्चात्स एवोत्तरतः स एव दक्षिणतः स एवाधस्तात्स एवोपरिष्टात्स एव सर्वम्।

अथास्य देवस्यात्मशक्तेरात्मक्रीडस्य भक्तानुकम्पिनो दत्तात्रेयरूपा सुरूपा तनूरवासा इन्दीवरलप्रख्या चतुर्बाहुरधोरापापकाशिनी। तदिदमस्य सकलं रूपम् ॥१॥

अथ हैनमथर्वाणं शाण्डिल्यः पप्रच्छ भगवन्सन्मात्रं चिदानन्दैकरसं कस्मादुच्यते परं ब्रह्मेति। स होवाचाथर्वा यस्माच्च बृहति बृंहयति च सर्वं तस्मादुच्यते परंब्रह्मेति। अथ कस्मादुच्यते आत्मेति। यस्मात्सर्वमाप्नोति सर्वमादत्ते सर्वमत्ति च तस्मादुच्यते आत्मेति। अथ कस्मादुच्यते महेश्वर इति। यस्मान्महत ईशः शब्दध्वन्या चात्मशक्त्या च महत ईशते तस्मादुच्यते महेश्वर इति। अथ कस्मादुच्यते दत्तात्रेय इति। यस्मात्सुदुश्चरं तपस्तप्यमानायात्रये पुत्रकामायातितरां तुष्टेन भगवता ज्योतिर्मयेनात्मैव दत्तो यस्माच्चानसूयायामत्रेस्तनयोऽभवत्तस्मादुच्यते दत्तात्रेय इति।

अथ योऽस्य निरुक्तानि वेद स सर्वं वेद। अथ यो ह वै विद्ययैनं परमुपास्ते सोऽहमिति स ब्रह्मविद्भवति ॥ अत्रैते श्लोका भवन्ति ॥ दत्तात्रेयं शिवं शान्तमिन्द्रनीलनिभं प्रभुम्। आत्ममायारतं देवमवधूतं गिदम्बरम् ॥१॥ भस्मोद्धूलितसर्वाङ्गं जटाजूटधरं विभुम्। चतुर्बाहुमुदाराङ्गं प्रफुल्लकमलेक्षणम् ॥२॥

ज्ञानयोगनिधिं विश्वगुरुं योगिजनप्रियम्। भक्तानुकम्पिनं सर्वसाक्षिणं सिद्धसेवितम् ॥३॥ एवं यः सततं ध्यायेद्देवदेवं सनातनम्। स मुक्तः सर्वपापेभ्यो निःश्रेयसमवाप्नुयात् ॥४॥ इत्योंसत्यमित्युपनिषत् ॥ इति तृतीयोऽध्यायः ॥३॥ भद्रं कर्णेभिरिति शान्तिः ॥

इति शाण्डिल्योपनिषत्समाप्ता ॥

२३. योगतत्त्वोपनिषत्

योगैश्वर्यं च कैवल्यं जायते यत्प्रसादतः।

तद्वैष्णवं योगतत्त्वं रामचन्द्रपदं भजे ॥

ॐ सह नाववत्विति शान्तिः ॥

योगतत्त्वं प्रवक्ष्यामि योगिनां हितकाम्यया। यच्छ्रुत्वा च पठित्वा च सर्वपापैः प्रमुच्यते ॥१॥ विष्णुर्नाम महायोगी महाभूतो महातपाः। तत्त्वमार्गे यथा दीपो दृश्यते पुरुषोत्तमः ॥२॥ तमाराध्य जगन्नाथं प्रणिपत्य पितामहः। पप्रच्छ योगतत्त्वं मे ब्रूहि चाष्टाङ्गसंयुतम् ॥३॥

तमुवाच हृषीकेशो वक्ष्यामि शृणु तत्त्वतः। सर्वे जीवाः सुखैर्दुःखैर्मायाजालेन वेष्टिताः ॥४॥ तेषां मुक्तिकरं मार्गं मायाजालनिकृन्तनम्। जन्ममृत्युजराव्याधिनाशनं मृत्युतारकम् ॥५॥ नानामार्गैस्तु दुष्प्रापं कैवल्यं परमं पदम्। पतिताः शास्त्रजालेषु प्रज्ञया तेन मोहिताः ॥६॥

अनिर्वाच्यं पदं वक्तुं न शक्यं तैः सुरैरपि। स्वात्मप्रकाशरूपं तत्किं शास्त्रेण प्रकाश्यते ॥७॥ निष्कलं निर्मलं शान्तं सर्वातीतं निरामयम्। तदेव जीवरूपेण पुण्यपापफलैर्वृतम् ॥८॥ परमात्मपदं नित्यं तत्कथं जीवतां गतम्। सर्वभावपदातीतं ज्ञानरूपं निरञ्जनम् ॥९॥

वारिवत्स्फुरितं तस्मिंस्तत्राहंकृतिरुत्थिता। पञ्चात्मकमभूतिपिण्डं धातुबद्धं गुणात्मकम् ॥१०॥ सुखदुःखैः समायुक्तं जीवभावनया कुरु। तेन जीवाभिधा प्रोक्ता

विशुद्धैः परमात्मनि ॥११॥ कामक्रोधभयं चापि मोहलोभमदो रजः। जन्म मृत्युश्च कार्पण्यं शोकस्तन्द्रा क्षुधा तृषा ॥१२॥

तृष्णा लज्जा भयं दुःखं विषादो हर्ष एव च। एभिर्दोषैर्विनिर्मुक्तः स जीवः केवलो मतः ॥१३॥ तस्माद्दोषविनाशार्थमुपायं कथयामि ते। योगहीनं कथं ज्ञानं मोक्षदं भवति ध्रुवम् ॥१४॥ योगो हि ज्ञानहीनस्तु न क्षमो मोक्षकर्मणि। तस्माज्ज्ञानं च योगं च मुमुक्षुर्दृढमभ्यसेत् ॥१५॥ अज्ञानादेव संसारो ज्ञानादेव विमुच्यते। ज्ञानस्वरूपमेवादौ ज्ञानं ज्ञेयैकसाधनम् ॥१६॥ ज्ञातं येन निजं रूपं कैवल्यं परमं पदम्। निष्कलं निर्मलं साक्षात्सच्चिदानन्दरूपकम् ॥१७॥ उत्पत्तिस्थितिसंहारस्फूर्तिज्ञानविवर्जितम्। एतज्ज्ञान-मिति प्रोक्तमथ योगं ब्रवीमि ते ॥१८॥

योगो हि बहुधा ब्रह्मन्भिद्यते व्यवहारतः। मन्त्रयोगो लयश्चैव हठोऽसौ राजयोगतः ॥१९॥ आरम्भश्च घटश्चैव तथा परिचयः स्मृतः। निष्पत्तिश्चेत्यवस्था च सर्वत्र परिकीर्तिता ॥२०॥ एतेषां लक्षणं ब्रह्मन्वक्ष्ये शृणु समासतः। मातृकादियुतं मन्त्रं द्वादशाब्दं तु यो जपेत् ॥२१॥ क्रमेण लभते ज्ञानमणिमादिगुणान्वितम् ॥ अल्पबुद्धिरिमं योगं सेवते साधकाधमः ॥२२। लययोगश्चित्तलयः कोटिशः परिकीर्तितः। गच्छंस्तिष्ठन्स्वपन्भुञ्जन्ध्यायेन्निष्कलमीश्वरम् ॥२३॥ स एव लययोगः स्याद्धठयोगमतः शृणु। समश्च नियमश्चैव आसनं प्राणसंयमः ॥२४॥

प्रत्याहारो धारणा च ध्यानं भ्रूमध्यमे हरिम्। समाधिः समतावस्था साष्टाङ्गो योग उच्यते ॥२५॥ महामुद्रा महाबन्धो महावेधश्च खेचरी। जालंधरोड्डियाणश्च मूलबन्धस्तथैव च।२६॥ दीर्घप्रणवसंधानं सिद्धान्तश्रवणं परम्। वज्रोली चामरोली च सहजोली त्रिधा मता ॥२७॥

एतेषां लक्षणं ब्रह्मन्प्रत्येकं शृणु तत्त्वतः। लघ्वाहारो यमेष्वेको मुख्या भवति नेतरः ॥२८॥ अहिंसा नियमेष्वेका मुख्या वै चतुरानन। सिद्धं पद्मं तथा सिंहं भद्रं चेति चतुष्टयम् ॥२९॥ प्रथमाभ्यासकाले तु विघ्नाः स्युश्चतुरानन्। आलस्य कत्थनं धूर्तगोष्टी मन्त्रादिसाधनम् ॥३०॥

धातुस्त्रीलौल्यकादीनि मृगतृष्णामयानि वै। ज्ञात्वा सुधीस्त्यजेत्सर्वा-न्विघ्नान्पुण्यप्रभावतः ॥३१॥ प्राणायामं ततः कुर्यात्पद्मासनगतः स्वयम्। सुशोभनं मठं कुर्यात्सूक्ष्मद्वारं तु निर्व्रणम् ॥३२॥ सुष्ठुं लिप्तं गोमयेन सुधया वा प्रयत्नतः। मत्कुणैर्मशवैर्लूतैर्वर्जितं च प्रयत्नतः ॥३३॥

दिने दिने च संमृष्टं संमार्जन्या विशेषतः। वासितं च सुगन्धेन धुपितं गुग्गुलादिभिः ॥३४॥ नात्युच्छ्रितं नातिनीचं चैलाजिनकुशोत्तरम्। तत्रोपविश्य मेधावी पद्मासनसमन्वितः ॥३५॥ ऋजुकायः प्राञ्जलिश्च प्रणमेदिष्टदेवताम्। ततो दक्षिणहस्तस्य अङ्गुष्ठेनैव पिङ्गलाम् ॥३६॥

निरुध्य पूरयेद्वायुमिडया तु शनैः शनैः। यथाशक्त्यविरोधेन ततः कुर्याच्च कुम्भकम् ॥३७॥ पुनस्त्यजेत्पिङ्गलया शनैरेव न वेगतः। पुनः पिङ्गलयापूर्य पूरयेदुदरं शनैः ॥३८॥ धारयित्वा यथाशक्ति रेचयेदिडया शनैः। यया त्यजेत्तयापूर्य धारयेदविरोधतः ॥३९॥

जानु प्रदक्षिणीकृत्य न द्रुतं न विलम्बितम्। अङ्गुलिस्फोटनं कुर्यात्सा मात्रा परिगीयते ॥४०॥ इडया वायुमारोप्य शनैः षोडशमात्रया। कुम्भयेत्पूरितं पश्चाच्चतुः षष्ट्या तु मात्रया ॥४१॥ रेचयेत्पिङ्गलानाड्या द्वात्रिंशन्मात्रया पुनः। पुनः पिङ्गलयापूर्य पूर्ववत्सुसमाहितः ॥४२॥

प्रातर्मध्यांदिने सायमर्धरात्रे च कुम्भकान्। शनैरशीतिपर्यन्तं चतुर्वारं समभ्यसेत् ॥४३॥ एवं मासत्रयाभ्यासान्नाडीशुद्धिस्ततो भवेत्। यदा तु नाडीशुद्धिः स्यात्तदा चिह्नानि बाह्यतः ॥४४॥

जायन्ते योगिनो देहे तानि वक्ष्याम्यशेषतः। शरीरलघुता दीप्तिर्जाठराग्निविवर्धनम् ॥४५॥ कृशत्वं च शरीरस्य तदा जायेत निश्चितम्। योगाविघ्नकराहारं वर्जयेद्योगवित्तमः ॥४६॥ लवणं सर्षपं चाम्लमुष्णं रूक्षं च तीक्ष्णकम्। शाकजातं रामठादि वह्निस्त्रीपथसेवनम् ॥४७॥

प्रातः स्नानोपवासादिकायक्लेशांश्च वर्जयेत्। अभ्यासकाले प्रथमं शस्तं क्षीराज्यभोजनम् ॥४८॥ गोधूममुद्गशाल्यन्नं योगवृद्धिकरं विदुः। ततः परं यथेष्टं तु शक्तः स्याद्वायुधारणे ॥४९॥ यथेष्टधारणाद्वायोः सिध्येत्केवलकुम्भकः। केवले कुम्भक सिद्धे रेचपूरविवर्जिते ॥५०॥

न तस्य दुर्लभं किंचिन्त्रिपु लोकेषु विद्यते। प्रस्वेदो जायते पूर्वं मर्दनं तेन कारयेत् ॥५१॥ ततोऽपि धारणाद्वायोः क्रमेणैव शनैः शनैः। कम्पो भवात देहस्य आसनस्थस्य देहिंनः ॥५२॥ ततोऽधिकतराभ्यासाद्दार्दुरी स्वेन जायते। यथा च दर्दुरो भाव उत्प्लुत्योत्प्लुत्य गच्छति ॥५३॥

पद्मासनस्थितो योगी तथा गच्छति भूतले। ततोऽधिकतराभ्यासाद्भूमित्यागश्च जायते ॥५४॥ पद्मासनस्थ एवासो भूमि हत्सृज्य वर्तते। आतमानुपचष्टाद्ध तथा सामर्थ्यमुद्भवेत् ॥५५॥ न दर्शयेच्च सामर्थ्यं दर्शन वीर्यवत्तरम्। स्वल्पं वा बहुधा दुःखं योगी न व्यथते तदा ॥५६॥

अल्पमूत्रपुरीषश्च स्वल्पनिद्रश्च जायते। कीलवो दृषिका लाला स्वेददुर्गन्धतानने ॥५७॥ एतानि सर्वथा तस्य न जायन्ते ततः परम्। ततोऽधिकतराभ्यासाद्बलमुत्पद्यते बहु ॥५८॥ येन भुचर सिद्धिः स्याद्भूचराणां जये क्षमः। व्याघ्रो वा शरभो वापि गजो गवय एव वा ॥५९॥ सिंहो वा योगिना तेन म्रियन्ते हस्तताडिताः। कन्दर्पस्य यथा रूपं तथा स्यादपि योगिनः ॥६०॥

तद्रूपवशगा नार्यः काङ्क्षन्ते तस्य सङ्गमम्। यदि सङ्गं करोत्येष तस्य बिन्दुक्षयो भवेत् ॥६१॥ वर्जयित्वा स्त्रियाः सङ्गं कुर्यादभ्यासमादरात्। योगिनोऽङ्गे सुगन्धश्च जायते बिन्दुधारणात् ॥६२॥ ततो रहस्युपाविष्टः प्रणवं प्लुतमात्रया। जपेत्पूर्वार्जितानां तु पापानां नाशहेतवे ॥६३॥

सर्वविघ्नहरो मन्त्रः प्रणवः सर्वदोषहा। एवमभ्यासयोगेन सिद्धिरारम्भसंभवा ॥६४॥ ततो भवेद्धठावस्था पवनाभ्यासतत्परा। प्राणोऽपानो मनो बुद्धिर्जीवात्मपरमात्मनोः ॥६५॥ अन्योन्यस्याविरोधेन एकता घटते यदा। घटावस्थेति सा प्रोक्ता तच्चिह्नानि ब्रवीम्यहम् ॥६६॥

पूर्वं यः कथितोऽभ्यासश्चतुर्थांशं परिग्रहेत्। दिवा वा यदि वा सायं याममात्रं समभ्यसेत् ॥६७॥ एकवारं प्रतिदिनं कुर्यात्केवलकुम्भकम्। इन्द्रियाणीन्द्रियार्थेभ्यो यत्प्रत्याहरणं स्फुटम् ॥६८॥ योगी कुम्भकमास्थाय प्रत्याहारः स उच्यते। यद्यत्पश्यति चक्षुर्भ्यां तत्तदात्मेति भावयेत् ॥६९॥

यद्यच्छृणोति कर्णाभ्यां तत्तदात्मेति भावयेत्। लभते नासया यद्यत्तत्तदात्मेति भावयेत् ॥७०॥ जिह्वया यद्रसं ह्यत्ति तत्तदात्मेति भावयेत्। त्वचा यद्यत्स्पृशेद्योगी तत्तदात्मेति भावयेत् ॥७१॥ एवं ज्ञानेन्द्रियाणां तु तत्तत्सौख्यं सुसाधयेत्। याममात्रं प्रतिदिनं योगी यत्नादतन्द्रितः ॥७२॥ यथा वा चित्तसामर्थ्यं जायते योगिनो ध्रुवम्। दूरश्रुतिर्दूरदृष्टिः क्षणाद्दूरागमस्तथा ॥७३॥

वाक्सिद्धिः कामरूपत्वमदृश्यकरणी तथा। मलमूत्रप्रलेपेन लोहादेः स्वर्णता भवेत् ॥७४॥ खे गतिस्तस्य जायेत संतताभ्यासयोगतः। सदा बुद्धिमता भाव्यं योगिना योगसिद्धये ॥७५॥ एते विघ्ना महासिद्धेर्न रमेत्तेषु बुद्धिमान्। न दर्शयेत्स्वसामर्थ्यं यस्यकस्यापि योगिराट् ॥७६॥

यथा मूढो यथा मूर्खो यथा बधिर एव वा। तथा वर्तेत लोकस्य स्वसामर्थ्यस्य गुप्तये ॥७७॥ शिष्याश्च स्वस्वकार्येषु प्रार्थयन्ति न संशयः। तत्तत्कर्मकरव्यग्रः स्वाभ्यासेऽविस्मृतो भवेत् ॥७८॥ अविस्मृत्य गुरोर्वाक्यमभ्यसेत्तदहर्निशम्। एवं भवेद्घठावस्था संतताभ्यासयोगतः ॥७९॥ अनभ्यासवतश्चैव वृथागोष्ठ्या न सिद्ध्यति। तस्मात्सर्वप्रयत्नेन योगमेव सदाभ्यसेत् ॥८०॥

ततः परिचयावस्था जायतेऽभ्यासयोगतः। वायुः परिचितो यत्नादग्निना सह कुण्डलीम् ॥८१॥ भावयित्वा सुषुम्नायां प्रविशेदनिरोधतः। वायुना सह चित्तं च प्रविशेच्च महापथम् ॥८२॥ यस्य चित्तं स्वपवनं सुषुम्नां प्रविशेदिह। भूमिरापोऽनलो वायुराकाशश्चेति पञ्चकः ॥८३॥ येषु पञ्चसु देवानां धारणा पञ्चधोच्यते। पादादिजानुपर्यन्तं पृथिवीस्थानमुच्यते ॥८४॥

पृथिवी चतुरस्रं च पीतवर्णं लवर्णकम्। पार्थिवे वायुमारोप्य लकारेण समन्वितम् ॥८५॥ ध्यायंश्चतुर्भुजाकारं चतुर्वक्त्रं हिरण्मयम्। धारयेत्पञ्च घटिकाः पृथिवीजयमाप्नुयात् ॥८६॥ पृथिवीयोगतो मृत्युर्न भवेदस्य योगिनः। आजानोः पायुपर्यन्तमपां स्थानं प्रकीर्तितम् ॥८७॥

आपोऽर्धचन्द्रं शुक्लं च वंबीजं परिकीर्तितम्। वारुणे वायुमारोप्य वकारेण समन्वितम् ॥८८॥ स्मरन्नारायणं देवं चतुर्बाहुं किरीटिनम्। शुद्धस्फटिकसंकाशं पीतवाससमच्युतम् ॥८९॥ धारयेत्पञ्च घटिकाः सर्वपापैः प्रमुच्यते। ततो जलाद्भयं नास्ति जले मृत्युर्न विद्यते ॥९०॥

आपायोर्हृदयान्तं च वह्निस्थानं प्रकीर्तितम्। वह्निस्त्रिकोणं रक्तं च रेफाक्षरसमुद्भवम् ॥९१॥ वह्नौ चानिलमारोप्य रेफाक्षरसमुज्ज्वलम्। त्रियक्षं वरदं रुद्रं तरुणादित्यसंनिभम् ॥९२॥

भस्मोद्धूलितसर्वाङ्गं सुप्रसन्नमनुस्मरन्। धारयेत्पञ्च घटिका वह्निनासौ न दाह्यते ॥९३॥ न दह्यते शरीरं च प्रविष्टस्याग्निमण्डले। आहृदयाद्भ्रूवोर्मध्यं वायुस्थानं

प्रकीर्तितम् ॥९४॥ वायुः षट्कोणकं कृष्णं यकाराक्षरभासुरम् मारुतं मरुतां स्थाने यकाराक्षरभासुरम् ॥९५॥ धारयेत्तत्र सर्वज्ञमीश्वरं विश्वतोमुखम्। धारयेत्पञ्च घटिका वायुवद्व्योमगो भवेत् ॥९६॥

मरणं न तु वायोश्च भयं भवति योगिनः। आभ्रूमध्यात्तु मूर्धान्तमाकाशस्थानमुच्यते ॥९७॥ व्योम वृत्तं च धूम्रं च हकाराक्षरभासुरम्। आकाशे वायुमारोप्य हकारोपरि शंकरम् ॥९८॥ बिन्दूरूपं महादेवं व्योमाकारं सदाशिवम्। शुद्धस्फटिकसंकाशं धृतबालेन्दुमौलिनम् ॥९९॥

पञ्चवक्त्रयुतं सौम्यं दशबाहुं त्रिलोचनम्। सर्वायुधैर्धृताकारं सर्वभूषणभूषितम् ॥१००॥ उमार्धदेहं वरदं सर्वकारणकारणम्। आकाशधारणात्तस्य खेचरत्वं भवेद्ध्रुवम् ॥१०१॥ यत्रकुत्र स्थितो वापि सुखमत्यन्तमश्नुते। एवं च धारणाः पञ्च कुर्याद्योगी विचक्षणः ॥१०२॥

ततो दृढशरीरः स्यान्मृत्युस्तस्य न विद्यते। ब्रह्मणः प्रलयेनापि न सीदति महामतिः ॥१०३॥ समभ्यसेत्तथा ध्यानं घटिकाषष्टिमेव च। वायुं निरुध्य चाकाशे देवतामिष्टदामिति ॥१०४॥ सगुणं ध्यानमेतत्स्यादणिमादिगुणप्रदम्। निर्गुणध्यानयुक्तस्य समाधिश्च ततो भवेत् ॥१०५॥

दिनद्वादशकेनैव समाधिं समवाप्नुयात्। वायुं निरुध्य मेधावी जीवन्मुक्तो भवत्ययम् ॥१०६॥ समाधिः समतावस्था जीवात्मपरमात्मनोः। यदि स्वदेहमुत्स्रष्टुमिच्छा चेदुत्सृजेत्स्वयम् ॥१०७॥ परब्रह्मणि लीयेत न तस्योत्क्रान्तिरिष्यते। अथ नो चेत्समुत्स्रष्टुं स्वशरीरं प्रियं यदि ॥१०८॥

सर्वलोकेषु विहरन्नणिमादिगुणान्वितः। कदाचित्स्वेच्छया देवो भूत्वा स्वर्गे महीयते ॥१०९॥ मनुष्यो वापि यक्षो वा स्वेच्छयापीक्षणाद्भवेत्। सिंहो व्याघ्रो गजो वाश्वः स्वेच्छया बहुतामियात् ॥११०॥ यथेष्टमेव वर्तेत यद्वा योगी महेश्वरः। अभ्यासभेदतो भेदः फलं तु सममेव हि ॥१११॥ पार्ष्णिं वामस्य पादस्य योनिस्थाने नियोजयेत्। प्रसार्य दक्षिणं पादं हस्ताभ्यां धारयेद्दृढम् ॥११२॥

चुबुकं हृदि विन्यस्य पूरयेद्वायुना पुनः। कुम्भकेन यथाशक्ति धारयित्वा तु रेचयेत् ॥११३॥ वामाङ्गेन समभ्यस्य दक्षाङ्गेन ततोऽभ्यसेत्। प्रसारितस्तु यः पादस्तमूरूपरि नामयेत् ॥११४॥ अयमेव महाबन्ध उभयत्रैवमभ्यसेत्। महाबन्धस्थितो योगी कृत्वा पूरकमेकधीः ॥११५॥

वायुना गतिमावृत्य निभृतं कर्णमुद्रया। पुटद्वयं समाक्रम्य वायुः स्फुरति सत्वरम् ॥११६॥ अयमेव महावेधः सिद्धैरभ्यस्यतेऽनिशम्। अन्तःकपालकुहरे जिह्वां व्यावृत्य धारयेत् ॥११७॥

भ्रूमध्यदृष्टिरप्येषा मुद्रा भवति खेचरी कण्ठमाकुञ्चय हृदये स्थापयेद्दृढया धिया ॥११८॥ बन्धो जालंधराख्योऽयं मृत्युमातङ्गकेसरी। बन्धो येन सुषुम्नायां प्राणस्तूड्डीयते यतः ॥११९॥ उड्यानाख्यो हि बन्धोऽयं योगिभिः समुदाहृतः। पार्ष्णिभागेन संपीड्य योनिमाकुञ्चयेद्दृढम् ॥१२०॥

अपानमूर्ध्वमुत्थाप्य योनिबन्धोऽयमुच्यते। प्राणापानौ नादबिन्दू मूलबन्धेन चैकताम् ॥१२१॥ गत्वा योगस्य संसिद्धिं यच्छतो नात्र संशयः। करणी विपरीताख्या सर्वव्याधिविनाशिनी ॥१२२॥ नित्यमभ्यासयुक्तस्य जाठराग्निविवर्धनी। आहारो बहुलस्तस्य संपाद्यः साधकस्य च ॥१२३॥

अल्पाहारो यदि भवेदग्निर्देहं हरेत्क्षणात्। अधःशिरश्चोर्ध्वपादः क्षणं स्यात्प्रथमे दिने ॥१२४॥ क्षणाच्च किंचिदधिकमभ्यसेत्तु दिनेदिने। वली च पलितं चैव षण्मासार्धान्न दृश्यते ॥१२५॥ याममात्रं तु यो नित्यमभ्यसेत्स तु कालजित्। वज्रोलीमभ्यसेद्यस्तु स योगी सिद्धिभाजनम् ॥१२६॥ लभ्यते यदि तस्यैव योगसिद्धिः करे स्थिता। अतीतानागतं वेत्ति खेचरी च भवेद्ध्रुवम् ॥१२७॥

अमरीं यः पिबेन्नित्यं नस्यं कुर्वन्दिने दिने। वज्रोलीमभ्यसेन्नित्यममरोलीति कथ्यते ॥१२८॥ ततो भवेद्राजयोगो नान्तरा भवति ध्रुवम्। यदा तु राजयोगेन निष्पन्ना योगिभिः क्रिया ॥१२९॥ तदा विवेः क्वैराग्यं जायते योगिनो ध्रुवम्। विष्णुर्नाम महायोगी महाभूतो महातपा ॥१३०॥

तत्त्वमार्गे यथा दीपो दृश्यते पुरुषोत्तमः। यः स्तनः पूर्वपीतस्तं निष्पीड्य मुदमश्नुते ॥१३१॥ यस्माज्जातो भगात्पूर्वं तस्मिन्नेव भगे रमन्। या माता सा पुनर्भार्या या भार्या मातरेव हि ॥१३२॥ यः पिता स पुनः पुत्रो यः पुत्रः स पुनः पिता। एवं संचारचक्रं कूपचक्रेण घटा इव ॥१३३॥

भ्रमन्तो योनिजन्मानि श्रुत्वा लोकान्समश्नुते। त्रयो लोकास्त्रयो वेदास्तिस्रः संध्यास्त्रयः स्वराः ॥१३४॥ त्रयोऽग्नयश्च त्रिगुणाः स्थिताः सर्वे त्रयाक्षरे। त्रयाणामक्षराणां च योऽधीतेऽप्यर्धमक्षरम् ॥१३५॥

तेन सर्वमिदं प्रोतं तत्सत्यं तत्परं पदम्। पुष्पमध्ये यथा गन्धः पयोमध्ये यता घृतम् ॥१३६॥ तिलमध्ये यथा तैलं पाषाणेष्विव काञ्चनम्। हृदि स्थाने स्थितं पद्मं तस्य वक्रमधोमुखम् ॥१३७॥

ऊर्ध्वनालमधोबिन्दूस्तस्य मध्ये स्थितं मनः। अकारे रेचितं पद्ममुकारेणैव भिद्यते ॥१३८॥ मकारे लभते नादमर्धमात्रा तु निश्चला। शुद्धस्फटिकसंकाशं निष्कलं पापनाशनम् ॥१३९॥ लभते योगयुक्तात्मा पुरुषस्तत्परं पदम्। कूर्मः स्वपाणिपादादिशिरश्चात्मनि धारयेत् ॥१४०॥

एवं द्वारेषु सर्वेषु वायुपूरितरेचितः। निषिद्धं तु नवद्वारे ऊर्ध्वं प्राङ्निश्वसंस्तथा ॥१४१॥ घटमध्ये यथा दीपो निवातं कुम्भकं विदुः। निषिद्धैर्नवभिद्वरिर्निर्जने निरुपद्रवे ॥१४२॥

निश्चितं त्वात्ममात्रेणावशिष्टं योगसेवयेत्युपनिषत् ॥ ॐ सह नाववत्विति शान्तिः ॥

इति योगतत्त्वोपनिषत्समाप्ता ॥

२४. ध्यानबिन्दूपनिषत्

ध्यात्वा यद्ब्रह्ममात्रं ते स्वावशेषधिया ययुः ।
योगतत्त्वज्ञानफलं तत्स्वमात्रं विचिन्तये ॥

ॐ सह नाववत्विति शान्तिः ॥

यदि शैलसमं पापं विस्तीर्णं बहुयोजनम् । भिद्यते ध्यानयोगेन नान्यो भेदः कदाचन ॥१ ॥ बीजाक्षरं परं बिन्दुं नादं तस्योपरि स्थितम् । सशब्दं चाक्षरे क्षीणे निःशब्दं परमं पदम् ॥२ ॥ अनाहतं तु यच्छब्दं तस्य शब्दस्य यत्परम् । तत्परं बिन्दते यस्तु स योगी छिन्नसंशयः ॥३ ॥ वालाग्रशतसाहस्रं तस्य भागस्य भागिनः । तस्य भागस्य भागार्धं तत्क्षये तु निरञ्जनम् ॥४ ॥

पुष्पमध्ये यथा गन्धः पयोमध्ये यथा घृतम् । तिलमध्ये यथा तैलं पाषाणेष्विव काञ्चनम् ॥५ ॥ एवं सर्वाणि भूतानि मणौ सूत्र इवात्मनि । स्थिरबुद्धिरसंसूढो ब्रह्मविद्ब्रह्मणि स्थितः ॥६ ॥ तिलानां तु यथा तैलं पुष्पे गन्ध इवाश्रितः । पुरुषस्य शरीरे तु सबाह्याभ्यन्तरे स्थितः ॥७ ॥

वृक्षं तु सकलं विद्याच्छाया तस्यैव निष्कला । सकले निष्कले भावे सर्वत्रात्मा व्यवस्थितः ॥८ ॥ ओमित्येकाक्षरं ब्रह्म ध्येयं सर्वमुमुक्षुभिः । पृथिव्यग्निश्च ऋग्वेदो भूरित्येव पितामहः ॥९ ॥ अकारे तु लयं प्राप्ते प्रथमे प्रणवांशके अन्तरिक्षं यजुर्वायुर्भुवो विष्णुर्जनार्दनः ॥१० ॥ उकारे तु लयं प्राप्ते द्वितीये प्रणवांशके । द्यौः सूर्यः सामवेदश्च स्वरित्येव महेश्वरः ॥११ ॥

मकारे तु लयं प्राप्ते तृतीये प्रणवांशके । अकारः पीतवर्णः स्याद्रजोगुण उदीरितः ॥१२ ॥ उकारः सात्त्विकः शुक्लो मकारः कृष्णतामसः । अष्टाङ्गं च चतुष्पादं त्रिस्थानं पञ्चदैवतम् ॥१३ ॥ ओंकारं यो न जानाति ब्राह्मणो न भवेत्तु सः । प्रणवो धनुः शरो ह्यात्मा ब्रह्म तल्लक्ष्यमुच्यते ॥१४ ॥

अप्रमत्तेन वेद्धव्यं शरवत्तन्मयो भवेत् । निवर्तन्ते क्रियाः सर्वास्तस्मिन्दृष्टे परावरे ॥१५ ॥ ओंकारप्रभवा देवा ओंकारप्रभवाः स्वराः । ओंकारप्रभवं सर्वं त्रैलोक्यं सचराचरम् ॥१६ ॥ ह्रस्वो दहति पापानि दीर्घः संपत्प्रदोऽव्ययः । अर्धमात्रासमा युक्तः प्रणवो मोक्षदायकः ॥१७ ॥

तैलधारामिवाच्छिन्नं दीर्घघण्टानिनादवत् । अवाच्यं प्रणवस्याग्रं यस्तं वेद स वेदवित् ॥१८ ॥ हृत्पद्मकर्णिकामध्ये स्थिरदीपनिभाकृतिम् । अङ्गुष्ठमात्रमचलं ध्यायेदोंकारमीश्वरम् ॥१९ ॥ इडया वायुमापूर्य पूरयित्वोदरस्थितम् । ओंकारं देहमध्यस्थं ध्यायेज्ज्वालावलीवृतम् ॥२० ॥

ब्रह्मा पूरक इत्युक्तो विष्णुः कुम्भक उच्यते । रेचो रुद्र इति प्रोक्तः प्राणायामस्य देवताः ॥२१ ॥ आत्मानमरणिं कृत्वा प्रणवं चोत्तरारणिम् । ध्याननिर्मथनाभ्यासादेव पश्येन्निगूढवत् ॥२२ ॥ ओंकारध्वनिनादेन वायोः संहरणान्तिकम् । यावद्बलं समादध्यात्सम्यङ्नादलयावधि ॥२३ ॥ गमागमस्थं गमनादिशून्यमोंकारमेकं रविकोटिदीप्तिम् । पश्यन्ति ये सर्वजनान्तरस्थं हंसात्मकं ते विरजा भवन्ति ॥२४ ॥

यन्मनस्त्रिजगत्सृष्टिस्थितिव्यसनकर्मकृत्। तन्मनो विलयं याति तद्विष्णोः परम पदम् ॥२५॥ अष्टपत्रं तु हृत्पद्मं द्वात्रिंशत्केसरान्वितम्। तस्य मध्ये स्थितो भानुर्भानुमध्यगतः शशी ॥२६॥ शशिमध्यगतो वह्निर्वह्निमध्यगता प्रभा। प्रभामध्यगतं पीठं नानारत्नप्रवेष्टितम् ॥२७॥ तस्य मध्यगतं देवं वासुदेवं निरञ्जनम्। श्रीवत्सकौस्तुभोरस्कं मुक्तामणिविभूषितम् ॥२८॥ शुद्धस्फटिकसंकाशं चन्द्रकोटिसमप्रभम्। एवं ध्यायेन्महाविष्णुमेवं वा विनयान्वितः ॥२९॥

अतसीपुष्पसंकाशं नाभिस्थाने प्रतिष्ठितम्। चतुर्भुजं महाविष्णुं पूरकेण विचिन्तयेत् ॥३०॥ कुम्भकेन हृदि स्थाने चिन्तयेत्कमलासनम्। ब्रह्माणं रक्तगौराभं चतुर्वक्रं पितामहम् ॥३१॥ रेचकेन तु विद्यात्मा ललाटस्थं त्रिलोचनम्। शुद्धस्फटिकसंकाशं निष्कलं पापनाशनम् ॥३२॥

अब्जपत्रमधःपुष्पमूर्ध्वनालमधोमुखम्। कदलीपुष्पसंकाशं सर्ववेदमयं शिवम् ।३३। शतारं शतपत्राढयं विकीर्णाम्बुजकर्णिकम्। तत्रार्कचन्द्रवह्नीनामुपर्यु-परिचिन्तयेत् ॥३४॥ पद्मस्योद्घाटनं कृत्वा बोधचन्द्राग्निसूर्यकम्। तस्य हृद्बीजमाहृत्य आत्मानं चरते ध्रुवम् ॥३५॥ त्रिस्थानं च त्रिमात्रं च त्रिब्रह्म च त्रयाक्षरम्। त्रिमात्रमर्धमात्रं वा यस्तं वेद स वेदवित् ॥३६॥

तैलधारामिवाच्छिन्नदीर्घघण्टानिनादवत्। बिन्दुनादकलातीतं यस्तं वेद स वेदवित् ॥३७॥ यथैवोत्पलनालेन तोयमाकर्षयेन्नरः। तथैवोत्कर्षयेद्वायुं योगी योगपथे स्थितः ॥३८॥ अर्धमात्रात्मकं कृत्वा कोशीभूतं तु पङ्कजम्। कर्षयेन्नालमात्रेण भ्रुवोर्मध्ये लयं नयेत् ॥३९॥ भ्रुवोर्मध्ये ललाटे तु नासिकायास्तु मूलतः। जानीयादमृतं स्थानं तद्ब्रह्मायतनं महत् ॥४०॥ आसनं प्राणसंरोधः प्रत्याहारश्च धारणा। ध्यानं समाधिरेतानि योगाङ्गानि भवन्ति षट् ॥४१॥ आसनानि च तावन्ति यावन्त्यो जीवजातयः। एतेषामतुलान्भेदा- न्विजानाति महेश्वरः ॥४२॥

छिद्रं भद्रं तथा सिंहं पद्मं चेति चतुष्टयम्। आधारं प्रथमं चक्रं स्वाधिष्ठानं द्वितीयकम् ॥४३॥ योनिस्थानं तयोर्मध्ये कामरूप निगद्यते। आधाराख्ये गुदस्थाने पङ्कजं यच्चतुर्दलम् ॥४४॥ तन्मध्ये प्रोच्यते योनिः कामाख्या सिद्धवन्दिता। योनिमध्ये स्थितं लिङ्गं पश्चिमाभिमुखं तथा ॥४५॥

मस्तके मणिवद्भिन्नं यो जानाति स योगवित्। तप्तचामीकराकारं तडिल्लेखेव विस्फुरत् ॥४६॥ चतुरस्रमुपर्यग्नेरधो मेढ्रात्प्रतिष्ठितम्। स्वशब्देन भवेत्प्राणः स्वाधिष्ठानं तदाश्रयम् ॥४७॥ स्वाधिष्ठानं ततश्चक्रं मेढ्रमेव निगद्यते। मणिवत्तन्तुना यत्र वायुना पूरितं वपुः ॥४८॥ तन्नाभिमण्डलं चक्रं प्रोच्यते मणिपूरकम्। द्वादशारमहाचक्रे पुण्यपापनियन्त्रितः ॥४९॥ तावज्जीवो भ्रमत्येवं यावत्तत्त्वं न विन्दति। ऊर्ध्वं मेढ्रादथो नाभेः कन्दो योऽस्ति खगाण्डवत् ॥५०॥ तत्र नाड्यः समुत्पन्नाः सहस्राणि द्विसप्ततिः। तेषु नाडीसहस्रेषु द्विसप्ततिरुदाहृताः ॥५१॥

प्रधानाः प्राणवाहिन्यो भूयस्तत्र दश स्मृताः। इडा च पिङ्गला चैव सुषुम्ना च तृतीयका ॥५२॥ गान्धारी हस्तिजिह्वा च पूषा चैव यशस्विनी। अलम्बुसा कुहूरत्र शङ्खिनी दशमी स्मृता ॥५३॥ एवं नाडीमयं चक्रं विज्ञेयं योगिना सदा। सततं प्राणवाहिन्यः सोमसूर्याग्निदेवताः ॥५४॥

इडापिङ्गलासुषुम्नास्तिस्रो नाड्यः प्रकीर्तिताः । इडा वामे स्थिता भागे पिङ्गला दक्षिणे स्थिता ॥५५ ॥ सुषुम्ना मध्यदेशे तु प्राणमार्गास्त्रयः स्मृताः । प्राणोऽपानः समानश्चोदानो व्यानस्तथैव च ॥५६ ॥ नागः कूर्मः कृकरको देवदत्तो धनंजयः । प्राणाद्याः पञ्च विख्याता नागाद्याः पञ्च वायवः ॥५७ ॥ एते नाडीसहस्रेषु वर्तन्ते जीवरूपिणः । प्राणापानवशो जीवो ह्यधश्चोर्ध्वं प्रधावति ॥५८ ॥

वामदक्षिणमार्गेण चञ्चलत्वान्न दृश्यते। आक्षिप्तो भुजदण्डेन यथोच्चलति कन्दुकः ॥५९ ॥ प्राणापानसमाक्षिप्तस्तद्वज्जीवो न विश्रमेत्। अपानात्कर्षति प्राणोऽपानः प्राणाच्च कर्षति ॥६० ॥ खगरज्जुवदित्येतद्यो जानाति स योगवित्। हकारेण बहिर्याति सकारेण विशेत्पुनः ॥६१ ॥ हंसहंसेत्यमुं मन्त्रं जीवो जपति सर्वदा । शतानि षट्दिवारात्रं सहस्राण्येकविंशतिः ॥६२ ॥ एतत्संख्यान्वितं मन्त्रं जीवो जपति सर्वदा। अजपा नाम गायत्री योगिनां मोक्षदा सदा ॥६३ ॥ अस्याः संकल्पमात्रेण नरः पापैः प्रमुच्यते । अनया सदृशी विद्या अनया सदृशो जपः ॥६४ ॥

अनया सदृशं पुण्यं न भूतं न भविष्यति। येन मार्गेण गन्तव्यं ब्रह्मस्थानं निरामयम् ॥६५ ॥ मुखेनाच्छाद्य तद्द्वारं प्रसुप्ता परमेश्वरी। प्रबुद्धा वह्नियोगेन मनसा मरुता सह ॥६६ ॥ सूचिवद्गुणमादाय व्रजत्यूर्ध्वं सुषुम्नया। उद्घाटयेत्कपाटं तु यथा कुञ्चिकया हठात् ॥६७ ॥ कुण्डलिन्या तया योगी मोक्षद्वारं विभेदयेत् ॥६८ ॥

कृत्वा संपुटितौ करौ दृढतरं बध्वाथ पद्मासनं गाढं वक्षसि सन्निधाय चुबुकं ध्यानं च तच्चेतसि। वारंवारमपातमूर्ध्वमनिलं प्रोच्चारयन्पूरितं मुञ्चन्प्राणमुपैति बोधमतुलं शक्तिप्रभावान्नरः ॥६९ ॥ पद्मासनस्थितो योगी नाडीद्वारेषु पूरयन् । मारुतं कुम्भयन्यस्तु स मुक्तो नात्र संशयः ॥७० ॥ अङ्गानां मर्दनं कृत्वा श्रमजातेन वारिणा । कट्वम्ललवणत्यागी क्षीरपानरतः सुखी ॥७१ ॥ ब्रह्मचारी मिताहारी योगी योगपरायणः । अब्दादूर्ध्वं भवेत्सिद्धो नात्र कार्या विचारणा ॥७२ ॥

कन्दोर्ध्वकुण्डली शक्तिः स योगी सिद्धिभाजनम्। अपानप्राणयोरैक्यं क्षयान्मूत्र-पुरीषयोः ॥७३ ॥ युवा भवति वृद्धोऽपि सततं मूलबन्धनात्। पार्ष्णिभागेन संपीड्य योनिमाकुञ्चयेद्गुदम् ॥७४ ॥ अपानमूर्ध्वमुत्कृष्य मूलबन्धोऽयमुच्यते। उड्याणं कुरुते यस्मादविश्रान्तमहाखगः ॥७५ ॥ उड्डियाणं तदेव स्यात्तत्र बन्धो विधीयते । उदरे पश्चिमं ताणं नाभेरुर्ध्वं तु कारयेत् ॥७६ ॥

उड्डियाणोऽप्ययं बन्धो मृत्युमातङ्गकेसरी। बध्नाति हि शिरोजातमधोगामिन-भोजलम् ॥७७ ॥ ततो जालन्धरो बन्धः कर्मदुःखौघनाशनः। जालन्धरे कृते बन्धो कर्णसंकोचलक्षणे ॥७८ ॥ न पीयूषं पतत्यग्नो न च वायुः प्रधावति। कपालकुहरे जिह्वा प्रविष्टा विपरीतगा ॥७९ ॥

भ्रुवोरन्तर्गता दृष्टिर्मुद्रा भवति खेचरी। न रोगो मरणं तस्य न निद्रा न क्षुधा तृषा ॥८० ॥ न च मूर्च्छा भरेत्तस्य यो मुद्रा वेत्ति खेचरीम् पीड्यते न च रोगेण लिप्यते न च कर्मणा ॥८१ ॥ बध्यते न च कालेन यस्य मुद्रास्ति खेचरी। चित्तं चरति खे यस्माज्जिह्वा भवति खेगता ॥८२ ॥

तेनैषा खेचरी नाम मुद्रा सिद्धनमस्कृता। खेचर्या मुद्रया यस्य लम्बिकोर्ध्वतः ॥८३ ॥ बिन्दुः क्षरति नो यस्य कामिन्यालिङ्गितस्य च। यावद्बिन्दुः स्थितो देहे तावन्मृत्युभयं कुतः ॥८४ ॥ यावद्बद्धा नभोमुद्रा तावद्बिन्दुर्न गच्छति। गलितोऽपि यदा बिन्दुः संप्राप्तो योनिमण्डले ॥८५ ॥

व्रजत्यूर्ध्वं हठाच्छक्त्या निबद्धो योनिमुद्रया। स एव द्विविधो बिन्दुः पाण्डरो लोहितस्तथा ॥८६ ॥ पाण्डरं शुक्रमित्याहुर्लोहिताख्यं महारजः। विद्रुमद्रुमसंकाशं योनिस्थाने स्थितं रजः ॥८७ ॥ शशिस्थाने वसेद्बिन्दुस्तयोरैक्यं सुदुर्लभम्। बिन्दुः शिवो रजः शक्तिर्बिन्दुरिन्दु रजो रविः ॥८८ ॥

उभयोः संगमादेव प्राप्यते परमं वपुः। वायुना शक्तिचालेन प्रेरितं खे यथा रजः ॥८९ ॥ रविणैकत्वमायाति भवेद्दिव्यं वपुस्तदा। शुक्लं चन्द्रेण संयुक्तं रजः सूर्यसमन्वितम् ॥९० ॥ द्वयोः समरसीभावं यो जानाति स योगवित्। शोधनं मलजालानां घटनं चन्द्रसूर्ययोः ॥९१ ॥ रसानां शोषणं सम्यङ्महामुद्राभिधीयते ॥९२ ॥

वक्षोन्यस्तहनुर्निपीड्य सुषिरं योनेश्च वामाङ्घ्रिणा हस्ताभ्यामनुधारयन्प्रविततं पादं तथा दक्षिणम्। आपूर्य श्वसनेन कुक्षियुगलं बध्वा शनै रेचयेदेषा पातकनाशिनी ननु महामुद्रा नृणां प्रोच्यते ॥९३ ॥ अथात्मनिर्णयं व्याख्यास्ये ॥ हृदिस्थाने अष्टदलपद्मं वर्तते तन्मध्ये रेखावलयं कृत्वा जीवात्मरूपं ज्योतीरूपमणुमात्रं वर्तते तस्मिन्सर्वं प्रतिष्ठितं भवति सर्वं जानाति सर्वं करोति सर्वमेतच्चरितमहं कर्ताऽहं भोक्ता सुखी दुःखी काणः खञ्जो बधिरो मूकः कृशः स्थूलोऽनेन प्रकारेण स्वतन्त्रवादेन वर्तते ॥

पूर्वदले विश्रमते पूर्वं दलं श्वेतवर्णं तदा भक्तिपुरःसरं धर्मे मतिर्भवति ॥ यदाऽग्नेयदले विश्रमते तदाग्नेयदलं रक्तवर्णं तदा निद्रालस्यमतिर्भवति ॥ यदा दक्षिणदले विश्रमते तद्दक्षिणदलं कृष्णवर्ण तदा द्वेषकोपमतिर्भवति ॥ यदा नैर्ऋतदले विश्रमते तन्नैर्ऋतदलं नीलवर्णं तदा पापकर्महिंसामतिर्भवति ॥

यदा पश्चिमदले विश्रमते तत्पश्चिमदलं स्फटिकवर्णं तदा क्रीडाविनोदे मतिर्भवति ॥ यदा वायव्यदले विश्रमते वायव्यदलं माणिक्यवर्णं तदा गमनचलनवैराग्यमतिर्भवति ॥ योदत्तरदले विश्रमते तदुत्तरदलं पीतवर्णं तदा सुखशृङ्गारमतिर्भवति ॥ यदेशानदले विश्रमते तदीशानदलं वैडूर्यवर्णं तदा दानादिकृपामतिर्भवति ॥

यदा संधिसंधिषु मतिर्भवति तदा वातपित्तश्लेष्ममहाव्याधिप्रकोपो भवति ॥ यदा मध्ये तिष्ठति तदा सर्वं जानाति गायति नृत्यति पठत्यानन्दं करोति ॥ यदा नेत्रश्रमो भवति श्रमनिर्भरणार्थं प्रथमरेखावलयं कृत्वा मध्ये निमज्जनं कुरुते प्रथमरेखाबन्धूकपुष्पवर्णं तदा निद्रावस्था भवति ॥

निद्रावस्थामध्ये स्वप्नावस्था भवति ॥ स्वप्नावस्थामध्ये दृष्टं श्रुतमनुमानसंभववार्ता इत्यादिकल्पनां करोति तदादिश्रमो भवति ॥ श्रमनिर्हरणार्थं द्वितीयरेखावलयं कृत्वा मध्ये निमज्जनं कुरुते द्वितीयरेखा इन्द्रकोपवर्णं तदा सुषुप्त्यवस्था भवति सुषुप्तौ केवलपरमेश्वरसंबन्धिनी बुद्धिर्भवति नित्यबोधस्वरूपा भवति पश्चात्परमेश्वरस्वरूपेण प्राप्तिर्भवति ॥

तृतीयरेखावलयं कृत्वा मध्ये निमज्जनं कुरुते तृतीयरेखा पद्मरागवर्णं तदा तुरीयावस्था भवति तुरीये केवलपरमात्मसंबन्धिनी भवति नित्बोधस्वरूपा भवति तदा शनैः

शनैरुपरमेद्बुद्ध्या धृतिगृहीतयात्मसंस्थं मनः कृत्वा न किंचिदपि चिन्तयेत्तदा प्राणापानयोरैक्यं कृत्वा सर्वं विश्वमात्मस्वरूपेण लक्ष्यं धारयति। यदा तुरीयातीतावस्था तदा सर्वेषामानन्दस्वरूपो भवति द्वन्द्वातीतो भवति यावद्देहधारणा वर्तते तावत्तिष्ठति पश्चात्परमात्मस्वरूपेण प्राप्तिर्भवति इत्यनेन प्रकारेण मोक्षो भवतीदमेवात्मदर्शनोपाया भवन्ति ॥ चतुष्पथसमायुक्तमहाद्वारगवायुना। सहस्थितत्रिकोणार्धगमने दृश्यतेऽच्युतः ॥९४।

पूर्वोक्तत्रिकोणस्थानादुपरि पृथिव्यादिपञ्चवर्णकं ध्येयम्। प्राणादिपञ्चवायुश्च बीजं वर्णं च स्थानकम्। यकारं प्राणबीजं च नीलजीमूतसन्निभम्। रकारमग्निबीजं च अपानादित्यसंनिभम् ॥९५ ॥ लकारं पृथिवीरूपं व्यानं बन्धूकसंनिभम्। वकारं जीवबीजं च उदानं शङ्खवर्णकम् ॥९६ ॥

हकारं वियत्स्वरूपं च समानं स्फटिकप्रभम्। हृन्नाभिनासाकर्णं च पादाङ्गुष्ठादिसंस्थितम् ॥९७ ॥ द्विसप्ततिसहस्राणि नाडीमार्गेषु वर्तते। अष्टाविंशतिकोटीषु रोमकूपेषु संस्थिताः ॥९८ ॥ समानप्राण एकस्तु जीवः स एक एव हि। रेचकादि त्रयं कुर्याद्दृढचित्तः समाहितः ॥९९ ॥ शनैः समस्तमाकृष्य हृत्सरोरुहकोटरे। प्राणापानौ च बध्वा तु प्रणवेन समुच्चरेत् ॥१०० ॥

कर्णसंकोचनं कृत्वा लिङ्गसंकोचनं तथा। मूलाधारात्सुषुम्ना च पद्मतन्तुनिभा सुभा ॥१०१ ॥ अमूर्तो वर्तते नादो वीणादण्डसमुत्थितः। शङ्खनादादिभिश्चैव मध्यमेव ध्वनिर्यथा ॥१०२ ॥ व्योमरन्ध्रगतो नादो मायूरं नादमेव च। कपालकुहरे मध्ये चतुर्द्वारस्य मध्यमे ॥१०३ ॥

तदात्मा राजते तत्र यथा व्योम्नि दिवाकरः। कोदण्डद्वयमध्ये तु ब्रह्मरन्ध्रेषु शक्ति च ॥१०४॥ स्वात्मानं पुरुषं पश्येन्मनस्तत्र लयं गतम्। रत्नानि ज्योत्स्निनादं तु बिन्दुमाहेश्वरं पदम्। य एवं वेद पुरुषः स कैवल्यं समश्नुत इत्युपनिषत् ॥१०५ ॥ ॐ सह नाववत्विति शान्तिः ॥

इति ध्यानबिन्दूपनिषत्समाप्ता ॥

२५. हंसोपनिषत्

हंसाख्योपनिषत्प्रोक्तनादालिर्यत्र विश्रमेत्।

तदाधारं निराधारं ब्रह्ममात्रमहं महः ॥

ॐ पूर्णमद इति शान्तिः ॥

गौतम उवाच। भगवन्सर्वधर्मज्ञ सर्वशास्त्रविशारद। ब्रह्मविद्याप्रबोधो हि केनोपायेन जायते ॥१ ॥ सनत्कुमार उवाच। विचार्य सर्ववेदेषु मतं ज्ञात्वा पिनाकिनः। पार्वत्या कथितं तत्त्वं शृणु गौतम तन्मम ॥२॥ अनाख्येयमिदं गुह्यं योगिनां कोशसंनिभम्। हंसस्याकृतिविस्तारं भुक्तिमुक्तिफलप्रदम् ॥३ ॥ अथ हंसपरमहंसनिर्णयं व्याख्यास्यामः। ब्रह्मचारिणे शान्ताय दान्ताय गुरुभक्ताय। हंसहंसेति सदा ध्यायन्सर्वेषु देहेषु व्याप्य वर्तते ॥ यथा ह्यग्निः काष्ठेषु तिलेषु तैलमिव तं विदित्वा मृत्युमत्येति। गुदम-

वष्टभ्याधाराद्वायुमुत्थाप्य स्वाधिष्ठानं त्रिः प्रदक्षिणीकृत्य मणिपूरकं च गत्वा अनाहतमतिक्रम्य विशुद्धौ प्राणान्निरुध्याज्ञामनुध्यायन्ब्रह्मरन्ध्रं ध्यायन् त्रिमात्रोऽहमित्येवं सर्वदा ध्यायन्। अथो नादमाधाराद्ब्रह्मरन्ध्रपर्यन्तं शुद्धस्फटिकसंकाशं स वै ब्रह्म परमात्मेत्युच्यते ॥१ ॥

अथ हंस ऋषिः । अव्यक्ता गायत्री छन्दः । परमहंसो देवता । अहमिति बीजम् । स इति शक्तिः । सोऽहमिति कीलकम् । षट्संख्यया अहोरात्रयोरेकविंशतिसहस्राणि षट्शतान्यधिकानि भवन्ति । सूर्याय सोमाय निरञ्जनाय निराभासाय तनु सूक्ष्मं प्रचोदयादिति अग्नीषोमाभ्यां वौषट् हृदयाद्यङ्गन्यासकरन्यासौ भवतः । एवं कृत्वा हृदये अष्टदले हंसात्मानं ध्यायेत् । अग्नीषोमौ पक्षावोंकारः शिरो बिन्दुस्तु नेत्रं मुखं रुद्रो रुद्राणी चरणौ बहू कालश्चाग्निश्चोभे पार्श्वे भवतः । पश्यत्यनागारश्च शिष्टोभयपार्श्वे भवतः । एषोऽसौ परमहंसो भानुकोटिप्रतीकाशः येनेदं व्याप्तम् । तस्याष्टधा वृत्तिर्भवति । पूर्वदले पुण्ये मतिः आग्नेये निद्रालस्यादयो भवन्ति याम्ये क्रूरे मतिः नैर्ऋते पापे मनीषा वारुण्यां क्रीडा वायव्ये गमनादौ बुद्धिः सौम्ये रतिप्रीतिः ईशाने द्रव्यादानं मध्ये वैराग्यं केसरे जाग्रदवस्था कर्णिकायां स्वप्नं लिङ्गे सुषुप्तिः पद्मत्यागे तुरीयं यदा हंसो नादे लीनो भवति तदा तुर्यातीतमुन्मननमजपोपसंहारमित्यभिधीयते ।

एवं सर्वं हंसवशात्तस्मान्मनो हंसो विचार्यते । स एव जपकोट्या नादमनुभवति एवं सर्वं हंसवशान्नदो दशविधो जयते । चिणीति प्रथमः चिञ्चिणीति द्वितीयः । घण्टानादस्तृतीयः शङ्खनादश्चतुर्थः पञ्चमस्तन्त्रीनादः । षष्ठस्तालनादः । सप्तमो वेणुनादः । अष्टमो मृदङ्गनादः । नवमो भेरीनादः । दशमो मेघनादः । नवमं परित्यज्य दशममेवाभ्यसेत् । प्रथमे चिञ्चिणीगात्रं द्वितीये गात्रभञ्जनम् । तृतीये खेदनं याति चतुर्थे कम्पते शिरः ॥ पञ्चमे स्रवते तालु षष्ठेऽमृतनिषेवणम् । सप्तमे गूढविज्ञानं परा वाचा तथाष्टमे ॥ अदृश्यं नवमे देह दिव्यं चक्षुस्तथामलम् । दशमे परमं ब्रह्म भवेद्ब्रह्मात्मसंनिधौ ॥ तस्मिन्मनो विलीयते मनसि संकल्पविकल्पे दग्धे पुण्यपापे सदाशिवः शक्त्यात्मा सर्वत्रावस्थितः सवयंज्योतिः शुद्धो बुद्धो नित्यो निरञ्जनः शान्तः प्रकाशत इति ॥ इति वेदप्रवचनं वेदप्रवचनम् ॥२ ॥ ॐ पूर्णमद इति शान्तिः ॥

इत्यथर्ववेदे हंसोपनिषत्समाप्ता ॥१५ ॥

२६. अमृतनादोपनिषत्

अमृतनादोपनिषत्प्रतिपाद्यं पराक्षरम् ।

त्रैपदानन्दसाम्राज्यं हृदि मे भातु संततम् ॥

ॐ सह नाववत्विति शान्तिः ॥ शास्त्राण्यधीत्य मेधावी अभ्यस्य च पुनः पुनः । परमं ब्रह्म विज्ञाय उल्कावत्तान्यथोत्सृजेत् ॥१ ॥ ओंकाररथमारुह्य विष्णुं कृत्वाथ सारथिम् । ब्रह्मलोकपदान्वेषी रुद्राराधनतत्परः ॥२ ॥ तावद्रथेन गन्तव्यं यावद्रथपथि स्थितः । स्थाता रथपतिस्थानं रथमुत्सृज्य गच्छति ॥३ ॥ मात्रालिङ्गपदं त्यक्त्वा शब्दव्यञ्जनवर्जितम् । अस्वरेण मकारेण पदं सूक्ष्मं हि गच्छति ॥४ ॥ शब्दादि विषयान्पञ्च मनश्चैवातिचञ्चलम् । चिन्तयेदात्मनो रश्मीन्प्रत्याहारः स उच्यते ॥५ ॥ प्रत्याहारस्तथा ध्यानं प्राणायामोऽथ

धारणा। तर्कश्चैव समाधिश्च षडङ्गो योग उच्यते ॥६ ॥ यथा पर्वतधातूनां दह्यन्ते धमनान्मलाः। तथेन्द्रियकृता दोषा दह्यन्ते प्राणधारणात् ॥७ ॥ प्राणायामैर्दहेद्दोषान्धारणाभिश्च किल्बिषम्। प्रत्याहारेण संरार्गान्ध्यानेनानीश्वरान्गुणान् ॥८ ॥ किल्बिषं हि क्षयं नीत्वा रुचिरं चैव चिन्तयेत् ॥९ ॥ रुचिरं रेचकं चैव वायोराकर्षणं तथा। प्राणायामास्त्रयः प्रोक्ता रेचपूरककुम्भकाः ॥१० ॥

सव्याहृतिं सप्रणवां गायत्रीं शिरसा सह। त्रिः पठेदायतप्राणः प्राणायामः स उच्यते ॥११ ॥ उत्क्षिप्य वायुमाकाशं शून्यं कृत्वा निरात्मकम्। शून्यभावे नियुञ्जीयाद्रेचकस्येति लक्षणम् ॥१२ ॥ वक्त्रेणोत्पलनालेन तोयमाकर्षयेन्नरः। एवं वायुर्ग्रहीतव्यः पूरकखेति लक्षणम् ॥१३ ॥ नोच्छ्रसेन्न च निश्वसेन्नैव गात्राणि चालयेत्। एवं भावं नियुञ्जीयात्कुम्भकस्येति लक्षणम् ॥१४ ॥ अन्धवत्पश्य रूपाणि शब्दं बधिरवच्छृणु। काष्ठवतपश्य वै देहं प्रशान्तस्यैति लक्षणम् ॥१५ ॥ मनः संकल्पकं ध्यात्वा संक्षिप्यात्मनि बुद्धिमान्। धारयित्वा तथात्मानं धारणा परिकीर्तिता ॥१६ ॥ आगमस्याविरोधेन ऊहनं तर्क उच्यते। समं मन्येत यल्लब्ध्वा स समाधिः प्रकीर्तितः ॥१७ ॥ भूमौ दर्भासने रम्ये सर्वदोषविवर्जिते। कृत्वा मनोमयीमृक्षां जहवा वै रथमण्डले ॥१८ ॥

पद्मकं स्वस्तिकं वापि भद्रासनमथापि वा। बद्ध्वा योगासनं सम्यगुत्तराभिमुखः स्थितः ॥१९ ॥ नासिकापुटमङ्गुल्या पिधायैकेन मारुतम्। आकृष्य धारयेदग्निं शब्दमेव विचिन्तयेत् ॥२० ॥ ओमित्येकाक्षरं ब्रह्म ओमित्येतेन रेचयेत्। दिव्यमन्त्रेण बहुधा कुर्यादामलमुक्तये ॥२१ ॥ पश्चाद्ध्यायीत पूर्वोक्तक्रमशो मन्त्रविद्बुधः। स्थूलादिस्थूलसूक्ष्मं च नाभेरूर्ध्वमुपक्रमः ॥२२ ॥ तिर्यगूर्ध्वमधोदृष्टिं विहाय च महामतिः। स्थिरस्थायी विनिष्कम्पः सदा योगं समभ्यसेत् ॥२३ ॥ नालमात्रविनिष्कम्पो धारणायोजनं तथा। द्वादशमात्रो योगस्तु कालतो नियमः स्मृतः ॥२४ ॥ अघोषमव्यञ्जनमस्वरं च यत्तालुकण्ठोष्ठमनासिकं च यत्। अरेफजातमुभयोष्मवर्जितं यदक्षरं न क्षरते कथंचित् ॥२५ ॥ येनासो गच्छते मार्गं प्राणस्तेनाभिगच्छति। अतस्तमभ्यसेन्नित्यं यन्मार्गगमनाय वै ॥२६ ॥

हृद्द्वारं वायुद्वारं च मूर्ध्नि द्वारमथापरम्। मोक्षद्वारं बिलं चैव सुषिरं मण्डलं विदुः ॥२७ ॥ भयं क्रोधमथालस्यमतिस्वप्नातिजागरम्। अत्याहारमनाहारं नित्यं योगी विवर्जयेत् ॥२८ ॥ अनेन विधिना सम्यङ्नित्यनभ्यस्यते क्रमात्। स्वयमुत्पद्यते ज्ञानं त्रिभिर्मासैर्न संशयः ॥२९ ॥ चतुर्भिः पश्यते देवान्पञ्चभिर्विततक्रमान्। इच्छयाप्नोति कैवल्यं षष्ठे मासि न संशयः ॥३० ॥ पार्थिवः पञ्चमात्रस्तु चतुर्मात्रस्तु वारुणः। आग्नेयस्तु त्रिमात्रोऽसौ वायव्यस्तु द्विमात्रकः ॥३१ ॥ एकमात्रस्तथाकाशो ह्यमात्रं तु विचिन्तयेत्। संधिं कृत्वा तु मनसा चिन्तयेदात्मनात्मनि ॥३२ ॥ त्रिंशत्पर्वाङ्गुलः प्राणो यत्र प्राणैः प्रतिष्ठितः। एष प्राण इति ख्यातो बाह्यप्राणस्य गोचरः ॥३३ ॥ अशीतिश्च शतं चैव सहस्राणि त्रयोदश। लक्षश्चैको विनिश्वास अहोरात्रप्रमाणतः ॥३४ ॥ प्राण आद्यो हृदि स्थाने अपानस्तु पुनर्गुदे। समानो नाभिदेशे तु उदानः कण्ठमाश्रितः ॥३५ ॥ व्यानः सर्वेषु चाङ्गेषु व्याप्य तिष्ठति सर्वदा। अथ वर्णास्तु पञ्चानां प्राणादीनामनुक्रमात् ॥३६ ॥ रक्तवर्णो मणिप्रख्यः प्राणवायुः प्रकीर्तितः। अपानस्तस्य मध्ये तु इन्द्रगोपसमप्रभः ॥३७ ॥ समानस्तु

द्वयोर्मध्ये गोक्षीरधवलप्रभः । आपाण्डर उदानश्च व्यानो ह्यर्चिःसमप्रभः ॥३८ ॥ यस्येदं मण्डलं भित्त्वा मारुतो याति मूर्धनि । यत्र यत्र म्रियेद्वापि न स भूयोऽभिजायते न स भूयोऽभिजायत इत्युपनिषत् ॥३९ ॥ ॐ सह नाववत्विति शान्तिः ॥

इत्यमृतनादोपनिषत्समाप्ता ॥

२७. वराहोपनिषत्

श्रीमद्वाराहोपनिषद्वेद्याखण्डसुखाकृति ।

त्रिपान्नारायणाख्यं तद्रामचन्द्रपदं भजे ॥१ ॥

ॐ सह नाववत्विति शान्तिः ॥

हरिः ॐ । अथ ऋभुर्वै महामुनिर्देवमानेन द्वादशवत्सरं तपश्चचार । तदवसाने वराहरूपी भगवान्प्रादुरभूत् । स होवाचोत्तिष्ठोत्तिष्ठ वरं वृर्णाष्वेति । सोदतिष्ठत् । तस्मै नमस्कृत्योवाच भगवन्कामिभिर्यद्यत्कामितं तत्तत्त्वत्सकाशात्स्वप्नेऽपि न याचे । समस्तवेदशास्त्रेतिहासपुराणानि समस्तविद्याजालानि ब्रह्मादयः सुराः सर्वे त्वद्रूपज्ञानान्मुक्तिमाहुः । अतस्त्वद्रूपप्रतिपादिकां ब्रह्मविद्यां ब्रूहीति होवाच । तथेति स होवाच वराहरूपी भगवान् । चतुर्विंशतितत्त्वानि केचिदिच्छन्ति वादिनः । केचित्षट्त्रिंशत्तत्त्वानि केचित्षण्णवतीनि च ॥१ ॥

तेषां क्रमं प्रवक्ष्यामि सावदानमनाः शृणु । ज्ञानेन्द्रियाणि पञ्चैव श्रोत्रत्वग्लोचनादयः ॥२ ॥ कर्मेन्द्रियाणि पञ्चैव वाक्पाण्यङ्घ्र्यादयः क्रमात् । प्राणादयस्तु पञ्चैव पञ्च शब्दादयस्तथा ॥३ ॥ मनोबुद्धिरहंकारश्चित्तं चेति चतुष्टयम् । चतुर्विंशतितत्त्वानि तानि ब्रह्मविदो विदुः ॥४ ॥ एतैस्तत्त्वैः समं पञ्चीकृतभूतानि पञ्च च । पृथिव्यापस्तथा तेजो वायुराकाशमेव च ॥५ ॥

देहत्रयं स्थूलसूक्ष्मकारणानि विदुर्बुधाः । अवस्था त्रितयं चैव जाग्रत्स्वप्नसुषुप्तयः ॥६ ॥ आहत्य तत्त्वजातानां षट्त्रिंशन्मुनयो विदुः । पूर्वोक्तैस्तत्त्वजातैस्तु समं तत्त्वानि योजयेत् ॥७ ॥ षड्भावविकृतिश्चास्ति जायते वर्धतेऽपि च । परिणामं क्षयं नाशं षड्भावविकृतिं विदुः ॥८ ॥ अशना च पिपासा च शोकमोहौ जरा मृतिः । एते षडूर्मयः प्रोक्ताः षट्कोशानथ वच्मि ते ॥९ ॥ त्वक्च रक्तं मांसमेदोमज्जास्थानी निबोधत । कामक्रोधौ लोभमोहौ मदो मात्सर्यमेव च ॥१० ॥ एतेऽरिषड्वा विश्वश्च तैजसः प्राज्ञ एव च । जीवत्रयं सत्त्वरजस्तमांसि च गुणत्रयम् ॥११ ॥ प्रारब्धागाम्यर्जितानि कर्मत्रयमितीरितम् । वचनादामगमनविसर्गानन्दपञ्चकम् ॥१२ ॥ संकल्पोऽध्यवसायश्च अभिमानोऽवधारणा । मुदिता करुणा मैत्री उपेक्षा च चतुष्टयम् ॥१३ ॥

दिग्वातार्कप्रचेतोऽश्विवह्नीन्द्रोपेन्द्रमृत्युकाः । तथा चन्द्रश्चतुर्वक्त्रो रुद्रः क्षेत्रज्ञ ईश्वरः ॥१४ ॥ आहत्य तत्त्वजातानां षण्णवत्यस्तु कीर्तिताः । पूर्वोक्ततत्त्वजातानां वैलक्षण्यमनामयम् ॥१५ ॥ वराहरूपिणं मां ये भजन्ति मयि भक्तितः । विमुक्ताज्ञानतत्कार्या जीवन्मुक्ता भवन्ति ते ॥१६ ॥ ये षण्णवतितत्त्वज्ञा यत्र कुत्राश्रमे रताः । जटी मुण्डी शिखी वापि मुच्यते नात्र संशयः ॥१७ ॥ इति ॥ इति प्रथमोऽध्यायः ॥१ ॥

ऋभुर्नाम महायोगी क्रोडरूपं रमापतिम्। वरिष्ठां ब्रह्मविद्यां त्वमधीहि भगवन्मम। एवं स पृष्टो भगवान्प्राह भक्तार्तिभञ्जनः ॥१॥ स्ववर्णाश्रमधर्मेण तपसा गुरुतोषणात्। साधनं प्रभवेत्पुंसां वैराग्यादिचतुष्टयम् ॥२॥ नित्यानित्यविवेकश्च इहामुत्र विरागता। शमादिषड्कसंपत्तिर्मुमुक्षा तां समभ्यसेत् ॥३॥

एवं जितेन्द्रियो भूत्वा सर्वत्र ममतामतिम्। विहाय साक्षिचैतन्ये मयि कुर्यादहंमतिम् ॥४॥ दुर्लभं प्राप्य मानुष्यं तत्रापि नरविग्रहम्। ब्राह्मण्यं च महाविष्णोर्वेदान्तश्रवणादिना ॥५॥ अतिवर्णाश्रमं रूपं सच्चिदानन्दलक्षणम्। यो न जानाति सोऽविद्वान्कदा मुक्तो भविष्यति ॥६॥ अहमेव सुखं नान्यदन्यच्चेन्नैव तत्सुखम्। अमदर्थं न हि प्रेयो मदर्थं न स्वतः प्रियम् ॥७॥

परप्रेमास्पदतया मा न भूवमहं सदा। भूयासमिति यो द्रष्टा सोऽहं विष्णुर्मुनीश्वर ॥८॥ न प्रकाशोऽहमित्युक्तिर्यत्प्रकाशैकबन्धना। स्वप्रकाशं तमात्मानमप्रकाशः कथं स्पृशेत् ॥९॥ स्वयं भातं निराधारं ये जानन्ति सुनिश्चितम्। ते हि विज्ञानसंपन्ना इति मे निश्चिता मतिः ॥१०॥ स्वपूर्णात्मातिरेकेण जगज्जीवेश्वरादयः। न सन्ति नास्ति माया च तेभ्यश्चाहं विलक्षणः ॥११॥

अज्ञानान्धतमोरूपं कर्मधर्मादिलक्षणम्। स्वयंप्रकाशमात्मानं नैव मां स्प्रष्टुमर्हति ॥१२॥ सर्वसाक्षिणमात्मानं वर्णाश्रमविवर्जितम्। ब्रह्मरूपतया पश्यन्ब्रह्मैव भवति स्वयम् ॥१३॥ भासमानमिदं सर्वं मानरूपं परं पदम्। पश्यन्वेदान्तमानेन सद्य एव विमुच्यते ॥१४॥ देहात्मज्ञानवज्ज्ञानं देहात्मज्ञानबाधकम्। आत्मन्येव भवेद्यस्य स नेच्छन्नपि मुच्यते ॥१५॥

सत्यज्ञानानन्दपूर्णलक्षणं तमसः परम्। ब्रह्मानन्दं सदा पश्यन्कथं बध्येत कर्मणा ॥१६॥ त्रिधामसाक्षिणं सत्यज्ञानानन्दादिलक्षणम्। तवमहंशब्दलक्ष्यार्थमसक्तं सर्वदोषतः ॥१७॥ सर्वगं सच्चिदात्मानं ज्ञानचक्षुर्निरीक्षते। अज्ञानचक्षुर्नेक्षेत भास्वन्तं भानुमन्धवत् ॥१८॥ प्रज्ञानमेव तद्ब्रह्म सत्यप्रज्ञानलक्षणम्। एवं ब्रह्मपरिज्ञानादेव मर्त्योऽमृतो भवेत् ॥१९॥ तद्ब्रह्मानन्दमद्वन्द्वं निर्गुणं सत्यचिद्घनम्। विदित्वा स्वात्मनो रूपं न बिभेति कुश्चन ॥२०॥

चिन्मात्रं सर्वगं नित्यं संपूर्णं सुखमद्वयम्। साक्षाद्ब्रह्मैव नान्योऽस्तीत्येवं ब्रह्मविदां स्थितिः ॥२१॥ अज्ञस्य दुःखौघमयं ज्ञस्यानन्दमयं जगत्। अन्धं भुवनमन्धस्य प्रकाशं तु सुचक्षुषाम् ॥२२॥ अनन्ते सच्चिदानन्दे मयि वाराहरूपिणि। स्थितेऽद्वितीयभावः स्यात्को बन्धः कश्च मुच्यते ॥२३॥ स्वस्वरूपं तु चिन्मात्रं सर्वदा सर्वदेहिनाम्। नैव देहादिसंघातो घटवद्दृशिगोचरः ॥२४॥ स्वात्मनोऽन्यदिवाभातं चराचरमिदं जगत्। स्वात्ममात्रतया बुद्ध्वा तदस्मीति विभावय ॥२५॥

स्वस्वरूपं स्वयं भुङ्क्ते नास्ति भोज्यं पृथक् स्वतः। अस्ति चेदस्तितारूपं ब्रह्मैवास्तित्वलक्षणम् ॥२६॥ ब्रह्मविज्ञानसंपन्नः प्रतीतमखिलं जगत्। पश्यन्नपि सदा नैव पश्यति स्वात्मनः पृथक् ॥२७॥ मत्स्वरूपपरिज्ञानात्कर्मभिर्न स बध्यते ॥२८॥

यः शरीरेन्द्रियादिभ्यो विहीनं सर्वसाक्षिणम्। परमार्थैकविज्ञानं सुखात्मानं स्वयंप्रभम् ॥२९॥ स्वस्वरूपतया सर्वं वेद स्वानुभयेन यः। स धीरः स तु विज्ञेयः सोऽहं तत्त्वं ऋभो भव ॥३०॥ अतः प्रपञ्चानुभवः सदा न हि स्वरूपबोधानुभवः सदा खलु। इति

प्रपश्यन्परिपूर्णवेदनो न बन्धमुक्तो न च बद्ध एव तु ॥३१ ॥ स्वस्वरूपानुसंधानान्नृत्यन्तं सर्वसाक्षिणम् । मुहूर्तं चिन्तयेन्मां यः सर्वबन्धैः प्रमुच्यते ॥३२ ॥

सर्वभूतान्तरस्थाय नित्यमुक्तचिदात्मने । प्रत्यक्चैतन्यरूपाय मह्यमेव नमोनमः ॥३३ ॥ त्वं वाहमस्मि भगवो देवतेऽहं वै त्वमसि । तुभ्यं मह्यमनन्ताय मह्यं तुभ्यं चिदात्मने ॥३४ ॥ नमो मह्यं परेशाय नमस्तुभ्यं शिवाय च । किं करोमि क्व गच्छामि किं गृह्णामि त्यजामि किम् ॥३५ ॥ यन्मया पूरितं विश्वं महाकल्पाम्बुना यथा । अन्तःसङ्गं बहिःसङ्गमात्मसङ्गं च यस्त्यजेत् । सर्वसङ्गनिवृत्तात्मा स मामेति न संशयः ॥३६ ॥ अहिरिव जनयोगं सर्वदा वर्जयेद्यः कुणपमिव सुनारीं त्यक्तुकामो विरागी । विषमिव विषयादीन्मन्यमानो दुरन्ताञ्जगति परमहंसो वासुदेवोऽहमेव ॥३७ ॥

इदं सत्यमिदं सत्यं सत्यमेतदिहोच्यते । अहं सत्यं परं ब्रह्म मत्तः किंचिन्न विद्यते ॥३८ ॥ उप समीपे यो वासो जीवात्मपरमात्मनोः । उपवासः स विज्ञेयो न तु कायस्य शोषणम् ॥३९ ॥ कायशोषणमात्रेण का तत्र ह्यविवेकिनाम् । वल्मीकताडनादेव मृतः किं नु महोरगः ॥४० ॥

अस्ति ब्रह्मेति चेद्वेद परोक्षज्ञानमेव तत् । अहं ब्रह्मेति चेद्वेद साक्षात्कारः स उच्यते ॥४१ ॥ यस्मिन्काले स्वमात्मानं योगी जानाति केवलम् । तस्मात्कालात्समारभ्य जीवन्मुक्तो भयेदसौ ॥४२ ॥ अहं ब्रह्मेति नियतं मोक्षहेतुर्महात्मनाम् । द्वे पदे बन्धमोक्षाय निर्ममेति ममेति च ॥४३ ॥ ममेति बध्यते जन्तुर्निर्ममेति विमुच्यते । बाह्यचिन्ता न कर्तव्या तथैवान्तरचिन्तिका । सर्वचिन्तां समुत्सृज्य स्वस्थो भव सदा ऋभो ॥४४ ॥

संकल्पमात्रकलनेन जगत्समग्रं संकल्पमात्रकलने हि जगद्विलासः । संकल्पमात्रमिदमुत्सृज निर्विकल्पमाश्रित्य मामकपदं हृदि भावयस्व ॥४५ ॥ मच्चिन्तनं मत्कथनमन्योन्यं मत्प्रभाषणम् । मदेकपरमो भूत्वा कालं नय महामते ॥४६ ॥ चिदिहास्तीति चिन्मात्रमिदं चिन्मयमेव च । चित्त्वं चिदहमेते च लोकाश्चिदिति भावय ॥४७ ॥

रागं नीरागतां नीत्वा निर्लेपो भव सर्वदा । अज्ञानजन्यकर्त्रादिकारकोत्पन्नकर्मणा ॥४८ ॥ श्रुत्युत्पन्नात्मविज्ञानप्रदीपो बाध्यते कथम् । अनात्मतां परित्यज्य निर्विकारो जगत्स्थितौ ॥४९ ॥ एकनिष्ठतयान्तस्थसंदविन्मात्रपरो भव । घटाकाशमठाकाशौ महाकाशे प्रतिष्ठितौ ॥५० ॥ एवं मयि चिदाकशे जीवेशौ परिकल्पितौ । या च प्रागात्मनो माया तथान्ते च तिरस्कृता ॥५१ ॥

ब्रह्मवादिमिरुद्गीता सा मायेति विवेकतः । मायातत्कार्यविलये नेश्वरत्वं न जीवता ॥५२ ॥ ततः शुद्धश्चिदेवाहं व्योमवन्निरुपाधिकः । जीवेश्वरादिरूपेण चेतनाचेतनात्मकम् ॥५३ ॥ ईक्षणादिप्रवेशान्ता सृष्टिरीशेन कल्पिता । जाग्रदादिविमोक्षान्तः संसारो जीवकल्पितः ॥५४ ॥ त्रिणाचिकादियोगान्ता ईश्वरभ्रान्तिमाश्रिताः । लोकायतादिसांख्यान्ता जीवविश्रान्तिमाश्रिताः ॥५५ ॥

तस्मान्मुमुक्षुभिर्नैव मतिर्जीवेशवादयोः । कार्या किंतु ब्रह्मतत्त्वं निश्चलेन विचार्यताम् ॥५६ ॥ अद्वितीयब्रह्मतत्त्वं न जानन्ति यथा तथा । भ्रान्ता एवाखिलास्तेषां क्व मुक्तिः क्वेह वा सुखम् ॥५७ ॥ उत्तमाधमभावश्चेत्तेषां स्यादस्ति तेन किम् । स्वप्नस्थराज्यभिक्षाभ्यां प्रबुद्धः स्पृशते खलु ॥५८ ॥ अज्ञाने बुद्धिविलये निद्रा सा भण्यते बुधैः । विलीनाज्ञानतत्कार्ये मयि निद्रा कथं भवेत् ॥५९ ॥

बुद्धेः पूर्णविकासोऽयं जागरः परिकीर्त्यते। विकारादिविहीनत्वाज्जागरो मे न विद्यते ॥६०॥ सूक्ष्मनाडिषु संचारो बुद्धेः स्वप्नः प्रजायते। संचारधर्मरहिते मयि स्वप्नो न विद्यते ॥६१॥ सुषुप्तिकाले सकले विलीने तमसावृते। स्वरूपं महदानन्दं भुङ्क्ते विश्वविवर्जितः ॥६२॥ अविशेषेण सर्वं तु यः पश्यति चिदन्वयात्। स एव साक्षाद्विज्ञानी स शिवः स हरिर्विधिः ॥६३॥ धीर्घस्वप्नमिदं यत्तद्दीर्घं वा चित्तविभ्रमम्। दीर्घं वापि मनोराज्यं संसारं दुःखमागरम्। सुप्तेरुत्थाय सुप्त्यन्तं ब्रह्मैकं प्रविचिन्त्यताम् ॥६४॥

आरोपितस्य जगतः प्रविलापनेन चित्तं मदात्मकतया परिकल्पितं नः। शत्रून्निहस्य गुरुषट्कगणान्निपाताद्गन्धद्विपो भवति केवलमद्वितीयः ॥६५॥ अद्यास्तमेतु वपुराशक्षि-तारमास्तां कस्तावत्तापि मम चिद्वपुषो विशेषः। कुम्भे विनश्यति चिरं समवस्थिते वा कुम्भाम्बरस्य नहि कोऽपि विशेषलेशः ॥६६॥

अहिनिर्ल्वयनी सर्पनिर्मोको जीववर्जितः। वल्मीके पतितस्तिष्ठेत्तं सर्पो नाभिमन्यते ॥६७॥ एवं स्थूलं च सूक्ष्मं च शरीरं नाभिमन्यते। प्रत्यग्ज्ञानशिखिध्वस्ते मिथ्याज्ञाने सहेतुके। नेति नेतीति रूपत्वादशरीरो भवत्ययम् ॥६८॥ शास्त्रेण न स्यात्परमार्थदृष्टिः कार्यक्षमं पश्यति चापरोक्षम्। प्रारब्धनाशात्प्रतिभाननाश एवं त्रिधा नश्यति चात्ममाया ॥६९॥

ब्रह्मत्वे योजिते स्वामिञ्जीवभावो न गच्छति। अद्वैते बोधिते तत्त्वे वासना विनि-वर्तते ॥७०॥ प्रारब्धान्ते देहहानिर्मायेति क्षीयतेऽखिला। अस्तीत्युक्ते जगत्सर्वं सद्रसं ब्रह्म तद्भवेत् ॥७१॥ भातीत्युक्ते जगत्सर्वं भानं ब्रह्मैव केवलम्॥ मरुभूमौ जलं सर्वं मरुभू-मात्रमेव तत्। जगत्त्रयमिदं सर्वं चिन्मात्रं स्वविचारतः ॥७२॥ अज्ञानमेव न कुतो जगतः प्रसङ्गो जीवेशदेशिकविकल्पकथातिदूरे। एकान्तकेवलचिदेकरसस्वभावे ब्रह्मैव केवलमहं परिपूर्णमस्मि ॥७३॥

बोधचन्द्रमसि पूर्णविग्रहे मोहराहुमुषितात्मतेजसि। स्नानदानयजनादिकाः क्रिया मोचनावधि वृथैव तिष्ठते ॥७४॥ सलिले सैन्धवं यद्वत्साम्यं भवति योगतः। तथात्ममनसोरैक्यं समाधिरिति कथ्यते ॥७५॥ दुर्लभो विषयत्यागो दुर्लभं तत्त्वदर्शनम्। दुर्लभा सहजावस्था सद्गुरोः करुणां विना ॥७६॥ उत्पन्नशक्तिबोधस्य त्यक्तनिःशेषकर्मणः। योगिनः सहजावस्था स्वयमेव प्रकाशते ॥७७॥

रसस्य मनसश्चैव चञ्चलत्वं स्वभावतः। रसो बद्धो मनो बद्धं किं न सिद्ध्यति भूतले ॥७८॥ मूर्च्छितो हरति व्याधिं मृतो जीवयति स्वयम्। बद्धः खेचरतां धत्ते ब्रह्मत्वं रसचेतसि ॥७९॥ इन्द्रियाणां मनो नाथो मनोनाथस्तु मारुतः। मारुतस्य लयो नाथस्तन्नाथं लयमाश्रय ॥८०॥ निश्चेष्टो निर्विकारश्च लयो जीवति योगिनाम्। उच्छिन्नसर्वसंकल्पो निःशेषाशेषचेष्टितः। स्वावगम्यो लयः कोऽपि मनसां वागगोचरः ॥८१॥

पुङ्खानुपुङ्खविषयेक्षणतत्परोऽपि ब्रह्मावलोकनधियं न जहाति योगी। सङ्गीततालयावाद्यवशं गतापि मौलिस्थकुम्भपरिरक्षणधीर्नटीव ॥८२॥ सर्वचिन्तां परित्यज्य सावधानेन चेतसा। नाद एवानुसंधेयो योगसाम्राज्यमिच्छता ॥८३॥ इति द्वितीयोऽध्यायः ॥२॥

नहि नानास्वरूपं स्यादेकं वस्तु कदाचन। तस्मादखण्ड एवास्मि यन्मदन्यत्र किंचन ॥१॥ दृश्यते श्रूयते यद्यद्ब्रह्मणोऽन्यन्न तद्भवेत्।

नित्यशुद्धविमुक्तैकमखण्डानन्दमद्वयम्। सत्यं ज्ञानमनन्तं यत्परं ब्रह्माहमेव तत् ॥२॥ आनन्दरूपोऽहमखण्डबोधः परात्परोऽहं घनचित्प्रकाशः। मेघा यथा व्योम न च स्पृशन्ति संसारदुःखानि न मां स्पृशन्ति ॥३॥

सर्वं सुखं विद्धि सुदुःखनाशात्सर्वं सद्रूपमसत्यनाशात्। चिद्रूपमेव प्रतिभानयुक्तं तस्मादखण्डं मम रूपमेतत् ॥४॥ न हि जनिर्मरणं गमनागमौ न च मलं विमलं न च वेदनम्। चिन्मयं हि सकलं विराजते स्फुटतरं परमस्य तु योगिनः ॥५॥ सत्यचिद्घनमखण्डमद्वयं सर्वदृश्यरहितं निरामयम्। यत्पदं विमलमद्वयं शिवं तत्सदाहमिति मौनमाश्रय ॥६॥

जन्ममृत्युसुखदुःखवर्जितं जातिनीतिकुलगोत्रदूरगम्। चिद्विवर्तजगतोऽस्य कारणं तत्सदाहमिति मौनमाश्रय ॥७॥ पूर्णमद्वयमखण्डचेतनं विश्वभेदकलनादिवर्जितम्। अद्वितीयपरसंविदंशकं तत्सदाहमिति मौनमाश्रय ॥८॥ केनाप्यबाधितत्वेन त्रिकालेऽप्येकरूपतः। विद्यमानत्वमस्त्येतत्सद्रूपत्वं सदा मम ॥९॥

निरुपाधिकनित्यं यत्सुप्तौ सर्वसुखात्परम्। सुखरूपत्वमस्त्येतदानन्दत्वं सदा मम ॥१०॥ दिनकरकिरणैर्हि शार्वरं तमो न निबिडतरं झटिति प्राणशमेति। घनतरभवकारणं तमो यद्धरिदिनकृत्प्रभया न चान्तरेण ॥११॥ मम चरणस्मरणेन पूजया च स्वकतमसः परिमुच्यते हि जन्तुः। न हि मरणप्रभवप्रणाशहेतुर्मम चरणस्मरणादृतेऽस्ति किंचित् ॥१२॥

आदरेण यथा स्तौति धनवन्तं धनेच्छया। तथा चेद्विश्वकर्तारं को न मुच्येत बन्धनात् ॥१३॥ आदित्यसंनिधौ लोकश्चेष्टते स्वयमेव तु। तथा मत्संनिधावेव समस्तं चेष्टते जगत ॥१४॥ शुक्तिकाया यथा तारं कल्पितं मायया तथा। महदादि जगन्मायामयं मय्येव केवलम् ॥१५॥ चण्डालदेहे पश्वादिस्थावरे ब्रह्मविग्रहे। अन्येषु तारतम्येन स्थितेषु न तथा ह्यहम् ॥१६॥

विनष्टदिग्भ्रमस्यापि यथापूर्वं विभाति दिक्। तथा विज्ञानविध्वस्तं जगन्मे भाति तन्न हि ॥१७॥ न देहो नेन्द्रियप्राणो न मनोबुद्ध्यहंकृति। न चित्तं नैव माया च न च व्योमादिकं जगत् ॥१८॥ न कर्ता नैव भोक्ता च न च भोजयिता तथा। केवलं चित्सदानन्दब्रह्मैवाहं जनार्दनः ॥१९॥ जलस्य चलनादेव चञ्चलत्वं यथा रवेः। तथाहंकारसंबन्धादेव संसार आत्मनः ॥२०॥

चित्तमूलं हि संसारस्तत्प्रयत्नेन शोधयेत्। हन्त चित्तमहत्तायां कैषा विश्वासता तव ॥२१॥ क्व धनानि महीपानां ब्राह्मणः क्व जगन्ति वा। प्राक्तनानि प्रयातानि गताः सर्गपरम्पराः। कोटयो ब्रह्मणां याता भूपा नष्टाः परागवत् ॥२२॥ स चाध्यात्माभिमानोऽपि विदुषोऽयासुरत्वतः। विदूषोऽप्यासुरश्चेत्स्यान्निष्फलं तत्त्वदर्शनम् ॥२३॥ उत्पाद्यमाना रागाद्या विवेकज्ञानवह्निना। यदा तदैव दह्यन्ते कुतस्तेषां प्ररोहणम् ॥२४॥

यथा सुनिपुणः सम्यक् परदोषेक्षणे रतः। तथा चेन्निपुणः स्वेषु को न मुच्यते बन्धनात् ॥२५॥ अनात्मविदमुक्तोऽपि सिद्धिजालानि वाञ्छति। द्रव्यमन्त्र-क्रियाकालयुक्त्याप्नोति मुनीश्वरः ॥२६॥ नात्यमज्ञस्यैष विषय आत्मज्ञो ह्यात्ममात्रदृक्। आत्मनात्मनि संतृप्तो नाविद्यामनुधावति ॥२७॥ ये केचन जगद्भावस्तानविद्यामयान्विदुः। कथं तेषु किलात्मज्ञस्त्यक्ताविद्यो निमज्जति ॥२८॥

द्रव्यमन्त्रक्रियाकालयुक्तयः साधुसिद्धिदाः। परमात्मपदप्राप्तौ नोपकुर्वन्ति काश्चन ॥२९॥ सर्वेच्छाकलनाशान्तावात्मलाभोदयाभिधः। स पुनः सिद्धिवाच्छायां कथमर्हत्यचित्ततः ॥३०॥ इति ॥ इति तृतीयोऽध्यायः ॥३॥

अथ ह ऋभुं भगवन्तं निदाघः पप्रच्छ जीवन्मुक्तिलक्षणमनुब्रूहीति। तथेति स होवाच। सप्तभूमिषु जीवन्मुक्ताश्चत्वारः। शुभेच्छा प्रथमा भूमिका भवति। विचारणा द्वितीया। तनुमानसी तृतीया। सत्त्वापत्तिस्तुरीया। असंसक्तिः पञ्चमी। पदार्थभावना षष्ठी। तुरीयगा सप्तमी। प्रणवात्मिका भूमिका अकारोकारमकारार्धमात्रात्मिका। स्थूलसूक्ष्मबीजसाक्षिभेदेनाकारादयश्चतुर्विधाः।

तदवस्था जाग्रत्स्वप्नसुषुप्तितुरीयाः। अकारस्थूलांशे जाग्रद्विश्वः। सूक्ष्मांशे तत्तैजसः। बीजांशे तत्प्राज्ञः। साक्ष्यंसे तत्तुरीयः। उकारस्थूलांशे स्वप्नविश्वः। सूक्ष्मांशे तत्तैजसः। बीजांशे तत्प्राज्ञः। साक्ष्यंसे तत्तुरीयः। मकारस्थूलांशे सुषुप्तविश्वः। सूक्ष्मांशे तत्तैजसः। बीजांशे तत्प्राज्ञः। साक्ष्यंशे तत्तुरीयः। अर्धमात्रास्थूलांशे तुरीयविश्वः। सूक्ष्मांसे तत्तैजसः। बीजांशे तत्प्राज्ञः। साक्ष्यंशे तुरीयतुरीयः।

अकारतुरीयांशाः प्रथमद्वितीयतृतीयभूमिकाः। उकारतुरीयांशा चतुर्थी भूमिका। मकारतुरीयांशा पञ्चमी। अर्धमात्रातुरीयांशा षष्ठी। तदतीता सप्तमी। भूमित्रयेषु विहरन्मुमुक्षुर्भवति। तुरीयभूम्यां विहरन्ब्रह्मविद्भवति। पञ्चमभूम्यां विहरन्ब्रह्मविद्वरो भवति। षष्ठभूम्यां विह-रन्ब्रह्मविद्वरीयान्भवति। सप्तमभूम्यां विरहन्ब्रह्मविद्वरिष्ठो भवति। तत्रैते श्लोका भवन्ति। ज्ञानभूमिः शुभेच्छा स्यात्प्रथमा समुदीरिता। विचारणा द्वितीया तु तृतीया तनुमानसा ॥१॥

सत्त्वापत्तिश्चतुर्थी स्यात्ततोऽसंसक्तिनामिका। पदार्थभावना षष्ठी सप्तमी तुर्यगा स्मृता ॥२॥ स्थितः किं मूढ एवास्मि प्रेक्ष्योऽहं शास्त्रसज्जनैः। वैराग्यपूर्वमिच्छेति शुभेच्छेत्युच्यते बुधैः ॥३॥ शास्त्रसज्जनसंपर्कवैराग्याभ्यासपूर्वकम्। सदाचार प्रवृत्तिर्या प्रोच्यते सा विचारणा ॥४॥ विचारणाशुभेच्छामिन्द्रियार्थेषुरक्तता। यत्र सा तनुतामेति प्रोच्यते तनुमानसी ॥५॥

भूमिकात्रितयाभ्यासाच्चित्तेऽर्थविरतेर्वशात्। सत्वात्मनि स्थिते शुद्धे सत्त्वापत्तिरूदाहृता ॥६॥ दशाचतुष्टयाभ्यासादसंसर्गफला तु या। रूढसत्वचमत्कारा प्रोक्ता संसक्तिनामिका ॥७॥ भूमिकापञ्चकाभ्यासात्स्वात्मारामतया भृशम्। आभ्यन्तराणां बाह्यानां पदार्थानामभावनात् ॥८॥ परप्रयुक्तेन चिरं प्रत्ययेनावबोधनम्। पदार्थभावना नाम षष्ठी भवति भूमिका ॥९॥ षड्भूमिकाचिराभ्यासाद्भेदस्यानुपलम्भनात्। यत्स्वभावैकनिष्ठत्वं सा ज्ञेया तुर्यगा गतिः ॥१०॥

शुभेच्छादित्रयं भूमिभेदाभेदयुतं स्मृतम्। यथावद्वेद बुद्ध्येदं जगज्जाग्रति दृश्यते ॥११॥ अद्वैते स्थैर्यमायाते द्वैते च प्रशमं गते। पश्यन्ति स्वप्नवल्लोकं तुर्यभूमिसुयोगतः ॥१२॥ विच्छिन्नशरदभ्रांशविलयं प्रविलीयते। सत्वावशेष एवास्ते हे निदाघ दृढीकुरु ॥१३॥

पञ्चभूमिं समारुह्य सुषुप्तिपदनामिकाम्। शान्ताशेषविशेषांशस्तिष्ठत्यद्वैतमात्रके ॥१४॥ अन्तर्मुखतया नित्यं बहिर्वृत्तिपरोऽपि सन्। परिश्रान्ततया

नित्यं निद्रालुरिव लक्ष्यते ॥१५॥ कुर्वन्नभ्यासमेतस्यां भूम्यां सम्यग्विवासनः। सप्तमी गाढसुप्त्याख्या क्रमप्राप्ता पुरातनी ॥१६॥ यत्र नासन्न सद्रूपो नाहं नाप्यनहंकृतिः। केवलं क्षीणमनन आस्तेऽद्वैतेऽतिनिर्भयः ॥१७॥

अन्तःशून्यो बहिःशून्यः शून्यकुम्भ इवाम्बरे। अन्तःपूर्णो बहिःपूर्णः पूर्णकम्भ इवार्णवे ॥१८॥ मा भव ग्राह्यभावात्मा ग्राहकात्मा च मा भव। भावनामखिलां त्यक्त्वा यच्छिष्टं तन्मयो भव ॥१९॥ द्रष्टृदर्शनदृश्यानि त्यक्त्वा वासनया सह। दर्शनप्रथमाभासमात्मानं केवलं भज ॥२०॥ यथास्थितमिदं यस्य व्यवहारवतोऽपिच। अस्तंगतं स्थितं व्योम स जीवन्मुक्त उच्यते ॥२१॥

नोदेति नास्तमायाति सुखे दुःखे मनःप्रभा। यथाप्राप्तस्थितिर्यस्य स जीवन्मुक्त उच्यते ॥२२॥ यो जागर्ति सुषुप्तिस्थो यस्य जाग्रन्न विद्यते। यस्य निर्वासनो बोधः स जीवन्मुक्त उच्यते ॥२३॥ रागद्वेषभयादीनामनुरूपं चरन्नपि। योऽन्तर्व्योमवदच्छन्नः स जीवन्मुक्त उच्यते ॥२४॥ यस्य नाहंकृतो भावो बुद्धिर्यस्य न लिप्यते। कुर्वतोऽकुर्वतो वापि स जीवन्मुक्त उच्यते ॥२५॥ यस्मान्नोद्विजते लोको लोकान्नोद्विजते च यः। हर्षामर्षभयोन्मुक्तः स जीवन्मुक्त उच्यते ॥२६॥

यः समस्तार्थजालेषु व्यवहार्यपि शीतलः। परार्थेष्विव पूर्णात्मा स जीवन्मुक्त उच्यते ॥२७॥ प्रजहाति यदा कामान्सर्वांश्चित्तगतान्मुने। मयि सर्वात्मके तुष्टः स जीवन्मुक्त उच्यते ॥२८॥ चैत्यवर्जितचिन्मात्रे पदे परमपावने। अक्षुब्धचित्तो विश्रान्तः स जीवन्मुक्त उच्यते ॥२९॥ इदं जगदहं सोऽयं दृशयजातमवास्तवम्। यस्य चित्ते न स्फुरति स जीवन्मुक्त उच्यते ॥३०॥ सद्ब्रह्मणि स्थिरे स्फारे पूर्णे विषयवर्जिते। आचार्यशास्त्रमार्गेण प्रविश्याशु स्थिरो भव ॥३१॥

शिवो गुरुः शिवो वेदः शिव देवः शिवः प्रभुः। शिवोऽस्म्यहं शिवः सर्वं शिवादन्यन्न किंचन ॥३२॥ तमेव धीरो विज्ञाय प्रज्ञां कुर्वीत ब्राह्मणः। नानुध्यायाद्बहूञ्छब्दान्वाचो विग्लापनं हि तत् ॥३३॥ शुको मुक्तो वामदेवोऽपि मुक्तस्ताभ्यां विना मुक्तिभाजो न सन्तिः। शुकमार्गं येऽनुसरन्ति धीराः सद्यो मुक्तास्ते भवन्तीह लोके ॥३४॥

वामदेवं येऽनुसरन्ति नित्यं मृत्वा जनित्वा च पुनःपुनस्तत्। ते वै लोके क्रममुक्ता भवन्ति योगैः सांख्यैः कर्मभिः सत्त्वयुक्तैः ॥३५॥ शुकश्च वामदेवश्च द्वे सृती देवनिर्मिते। शुको विहङ्गमः प्रोक्तो वामदेवः पिपीलिका ॥३६॥ अतद्व्यावृत्तिरूपेण साक्षाद्विधिमुखेन वा। महावाक्यविचारेण सांख्ययोगसमाधिना ॥३७॥

विदित्वा स्वात्मनो रूपं संप्रज्ञातसमाधितः। शुकमार्गेण विरजाः प्रयान्ति परमं पदम् ॥३८॥ यमाद्यासनजायासहठाभ्यासात्पुनःपुनः। विघ्नबाहुल्यसंजात अणिमादि-वशादिह ॥३९॥ अलब्ध्वापि फलं सम्यक्पुनर्भूत्वा महाकुले। पुनर्वासनवैवायं योगाभ्यासं पुनश्चरन् ॥४०॥ अनेकजन्माभ्यासेन वामदेवेन वे पथा। सोऽपि मुक्तिं समाप्नोति तद्विष्णो परमं पदम् ॥४१॥ द्वाविमावपि पन्थानौ ब्रह्मप्राप्तिकरौ शिवौ। सद्यो-मुक्तिप्रदश्चैकः क्रममुक्तिप्रदः परः। अत्र को मोहः कः शोक एकत्वमनुपश्यतः ॥४२॥

यस्यानुभवपर्यन्ता बुद्धिस्तत्त्वे प्रवर्तते। तद्दृष्टिगोचराः सर्वे मुच्यन्ते सर्वपातकैः ॥४३॥ खेचरा भूचराः सर्वे ब्रह्मविद्दृष्टिगोचराः। सद्य एव विमुच्यन्ते कोटिजन्मार्जितैरघैः ॥४४॥ इति चतुर्थोऽध्यायः ॥४॥

अथ हैनं ऋभुं भगवन्तं निदाघः पप्रच्छ योगाभ्यासविधिमनुब्रूहिति। तथेति स होवाच। पञ्चभूतात्मको देहः पञ्चमण्डलपूरितः। काठिन्यं पृथिवीमेका पानीयं तद्द्रवाकृति ॥१॥ दीपनं च भवेत्तेजः प्रचारो वायुलक्षणम्। आकाशः सत्त्वतः सर्वं ज्ञातव्यं योगमिच्छता ॥२॥ षट्शतान्यधिकान्यत्र सहस्राण्येकविंशतिः। अहोरात्रवहैः श्वासैर्वायुमण्डलघाततः ॥३॥ तत्पृथ्वीमण्डले क्षीणे वलिरायाति देहिनाम्। तद्वदापो गणापाये केशाः स्युः पाण्डुराः क्रमात् ॥४॥

तेजःक्षये क्षुधा कान्तिर्नश्यते मारुतक्षये। वेपथुः संभवेन्नित्यं नाम्भसेनैव जीवति ॥५॥ इत्थंभूतं क्षयान्नित्यं जीवितं भूतधारणम्। उड्डाणं कुरुते यस्मादविश्रान्तं महाखगः ॥६॥ उड्डियाणं तदेव स्यात्तत्र बन्दोऽभिधीयते। उड्डियाणे ह्यसौ बन्धो मृत्युमातङ्गकेशरी ॥७॥ तस्य मुक्तिस्तनोः कायात्तस्य बन्धो हि दुष्करः। अग्नौ तु चालिते कुक्षौ वेदना जायते भृशम् ॥८॥

न कार्या क्षुधि तेनापि नापि विण्मूत्रवेगिना। हितं मितं च भोक्तव्यं स्तोकं स्तोकमनेकधा ॥९॥ मृदुमध्यममन्त्रेषु क्रमान्मन्त्रं लयं हठम्। लयमन्त्रहठा योगा योगो ह्यष्टाङ्गसंयुतः ॥१०॥ यमश्च नियमश्चैव तथा चासनमेव च। प्राणायामस्तथा पश्चात्प्रत्याहारस्तथा परम् ॥११॥ धारणा च तथा ध्यानं समाधिश्चाष्टमो भवेत्। अहिंसा सत्यमस्तेयं ब्रह्मचर्यं दयार्जवम् ॥१२॥ क्षमा धृतिर्मिताहारः शौचं चेति समा दश। तपः सन्तोषमास्तिक्यं दानमीश्वरपूजनम् ॥१३॥

सिद्धान्तश्रवणं चैव ह्रीर्मतिश्च जपो व्रतम्। एते हि नियमाः प्रोक्ता दशधैव महामते ॥१४॥ एकादशासनानि स्युश्चक्रादि मुनिसत्तम। चक्रं पद्मासनं कूर्मं मयूरं कुक्कुटं तथा ॥१५॥ वीरासनं स्वास्तिकं च भद्रं सिंहासनं तथा। मुक्तासनं गोमुखं च कीर्तितं योगवित्तमैः ॥१६॥ सव्योरु दक्षिणे गुल्फे दक्षिणं दक्षिणेतरे। निदध्यादृजुकायस्तु चक्रासनमिदं मतम् ॥१७॥ पूरकः कुम्भकस्तद्वद्रेचकः पूरकः पुनः। प्राणायामः स्वनाडी-भिस्तस्मान्नाडीः प्रचक्षते ॥१८॥

शरीरं सर्वजन्तूनां षण्णवत्यङ्गुलात्मकम्। तन्मध्ये पायुदेशात्तु द्व्यङ्गुलात्परतः परम् ॥१९॥ मेढ्रदेशादधस्तात्तु द्व्यङ्गुलान्मध्यमुच्यते। मेढ्रान्नवाङ्गुलादूर्ध्वं नाडीनां कन्दमुच्यते ॥२०॥ चतुरङ्गुलमुत्सेधं चतुरङ्गुलमायतम्। अण्डाकारं परिवृतं मेदोमज्जास्थिशोणितैः ॥२१॥ तत्रैव नाडीचक्रं तु द्वादशारं प्रतिष्ठितम्। शरीरं ध्रियते येन वर्तते तत्र कुण्डली ॥२२॥ ब्रह्मरन्ध्रं सुषुम्णा या वदनेन पिधाय सा। अलम्बुसा सुषुम्णायाः कुहूर्नाडी वसत्यसौ ॥२३॥

अनन्तरारयुग्मे तु वारुणा च यशस्विनी। दक्षिणारे सुषुम्णायाः पिङ्गला वर्तते क्रमात् ॥२४॥ तदन्तरारयोः पूषा वर्तते च पयस्विनी। सुषुम्ना पश्चिमे चारे स्थिता नाडी सरस्वती ॥२५॥ शङ्खिनी चैव गान्धारी तदनन्तरयोः स्थिते। उत्तरे तु सुषुम्नाया इडाख्या निवसत्यसौ ॥२६॥ अनन्तरं हस्तिजिह्वा ततो विश्वोदरी स्थिता। प्रदक्षिणक्रमेणैव चक्रस्यारेषु नाड्यः ॥२७॥ वर्तन्ते द्वादश ह्येता द्वादशानिलवाहकाः। पटवत्संस्थिता नाड्यो नानावर्णाः समीरिताः ॥२८॥

पटमध्यं तु यत्स्थानं नाभिचक्रं चदुच्यते। नादाधारा समाख्याता ज्वलन्ती नाद-रूपिणी ॥२९॥ पररन्ध्रा सुषुम्ना च चत्वारो रत्नपूरिताः। कुण्डल्या पिहितं

शश्वद्ब्रह्मरन्ध्रस्य मध्यमम् ॥३०॥ एवमेतासु नाडीषु धरन्ति दश वायवः। एवं नाडीगतिं वायुगतिं ज्ञात्वा विचक्षणः ॥३१॥ समग्रीवशिरःकायः संवृतास्यः सुनिश्चलः। नासाग्रे चैव हृन्मध्ये बिन्दुमध्ये तुरीयकम् ॥३२॥ स्रवन्तममृतं पश्येन्नेत्राभ्यां सुसमाहितः। अपानं मुकुलीकृत्य पायुमाकृष्य चौन्मुखम् ॥३३॥ प्रणवेन समुत्थाप्य श्रीबीजेन निवर्तयेत्। स्वात्मानं च श्रियं ध्यायेदमृतप्लावनं ततः ॥३४॥

कालवञ्चनमेतद्धि सर्वमुख्यं प्रचक्षते। मनसा चिन्तितं कार्यं मनसा येन सिध्यति ॥३५॥ जलेऽग्निज्वलनाच्छाखापल्लवानि भवन्ति हि। नाधन्यं जागतं वाक्यं विपरीता भवेत्क्रिया ॥३६॥ मार्गे बिन्दुं समाबध्य वह्निं प्रज्वाल्य जीवने। शोषयित्वा तु सलिलं तेन कायं दृढं भवेत् ॥३७॥ गुदयोनिसमायुक्त आकुञ्चत्येककालतः। अपानमूर्ध्वगं कृत्वा समानोऽन्ने नियोजयेत् ॥३८॥ स्वात्मानं च श्रियं ध्यायेदमृतप्लावनं ततः। बलं समारभेद्योगं मध्यमद्वारभागतः ॥३९॥

भावयेदूर्ध्वगत्यर्थं प्राणापानसुयोगतः। एष योगो वरो देहे सिद्धि-मार्गप्रकाशकः ॥४०॥ यथैवापाङ्गतः सेतुः प्रवाहस्य निरोधकः। तथा शरीरगा च्छाया ज्ञातव्या योगिभिः सदा ॥४१॥ सर्वासामेव नाडीनामेष बन्धः प्रकीर्तितः। बन्धस्यास्य प्रसादेन स्फुटीभवति देवता ॥४२॥ एवं चतुष्पथो बन्धो मार्गत्रयनिरोधकः। एक विकासयन्मार्गं येन सिद्धाः सुसङ्गताः ॥४३॥ उदानमूर्ध्वगं कृत्वा प्राणेन सह वेगतः। बन्धोऽयं सर्वनाडीनामूर्ध्वं याति निरोधकः ॥४४॥

अयं च संपुटो योगो मूलबन्धोऽप्ययं मतः। बन्धत्रयमनेनैव सिद्ध्यत्यभ्यासयोगतः ॥४५॥ दिवारात्रमविच्छिन्नं यामेयामे यदा यदा। अनेनाभ्यासयोगेन वायुरभ्यसितो भवेत् ॥४६॥ वायावभ्यसिते वह्निः प्रत्यहं वर्धते तनौ। वह्नौ विवर्धमाने तु सुखमन्नादि जीर्यते ॥४७॥ अन्नस्य परिपाकेन रसवृद्धिः प्रजायते। रसे वृद्धिं गते नित्यं वर्धन्ते धातवस्तथा ॥४८॥

धातूनां वर्धनेनैव प्रबोधो वर्धते तनौ। दह्यन्ते सर्वपापानि जन्मकोट्यर्जितानि च ॥४९॥ गुदमेढ्रान्तरालस्थं मूलाधारं त्रिकोणकम्। शिवस्य बिन्दुरूपस्य स्थानं तद्धि प्रकाशकम् ॥५०॥

यत्र कुण्डलिनि नाम परा शक्तिः प्रतिष्ठिता। यस्मादुत्पद्यते वायुर्यस्माद्वह्निः प्रवर्धते ॥५१॥ यस्मादुत्पद्यते बिन्दुर्यस्मान्नादः प्रवर्धते। यस्मादुत्पद्यते हंसो यस्मादुत्पद्यते मनः ॥५२॥ मूलाधारादिषटचक्रं शक्तिस्थानमुदीरितम्। कण्ठादुपरि मूर्धान्तं शांभवं स्थानमुच्यते ॥५३॥ नाडीनामाश्रयः पिण्डो नाड्यः प्राणस्य चाश्रयः। जीवस्य निलयः प्राणो जीवो हंसस्य चाश्रयः ॥५४॥ हंसः शक्तेरधिष्ठानं चराचरमिदं जगत्। निर्विकल्पः प्रसन्नात्मा प्राणायामं समभ्यसेत् ॥५५॥

सम्यग्बन्धत्रयस्थोऽपि लक्ष्यलक्षणकारणम्। वेद्यं समुद्धरेन्नित्यं सत्यसंधानमानसः ॥५६॥ रेचकं पूरकं चैव कुम्भमध्ये निरोधयेत्। दृश्यमाने परे लक्ष्ये ब्रह्मणि स्वयमाश्रितः ॥५७॥ बाह्यस्थविषयं सर्वं रेचकः समुदाहृतः। पूरकं शास्त्रविज्ञानं कुम्भकं स्वगतं स्मृतम् ॥५८॥ एवमभ्यासचित्तश्चेत्स मुक्तो नात्र संशयः। कुम्भकेन समारोप्य कुम्भकेनैव पूरयेत् ॥५९॥ कुम्भेन कुम्भयेत्कुम्भं तदन्तस्थः परं शिवम्। पुनरास्फालयेदद्य सुस्थिरं कण्ठमुद्रया ॥६०॥

वायूनां गतमावृत्य धृत्वा पूरककुम्भकौ। समहस्तयुगं भूमौ समं पादयुगं तथा ॥६१ ॥ वेधकक्रमयोगेन चतुष्पीठं तु वायुना। आस्फालयेन्महामेरुं वायुवक्त्रे प्रकोटिभिः ॥६२ ॥ पुटद्वयं समाकृष्य वायुः स्फुरति सत्वरम्। सोमसूर्याग्निसंबन्धाज्जानीयादमृताय वै ॥६३ ॥ मेरुमध्यगता देवाश्चलन्ते मेरुचालनात्। आदौ संजायते क्षिप्रं वेधोऽस्य ब्रह्मग्रन्थितः ॥६४ ॥ ब्रह्मग्रन्थिं ततो भित्त्वा विष्णुग्रन्थिं भिनत्त्यसौ। विष्णुग्रन्थिं ततो भित्त्वा रुद्रग्रन्थिं भिनत्त्यसौ ॥६५ ॥

रुद्रग्रन्थिं ततो भित्त्वा छित्त्वा मोहमलं तथा। अनेकजन्मसंस्कारगुरुदेवप्रसादतः ॥६६ ॥ योगाभ्यासात्ततो वेधो जायते तस्य योगिनः। इडापिङ्गलयोर्मध्ये सुषुम्नानाडिमण्डले ॥६७ ॥ मुद्राबन्धविशेषेण वायुमूर्ध्वं च कारयेत्। ह्रस्वो दहति पापानि दीर्घो मोक्षदायकः ॥६८ ॥ आप्यायनः प्लुतो वापि त्रिविधोच्चारणेन तु। तैलधारामिवाच्छिन्नं दीर्घघण्टानिनादवत् ॥६९ ॥

अवाच्यं प्रणवस्याग्रं यस्तं वेद स वेदवित्। ह्रस्वं बिन्दुगतं दैर्घ्यं ब्रह्मरन्ध्रगतं प्लुतम्। द्वादशान्तगतं मन्त्रं प्रसादं मन्त्रसिद्धये ॥७० ॥ सर्वविघ्नहरश्चायं प्रणवः सर्वदोषहा। आरम्भश्च घटश्चैव पुनः परिचयस्तथा ॥७१ ॥ निष्पत्तिश्चेति कथिताश्चतस्रस्तस्य भूमिकाः। कारणत्रयसंभूतं बाह्यं कर्म परित्यजन् ॥७२ ॥ आन्तरं कर्म कुरुते यत्रारम्भः स उच्यते। वायुः पश्चिमतो वेधं कुर्वन्नापुर्य सुस्थिरम् ॥७३ ॥ यत्र तिष्ठति सा प्रोक्ता घटाख्या भूमिका बुधैः। न सजीवो न निर्जीवः काये तिष्ठति निश्चलम्। यत्र वायुः स्थिरः खे स्यात्सेयं प्रथमभूमिका ॥७४ ॥

यत्रात्मना सृष्टिलयौ जीवन्मुक्तिदशागतः। सहजः कुरुते योगं सेयं निष्पत्तिभूमिका ॥७५ ॥ इति। एतदुपनिषदं योऽधीते सोऽग्निपूतो भवति। स वायुपूतो भवति। सुरापानात्पूतो भवति। स्वर्णस्तेयात्पूतो भवति। स जीवन्मुक्तो भवति। तदेतदृचाभ्युक्तम्। तद्विष्णोः परमं पदं सदा पश्यन्ति सूरयः। दिवीव चक्षुराततम्। तद्विप्रासो विपन्यवो जागृवांसः समिन्धते। विष्णोर्यत्परमं पदमित्युपनिषत्। इति पञ्चमोऽध्यायः ॥५ ॥ ॐ सह नाववत्विति शान्तिः ॥ हरि ॐ तत्सत् ॥

इति वराहोपनिषत्समाप्ता ॥

२८. मण्डलब्राह्मणोपनिषत्

ब्राह्मान्तस्तारकाकारं व्योमपञ्चकविग्रहम्।
राजयोगैकसंसिद्धं रामचन्द्रमुपास्महे ॥१ ॥

ॐ पूर्णमद इति शान्तिः।

ॐ याज्ञवल्क्यो ह वै महामुनिरादित्यलोकं जगाम। तमादित्यं नत्वा भो भगवन्नादित्यात्मतत्त्वमनुब्रूहीति। सहोवाच नारायणः। ज्ञानयुक्तयमाद्यष्टाङ्गयोग उच्यते। शीतोष्णाहारनिद्राविजयः सर्वदा शान्तिर्निश्चलत्वं विषयेन्द्रियनिग्रहश्चैते यमाः। गुरुभक्तिः सत्यमार्गानुरक्तिः सुखागतवस्त्वनुभवश्च तद्वस्त्वनुभवेन तुष्टिर्निः सङ्गता एकान्तवासो मनो-

निवृत्तिः फलानभिलाषो वैराग्यभावश्च नियमाः। सुखासनवृत्तिश्चीरवासाश्चैवमासननियमो भवति। पुरककुम्भकरेचकैः षोडशचतुष्षष्टिद्वात्रिंशत्संख्यया यथाक्रमं प्राणायामः। विषयेभ्य इन्द्रियार्थेभ्यो मनोनिरोधनं प्रत्याहारः सर्वशरीरेषु चैतन्यैकतानता ध्यानम्। विषयव्यावर्तनपूर्वकं चैतन्ये चेतःस्थापनं धारणं भवति। ध्यानविस्मृतिः समाधिः। एवं सूक्ष्माङ्गानि। य एवं वेद स मुक्तिभाग्भवति॥१॥

देहस्य पञ्च दोषा भवन्ति कामक्रोधनिःश्वासभयनिद्राः। तन्निरासस्तु निःसंकल्पक्षमालध्वाहराप्रमादतातत्त्वसेवनम्। निद्राभयसरीसृपं हिंसादितरङ्गं तृष्णावर्तं दारपङ्कं संसारवार्धिं तर्तुं सूक्ष्ममार्गमवलम्ब्य सत्त्वादिगुणानतिक्रम्य तारकमवलोकयेत्। भ्रूमध्ये सच्चिदानन्दतेजः कूटरूपं तारकं ब्रह्म। तदुपायं लक्ष्यत्रयावलोकनम्। मूलाधारादारभ्य ब्रह्मरन्ध्रपर्यन्तं सुषुम्ना सूर्याभा। मृणालतन्तुसूक्ष्मा कुण्डलिनी। तत्र तमोनिवृत्तिः। तद्दर्शनात्सर्वपापनिवृत्तिः। तर्जन्यग्रोन्मीलितकर्णरन्ध्रद्वये फूत्कारशब्दो जायते।

तत्र स्थिते मनसि चक्षुर्मध्यनीलज्योतिः पश्यति। एवं हृदयेऽपि। बहिर्लक्ष्यं तु नासाग्रे चतुःषडष्टदशद्वादशाङ्गुलीभिः क्रमान्नीलद्युतिश्यामत्वसदृग्रक्तभङ्गी-स्फुरत्पीतवर्णद्वयोपेतं व्योमत्वं पश्यति स तु योगी चलनदृष्ट्या व्योमभागवीक्षितुः पुरुषस्य दृष्ट्यग्रेज्योतिर्मयूखा वर्तन्ते।

तद्दृष्टि स्थिरा भवति। शीर्षोपरि द्वादशाङ्गुलिमानज्योतिः पश्यति तदाऽमृतत्वमेति। मध्यलक्ष्यं तु प्रातश्चित्रादिवर्णसूर्यचन्द्रवह्निज्वालावलीवत्तद्विहीनान्तरिक्षवत्पश्यति। तदाकाराकारी भवति। अभ्यासान्निर्विकारं गुणरहिताकाशं भवति। विस्फुरत्तारकाकारगाढतमोपमं पराकाशं भवति। कालानलसमं द्योतमानं महाकाशं भवति।

सर्वोत्कृष्टपरमाद्वितीयप्रद्योतमानं तत्त्वाकाशं भवति। कोटिसूर्यप्रकाशं सूर्याकाशं भवति। एवमभ्यासात्तन्मयो भवति। य एवं वेद॥२॥ तद्योगं च द्विधा विद्धि पूर्वोत्तरविभागतः। पूर्वं तु तारकं विद्यादमनस्कं तदुत्तरमिति। तारकं द्विविधम्। मूर्तितारकममूर्तितारकमिति।

यदिन्द्रियान्तं तन्मूर्तितारकम्। यद्भ्रूयुगातीतं तदमूर्तितारकमिति। उभयमपि मनोयुक्तमभ्यसेत्। मनोयुक्तान्तरदृष्टिस्तारकप्रकाशाय भवति। भ्रूयुगमध्यबिले तेजस आविर्भावः। एतत्पूर्वतारकम्। उत्तरं त्वमनस्कम्। तालुमूलोर्ध्वभागे महाज्योतिर्विद्यते।

तद्दर्शनादणिमादिसिद्धिः। लक्ष्येऽन्तर्बाह्यायां दृष्टौ निमेपोन्मेषवर्जितायां च इयं शाम्भवी मुद्रा भवति। सर्वतन्त्रेषु गोप्यमहाविद्या भवति। तज्ज्ञानेन संसारनिवृत्तिः। तत्पूजनं मोक्षफलदम्। अन्तर्लक्ष्यं जलज्योतिःस्वरूपं भवति। महर्षिवेद्यं अन्तर्बाह्येन्द्रियैरदृशयम्॥३॥

सहस्रारे जलज्योतिरन्तर्लक्ष्यम्। बुद्धिगुहायां सर्वाङ्गसुन्दरं पुरुषरूपमन्तर्लक्ष्यमित्यपरे। शीर्षान्तर्गतमण्डलमध्यगं पञ्चवक्त्रमुमासहायं नीलकण्ठं प्रशान्तमन्तर्लक्ष्यमिति केचित्। अङ्गुष्ठमात्रः पुरुषोऽन्तर्लक्ष्यमित्येके। उक्तविकल्पं सर्वमात्मैव। तल्लक्ष्यं शुद्धात्मदृष्टया वा यः पश्यति स एव ब्रह्मनिष्ठो भवति। जीवः पञ्चविंशकः स्वकल्पितचतुर्विंशतितत्त्वं परित्यज्य षड्विंशः परमात्माहामेति निश्चयाज्जीवन्मुक्तो भवति। एवमन्तर्लक्ष्यदर्शनेन जीवन्मुक्तिदशायां स्वयमन्तर्लक्ष्यो भूत्वा परमाकाशाखण्डराण्लो भवति॥४॥ इति प्रथम ब्राह्मणम्॥

अथ ह याज्ञवल्क्य आदित्यमण्डलपुरुषं पप्रच्छ । भगवन्नन्तर्लक्ष्यादिकं बहुधोक्तम् । मया तन्न ज्ञातम् । तद्ब्रूहि मह्यम् । तदुहोवाच पञ्चभूतकारणं तडित्कूटाभं तद्वच्चतुः पीठम् । तन्मध्ये तत्त्वप्रकाशो भवति । सोऽतिगूढ अव्यक्तश्च । तज्ज्ञानप्लवाधिरूढेन ज्ञेयम् ।

तद्बाह्याभ्यन्तर्लक्ष्यम् । तन्मध्ये जगल्लीनम् । तन्नादबिन्दुकलातीतमखण्डमण्डलम् । तत्सगुणनिर्गुणस्वरूपम् । तद्वेत्ता विमुक्तः । आदावग्निमण्डलम् । तदुपरि सूर्यमण्डलन् । तन्मध्ये सुधाचन्द्रमण्डलम् । तन्मध्येऽखण्डब्रह्मतेजोमण्डलम् । तद्विद्युल्लेखावच्छुक्लभास्वरम् । तदेव शाम्भवीलक्षणम् । तद्दर्शने तिस्रो मूर्तय अमा प्रतिपत्पूर्णमः चेति । निमीलितदर्शनमामादृष्टिः । अर्धोन्मीलितं प्रतिपत् ।

सर्वोन्मीलनं पूर्णिमा भवति । तासु पूर्णिमाभ्यासः कर्तव्यः तल्लक्ष्यं नासाग्रम् । तदा तालुमूले गाढतमो दृश्यते । तदभ्यासादखण्डमण्डलाकारज्योतिर्दृश्यते । तदेव सच्चिदानन्दं ब्रह्म भवति ।

एवं सहजानन्दे यदा मनो लीयते तदा शान्तो भवी भवति । तामेव खेचरीमाहुः । तदभ्यासान्मनःस्थैर्यम् । ततो वायुस्थैर्यम् । तच्चिह्नानि । आदौ तारकवद्दृश्यते । ततो बज्रदर्पणन् । तत उपरि पूर्णचन्द्रमण्डलम् । ततो नवरत्नप्रभामण्डलम् । ततो मध्याह्नार्क मण्डलम् । ततो वह्निशिखामण्डलं कमाद्दृश्यते ॥१ ॥

तदा पश्चिमाभिमुखप्रकाशः स्फटिकधूम्रबिन्दुनादकलानक्षत्रखयोतदीपनेत्रसवर्णनवरत्नादिप्रभःदृश्यन्ते । तदेव प्रणवस्वरूपम् । प्राणापानयोरैक्यं कृत्वा धृतकुम्भको नासाग्रदर्शनदृढभावनया द्विकराङ्गुलिभिः पण्मुकी करणेन प्रणवध्वनिं निशम्य मनस्तत्र लीनं भवति ।

तस्य न कर्मलेपः । रवेरुदयास्तमययोः किल कर्म कर्तव्यम् । एवंविदश्चिदादित्यस्योदयास्तमयाभावात्सर्वकर्माभावः । शब्दकाललयेन दिवारात्र्यवीतो भूत्वा सर्वपरिपूर्णज्ञानेनोन्तन्यवस्थावशेन ब्रह्मैवयं भवति । उन्मन्या अमनस्कं भवति । तस्य निश्चिन्ता ध्यानम् । सवकर्मनिराकरणमावाहनम् । निश्चयज्ञानमासनम् उन्मनीभावः पाद्यम् । सदाऽमनस्कमर्घ्यम् । सदादीप्तिरपारामृतवृत्तिः स्नानम् । सर्वत्र भावना गन्धः दृक्स्वरूपातस्थानमक्षताः । चिदाप्तिः पुष्पम् । जिदग्निस्वरूपं धूपः । चिदादित्यस्वरूपं दीपः । परिपूर्णचन्द्रामृतरसस्यैकीकरणं नैवेद्यम् । निश्चलत्वं प्रदक्षिणम् ।

सोहंभावो नमस्कारः । मौनं स्तुतिः । सर्वसंतोषो विसर्जनमिति य एवं वेद ॥२ ॥ एवं त्रिपुठ्या निरस्तायां निस्तरङ्गसमुद्रवन्निवातस्थितदीपवदचलसंपूर्णभावाभावविहीनकैवल्यद्योतिर्भवति । जाग्रन्निन्दान्तः परिज्ञानेन ब्रह्मविद्भवति । सुषुप्तिसमाध्योर्मनोलयाविशेषेऽपि महदस्त्युभयोर्भेदस्तमसि लीनत्वान्मुक्तिहेतुत्वाभावाच्च । समाधौ मृदिततमोविकारस्य तदाकाराकारिताखण्डाकारवृत्त्यात्मकसाक्षिचैतन्ये प्रपञ्चलयः संपद्यते प्रपञ्चस्य मनः कल्पितत्वात् । ततो भेदाभावात् कदाचिद्बहिर्गतेऽपि मिथ्यात्वभानात् । सकृद्विभातसदानन्दानुभवैकगोचरो ब्रह्मवित्तदेव भवति ।

यस्य संकल्पनाशः स्यात्तस्य मुक्तिः करे स्थिता । तस्माद्भावाभावौ परित्यज्य परमात्मध्यानेन मुक्तो भवति । पुनःपुनः सर्वावस्थासु ज्ञानज्ञेयौ ध्यानध्येयौ लक्ष्यालक्ष्ये दृश्यादृश्ये चोहापोहादि परित्यज्य जीवन्मुक्तो भवेत् । य एवं वेद ॥३ ॥

पञ्चावस्थाः जाग्रत्स्वप्नसुषुप्तितुरीयतुरीयातीताः। आग्रति प्रवृत्तो जीवः प्रवृत्तिमार्गासक्तः। पापफलनरकादिमांस्तु शुभकर्मफलस्वर्गमस्त्विति काङ्क्षते। स एव स्वीकृतवैराग्यात्कर्मफलजन्माऽलं संसारबन्धनमलमिति विमुक्त्यभिमुखो

निवृत्तिमार्गप्रवृत्तो भवति। स एव संसारतारणाय गुरुमाश्रित्य कामादि त्यक्त्वा विहितकर्माचरन्साधनचतुष्टयसंपन्नो हृदयकमलमध्ये भगवत्सत्तामात्रान्तर्लक्ष्यरूपमासाद्य सुषुप्त्यवस्थाया मुक्तब्रह्मानन्दस्मृतिं लब्ध्वा एक एवाहमद्वितीयः कंचित्कालमज्ञानवृत्त्या विस्मृतजाग्रद्वासनानुफलेन तैजसोऽस्मीति तदुभयनिवृत्त्या प्राज्ञ इदानीमस्मीत्यहमेक एव स्थानभेदादवस्थाभेदस्य परंतु नहि मदन्यदिति जातविवेकः शुद्धाद्वैतब्रह्माहमिति भिदागन्धं निरस्य स्वान्तर्विजृम्भितभानुमण्डलध्यानतदाकाराकारितपरंब्रह्माकारितमुक्तिमार्गमारुढः परिपक्वो भवति।

संकल्पादिकं मनो बन्धहेतुः। तद्वियुक्तं मनो मोक्षाय भवति। तद्वांश्चक्षु-रादिबाह्यप्रपञ्चोपरतो विगतप्रपञ्चगन्धः सर्वजगदात्मत्वेन पश्यंस्त्यक्ताहंकारो ब्रह्माहमस्मीति चिन्तयन्निदं सर्वं यदयमात्मेति भावयन्कृतकृत्यो भवति ॥४॥

सर्वपरिपूर्णतुरीयातीतब्रह्मभूतो योगी भवति। तं ब्रह्मेति स्तुवन्ति। सर्वलोकस्तुतिपात्रः सर्वदेशसंचारशीलः परमात्मगगने बिन्दुं निक्षिप्य शुद्धाद्वैताजाड्यसहजामनस्कयोगनिद्राखण्डानन्दपदानुवृत्त्या जीवन्मुक्तो भवति। तच्चानन्दसमुद्रमग्ना योगिनो भवन्ति। तदपेक्षया इन्द्रादयः स्वल्पानन्दाः। एवं प्राप्तानन्दः परमयोगी भवतीत्युपनिषत् ॥५॥ इति द्वितीयं ब्राह्मणम् ॥२॥

याज्ञवल्क्यो महामुनिर्मण्डलपुरुषं पप्रच्छ स्वामिन्नमनस्कलक्षणमुक्तमपि विस्मृतं पुनस्तल्लक्षणं ब्रूहीति। तथेति मण्डलपुरुषोऽब्रवीत्। इदममनस्कमतिरहस्यम्। यज्ज्ञानेन कृतार्थो भवति तन्नित्यं शांभवीमुद्रान्वितम्। परमात्मदृष्ट्या तत्प्रत्यलक्ष्याणि दृष्ट्वा तदनु सर्वेशमप्रमेयमजं शिवं परमाकाशं निरालम्बमद्वयं ब्रह्मविष्णुरुद्रादीनामेकलक्ष्यं सर्वकारणं परंब्रह्मात्मन्येव पश्यमानो गुहाविहरणमेव निश्चयेन ज्ञात्वा भावाभावादिद्वन्द्वातीतः

संविदितमनोन्मन्यनुभवस्तदनन्तरमखिलेन्द्रियक्षयवशादमनस्कसुखब्रह्मानन्दसमुद्रे मनःप्रवाहयोगरूपनिवातस्थितदीपवदचलं परंब्रह्म प्राप्नोति। ततः शुष्कवृक्षवन्मूर्च्छा-निद्रामयनिः श्वासोच्छ्वासाभावान्नष्टद्वन्द्वः सदाचञ्चलगात्रः परमशान्तिं स्वीकृत्य मनः प्रचारशून्यं परमात्मनि लीनं भवति। पयः स्रावानन्तरं धेनुस्तनक्षीरमिव सर्वेन्द्रियवर्गे परिनष्टे मनोनाशं भवति तदेवामनस्कम्। तदनु नित्यशुद्धः परमात्माहमेवेति तत्त्वमसीत्युपदेशेन त्वमेवाहमहमेव त्वमिति तारकयोगमार्गेणाखण्डानन्दपूर्णः कृतार्थो भवति ॥१॥

परिपूर्णपराकाशमग्नमनाः प्राप्तोन्मन्यवस्थः संन्यस्तसर्वेन्द्रियवर्गः अनेकजन्मार्जित-पुण्यपुञ्जपक्वकैवल्यफलोऽखण्डानन्दनिरस्तसर्वक्लेशकश्मलो ब्रह्माहमस्मीति कृतकृत्यो भवति। त्वमेवाहं न भेदोऽस्ति पूर्णत्वात्परमात्मनः। इत्युच्चरन्त्समालिङ्ग्य शिष्यं ज्ञप्तिमनीनयत् ॥२॥ इति तृतीय ब्राह्मणम् ॥३॥

अथ ह याज्ञवल्क्यो मण्डलपुरुषं पप्रच्छ व्योमपञ्चकलक्षणं विस्तरेणानुब्रूहीति। स होवाचाकाशं पराकाशं महाकाशं सूर्याकाशं परमाकाशमिति पञ्च भवन्ति।

बाह्याभ्यन्तरमन्धकारमयमाकाशम्। बाह्यस्याभ्यन्तरे कालानलसदृशं पराकाशम्। सबाह्याभ्यन्तरेऽपरिमितद्युतिनिभं तत्त्वं महाकाशम्।

सबाह्याभ्यन्तरे सूर्यनिभं सूर्याकाशम्। अनिर्वचनीयज्योतिः सर्वव्यापकं निरतिशयानन्दलक्षणं परमाकाशम्। एवंतत्तल्लक्ष्यदर्शनात्तत्तद्रूपो भवति। नवचक्रं षडाधारं त्रिलक्ष्यं व्योमपञ्चकम्। सम्यगेतन्न जानाति स योगी नामतो भवेत् ॥१ ॥ इति चतुर्थं ब्राह्मणम्।

सविषयं मनो बन्धाय निर्विषयं मुक्तये भवति। अतः सर्वं जगच्चित्तगोचरम्। तदेव चित्तं निराश्रयं मनोन्मन्यवस्थापरिपक्वं लययोग्यं भवति। तल्लयं परिपूर्णे मयि समभ्यसेत्। मनोलयकारणमहमेव। अनाहतस्य शब्दस्य तस्य शब्दस्य यो ध्वनिः। ध्वनेरन्तर्गतं ज्योतिर्ज्योतिरन्तर्गतं मनः। यन्मनस्त्रिजगत्सृष्टिस्थितिव्यसनकर्मकृत्। तन्मनो विलयं याति तद्विष्णोः परमं पदम्। तल्लयाच्छुद्धाद्वैतसिद्धिर्भेदाभावात्। एतदेव परमतत्त्वम्। स तज्ज्ञो बालोन्मत्तपिशाचवज्जडवृत्त्या लोकमाचरेत् एवममनस्काभ्यासेनैव नित्यतृप्तिरल्पमूत्रपुरीषमितभोजनदृढाङ्गाजाड्यनिद्रादृग्वायुचलनाभावब्रह्मदर्शनाज्ज्ञातसुखस्वरूपसिद्धिर्भवति। एवं चिरसमाधिजनितब्रह्मामृतपानपरायणोऽसौ संन्यासी परमहंस अवधूतो भवति। तद्दर्शनेन सकलं जगत्पवित्रं भवति। तत्सेवापरोऽज्ञोऽपि मुक्तो भवति। तत्कुलमेकोत्तरशतं तारयति। तन्मातृपितृजायापत्यवर्गं च मुक्तं भवतीत्युपनिषत् ॥ ॐ पूर्णमद इति शान्तिः ॥

इति मण्डलब्राह्मणोपनिषत्समाप्ता ॥

२९. नादबिन्दूपनिषत्

वैराजात्मोपासनया संजातज्ञानवह्निना।
दग्ध्वा कर्मत्रयं योगी यत्पदं याति तद्भजे ॥

ॐ वाङ्मे मनसीति शान्तिः ॥

ॐ अकारो दक्षिणः पक्ष उकारस्तूत्तरः स्मृतः। मकारं पुच्छमित्याहुरर्धमात्रा तु मस्तकम् ॥१ ॥ पादादिकं गुणास्तस्य शरीरं तत्त्वमुच्यते। धर्मोऽस्य दक्षिणं चक्षुरधर्मोऽथो परः स्मृतः ॥२ ॥ भूर्लोकः पादयोस्तस्य भुवर्लोकस्तु जानुनि। सुवर्लोकः कटीदेशे नाभिदेशे महर्जगत् ॥३ ॥

जनोलोकस्तु हृद्देशे कण्ठे लोकस्तपस्ततः। भ्रुवोर्ललाटमध्ये तु सत्यलोको व्यवस्थितः ॥४ ॥ सहस्रार्णमतीवात्र मन्त्र एष प्रदर्शितः। एवमेतां समारूढो हंसयोगविचक्षणः ॥५ ॥ न भिद्यते कर्मचारैः पापकोटिशतैरपि। आग्नेयी प्रथमा मात्रा वायव्येषा तथापरा ॥६ ॥

भानुमण्डलसंकाशा भवेन्मात्रा तथोत्तरा। परमा चार्धमात्रा या वारुणीं तां विदुर्बुधाः ॥७ ॥ कालत्रयेऽपि यस्येमा मात्रा नूनं प्रतिष्ठिताः। एष ओंकार आख्यातो धारणाभिर्निबोधत ॥८ ॥ घोषिणी प्रथमा मात्रा विद्या मात्रा तथापरा। पतङ्गिनी तृतीया स्याच्चतुर्थी

वायुवेगिनी ॥९ ॥ पञ्चमी नामधेया तु षष्टी चैन्द्र्यभिधीयते । सप्तमी वैष्णवी नाम अष्टमी शांकरीति च ॥१० ॥

नवमी महती नाम धृतिस्तु दशमी मता। एकादशी भवेन्नारी ब्राह्मी तु द्वादशी परा ॥११ ॥ प्रथमायां तु मात्रायां यदि प्राणैर्वियुज्यते । भरते वर्षराजासौ सार्वभौमः प्रजायते ॥१२ ॥ द्वितीयायां समुत्क्रान्तो भवेद्यक्षो महात्मवान्। विद्याधरस्तृतीयायां गान्धर्वस्तु चतुर्थिका ॥१३ ॥ पञ्चम्यामथ मात्रायां यदि प्राणैर्वियुज्यते । उषितः सह देवत्वं सोमलोके महीयते ॥१४ ॥ षष्ठ्यामिन्द्रस्य सायुज्यं सप्तम्यां वैष्णवं पदम् । अष्टम्यां व्रजते रुद्रं पशूनां च पतिं तथा ॥१५ ॥

नवम्यां तु महर्लोकं दशम्यां तु जनं व्रजेत्। एकादश्यां तपोलोकं द्वादश्यां ब्रह्म शाश्वतम् ॥१६ ॥ ततः परतरं शुद्धं व्यापकं निर्मलं शिवम्। सदोदितं परं ब्रह्म ज्योतिषामुदयो यतः ॥१७ ॥ अतीन्द्रियं गुणातीतं मनो लीनं यदा भवेत्। अनूपमं शिवं शान्तं योगयुक्तं सदाविशेत् ॥१८ ॥ तद्युक्तस्तन्मयो जन्तुः शनैर्मुञ्चेत्कलेवरम् । संस्थितो योगचारेण सर्वसङ्गविवर्जितः ॥१९ ॥

ततो विलीनपाशोऽसौ विपलः कमलाप्रभुः। तेनैव ब्रह्मभावेन परमानन्दमश्नुते ॥२० ॥ आत्मानं सततं ज्ञात्वा कालं नय महामते प्रारब्धमखिलं भुञ्जन्नोद्वेगं कर्तुमर्हसि ॥२१ ॥ उत्पन्ने तत्त्वविज्ञाने प्रारब्धं नैव मुञ्चति । तत्त्वज्ञानोदयादूर्ध्वं प्रारभ्धं नैव विद्यते ॥२२ ॥

देहादीनामसत्त्वात्तु यथा स्वप्ने विबोधतः। कर्म जन्मान्तरीयं यत्प्रारब्धमिति कीर्तितम् ॥२३ ॥ तत्तु जन्मान्तराभावात्पुंसो नैवास्ति कर्हिचित्। स्वप्नदेहो यथाध्यस्तस्तथैवायं हि देहकः ॥२४ ॥ अध्यस्तस्य कुतो जन्म जन्माभावे कुतः स्थितिः । उपादानं प्रपञ्चस्य मृद्भाण्डस्येव पश्यति ॥२५ ॥

अज्ञानं चेति वेदान्तैस्तस्मिन्नष्टे क्व विश्वता । यथा रज्जुं परित्यज्य सर्पं गृह्णाति वै भ्रमात् ॥२६ ॥ तद्वत्सत्यमविज्ञाय जगत्पश्यति मूढधीः । रज्जुखण्डे परिज्ञाते सर्परूपं न तिष्ठति ॥२७ ॥ अधिष्ठाने तथा ज्ञाते प्रपञ्चे शून्यतां गते। देहस्यापि प्रपञ्चत्वात्प्रारब्धावस्थितिः कुतः ॥२८ ॥ अज्ञानजनबोधार्थं प्रारब्धमिति चोच्यते । ततः कालवशादेव प्रारब्धे तु क्षयं गते ॥२९ ॥

ब्रह्मप्रणवसंधानं नादो ज्योतिर्मयः शिवः। स्वयमाविर्भवेदात्मा मेघापायेंऽशुमानिव ॥३० ॥ सिद्धासने स्थितो योगी मुद्रां संधाय वैष्णवीम् । शृणुयाद्दक्षिणे कर्णे नादमन्तर्गतं सदा ॥३१ ॥ अभ्यस्यमानो नादोऽयं बाह्यमावृणुते ध्वनिः । पक्षाद्विपक्षमखिलं जित्वा तुर्यपदं व्रजेत् ॥३२ ॥ श्रूयते प्रथमाभ्यासे नादो नानाविधो महान्। वर्धमाने तथाभ्यासे श्रूयते सूक्ष्मसूक्ष्मतः ॥३३ ॥

आदौ जलधिजीमूतभेरीनिर्झरसंभवः। मध्ये मर्दलशब्दाभो घण्टाकाहलजस्तथा ॥३४ ॥ अन्ते तु किंकिणीवंशवीणाभ्रमरनिस्वनः । इति नानाविधा नादाः श्रूयन्ते सूक्ष्मसूक्ष्मतः ॥३५ ॥ महति श्रूयमाणे तु महाभेर्यादिकध्वनौ । तत्र सूक्ष्मं सूक्ष्मतरं नादमेव परामृशेत् ॥३६ ॥ घनमुत्सृज्य वा सूक्ष्मे सूक्ष्ममुत्सृज्य वा घने । रममाणमपि क्षिप्तं मनो नान्यत्र चालयेत् ॥३७ ॥

यत्र कुत्रापि वा नादे लगति प्रथमं मनः। तत्र तत्र स्थिरीभूत्वा तेन सार्धं विलीयते ॥३८॥ विस्मृत्य सकलं बाह्यं नादे दुग्धाम्बुवन्मनः। एकीभूयाथ सहसा चिदाकाशे विलीयते ॥३९॥ उदासीनस्ततो भूत्वा सदाभ्यासेन संयमी। उन्मनीकारकं सद्यो नादमेवावधारयेत् ॥४०॥ सर्वचिन्तां समुत्सृज्य सर्वचेष्टाविवर्जितः। नादमेवानुसंदध्यान्नादे चित्तं विलीयते ॥४१॥ मकरन्दं पिबन्भृङ्गो गन्धान्नापेक्षते यथा। नादासक्तं सदा चित्तं विषयं न हि काङ्क्षति ॥४२॥

बद्धः सुनादगन्धेन सद्यः संत्यक्तचापलः। नादग्रहणतश्चित्तमन्तरङ्गभुजङ्गमः ॥४३॥ विस्मृत्य विश्वमेकाग्रः कुत्रचिन्न हि धावति। मनोमत्तगजेन्द्रस्य विषयोद्यानचारिणः ॥४४॥ नियामनसमर्थोऽयं निनादो निशिताङ्कुशः। नादोऽन्तरङ्गसारङ्गबन्धने वागुरायते ॥४५॥ अन्तरङ्गसमुद्रस्य रोधे वेलायतेऽपि वा। ब्रह्मप्रणवसंलग्ननादो ज्योतिर्मयात्मकः ॥४६॥

मनस्तत्र लयं याति तद्विष्णोः परमं पदम्। तावदाकाशसंकल्पो यावच्छब्दः प्रवर्तते ॥४७॥ निःशब्दं तत्परं ब्रह्म परमात्मा समीयते। नादो यावन्मनस्तावन्नादान्तेऽपि मनोन्मनी ॥४८॥ सशब्दश्चाक्षरे क्षीणे निःशब्दं परमं पदम्। सदा नादानुसंधानात्संक्षीणा वासना तु या ॥४९॥ निरञ्जने विलीयेते मनोवायू न संशयः। नादकोटिसहस्राणि बिन्दुकोटिशतानि च ॥५०॥ सर्वे तत्र लयं यान्ति ब्रह्मप्रवनादके। सर्वावस्थाविनिर्मुक्तः सर्वचिन्ताविवर्जितः ॥५१॥

मृतवत्तिष्ठते योगी स मुक्तो नात्र संशयः। शङ्खदुन्दुभिनादं च न शृणोति कदाचन ॥५२॥ काष्ठवज्ज्ञायते देह उन्मन्यावस्थया ध्रुवम्। न जानाति स शीतोष्णं न दुःखं न सुखं तथा ॥५३॥ न मानं नावमानं च संत्यक्त्वा तु समाधिना। अवस्थात्रयमन्वेति न चित्तं योगिनः सदा ॥५४॥

जाग्रन्निद्राविनिर्मुक्तः स्वरूपावस्थतामियात् ॥५५॥ दृष्टिः स्थिरा यस्य विनासदृश्यं वायुः स्थिरो यस्य विनाप्रयत्नम्। चित्तं स्थिरं यस्य विनावलम्बं स ब्रह्मतारान्तरनादरूप इत्युपनिषत् ॥५६॥ ॐ वाङ्मे मनसीति शान्तिः ॥

इति नादबिन्दूपनिषत्समाप्ता।

३०. योगकुण्डल्युपनिषत्

योगकुण्डल्युपनिषद्योगसिद्धिहृदासनम्।
निर्विशेषब्रह्मतत्त्वं स्वमात्रमिति चिन्तये ॥१॥

ॐ सह नाववत्विति शान्तिः ॥

हरिः ॐ ॥ हेतुद्वयं हि चित्तस्य वासना च समीरणः। तयोर्विनष्ट एकस्मिंस्तद्द्वावपि विनश्यतः ॥१॥ तयोरादौ समीरस्य जय कुर्यान्नरः सदा। मिताहारश्चासनं च शक्तिचालस्तृतीयकः ॥२॥ एतेषां लक्षणं वक्ष्ये शृणु गौतम सादरम्। सुस्निग्धमधुराहारश्चतुर्थांशविवर्जितः ॥३॥ भुज्यते शिवसंप्रीत्यै मिताहारः स उच्यते। आसनं द्विविधं प्रोक्तं पद्मं वज्रासनं तथा ॥४॥

ऊर्वोरुपरि चेद्धत्ते उभे पादतले यथा। पद्मासनं भवेदेतत्सर्वपापप्रणाशनम् ॥५॥ वामाङ्घ्रिमूलकन्दाधो ह्यन्यं तदुपरि क्षिपेत्। समग्रीवशिरः कायो वज्रासनमितीरितम् ॥६। कुण्डल्येव भवेच्छक्तिस्तां तु संचालयेद्बुध। स्वस्थानादा भ्रुवोर्मध्यं शक्तिचालनमुच्यते ॥७॥ तत्साधने द्वयं मुख्यं सरस्वत्यास्तु चालनम्। प्राणरोधमथाभ्यासादृज्वी कुण्डलिनी भवेत् ॥८॥

तयोरादौ सरस्वत्याश्चालनं कथयामि ते। अरुन्धत्येव कथिता पुराविद्भिः सरस्वती ॥९॥ यस्याः संचालनेनैव स्वयं चलति कुण्डली। इडायां वहति प्राणे बद्ध्वा पद्मासनं दृढम् ॥१०॥ द्वादशाङ्गुलदैर्ध्यं च अम्बरं चतुरङ्गुलम्। विस्तीर्य तेन तनानाडीं वेष्टयित्वा ततः सुधीः ॥११॥ अङ्गुष्ठतर्जनीभ्यां तु हस्ताभ्यां धारयेद्दृढम्। स्वशक्त्या चालयेद्वामे दक्षिणेन पुनःपुनः ॥१२॥ मुहूर्तद्वयपर्यन्तं निर्भयाच्चालयेत्सुधीः। ऊर्ध्वमाकर्षयेत्किंचित्सुषुम्नां कुण्डलीगताम् ॥१३॥

तेन कुण्डलिनी तस्याः सुषुम्नाया मुखं व्रजेत्। जहाति तस्मात्प्राणोऽयं सुषुम्नां व्रजति स्वतः ॥१४॥ तुन्दे तु ताणं कुर्याच्च कण्ठसंकोचने कृते। सरस्वत्यां चालनेन वक्षसश्चोर्ध्वगो मरुत् ॥१५॥ सूर्येण रेचयेद्वायुं सरस्वत्यास्तु चालने। कण्ठसंकोचनं कृत्वा वक्षसश्चोर्ध्वगो मरुत् ॥१६॥ तस्मात्संचालयेन्नित्यं शब्दगर्भा सरस्वतीम्। यस्याः संचालनेनैव योगी रोगैः प्रमुच्यते ॥१७॥

गुल्मं जलोदरः प्लीहा ये चान्ये तुन्दमध्यगाः। सर्वे ते शक्तिचालेन रोगा नायन्ति निश्चयम् ॥१८॥ प्राणरोधमथेदानीं प्रवक्ष्यामि समासतः। प्राणश्च दहयो वायुरायामः कुम्भकः स्मृतः ॥१९॥ स एव द्विविधः प्रोक्तः सहितः केवलस्तथा। यावत्केवलसिद्धिः स्यात्तावत्सहितमभ्यसेत् ॥२०॥

सूर्योज्जायी शीतली च भस्त्री चैव चतुर्थिका। भेदैरेव समं कुम्भो यः स्यात्सहितकुम्भकः ॥२१॥ पवित्रे निर्जने देशे शर्करादिविवर्जिते। धनुःप्रमाणपर्यन्ते शीताग्निजलवर्जिते ॥२२॥ पवित्रे नात्युच्चनीचे ह्यासने सुखदे सुखे। बद्धपद्मासनं कृत्वा सरस्वत्यास्तु चालनम् ॥२३॥ दक्षनाड्या समाकृष्य बहिष्ठं पवनं शनैः। यथेष्टं पूरयेद्वायुं रेचयेदिडया ततः ॥२४॥

कपालशोधने वापि रेचयेत्पवनं शनैः। चतुष्कं वातदोषं तु कृमिदोषं निहन्ति च ॥२५॥ पुनः पुनरिदं कार्यं सूर्यभेदमुदाहृतम्। मुख संयम्य नाडिभ्यामाकृष्य पवनं शनैः ॥२६॥ यथा लगति कण्ठात्तु हृदयावधि सस्वनम्। पूर्ववत्कुम्भयेत्प्राणं रेचयेदिडया ततः ॥२७॥ शीर्षोदितानलहरं गलश्लेष्महरं परम्। सर्वरोगहरं पुण्यं देहानलविवर्धनम् ॥२८॥

नाडीजलोदरं धातुगतदोषविनाशनम्। गच्छतस्तिष्ठतः कार्यमुज्जायाख्यं तु कुम्भकम् ॥२९॥ जिह्वया वायुमाकृष्य पूर्ववत्कुम्भकादनु। शनैस्तु घ्राणरन्ध्राभ्यां रेचयेदनिलं सुधीः ॥३०॥ गुल्मप्लीहादिकान्दोषान्क्षयं पित्तं ज्वरं तृषाम्। विषाणि शीतली नाम कुम्भकोऽयं निहन्ति च ॥३१॥ ततः पद्मासनं बद्ध्वा समग्रीवोदरः सुधीः। मुखं संयम्य यत्नेन प्राणं घ्राणेन रेचयेत् ॥३२॥ यथा लगति कण्ठात्तु कपाले सस्वनं ततः। वेगेन पूरयेत् किंचिद्धृत्पद्मावधि मारुतम् ॥३३॥

पुनर्विरेचयेत्तद्वत्पूरयेच्च पुनः पुनः । यथैव लोहकाराणां भस्त्रा वेगेन चाल्यते ॥३४ ।। तथैव स्वशरीरस्थं चालयेत्पवनं शनैः । यथा श्रमो भवेद्देहे तथा सूर्येण पूरयेत् ॥३५ ॥ यथादरं भवेत्पूर्णं पवनेन तथा लघु । धारयन्नासिकामध्यं तर्जनीभ्यां विना दृढम् । ।३६ ॥ कुम्भकं पूर्ववत्कृत्वा रेचयेदिडयानिलम् । कण्ठोत्थितानलहरं शरीराग्निविवर्दनम् ॥३७ ॥

कुण्डलीबोधकं पुण्यं पापघ्नं शुभदं सुखम् । ब्रह्मनाडीमुखान्तस्थकफाद्यर्गल-नाशनम् ॥३८ ॥ गुणत्रयसमुद्भूतग्रन्थित्रयविभेदकम् । विशेषेणैव कर्तव्यं भस्त्राख्यं कुम्भकं त्विदम् ॥३९ ॥ चतुर्णामपि भेदानां कुम्भके समुपस्थिते । बन्धत्रयमिदं कार्यं योगिभिर्वीतकल्मषैः ॥४० ॥ प्रथमो मूलबन्धस्तु द्वितीयोड्डीयणाभिधः । जालन्धर-स्तृतीयस्तु तेषां लक्षणमुच्यते ॥४१ ॥ अधोगतिमपानं वै ऊर्ध्वगं कुरुते बलात् । आकुञ्चनेन तं प्राहुर्मूलबन्धोऽयमुच्यते ॥४२ ॥ अपाने चोर्ध्वगे याते संप्राप्ते वह्निमण्डले । ततोऽनलशिखा दीर्खा वर्धते वायुनाहता ॥४३ ॥

ततो यातौ वह्न्वमानौ प्राणमुष्णस्वरूपकम् । तेनात्यन्तप्रदीप्तेन ज्वलनो देहज-स्तथा ॥४४ ॥ तेन कुण्डलिनी सुप्ता संतप्ता संप्रबुध्यते । दण्डाहतभुजङ्गीव निःश्वस्य ऋजुतां व्रजेत् ॥४५ ॥ बिलप्रवेशतो यत्र ब्रह्मनाड्यन्तरं व्रजेत् । तस्मान्नित्यं मूलबन्धः कर्तव्यो योगिभिः सदा ॥४६ ॥ कुम्भकान्ते रेचकादौ कर्तव्यस्तूड्डियाणकः । बन्धो येन सुषुम्नायां प्राणस्तूड्डीयते यतः ॥४७ ॥

तस्मादुड्डीयणाख्योऽयं योगिभिः समुदाहृतः । सति वज्रासने पादौ कराभ्या धारयेद्दृढम् ॥४८ ॥ गुल्फदेशसमीपे च कन्दं तत्र प्रपीडेत् । पश्चिमं ताणमुदरे धारयेद्धृदये गले ॥४९ ॥ शनैः शनैर्यदा प्राणस्तुन्दसन्धिं निगच्छति । तुन्ददोषं विनिर्धूय कर्तव्यं सततं शनैः ॥५० ॥ पूरकान्ते तु कर्तव्यो बन्धो जालन्धराभिधः । कण्ठसंकोचरूपोऽसौ वायुमार्गनिरोधकः ॥५१ ॥

अधस्तात्कुञ्चनेनाशु कण्ठसंकोचने कृते । मध्ये पश्चिमताणेन स्यात्प्राणो ब्रह्मनाडिगः ॥५२ ॥ पूर्वोक्तेन क्रमेणैव सम्यगासनमास्थितः । चालनं तु सरस्वत्याः कृत्वा प्राणं निरोधयेत् ॥५३ ॥ प्रथमे दिवसे कार्यं कुम्भकानां चुतष्यम् । प्रत्येकं दशसंख्याकं द्वितीये पञ्चभिस्तथा ॥५४ ॥ विंशत्यलं तृतीयेऽह्नि पञ्चवृद्ध्या दिनेदिने । कर्तव्यः कुम्भको नित्यं बन्धत्रयसमन्वितः ॥५५ ॥

दिवा सुप्तिर्निशायां तु जागरादतिमैथुनात् । बहुसंक्रमणं नित्यं रोधान्मूत्र-पुरीषयोः ॥५६ ॥ विषमाशनदोषाच्च प्रयासप्राणचिन्तनात् । शीघ्रमुत्पद्यते रोगः स्तम्भयेद्यदि संयमी ॥५७ ॥ योगाभ्यासेन मे रोग उत्पन्न इति कथ्यते । ततोऽभ्यासं त्यजेदेवं प्रथमं विघ्नाच्यते ॥५८ ॥ द्वितीय संशयाख्यं च तृतीयं च प्रमत्तता । आलस्याख्यं चतुर्थं च निद्रारूपं तु पञ्चमम् ॥५९ ॥

षष्ठं तु विरतिर्भ्रान्तिः सप्तमं परिकीर्तितम् । विषमं चाष्टमं चैव अनाख्यं नवमं स्मृतम् ॥६० ॥ अलब्धिर्योगतत्त्वस्य दशमं प्रोच्यते बुधैः । इत्येतद्विघ्नदशकं विचारेण त्यजेद्बुधः ॥६१ ॥ प्राणाभ्यासस्ततः कार्यो नित्यं सत्त्वस्थया धिया । सुषुम्ना लीयते चित्तं तथा वायुः प्रधावति ॥६२ ॥ शुष्के मले तु योगी च स्याद्गतिश्चलिता ततः । अधोगतिमपानं वै ऊर्ध्वगं कुरुते बलात् ॥६३ ॥ आकुञ्चनेन तं प्राहुर्मूलबन्धोऽयमुच्यते । अपानश्चोर्ध्वगो भूत्वा वह्निना सह गच्छति ॥६४ ॥

प्राणस्थानं ततो वह्निः प्राणापानौ च सत्वरम्। मिलित्वा कुण्डलीं याति प्रसुप्ता कुण्डलाकृतिः ॥६५ ॥ तेनाग्निना च संतप्ता पवनेनैव चालिता। प्रसार्य स्वशरीरं तु सुषुम्ना वदनान्तरे ॥६६ ॥ ब्रह्मग्रन्थिं ततो भित्त्वा रजोगुणसमुद्भवम्। सुषुम्ना वदने शीघ्रं विद्युल्लेखेव संस्फुरेत् ॥६७ ॥ विष्णुग्रन्थिं प्रयात्युच्चैः सत्वरं हृदि संस्थिता। ऊर्ध्वं गच्छति यच्चास्ते रुद्रग्रन्थिं तदुद्भवम् ॥६८ ॥ भ्रुवोर्मध्यं तु संभिद्य याति शीतांशु-मण्डलम्। अनाहताख्यं यच्चक्रं दलैः षोडशभिर्युतम् ॥६९ ॥

तत्र शीतांशुसंजातं द्रवं शोषयति स्वयम्। चलिते प्राणवेगेन रक्तं पित्तं रवेर्ग्रहात् ॥७० ॥ यातेन्दुचक्रं यत्रास्ते शुद्धश्लेष्मद्रवात्मकम्। तत्र सिक्तं ग्रसत्युष्णं कथं शीतस्वभावकम् ॥७१ ॥ तथैव रभसा शुक्लं चन्द्ररूपं हि तप्यते। ऊर्ध्वं प्रवहति क्षुब्धा तदैवं भ्रमतेतराम् ॥७२ ॥ तस्यास्वादवशाच्चित्तं बहिष्ठं विषयेषु यत्। तदेव परमं भुक्त्वा स्वस्थः स्वात्मरतो युवा ॥७३ ॥

प्रकृत्यष्टकरूपं च स्थानं गच्छति कुण्डली। क्रोडीकृत्य शिवं याति क्रोडीकृत्य विलीयते ॥७४ ॥ इत्यधोर्ध्वरजः शुक्लं शिवे तदनु मारुतः। प्राणापानौ समौ याति सदा जातौ तथैव च ॥७५ ॥ भूतेऽल्पे चाप्यनल्पे वा वाचके त्वतिवर्धते। धावयत्यखिला वाता अग्निमूषाहिरण्यवत् ॥७६ ॥ आधिभौतिकदेहं तु आधिदैविकविग्रहे। देहोऽतिविमलं याति चातिवाहिकतामियात् ॥७७ ॥

जाड्यभावविनिर्मुक्तममलं चिन्मयात्मकम्। तस्यातिवाहिकं मुख्यं सर्वेषां तु मदात्मकम् ॥७८ ॥ जायाभवविनिर्मुक्तिः कालरूपस्य विभ्रमः। इति तं स्वस्वरूपा हि मती रज्जुभुजङ्गवत् ॥७९ ॥ मृषैवोदेति सकलं मृषैव प्रविलीयते। रौप्यबुद्धिः शुक्तिकायां स्त्रीपुंसोर्भ्रमतो यथा ॥८० ॥ पिण्डब्रह्माण्डयोरैक्यं लिङ्गसूत्रात्मनोरपि। स्वापाव्याकृतयोरैक्यं स्वप्रकाशचिदात्मनोः ॥८१ ॥

शक्तिः कुण्डलिनी नाम बिसतन्तुनिभा शुभा। मूलकन्दं फणाग्रेण दृष्ट्वा कमलकन्दवत् ॥८२ ॥ मुखेन पुच्छं संगृह्य ब्रह्मरन्ध्रसमन्विता। पद्मासनगतः स्वस्थो गुदमाकुञ्च्य साधकः ॥८३ ॥ वायुमूर्ध्वगतं कुर्वन्कुम्भकाविष्टमानसः। वाय्वाघातवशादग्निः स्वाधिष्ठानगतो ज्वलन् ॥७४ ॥ ज्वलनाघातपवना-घातोरुन्निद्रितोऽहिराट्। ब्रह्मग्रन्थिं ततो भित्त्वा विष्णुग्रन्थिं भिनत्त्यतः ॥८५ ॥ रुद्रग्रन्थिं च भित्त्वैव कमलानि भिनत्ति षट्। सहस्रकमले शक्तिः शिवेन सह मोदते ॥८६ ॥ सैवावस्था परा ज्ञेया सैव निर्वृतिकारिणी इति ॥ इति प्रथमोऽध्यायः ॥१ ॥

अथाहं संप्रवक्ष्यामि विद्यां खेचरिसंज्ञिकाम्। यथा विज्ञानवानस्या लोकेऽस्मिन्नजरोऽमरः ॥१ ॥ मृत्युव्याधिजराग्रस्तो दृष्ट्वा विद्यामिमां मुने। बुद्धिं दृढतरां कृत्वा खेचरीं तु समभ्यसेत् ॥२ ॥ जरामृत्युगदघ्नो यः खेचरीं वेत्ति भूतले। ग्रन्थ-तश्चार्थतश्चैव तदभ्यासप्रयोगतः ॥३ ॥

तं मुने सर्वभावेन गुरुं मत्वा समाश्रयेत्। दुर्लभा खेचरी विद्या तदभ्यासोऽपि दुर्लभः ॥४ ॥ अभ्यासं मेलनं चैव युगपन्नैव सिध्यति। अभ्यासमात्रनिरता न विन्दन्ते ह मेलनम् ॥५ ॥ अभ्यासं लभते ब्रह्मञ्जन्मजन्मान्तरे क्वचित्। मेलनं तत्तु जन्मनां शतान्तेऽपि न लभ्यते ॥६ ॥ अभ्यासं बहुजन्मान्ते कृत्वा तद्भावसाधितम्। मेलनं लभते कश्चिद्योगी जन्मान्तरे क्वचित् ॥७ ॥

यदा तु मेलनं योगी लभते गुरुवक्त्रतः। तदा तत्सिद्धिमाप्नोति यदुक्ता शास्त्रसंततौ ॥८॥ ग्रन्थतश्चार्थतश्चैव मेलनं लभते यदा। तदा शिवात्वमाप्नोति निर्मुक्तः सर्वसंसृतेः ॥९॥ शास्त्रं विनापि संबोद्धुं गुरवोऽपि न शक्नुयुः। तस्मात्सुदुर्लभतरं लभ्यं शास्त्रमिदं मुने ॥१०॥ यावन्न लभ्यते शास्त्रं तावद्गां पर्यटेद्यतिः। यदा संलभ्यते शास्त्रं तदा सिद्धिः करे स्थिता ॥११॥

न शास्त्रेण विना सिद्धिर्दृष्टा चैव जागन्त्रये। तस्मान्मेलनदातारं शास्त्रदातारमचातुम् ॥१२॥ तदभ्यासप्रदातारं शिवं मत्वा समाश्रयेत्। लब्ध्वा शास्त्रमिदं मह्यमन्येषां न प्रकाशयेत् ॥१३॥ तस्मात्सर्वप्रयत्नेन गोपनीयं विजानता। यत्रास्ते च गुरुर्ब्रह्मन्दिव्ययोगप्रदायकः ॥१४॥ तत्र गत्वा च तेनोक्तविद्यां संगृह्य खेचरीम्। तेनोक्तः सम्यगभ्यासं कुर्यादादावतन्द्रितः ॥१५॥

अनया विद्यया योगी खेचरीसिद्धिभाग्भवेत्। खेचर्या खेचरीं युञ्जन्खेचरीबीजपूरया ॥१६॥ खेचराधिपतिर्भूत्वा खेचरेषु सदा वसेत्। खेचरावसथं वह्निमम्बुमण्डलभूषितम् ॥१७॥ आख्यातं खेचरीबीजं तेन योगः प्रसिध्यति। सोमांशनवकं वर्णं प्रतिलोमेन चोद्धरेत् ॥१८॥ तस्मान्त्र्यंशकमाख्यातमक्षरं चन्द्ररूपकम्। तस्मादप्यष्टमं वर्णं विलोमेन परं मुने ॥१९॥

तथा तत्परमं विद्धि तदादिरपि पञ्चमी। इन्दोश्च बहुभिन्ने च कूटोऽयं परिकीर्तितः ॥२०॥ गुरूपदेशलभ्यं च सर्वयोगप्रसिद्धिदम्। यत्तस्य देहजा माया निरुद्धकरणाश्रया ॥२१॥ स्वप्नेऽपि न लभेत्तस्य नित्यं द्वादशजप्यतः। य इमां पञ्च लक्षाणि जपेदपि सुयन्त्रितः ॥२२॥ तस्य श्रीखेचरीसिद्धिः स्वयमेव प्रवर्तते। नश्यन्ति सर्वविघ्नानि प्रसीदन्ति च देवताः ॥२३॥ वलीपलितनाशश्च भविष्यति न संशयः। एवं लब्ध्वा महाविद्यामभ्यासं कारयेत्ततः ॥२४॥

अन्यथा क्लिश्यते ब्रह्मन्न सिद्धिः खेचरीपथे। यदभ्यासविधौ विद्यां न लभेद्यः सुधामयीम् ॥२५॥ ततः संमेलकादौ च लब्ध्वा विद्यां सदा जपेत्। नान्यथा रहितो ब्रह्मन्न किंचित्सिद्धिभाग्भवेत् ॥२६॥ यदिदं लभ्यते शास्त्रं तदा विद्यां समाश्रयेत्। ततस्तदोदितां सिद्धिमाशु तां लभते मुनिः ॥२७॥ तालुमूलं समुत्कृष्य सप्तवासरमात्मवित्। स्वगुरूक्त-प्रकारेण मलं सर्वं विशोधयेत् ॥२८॥

स्नुहिपत्रनिभं शस्त्रं सुतीक्ष्ण स्निग्धनिर्मलम्। समादाय ततस्तेन रोममात्रं समुच्छिनेत् ॥२९॥ हित्वा सैन्धवपथ्याभ्यां चूर्णिताभ्यां प्रकर्षयेत्। पुनः सप्तदिने प्राप्ते रोममात्रं समुच्छिनेत् ॥३०॥ एवं क्रमेण षण्मासं नित्योद्युक्तः समाचरेत्। षण्मासाद्रसनामूलं सिराबद्धं प्रणश्यति ॥३१॥ अथ वागीश्वरीधाम शिरो वस्त्रेण वेष्टयेत्। शनैरुत्कर्षयेद्योगी कालवेलाविधानवित् ॥३२॥ पुनः षण्मासमात्रेण नित्यं संघर्षणान्मुने। भ्रूमध्यावधि चाप्येति तिर्यक्कणबिलावधिः ॥३३॥

अधश्च चुबुकं मूलं प्रयाति क्रमचारिता। पुनः संवत्सराणां तु तृतीयादेव लीलया ॥३४॥ केशान्तमूर्ध्वं क्रमति तिर्यक्शाखावधिर्मुने। अधस्तात्कण्ठकूपान्तं पुनर्व-र्षत्रयेण तु ॥३५॥ ब्रह्मरन्ध्रं समावृत्य तिष्ठेदेव न संशयः। तिर्यक् चूलितलं याति अधः कण्ठबिलावधि ॥३६॥ शनैः शनैर्मस्तकाच्च महावज्रकपाटभित्। पूर्वं बीजयुता विद्या ह्याख्याता यातिदुर्लभा ॥३७॥

तस्याः षडङ्गं कुर्वीत तया षट्स्वरभिन्नया। कुर्यादेवं करन्यासं सर्वसिद्ध्यादिहेतवे ॥३८ ॥ शनैरेवं प्रकर्तव्यमभ्यासं युगपन्नहि। युगपद्वर्तते यस्य शरीरं विलयं व्रजेत् ॥३९ ॥ तस्माच्छनैः शनैः कार्यमभ्यासं मुनिपुङ्गव। यदा च बाह्यमार्गेण जिह्वा ब्रह्मबिलं व्रजेत् ॥४० ॥ तदा ब्रह्मार्गलं ब्रह्मन्दुर्भेद्यं त्रिदशनैरपि। अङ्गुल्यग्रेण संघृष्य जिह्वामात्रं निवेशयेत् ॥४१ ॥ एवं वर्षत्रयं कृत्वा ब्रह्मद्वारं प्रविश्यति। ब्रह्मद्वारे प्रविष्टे तु सम्य अथनमाचरेत् ॥४२ ॥

मथनेन विना केचित्साधयन्ति विपश्चितः। खेचरीमन्त्रसिद्धस्य सिध्यां मथनं विना ॥४३ ॥ जपं च मथनं चैव कृत्वा शीघ्रं फलं लभेत्। स्वर्णजां रौप्यजां वापि लोहजां वा शलाकिकाम् ॥४४ ॥ नियोज्य नासिकारन्ध्रं दुग्ध सिक्तेन तन्तुना। प्राणान्निरुध्य हृदये सुखमासनमात्मनः ॥४५ ॥ शनैः सुमथनं कुर्याद्भ्रूमध्ये न्यस्य चक्षुषी। षण्मासं मथनावस्था भावेनैव प्रजायते ॥४६ ॥ यथा सुषुप्तिर्बालानां यथा भावस्तथा भरेत्। न सदा मथनं शस्तं मासे मासे समाचरेत् ॥४७ ॥

सदा रसनया योगी मार्गं न परिसंक्रमेत्। एवं द्वादशवर्षान्ते संसिद्धिर्भवति ध्रुवा ॥४८ ॥ शरीरे सकलं विश्वं पश्यत्यात्माविभेदतः। ब्रह्माण्डोऽयं महामार्गो राजदन्तोर्ध्वकुण्डली ॥४९ ॥ इति ॥ इति द्वीतीयोऽध्यायः ॥२ ॥

मेलनमनुः। हीं भं सं पं फं सं क्षम्। पद्मज उवाच। अमावास्या च प्रतिपत्पौर्णमासी च शंकर। अस्याः का वर्ण्यते संज्ञा एतदाख्याहि तत्त्वतः ॥१ ॥ प्रतिपद्दिनतीऽकाले अमावास्या तथैव च। पौर्णमास्यां स्थिरीकुर्यात्स च पन्था हि नान्यथा ॥२ ॥ कामेन विषयाकाङ्क्षी विषयात्काममोहितः। द्वावेव संत्यजेन्नित्यं निरञ्जनमुपाश्रयेत् ॥३ ॥ अपरं संत्यजेत्सर्वं यदिच्छेदात्मनो हितम्। शक्तिमध्ये मनः कृत्वा मनः शक्तेश्च मध्यगम् ॥४ ॥

मनसा मन आलोक्य तत्त्यजेत्परमं पदम्। मन एव हि बिन्दुश्च उत्पत्तिस्थितिकारणम् ॥५ ॥ मनसोत्पद्यते बिन्दुर्यथा क्षीरं घृतात्मकम्। न च बन्धनमध्यस्थं तद्वै कारणमानसम् ॥६ ॥ चन्द्रार्कमध्यमा शक्तिर्यत्रस्था तत्र बन्धनम्। ज्ञात्वा सुषुम्नां तद्भेदं कृत्वा वायुं च मध्यगम् ॥७ ॥ स्थित्वासौ वैन्दवस्थाने घ्राणरन्ध्रे निरोधयेत्। वायुं बिन्दु समाख्यातं सत्वं प्रकृतिमेव च ॥८ ॥

षट् चक्राणि परिज्ञात्वा प्रविशेत्सुखमण्डलम्। मूलाधार स्वाधिष्ठानं मणिपूरं तृतीयकम् ॥९ ॥ अनाहतं विशुद्धं च आज्ञाचक्रं च षष्ठकम्। आधारं गुदमित्युक्तं स्वाधिष्ठानं तु लैङ्गिकम् ॥१० ॥ मणिपुरं नाभिदेशं हृदयस्थमनाहतम्। विशुद्धिः कण्ठमूले च आज्ञाचक्रं च मस्तकम् ॥११ ॥ षट् चक्राणि परिज्ञात्वा प्रविशेत्सुखमण्डले। प्रविशेद्वायुमाकृष्य तयैवोर्ध्वं नियोजयेत् ॥१२ ॥

एवं समभ्यसेद्वायुं स ब्रह्माण्डमयो भवेत्। वायुं बिन्दुं तथा चक्रं चित्तं चैव समभ्यसेत् ॥१३ ॥ समाधिमेकेन सममममृतं यान्ति योगिनः। यथाग्निर्दारुमध्यस्थो नोत्तिष्ठेन्मथनं विना ॥१४ ॥ विना चाभ्यासयोगेन ज्ञानदीपस्तथा न हि। घटमध्यगतो दीपो बाह्ये नैव प्रकाशते ॥१५ ॥ भिन्ने तस्मिन्घटे चैव दीपज्वाला च भासते। स्वकायं घटमित्युक्तं यथा दीपो हि तत्पदम् ॥१६ ॥

गुरुवाक्यसमाभिन्ने ब्रह्मज्ञानं स्फुटीभवेत्। कर्णधारं गुरुं प्राप्य कृत्वा सूक्ष्मं तरन्ति च ॥१७ ॥ अभ्यासवासनाशक्त्या तरन्ति भवसागरम्। परायामङ्कुरीभूय पश्यन्त्यां

द्विदलीकृता ॥१८॥ मध्यमायां मुकुलिता वैखर्यां विकसीकृता। पूर्वं यथोदिता या वाग्वि- लोमेनास्तगा भवेत् ॥१९॥ तस्या वाचः परो देवः कूटस्थो वाक्प्रबोधकः। सोहमस्मीति निश्चित्य यः सदा वर्तते पुमान् ॥२०॥ शब्दैरुच्चावचैर्नीचैर्भाषितोऽपि न लिप्यते। विश्वश्च तैजसश्चैव प्राज्ञश्चेति च ते त्रयः ॥२१॥

विराड्हिरण्यगर्भश्च ईश्वरश्चेति ते त्रयः। ब्रह्माण्डं चैव पिण्डाण्डं लोका भूरादयः क्रमात् ॥२२॥ स्वस्वोपाधिलयादेव लीयन्ते प्रत्यगात्मनि। अण्डं ज्ञानाग्निना तप्तं लीयते कारणैः सह ॥२३॥ परमात्मनि लीनं तत्परं ब्रह्मैव जायते। ततः स्तिमितगम्भीरं तेजो न तमस्ततम् ॥२४॥ अनाख्यमनभिव्यक्तं सत्किंचिदवशिष्यते। ध्यात्वा मध्यस्थमात्मानं कलसान्तरदीपवत् ॥२५॥ अङ्गुष्ठमात्रमात्मानमधूमज्योतिरूपकम्। प्रकाशयन्तमन्तस्थं ध्यायेत्कूटस्थमव्ययम् ॥२६॥

विज्ञानात्मा तथा देहे जाग्रत्स्वप्नसुषुप्तितः। मायया मोहितः पश्चाद्बहुजन्मान्तरे पुनः ॥२७॥ सत्कर्मपरिपाकात्तु स्वविकारं चिकीर्षति। कोऽहं कथमयं दोषः संसाराख्य उपागतः ॥२८॥ जाग्रत्स्वप्ने व्यवहरन्त्सुषुप्तौ क्व गतिर्मम। इति चिन्तापरो भूत्वा स्वभासा च विशेषतः ॥२९॥ अज्ञानात्तु चिदाभासो बहिस्तापेन तापितः। दग्धं भवत्येव तदा तूलपिण्डमिवाग्निना ॥३०॥

दहरस्थः प्रत्यगात्मा नष्टे ज्ञाने ततः परम्। विततो व्याप्य विज्ञानं दहत्येव क्षणेन तु ॥३१॥ मनोमयज्ञानमयान्त्सम्यग्दध्वा क्रमेण तु। घटस्थदीपवच्छश्वदन्तरेव प्रकाशते ॥३२॥ ध्यायन्नास्ते मुनिश्चैवमासुप्तेरामृतेस्तु यः। जीवन्मुक्तः स विज्ञेयः स धन्यः कृतकृत्यवान् ॥३३॥

जीवन्मुक्तपदं त्यक्त्वा स्वदेहे कालसात्कृते। विशत्यदेहमुक्तत्वं पवनोऽस्पन्दतामिव ॥३४॥ अशब्दमस्पर्शमरूपमव्ययं तथारसं नित्यमगन्धवच्च यत्। अनाद्यनन्तं महतः परं ध्रुवं तदेव शिष्यत्यमलं निरामयम् ॥३५॥ इत्युपनिषत् ॥

ॐ सह नाववत्विति शान्तिः ॥ हरि ॐ तत्सत् ॥

इति योगकुण्डल्युपनिषत्समाप्ता ॥

संपूर्णोऽयमुपनिषत्समुच्चयः ॥

ॐ तत्सद्ब्रह्मार्पणमस्तु ।